United States
Naval Aviation

1910-1918

Noel C. Shirley

Schiffer Military History
Atglen, PA

Acknowledgments

Over the years that it has taken to prepare the manuscript for this book, there are many individuals and organizations without whose help this effort could never have been completed. To begin with, thanks must be provided to the staff of the office of the Historian for the Deputy Chief of Naval Operations (Air) of the United States Navy. Through their generosity, both the principal reference source and principal photographs used in the book were obtained. Likewise, the staff of the National Archives in Washington D.C. where extremely accommodating in allowing copying of relevant photographs from their collection. Further, the staff of the Naval Historical Center at the Washington Navy Yard was very helpful in providing photographs. Other individuals associated with various organizations provided inestimable help: Mr. Dennis R. Kenson of the Dunwoody Institute, Minneapolis, opened his files on the naval aviation ground school at Dunwoody, thereby allowed the filling of a major void in the text; Mr. Kurt House of the Curtiss Museum of Hammondsport, New York, was very generous in allowing the copying of photographs from the Curtiss collection; Mr. Colin Owers provided numerous photographs, and Mr. Hill Goodspeed was very helpful in providing photographs from the collection of the Emil H. Buhler Library within United States Naval Aviation Museum in Pensacola, Florida. Individuals who often pushed, cajoled, and otherwise encouraged this effort—often by providing input to the book—include Peter Kilduff and Pat Mallahan who each provided valuable input to this effort; both the late R.D. Layman and Jim Davilla each provided constant encouragement. Without their efforts this book would never have been completed. And finally, I must give the biggest vote of appreciation to my wife, Sue, who had to put up with my fixation on doing research on this subject, my often disappearing for extended periods of time into yet another archival source, plus subjecting our family budget to a continual accumulation of charges for more photographs and copying fees.

Book Design by Ian Robertson.

Library of Congress Catalog Number: 00-101411

Printed in China.
ISBN: 0-7643-1179-4

We are interested in hearing from authors with book ideas on related topics.

Published by Schiffer Publishing Ltd.
4880 Lower Valley Road
Atglen, PA 19310
Phone: (610) 593-1777
FAX: (610) 593-2002
E-mail: Schifferbk@aol.com.
Visit our web site at: www.schifferbooks.com
Please write for a free catalog.
This book may be purchased from the publisher.
Please include $3.95 postage.
Try your bookstore first.

In Europe, Schiffer books are distributed by:
Bushwood Books
6 Marksbury Avenue
Kew Gardens
Surrey TW9 4JF
England
Phone: 44 (0)208 392-8585
FAX: 44 (0)208 392-9876
E-mail: Bushwd@aol.com.
Free postage in the UK. Europe: air mail at cost.
Try your bookstore first.

Contents

Introduction

This book has been prepared both on the basis of the author's interest in the subject as well as a sense of frustration associated with researching the subject of WWI naval aviation. The author's interest in the subject goes back for over 30 years and is based not only on his interest in history, but also his interest in aviation. Researching and writing about the subject has generated a great deal of frustration due to the lack of a single complete reference source of information. It has been said that the aviation activities of the U.S. Navy during World War I have been underestimated, often ignored, and unrealized. This is in spite of the situation that a strong case can be made that naval aviation had as large an impact on the final outcome of the hostilities as that provided by the Aviation Section of the United States Army Signal Corps. What many readers of WWI aviation history do not remember is: 1) the Navy's First Aeronautic Detachment was the first organized arm of the American armed forces to arrive in France following the outbreak of hostilities in April 1917; 2) the Marine Corps' First Marine Aeronautic Company became the first fully operational aviation organization to undertake routine patrols in European waters as part of America's War effort; and 3) in November 1917, the Navy was given priority over the Army for materials due to the need to combat the German submarine menace before being able to transport the troops to France. The success of the Navy's efforts was such that no convoy vessel escorted by a Navy aircraft or dirigible was lost to submarine attack. This allowed the men and materials supplied by America to reach the front in order to perform their intended roles. Hopefully, this book will be a positive step improving the perception of naval aviation during WWI.

The book is organized into chapters and a multitude of appendices. Chapter 1 discusses the birth and evolution of naval aviation. In particular, emphasis is placed upon the early efforts of junior and senior officers to establish a viable flying presence within the Navy, inspite of often overwhelming resistance, and outright hostility, from more traditional "blue-water" officers. Chapter 2 addresses the Navy's efforts to enlarge its aviation program in light of the inevitable entry of America into the European war. Details are provided both on the political rivalries and inter-service strife as America geared up for war and the enlarged training programs thus necessitated. The expansion of the naval air stations in this country is also covered. An introduction is also provided covering the expansion of naval aviation into the areas of Lighter-than-Air activities and aviation support functions. Chapter 3 provides a detailed discussion of the development and procurement by the Navy of a Lighter-than-Air program. Chapter 4 covers the development and procurement of Heavier-than-Air craft— from the first aircraft purchased by the Navy through 1918. Chapter 5 provides an in-depth discussion of the invaluable contribution of the Marine Corps to the overall naval aviation effort, beginning in 1912 and culminating in the operations of the Day Wing of the Northern Bombing Group in France in 1918. Chapter 6 addresses the war efforts and assignments of the Navy and contains a discussion of each of the naval air stations established in Canada, England, Ireland, France, and Italy during the War. The remaining portion of the book consists of appendices. Most of the appendices are detailed histories of the formation and operation of individual naval air stations operated in Foreign Service by the Navy during the War. Three other appendices discuss the formation and implementation of the naval aviation training programs instituted at the Massachusetts Institute of Technology, University of Washington, and the Dunwoody Institute in Minneapolis.

1

Evolution of Naval Aviation

The early history of naval aviation in the United States is marked by the attempts of a few farsighted naval officers striving to overcome the at times myopic perception of the military usefulness of the airplane which was held not only by many members of the senior naval organization, but also by many appointed officials associated with naval activities. This chapter is an overview of the people and events that led from the initial interests of a dedicated few, through the embryonic beginnings, to the establishment of a formalized aviation organization within the Department of the Navy.

The U.S. Navy first fully investigated the feasibility of aviation for naval purposes in 1908 when Lieutenant George C. Sweet and Naval Constructor William McEntee were detailed as observers for the flight of the Wright plane at Fort Myer, VA, on 17 September 1908. Tragically, the test resulted in the death of Lieutenant Selfridge of the U.S. Army when Orville crashed due to the failure of a propeller. In spite of the accident, Lieutenant Sweet was sufficiently impressed with aviation that in his report to the Navy Department he endeavored to stimulate interest in the subject of aviation and suggested the use of pontoons in lieu of wheels or skids, but no action was taken. On 2 December 1908, Rear Admiral William S. Cowles, Chief of the Bureau of Steam Engineering, on the basis of a report on aviation prepared by Lieutenant Sweet, recommended to the Secretary of the Navy that "a number of aeroplanes be purchased to operate from a ship's deck, carry a wireless telegraph, operate in weather other than a dead calm, maintain a high rate of speed, and be of such a design as to permit convenient storage on-board ship." The recommendation was not acted upon. In July 1909 the Wright Brothers completed the flights required by the Army for the purchase of their machine. On 16 August 1909, the Bureau of Equipment requested authority to advertise for the construction of two planes. The request was disapproved. On 1 September Commander F.L. Chapin, U.S. Naval Attaché in Paris, was an observer at the Rheims Aviation Meet. In his report he expressed the opinion that "the airplane could have a present usefulness in naval warfare" and that "the limits of the field will be extended in the near future." He went on to prophetically note that a use of aircraft to be operated from naval vessels could be via "the construction of a floor over the deckhouses of auxiliary ships to provide the clean space required for takeoff runs and landing aboard."[1] On 3 November 1909, Lieutenant Sweet, at College Park,

The AH of 1911. Individual is unidentified. (source: Glenn H. Curtiss Museum of Hammondsport)

The AH of 1911 in flight. Pilot is unidentified. (source: Glenn H. Curtiss Museum of Hammondsport)

The AH of 1911 on the water. View shows the floats on the lower wings to advantage. (source: Glenn H. Curtiss Museum of Hammondsport)

Preparation for the launching of a Curtiss Hydro-plane for its flight from water. The photo was taken on January 25,1911 at San Diego. (source: Glenn H. Curtiss Museum of Hammondsport)

MD, was taken up in a Wright machine by Lieutenant Frank P. Lahm, U.S.A., thus becoming the first navy officer to fly.

On 1 October 1910, the General Board, with Adm. George Dewey as President, ordered that the Navy consider providing space for airplanes or dirigibles in all new designs. On 7 October, Captain Hutch I. Cone requested authority to requisition an airplane for the cruiser U.S.S. *Chester* and the services of an instructor to teach one or more officers to fly. While the General Board concurred in the recommendation, the Secretary of the Navy was not disposed to purchase any airplanes at this time. On 13 October, the Secretary of the Navy approved the recommendation of 11 October of the Chief Constructor that officers from the Bureau of Steam Engineering and the Bureau of Construction and Repair be appointed to investigate the subject of aviation. Acting Secretary of the Navy Beekman Winthrop approved. Naval Constructor McEntree and Lieutenant Nathaniel H. Wright were appointed by the Bureau of Construction and Repair and the Bureau of Steam Engineering, respectfully. And finally, on 31 October, the Chief of the Bureau of Construction and Repair suggested that steps be taken to obtain one or more planes for naval purposes, and that the battleship U.S.S. *Texas* be modified to handle planes.

In 1910 Captain Washington Irving Chambers, USN, a 54-year-old nonpilot who was at this time assistant to the Aid for Material in the Bureau of Equipment, attended the aviation meets at Belmont Park, NY (22 October), and at Halethorpe, near Baltimore, as an official navy observer. Captain Chambers, as a result of an increasing volume of mail received by the Navy on the subject of aviation from both private citizens and the U.S. Aeronautical Reserve, had been assigned, on 26 September 1910, by the Secretary of the Navy as the individual to whom all such questions should be addressed—the first reference to a provision for aviation in the Navy Department organization. In this capacity he became the first of what would eventually become the Director of Naval Aeronautics. He was not, however, given either staff, authority, or money with which to perform his duties. What he was given was little backing. Appreciating the potential value of the airplane in naval warfare, Captain Chambers endeavored to interest the Wright Co. in arranging for a flight off a United States war ship. Wilbur Wright declined to make the attempt. The Curtiss Co. was then approached, and they agreed to try it. The necessary arrangements were thereupon made by Captain Chambers, and on 14 November 1910, the Curtiss representative, Eugene B. Ely, successfully flew a 50-horsepower Curtiss

Curtiss Pusher at North Island in 1911. (source: Glenn H. Curtiss Museum of Hammondsport)

Curtiss Pusher at North Island in 1911. (source: Glenn H. Curtiss Museum of Hammondsport)

Eugene Ely landing on the cruiser U.S.S. Pennsylvania (ARC-4) in San Francisco Bay. (source: Glenn H. Curtiss Museum of Hammondsport)

Eugene Ely after landing on the cruiser U.S.S. Pennsylvania (ARC-4) in San Francisco Bay. Photo shows good detail of the flotation bags on the lower wings and the make-shift life preserver made of the inner tubes of bicycle tires. (source: Glenn H. Curtiss Museum of Hammondsport)

landplane (the Albany Flyer) from a platform hastily constructed by Naval Constructor McEntree on the bow of the cruiser U.S.S. *Birmingham*, anchored at Hampton Roads, VA. Captain Chambers, in a very "Politic" report on Ely's success, took the position that while the airplane would never supplant the scouting cruiser, the airplane would significantly expand the capability of the cruiser, and therefore the Navy should proceed in procuring and developing the aircraft for naval application.

Captain Chambers, in his capacity as an assistant to the Aide for Materials had no authority, but instead worked with the Bureaus, several aero clubs, and interested fraternities of private citizens in an advisory and coordinating capacity. Naval Construction McEntree and Lieutenant N.H. Wright were assigned to work with Captain Chambers as the bureau system began to educate itself and to acquire competence in this new field. The assignment of Naval Constructor McEntree and Lieutenant Wright to assist Captain Chambers in the fall of 1910 marked the beginning of the Aeronautical Engineering Duty Officer movement in the Navy.

Two weeks following Ely's successful experiment (29 November), Glenn H. Curtiss sent a letter volunteering to instruct several naval officers free of charge, as no money had as yet been appropriated by Congress for the development of naval aviation. At this time the Secretary of the Navy, George von Lengerke Meyer, had no perception of the naval use for aviation. Upon receipt of the Curtiss letter Captain Chambers waited until von Lengerke Meyer was out of town. He then asked Acting Secretary Beekman Winthrop to sign a letter of acceptance. The acceptance letter is dated 13 December. It just happened that Lieutenant (j.g.) Theodore Gordon

Eugene Ely taking off from the cruiser U.S.S. Pennsylvania (ARC-4) in San Francisco Bay. (source: Glenn H. Curtiss Museum of Hammondsport)

Glenn H. Curtiss and his first military class. (Left to Right: Lt. J.C. Walker, Lt. P.W. Beck, Lt. T.G. Ellyson, and Lt. Kelly. Apparently only Ellyson of the naval officers shown pursued an aviation career after this course was completed. (source: Glenn H. Curtiss Museum of Hammondsport)

At North Island, standing are (left to right) McClosky and Glenn Curtiss (at controls); seated (left to right) are John H. Towers, Paul Beck, and T.G. Ellyson. (source: Glenn H. Curtiss Musuem at Hammondsport)

Group photo taken at North Island. In the rear are Beck and Kelly; in front are Ellyson, Curtiss, and Walker. (source: Glenn H. Curtiss Museum of Hammondsport)

("Spuds") Ellyson, USN (U.S. Naval Academy Class of 1905), had, on 16 December 1910, requested "duty in connection with aeroplanes" at the suggestion of Kenneth Whiting, a former Academy roommate. When, on 23 December, the detail officer was told by Winthrop to select a candidate, Lieutenant (j.g.) Ellyson's request was at the top of his stack of paper. As a result of this offer, Ellyson was ordered to the Curtiss camp at San Diego, CA. On 23 December Ellyson was promoted to full Lieutenant, sent $100 in back pay, and issued orders to San Diego. Ellyson received his orders on 27 December and reached Dominguez Field, south of Los Angeles, on 2 January 1911. The next day he and Curtiss moved to San Diego, the winter quarters for the Curtiss School. After spending two weeks in San Francisco with Curtiss at an aviation meet, Lieutenant Ellyson and Curtiss went back to San Diego for the opening of the Curtiss Flying School on 17 January. Curtiss' method of training was to forego the use of an instructor sitting with the student; he preferred to limit the power of the engine and thus allow the student, who was by himself in the plane, to get the feel of the plane before taking off. Lieutenant Ellyson, on his second trip in a plane, on 18 January, found the throttle blockage mechanism failed, inadvertently took off, and from 15 feet altitude crashed. For the next nine days Lieutenant Ellyson worked as a mechanic on the field, learning the details of the plane.

Lieutenant Ellyson soloed a little over one month after reporting to what was to become the naval station at North Island, and thus went on to become Naval Aviator No. 1. On 18 January 1911, Ely, then attached to the Curtiss camp at San Diego, at 1100 hours made a successful landing with a Curtiss D.IV model pusher on the deck of the armored cruiser U.S.S. *Pennsylvania* (ACR 4) laying in San Francisco harbor. The landing deck on the *Pennsylvania* was configured such that there were 22 landing wires evenly spaced and stretched across the deck at right angles to the flight path of the aircraft. On each end of each wire was secured a weighted sandbag.

Capte. DeFilippi of the Royal Italian Navy. Photo is believed to have been taken at North Island. It shows the Curtiss shoulder yoke controls to good advantage. (source: Glenn H. Curtiss Museum of Hammondsport)

At the end of the landing deck was a canvas crash curtain in case Ely missed all of the landing wires. Landing downwind, Ely caught the number 11 wire! Captain C.F. Pond of the *Pennsylvania* has been quoted as describing the feat as "the most important landing of a bird since the dove flew back to the ark!" At 11:58 Ely flew this plane from the deck on which he had landed and returned to Selfridge Field (San Francisco), completing the earliest demonstration of the adaptability of aircraft to shipboard operations.

During the same month, Glenn Curtiss and Lieutenant Ellyson perfected a hydroairplane attachment for airplanes. The impetus behind this effort was the resistance of Secretary of the Navy von Lengerke Meyer to aviation in general. In January Meyer had basically challenged Curtiss to develop a meaningful and useable aircraft. In a letter to Curtiss, he stated "when you show me that it is feasible for an aeroplane to alight on the water alongside a battleship and be hoisted aboard without any false deck to receive it, I shall believe the aeroplane is of practical value to the Navy."

On 1 February Curtiss made two successful takeoffs from the water at San Diego using a single main float to support the aircraft on the water. On 17 February 1911, Mr. Curtiss flew a model D.IV from the water at his San Diego base, taxied alongside the *Pennsylvania*, was hoisted aboard ship, subsequently hoisted out again, and went back to his camp. A week later Curtiss took up Lieutenant Ellyson for a flight in the hydroairplane. For the first time it was demonstrated that a crew of a pilot and an observer could be launched from a ship, perform reconnaissance functions, and return to the ship's commanding officer with the information. The day of naval aviation was at hand. Curtiss' performance, together with the previous feat of Ely, gave a very decided impetus to the development of naval aviation.

The Navy during this period was not limiting itself to investigations dealing just with aircraft. On 24 January 1911 an experiment was conducted in the Santa Barbara Channel, off the Southern California coast, in which Lieutenant John Rodgers, seated in a "boatswain's chair" attached to a box kite designed by Samuel F. Perkins, was sailed from the stern of the *Pennsylvania*. The box kite reached an altitude of 400 feet, from which Rodgers signaled his observations to the crew below. It was reported that the box-kite method of hoisting a spotter aloft was wholly impractical. This was the last attempt by the Navy to use non-lifting kites. At the end of February 1911 Perkins towed Lieutenant Rodgers and Ensign Alexander M. Charlton in a balloon of his making.

John H. Towers and Godfrey Chevalier. (source: Naval Historical Foundation)

Left to right: unidentified, Lt. Ellyson (in hat with a band), Wiegard (navy mechanic), and John H. Towers. (source: Naval Historical Foundation)

U.S. Navy representatives at Hammondsport. Left to right: T.G. Ellyson, J.C. "Bud" Mass, Glenn Curtiss, unidentified, unidentified, and unidentified.

Ellyson's launch at Hammondsport from a wire suspension system. (source: Glenn H. Curtiss Museum of Hammondsport)

As a result of Captain Chambers' reports and recommendations on aviation, the first aviation appropriation for $25,000 was included for experimental work in the development of aviation for naval purposes in the 1911-1912 Naval Appropriations Act. This money was appropriated on 4 March 1911. On 9 March 1911 the Wright Brothers made a formal offer to train one pilot for the Navy contingent upon the purchase of one airplane for the sum of $5,000. Lieutenant Rodgers was therefore ordered to Dayton for flight training. Lieutenant Rodgers reported to Dayton on 17 March. On his first day there he had 8 lessons. On 18 April he soloed at the Wright School, thus becoming (in August) both the first Wright trained Naval Aviator and Naval Aviator No. 2 (Aero Club of America License No. 48). On 13 March 1911, Captain Chambers was assigned to the Bureau of Navigation and directed to devote his efforts exclusively to aviation and to the coordination of the aeronautical work of the various bureaus. His reception upon reporting to the Bureau of Navigation on 17 April 1911 was not encouraging; in fact, at one point it was suggested that he do his work at home. This officer struggled with the many difficulties which always present themselves to those to whom fate assigns the difficult task of injecting new ideas and a new activity into a staid and archly conservative organization. The Navy as a whole lacked interest, and Captain Chambers worked virtually alone and unassisted to build up a naval aviation establishment.

Early in 1911, Lieutenant (j.g.) John Towers, USN (Naval Aviator No. 3) and Ensign V.D. Herbster, U.S.N. (Naval Aviator No. 4) were ordered to the Curtiss Co. for instruction in the art of flying. On 31 March Lieutenant Ellyson reported, "in obedience to the Department Order No. 5021-42 of 23 December 1910" that, in the opinion of Mr. Curtiss, he was qualified to fly in fair weather. In April, Lieutenant Ellyson accompanied the Curtiss School in its move to Hammondsport, NY. Enroute the two took part in an air meet in Salt Lake City from 4 April to 10 April. On 12 April 1911 Glenn Curtiss wrote to the Secretary of the Navy regarding the qualifications of Lieutenant Ellyson. He reported "I have the honor to report that Lt. Ellyson is now competent to care for and operate Curtiss seaplanes and instruct others in the operation of these machines. Mr. Ellyson is a hard worker and has acquired considerable knowledge of the art of aviation. He has been especially successful in operating the machine and is easily capable of qualifying for a pilot's license. It is a pleasure for me to recommend Mr. Ellyson as a man who will make success in aviation." Captain Chambers, on 1 April 1911, reported for duty with the General Board, a move suggested by Admiral George Dewey, when space for aviation was no

Crash of naval Constructor Holden C. Richardson at Hammondsport. (source: Glenn H. Curtiss Museum of Hammondsport)

W.B. Atwater in a Curtiss Hydroplane at North Island. (source: Glenn H. Curtiss Museum of Hammondsport)

Naval Constructor Holden C. Richardson. (source: Glenn H. Curtiss Museum of Hammondsport)

W.B. Atwater and John Lansing Callan. (source: Glenn H. Curtiss Museum of Hammondsport)

longer available in the Office of the Aid for Operation. On 14 April 1911 the embryo Office of Naval Aviation was transferred from the General Board to the Bureau of Navigation. Two Curtiss E Model planes (A-1 Triad and A-2) and one Wright plane (B-1) were purchased on 8 May 1911 (on 25 June 1959, in Sec Nav. Instr. 5060.17, the date of 8 May 1911 was established as the official birthday of Naval Aviation). The Wright B-1 was built at Dayton and made its first flights on 15 July. The Triad, first aircraft of the U.S. Navy, was ordered from Glenn Curtiss at the cost of $5,500. The machine was called "Triad" because of its three-fold ability to fly and land on either land, water, or the sea. Specifications, written by Captain Chambers, called for:

One Curtiss eight cylinder biplane, or "Triad," fitted for rising from or alighting on land or water, including land equipment, water equipment, and combination equipment, fitted with engine panels and chassis, and four interchangeable wing panels, covered with rubberized linen on top and tight woven special sail cloth on the bottom. One main pontoon and pair of balancing hydroplanes, with pontoons and hydrosurface to enable the machine to float when alighting on the water with land equipment attached. Landing wheels with suitable rims and clincher tires, capable of being housed above or extended beneath the line of the main pontoon by the aviator during flight. Subject to alterations if approved by the naval inspector at the factory. All complete with metal tipped propeller de signed for a speed of at least 45 miles per hour. The same to be fitted with a capacity for one passenger seated alongside the pilot with double controls so that either pilot or the passenger may operate the machine.

The contract for these planes stipulated that it was the responsibility of the manufacturer to train one pilot and one mechanic for each of the aircraft.

Curtiss School at San Diego on January 1912. Left to right: John Lansing Callan, W.B. Atwater, J.W.M. McClasky, G.E. Mallick, and G.E. Underwood. (source: Glenn H. Curtiss Museum of Hammondsport)

Curtiss School at San Diego in 1912. Standing, left to right, are: H.E.S. Shreve, Lt. J.W. McClasky, Lt. J.H. Tower, C.C. Perkins, G.E. Malick, A. Schaarff, A. Mayo, A. Solbrig, R.G. McMilllan, G.E. Underwood, T.D. Spaulding, F.J. Terrill, F.A. Hoover, C.A. Berlin, J. Bailey, C. Barvoith (Aero referee), W.B. Atwater, W.H. Harrison, and Mrs. W. Fisher. Seated, left to right, are: M. Kando, M. Stark, H. Park, and G.H. Curtiss. (source: Glenn H. Curtiss Museum of Hammondsport)

Curtiss School at San Diego, Class of 1912 at North Island. Left to right: J.C. Kaminski, unknown, C.A. Berlin, M. Dumlop 'French' Schaffer, John Lansing Callan, Komo Takoiski, Mohan Singh, and C. Capitsini. (source: Glenn H. Curtiss Museum of Hammondsport)

On 20 June 1911 Lieutenant (j.g.) Towers received orders for "Aviation Instruction." On 27 June he reported for duty and instruction in flying at the Curtiss School, Hammondsport, NY. His instructor, much to his surprise, since he was anticipating Curtiss, was Lieutenant Ellyson. The next morning Lieutenant Ellyson, using the Curtiss method, fashioned a wooden block to be fitted under the throttle of the training plane. By restricting throttle movement the engine was not given enough power to enable the machine to fly. He, however, forgot to take into consideration the 20-pound weight difference between he and Towers. Towers got into the seat and pushed the throttle wide open. The plane leapt 20 feet into the air, stalled, and crashed. Towers escaped bruised and with a broken foot. Towers qualified for a pilot's license on 14 September, thus becoming Naval Aviator No. 3.

The Navy's first aircraft, the A-1 and A-2, were built at Hammondsport and first flown and delivered on 1 and 13 July, respectively. Capt. Chambers and Dr. A. Francis Zahn of the Smithsonian Institution and the Aero Club of America arrived at Hammondsport on 1 July. Chambers was to witness the acceptance trials of the A-1, and Zahn was to evaluate Ellyson for his Aero Club license. After a five-minute demonstration ride by Curtiss in the A-1 at 1850 hrs. at Lake Keuka, Lieutenant Ellyson flew solo to qualify for his license. He had waited so that the Navy's first aviator could qualify in the Navy's first plane. Dr. Zahn failed to certify Lieutenant Ellyson because he failed to stop his engine before he touched down on the lake. On 2 July Lieutenant Ellyson retook the test and passed (Aero Club of America License #28 and Military Aviator's Certificate No. 26, and Naval Aviator No. 1). Curtiss then took Captain Chambers up for his first ride. That evening Lieutenant Ellyson flew the A-1 from Keuka to Hammondsport, landing on the water without the aid of lights, and thus making the Navy's first night flight. Lieutenant Rodgers qualified for his pilot's license under the Aero Club of America on 7 August 1911; he remained at Dayton until September when he was ordered to Annapolis. On 6 July 1911 Captain Chambers was ordered to the Naval Academy on temporary duty in connection with the establishment of an aviation experimental station at Greenbury Point. This station thus became the first base for naval aviation. On 10 July Curtiss, in the A-1, demonstrated the amphibious nature of the Navy's first plane when he took off from land, raised the wheels while in the air, and

Curtiss School at North Island after a 70 mph storm in March 1912. (source: Glenn H. Curtiss Museum of Hammondsport)

Curtiss School at North Island after a 70 mph storm in March 1912. (source: Glenn H. Curtiss Museum of Hammondsport)

Curtiss School at North Island after a 70 mph storm in March 1912. (source: Glenn H. Curtiss Museum of Hammondsport)

A catapult launching at the Washington Navy Yard on 12 November 1912. (source: Glenn H. Curtiss Museum of Hammondsport)

landed on water. On the morning of 12 July Ellyson took up Towers in the A-1 that had been rigged with three wheels (Triad) for land use. Four short flights were made in order to introduce Towers to the sensation of flying.

Lieutenants Ellyson, Rodgers, and Towers were ordered to Annapolis, MD, along with their mechanics and aircraft, on 23 August 1911. On 7 September 1911 the first naval aviation unit was organized and an aviation camp established at Greenbury Point on Government land near Annapolis. The camp was at the site of the Engineering Experiment Station commanded by Captain T.W. Kinkaid. Lieutenant Ellyson was in command, but Lieutenant Rodgers (Naval Aviator No. 2) was the first to arrive with the Wright B-1 in packing crates. The airplane was quickly assembled in Dahlgren Hall on the Academy grounds. When the airplane was fully assembled Lieutenant Rodgers made the first flight at Annapolis from Farragut Field. After warming up the engine, Lieutenant Rodgers made an uneventful ascent and stayed airborne for approximately fifteen minutes. Lieutenant Ellyson didn't arrive at Annapolis until 4 October, as he had taken leave to participate in an air meet in Brooklyn. For the first time the entire naval air element—two officers qualified as pilots, one student pilot, and three aircraft—was assembled in one location on Navy ground. One interesting aspect of this field was that the hangar was located right in the line of fire behind the Academy's rifle butts. At one time Lieutenant Ellyson had to order everybody off the field whenever the midshipmen were firing. It was here over the next several years that the original nine Naval Aviators and their crews conducted some extremely important tests. Tests that, in essence, determined the entire future of Naval Aviation.

Also, on 7 September 1911 the first naval seaplane was flown off a suspended cable, Lieutenant Ellyson acting as pilot when, at Hammondsport, NY, he made a successful takeoff from an inclined wire rigged from the beach down to the water. A brief explanation is perhaps in order here. The Ely demonstration off of the *Pennsyl-*

A catapult launching at the Washington Navy Yard on 12 November 1912. (source: Glenn H. Curtiss Museum of Hammondsport)

1912 crash of machine piloted by Roy Geiger which, on landing, ran off the field into Keuka Lake at Hammondsport. (source: Glenn H. Curtiss Museum of Hammondsport)

The U.S. Navy A-2, remodeled to O.W.L. configuration and designated E-1, when fited with the new float "hull" designed by Constructor Holden Richardson and built and tested at Hammondsport in 1913. Note the 3-blade Paragon propeller. The only identified individual is Holden C. Richardson who is in the right seat of the aircraft. (source: Glenn H. Curtiss Museum of Hammondsport)

The A-2 taxing on the water. (source: Glenn H. Curtiss Museum of Hammondsport)

vania demonstrated the capability of a plane to takeoff from a Navy ship. The problem with Ely's effort was that the deck masked the cruiser's guns, and was obviously unacceptable in light of the infrequent use of a scout at sea. A proposed second approach was the use of a taut wire upon which the plane would be supported and upon which the plane could use as a takeoff surface. The third possibility was that of a catapult—more of which will be discussed shortly. After giving the matter much thought, Lieutenant Ellyson conceived of the idea of launching a hydroplane down a 250 foot long cable, 3/4-inch in diameter, secured at one end to a submerged piling in Lake Keuka and, at the other end, to a 16-foot high tripod on the shore of the lake. In the keel of the pontoon of the plane was cut a 1-inch groove. The plane was held in place on the wire via a toggle, while lateral control was provided by two wires parallel to the main wire on which the wings, outfitted with special fittings, rested. Lieutenant Ellyson's report contained the following description of the run: "The engine was started and run at full speed and then I gave the signal to release the machine...I held the machine on the wire as long as possible as I wanted to be sure that I had enough headway to rise and not run the risk of the machine partly rising and then falling on the wire outside of the groove. Everything happened so quickly and went off so smoothly that I hardly know what happened except that I did have to use the ailerons, and that the machine was so sensitive to their action." Even though the test was successful, Captain Chambers began to have second thoughts about the applicability of such a launching mechanism from a rolling ship at sea. He contacted Naval Constructor Holden Chester Richardson about the concept of the use of a catapult for such takeoffs.

On 10 September 1911 Lieutenant (j.g.) Towers attempted to qualify for his Aero Club of America certificate. Following an unsuccessful attempt he succeeded in making the first of two required flights. The onset of high winds prevented completion of the effort until the 13th. Here again his first attempt was unsuccessful, but he

Ens. Godfrey Chevalier at Pensacola in February 1914. (source: Glenn H. Curtiss Museum of Hammondsport)

Lt.Cdr. Henry C. Mustin, Commanding Officer of the U.S.S. *Mississippi*. Photo was taken at Pensacola in February 1914. (source: Glenn H. Curtiss Museum of Hammondsport)

eventually completed the efforts satisfactorily. On 14 September Towers was issued Aero Certificate No. 62, and became Naval Aviator No. 3.

On 10 October Naval Constructor Richardson reported to Naval Aviation at the Washington Navy Yard. Naval Constructor Richardson was to become the Navy's first engineering and maintenance officer. The first notable long-distance flight by a naval aviator was accomplished on 25 October 1911 by Lieutenant Rodgers, who flew from Annapolis to Washington and then to College Park, MD, from which place he later returned to Annapolis via Baltimore and Havre de Grace. Lieutenants Ellyson and Towers made a memorable record flight over the water of Chesapeake Bay from Annapolis to Fortress Monroe, VA, and return, on 25 October of 1911. After flying 112 miles in 122 minutes the pair was forced down somewhat short of their goal by mechanical problems. Although a failure in part, the flight paved the way for successful durability tests in the ensuing months. On 8 November 1911 Ensign V.D. Herbster reported to Annapolis for flight instruction after having spent some time in France studying aviation developments abroad. His work, after having qualified, consisted of testing the Wright's first hydroplane, which was fitted with the new Burges pontoons.

On 20 December Ensign C.H. Maddox in the A-1, flown by Lieutenant (j.g.) Towers, while over the Severn River conducted the Navy's first airborne wireless transmission experiments. On 29 December the camp at Annapolis was transferred to San Diego on land adjoining the Curtiss camp for the duration of the winter of 1911-1912. Due to the financial institution in place in the Navy at this time, Officers making domestic moves had to pay their own expenses and then be reimbursed. At this time Lieutenant Ellyson was broke. The commanding officer of the air element had to make special arrangements with Captain Chambers in order to follow his command to San Diego from Annapolis, where there were separate facilities for the Wright and the Curtiss machines, necessitated both by the patent infringement suit which had been brought by Wright against Curtiss and the controversy between Lieutenant Ellyson and Lieutenant Rodgers over seniority (Rodgers' commission predated Ellyson's by several months, but Ellyson took the position that the date of pilot qualification was controlling for aviators).

By 25 January the Curtiss Camp at San Diego was set up. At San Diego there was keen competition between the Army and the Navy for flying time. Damage to any aircraft significantly limited available flying time. Lieutenant Ellyson got into a mode of secretly arising before dawn and going to the flying field to get in flying time. Following this practice he would then go back to the Navy camp and come back later, pretending it was his first appearance of the day. On 14 March Lieutenant Ellyson was injured in a crash of the A-2 at North Island. In April the camp was moved back to Annapolis, where tent hangars were again set up fronting the Severn River near the Engineering Experiment Station. Again the Wright and Curtiss camps were kept separate. It was not until 24 May that Lieutenant Ellyson rejoined the other flyers. The first aerial reconnaissance by a U.S. Naval officer occurred on 2 May 1912, when, under the direction of Rear Admiral Bradley A. Fiske, the commander of the 2nd Squadron of the Atlantic Fleet, a plane landed alongside the U.S.S. *Georgia* in Salem harbor. Rear Admiral Fiske was both an early and a strong advocate of naval aviation. As early as the winter of 1910-1911 Fiske was contemplating the concept of an aerial defense of the Philippines using a torpedo carrying aircraft. As Head of the "War Plans Section" of the General Board, U.S. Navy, he originated the idea of a fleet of torpedo carrying aircraft intended to attack and sink both troop ships and landing craft associated with an attack on the Philippines. In April 1912 Fiske applied for a patent on the concept of a torpedo carrying aircraft. The patent was granted in July 1912.

In the spring of 1912 Lieutenant Ellyson demonstrated a double control system devised by Curtiss for the A-1 in seaplane form. For the first time dual instruction could be offered in a seaplane. On 1 July Captain Chambers ordered a new hydroplane and the first flying boat from Curtiss. Later he added another boat from W. Starling Burgess, a Marblehead yacht builder who was building planes under a Wright license. Lieutenant Ellyson, in addition to his duties at Annapolis, then made periodic inspection trips to Hammondsport and Marblehead. The hydro was delivered in October 1912, but

A staged photo of Lt. Victor Hebster at Pensacola in January 1914. Good detail is provided of the Curtiss shoulder yoke control system. (source: Glenn H. Curtiss Museum of Hammondsport)

Burgess missed his delivery date of 1 January 1913 by several months. Eventually these inspection trips so interfered with the instruction Lieutenant Ellyson was giving Isaac (Ike) Dortch and Laurence North (Fuzzy) McNair at Annapolis that he turned the instruction over to Lieutenant (j.g.) Towers. In the fall, when Dortch and McNair were ready for their Aero Club licenses, the Aero Club of America declined to provide observers on the grounds that since these students had been trained only on hydros they were not ready to meet the new Aero Club rule requiring at least one landing on land. On 26 July 1912, in the Wright B-1, Lieutenant Rodgers, with technical assistance by Ensign C.H. Maddox, succeeded in sending wireless messages to the U.S.S. *Stringham* in Chesapeake Bay. Also, on 20 July 1912, the first recorded tests of aircraft structural material were made at Annapolis when Naval Constructor Holden Chester Richardson (Naval Aviator No. 13), in comparative tests, proved that Monel wire was stronger and more corrosive resistant than the Wright steel wire which had been used up to that time.

The first week in August 1912 Lieutenant Rodgers was suddenly sent to nonflying sea duty. Lieutenant Ellyson became the undisputed senior officer and inherited both the incomplete radio and engine tests Lieutenant Rodgers had been doing, as well as the administration of both of the camps.

On 6 October 1912 Lieutenant (j.g.) Towers in a Curtiss A-2 took off from the water at Annapolis at 0650 hrs. and established a new American endurance record for seaplanes by remaining in the air 6 hours and 20 minutes. Lieutenant (j.g.) Towers was also involved in the first work done toward using naval aviation in antisubmarine warfare. Experiments were conducted on the Chesapeake Bay east of Annapolis to determine whether aviators could spot submerged submarines from the air. Lieutenant (j.g.) Towers found that submarines could be seen easily when running anywhere near the surface, and that 800 feet was the best altitude. On 8 October 1912 the Bureau of Medicine and Surgery, in Circular 125221, established for the first time, the physical requirements for perspective naval aviators.

During the year 1912, the following officers were ordered to the naval aviation camp for flying instruction: Naval Constructor Richardson; Lieutenant (j.g.) Godfrey de Courcelles Chevalier (Naval Aviator No. 7 who reported on 25 October); Lieutenant (j.g.) Pat N.L. Bellinger (Naval Aviator No. 8 who reported on 26 November); Ensign W.D. Billingsley (Naval Aviator No. 9 who reported on 2 December); First Lieutenant Alfred A. Cunningham, USMC (Naval Aviator No. 5 and Marine Aviator No. 1 who reported on 22 May); and First Lieutenant Barry L. Smith, USMC (Naval Aviator No. 6 and Marine Aviator No. 2 who reported 18 September 1912). 22 May is celebrated as the Birthday of Marine Corps Aviation. First Lieutenant Cunningham was to receive his initial instruction at the Burgess-Curtiss air factory at Marblehead Massachusetts. He was to solo after two hours, 40 minutes of training, and, in a long and illustrious career among many other things, made the first takeoff using a compressed air catapult from a battleship underway. First Lieutenant Smith eventually became a pioneer in aerial bombing. Lieutenant (j.g.) Chevalier was to become famous in Naval Aviation history for both the development of the first landing deck gear and for making the first carrier landing in the U.S. Navy. During the year four additional aircraft were ac-

Lt.(j.g.) Melvin L. Stolz at Pensacola in February 1914. Stolz was killed in the crash of AH-9 at Pensacola on 8 May 1915. (source: Glenn H. Curtiss Museum of Hammondsport)

quired; and one, the A-1, was expended. Ensign Billingsley would be assigned the Wright B-2, in the subsequent crash of which he would become the first fatality of Naval Aviation.

The year 1912 saw the invention by the Navy of the compressed gas aircraft catapult. In January Captain Chambers, after having written both to Curtiss and to Orville Wright concerning the practicality of the catapult launching of an airplane, wrote to Curtiss on the concept of a catapult launch as opposed to a wire launch mechanism. Naval Constructor Richardson, under the supervision of Captain Chambers, designed the first catapult at the Naval Gun Factory, Washington D.C. The first shot that was attempted, with Lieutenant Ellyson as pilot in the Curtiss A-1 Triad from the Santee Dock at the Academy on 31 July 1912, at 1100 hrs, proved unsuccessful, as the aircraft lifted off prematurely and became caught in a cross-wind. Lieutenant Ellyson, who usually wore greasy overalls for flight testing, had been forced to wear his Naval uniform by the Superintendent of the Academy, Captain Gibbons, for this test, since the Santee Dock was inside the grounds of the Academy, and "all officers had to establish a proper image with the midshipmen by wearing the uniform of the day." The Triad ended up upside down in the Severn River. The redesign of the catapult was assigned to Naval Constructor Richardson (Naval Academy Class of 1901). Lieutenant Ellyson, in Curtiss hydroplane AH-3, was successfully catapulted from this second catapult on 12 October 1912. This feat was accomplished from a barge at the Washington Navy Yard. Curtiss, who viewed this test, has been quoted as stating "This device is the most important achievement since wheels were put on land machines." On 30 November 1912 Lieutenant Ellyson tested the Navy's first flying boat, the C-1, at Hammondsport. Lieutenant Ellyson flew the C-1 from the catapult on 17 December. Even though the demonstrations were successful, the catapult would not be mounted aboard a ship until 1915.

Another important naval aviation accomplishment which occurred in 1912 was the construction of the United States Navy Aerodynamical Laboratory at the Washington Navy Yard. This aerodynamical laboratory, or wind tunnel, was constructed under the supervision of Naval Constructor David W. Taylor in order to provide a means for determining the engineering basis for the design of naval aircraft and was the first wind tunnel of modern type to be built in the United States. It is of interest to observe Naval Constructor Taylor's foresight and enterprise in providing, immediately after the purchase of the Navy's first seaplane in 1911, the scientific apparatus for its analysis and improvement. This wind tunnel was then, and remained for many years thereafter, the largest and most powerful in the world.

During 1912 Naval Constructor Richardson conducted a series of model basin tests on the planing properties of seaplane floats and hulls. Richardson for the first time showed the effect of the form of the float on its water performance, and from these tests he evolved the lines of the United States Navy seaplane floats and hulls, which since that date made them a standard for others to follow. Richardson's tests showed the advantages of Vee bottom, long easy form, spray stripes, and single step with a sharp rise of after body. Naval Constructor J.C. Hunsaker was sent to Europe during the summer of this year to make a study of European aviation. He was then ordered to the Massachusetts Institute of Technology, where he installed a wind tunnel and where a course in aeronautical engineering was established under his supervision.

In 1913 Lieutenant (j.g.) G.D. Murray, USN (Naval Aviator No. 22), Second Lieutenant William McIlvaine, USMC (Naval Aviator No. 12 and Marine Aviator No. 3), Lieutenant (j.g.) Saufley (Naval Aviator No. 14), Lieutenant (j.g.) M.L. Stolz, and Ensign W.D. La Mont joined the ranks of naval aviators. In addition, Lt. Alfred Cunningham, who had joined the Naval Aviation Camp at Annapolis on 22 May 1912, had soloed on 1 August, and was designated a Naval Aviator on 5 March 1913.

Air operations in the fleet were inaugurated on 6 January 1913 when the entire naval aviation detachment was transported by the Navy colliers U.S.S. *Cyclops* and *Orion* to Guantanamo for its first operation with the fleet. The purpose of this exercise was "to familiarize the officers and men of the fleet with the peculiarities of the machines and to enable as many as could be spared to obtain instruction (as aviators)." The Cuban camp, located at Fisherman's Point, was commanded by Lieutenant (j.g.) J.H. Towers and subject to orders from the commander in chief of the fleet. Pilots included Lieutenants (j.g.). J.M. Murray, Saufly, Belinger, and Stolz, and Ensigns La Mont and Chevalier. The air element remained here for eight weeks. Numerous interesting and practical tests were made of the employment of planes in cooperation with ships, and many of the fleet officers became more or less familiar with aviation. At this time several notable flights were made along the Cuban coast, and the usefulness of aircraft as scouts in discovering the approach of a distant fleet and in detecting mine fields and submerged submarines was amply and practically demonstrated. Such activities served to demonstrate the operational capabilities of the aircraft and to stimulate an interest in aviation among the personnel. During the eight weeks in Cuba more than 100 fleet personnel were given flights. With the return of the fleet to the United States after these winter maneuvers, the aviation detachment was transferred

Aviators of the regular Navy and Marine Corps at Pensacola in 1914. Back row (left to right): R.R. Paunack, E.W. Spenser, H.T. Bartlett, Edwards, C.K. Bronson, W.M. Corry, J.P. Norfleet, E.O. McDonnell, and H.W. Schofield. Seated (left to right): R.C. Saufley, P.N. Bellinger, K. Whiting, Commander H.C. Mustin, A.C.Read, E,F, Johnson, A.A. Cunningham, F.T. Evans, and Haas. Note that Haas was assigned to aviation, but is not identified as a naval aviator).

back to Annapolis again in mid-March and continued under the command of Towers.

On 4 March 1913 Congress passed the Naval Appropriations Act for fiscal 1914. Significant aspects of the Act were: 1) the establishment of a 35% bonus for qualified aviators as flight pay; 2) a limit of 30 men to receive flight pay; and 3) a stipulation that no officer above the rank of Lieutenant Commander in the Navy or Major in the Marine Corps was to fly. Lt. (j.g.) Towers, while at Guantanamo, worked on the senior officers of the Atlantic Fleet to develop an interest and appreciation for aviation. One of his biggest skeptics was R.Adm. Charles J. Badger, the Fleet Commander. With the growing unrest in Mexico, Towers was able to convince Lieutenant Commander. Henry C. Mustin, the Executive Officer of the cruiser U.S.S. *Minnesota*, of the ability of aviation to perform scouting duties for the fleet. On 6 March 1913 Adm. Badger ordered Towers to prepare for the aerial search for a "hostile fleet"—the first tactical maneuver involving aircraft of the U.S. Navy. Towers and Chevalier, in the C-1, were successful in their effort.[2]

On 10 April 1913 performance standards for qualification as a "Navy Air Pilot" were determined for the first time, and issuance of a certificate to all officers qualifying was approved by the Secretary of the Navy. The requirements were different from those of a land pilot and more exacting than those of the F.A.I., but no one pointed out that qualification as a pilot had no Navy recognition up to this point, and that some official evidence of qualification was needed to collect the flight pay authorized the previous month.[3] On 29 April 1913 "Spuds" Ellyson was detailed from naval aviation for sea duty. He would not return until January 1921. The reason for his departure, as with that associated with Lieutenant Rodgers in August 1912, lay with the naval policy that promotion depended to a great extent on time at sea. Command of an aviation unit did not count toward promotion.

On 12 June the Secretary of the Navy approved the assignment of Assistant Naval Constructor Hunaker to M.I.T. to develop a course of lectures and experiments on the design of aeroplanes and dirigibles and to undertake research in this field. On 13 June of this year Lieutenant (j.g.) Bellinger achieved a world's seaplane record for altitude by ascending to 6,200 feet in 45 minutes in a Curtiss A-2 seaplane. First Lieutenant Smith, USMC, by starting from the water, alighting on the land, and then returning to the water, made the first successful flight in an amphibian in the summer of 1913. June also saw the first fatality in Naval Aviation history when, on the 20th, Ensign Billingsley, who was piloting the Wright B-2 with Lieutenant (j.g.) Towers as a passenger, was thrown from the aircraft due to turbulence and fell some 1200 feet to the water below. Towers managed to hang on to the airplane and stayed with it all the way to the water, suffering serious injuries. This incident provided the impetus for the requirement of safety belts on all Navy aircraft. General Order No. 41 of 23 June 1913 fixed the cognizance of the various Bureaus in aeronautical matters. To Construction and Repair it allocated responsibility for airframes; to Steam Engineering went power plants; and to Navigation went instruments and flight clothing.

Prior to his accident, Lieutenant (j.g.) Towers had also made the first night landings and takeoffs from the Severn River, using buckets of burning gasoline in rowboats to guide him to his landing area. During those early years at Annapolis, the first autopilot was designed, as was the first airspeed indicator and the electric stabilizer, as well as other navigational instruments. Unfortunately, none of them were really developed due to a lack of funds.

Without any warning, on 1 July 1913 Adm. Bradly Fiske retired Capt. Chambers from active duty. This was apparently done "in order to infuse new blood" into the system. However, with Towers on medical leave, there was no one knowledgeable enough to replace Chambers. This, plus the fact that there were no naval aviators of rank comparable to Capt. Chambers, forced Adm. Fiske to keep Chambers in the position of being in charge of naval aviation, even though retired.[4]

In order to provide some specific details on the tenuous conditions in which naval aviation functioned in these days, the following excerpt is quoted from a 25 July 1913 letter from Alfred A. Cunningham at the Naval Aviation Camp at Annapolis to Captain Chambers: "My machine, as I told you and as Mr. Towers probably told you, is not in my opinion fit for use. I built it from parts of the Burgess F and Wright B, which are not exactly alike and nothing fitted. Had to cut off and patch up parts and bore additional holes in beams in order to make them fit. The engine bed, made by Burgess, was not exactly square with the front beam, so the engine had to be mounted a little out of true (with reference to the engine bed). I have made over two hundred flights in this machine and recently, in spite of unusual care of men and myself something seems to vibrate loose or off a majority of the flights made. One of the propeller shafts is the same one used with the Gyro motor in the old machine. It is the only left-hand shaft here. While the engine runs smoothly, it does not deliver nearly as much power as when it was newer, and even then, it did not have enough power to fly safely in any but smooth weather. It is impossible to climb over a few hundred feet with a passenger. The whole machine has just about served its usefulness, and I would like very much to have a new machine of the single propeller type. Lieutenant Arnold, of the Army, after seeing the machine run and examining it, said that none of the Army

Lt. P.N.L. Bellinger in a Curtiss single-seater at Pensacola in 1915. Note that the trim indicator consists of a string tied to a mast mounted on the foreward part of the float. (source: Glenn H. Curtiss Museum of Hammondsport)

flyers would go up in it. Will you kindly let me know what the prospects are for my getting a new machine."

On 30 August 1913 the General Board recommended the establishment of an Air Department in the Navy. It opined that the "organization of an efficient naval air service should be immediately taken in hand and pushed to fulfillment." This is apparently the first proposal that aviation be given official status. Also, on 30 August 1913, Lieutenant (j.g.) Bellinger, in the C-2 Flying Boat at Hammondsport, conducted the initial test of the Speery gyroscopic stabilizer, or automatic pilot. These tests were the results of a proposal, approved on 28 April by Rear Admiral Victor Blue of the Bureau of Navigation, that Curtiss and the Sperry Company cooperate in testing a gyroscopic stabilizer on a Navy plane.

On 7 October 1913, Assistant Secretary of the Navy Franklin D. Roosevelt appointed a Board of Aeronautics. Its charter was both to report on the needs of a suitable aeronautical organization and establishment for the Navy, and to prepare a comprehensive plan for the organization of a Naval Aeronautical Service. Capt. W.I. Chambers, as senior member, was made Chairman of the Board, with other members being Lieutenant (j.g.) J.H. Towers, Naval Constructor H.C. Richardson, First Lieutenant Alfred A. Cunningham, Commander Carlo B. Briltan (Bureau of Navigation), Commander S.S. Robinson (Bureau of Stean Engineering), and Lieutenant Manley H. Simons (Bureau of Ordnance). After 12 days of deliberation the board, in outlining a policy of development, made a number of recommendations: 1) 50 planes for the fleet and six planes for shore bases; 2) Dirigibles to be regarded as non-essential (to be used for purposes for which the airplane is currently unfit, a dirigible should be purchased for evaluation; 3) A flying school to be established at Pensacola; 4) The Washington Navy Yard Laboratory, in cooperation with the Model Basin at the proposed national laboratory, to be used for research in the field of aerodynamics; and 5) An Office of Naval Aeronautics to be established. With respect to recommendation number 1 the Board foresaw the need for every first line naval ship to have assigned to it an airplane. Of these recommendations one of the most important was that for the establishment of an aviation station at Pensacola, Florida. This recommendation was approved. One of the most prophetic recommendations from this Board was that special ships for aeroplanes and other types of flying machines should be considered, but not in the immediate future.

On 17 December 1913, Captain Chambers was relieved of his duties in charge of naval aviation activities by Captain Mark L. Bristol. Captain Chambers had come due for promotion, and even though his duties associated with aviation had been performed under special orders, it was determined that his ashore time did not qualify as sufficient sea service. He was therefore placed on the involuntarily retired list. One stated reason for Captain Chambers' dismissal, as given by Rear Admiral Fiske, was the perception that Captain Chambers was more interested in developing the aeroplane than he was in developing an aeronautical service. There is some suspicion here that this decision was taken by Naval officials who did not perceive the importance of air power in the same light as did Captain Chambers and felt their position/organization threatened by his advocacy of aviation.

1914 saw the Bureau of Aeronautics formed, the first employment of naval aviation in active service, and the establishment by Congress of a naval air militia (April 1914). Meanwhile, work at Pensacola continued, with Lieutenants Smith and McIlvain of the Marine Corps conducting spotting and bombing tests off Culebra, Puerto Rico, using a flying boat and an amphibian. During 1914 additional officers were assigned to aviation duty in the following sequence: Ensigns C.K. Bronson (Naval Aviator No. 15) and W.A. Edwards, Lieutenant Kenneth Whiting (Naval Aviator No. 16), Lieutenant Maxfield (Naval Aviator No. 71), and Ensigns E.O. McDonnel (Naval Aviator No. 18), Wadleigh Capehart, E.W. Spencer (Naval Aviator No. 20), H.T. Bartlett (Naval Aviator No. 21), and G.D. Murray (Naval Aviator No. 22). Classes were then ordered more or less regularly until the entry of the U.S. in the war. And 1914 heard Josephus Daniels, the Secretary of the Navy, announce that "the science of aerial navigation has reached the point where aircraft must form a large part of our naval force for offensive and defensive operations."

On 7 January 1914 Captain Bristol moved from the Bureau of Navigation to the Division of Operations, headed by Rear Admiral Fiske, who was directly responsible to the Secretary of the Navy. On 20 January 1914, the first United States Navy Air Station was established on the site of the abandoned navy yard at Pensacola, FL. At the same time, the Annapolis aviation camp was broken up, and all aviation personnel—nine officers, 23 men, seven aircraft, portable hangars, and other equipment were transferred to the cruiser U.S.S. *Mississippi,* commanded by Lieutenant Commander H.C. Muslin, and the *Orion*, which were ordered to Pensacola. Upon arrival the *Mississippi* was turned over to naval aviation in order that aviation might keep in touch with ships. Lieutenant Commander Mustin (Naval Aviator No. 11) was assigned to aviation and became the first commanding officer of the Pensacola Air Station, with direction from Captain Bristol "to plan the aeronautic station with the future in mind." Lieutenant (j.g.) Towers and Ensign Chevalier made the first flight from the station on 2 February, just 13 days after their arrival at Pensacola. The flight-training program at the station was informal, although in the next three years some progress was made toward developing a formal curriculum. Personnel were assigned individually, rather than in groups. In consequence, training was sporadic, and although men assigned in the summer of 1915 were generally considered the first class at Pensacola, the station still lacked the formality of class organization. Ground school for prospective pilots stressed the technical aspects of aviation, but, because all the students were Annapolis graduates, omitted entirely such subjects as navigation and fundamentals of seamanship. These courses were added later when officers were recruited from civilian status.

February saw the first death of a naval aviator at Pensacola when on the 16th Lieutenant (j.g.) J. McCurray was killed at 1600 hrs. in the crash of his Burgess D-1 flying boat. McCurray was posthumously awarded the designation of Naval Aviator No. 10. On 17 February 1914 Lieutenant (j.g.) Towers was ordered, by Captain Mark Bristol, to discuss with Glenn Curtiss the concept of building a plane designed to fly the Atlantic. The beginning of hostilities in Europe virtually ended the original purpose of the machine. However, it was realized that the design had military potential. The eventual design (called the "America"), after being shipped to England where it was to be modified by the British, became the F-5. The seed of Aviation Medicine was planted in a 20 February letter to the Commanding Officer at Pensacola on the subject of physical requirements for aviator candidates. The opinion was laid down that useful information could be obtained by observing pilots during flights and by physical examination both prior to and following flights. The letter directed that such a program be developed.[5]

On 27 March 1914, in General Order No. 88, the designation of naval aircraft was established as two letters and a number, of which the first letter denoted class, the second the type within a class, and the number the order in which the aircraft within a class was acquired. Four Classes were set up: "A" for all heavier-than-air; "D" for airships and dirigibles; "B" for balloons; and "K" for Kites. Within the A Class the letters "L," "H," 'IBI," "X," and "C" represented land planes, hydroplanes, flying boats, combination land and water machines, and convertibles, respectively.

On 18 April, Lieutenants (j.g.) Towers and Bellinger, the Navy's observers at Curtiss' Hammondsport facility during the construction of the flying boat to be used by Rodman Wanamaker for the London Daily Mail transatlantic flight prize, were recalled. On 19 April 1914, a U.S. aviation unit was first called into action with the Fleet. At noon orders were received for duty in Mexican waters. Within six hours the planes, parts, crews, and equipment were on the dock alongside the U.S.S. *Birmingham*. Twenty-four hours after receiving orders, the unit, commanded by Lieutenant (j.g.) John H. Towers and consisting of three pilots (Towers, Smith, and Chevalier), 12 enlisted men, and three aircraft (two Curtiss flying boats and a Curtiss hydroplane) sailed from Pensacola aboard the *Birmingham* to join Atlantic Fleet forces operating off Tampico in the Mexican crisis. The next day, a second aviation detachment, commanded by Bellinger—one pilot (Bellinger), three student pilots (Saufley, La Mont, and Stolz), and two aircraft (One hydroplane and one flying boat)—also from Pensacola, embarked in the U.S.S. *Mississippi* upon the same mission, but this time to Vera Cruz. She arrived at Vera Cruz on 25 April, and within five minutes of dropping anchor a plane (AB-3) was in the air for observation of the city and mine searching activities. On 28 April Lieutenant (j.g.) Bellinger and Ensign La Mont, in the AB-3, photographed the harbor at Vera Cruz. The machines commanded by Towers and Bellinger thus became the first planes to be used by the Navy in a combat operational situation.

On 2 May Lieutenant (j.g.) Bellinger, with Ensign LaMont as observer, flew the AH-3 hydroaeroplane in the Navy's first mission in direct support of ground troops when requested by the Marines who were under attack near Tejar.[6] In the vicinity of Vera Cruz on 6 May, the Curtiss AH-3 hydroplane, piloted by Bellinger, with Saufley as observer, was hit by rifle fire while making a reconnaissance flight over enemy positions—the first marks of combat on a Navy plane. The two airplanes at Vera Cruz were used continually, and although these planes were not fitted for land work, for 43 days they did considerable reconnoitering over the trenches protecting the city of Vera Cruz. Other missions included searching for mines

Lt.(j.g.) P.N.L. Bellinger, in the AB-2, being catapulted from a barge in Pensacola Bay on 16 April 1915.

and photographing the harbor of Vera Cruz. To every call made upon them, the naval aviators attached to the cruiser *Mississippi* made ready and cheerful response, and their scout work in the air was of much value in the combined Army and Navy operations at Vera Cruz. On 24 May the aero detachment aboard the cruiser *Birmingham* arrived at Vera Cruz to join that aboard the *Mississippi* in routine school flight instruction. In the summer of 1914, the *Mississippi* was relieved by the cruiser U.S.S. *North Carolina* as the naval aviation ship, the Government having sold the former ship to Greece. While the contingents were gone the Bureau of Navigation, on 22 April, approved the formal course of instruction for student aviators and student mechanics at Pensacola. On 15 May, Clifford Webster, factory pilot of the Burgess-Dunne Company, gave rides in the Burgess-Dunne 1B to Lieutenant (j.g.) Herbster and Naval Constructor Richardson. Richardson was sufficiently impressed with the performance of the IB that he recommended to the Navy Department that two Burgess-Dunne's be purchased "as it appears to be only the beginning of an important development in aeronautical design."

Upon the Navy's return from Mexican waters Lieutenant (j.g.) Herbster and First Lieutenant Smith conducted experiments at Pensacola in bombing. Their conclusion was that there was a need for better bombs (a design to stop tumbling of the bomb), better sights (a reliable lightweight mechanism), and a better release mechanism (at this time the bombardier had to have his left arm secured to the plane so as to prevent falling out of the plane while he released the bomb with his right hand). In June 1914, the Navy Department once again ordered Lieutenant (j.g.) Towers to Hammondsport for duty in connection with the construction and proposed flight to Europe of the twin-engined seaplane *America*, with the understanding that he would be permitted to participate in that flight if success seemed feasible. The *America* marked the beginning of big flying boat development by the Navy. In June the Bureau of Navigation issued the first formal training syllabus for naval pilots.

The first formal recognition of Naval Aviation was the establishment of an Office of Naval Aeronautics in the Division of Operations, under the Secretary of the Navy, on 1 July 1914.[7] By the

28th of July, Lieutenant (j.g.) Herbster and First Lieutenant Smith had moved their bombing experiments to the Indian Head Proving Ground at Stumpneck, Maryland. At this point naval aviation suffered a serious setback. The war in Europe broke out, and the cruiser U.S.S. *North Carolina*, commanded by Lieutenant Commander Mustin, with its complement of aviation officers and men, augmented by other naval personnel, was ordered to Europe (Chevaliers, McIlvain, and Bronson were left at Pensacola). The ship remained in Europe until the summer of 1915, performing various duties in connection with the relief of Americans there. While in France, Mustin, with Lieutenant (j.g.) Bellinger and First Lieutenant Smith, took the time, on 21 August, to compare French designs with the American designs. His 2-day comparison was not favorable to the U.S. designs. In addition, in September Lieutenant (j.g.) Towers was ordered as assistant Naval Attaché, London, and Lieutenant (j.g.) Herbster and First Lieutenant Smith to Berlin and Paris, respectively, for the same duties. This was the first use of Naval Aviators as observers in foreign lands and was the precedent for the assignment of naval personnel as Naval Attachés. Work at Pensacola was brought practically to a standstill for many months. Also in September, the official title of Director of Naval Aviation was assigned. Captain Bristol, who was performing this function, was designated on 23 September.

The overall command of the Flying School at Pensacola was shifted from the Station Ship *Mississippi* to a Headquarters ashore.[8] With this reorganization, Pensacola, on 16 November, however, became finally known as a Naval Aeronautic Station. Lieutenant Kenneth Whiting took command at Pensacola in late 1914. On 23 November 1914 Captain Bristol became officially "Director of Naval Aeronautics." Under this new title he reported directly to the Secretary of the Navy.

During 1915 the first Navy designed seaplane was built at the Washington Navy Yard. Naval Constructor H.C. Richardson designed this plane. During the year Lieutenant Commander Mustin became commandant at Pensacola when the station was again administratively reorganized. One of the early proposals put forth by Captain Bristol was the establishment of coastal patrol stations at Narragansatt, the Chesapeake, Guantanamo, Panama, San Francisco, Hawaii, and Manilla. No action was to be taken on this recommendation, or similar recommendations, for several years. In 1915 the Coast Guard became interested in the use of aircraft to locate ships in distress. Lieutenant Elmer F. Stone of the Coast Guard was sent to Pensacola for flight training (becoming eventually Naval Aviator No. 38), and Lieutenant Norman B. Hall of the Coast Guard was sent to Hammondsport for technical instruction. Also, in 1915, by congressional action, the Office of the Chief of Naval Operations was created. This action had a direct impact on the General Board of the Navy, as the new entity assumed many responsibilities previously endowed to the Board. In effect, the General Board became the consultative body on matters of general policy for use by the Navy Department at its discretion.

On 9 January 1915, the Aide for Operations, Rear Admiral Fiske, called attention to the fact that although the Secretary's order to issue "Navy Air Pilot" certificates was over a year and a half old, none had been issued for the simple reason that there were no officers qualified to sit in judgement on the applicants. He then recommended that the qualifications of seven officers be recognized and that they be issued certificates, and thus be made eligible to judge the qualifications of the others. Those he recommended were: Ellyson, Towers, Mustin, Bellinger, Herbster, Smith, and Chevalier, who were subsequently issued Certificates numbered One through Seven, with dates ranging after the 1 January 1914 assigned to Ellyson.[9]

The Division of Naval Militia Affairs in the Bureau of Navigation directed, on 1 February 1915, that an aeronautic corps be organized in each of the State Naval Militia. And, on 22 March, the title of Naval Aviator replaced the former Navy Air Pilot. Congress, in the Naval Appropriations Act for fiscal 1916 (passed on 3 March 1915), appropriated $1,000,000 for Naval Aviation, established, in a rider to the authorization, the National Advisory Committee for Aeronautics (NACA), modified flight pay for aviators, and, over the objection of the Secretary of the Navy, provided for the establishment of the Office of Chief of Naval Operation. The NACA was to consist of two Navy men, two men from the War Department, one man each from the Smithsonian, the Weather Bureau, and the Bureau of Standards, and five civilians. Flight pay, which up to this time had been assigned only to those qualified officers directly involved in flying and hence ignored student pilots, qualified pilots performing desk functions, and flying enlisted men was established at 50% for all qualified pilots and enlisted men (flight pay was now to be allotted to 48 officers and 96 enlisted men of the Navy and 12 officers and 24 men of the Marine Corps). On 22 March the title "Naval Aviator" replaced the former "Naval Air Pilot" designation for qualified pilots. This change was necessary to make the designation consistent with the wording of the 1916 Appropriations Act, which used the word "aviator" in place of "pilot." It would, however, be an additional three years before they would be ranked according to the date on which they received their license.

In April 1915 Lieutenant Warren G. Child was detailed to the Bureau of Steam Engineering to specialize in the development of aircraft motors. On 16 April 1915 the AB-2 Flying Boat, flown by Lieutenant (j.g.) Bellinger, was successfully catapulted from a barge in Pensacola Bay. It was the first such launching by the U.S. Navy of a Flying Boat. A week later, on 23 April, the same pilot established an American altitude record for seaplanes by ascending to 10,000 ft. in the Burgess-Dunne AH-10. On 28 May the Naval Militia was informed that refresher flight training at Pensacola was available for a limited number of its aviators.

On 1 June 1915, the Navy bought its first airship, the "DN-l," from the Connecticut Aircraft Company of New Haven, CT, for $45,636.25. Also on 1 June 1915, Lieutenant Frank R. McCrary was told by Captain Bristol to devote full time to Lighter-than-Air activities. McCrary hence became the inspector for the Navy for the construction of the DN-1. Also in June, General Order No. 133 was issued, which authorized the loan of Navy planes to naval militia units. Nothing was to be done in this area for over a year, when the Naval Appropriations of 1916 was authorized.

In July the first new class at Pensacola consisted of eight Navy and two Marine officers reporting for flight training, plus 20 Navy and Marine enlisted men reporting for ground work training. On 1 July 1915 the Office of Naval Aeronautics came under the cognizance of Admiral W.E. Benson, the Chief of Naval Operations. Admiral Benson, an old "blue-water sailor," replaced the Aide for Operations, Rear Admiral Fiske, when the Office of Chief of Naval Operations was created. Rear Admiral Fiske left Washington on 1 July to become President of the Naval War College at Newport. With this transfer naval aviation lost an advocate who as early as 12 April 1911 was suggesting naval air stations, each to support 100 planes, on Luzon in the Philippines, and gained a sailor whose perspective on aviation was "a plane should be viewed in the same light as any other ship!"

On 22 July 1915 the Director of Naval Aeronautics established the following instrument allowance for each Navy plane: airspeed, incidence indicator, tachometer, skidding and side slipping meter, altitude barometer, oil gauge, fuel gauge, compass, course and distance indicator, magazine camera, binoculars, clock, and sextant. All except the navigational instruments, camera, binoculars, and clock were also required for school machines.

In 1915 the Naval Observatory became involved with aviation when, on 11 August, it requested the Eastman Kodak Co. to develop an aerial camera. The specifications called for a camera with a high-speed lens, suitable for photography at 1000 to 2000 yard altitudes, and so constructed that the pressure of the air during flight would not distort the camera. On 10 January 1917 the first production order for aerial photographic equipment was initiated by the Observatory, with Kodak, for 20 aerial cameras and accessories.[10]

On 12 October 1915 a directive was issued that abolished the Office of Naval Aeronautics, returning most of its functions to the Bureaus, and transferring the remainder to the Material Branch of CNO (U.S. Navy Dept. Office of the Secretary, Directive, 12 October 1915), headed by Captain Josiah S. McKean. Aeronautics, so far as it had any central direction, came under a Lieutenant Junior Grade (Clarence K. Bronson) who became an assistant in Captain McKean's Office. The move effectively removed from the "Director" of Naval Aviation all real planning functions and all real authority. In a Memorandum to the Navy Department dated 12 October 1915 the Secretary of the Navy specified:

1. There shall be an Officer in Charge of Naval Aeronautics under the Chief of Naval Operations.

2. This officer will submit to the Chief of Naval Operations (Materials), as required, the types, numbers, and general characteristics of aircraft desired for the naval service, and, after conference with the technical bureaus concerned as to the practicability of desired characteristics, the Chief of Naval Operations will recommend to the Secretary of the Navy a program in this connection.

3. Upon approval by the Secretary of the Navy this program will be forwarded to the various bureaus and offices of the Navy Department concerned. They will carry into effect such work as comes under their cognizance in accordance with the provisions of General Order No. 41, of June 23, 1913, which General Order is hereby made to apply to all types of aircraft. In planning experimental and research work the advice of the National Advisory Committee for Aeronautics shall be obtained.

4. Funds appropriated under title "Aeronautics, 1916" will be allotted by the Secretary of the Navy for expenditure upon approved requests submitted by the bureaus and aeronautical stations through the bureaus engaged in aeronautical work. One copy of all statements of the status of the appropriation "Aeronautics" and of allotments or expenditures thereunder shall be sent direct to the Officer in Charge of Naval Aeronautics.

5. Correspondence intended for the Officer in Charge of Naval Aeronautics shall be addressed "Navy Department (Aeronautics)," and in accordance with Naval Instructions I 35 (3), P A S shall be the abbreviation for the Aeronautic Station, Pensacola.

The changes, however, only became effective when Captain Bristol was detached to sea duty.

As noted earlier, the Navy's Aeronautic Detachment was transferred in 1914 from Annapolis to Pensacola. Aboard the cruiser *Mississippi* when she arrived at Pensacola was the catapult designed by Lieutenant Commander Richardson and used in the experiments at the Washington Navy Yard. Because of a number of circumstances, not the least of which were the intervention in Mexico and the fact that the primary charter of the Detachment was that of training future aviators, nothing was done with the catapult. In 1915, however, Lieutenant Commander Mustin assigned W.M. Fellers to redesign the catapult. The modified catapult was placed aboard the armored cruiser U.S.S. *North Carolina* during the summer of 1915. On 5 November 1915 Commandant Mustin, in the AB-2 Flying Boat, made the first catapult launching from a ship underway, flying off the stern of the *North Carolina* in Pensacola Bay. The next day Naval Constructor Richardson and Lieutenant (j.g.) Bellinger made similar launches. The catapult tests were ended on the 8th when First Lieutenant Cunningham crashed and was injured as a result of a failure of the catapult system. Cunningham thus became the first Marine Corps Aviation casualty.

On 3 December 1915, Lieutenant (j.g.) Saufley, flying the Curtiss AH-14, set an American altitude record for hydroplanes, reaching 11,975 feet over Pensacola and surpassing his own record of 11,056 feet which he had set only three days before. In this year Saufley ascended to an altitude of 14,500 feet in a Curtiss seaplane, and shortly afterwards made an endurance record of 8 hours and 20 minutes in the same type of plane.

In the early part of 1916, the aviation ship *North Carolina*, with five planes abroad, operated with the fleet during the winter maneuvers based on Guantanamo. An attempt was made in 1916 to establish a combined experimental station for the Army, the Navy, and the NACA at Langley Field, VA, but as this field was unsuitable for naval purposes because of the lack of deep-water access for ships, the project was abandoned.

On 6 January 1916 instruction began for the first group of enlisted men at Pensacola to receive flight training. They were: P.J. Dunleavy, CBM; E. Grompe, CMAA; A.A. Bressman, CTC (Naval Aviator No. 44); L.A. Welty, CTC; A. Hayes, CTC (Naval Aviator No. 609); A.P. Bauer, GMlc; J. Markolin, 1st Sgt., USMC; W.E. McCaughtry, Gun.Sgt., USMC (Naval Aviator No. 1310); and later, A.F. Dietrich, BM2c (Naval Aviator No. 90 1/2).[11]

On 10 February orders were issued implementing serial numbers on all Navy planes until the aircraft were tested or placed in service, at which time the standard designations provided by the Order of 27 March 1914 were to be used. This is the introduction of serial numbers henceforth assigned to all aircraft.[12] On 25 February 1916 orders were requested for Captain Bristol, which detached him for duty with the Fleet as Commanding Officer aboard the *North Carolina*.

On 1 March 1916 Captain Bristol was relieved from his duties in the Bureau of Navigation, and the direction of aviation activities, as noted above, was transferred to the Office of the Chief of Naval Operations, where an aviation desk was placed under the Aide for Material. Captain Bristol formerly ceased functioning as the Director of Naval Aviation on 4 March 1916. As part of the reassignment of responsibilities the title of Director of Naval Aviation was abolished. Aviation work was moved from its separate office on the first floor of the State, War, and Navy Building, and was officially and physically incorporated in the Bureau of Material. As noted above, Lieutenant Bronson (Naval Aviator No. 15) filled this newly created position. He continued in the capacity until November 1916, at which time his death occurred from an aviation accident at Indianhead. Lieutenant (j.g.) Towers was then assigned as assistant for aviation in the office of the Chief of Naval Operations, and this officer was occupying this position when the United States declared war against Germany on April 6, 1917. Captain Bristol, as well as being assigned the command of the *North Carolina*, was given supervision, not only of all aircraft and aircraft stations, but also the further development of aeronautics. Before he left his post as Director of Naval Aeronautics, Captain Bristol took some rather significant actions: 1) He ordered Lieutenant Commander Mustin at Pensacola to select eight Petty Officers and two Sergeants from the Marine Corps for flight instruction, 2) He requested that the special aviation rating for enlisted men be established on a permanent basis; 3) He insisted that more orders be placed with domestic manufacturers in order both to keep their factories busy and to increase the technology of aviation in the U.S.; 4) He saw to it that the Navy started work on bigger planes; and 5) He adopted the double Deperdussin control for all Navy planes. On this last item he subsequently changed his mind to the "straight" Deperdussin, since that was what the Army had adopted.

Lt. Chevalier, in the AB-3, flying off the catapult of the U.S.S. *North Carolina* at Pensacola in July 1916. The North Carolina was the first U.S. Navy ship to become operational with a catapult.

In March 1916 General Order No. 198 established a new three-month course for naval militia aviators established at Pensacola. The course was offered as a result of a General Order, which specified a minimum level of aeronautical knowledge for each rank, held in the Naval Militia. This course covered: Navy Regulations and all general special orders; care of clothing, bedding, and equipment; knowledge of navigation and the principle of scouting; and familiarity with aircraft and their fitting. For officers of and above the rank of Lieutenant Commander, a class in naval administration and business methods was involved. The Pensacola class could accommodate four officers and 16 enlisted men at a time. Due to limitations in the coverage content and duration of the class, graduates of the course were never designated as naval aviators. On 4 March 1916 Captain Bristol, in a Memorandum to the Secretary of the Navy, discussed the current status of matters in aeronautics. Highlights of this Memorandum are as follows:

a. There were at the aeronautical station 16 aeroplanes, seven of which were being rebuilt or overhauled—this is consistent with the usual ratio of one-third of the machines being under repair, being rebuilt, or being overhauled.

b. There were 24 officers at the aeronautical station, 10 of which were expert aviators and held Navy Pilot Certificates. The other 14 were under instruction and consisted of officers who had been ordered to the station since the 1st of July 1915. According to the plan to have 10 officers ordered every three-month, there should be 30 under instruction instead of 14. On account of shortage of officers, only eight were ordered on the 1st of July, seven on the 1st of October, two on the 1st of January, and one recently. Of this number, one had been dismissed, and two have been detached for ineptitude for air service.

c. On the 1st of January 1916, a class of 10 enlisted men was formed and placed under instruction in flying. It was planned to order a class of such men every three-month hereafter.

d. The dirigible ordered in May 1915 has not yet been delivered. The hydrogen plant is in full operation, and in the near future operations with free balloons will begin.

e. The manufacturers of seaplanes in this country are meeting with a good deal of difficulty in producing machines that are suitable to Navy use. The ordinary flying boat type that has been produced is all right for smooth water and inland water, but it is not strong enough for deep-water work, and its form makes it hard to get off the water in rough water.

f. The Navy Department is trying to encourage the manufacturers to produce a satisfactory type of hydroplane, but so far has not met with any success. A contract was placed with the Wright Co. two years ago. An aeroplane that could be accepted has not yet been produced. The difficulties being encountered by the manufacturers are in a large part due to the inexperience of the manufacturers in this area. The manufacturers should not be blamed for the delays, for like anything new it takes time to develop it.

An acceptance motor testing laboratory was completed at the Washington Navy Yard during March 1916. Various motors, which had been contracted for, were submitted to test. The results were not encouraging. Up to 15 October 1916 only two types of motors had passed their contractual tests at this laboratory.

On 29 March 1916 Lieutenant Saufley, again flying a Curtiss hydroplane at Pensacola, bettered his earlier record with a flight to 16,010 feet, and, on 2 April, extended it again, this time to 16,072 feet. On 30 March 1916 the Secretary of the Treasury informed the Secretary of the Navy that in accordance with a previous agreement that the Navy would provide flight instruction to officers of the Coast Guard, Second Lieutenant of Engineers Charles E. Sugden (Naval Aviator No. 43 and USCG Aviator No. 2) and Third Lieutenant Elmer F. Stone (Naval Aviator No. 38 and USCG Aviator No. 1) were being ordered to Pensacola.[13]

On 15 April an anchor and a two digit number, both in dark blue on a white background, were prescribed as "distinguishing marks for Naval Aeroplanes" in a Bureau of Construction and Repair drawing. Also, the aircraft number was to be displayed forward and aft on both sides of the fuselage and under the wings. The CNO, on 13 May 1916, authorized the development of gyroscopic attachments for aircraft instruments and equipment, including compass, bombsights, and base lines (the forerunner of the turn and bank indicator).[14]

By the spring of 1916 it was apparent that a conflict within the ranks of naval aviation was brewing between Captain Bristol and Lieutenant Commander Mustin over the issue of "supervision of all aircraft and aircraft stations and the further development of aeronautics in the Navy." Therefore, on 25 May 1916 the CNO, unhappy with the rate of change in designs "which result in delays and disappointments," proposed an organization for Aeronautics (see Appendix A). The result of this organization was that Lieutenant Commander Mustin was to head "work at stations," while Captain Bristol was responsible for "tactics and use of aircraft afloat."

Lt. Richard C. Saufley. Saufley was killed at Pensacola on 9 June 1916 while attempting an endurance record in the AH-9. The accident was attributed to a structural failure in the tail of the aircraft. The resultant of the crash was a halt in all instruction at Pensacola until November 1916 when the first of the Curtiss N-9s arrived.

On 3 June 1916 instruction in free and captive balloon was instituted at Pensacola when the Secretary of the Navy approved a course prepared by Lieutenant Commander McCrary. Also on 3 June the National Defense Act provided for a census of American industry; the purpose of the census was an investigation of the effort which would be required to put American industry on a war time production basis. The census did not effect aircraft manufacturers, since they were already working on government contracts. The principle benefit to naval aviation was the knowledge gained in the area of the conversion of other manufacturing facilities to aviation components. A little over two months later—9 June 1916—on an endurance flight in the AH-9 over Santa Rosa Island, Lieutenant Saufley crashed to his death after being in the air eight hours, 51 minutes. Since the AH-9 was also the type of plane in which Civil Engineer Rockwell was killed it was decided to abandon this type. This reduced to four the number of aeroplanes then in commission. Furthermore, none of the four were of a type considered suitable for preliminary instruction in flying. Consequently, all schoolwork except shop and theoretical instruction in aeronautics ceased. On 20 June a General Order, superceding that of 23 January 1913, defined the cognizance of aeronautics in the Navy Department. On 24 June a General Board report on "the possible use of naval aircraft" was issued. It was not complimentary. It stated that aviation was downgraded based on reliability, weight carrying capacity, and the number of planes in the Navy. It proposed the use of three small non-rigids for coastal patrol. And it recommended a standardized air division ashore and afloat. Also in June contracts for three more aeroplanes were let.

On 12 July Lieutenant Chevalier, in the AB-3 Flying Boat, was catapulted from the *North Carolina* while she was underway in Pensacola Bay. As a result of this achievement the *North Carolina* became the first U.S. Navy ship equipped to carry and operate aircraft. On 18 July an allowance for flight clothing was established by the Secretary of the Navy. It consisted of helmets, goggles, and a safety jacket. Enlisted men involved with aircraft were to receive a wool head cover, a suit, gauntlets, and boots.

In August the Secretary of the Navy directed the Officer of Naval Operations to consider all the recommendations of the General Board and then to distribute measures to the appropriate bureaus. In this vein Dr. A.H. Zahn was secured by Rear Admiral Taylor to head his Bureau's research into planes, instruments, and wind tunnels. On 3 August 1916 the Commandant of Naval Aviation proposed to the Secretary of the Navy a formalized development of the U.S. Aeronautic Station (see Appendix B). On 8 August the Secretary of the Navy made the Bureau of Construction and Repair a lead Bureau for aircraft development and procurement. On 10 August the Navy initiated contact with Glenn Curtis for what was to become the first aircraft production contract. The training machine which resulted from these discussions was the N-9, the Navy's most popular training machine during WWI. On 12 August 1916 agreement was reached between the Secretary of the Navy and the Secretary of War that the Deperdussin system of aircraft control be adopted, as standard, for use in all aircraft of both services. On 17 August Pensacola was again reorganized, though it now had training as its primary mission. It was to be an aeronautical school with departments of Manufacturing, Experimental test and inspection, Public Works, and Supply and Medical.

As the nation began to prepare for war in the summer of 1916, Congress voted $3,500,000 for naval aviation in the Naval Appropriations Act for fiscal year 1917, signed by President Wilson on 29 August 1916. This figure was a million and a half more than Admiral Benson and Secretary Daniels had requested, but some $9,500,000 less than Captain Bristol had originally requested. It authorized the establishment of a separate Naval Flying Corps, consisting of 150 officers and 350 enlisted men. The authorization was never implemented because of the opposition of the recently formed Office of the Chief of Naval Operations. It also provided for a Reserve Flying Corps and for the purchase of aircraft, including 10 planes to be lent to the naval militia. This Reserve Corps was eventually to provide the overwhelming majority of WWI naval aviators. Beyond the issue of money to be allocated to naval aviation, this bill focused the diverse opinions, on a variety of issues, of several major players in the saga of the development of naval aviation. Mustin, at Pensacola, for some time had been advocating the creation of a separate and distinct Naval Flying Corps. His chief opponent on this subject was Towers. Lieutenant Commander Mustin felt that only with a separate Corps could naval aviation be free to grow and develop without the hindrance of the surface navy. Lieutenant (j.g.) Towers, on the other hand, felt that aviation was being promoted for the good of the fleet, and only by keeping the organizations together could the original purpose of naval aviation be achieved. Other aspects of the Bill which generated controversy were CNO Benson's opposition to taking in civilians and giving them commissions. He preferred to see enlisted men taught to "chauffeur" officers. Captain Bristol, on the other hand, insisted that the command of aircraft required the same skill as that required to command a ship. And finally, Rear Admiral Blue, Chief of the Bureau of Navigation, and hence the officer responsible for obtaining men for all branches of the Navy, came out strongly for a separate Corps with only a nucleus of "regular" Navy officers.

It is interesting to compare this appropriations figure with the fact that for the three years prior to July 1914 aviation had been handled as a matter of experiment in the Bureau of Navigation, with small appropriations of approximately $10,000 per annum. Another facet of the 1916 Naval Appropriations Act was the establishment of a Special Board chartered with the issue of selecting coastal air bases. The created board, chaired, at the direction of the Secretary of the Navy, by Rear Admiral James H. Helm, decided to leave the final site selection up to the Army and the Navy. Also in the summer of 1916 the Congress reported out two new laws which were important to the Navy; one established the process of promotion by selection as opposed to strict seniority; the other established a new category of officers in the line who were to be carried as additional numbers in grade. The latter step was of critical importance to officers contemplating careers in naval aviation. Prior to this time officers either volunteering for, or being ordered to, aviation duty were faced with having their careers jeopardized by the time they spent in aviation, since it did not count as sea duty. With new legislation officers could plan on a full uninterrupted career in aviation without the need for interruption for sea duty in order to qualify for promotion.

On 17 August 1916 a reorganization of the Naval Aeronautic Station at Pensacola was approved by the Secretary of the Navy. Its primary mission was now to train officers and enlisted men for aviation duties with the fleet. Specific specialties included courses for seaplane pilots, dirigible pilots, kite balloon pilots, Quartermaster (Aviation), Carpenter Mate, Radio Operator, Instrument Man, and Machinist Mate. Also ordered was the establishment of Departments for Manufacturing, Experimental Test and Inspection, Public Works, Supply, and Medicine.

On 9 September the Navy initiated, by the order of the Secretary of the Navy, the concept of formal flight testing as a basis for accepting new aircraft. On 20 September the first instructions were issued on the color of Navy aircraft. The use of slate color was canceled, and the use of opaque yellow varnish specified for wings, body, and pontoon of the N-9 specified. These were to change many times over the next several years.

During the first two years of the war Lieutenant (j.g.) John H. Towers served in London as Assistant Naval Attaché. Returning to the United States in September 1916, Towers reported to the State-War-Navy Building in Washington on 3 October. At this time the naval aviation program was administered by Lieutenant (j.g.) Bronson, who reported to Captain Josiah S. McKean, Material Director. A more experienced aviator was desired. The initial choice was the promoted Captain Henry Mustin; however, his clashes with Captain Bristol leveraged against his selection. Towers was ordered to the Bronson position on 17 October.[15]

On 11 October 1916 the Acting Secretary of War proposed to the Secretary of the Navy that they each nominate officers to consider methods of organizing Lighter-than-Air construction. The proposal was agreed to, and the General Board named Captains Hugh Rodmann and Josiah S. McKean, with Lieutenant (j.g.) Towers. Their counterparts were Lieutenant Colonel G.O. Squier of the Signal Corps, Major S.D. Embrick of the Coast Artillery, and Major D.T. Moore of the Field Artillery. This so-called "Cognizance Board"

A posed photo of Elmer F. Stone at Pensacola in 1916. Photo shows good detail of the Curtiss shoulder yoke system. Following the war Stone became the first pilot of the NC-4, the only plane of the four NCs to complete the transatlantic flight in May 1919.

was officially known as the Joint Army and Navy Board on Aeronautic Cognizance. It was different from the already existing Joint Army and Navy Board. The "Cognizance Board" dodged the issue for which it was chartered and passed it to a group of "3 Officers from each service who most thoroughly understood it to supervise the building of a Zeppelin." While this Board was unable to successfully address the issue which generated its origin, it did successfully address a second, and significant issue placed before it—the lines of demarcation between the Army and Navy air services. On this issue the finally accepted divisions were to be:

Army:
- Aircraft operating in conjunction with the mobile army
- Aircraft required for fire control for coast defenses
- Aircraft required for the defense of fortifications, navy yards, arsenals, cities, ship building plants, powder works, or other similar important utilities, whether public or private, that are located ashore.

Navy:
- Aircraft operating in conjunction with the fleets
- Aircraft operating from shore bases for overseas scouting
- Aircraft operating under the command of naval districts and advanced bases.

By November eight planes had been borrowed by the naval militia pursuant to the Naval Appropriations Act of 1916 (one by California, two by Massachusetts, two by New Jersey, two by New York; and one by Rhode Island). These loans were made only after at least one officer had completed the three-month course at Pensacola established under General Order No. 198. On 3 November 1916, the Commandant of the Navy sent a letter to the Bureau of Navigation outlining the Organization of Naval Flying Corps (see Appendix C). On 8 November Lieutenant Bronson (Naval Aviator No. 15), piloting a Curtiss N-9 seaplane, and Lieutenant Luther Welsh, on an experimental bomb flight, were killed at Indianhead by the premature explosion of a bomb dropped by Welsh. As noted earlier, since the fatal crash of Lieutenant Saufley on 9 June, training at Pensacola had virtually ceased. Flight training was resumed on 26 November 1916 upon the delivery of the first Curtiss N-9 seaplanes. These machines, the counterpart to the Army's JN-4, were to continue in use in the Naval Training Program into 1927.

On 12 December 1916 Captain Bristol was detached as "Commander of the Air Service," and the functions of command, but not the title, were transferred to Captain Albert Cleaves, Commander of the Destroyer Force, Atlantic Fleet. On 31 January 1917 Captain Joseph L. Jayne, a non-aviator, relieved Commander H.C. Mustin of command at Pensacola. On 30 December the Commission on Navy Yards and Naval Stations, authorized by the Act of 29 August 1916—which had as one of its charters the selection of new sites for air bases along the coast—submitted its preliminary report. For aviation the Commission could only report that "the present development of aeronautical machines...and the practical experience so far obtained in the utilization of such machines to meet the tactical and strategic requirements of the fleet and the defense of the coast, is such as to preclude the determination at this time of any extensive system of aviation bases." A recommendation was made that a joint Army-Navy Board decide upon locations that might be used by both services.[16]

Notes:

[1] Van Vleet, Clarke and Wm. J. Armstrong, *United States Naval Aviation 1910-1980*, United States G.P.O., Washington, D.C., 1981
[2] Reynolds, Clark G., *Admiral Jack H. Towers*, Naval Institute Press, pages 57-61
[3] Arthur, Reginald White, *Contact! Careers of Naval Aviators Assigned Numbers 1 to 2000*, Naval Aviator Register, Washington, D.C., 1967
[4] Reynolds, Clark G., *Admiral John H. Towers*, Naval Institute Press, pages 57-61
[5] van Vleet, Clarke and Wm. J. Armstrong, *United States Naval Aviation 1910-1980*, U.S. Government Printing Office, Washington, D.C. 1981
[6] Arthur, Reginald, *CONTACT!, Careers of Naval Aviators Assigned Numbers 1 to 2000*, Naval Aviator Register, Washington, D.C. 1967
[7] ibid
[8] ibid.
[9] ibid.
[10] ibid
[11] ibid
[12] van Vleet, Clarke and Wm. J. Armstrong, *United States Naval Aviation 1910-1980*, U.S. Government Printing Office, Washington, D.C., 1981
[13] Arthur, Reginald White, *CONTACT! Careers of Naval Aviators Assigned Numbers 1 to 2000*, Naval Aviator Register, Washington, D.C.
[14] ibid
[15] Reynolds, Clark G. *Admiral John H Towers*, Naval Institute Press
[16] van Vleet, Clarke and Wm. J. Armstrong, United States Naval Aviation 1910-1980, U.S. Government Printing Office, Washington, D.C. 1981

2

Naval Aviation
Organization, Personnel, and Training

In the previous chapter the development of naval aviation was presented. In this chapter the evolution of a struggling peacetime air service into a war power will be explored. The discussion will cover not only actions taken by the Navy, but will also review the influence on the Navy of the various coordinating bodies established either jointly by the Army and the Navy, or by Congressional legislation.

As the military entered the year 1917 it was becoming increasingly obvious that the development of aviation in the U.S. was being severely restricted by the limitations and restrictions imposed by the Curtiss and Wright patents on the furthering of the technology of domestic aviation. On 10 February 1917 the National Advisory Committee for Aeronautics (NACA) established a Patent Committee, with Lieutenant Towers as a member. Its charter was to resolve the issue of patent infringements in the areas of aircraft airframe, engine design, and construction. The principle item of contention was that brought by the Wrights against Curtiss in the area of their design for wing warping versus the Curtiss design of the aileron. The Committee was chartered with developing a mechanism wherein the issue of patents and their potential infringement could be resolved "at a later time." By July 24th the Committee had producers organized into a Manufacturers Aircraft Association. The Association "pooled" both the basic Curtiss and Wright patents—plus others, for a total of 192—in a "cross-license" agreement. By the end of the war 50 companies had joined this association. This agreement allowed the individual manufacturers to proceed with their developmental activities without the threat of patent infringement being brought against them.

On 12 March 1917, the first in-service agreement regarding the development of aeronautic resources and the operations of aircraft was submitted by a Board of Army and Navy Officers and approved by the Secretaries of War and Navy. The agreement recognized a general division of aeronautical functions along lines traditional to the services, but stressed the importance of joint development, organization, and operation, and enunciated basic principles whereby joint effort could be achieved in those cases.[1]

The Secretary of War and the Secretary of the Navy created the Joint Technical Board on Aircraft on May 5, 1917. This Board, also formed at the suggestion of Charles D. Walkout, had as its purpose the determining of specifications and methods of inspec-

Group photo of the First Yale Unit. Personnel are not identified. Photo was likely taken in Florida.

Curtiss F-Boat believed to have been used by the First Yale Unit.

Members of the First Yale unit launching a seaplane

Aircraft used by the First Yale Unit at the Yale University Aviation Station at Huntington Beach, Long Island

tion of all aircraft for the two services. It was also to advise on the types of planes and motors to be procured. The original members of this board were: Major Benjamin F. Foulois, Captain V.E. Clark, and Captain Edgar S. Gorrell of the Army; and Lieutenant A.K. Atkins, Lieutenant Towers, and Lieutenant Hunsaker (Construction Corps) of the Navy. As no official name was given to the board by its precepts, and to avoid confusion with the Aircraft Production Board and the Joint Army and Navy Airship Board, the board de-

Personnel of the First Yale Unit hauling out a seaplane at Huntington Beach. (source: Official U.S. Navy Photo)

Yale University Aviation Station at Huntington Beach, Long Island.

Cord Meyer and Seth Low who were members of the First Yale Unit.

Formal portrait of F. Trubee Davison. (source:Davison collection)

R.Adm. Colby M. Chester, USN, Superintendent of Naval Training Units at Yale and Brown Universities during WWI. (source: Naval Historical Center)

cided to call itself the Joint Technical Board on Aircraft upon organizing. The function of this board was to advise the War and Navy Departments on the purchase of types of aircraft and engines. A vast number of miscellaneous technical matters were also referred to the Board by the War and Navy Departments, and by the Aircraft Board for recommendation. The Joint Army and Navy Technical Board on Aircraft framed the initial aircraft building program for the Army and Navy on 23 May 1917, which was approved by the War and Navy Departments for execution. The recommended naval program was for 300 school machines, 200 service seaplanes, 100 speed scouts, and 100 large seaplanes (The Curtiss N-9 and R-6 were acceptable for the first two categories, but there was nothing available for the other categories). The Board also drew up a set of specifications entitled "General Specifications for Building Airplanes," which was adopted by the Navy, and a revision of it is still the standard practice of the Bureau of Aeronautics. On 18 September 1917 the Board proposed a production plan of 1700 operational type aircraft. As noted above in October the Air Board recommended the program. On July 24, 1918, the last formal meeting of the Board was held, and after that date it died a natural death as the War and Navy Departments went ahead with their approved programs without further questions of technical policy. The Aircraft Production Board, which was created on May 16, 1917, functioned during the

Second Yale Unit at Buffalo, NY, in the summer of 1917. Personnel are not identified.

Members of the Second Yale Unit (left to right): Stephen Potter NA No. 130), Chauncey Lufkin (NA No. 129), Edward Traver Smith (NA No. 126), Harold Kanter, and an unspecified instructor (seated).

war as the supreme authority with regard to aircraft production by and for the Army and Navy. The Council of National Defense, on the recommendation of the NACA, and at the instigation of Charles D. Wolcott, Secretary of the Smithsonian and Chairman of the NACA, created the Board. Its advisory charter was to "consider the quantity production of aircraft....and to cooperate with offices of the Amy and Navy and other Departments." The first members were: Howard Coffin, chairman; General G.O. Squier, United States Army; Admiral Taylor (Construction Corps), United States Navy; Lieutenant Towers; S.D. Waldon; E.A. Deeds; and R.L. Montgomery. The Aircraft Production Board was transferred from the control of the Council of National Defense to the Secretary of War and the Secretary of the Navy by act of Congress[2] approved October 1, 1917, which act changed the name to Aircraft Board. At the same time, additional members were added from the Army and Navy. The Navy members of the enlarged board, in addition to Admiral Taylor, chief constructor, were Captain N.E. Irwin (Naval Aviator No. 1104), Director of Naval Aviation, and Lieutenant Commander Atkins of the Bureau of Steam Engineering. Mr. Coffin continued

Henry Hutton Landon, Naval Aviator No. 93, a member of the 2nd Yale Unit. Photo taken while Landon was in training.

Alexander H. McCormick (NA No. 895) of the Second Yale Unit. (source: J. Schieffelin Collection)

Naval personnel training in Canada. Rear row (left to right): Richard McCann, Richard Randolph, Thomas H. Chapman, James Forrestal, Gavin Brackenridge, and William Mudge. Middle row (left to right): Floyd Clarkson, Stewart Butler, Paul McCoid, Henry Swift, Frank Zunino, Edward Shea, and Robert Matter. Bottom row (left to right): Peter Gibson, Harry Gordon, Ens. Frederick H. Allen (Office in Command), Ens Francis I. Amroy (AOIC), Duval Goldthwaite, and Duncan Read. Enlisted personnel are not identified. Not included in the photo were: Philip Frothingham, Rettig Grisweld, Arthur Wright, Frank Tenney, John Warburton, Stewart Esty, and Jacob Halstead. (source: Gibson Collection)

as chairman of the enlarged board. The legislative standing assigned the Board by Congress, however, allowed the Board only to "supervise and direct." All contracts could only be made by already constituted authorities of the respective departments. The Board thus became an advisory organization concentrating on the industrial aspects, as opposed to the military aspects, of aircraft production. The so-called aircraft scandals (based on the fall down in the Army program) forced the resignation of Mr. Coffin as chairman in the spring of 1918, and John D. Ryan was appointed by the President as his successor. The Aircraft Board was dissolved by Executive Order on March 19, 1919.

The influence of the Aircraft Board on the Navy's program of aircraft production was not very frequent or detailed, but in its large aspects was most beneficial. The greatest single benefit to the Navy from the Aircraft Board was the resolution adopted November 6, 1917, to the effect that all air measures taken against submarines should have precedence over all other air measures. This gave the Navy priority in the War Industries Board over controlled raw materials, on the railroads for cars and trains, and in general made the Navy's task of creating a great antisubmarine fleet of flying boats possible. On 14 November 1917 the Secretary of War, Newton D.

Harold R. "Pete" Gibson, Naval Aviator No. 156, who trained in Canada. The insignia on the fuselage of the Curtiss JN is that of the training squadron.

Edward L Shea, Naval Aviation No. 153 who trained in Canada. (source: Gibson Collection)

Army and Navy students in training in Canada. From left to right: Halstead, McCoid, Goldthwaite, Swift (hidden), Wright, Forrestal, Tenney, Matter, Mudge, Butler, Clarkson, McCain, Gibson, Randolph, Brackenridge, and Gordon.

Baker, approved a recommendation "that priority be given by the War Department to naval needs for aviation material necessary to equip and man seaplane bases." This was a major concession by the Army and went a long way toward resolving the constant inter-service rivalry over availability of the sources of raw materials each service needed to fulfill their respective missions. Taylor also convinced the Aircraft Board to agree that the Navy should get part of the output of the Standard Aircraft Plant at Elizabeth, NJ, and the full output of the following: Aeromarine Plane and Motor Co., Keyport, NJ; Boeing Airplane Co., Seattle, WA; Burgess Co., Marblehead, MA; Canadian Aeroplanes Ltd., Toronto, Canada; Curtiss Engineering Corp., Garden City, NJ; Curtiss Aeroplanes Ltd., Toronto, Canada; Gallaudet Aircraft Corp., East Greenwhich, RI; L.W.F. Engineering Corp., College Point, NJ; and Victor Talking Machine Co., Camden, NJ. Another important feature of the Board which was of great benefit to the Navy was the creation and quantity production of the Liberty engine. In May the Board decided that a new American design of an aircraft motor was needed. This engine was started by E.A. Deed of the Aircraft Board, designed by engineers selected by him, and developed by the automobile industry of the country working under the control of the Aircraft Board. Lieutenant Harold Emmons, United States Naval Reserve Force (formerly of the Ford Motor Co.), was assigned to the War Department to take charge of the production of the Liberty engines. The first 12-cylinder Liberty engine underwent initial flight testing on 10 October 1917 in a Curtiss HS-1 Flying Boat at Buffalo, NY. The complete success of the Liberty engine was of vital

Stuart M. Butler (NA No. 150) while training in Canada. (source: Official U.S. Navy Photo)

W.J. Warburton (NA No. 163), W.F. Clarkson (NA No. 158), and H.F. Gibson (NA No. 156) while training in Canada.

Aerial view of Camp Borden. (source: Gibson Collection)

assistance in making the Navy aircraft program possible, as every flying boat intended for overseas duty, whether single or twin-engined, was designed for the Liberty.

In the summer of 1917 the Aircraft Production Board (with the approval of the Army and the Navy) sent to Europe an expert commission to study the aeronautical situation overseas, and to arrange with our Allies and our military and naval commanders abroad for the necessary design and production data for such foreign aircraft and engines as the United States should build. This commission was commonly known as the Bolling Commission. The head of the commission was R.C. Bolling (an attorney for the United States Steel Corporation), and the other members were: Captains Clark and Gorrell of the Army; Naval Constructor G.C. Westervelt and Lieutenant W.S. Child of the Navy; Howard Marmon of the Nordyke-Marmon Co.; and Herbert Hughes of the Packard Co. The Bolling Commission had as a charter "to study allied progress in the design and building of aircraft and to recommend a complimentary program in the U.S." Its report, as it impacted the Navy, was: 1) recommend that air power of the Navy might be most quickly and effectively applied through Kite Balloons on destroyers, with flying boats for patrol or anti-submarine attacks; 2) the purchase of the DH-4; 3) a recommendation on motors (which was too late to impact the Liberty engine); and 4) stressed that the U.S. should build training planes, heavy bombers, and flying boats with fighters to be left to European manufacturers. Perhaps the most important and useful accomplishment of the Bolling Commission abroad was the so-called Bolling Agreement entered into with the British, French, and Italian Governments to the effect that any country had the right to produce any aircraft, aircraft engine, or accessory to be found in any other country. The compensation for any national on account of patent infringement, royalties, etc., should be made by his own government. This agreement was for the "duration of the war," and effectively stopped the activities of foreign manufactur-

Harry Gordon (NA No. 151) and Duncan H. Read (NA No. 145) while training in Canada.

Richard H. McCann, Naval Aviation No. 147, while training in Canada.

A line-up of Curtiss JNs of a Canadian Training Squadron commanded by Capt. John Aird. (source: Gibson Collection)

Student Naval Aviators training in Canada. Back row (left to right): Forrestal, Shea, Goldthwaite, Chapman, Halstead, Tenney, Clarkson, and McCain. Middle row (left to right): Zunnio, Randolph, Gordon, Read, Brackenridge, and Matter. Bottom row (left to right): Frothingham, Butler, Wright, Swift, and Warburton.

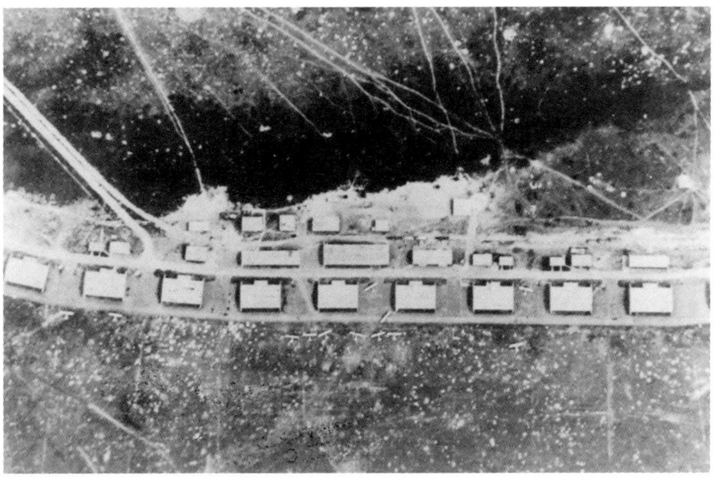

Hoar Field within Camp Borden. (source: Official U.S. Navy Photo)

Aerial view of Camp Borden. (source: Gibson Collection)

Harry Swift in the cockpit of a Curtiss JN. The non-flying officer in front of the fuselage is not identified. (source: Gibson Collection)

ers' agents in Washington, who swarmed about the Aircraft Board. In October 1917 the Air Board established a "Seventeen Hundred Program" of aircraft production. For the Navy this plan called for:

235 H-16 Flying Boats
832 HS-1 Flying Boats
640 R-6 Aircraft
2289 Liberty engines
200 Curtiss V-1 engines
600 Kite Balloons (mostly Cacquot M-types)

In an additional action, on 8 November 1917 the Board established a policy that air offensives against U-boats were to take precedence over all other aviation measures.

A Naval presence was first established in Europe in March of 1917 when Admiral William Sims, then President of the Naval War College, was ordered overseas. His mission in England was to begin to establish the basis for a naval command base in that country. Since the U.S. was not technically then at war, Admiral Sims traveled aboard the S.S. *New York* in his capacity at the Naval War College, but in mufti and under the assumed name of V.J. Richardson. His aide, Commander J.V. Babcock, also traveled in mufti and under the assumed name of S.W. Davidson. Once this office was established, Sims was to become the Officer in Charge of U.S. Naval Forces in Foreign Waters. On 9 April Sims reported to the British Admiralty in this capacity. Shortly after his arrival in Europe Sims forwarded to the Navy Department a recommendation for building planes to reinforce the British patrols over the coastline and over the English Channel. His position was "the sooner

Aerial view of NAS Bay Shore.

Harry Swift, Naval Aviation No. 149, while in training in Canada. (source: Gibson Collection)

Duncan Read, Naval Aviator No. 145, while training in Canada. (source: Gibson Collection)

Aerial view of NAS Bay Shore.

Unidentified enlisted personnel at the U.S. Naval Training base, Long Island (NAS Bay Shore).

they get there the better." He did, however, place small fast convoy ships as a priority over airplanes.

On 26 March 1917, the first aerial U-boat hunt in the U.S. occurred when four flyers arose from Mineola and Governor's Island on a false alarm of a U-boat being sighted off Long Island. The combined air-sea search lasted for three days. On 27 March 1917, in a letter to the Commander-in-Chief, Atlantic Fleet, the Commander Destroyer Force proposed a major philosophical change in the organization of Navy Aviation—the establishment of a separate, and permanent, Navy Aviation Corps. The basis for this recommendation were that there was a shortage of qualified officers, and that the available supply of officers should not be diverted to duties which could be performed by civilians. An aviator's entire time should be given to aviation, for he could not be a satisfactory sea officer at the same time, and flying needs to be done by younger men and was not suitable for older men who might be transferred into that Branch. The eventual establishment of an independent Bureau of Aeronautics, however, would not come into being until 1922.

Ens. Spencer T. Alden, Naval Aviator No. 482, was killed in the crash of this aircraft at NAS Bay Shore on 4 May 1918

Hangar #5 at NAS Bay Shore.

Training at NAS Bay Shore.

Aerial view of NAS Chatham taken in about 1918. (source: Naval Historical Center)

Aerial view of NAS Rockaway showing both the Blimp hangar and the seaplane hangars. (source: National Archives 80G-454992)

In April 1917, the Navy's training program was just recovering from the effects of a six-month hiatus that had begun in June 1916 when a series of accidents underscored the unsatisfactory nature of the aircraft then in use. The effect of the $3.5 million provided for aviation in the Naval Appropriations Act of August 29, 1916, had not been felt. The Naval Flying Corps, authorized by the same act, had not been established. Aircraft manufacturing was undergoing some measure of expansion as a result of orders from abroad, but not as a result of Navy orders. Although suitable sites for air bases along the East Coast had been selected, their establishment and construction were still in the planning stage. Some advance had been made in flight training after the delivery of Curtiss N-9's late in 1916, and the experiments conducted with shipboard catapults had borne some fruit. The *North Carolina* was equipped with gear necessary to carry and operate aircraft; the *Huntington* and the *Seattle* were being similarly equipped.

The strength of the commissioned and enlisted personnel of the Navy assigned to aviation duty on 6 April 1917 was as follows:

Officers:	
Naval Aviators	48
Student naval aviators	0
Ground Personnel	0
Student Officers (under training for commission)	0
Total Officer personnel	48
Men:	
Aviation ratings	163
General ratings assigned to aviation duty	0
Total enlisted personnel	163
Total Personnel	211

In addition, the Navy had 54 training-type planes, three balloons, one blimp, and one Naval Aeronautic Station. By the end of

Aerial view of blimp over NAS Rockaway. (source: National Archives 111-SG-95866)

Aerial view of NAS Rockaway photographed on 27 January 1919. (source: Naval Historical Center Photo NH 95396)

Aerial view of NAS Rockaway photographed 24 April 1919. A number of Curtiss HS-type seaplanes are on the water front and an Army sea-coast mortar battery is in the bottom center. (source: Naval Historical Center Photo NH 95539)

Curtiss NC-1 seaplane which, on 27 November 1918, established a world record by carrying 51 men (including a stowaway) into the air. Show here outside the hangar at NAS Rockaway with unidentified men lined up on each side of her. (source: Naval Historical Center Photo NH 42552)

the war naval aviation had 500 planes in commission, 2,500 officers, and 22,000 enlisted men.

When the U.S. did enter the war the perception of both Congress and the military on the need for aviation funds changed drastically. The Appropriations Act of 17 April 1917 added $3,000,000 for Naval Aviation to the $3.5 million provided on 24 August 1916. More funds were provided in the Deficiency Act of 15 June 1917 ($11,000,000), and a further increase on 6 October ($45,000,000).

When the United States entered the World War, naval aviation was under the general supervision of the Aide for Material, Captain McKean, USN. Lieutenant Towers was on duty in the office of the Aide for Materials as Assistant for Aviation, and in this capacity had direct charge of all naval aviation activities. On 17 May 1917 Towers was relieved by Commander Noble E. Irwin, USN, who was ordered to aviation duty in the Bureau of Material. In this capacity Irwin was assigned the reinstituted title of Director of Naval Aviation. It was to be Irwin who carried the load of responsibility for naval aviation during the period of hostilities. Towers initially remained on duty as his assistant, and later assumed responsibility for supervision of the Naval Reserve Flying Corps in the Bureau of Navigation. In July of 1917 aviation work was segregated and moved to the Navy Annex. Irwin continued being assistant for aviation under the Aide for Materials until 7 March 1918, on which date Navy General Order No. 375, creating the Office of the Director of Naval Aviation, was signed by the Secretary of the Navy, and the then Captain Irwin was ordered to duty as the first director. This general order made the Director of Naval Aviation directly responsible to the Chief of Naval Operations. Within the Naval Aviation organization three Sections were established: Training—Lieutenant Johnson; Information and Planning—Captain B.L. Smith, USMC; and LTA—Lieutenant Norfleet, and later Lieutenant Zachary Landsdowne. In order to maximize the number of personnel in the Navy aviation service, Towers, newly promoted to Lieutenant Commander, was appointed Supervisor of the Naval Reserve Flying Corps while still staying at his desk in aviation (this was with the agreement of Rear Admiral Leigh C. Palmer, Chief of

A Navy Curtiss NC seaplane taxies off from the NAS Rockaway ramp on its first flight (4 October 1918). (source: Naval Historical Center Photo NH 42558)

Officers at NAS Rockaway with Curtiss HS-1 flying boat. Ens. Stephen A. Freeman is fifth from left. Others are unidentified. (source: Freeman Collection)

Curtiss HS-12L at NAS Rockaway in December 1918. (source: Freeman Collection)

Navigation, who would normally have had this responsibility). It is to Towers' credit that the NRFC was to supply the majority of the Naval Aviators for the war (200 to the Navy, out of a total of 243, and 30 to the Marine Corps, out of a total of 35). One of the major steps Irwin took in order to achieve better coordination between the Bureaus was to institute a weekly conference between the cognizant aviation personnel in the Bureaus having cognizance over some phase of the Navy's aviation program. The purpose of these meetings, which were requested in a 5 November 1917 Memo, was the discussion, coordination, and expediting of all matters pertaining to naval aviation. Eventually, Flight Commander H.B Hobbs of the RAF would be invited to these weekly coordination meetings.

On 7 April, by Executive Order, the President directed that the Coast Guard be transferred from the Treasury Department to operate as part of the Navy. Also in April, several privately owned fields and schools, plus those of the Naval Militia at Squantum, MA, and Bayshore, Long Island, were placed under the jurisdiction of the Navy. These facilities served as outlets for the initial expansion of aviation men and materials, and carried the load until stations of a more permanent nature could be built.

All Bureaus in the Navy were directly and immediately impacted by the declaration of war. In order to operate on a war footing major reorganizations within the Bureaus began to evolve. By the end of the war the following organizational changes had been implemented:

Bureau of-Construction and Repair—Hunsaker headed a larger aviation section concerned with the design, specifications, material supply, construction, and service of aircraft.

Bureau of Steam Engineering—Lieutenant Commander Atkins headed an Aviation Division of three Sections—Engineering, Production, and Operations Maintenance. This Division started with just Atkins and one typist, but grew to 40 officers, 60 clerks, and over 100 Inspectors.

Stephen A. Freeman, Naval Aviator No. 1091. Note lack both of shoulder boards and aviator wings indicating photo was taken prior to his receiving his commission. (source: Freeman Collection)

Formal portrait of Ens. Stephen A. Freeman who served at NAS Rockaway.

Bureau of Ordnance—A new desk marked "Aviation" took over machine guns, bombs, and sights for aircraft through three Sections—Experimental, Technical, and Production Distribution. This Bureau also operated a special storehouse in Philadelphia.

Bureau of Yards and Docks—Established its Aviation Section under Civil Engineer Kirby Smith. This Section was principally involved in the construction of foreign bases, but it would eventually grow to what was the forerunner of the WWII Seabees.

Bureau of Navigation—Due to its responsibility for the Naval Observatory, this Bureau became involved with precision aviation instruments.

On 19 May the Secretary of the Navy directed that the bureau number of each aircraft be placed in figures three inches high at the top of the white vertical band on each side of the rudder. The number was also to be placed on both sides of the fuselage. As a result of this order the practice of assigning numbers to aircraft, as AH, was discontinued, and the bureau number, or serial number, became the sole means of identifying a particular aircraft.[3] The General Order also established the National emblem on all planes to be a red disc within a five pointed white star on a blue circular field. On the upper wing the insignia was to be carried inboard of the ailerons. On the lower wing the insignia was to be in line with that on the upper wing, but was not to interfere with the ailerons. The insignia was to be carried on all wing positions. Red, White, and Blue vertical bars on the rudder, with blue forward was also prescribed. Also on 19 May 1917 the CNO requested that two small seaplanes and one pilot be detailed for duty in connection with radio experiments at Pensacola. In tests on 7 September 1917, which led to additional orders for Simon radio transmitters, radio signals sent from a Curtiss R-6 seaplane at Pensacola were clearly received by the Naval Radio Station at New Orleans, a distance of 140 miles. On 22 February 1918 the Director of Naval Communication was requested to provide wireless transmitting and receiving equipment at five naval air stations on the Atlantic coast and at San Diego and Coco Solo to permit pilots on patrol to communicate with their bases.

Left to right: Lt.Cdr. Mustin, Rofer (non-aviator), unknown, unknown, and believed to be Warren Gerald Child who was the Commanding Officer of NAS Rockaway in 1917. (source: Freeman Collection)

Aerial view of NAS Cape May. HS-2L seaplanes (including Bu#'s A-1210 and A-1925) on the water front. (source: Naval Historical Center Photo NR&L (M) 13007)

Repairing a HS-2L seaplane (Bu# A-2256) at the Gallaudet Factory on 3 March 1919. Aircraft was assigned to NAS Cape May. (source: Naval Historical Center Photo NR&L (M) 13005)

Aerial view of NAS Cape May taken from an altitude of 1,000 ft. on 17 March 1919. Note HS-2L seaplanes outside of hangars and one near the beach appears to be Bu# A-1357. (source: Naval Historical Center Photo NR&L (M) 5249)

On 28 May the *Huntington*, following her transfer from Mare Island to the East Coast, arrived at her new homeport at Pensacola. Between the 28th and 1 August she was used in various experiments associated with the operation of seaplanes and kite balloons.

Until June 1917 there was no specific approved uniform for Naval Aviators. On 22 June a summer service working uniform for officers assigned to aviation duty and officers of the Naval Reserve Flying Corps was prescribed. It was of khaki. Leggings of drab were to be worn with breeches and high laced leather shoes. The "prescribed" working dress uniform was a one piece overall suit made of canvas, khaki, or moleskin capable of being worn over the summer service uniform.

At the impetus of Rear Admiral Fiske, Lieutenant E.O. MacDonnel began testing with torpedoes at Hunnington Beach, L.I., on 14 August 1917. The evaluation of the military application of torpedo carrying aircraft in the U.S. got off to a very inauspicious start. On 16 July 1912 patent number 1,032,394 was obtained for "a method of delivery and directing them on the attack." When the Navy began to develop an aircraft capable of carrying torpedoes, the work was done under Capt. Chambers, and the holder of the patent brought suit. The suit was lost! The holder of the patent was Rear Admiral Fiske![4]

On 7 September 1917 a winter service flying uniform was prescribed; it was the same as the summer service design, but forestry green cloth was substituted for khaki. In October, brown gloves and an overcoat were added.

On 11 October the catapult, aircraft, and all aviation equipment were removed from the *North Carolina* at the Brooklyn Navy

Aerial photograph, taken from an altitude of 1,000 ft., on 17 March 1919 of NAS Cape May. Note HS-2L seaplanes outside of hangars and near the beach. (source: Naval Historical Center NR&L (M) 5247)

Beach and hangars of NAS Cape May as of 25 January 1919. Seaplane in the foreground is a HS 2L (Bu# A 2257). (source: Naval Historical Center Photo NR&L (M) 5256)

Aerial photograph of NAS Cape May from an altitude 1,000 ft. on 17 March 1919. Shown are minesweepers and submarine chasers alongside a pier. Note marine railway at right. (source: Naval Historical Center Photo NR&L (M) 52460

Aerial view of NAS Hampton Roads, looking east, taken on 16 August 1918. (source: Naval Historical Center Photo NH 2620)

Yard. The justification for this move was the fact that while on convoy duty, except for a single incident involving a kite balloon, the equipment was never used. The *Hunnington*, on 13 October 1917, also had her aeronautic gear removed. This ended the concept of operational testing on board combatant ships begun with the *North Carolina* in 1916.

Even though some Army aviators began to wear "badges" as early as 1913, when war was declared the Naval Aviator had no such emblem. On 29 June 1917 the G.F. Hemsley Co., in an unsolicited letter, offered a design of an aviation cap and collar ornament. While the CNO rejected the design, he did propose to the Bureau of Navigation a design of a Wing representative of what he wanted. On 7 September the Secretary of the Navy approved Change 12 to the Uniform Regulations. It stated "A Naval Aviator's device, a winged foul anchor with the letters 'U.S.,' is hereby adopted to be worn by qualified Naval Aviators. The device will be issued by the Bureau of Navigation to Officers and men of the Navy and Marine Corps who qualify as Naval Aviators, and will be worn of the left breast." On 12 October a change removed the letters "U.S." from the design. While several metals and combinations of metals for the pin were tried, it was decided in October that the design should be all gold. On 24 October Baily, Banks, and Biddle, in competition with a number of firms to make the pins, submitted its first sample. By early November it submitted other samples. On 21 November the Bureau of Navigation sent a letter to the Supply Officer selecting "the higher priced pin" ($1.15 each). While the company was not named, on 19 December Baily, Banks, and Biddle confirmed a telegram from which is quoted "balance aviation insignia shipped tomorrow." The Bureau of Navigation, on 26 December, confirmed in a letter to Pensacola the receipt of the pins with a statement "will be sent out as soon as they can be engraved to show the Aviator's number, his name, and branch of service." Distribution of the wings began on 19 January 1918. It seems likely that Lieutenant Commander Towers, as Senior Naval Aviator in Washington, DC, at the time was likely an early recipient. In January 1918 the first precedence list of Naval Aviators was compiled.

Curtiss R-6 (Bureau # A-968) seaplane at NAS Hampton Roads on 17 August 1918. (source: Naval Historical Center Photo NH 60783)

Hangars and ramp at NAS Hampton Roads. Photograph taken in about 1918. (source: Naval Historical Center Photo USN 903202)

Three Curtiss R-6's on the water at NAS Pensacola. (source: Emil Buehler Naval Aviation Library)

It numbered 284. The Navy does not seem to have considered the subject of appropriate insignia for enlisted personnel, who were on flying status until they were forced to do so by the issuance of "wings" to naval enlisted personnel completing training courses in Britain during the war. Up until that time, even though enlisted personnel had been authorized to fly since early 1915, there had been no specific emblem to show this status. Naval enlisted personnel graduating from the British Observer School seem to have been provided Royal Naval Air Service GE-N-4 Observer Wings. It was not until Change 13 to the Uniform Regulations, dated 18 March 1918, that badges for Machinist's Mate (Aviation)—a winged airplane propeller; Quartermaster (Aviation)—winged ships wheel; and Carpenter's Mate—crossed axes or hatchets—were authorized. The designation of RA (for Radio and Aviation) was established on 30 August 1918. The designation of GE (for Gunnery-Engineer) did not appear until 5 October 1918.

At the outbreak of hostilities the number of trained aviators, or of persons familiar in any way with naval aviation, was small. The early training pilots and mechanics had received covered only the flying and maintenance of aircraft, without particular attention to the requirements of aerial combat or other warlike operations. For the purposes of war, it immediately became necessary to obtain numerous trained crews composed of pilots, machine gunners, and observers, in order to operate successfully the bombs, machine guns, and radios making up the equipment of aircraft. In addition, a very large force of so-called trained ground personnel was required, and the enrollment and training of the tremendous numbers of officers and men required was in itself a task of stupendous magnitude. On 1 May 1917 an expansion of the training program was approved which called for assignment of new classes every three months, and the establishment of a course of 18 months duration to qualify regular navy officers as pilots of either seaplanes or dirigibles. The

Hangar for LTA airships at NAS Hampton Roads, circa 1918. Note: Blimp being inflated in the hangar. (source: Naval Historical Center Photo NH 44284)

Aircraft coming in for a landing in front of the blimp hangar at NAS Hampton Roads. (source: Emil Buehler Naval Aviation Library)

Curtiss F-boat (Bureau number A-2332) at NAS Pensacola. Photo taken on 24 November 1918.

Naval Officers at NAS Penasacola (left to right): Lt. W.M. McIlvain, Lt. Patrick, Lt. Bellanger, Lt. Saufley, Lt. Towers, Lt. Mustin, Lt.Cdr. Smith, Lt. Chevalier, and Lt. Stolz.. (source: Glenn H. Curtiss Museum of Hammondsport)

program also provided for training enlisted men as aviation mechanics and for selection of a few for pilot training and qualification as Quartermasters. No sooner was its implementation approved than it was abandoned as impractical once the expansion began. Heavier-Than-Air training was initially concentrated at Pensacola, and Lighter-Than-Air (for both balloons and dirigibles) was centered at Goodyear, at Akron. At the same time the Curtiss Exhibition Company was given a contract to give flying training at the Curtiss School at Newport News, VA.

To meet the growing needs, as noted above, a Training Section was organized in the Office of Aviation (Operations) and placed under the direction of Lieutenant Earle F. Johnson (Naval Aviator No. 25). This section not only supervised all aspects of aviation training, but also had responsibility for enrolling candidates for pilot training. In this capacity, Johnson directed the movement of personnel by coordination with the Supervisor of the Naval Reserve Flying Corps, Lieutenant Commander Towers. The multiple activities connected with these tasks combined to make this one of the most important sections at the start of the war, and one of the largest in the Aviation Office at the end. Plans for the training of student officers formulated in this Office were distributed on 10 July 1917. As then visualized, the training course was in three parts as suggested by British experience. The purpose of the division, which represented a radical change for the existing system, was to promote greater efficiency by narrowing the scope of each part and thereby reduce the problems of their development. The three divisions consisted of a ground school of roughly six weeks duration, a preliminary flight school to carry the student through between five and ten hours solo flying, and an advanced flight school in which the student would complete work toward qualifying as a Naval Aviator and for Commissioning in the Naval Reserve Flying Corps. The program as outlined provided for the general organization of schools for each part, and in particular a fairly detailed outline of the subjects to be studied in ground school.

The Naval Appropriations Act of August 1916 had made provisions for a Naval Reserve Flying Corps, including the provision for buying 12 planes for the naval militia. As soon as it became evident that the United States would enter the war in a few months,

Aerial view of NAS Pensacola taken on 22 August 1918. Note the camouflage painting of the buildings. (source: Emil Buehler Naval Aviation Library)

Aerial view of the hangars and ramp at NAS Pensacola taken on 17 January 1917. (source: Emil Buehler Naval Aviation Library)

Line up of various types of seaplanes flown at NAS Pensacola. The three machines in the foreground are Curtiss H-12s. Photo taken in 1917. (source: Emil Buehler Naval Aviation Library)

Curtiss H-16 of NAS Pensacola on its step on 24 November 1918

certain groups of college men got together and applied for enrollment. While groups of students from both Harvard and Yale formed into independent flying groups, the group from Yale was to become the first unit of reserve pilots in the Navy. F. Trubee Davidson, who was then a sophomore at Yale at the time when President Wilson ordered additional troops to the Mexican border in 1916, formed this group. The First Yale Unit was formed at Locust Valley in the summer of 1916 with the backing of Admiral Robert E. Perry, and with a Curtiss flying boat donated by Rodman Wanamaker. The flight instructor was David McCulloch. The idea of the unit was to be trained as pilots as the First Aerial Coastal Patrol Unit; thus meeting a portion of a recommendation of Henry Woodhouse and Admiral Perry for the formation of air stations along the East Coast. By 6 June 1916 the group was in training at Huntington Beach, Long Island, New York. Besides Davidson, the original members of this group were:

Allan Ames	Henry P. Davidson Jr.	John V. Farwell III
Artemus Gates	Erl Gould	Robert A. Lovett
Albert D. Sturtevant	John M. Vorys	Charles D. Wiman
Wellesley Laud-Brown		Albert J. Ditman Jr.

By summer's end four students had soloed. During the fall of 1916 the students, still civilians, participated in naval maneuvers off Sandy Hook with a fleet from the volunteer "Mosquito Fleet" in Gravesend Bay. To be closer to Yale during the fall semester the unit moved to the New London submarine base and operated there until snow and ice halted their efforts. Eventually, the group grew to a total of 30 aviators:[5]

Charles F. Beach	Graham M. Brush
Reginald C. Comb	David S. Ingots
Robert Livingston Ireland	Francis RV Lynch
Kenneth MacLeish	Archibald G. McIlwaine
Curtis S. Read	Russel Bartow Read
William A. Rockefeller	Kenneth R. Smith
William P. Thompson	Charles M. Stewart
Samuel S. Walker	Oliver B. James
Henry H. Landon	George Francklyn Lawrence Jr.

Curtiss F-boat at NAS Pensacola

Curtiss H-12 No. 767 at NAS Pensacola. (source: 80-HAN-63-11)

Curtiss HS-1 at NAS Pensacola. (source: 80-HAN-63-1)

Curtiss H-12 No. 767 at NAS Pensacola. (source: 80-HAN-57-1)

During this formative period the Yale Unit and the Navy had a number of conversations on the subject of how to go about having the Navy assimilate the Unit. The problem was that up until the passage of the 1916 Naval Appropriations Bill the Navy had no mechanism for formally recognizing any volunteer Aerial Coastal Patrol. With the passage of the Bill, including the provision for a Naval Reserve Flying Corps, volunteer units could enter the Navy via the aero branch of the State Naval Militia. On 24 March 1917 the unit transferred en masse to the Navy, and, four days later, under the command of Lieutenant E.O. McDonnell (Naval Aviator No. 18), to Palm Beach, FL, for more training. McDonnell, who reported to Palm Beach from Pensacola, was a holder of the Medal of Honor, which he had received prior to his involvement with aviation, and while assigned to duty at Vera Cruz. It was at Palm Beach that the unit was formally enrolled in the Navy. Receiving commissions were F.T. Davison (Lieutenant j.g.), as well as Gates, Lovett, Brown, Ames, Ditman, Gould, and H.P. Davison Jr. (all Ensigns). Those men almost ready to solo were rated at CPOs pending qualification, and the newer members were given rates of Machinists and Electricians. The group as a whole was very loosely organized, with rules and regulations being only loosely enforced. To sharpen up the group McDonnell ordered uniforms for the commissioned officers in May 1917. In June 1917, the unit moved back to Huntington Beach. Flight instruction was offered on a mix of Curtiss N-9, R-3, and R-6 machines and a Burgess-Dunne machine. It was here that the unit's civilian helpers (David McCulloch and Caleb Bragg) detached themselves from the unit. On 28 July 1917, flight tests for qualification as Naval Aviators were begun before a Board consisting of Commander A.C. Read, the promoted Lieutenant Commander Earle F. Johnson, and Lieutenant McDonnell. The first pilot to attempt to qualify was Trubee Davison. Davison crashed on this test and was so severely injured that he never flew again. Upon recovery he was assigned to the Bureau of Ordnance for work in connection with the development of a flying bomb. In February 1917, Davison was made a member of the Committee on Aeronautics. Davison was discharged from the Navy on 23 November 1918, and on 26 December 1918 Captain N.E. Irwin requested that he be designated as a Naval Aviator. This request was granted. Upon completion of their training the men of the First Yale Unit were widely dispersed. On 15 August 1917 Lovett and Gates went overseas. On 28 August Farwell was assigned to Buffalo to work with the Second Yale Unit. On 14 September Sturtevant and Vorys left for France. Walker, Smith, McIlwaine, Coomb, Landon, Ingalls, and Beach left for France on 23 September. Of the others, Ames, Ditman, Gould, Brown, and Rockefeller were assigned to the Naval station at Bay Shore. Lt. Curtiss Read, Bartow Read, MacLeish, and Lieutenant McDonnell were assigned to Hampton Roads. W.P. (Bill) Thompson was ordered to the Ground School at MIT. Harry

Curtiss H-12 at NAS Pensacola. (source: 80-HAN-57-3)

Curtiss H-12 No. 767 at NAS Pensacola.

Curtiss H-12 at NAS Pensacola.

Davison was initially ordered to Newport as OIC of enlistments, and then to Hampton Roads. Graham Bush was ordered to Washington as a technical expert in the Navy Department as an assistant to Lieutenant Commander Johnson. Lynch and Lawrence received orders for the Naval station at Squantum, NY, and then Rockaway Beach. Livingston Ireland, due to a mix up in papers, didn't receive his commission until 17 October. He was then ordered to Hampton Roads, VA, as an instructor. Foster Rockwell went into the Red Cross under H.P. Davison.

In February 1917 Admirals Perry and Fiske visited the Yale campus to extol the virtues of Naval Aviation to combat the submarine peril. As a result of this visit, 11 undergraduates and two recent graduates, under the leadership of Ganson Goodyear Depew, formed a unit styled as Aerial Coastal Patrol Unit #2. Depew broached the concept to CNO Admiral Benson, who approved it and had orders issued for the group to report to Lieutenant Wadleigh Capehart (Naval Aviator No. 19), who at the time was in Buffalo supervising the production of Naval aircraft at the Curtiss factory. Capehart convinced Curtiss to take on the Yale undergraduates as apprentices in his plant so that they could learn the essentials of aircraft and motor construction. Flight training began on 30 May 1917 on Lake Erie using a second hand Curtiss F-boat. On the fifth flight of the day the boat crashed, killing the instructor, Fred Zimmer, and so injuring the student, Seymour Knox, that he was eliminated from the program. To head off being sent to the ground school at MIT, Depew managed to obtain a new flying boat and the services of Harold Kanter as instructor. The remaining 12 members of the unit successfully completed their training in October 1917. On 2 November 1917, after receiving commissions as Ensigns, USNRF, five were ordered overseas, six were ordered to Pensacola, and one was ordered to Washington.

A third unit from Yale was formed, but a change in Navy policy prevented it from completing its training as a unit. Instead, it completed its training under navy supervision.

So far as the record is concerned, the idea of utilizing established civilian educational institutions for the initial stages of Military training seems to have sprung full-grown out of nowhere, as the program seems to have become effective without the benefit of formal directive. But the experience of the British established the precedent, and also appears to have planted the seed (reference the RFC school at the University of Toronto). The training problem was discussed at a meeting of the NACA held in Washington on 23 April 1917. This discussion led directly to a second meeting one week later, to which representatives of the following six scientific schools were invited: the Universities of Cornell, Ohio, Texas, California, Illinois, and the Massachusetts Institute of Technology. The outcome of this meeting was tentative agreement between the Army and the respective institutions to set up training programs and to begin by learning first hand about the Canadian program at Toronto. Army programs at these institutions began functioning in May, less than three weeks after the initial meeting. The Aircraft Production Board also considered the idea. In late June its chairman informed the Secretary of the Navy that, as a measure of increased efficiency and reduction of overhead, the Board considered that it would be well "to have both Army and Navy cadets undergo the same courses of technical training already arranged in many of the educational institutions giving Military training." The Secretary's reply indicated that the Navy was already thinking along these lines.

One of the Argentinean officers under training at NAS Pensacola off on gunnery practice in a HS-2L.

Curtiss N-9 at NAS Key West.

In order to initiate training as rapidly as possible the Navy, assisted by Lieutenant Commander Towers, reached agreement with the Canadian government and the RFC to allow Navy Aviation cadets to train at the RFC facilities outside of Toronto. Subsequently, a group of Navy Aviation volunteers, under the command of Ensign Frederick S. Allen (Naval Aviator No. 143), with Ensign Francis I. Amory (Naval Aviator No. 144), and expecting to be assigned to NAS Squantum, in Massachusetts, was instead ordered to the University of Toronto in July of 1917. This group, consisting of graduates and undergraduates from Princeton, Harvard, Yale, and Dartmouth, plus other universities, consisted of:

Gavin Breckenridge	William F. Clarkson
James V. Forrestal	Harold B. Gibson
Harry B. Gordon	Robert Matter
Richard H. McCann	William F. Mudge
Edward L. Shea	William J. Waraburton
Frank S. Zunino	Duval R. Goldthwaite
Paul S. McCoid	Duncan H. Read
J Sterling Halstead	Philip B. Frothingham
Stuart M. Butler	Thomas H. Chapman
Arthur H. Wright	Rettign A. Griswold
Henry Swift	Robert D. Randolph

Between reporting to the University of Toronto (Burwash Hall) on 9 July and August they drilled and attended classes. They were ordered to take copious notes, as the lessons they learned in Canada were to be incorporated into the training syllabus then being developed by the Navy for Ground Schools in the U.S. The first two weeks at Toronto consisted of 4-6 hours a day of drill conducted by Sergeant-Major Sedgewick and Flight-Sergeant Cooper. The Ground School covered the subjects of Theory of Flight, Rigging, Engines, Machine Gunnery, Bombing, Aerial Photography, Meteorology, Instruments, and Astronomy. Part of this instruction was provided by Canadian and British officers with front line experience. Following completion of the Ground School the detachment spent a week in tents at Long Branch awaiting openings at Deseronto for flight training. With time on their hands and no materials available, the British authorities decided to continue drill training. Ed Shea thought that anything would be better than more drill, so he convinced Sergeant-Major Sedgewick that in lieu of drill that Navy Cadets would wash dishes. To their dismay it was learned that in addition to the men already in camp that 300 Cadets were soon to arrive. For three days the Navy Cadets subsequently steadily washed dishes. At Deseronto the group was billeted at Camp Rathburn. In October, with the entire group having completed their ten hours of preliminary training the group was transferred to Camp Borden for advanced training. The group returned to the Boston Navy Yard at the end of October. At Boston the members received their commissions and the group was divided; some went to Bay Shore to train on seaplanes, and others to Hampton Roads to train in flying boats. Allen, Gibson, Gordon, Clarkson, and Swift eventually left Bayshore for Pensacola, where they helped develop both an advanced flying school and an aerial gunnery school patterned along the lines of Camp Bordon. Duncan Read was assigned to Miami to found an aerial gunnery school, which he commanded, for the duration of the war. Beckenridge, Butler, Frothingham, McCann, and Wright went overseas, with Frothingham and Wright not returning. Shea and Halstead, after a week at Hampton Roads, were ordered to San Diego, with Ensigns A.K. Warren and Bert Ames, to assist Commander E. Winfield Spencer in founding NAS North Island. Forrestal and Goldthwaite were sent to the Navy Department in Washington to help in the task of distributing the lessons learned in Canada.

Curtiss N-9 over Miami

Princeton and Yale were not the only universities with active naval aviation volunteers. On 19 May 1917 seven student aviators comprising the Harvard Unit, with Lieutenant H.B. Cecil (Naval Aviator No. 42) in charge, reported to the Curtiss Field at Newport News, VA, for flight instruction. Their training was conducted pursuant to a contract signed between Curtiss and the Navy for 20 men of the NRFC to be trained at the Curtiss Flying School at Newport News, VA.

The zeal and enthusiasm of the men of these groups resulted in the naval aviation having available, very shortly after war was declared, a nucleus of very capable young officers who proved of inestimable value in the building up of the big corps, which so soon became necessary to carry out the mission of naval aviation. This nucleus was augmented by officers of the Naval Militia, who were later transferred to the Naval Reserve Flying Corps, and by many men taken up directly from civil life for administrative duties. The problem which arose from this over abundance of anxious and willing volunteers was a corresponding dearth of training facilities—either for introductory training or for flight. At the same time the flow of training was difficult to maintain. Such facilities took time to develop, and supplies of volunteers did not dwindle.

On 15 May 1918 the Bureau of Steam Engineering reported that the Marconi SE 1100 radio transmitter had demonstrated dependability in voice communication at distances up to 50 nautical miles, and in code communication at up to 120 nautical miles. Initially designed for use in the H-16 Flying Boat, this was one of the first radio sets widely used in, and the first tube set to be developed for, naval aircraft. On 18 May 1918 the CNO scheduled training goals to provide pilots for Foreign Service. To meet this demand directly the goals called for 124 pilots and 62 gunners trained in night bombers by 1 July, and 552 pilots and 156 engineers trained in H-16 patrol planes by 1 August. To meet them it was directed that eight elementary training squadrons be formed—two at Key West, four at Miami, and two at Bay Shore—and that six advanced training squadrons be organized at Pensacola, where only advanced training would be given as soon as the elementary students on board were graduated.[6] On 1 November 1918 the night flight instruction program at Pensacola was terminated.

As it became increasingly obvious that the United States would soon become involved in the war, the Navy, in addition to making plans regarding manpower, also began to make plans regarding bases. On 5 February 1917 the CNO (Admiral Benson) recommended to the Secretary of the Navy that eight Coastal Patrol Stations be established in Massachusetts, Virginia, New York, New Jersey, Florida, Texas, and the Canal Zone (See Appendix D). On 12 February 1917 Josephus Daniels, the Secretary of the Navy, wrote to the Joint Army and Navy Board on Division of Aeronautic Cognizance requesting that Board consider the matter of the establishment of Coastal Air Stations in light of the questions of separate vis joint stations, location of such stations, and aircraft to equip such stations. On 14 February 1917 the Army and Navy Board on Aeronautics replied to the Secretary with the following positions: 1) The stations should be established with a view of joint occupancy; 2) The stations should be established as soon as practicable and in the following order (Atlantic Coast, Chesapeake Capes, Block Island or vicinity, Panama Canal Zone, New York, Boston or vicinity, Entrance to Delaware Bay, Key West, and Frenchman's Bay, ME, or vicinity; Pacific Coast—San Francisco, Puget Sound, San Diego, and Hawaii); and 3) The personnel to man the stations and the aircraft to equip the stations should be determined after consultation between the two Departments. The Board also recommended that two boards be established, one on the Atlantic coast and one on the Pacific coast, each consisting of two Army Officers and two Navy Officers, who would be chartered with the selection of the sites for the stations proposed on their respective coasts. The Atlantic panel, headed by Colonel Haan, USA, included the promoted Captain Alfred A. Cunningham, USMC, with Lieutenant Johnson, USN, for the First and Second Naval Districts, Lieutenant Commander Towers for the Third, Fourth, and Fifth Districts, and Lieutenant Bellinger for the Seventh and Eighth Districts. The East Coast Board selected some ten sites: Squantum, Massachusetts, was to be an Army base with provisions for naval use, if necessary; Provincetown was selected as a Naval base with provisions for Army use, if necessary; Rockaway Beach was to be a joint site; sites exclusively for naval use were selected at Montauk, Cape May, Hampton Roads, Savannah, Key West, Galveston, and Coco Solo in the Canal Zone. Prior to implementation Chatham replaced Provincetown and Savannah was abandoned. The West Coast Board, with again Captain Cunningham as the Naval representative, chose Ediz Point on Puget Sound and Tongue Point near Astoria, Oregon, as combined air and submarine bases, and San Diego as another major base. For operating bases the sites of Morro Bay, Montery, San Francisco, and Humbolt Bay in California, Coos Bay in Oregon, and Grays Harbor, Fort Townshend, Bellignham Bay, and Lake Ozetle in Washington were selected.[7] On 4 June 1917 the establishment of coastal patrol stations was initiated when the first base contract was let. Sites covered by the contract were all on Long Island, at Montauk Point, Rockaway Beach, and Bay Shore.

On 19 August Secretary of the Navy Daniels approved some 19 sites for naval air bases, most of which were on the list provided by the Rear Admiral J.H. Helm Board on Shore Establishments (the following focuses on Heavier-Than-Air bases; Lighter-Than-Air bases will be discussed in more detail in a later chapter). In addition to the single naval aviation training base at Pensacola, temporary training stations were to be established at East Greenwhich, RI; Miami, FL; Key West, FL; San Diego (North Island), CA; and at the Curtiss Exhibition School at Newport News, VA. At the Curtiss plant at Buffalo, Lieutenant W. Capehart and Naval Constructor E.L. Gayhart supervised the training of Naval Reservists, who provided their own expenses, as inspectors of machinery. In April James P. Knapp, President of the American Lithographic Company, presented to the Navy, through Rear Admiral Nathaniel R. Usher, Commandant of the Third Naval District, his seaplane base at Mastic, L.I., for training purposes. The property, on the south shore of Long Island, consisted of three hangars and a wireless station. The location of the station, half way between New York City and Montauk Point, allowed an area to be patrolled covering the coast line along the entire Third Naval District boundary. It was used until the autumn of 1917. The New York State militia station at Bay Shore and the Massachusetts State militia station at Squantum were also commandeered. A ground school for enlisted men was established at Great Lakes, IL, in 1918. Aviation gunners were trained at Miami, and radiomen at Miami and at Harvard University.

Stations suitable for supplementary patrols and training programs were built at Anacostia, DC, Morehead City, NJ, Brunswick, GA, and Miami, FL. Schools for ground personnel and mechanics were established at Hampton Roads, VA, Pensacola and Santa Rosa, FL, Charleston, SC, Great Lakes, IL, Dunwoody Institute (See Appendix F), Minneapolis, the University of Washington, Seattle (See Appendix Z), San Diego, and M.I.T. (See Appendix E). With the proliferation of schools, both for officer candidates and for enlisted personnel, the Navy began to become concerned over the wide variety and scope some of the schools were applying to common courses. To address this concern Dr. Charles E. Lucke of Columbia University was commissioned a Lieutenant Commander in the reserves and given the charge of overhauling course instruction to standardize the curriculum.

Curtiss JN-4s at Curtiss Flying Field at Miami. Photo was taken in either 1917 or 1918. (source: Glenn H. Curtiss Museum of Hammondsport)

Rest stations were established at Provincetown (authorized in June 1918 and used by NAS Chatham), Glouster (established in October 1918 and used by NAS Hampton Roads), Nantucket (authorized in October 1918 and used both by NAS Chatham and NAS Montauk), Waretown, NJ, Block Island (established in September 1918 and used by NAS Montauk), Barmegat Bay, NJ (authorized in September 1918 and used by NAS Rockaway and NAS Cape May), Atlantic City, NJ (authorized in September 1918 and used by NAS Cape May), Assateague, VA (established in September 1918 and used by NAS Cape May and NAS Hampton Roads), Morehead City and Manteo (Roanoke Island), NC (established in October 1918 and used by NAS Hampton Roads), Beaufort, NC, Charleston, SC, and St. Augustine, Edgemet (off Tampa), FL, Indian Pass, Sewall Point (Stewart), Isla Morada Key, Marathon Key, and Dry Tortugas, FL. These skeleton fields consisted of just a small landing beach and a supply of gasoline (up to 500 gallons), parts, tools, and oil. Personnel stationed at these bases were capable of making minor repairs. Quarters and food provided were suitable for a short rest of no more than overnight in duration. Few, if any, had anything approaching permanent quarters.

By the end of 1917 preliminary flight training was offered at Chatham, Bay Shore, Montauk Point, Rockaway Beach, Cape May, Hampton Roads, Colon (Canal Zone), Miami, Key West, and San Diego. The HTA Advanced Ground and Flight Schools were at Pensacola.

In addition to the above mentioned active duty stations, a naval aviation training station was opened at Marblehead, MA, for the naval reserve. 12 Officers and 100 men operated the station, which was commanded by Lieutenant Godfrey L. Cabot.

Prior to April 1917, the Massachusetts Naval Militia had established a small air base on the Squantum Peninsula, which separates Quincy and Dorchester Bays in Boston Harbor. The station served as a training field for the state's naval militia via the Massachusetts Public Safety Committee. On 4 May 1917 the Commandant of the First Naval District took possession of the property, which was then in the process of development. The Committee had spent more than $30,000 on equipment and buildings at the time of Navy acquisition. Lieutenant Earle W. Spencer (Naval Aviator No. 20) assumed command of the station on 15 June (Note: Other dates provided for this assumption are 11 May and 18 May). When the first class of students arrived, which was prior to the takeover by the Navy, the outlook was very unimpressive. What were seen were one old hangar, a row of tents and several buildings in various stages of construction, and a lone seaplane—a Burgess U-type—that was loaned by Mr. Godfrey L. Cabot. One student, Harry Swift, decided to leave the class and opted instead for training in Canada at Camp Borden. Swift successfully completed his training and became Naval Aviator No. 149. When instruction under naval auspices began at Squantum, it was conducted by Bradford and Page, the instructors of the Naval Militia group who had been commissioned as Ensigns in the Navy. When Clifford Webster arrived he was likewise commissioned and installed as an instructor. Instruction was begun on the Burgess, but shortly there arrived at the base three Curtiss N-9s and the U-type was retired. Of the 24 men who reported to Squantum, six did not go on to qualify; one transferred to Canada, and 17 received designations as naval aviators and were commissioned Ensigns in the Navy Reserve Corps. Those so designated were: Charles B. Ames (Naval Aviator No. 193); James R. Clements (Naval Aviator No. 208); Horace Schmerhorn (Naval Aviator No. 209); Dudley B. Murphy (Naval Aviator No. 210); Theodore O. Grosvenor (Naval Aviator No. 210 1/2); Leo W. Connolly (Naval Aviator No. 235); Winfield M. West (Naval Aviator No. 220 1/2); Justin D. Graves (Naval Aviator No. 234); Carlton M. Pike (Naval Aviator No. 293); William Gaston (Naval Aviator No. 294); Joshua Crane (Naval Aviator No. 296); Woldemar Crosscup (Naval Aviator No. 332); Basil O.J. Finnegan (Naval Aviator No. 336); Chauncy A. Golloupe (Naval Aviator No. 423); Leslie P. Jacobs (Naval Aviator No. 526); Thomas T. Hoopes (Naval Aviator No. 1094); and Henry C. Flower (Naval Aviator No. 1278). By October 1917 the prospect of the New England winter resulted in the shifting of the training activities to the warmer climate of Hampton Roads, VA. On 18 October the Navy abandoned the station as a training facility, transferring students to Norfolk and equipment to other Atlantic Coast Stations.[8] Squantum, however, continued in service as a Coastal patrol along the New England coast.

To expand their training facilities the Navy began to investigate potential additional sites for flight training. Obvious choices were those sites at which some form of flight training was currently being provided. In May contracts were made with private companies to provide instruction in both seaplane and airships (contracts were let 17 May 1917 to the Curtiss Co., for instruction in seaplanes at Newport News, VA, and on 29 May 1917 to the Goodyear Tire and Rubber Company for training as kite balloon and airship

Curtiss JN-4s at Curtiss Flying Field at Miami. Photo was taken in either 1917 or 1918. (source: Glenn H. Curtiss Museum of Hammondsport)

Instructors and students at the Curtiss Flying Field in Miami. (source: Glenn H. Curtiss Museum of Hammondsport)

pilots). The latter remained in use throughout the war, but the former operated only until October 1917, when the students were transferred to Hampton Roads for training under Navy jurisdiction. Fields operated by the Naval Militia at Squantum and Bay Shore were also placed under Navy jurisdiction. These served as outlets for the initial expansion and carried the load until stations of a more permanent nature could be built. Base construction began the same month (initial contracts were for construction at Rockaway, Bay Shore, and Montauk Point, all on Long Island).

The Naval Militia Aviation camp at Bay Shore had been established by the state of New York in May 1916. It was to grow to one of the Navy's four largest elementary flight training stations for heavier-than-air pilots. Bay Shore was chosen as the site of a training station, chiefly because an aviation camp that had reached a stage of considerable development before the war was located at that place. Much preliminary work had been done at that camp before the Navy took it over from the New York Naval Militia, which fact rendered the task of expanding it into a large training center in a short time comparatively easy. When completed, the station, with a cadre of 700 and capable of handling 50 students at a time—and graduating two qualified students per day—would become the largest naval primary seaplane training school for would-be aviators of the Reserve Force.

On 4 May 1917, a contract was entered into between the federal government and the owner of the site on which the naval militia camp stood, whereby the land was leased at the rate of one dollar a year for the duration on the war. Rapid arrangements were made in the course of the following two weeks for effecting the transfer of the station to the regular Navy. On 17 May 1917 the station was commissioned as a Naval Air Station, with Lieutenant Albert Cushing Read (Naval Aviator No. 24) in command. On 28 May Commander Irwin and Lieutenant Commander Towers visited and inspected the camp with a view of obtaining first hand information relative to the progress which had been made up to that date by the naval aviation unit of New York state. These officers found the situation to be as follows. The camp was located in the village of Bay Shore, west of the town, on a peninsula jutting out into Great South Bay. In area it was about eight acres. The property was originally a sandy spit only a few inches above water, but pumping sand out of a nearby creek and an inlet and covering this with topsoil had raised the level. Upon the site had been erected a dozen or more buildings, including three hangars and several shops. The expenses incidental to the construction of these buildings, which had been started before war was declared, when it was proposed to make a state camp only out of the station at Bay Shore, had been defrayed by public spirited citizens of the state who had generously subscribed funds from their private means. In addition to the hangars and shops a dock had been built and a crane erected. The flying equipment of the camp consisted of two Burgess-Dunn flying boats, one Curtiss flying boat, and one Curtiss N-9. At least two of these planes had been provided by private individuals of New York who were interested in naval aviation, Mr. Vincent Astor being among them. In the way of surface boats for use in connection with seaplane flights, the camp at this time had only one small power dory. A circular flying course having a diameter of about three miles and lying over water from seven to nine feet deep had been laid out over the Great South Bay. The personnel of the camp at this time consisted of six officers and 89 men, all of whom had enrolled in one of the first three battalions of the New York naval militia before war was declared. They came, in general, from the same class of young men as those who later enrolled in the aviation reserve force. Assuming that the United States would sooner or later be actively involved in the war and wishing in such an event to serve as naval aviators, they had joined the New York Naval Militia, in each of whose four battalions a flying unit was being organized. These men, many of them recent graduates or undergraduates of the colleges, took upon enrollment any rating they could get, such as electrician third class, carpenter's mate third class, or landsman. The greater number of them, however, hoped to qualify as pilots. Three of the officers were licensed pilots and capable of giving flight instruction. Other officers, and some of the men in camp at the time, were able to operate seaplanes, and were expected to qualify as instructors after a few days' flying. Two classes for flight instruction, which had begun on 17 May, were following regular courses by the last of the month, and those members of the compliment who had reported for flight work, but for whom there were no opportunities in the first two classes, were being trained as mechanics until such time as increased facilities would enable them to enter upon more advanced work. The entire detachment was under the command of Lieutenant Commander F.R. Lackey, NNV, who was the direct personnel representative of the Commandant of the Third Naval District. On 28 September 1917, the Navy signed a $13,000 contract for the construction of a timber framed seaplane hangar at Bay Shore capable of handling three seaplanes. On 13 October 1917 Charles P. Mason assumed the position of Commanding Officer at NAS Bay Shore.

The Station at Anacostia traces its history to a 25 September 1917 request of the Secretary of the Navy to the Secretary of War for authorization for the Navy to use the Army base at Anacostia "To occupy and use as an air plane landing site during the period 1 November 1917, and ending 6 months after termination of the war, the area of Anacostia Flats in the District of Columbia." On 6 October Secretary of War Newton D. Baker notified Secretary Daniels that the Navy could use the field in conjunction with the Army. The station was commissioned 19 January 1918 with Lieutenant George

D. Murray (Naval Aviator No. 22) as Commanding Officer. NAS Anacostia was established to provide a base for short test flights, to provide housing and repair services for seaplanes on test flights from Hampton Roads and Langley Field, and to display new seaplane types for study by key men working in the Navy Department offices concerned with their construction and improvements. Later in 1918 Lieutenant William E. Doherty became the Commanding Officer at Anacostia.

The Naval Air Station at Brunswick, Georgia, due to the immediate need for training facilities, was originally perceived as a two squadron training station, but with an ultimate goal of it being a 12 seaplane patrol station. As a preliminary training station its compliment was to consist of 18 tractor type aircraft, 12 Curtiss F-boat aircraft, and six Curtiss HS type flying boats. The station was not completed prior to the armistice.

On 16 August 1917 the Navy signed a $500,000 contract for a coastal air patrol station at Cape May, NJ. The station was to be similar to that which was being constructed at Montauk. A Naval presence was established at Cape May on 6 October 1917. A seaplane and LTA patrol station was commissioned at Cape May on 4 December 1917, with George S. Gillespie (Naval Aviator No. 32) as the commanding officer. The station was not deactivated until 1922.

The contract for the construction of a Naval Air Station at Chatham, MA, was signed on 8 September 1917. In January 1918 NAS Chatham was commissioned with Lieutenant E.H. McKitterick (Naval Aviator No. 39) in command. Originally intended as a base for seaplane patrols, LTA facilities were later added. On 19 June Phillip B. Eaton, USCG, became the Commanding Officer at NAS Chatham. On 21 July 1918 a surfaced U-boat, firing on a tug boat and three barges off Orleans, MA, and in full view of boaters on Nauset Beaches, Cape Cod, was attacked by two seaplanes from NAS Chatham, which dropped bombs that failed to explode. One of the machines was HS-1L No. 1695 with a crew of Ensigns Lingard (Naval Aviator No. 540) and E.M. Shields (Naval Aviator No. 452), and Mechanic E.H. Howard. By this action Lingard became the first Naval Aviator ever to engage an enemy vessel on this side of the Atlantic. Ensigns Thomas Durfree (Naval Aviator No. 415) and Fredrick B. Hicks (Naval Aviator No. 729) flew the other aircraft from Chatham. After firing on both aircraft the submarine submerged and escaped.

The contract for the construction of a Naval Air Station, at the existing Key West Naval Base, was signed on 24 August 1917. On 18 December 1917 a Naval Air Station was commissioned. Its first Commanding Officer was Captain Stanley V. Parker, USCG (Naval Aviator No. 57). In July 1918 Lieutenant Erl Gould (Naval Aviator No. 68 of the First Yale Unit) was given command of the station; he replaced Captain Parker, who was transferred to Rockaway Beach. At 22 Gould became the youngest officer in the Navy to command any of the four primary training stations in the U.S. Gould, in turn, was relieved of command on 1 February 1919. During the war the station was used chiefly for anti-submarine patrols and for elementary seaplane training. From 11 January 1918 to 11 June 1918, Ensign Noel Chadwick was the chief dirigible pilot—and only dirigible pilot—at NAS Key West. Students undergoing HTA elementary training at Key West did 10 hours solo in Curtiss N-9s; then they were given instruction in Curtiss F-boats, H-boats, and R-9s. Following the war the station was decommissioned.

The Great Lakes Naval Training Station was built between 1905 and 1911. During the war years Commandant Captain William A. Moffett oversaw a significant expansion, supervised in 1917 by Commander George A. McKay (Civil Engineering Corps), and in 1918 by Commander W.H. Allen (CEC). When construction was completed the base could handle 27,000 men. In 1918 Camp Lawrence was added, as well as an aviation school, several drill halls, and enlargement to two existing camps. This expanded the camp capacity to 48,000 men.

Montauk was commissioned early in August 1917 as a seaplane and LTA station. Its first commanding officer was Lieutenant Marc A. Mitscher.[9] (Naval Aviator No. 33). On 19 July 1918 pilots of two planes on patrol out of NAS Montauk sighted the *San Diego* after she had struck a mine off Fire Island and sent the first reports of her sinking. In September 1918 Harold W. Scofield (Naval Aviator No. 28) became the Commanding Officer. The station closed on 2 August 1919.

Miami was the site of the first continental naval station. Construction began in October 1917. It started out, in January 1918, as a patrol station based at Dinner Key. In March 1918 Lieutenant Marc A. Mitscher was the Commanding Officer. On 18 May 1918 the CNO directed that four elementary flight-training squadrons be added to the station's initial patrol functions. The first D.H.-4s assigned to American service were delivered to NAS Miami, for Marine use, on 4 June 1918. By the end of the war the stations operated 12 seaplanes and 2 dirigibles, and were commanded by Albert C. Read (Naval Aviator No. 24). The station closed on 28 May 1920.

In April 1917 Congress allowed the purchase of 143 acres of land at Norfolk, VA, for use by the Navy. The Navy began, on 8 September 1917, with an experimental station, but soon turned to the training of pilots and mechanics. Initially, the small facility had just seven students who had crossed Hampton Roads from the nearby Glenn Curtiss airfield at Newport News. Also in October, a detachment from Squantum arrived. The original officer cadre at the site was just five officers, with Lieutenant McDonnel commanding. By Thanksgiving 1917 the command consisted of 30 officers, 90 students, and several hundred enlisted men. Due to the remoteness of Pensacola, the Hampton Roads base, on 1 January 1918, assumed responsibility for the Experiment, Test, and Inspection Department, which had originally been at NAS Pensacola. The station contained

Curtiss N-9 No. 2789 at NAS Key West.

three hangars, a machine shop, and numerous storage houses, barracks, and tents, as well as 21 seaplanes. In November McDonnell was transferred to Washington. His successor was Lieutenant Commander Bellinger (Naval Aviator No. 8). The station was commissioned, after being in operation for almost a year, on 27 August, with Bellinger commanding. By then it had six canvas hangars to house seven seaplanes. In the middle of the war Pensacola absorbed most of the mission to train pilots. The Norfolk Air Station then concentrated on experimental work. During the war the station was to train some 168 officers and thousands of mechanics.

The North Island Naval Air Station traces its origins back to the field at Imperial Beach, which the Army established as a landing practice and gunnery field and called it initially "Aviation Field," and then "Oneonta Flying Field." On 5 October 1918 the name was changed to Ream Field in honor of Major William R. Ream, the first flight surgeon of the Army Air Service to be killed. In early 1918 Ream Field consisted of two dirt strips at a sub-station of Rockwell Field (which was adjacent to the current North Island Naval Air Station). The Navy did not return to North Island until 1917, when they moved in with some Army officers who were training at Rockwell Field. On 27 July 1917 Congress authorized the President to take possession of North Island, which was to be shared in joint tenancy by the Army and the Navy. NAS North Island was established by Lieutenant E. Winfield Spencer (Naval Aviator No. 20), then the Commanding Officer of an air mechanics school in Balboa Park, San Diego, following the arrival of Toronto trained Ensigns Ed Shea and J. Sterling Halstead, plus Ensigns A.K. Warren and Bert Ames. The station was commissioned on 8 November 1917. The station was established as a permanent air station for the training of pilots and mechanics in ground and flight schools. Air operations by military and marine personnel began in January 1918.

On 6 April 1917 Pensacola had a capacity of 64 pilots and 64 mechanics. Upon the declaration of war with Germany construction activity accelerated significantly at the base. By 11 November 1918 over 100 additional structures, ranging from seaplane hangars to barracks, had been built at the station. Some four temporary camps were established: Camp Bennett (west of the hospital) for incoming recruits; Camp Mustin (near the beach between the hospital and the yard) for additional quarters for enlisted men; Camp Saufley (on Santa Rosa Island) for gunnery; and Camp Bronson (at Magnalia Point on Escambia Bay, north of the city) for aerial bombing. Flight training at the station expanded to include instruction in aerial gunnery, bombing, navigation, photography, signaling, radio, aircraft rigging, and orientation in plane and engine structures. Elementary and advanced flight training were provided until May 1918 when the station was designated as the advanced training station for naval aviation (tailspins, Vrille, loops, etc.). By the end of 1917 the increase in student population at Pensacola had outstripped the number of available qualified instructors. On 9 November 1917 permission was received from the Argentine Government to use three Argentine Naval Officers—recently qualified as U.S. Naval Aviators—as instructors in the ground school at the base (Lieutenant Ricardo Fitzsimon, Naval Aviator No. 95a, Lieutenant Carlos F. Pichon, Naval Aviator No. 95b, and Jr. Lieutenant Marco A. Zax, Naval Aviator No. 95c). On 17 December 1917 the station's designation was changed from Naval Aeronautic Station to Naval Air Station. As noted above, on 1 January 1918 the Experimental and Test Department at Pensacola was transferred to the air station at Hampton Roads to overcome difficulties arising from the remoteness of Pensacola from principle manufacturers and industrial plants in the northern states. The following table depicts the growth of the station:

	5 April 1917	11 November 1918
Officers on Board	0	438
Enlisted Men on Board	431	5559
Seaplanes Assigned	39	215
Mechanics Trained	159	5382
Naval Aviators Trained	0	921
Dirigible Pilots Trained	0	63
Free Balloon Pilots Trained	0	15

The advanced training station was located at Pensacola, FL, and here the student naval aviators were taught gunnery, bombing, navigation, and big boat flying. As the flight program at NAS Pensacola was reoriented to concentrate on advanced training, the gunnery course was raised to the level of a School, and Ensign Raymond C. Mudge (Naval Aviator No. 298) placed in command.[10] By the end of hostilities NAS Pensacola was the largest station of its kind in the U.S., and perhaps the largest in the world.

A seaplane and LTA patrol station was commissioned at Rockaway, L.I., on 15 October 1917. Lieutenant Commander W.G. Child (Naval Aviator No. 29) was placed in command in November 1917. The base was decommissioned in 1922.

To extend the string of air patrol stations along the Atlantic Coast from Canada through the Caribbean, three U.S. naval air stations were constructed outside the continental shores of the U.S. at strategic points along the Atlantic seaboard. Two stations, one at Halifax and the other at Sydney, were built in Canada. The third station was built at Coco Solo in the Panama Canal Zone. The Canadian stations were to provide aerial surveillance of the shipping lanes along the northeast coast of the U.S., the entrance to the St. Lawrence River, and the western terminus of the shipping lanes from Canada to Europe. Originally intended to be eventually staffed by Canadian personnel, the war ended before the transition from U.S. to Canadian personnel could occur. As early as 1915 German submarine activity off the coast of Canada had resulted in steps

Hangars at North Island prior to the war.

being taken to combat the U-boat threat. As Halifax became an increasingly important and successful port for eastbound convoys, more and more concern and efforts were being placed to counter potential submarine attacks. Initially, the concept of transferring the British aircraft carriers H.M.S. *Engadine, Riveria*, and *Vindex* to Canada was considered, but on 2 April 1918 the Operations Committee of the Air Council decided that these vessels were more valuable operating in the Mediterranean. Instead, the British Admiralty proposed that there should be established in Canada land-based submarine patrol stations, and that assistance should be sought from the Americans. The initial investigation relating to potential Canadian bases began in March 1918 and culminated in a conference in Washington on 20 April 1918. From the conference a plan of cooperation was developed, which in turn was approved by the Secretary of the Navy on 29 April. The approval involved the establishment of two stations, each with a compliment of 54 officers and 450 enlisted men. Each station was intended to have three dirigibles, four kite balloons, and six Curtiss HS-12 seaplanes.

On 8 May 1918, a Board consisting of Lieutenant Commander Bellinger, USN, Flight Commander W.H. Greer, RN, and Flight Commander John Barron, RN, met in Ottawa. They proceeded to Halifax and Sydney, and selected the actual sites upon which the stations were to be built. Progress in developing these stations was rapid. By 27 July 1918 the Chief of Naval Operations requested the Bureau of Navigation to finalize the details of the manpower for each station. At the same time the Office of the Commanding Officer, U.S. Naval Air Forces' Canada was established, with Lieutenant Richard E. Byrd (Naval Aviator No. 608) detailed to this position in addition to being given command of the station at Halifax. Lieutenant Byrd assumed his duties on 15 August 1918.

The Station at Halifax, Nova Scotia, was commissioned for seaplane patrol on 19 August 1918 with Lieutenant Byrd commanding. The station compliment was four Ensigns and 145 men. The intention of this station was to conduct patrols over the northern approaches to the Atlantic coast. The first planes reached Halifax on 17 August. Seaplane operations at NAS Halifax began the week of 14 September 1918. For its operating history there were 200 patrols made from this station encompassing some 400 flying hours. While dirigibles never reached the base, the Canadian Government did supply two gunboats for Kite Balloon patrol. The first cruise with a kite balloon did not actually take place until 7 November.

The station at Sydney, Cape Breton Island, was commissioned as a seaplane patrol and kite balloon station on 31 July 1918, with Lieutenant Robert Donahue (Naval Aviator No. 54), USCG, commanding. The compliment of the station was three officers and 44 men. The first seaplane arrived at the station on 4 September. A short trial flight was conducted on 11 September. Patrol activities commenced on 25 September. Operations at this Canadian base were of a routine patrol nature. During its existence this station performed 149 flights consisting of 177 flying hours. Both of these stations were closed on 4 January 1919, and by 7 January the U.S. flag had been hauled down and material turned over to the Canadian Government.

On 6 June 1918 Lieutenant R.G. Pennoyer placed the NAS Coco Solo in commission. Coco Solo was two miles east of Colon on the Atlantic coast of Panama. U.S. military activity at Coco Solo had started with a Marine base, which gave way to an Army base, and finally to a Navy submarine base, prior to the joint occupancy by the air base. The missions of Coco Solo were to provide services and operating facilities; to aid in maintaining assigned aircraft squadrons to protect the eastern approaches to the Canal; and to maintain and overhaul assigned naval aircraft. To assist in the aerial observation over the Caribbean entrance to the Canal, an auxiliary seaplane base was established in the San Blas district in 1918. LTA facilities were added still later. By the end of the war there were 1183 men at Coco Solo. These stations carried out regular daily patrols, and aircraft were detailed from these points to accompany[11] all-important convoys.

When the training of personnel was begun it was soon found necessary to divide the training into three phases, namely ground school, elementary flight training, and advanced ground school and flight training. The first ground school was established at the Massachusetts Institute of Technology in September 1917 (See Appendix E). Ground schools were also established at the Dunwoody Institute, Minneapolis (31 July—see Appendix F) and the University of Washington (1 July—see Appendix Z); also, the subject of Aerology was added to the ground school curriculum. A revision of the training program to permit assignment of new classes every three month to a new course of eighteen months duration for both heavier-

Davis Gun carrier aircraft at NAS North Island with the Davis Gun in position.

than-air and lighter-than-air pilots was approved and then abandoned as impractical once expansion began.

The air training was two-fold, to give students academic instruction in aeronautical matters, and to inculcate in them the concept of strict military discipline. In May 1918 the training program was again revised. Since the threat of U-boats put heavy demands on the coastal stations, more emphasis was given to training at inland stations.

Before embarking on the program, however, two actions were taken which alleviated some of the jam created by the number of men on board. The first was the organization of the First Aeronautical Detachment under the command of Lieutenant Kenneth Whiting (Naval Aviator No. 16). Whiting had most recently been in command of the Aviation Detachment aboard the cruiser U.S.S. *Seattle*. This vessel carried four seaplanes, which operated from a deck-mounted catapult. Organized at Pensacola, the Detachment consisted of seven officers, four of whom were Naval Aviators, and one hundred twenty-two enlisted men, about half of whom were destined for pilot training. At the end of May 1917 the unit left from Baltimore and Hobken for France, thus becoming the first American military unit to leave the U.S. for France. Another chapter will discuss this group in detail. The second action was an agreement with the Army that prospective naval aviators would make up part of the contingent for which the Government of Canada had agreed to provide flight training. On 9 July 1917 this group, composed of 26 officers and prospective officers under Ensign Frederick S. Allen, reported at the University of Toronto for the start of their training under the RFC. In addition to qualifying as an aviator, each man was expected to gather material on teaching methods and course content that would be of help in developing U.S. Navy courses and in adjusting its training program to the needs of the war. This group completed training in November and was the only one trained in Canada.

To provide officer personnel to discharge other than flying duties, it became necessary to establish a class known as ground officers, which included ordnance, communication (intelligence), navigation, aerography, and administration officers. Such ground officers were at first trained simply by the expedient of giving them the pilot's course at the Massachusetts Institute of Technology and then detailing them to flight stations to become familiar with actual aviation work. More specialized training soon became necessary, however, with the result that a school for ground officers was established at the United States Naval Training Station, Great Lakes. Graduates of this school were divided into the various classifications mentioned above, according to their abilities, and detailed in the following manner: Ordnance officers to Pensacola to take gunnery and bombing courses, and thence for temporary duty to the Bureau of Ordnance to become familiar with the latest developments; Navigation officers detailed to Pensacola to take a special course in navigation; Communication officers to Hampton Roads for special instruction in communication work; Administration officers to Pensacola for training in executive work; and aerographers to Blue Hills Observatory, Boston, MA, for a special course under McAdie.

On 25 January 1918 the Supervisor, NFRC, requested that Dr. Alexander McAdie, Director of the Blue Hill Observatory, Harvard University, be enrolled as a Lieutenant Commander in the Naval Reserve and be assigned to the Aviation Office in CNO to direct the establishment of a Naval Aerological organization. On 26 February, acting largely on the recommendations of McAdie, the Chief of Naval Operations established an allowance list of aerographic equipment for air stations abroad. On 30 March 1918 a requirement was established for weekly reports from the Commanding Officers of all air stations in the U.S. of weather conditions experienced in flight operations. On 16 April 1918 the first formally trained Navy Aerologists, 9 officers and 15 enlisted men headed by McAdie, departed for duty at naval air stations in Europe. On 17 April 1918 Lieutenant W.F. Reed, Jr., reported to NAS Pensacola to provide meteorological services for flight operations, or for what was then called "Aerological" duty. On 19 June 1918 the practice of taking regular upper air soundings began at NAS Pensacola to provide information on wind velocity and direction needed for navigation training flights. Recording instruments were carried aloft in a kite balloon, a technique developed by the station Meteorological Officer Reed.

For the training of aviation mechanics, elementary trade schools were established at convenient points throughout the country, and an advanced training school was established at Great Lakes, IL. Aviation mechanics that had been selected at the various elementary schools because of their special ability and qualifications were sent to the Great Lakes School for advanced instruction. This school soon became one of the largest and most successful manual training schools in the country.

W.L. Hamlen, not yet enrolled in the Navy, arrived 1 June 1917 before Lieutenant Maxfield (Naval Aviator No. 17)—the Commanding Officer of the LTA School at Akron—for assignment. Hamlen was the first student of the first class at this school. At the time of his arrival the station, commissioned on 28 May 1917 and located at Fritsche's Lake, consisted of an almost completed hangar, shops, hydrogen plant, barracks, officer quarters, and a temporary mess hall. The first class, as members eventually arrived at Akron, consisted of:

Colley W. Bell	Arthur D. Brewer
Noel Chadwick	George Crompton
Merrill P. Delano	Richard C. Gortz
Warren L. Hamlen	Charles G. Little
Ralph M. Strader	Andrew W. Talbot
William P. Whitehouse	Arthur S. Williams

The agreement between the Navy and Goodyear was for the Navy to provide the trainees and Goodyear to do the rest. The Navy taught only navigation, seamanship, signaling, communications, and drill. Assisting Maxfield were Lieutenant (j.g.'s) Emory W. Coil (Naval Aviator No. 96) and Ralph G. Pennoyer (Naval Aviator No. 100 1/2), and Ensign Frederick P. Culbert (Naval Aviator No. 94). Flight training began with kite balloons, then advanced to free balloons, and finally to blimps (first the "A" type and then the "B" type). The course required 18 flights in a blimp—the first five as mechanic, the next five as the aide (controlling air to the balloonets

Newly-constructed pigeon loft at NAS Coco Solo, Panama Canal Zone. Photo taken on 1 October 1918. (source: Naval Historical Center Photo NR&L (M) 217)

and beginning dual instruction), and the last eight flights as pilot. At the start of the course nobody had a uniform. Finally Maxfield had to get a naval tailor from Washington to come to Akron to take measurements and orders. It was mid-July before the uniforms arrived. On 22 June Maxfield issued orders involving actual flying of naval aircraft to the group. Kite balloon training began on 16 June for a week then on the free balloons, and training on Blimps started about the middle of August. Maxfield qualified as an LTA pilot at Akron on 1 September 1917. The first eight men in the course qualified on 21 September. They were designated Naval Aviators on 5 October. By late October they were commissioned as Ensigns, USNRF. On 27 September the newly promoted Lieutenant Commander Maxfield and the promoted Lieutenant F.P. Cully were detached from the unit, whose command passed to Lieutenant W.E. Coil. On 7 October seven graduates designated for overseas duty were given leave to await further orders. On 2 November they were ordered overseas. On 9 November Strader, Talbot, Whitehouse, Brewer, Little, Delano, and Hamlen sailed aboard the *St. Louis* from the Brooklyn Navy Yard. Noel Chadwick, commissioned Ensign, USNRF, stayed at Akron to become "Dirigible Pilot in Charge" of the second class.

As the naval training programs subsequently evolved, pilots for lighter-than-air craft were first sent to the same ground school as heavier-than-air pilots at Massachusetts Institute of Technology, where a special lighter-than-air course was included in the curriculum. On completion of this course, all lighter-than-air students were sent to Akron, Ohio, for training in free and kite balloon work. From Akron the students designated as dirigible pilots were sent to Pensacola, and those designated as kite balloon pilots to Rockaway, Long Island, for advanced instruction.

On 3 February 1918 Aerial Gunnery training for prospective Naval Aviators and enlisted men began under Canadian RFC instructors at the Army Field at Camp Taliaferro, Fort Worth, Texas. Although the program was of short duration, 38 Officers and 80 enlisted men completed the course before its closing on 16 March 1918. On 8 February 1918 the Navy promulgated a change in national aircraft markings. The change was initiated at the urgings of the Allies, who pointed out that the white star could, in the heat of combat, be taken for the white bordered German Cross. It discarded the White Star design and replaced it with the concentric circles of red and blue around white (the former Imperial Russian markings), and reversed the order of red, white, and blue vertical bands on the rudder, placing red nearest the rudder post. This method of identification was to remain standard until August 1919, when the 1917 insignia was readapted. On 22 February the Director of Naval Communications was requested to provide wireless transmitting and receiving equipment at five naval air stations on the Atlantic coast, and at San Diego and Coco Solo, to permit pilots on patrol to communicate with their bases. In May this request was expanded to cover all naval air stations.[12]

On 6 March the Bureau of Navigation established instrument allowances for naval aircraft allotting a compass, two altimeters, and a clock for service seaplane and flying boats; a compass, altimeter, clock, and a statoscope for dirigibles and free balloons; and an altimeter and clock for kite balloons and training planes.[13] General Order 375, issued on 7 March 1918, established the Office of the

Chief Machinist Mate Francis Edward Ormsbee Jr.

Director of Naval Aviation in the Office of the Chief of Naval Operations, raising the status of aviation from a Section to one of the 13 Divisions within the office of the CNO.[14] Captain Irwin was to remain in this position until May 1919. On 9 March 1918 a revised Flight Training Program was initiated by the Navy, which divided the syllabus into elementary, advanced, and advanced specialization courses; it designated the stations at which each would be given, and provided that after a period of general training, all students would specialize in one of the three general types of seaplanes.

On 1 July an Act of Congress repealed all laws relating to the National Naval Volunteers, and authorized the President to transfer, as a Class, all its members, in their confirmed ranks and ratings, to the Naval Reserve, the Naval Reserve Flying Corps, or the Marine Corps Reserve.

In August 1918 the Navy Department moved from the State, War, and Navy Building to quarters in a temporary structure on Constitution Ave, which became known as "Main Navy." On 27 August 1918 the Secretary of the Navy signed General Order No. 418 directing that "Applicable alike to regulars and reservists, the uniform of any given rank or rating in the Navy shall here after be identical in every aspect throughout, except for necessary distinguishing corps devices, and every officer of the Navy shall be designated and addressed by the title of his rank without discrimination whatever."

On 25 September Chief Machinist Mate Francis E. Ormsbee, who was on a material test with Ens. J.A. Jova, went to the rescue of two men in Burgess N-9 seaplane #2422, which had crashed in Pensacola Bay. He was successful in saving the life of the student gunner (P.B. Parsons), but, after repeated dives into the wreckage of the plane, was unable to save the life of the pilot (Ens. Thomas C. McCharthy). For his heroism Chief Ormsbee was awarded the Medal of Honor—approved in General Order 436 dated 3 December 1918.

During the year 1918, United States Navy airplanes flew a total of 40,883 hours on patrol duty in home waters. Patrols during the last three months of the war covered 1,305,000 nautical miles. Lighter-than-air craft patrols in home waters flew a total of 5,145 hours. In the 19 months of U.S. participation, the strength of naval aviation had grown to a force of 6,716 officers and 30,693 enlisted men in Navy units, and 282 officers and 2180 men in the Marine Corps units, with 2107 aircraft (695 seaplanes, 1170 flying boats, and 242 landplanes), 15 dirigibles, and 215 kite and free balloons on hand. Of these number, 18,000 officers and men, and 570 aircraft had reached foreign shores.[15]

Notes:

[1] van Vleet, Clarke, and William J. Armstrong, *United States Naval Aviation 1910-1980*, G.P.O., Washington DC, 1980

[2] No. 48, 65th Congress

[3] van Vleet, Clarke, and William J. Armstrong, *United States Naval Aviation 1910-1980*, G.P.O., Washington, DC, 1981

[4] Arthur, Reginald, *Contact! Careers of Naval Aviators Assigned Numbers 1 to 2000*, Naval Aviator Register, Washington, DC 1967

[5] Paine, Ralph D., The First Yale Unit, "A Story of Naval Aivation" 1916-1919, The Riverside Press, 1935

[6] Van Vleet, Clarke, and William J. Armstrong, *United States Naval Aviation 1910-1918*, G.P.O., Washington, DC 1981

[7] Trumbull, Archibald D. and Clifford L. Lord, *History of the United States Naval Aviation*, Yale University Press

[8] Lewis, Henry P., *The Squantum Story*

[9] Mitscher was to go on to an illustrious career du;ring World War II

[10] Arthur, Reginald White, *Contact! Careers of Naval Aviators Assigned Numbers 1 to 2000*, Naval Aviator Register, Washington, DC, 1967

[11] Colleta, Paolo E., *United States Navy and Marine Corps. Bases, Overseas*. Greenwood Press

[12] Van Vleet, Clarke, and William J. Armstrong, United States Naval Aviation 1910-1980. G.P.O., Washington, DC, 1981

[13] ibid

[14] Arthur, Reginald White, *Contact! Careers of Naval Aviators Assigned Numbers 1 to 2000*, Naval Aviator Register, Washington, DC, 1967

[15] ibid

3

Development of Lighter-Than-Air Craft[1,2]

The Navy began to experiment with Lighter-Than-Air (LTA) apparatus in 1911. The purpose of these experiments was to achieve a more elevated spotting platform for gun fire from ships. As noted in a previous chapter, the armored cruiser U.S.S. *Pennsylvania* had been the ship used in San Francisco Bay by Ely as an aircraft carrier and by Glen Curtiss in San Diego harbor in the experiment with his hydroplane. In between these two events occurred an experiment with man-lifting kites, conducted by Mr. Samuel Perkins, aboard the *Pennsylvania* while she was off Santa Barbara. Initially, a sandbag weighing 160 pounds was used as ballast. Following a successful demonstration of the kite's performance, Lieutenant John Rodgers volunteered to ascend. The *Pennsylvania* steamed at 13 knots into a gentle to moderate breeze. Rodgers, riding in a "boatswain's chair," arose to an altitude of 400 feet. In the afternoon Ensign A.M. Charlton volunteered to be lifted. Due to a lessening of the wind he was only able to reach an altitude of 200 feet.

LTA craft activities of the Navy formally began on 1 June 1915, when the Navy Department contracted for one nonrigid airship with the Connecticut Aircraft Co. of New Haven, CT, a concern which had secured services of a German engineer, a German mechanic, and an Austrian pilot, all of whom were supposed to be experts in the field of airships (The Connecticut Aircraft Company Proposition No. DC16 was for a "Velette (sic) type" dirigible, and is dated 18 April 1915 with a revision date of September 1915). The contractual price was $45,636. The specifications for this ship were drawn up by Ensign Herbster, Naval Constructor Richardson, and Lieutenant Commander McCrary. The craft was designed for a useful load of 3800 pounds, was to have a maximum speed of 25-35 mph, a duration of five hours carrying a crew of eight, a ceiling of 3,000 ft., and was to be able to alight on water. The ship had a volume of 115,000 ft^3. The envelope was 175 ft. long by 35 ft. in diameter. It was powered by a 8-cylinder 140 hp. Sturtevant motor driving two propellers. This first dirigible, designed and built under the supervision of this imported talent, was a great disappointment, for when it was completed two years later (April 1917) it was so much overweight that it could barely lift itself off the ground. Its envelope leaked, and the power plant functioned badly. It did, however, actually fly, and since the firm had built the ship in good faith and at a cost greatly in excess of the contract price, it was formally accepted and designated the DN-1 on 16 May 1917. The DN-1 made its first flight at Pensacola on 20 April 1917 piloted by McCrary. It was found to lack both military value and were worthless as a training ship. Its performance was unsatisfactory on several counts, and after only two more flights in the same month it was grounded and

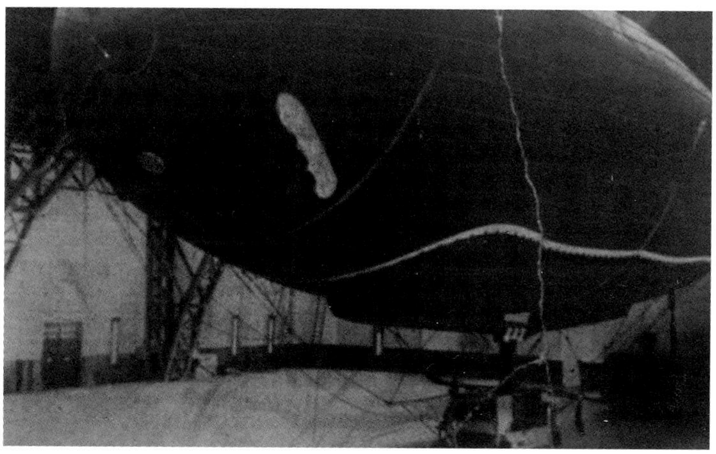

DN-1 under construction at the Connecticut Aircraft Company. She was 175 ft. long by 50 ft. high by 35 ft. wide.

DN-1 at NAS Pensacola in April 1917.

Lt.Cdr. J.P. Norfleet

never flown again. Its motor was poor, the envelope leaked, and when it was damaged while maneuvering into its hangar it was determined that it was not worth repairing. It was eventually deflated and broken up.

Two other LTA craft were ordered by the Navy in 1915—a free balloon from Goodyear in September, and a kite balloon which was purchased and put into commission at the Pensacola Aeronautic Station for instruction of personnel in "lighter-than-air" work on 5 April. The contract with Goodyear called for the training of two Naval Officers in LTA operations. Lieutenant Commander McCrary and Lieutenant Maxfield were subsequently ordered to Akron for training.

Even before the construction of the DN-1 was completed, the Bureau of Construction and Repair began studies on a future class of rigid airships (these studies were reinforced by a directive from Admiral Benson to prepare studies for two training dirigibles and one rigid dirigible). The concept was to be for a training airship capable of carrying six men, and with an endurance of four hours at 40 mph. On 22 July 1916 Chief Constructor Rear Admiral Taylor requested that the Aluminum Co. of America apply its resources to the development of a suitable alloy, and its fabrication into Zeppelin-type girders. On 19 October 1916 the General Board endorsed the development of LTA craft. With respect to planning by the Navy for the procurement of a rigid airship, the following is quoted from a 24 October 1916 Memo to Captain McKean: "All information available relative to rigid dirigibles has been compiled. Efforts have been and are being made to interest the various manufacturers of material which enter into the construction of rigid dirigibles, in the development of suitable materials. Computations have been made on which specifications for one dirigible of the rigid type are being prepared."

Lieutenant Maxfield accepted for the Navy the Goodyear free balloon on 14 December 1915 and the kite balloon on 22 December 1915. The kite balloon was immediately shipped to Pensacola, accompanied by a Goodyear representative. Instruction of officers and ground crew in the handling and inflating of the kite balloon was begun the next day. However, on 7 April a strong wind hit Pensacola and tore the kite balloon from its moorings, inflicting

LTA Training at Akron showing an airship in a hangar and another airship cruising above the hangar.

Quarters for LTA students at Akron.

Close-up view of an aircraft fuselage suspended from an airship.

Close-up view of an aircraft fuselage suspended from an airship.

significant damage. The balloon, however, was soon repaired, and two more were subsequently ordered late in the year. As a result of the damage to the kite balloon, planned tests aboard the U.S.S. *North Carolina* were postponed. Eventually, due to prodding by Captain Bristol, the balloon was tested aboard the U.S.S. *Nevada* and U.S.S. *Oklahoma*. Robert R. Paunack (Naval Aviator No. 27) was assigned to LTA duty aboard the *Nevada* for this activity (in November 1917 he was designated an LTA pilot). To train winchmen for the kite balloon ships, a training camp was established at Pelham Bay. The capacity of the school was 20 students per course.

The Navy purchased a total of 117 kite balloons of various volumes (Goodyear Tire and Rubber Company—65; Goodrich Tire and Rubber Company—29; Connecticut Aircraft Company—three; and Air Cruisers Inc.—two). In addition, 17 were obtained from the Allies—13 from England, and two each from France and Italy. A kite balloon was also purchased from the U.S. Army. In 1918 those kite balloons purchased from the Allies and most of those purchased from Goodyear and Goodrich were in use in Europe. Specifically, as referenced in the report *U.S. Naval Forces in Foreign Service*: 12 Goodrich type "M" of 33,000 ft.^{3} serial number A-727 to A-732 inclusive and A-734; 18 Goodyear type "R" of 37,500 ft.^{3} serial numbers 2659 to 2624 inclusive, and 2673 to 2684 inclusive (even numbered balloons were used as spares for the odd number balloons); and 18 Goodyear type "C" of 33,000 ft.^{3} serial numbers A-704 to 721 inclusive. All of these balloons had to be altered and repaired before they were fit for sea duty. Alterations and tests were made at the U.S. Naval Air Station at Brest, France, and all repairs as well, except for the first shipment of 14 Goodyear Type "R" balloons that were repaired at the U.S. naval air station at Pauilliac, France.

One Goodrich "M" balloon was surveyed and turned over to the U.S. Army for experimental work in August 1918. Eight Goodyear type "R" balloons and two Goodrich type "M" balloons were forwarded to the RAF in London in October 1918. The remainder were returned to the U.S. after the cessation of hostilities.

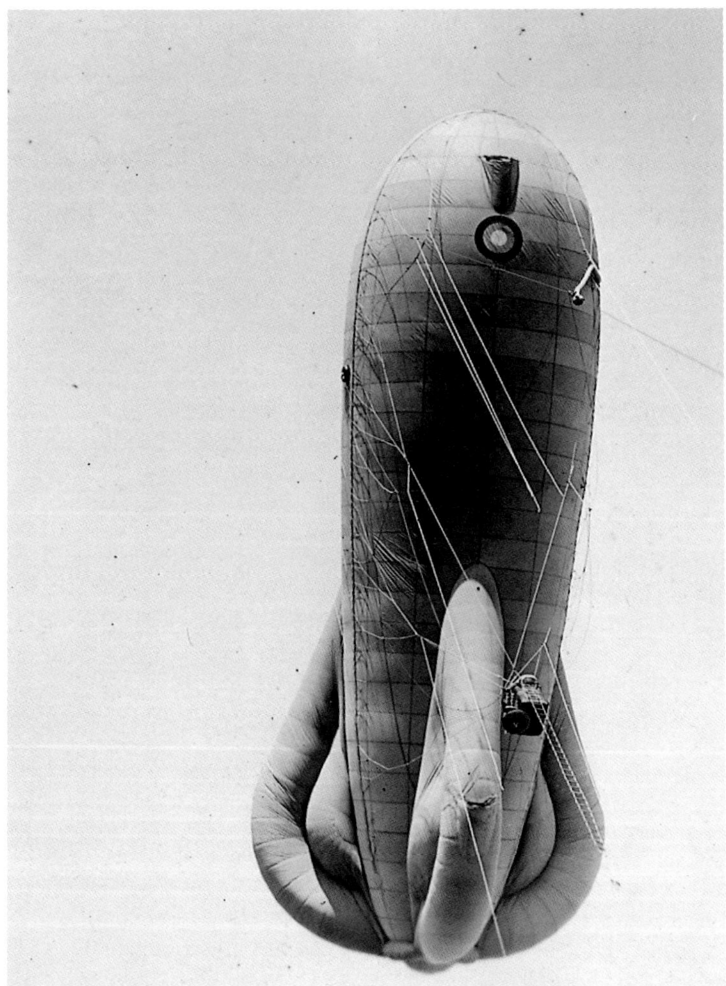

View of a Kite Balloon showing the rigging associated with both the balloon and the Observer's basket.

U.S. Navy Blimp B-8.

View of an unidentified naval blimp entering its hangar.

Four 2500 m^3 and two 750 m^3 Nourrice Balloons were also ordered from the French, but none were completed in time for use. To settle this contract, one 750 m^3 and two 2500 m^3 nourrices were completed, paid for, and shipped to the U.S. and the others canceled, an indemnity being paid.

In January 1916 Congress authorized the building of rigid airships. In December, 1916, the design of a coast patrol airship of 12 hours was modified. The maximum speed was revised to 45 mph, the endurance was to be 12 hours at 35 mph, the crew was to total three, a radio was added, and the capability for both landing at sea as well as being towed was added. On 6 January 1917 a Board of Army and Navy Officers recommended to the Secretaries of War and Navy that an airship of the Zeppelin type be designed and constructed under the direction of the Chief Constructor of the Navy, with funds provided equally by the two services, and that a board of three Army and three Navy officers be created to ensure interservice cooperation.[3] This interservice Board made the following recommendations:

1. That rigid ships be purchased in England to meet the U.S. needs in the war zone;
2. That ships that were needed at home be built so that America might develop a capability of her own;
3. That the responsibility for building rigids be assigned to the Navy, because the ships appeared to possess primarily a naval value; and
4. That the production of helium be accelerated.

In January 1917 Naval Constructor Hunsaker proposed that plans for a training LTA ship were met, and his plans were approved. This design, designated as Type B, was submitted by Admiral Taylor on 6 January 1917. It was approved by the Secretary of the Navy on 27 January 1917. This ship was of 77,000 ft.^{3} capacity, with a useful load of 2,000 lbs. A 100 hp Curtiss engine drove a tractor propeller. The cruising endurance of this design was 12 hours. It was only intended to build one airship to this design as an experiment, but, as relations with Germany were becoming acute, the Secretary, on 17 February 1917, ordered the construction of 16 "limp" airships of the B type instead of one. [Note: The acronym "Blimp" seems to have evolved from the phrase "B limp airship."] This order was a thunderbolt, as delivery in any reasonable time was out of the question with existing facilities. No firms had knowledge or experience, and no time could be allowed them for experiment and research. There was also no time to build one airship to prove the design; all 16 were wanted at once. On 6 February, the Office of Chief Constructor distributed plans and specifications to the five U.S. firms which had expressed an interest in providing their facilities for war work should the U.S. enter hostilities. Representatives of these firms met with the Chief Constructor on 12 February. Arrangements were finally made, during a conference in Taylor's office, for the production of these airships by a group of firms, pooling their knowledge, skill, materials, and information. Contracts were placed on 14 March 1917 for nine airships to the Goodyear Co., five to the Goodrich Co., two to the Connecticut Aircraft Co., and 14 cars and engines (for the Goodyear and Goodrich ships) to the Curtiss Aeroplane Co. Goodrich hired an engineer from Lebaudy in Paris to help with the design of their ship. Pigeon Frazer contracted to build the car for the Connecticut Aircraft Co. U.S. Rubber Co. was to make the fabric. And Hall-Scott was to build the motor. The design of the airship manufactured by Goodrich called for an envelope 160 ft. long with a diameter of 31.5 ft., and with a displacement of 77,000 ft.^{3} The car to be carried was for a pilot, an observer, and a 100 hp engine. The maximum speed was to be 45 mph at 600 ft. altitude for a duration of 10 hours. The useful load was 1941 lbs. The cost of the ship, arrived at prior to production, was $40,000. The Goodyear Co., at its own expense, also undertook to provide a flying field with shed and hydrogen plant, in order to conduct tests and trials, and to train naval airship personnel. Construction of these facilities began on 1 April. Goodyear completed the first B Class nonrigid in May 1917. Two short test flights were made with the ship on 24 May. On 30 May 1917 the Navy's first successful airship, the B-1, completed an overnight test flight to Akron from Chicago, where it had been assembled. (Inflation had taken place in the Goodrich facilities near

Chicago, since the Goodyear facilities at Akron were not yet completed.) The pilot was R.H. Upson of Goodyear. The airship unfortunately crashed into a tree a few miles short of Akron. Heavily damaged, it had to undergo extensive repairs. The B-1 was delivered to the Navy on 19 July and shipped to Pensacola on 7 August. The delivery of the remaining B class airships—designated B-2 thru B-16, and assigned Bureau numbers A-235 thru A-250—took place between July 1917 and June 1918, during which time the Goodyear Co. trained the first naval airship detachment under the command of the promoted Commander Maxfield (Naval Aviator No. 17), USN, at Akron, Ohio (based upon a contract of 29 May 1917 for a class of 20—See Chapter 2). The first Goodrich Type B airship was commissioned on 11 September 1917. It was initially used for extensive and secret night flight testing over Lake Michigan. Table 1 provides the dates of delivery of these craft:

Table 1

Number	Manufacturer	Date
B-1	Goodyear	19 July 1917
B-2	Goodyear	22 January 1918
B-3	Goodyear	22 October 1917
B-4	Goodyear	4 December 1917
B-5	Goodyear	11 August 1917
B-6	Goodyear	3 March 1918
B-7	Goodyear	27 February 1918
B-8	Goodyear	25 February 1918
B-9	Goodyear	31 January 1918
B-10	Goodrich	14 April 1918
B-11	Goodrich	8 May 1918
B-12	Goodrich	6 June 1918
B-13	Goodrich	11 September 1917
B-14	Goodrich	11 January 1918
B-15	Connecticut	14 December 1917
B-16	Connecticut	15 April 1918

While this effort was underway, a parallel effort was being carried out relating to the acquisition of free balloons by the Navy. The Goodyear Company, at its own expense, agreed to construct and erect a facility, consisting of an airship shed, a hydrogen facility, and quarters, at a field near Akron. The decision was reached 20 March 1917, and ground was broken on 1 April. The first free balloon was inflated 1 June 1917.

Ground crew handling the blimp C-8.

Kite Balloon hangar on a Kite Balloon ship.

On 18 April 1917 the Navy signed a $375,000 contract for the fabrication of steel work and the erection of eight LTA hangars "at points to be designated." Each hangar was to be 250 ft. long by 133 ft. wide by 66 ft. high. On 14 June 1917 the Navy entered into "cost plus" contracts for LTA base construction at Montauk, Bay Shore, and Rockaway Beach. The contracts specified that each base was to be equipped with: one LTA hangar; one seaplane hangar; one shelter for hydrogen production; one Officers Quarters; two Men's Quarters; and one Mess and Recreation Building. The funds for these stations were covered by the Appropriations Bill passed on 29 August 1916 for fiscal 1917. In addition to the established stations previously indicated, the Navy established Kite Balloon hangars at Marginal Parkway (Brooklyn) and at Charleston, South Carolina.

On 26 September 1917 Lieutenant Maxfield, Commanding the Naval Air Detachment at Akron, reported the qualification of 11 students, including himself, as LTA pilots, and requested their designation as Naval Aviators (Dirigibles). These men, the first trained specifically as dirigible pilots, were subsequently assigned Naval Aviator numbers ranging from 94 to 104. Training continued at Akron through the war period, and as more men acquired the necessary skills, the Navy gradually took over more of the responsibility for instruction and upkeep. When graduates of the Ground School at M.I.T. began arriving, some reduction in the length of the course was possible by eliminating some of the ground school subjects already covered at that school. Throughout the war Akron remained the main source of LTA pilots, although some were trained at other stations. Akron, however, was not the only station to provide primary dirigible training for prospective naval aviators. Initially, LTA training was offered domestically—in addition to Akron—at Pensacola, Chatham, Montauk, Rockaway, Cape May, Hampton Roads, and Key West. Eventually, training was concentrated at Akron, Pensacola, and Rockaway.

U.S. Naval Aviation's LTA activities in Europe began with the assignment of Lieutenant Lansdowne and Lieutenant (j.g.) Ralph Kiley to England for training as dirigible pilots in August 1917. Both men completed their training and were graduated from Cranwell, England, on 14 November. On 27 October 1917, a group of graduates of the naval ground school at M.I.T. left the U.S. for LTA training at RNAS Roehampton, England (Eugene I. Wolfe, Alfred Gardner, Ralph Hawthorne, Max J. Baehr, Donald H. Merrill, R.L. Piper, Jr., George Dana Anderson, Albert A. Bailey, Thomas R. Punnett, Addison C. Burnham, Jr., Thomas E. McCraken, Philip J. Barnes, N.J. Leonard, Joseph Warren Homer, Jr., and Harrison S. Goodspeed). These men, enrolled at M.I.T. as Seaman 2c, were the first U.S. Aviators to go as a body to England to become pilots and to assist the RNAS. Following completion of their training and subsequent commissioning as Ensigns, these men were assigned to various RNAS Dirigible stations for further training and patrol duties. Their achievements were such that on 22 June 1918, Brigadier-General E.M. Maitland, Superintendent of Airships, wrote to Admiral Sims commending the following U.S. Naval personnel assigned to RNAS Dirigible stations: G.D. Adams, H.E. Goodspeed, P.J. Barnes, L.A. Pope, R.L. Piper, N.J. Leonard, J.W. Homer, D.H. Morrill, and R.H. Norris.

In November 1917 the first contingent U.S. Naval dirigible pilots arrived in Europe—all were from the first LTA Class at Akron. The group included Ens. Strader, Talbot, Whitehouse, Brewer, Little, Deland, and Hamlen. Ensign Hamlen was ordered to Headquarters, Paris, for duty with dirigible operations, schools, and training, while the remainder were ordered to NAS Paimboeuf for LTA operations.

By the end of 1917 six B Class nonrigids were operating from stations on the Atlantic coast (Chatham, Montauk, Rockaway Beach, Cape May, and Key West, with a B Class ship assigned to Hampton Roads for experimentation purposes). These airships were successful in meeting their mission, and at least the equal of the foreign product of that date. They had little direct war experience, being all used on this side of the Atlantic. However, these B Class airships trained 170 pilots, and on coast patrol did 13,600 hours—some 400,000 miles—without a fatality. Designed for a 16-hour patrol, one ship at Key West was out 40 hours. One ship was in service for 15 months with its original envelope. Another kept a single inflation of gas for 9 months, and was in the air during this time 743 hours.

As airship construction began in earnest, the Navy began to experience problems with LTA inspectors. These men, supplied by the Bureau of Construction and Repair and/or the Bureau of Steam Engineering, were not always pilots—and if they were, they were HTA pilots—nor were they engineers. Hunsaker recommended the Navy follow the Army approach and hire civilian engineers as inspectors. This was done.

Once war was declared the Marine Corps became involved with LTA activities. A small detachment of Marines was sent to the Army Balloon School at St. Louis, and then to a second Army School at Fort Omaha, NE. For one reason or another, this detachment never received orders for overseas duty.

On 17 September a kite balloon from the U.S.S. *Huntington* was hit by a squall. While it was being hauled down to the ship it struck the water so hard that the Observer, Lieutenant (j.g.) H.W. Hoyt, was knocked out of the basket and entangled in its lines. As the balloon was pulled toward the ship SF1 Patrick McGunigal went over the side, cleared the tangle of lines, and put a line around Hoyt so that he could be hauled up on deck. For this act of heroism, McGunigal was later to receive the Medal of Honor. Early in August 1918 trial trips with Kite Balloons were begun in France by the destroyer U.S.S. *Cushing*.

In the spring of 1918 a larger and faster type of nonrigid airship to carry heavy depth charges was designed for anti-submarine activities overseas. The modification for a new design was a combination of experiences gained from the B-Class airships, as well as information received from British, French, and Italian sources. A key input was provided by Lieutenant Commander P.L. Reed, RNVR, who was attached to the British Naval Attaché in Washington. This design provided high speed to cope with head winds, great endurance to follow convoys, and a duplicated power plant to lessen the chance of complete breakdown at sea, and was designed Type C. The objective of this type was to have an airship with two engines, capable of çarrying four 270 lb. depth bombs and to be armed. The ship was powered by two 150 hp Hispano-Suiza engines. It had a useful load of 4760 lbs. and a volume of 182,000 ft^3. The design proved to be highly successful, and a full speed of 60 miles

Close-up view of the Kite Balloon Observer in his basket.

per hour was realized. Contracts were placed with Goodrich and Goodyear for 30 C-Class airships to be built in accordance with the bureau's design, with the cars for all 30 to be made by Curtiss Co. The first C-Class airship, the C-1, was completed in September 1918, and on its maiden flight, 22 October, flew a nonstop distance of 400 miles. The twin-engine airship C-1, commanded by the now Major Bernard L. Smith, USMC, with a Navy crew of Ensign Warner L. Hamlen, Lieutenant R.A.D. Preston, Lieutenant (j.g.) Donald T. Hood, Ensign M.H. Estorly, and two civilian mechanics (M. Roulette and James Royal), was delivered to NAS Rockaway after a one-day flight from Akron, Ohio, which included a stop at Washington, DC. The Aero Club of America later awarded Smith and Hamlen its Medal of Merit for this flight. As a result of the armistice, only 10 C-Class airships were completed, and the contracts for the other 20 ships were canceled.

Several features of the C-Class ships resulted in pilot objections. The resultant attempt to address these concerns resulted in the D-Class of airships. This design was authorized by the Secretary of the Navy on 16 July 1918. The car was lightened, gas tanks were relocated outside of the car, the engines were mounted so as to have the crew outside of the slipstream, and the control surfaces were balanced. Goodyear received a contract for three ships, Goodrich a contract of two, and the Naval Aircraft Factory a contract for one ship. The first D-Class ship flew on 13 July 1920.

Kite Balloon showing both the stabilizing tail and the observation basket.

The Observation basket of a Kite Balloon. Photo taken at the Naval Aviation Museum at Pensacola.

Two other "one-of-a-kind" ships were built—both of the B-Class, but of a smaller capacity. The E-1 was intended to be used for training. The F-1 was intended to be used as an engine test bed. Both of these ships were Goodyear design, which were offered to the Navy in 1918. The Navy procured the E-1, via a contract dated 5 June, and the F-1 via a contract dated 7 July. The E-1 flew at Akron and was then shipped to Pensacola on 16 December 1918. The F-1 first flew at Akron, on 11 February 1919.

In the Summer of 1918 plans were made for a G-Class of airship to be used on long-distance anti-submarine patrols. The design, originally conceived to have a 360,000 $ft.^3$ capacity, and later increased to 400,000 $ft.^3$, was to include an enclosed car, with sleeping quarters, and to be armed both with an anti-submarine gun (Davis Gun?), as well as depth bombs. This design was never built, but, if the war had continued, it is certain that something larger than the D-Class airships would have been used to replace the French non-rigids then in use at the French coastal air stations.

On 25 June the Secretary of War approved a recommendation by the Joint Army and Navy Airship Board, thus completing an inter-service agreement which assigned responsibility for development of rigid airships to the Navy.[4] This agreement established the foundation for the Navy's airship activities in the 1920s.

U.S. Navy Airships, 1915-1918:[5]

Class	No. Built	Volume (Ft^3.)	No. Engines	Hp.	Engine Type	Max. Speed
A	1	110,000	1	140	Sturtevant	30
B	16	77,000	2	100	Curtiss OXX	40
C	10	181,000	2	150	Hispano-Suiza	52
D	6	1990,000	2	125	Union	50
E	1	95,000	1	150	Thomas	48
F	1	95,000	1	125	Union	45

In October 1918 the Navy submitted to Congress a request for funding, both to allow the construction of four rigid airships of the zeppelin style, and to construct hangars for the ships. Two of the ships were to be built in England, and two in the United States. Before the request could be acted upon the war ended. Following the armistice, the requested program was cut in half. The funding allotted was for one ship to be built in the U.S. (ZR-I) and one ship (ZR-2) to be constructed in England. Without a proven experience base upon which to draw, the Navy decided that the most logical approach would be to duplicate a proven design. It was therefore decided that the design of the ZR-1 would be based upon the German Zeppelin L49, which had fallen on 20 October 1917 at Bourbonne-les-Baines, France. The ZR-1 (Shenandoah) was not completed until 1924.

While the caption on this photo states that it shows the first lot of pilots, instructors, and mechanics at Cranwell, it is more likely showing the group of 15 graduates of the naval aviation ground school at M.I.T. who were assigned to RNAS Roehampton, England, for LTA training.

TABLE 2

Partial Listing of Lighter-than-air Aircraft Purchased by the Navy Prior to 1919

Aircraft Number (First Series)	**Model/Type/Name Manufacturer**	**Power Plant/Capacity**	**Remarks**
BC-1	Kite Balloon, Goodyear		1916
DN-1	Dirigible, Goodyear		1916
A-94 (BC-3)	Kite Balloon	25,000 ft.^{3}	
A-95 (BC-2)	Kite Balloon	25,000 ft.^{3}	
A-151 (BC-4)	Kite Balloon	25,000 ft.^{3}	
A-160 - A-161	Kite Balloon	25,000 ft.^{3}	
A-235 - A-243	B-Class Dirigible, Goodyear	Curtiss OXX, 100 hp	
A-244 - A-246	B-Class Dirigible, Curtiss	Curtiss OXX, 100 hp	
A-247 - A-248	B-Class Dirigible, Goodrich	Curtiss OXX, 100 hp	
A-249 - A-250	B-Class Dirigible, Connecticut Airc.	Hall-Scott, 100 hp	
A-251	Free Balloon, Connecticut Aircraft Co.		Pensacola
A-252 - A-275			Canceled
A-276 - A-281	Kite Balloon, Goodyear	16,000 ft.^{3}	
A-282 - A-287	Kite Balloon, Goodyear	25,000 ft.^{3}	
A-372 - A-373	Kite Balloon, Goodyear		Canceled
A-700	Kite Balloon, Goodyear	19,000 ft.^{3}	
A-701	Kite Balloon, Goodrich	19,000 ft.^{3}	
A-702 - A-726	Kite Balloon, Goodyear	35,000 ft.^{3}	
A-727 - A-751	Kite Balloon, Goodrich	35,000 ft.^{3}	
A-763 - A-764	Cacquot "M" Kite Balloon (British)		From British Govt.
A-816 - A-817	Cacquot "P" Kite Balloon	25,000 ft.^{3}	From French Govt.
A-998	Type "M" (Henri Julliot) Kite Balloon, B.F. Goodrich	19,000 ft.^{3}	
A-1029 - A-1030	O-SS Dirigible (British Govt.)	Rolls-Royce, 75 hp	Adm. Sims purchase (A-1030 Canceled)
A-2208 - A-2214	Free Balloon, Goodyear	19,000 ft.^{3}	
A-2215 - A-2216	Free Balloon, Connecticut Airc.	35,000 ft.^{3}	
A-2655 - A-2929	Cacquot "R" Kite Balloon, Goodyear	37,500 ft.^{3}	A-2845 - A-2929 Canceled
A-2930 - A-3204	Cacquot Kite Balloon, Goodrich Type "R" (81) and Type "M" (10)	37,500 ft.^{3}	A-3021 - A-3204 Canceled

A-3383	"K" "Gastite" Kite, Balloon, Goodrich		
A-4109	E-1 Dirigible, Goodyear	Thomas Mod., 150 hp	
A-4118	C-1 Dirigible, Goodyear	2/Hispano-Suiza, 150 hp	
A-4119	C-2 Dirigible, Goodrich	2/Hispano-Suiza, 150 hp	
A-4120	C-3 Dirigible, Goodyear	2/Hispano-Suiza, 150 hp	
A-4121	C-10 Dirigible, Goodrich	2/Hispano-Suiza, 150 hp	
A-4122 - A-4123	C-4 and C-8 Dirigible, Goodyear	2/Hispano-Suiza, 150 hp	
A-4124 - A-4125	C-6 and C-9 Dirigible, Goodrich	2/Hispano-Suiza, 150 hp	
A-4126 - A-4127	C-5 and C-7 Dirigible, Goodyear	2/Hispano-Suiza, 150 hp	
A-4348	F-1 Dirigible, Goodyear	Union, 150 hp (Test)	
A-4450	D-1 Dirigible, Goodyear	2/Union, 150 hp	
A-4451	D-2 Dirigible, Goodrich	2/Union, 150 hp	
A-4452 - A-4453	D-3 and D-4 Dirigible, Goodyear	2/Union, 150 hp	
A-4454	D-5 Dirigible, Goodrich	2/Union, 150 hp	
A-4455 - A-4462	D-Class Dirigibles, Goodyear	2/Union, 150 hp	Canceled
A-4463 - A-4469	D-Class Dirigibles, Goodrich	2/Union, 150 hp	Canceled
A-5020	M-1 Type "R" Kite Balloon, Goodyear	20,000 ft.^{3}	
A-5022 - A-5023	Reduced "R" Kite Balloon, Goodrich	20,000 ft.^{3}	
A-5025 - A-5028	Cacquot "P" Kite Balloon, Goodyear	25,000 ft.^{3}	
A-5029	Experimental Kite Balloon, Goodyear	37,500 ft.^{3}	
A-5240	Cacquot Type "M" Kite Balloon, Brit. Admiralty		
A-5241 - A-5242	A.P. (Avorioi-Prasone) Kite Balloon, Avorio-Prasone	38,000 ft.^{3}	From Italian Government
A-5257	B-20 Dirigible, Goodyear	Curtiss OXX, 100 hp	
A-5463	Kite Balloon, Goodyear		
A-5464 - A-5465	B-17 and B-18 Dirigibles, Goodyear	Hispano-Suiza	Rebuilt cars
A-5466	Airship car, Goodyear		Canceled
A-5467	B-19 Dirigible, Goodyear	Hispano-Suiza, 150 hp	Rebuilt Car
A-5468	Airship car, Goodyear		Canceled
A-5472	AT-1 Dirigible, Astra-Torres	2/Renault, 150 hp	From French Government
A-5473 - A-5482	Kite Balloon (British)		From British Government
A-5563	SS-Z-23 (R-23)(Z-2), British Dirigible	Rolls-Royce, 75 hp	From British Government
A-5580	NS-1 (North Sea) British Dirigible	2/Fiat, 260 hp	From British Government
A-5587	O-1 Dirigible	2/Colombo, 230 hp	From Italian Government
A-5592 - A-5593	VZ-1 and VZ-2 Dirigible, Vedette Zodiac (Originally VZ-8 and VZ-13)	2/Renault, 80 hp	From French Government
A-5594 - A-5605	Free Balloon, Connecticut Airc.	35,000 ft.^{3}	

TABLE 3

Status of French Dirigibles Operated or Ordered by the Navy on November 11, 1918

Ship	Manufacturer	Type	Capacity	Located	Remarks
VZ-7	Zodiac	Tri-lobe, Envelope, Twin Engine	2800 m^3	Paimbouef	New in June
AT-1	Astra-Torres	Tri-lobe, Envleope	6000 m^3		Packaged and shipped to the U.S.
VZ-13	Zodiac	Plain Envelope, Twin Engine	2800 m^3	Paimboeuf	New in October
T-2	Chalais-Meudon	Plain Envelope, Twin Engine	9500 m^3	Guipavas	Ready for cession to U.S. Forces
AT-13	Astra-Torres	Tri-lobe Envelope, Twin Engine	8300 m^3	Paimboeuf	New in August
AT-17	Astra-Torres	Tri-lobe, Envelope, Twin Engine	8300 m^3	Factory	Delivery about January 1, 1919
AT-18	Astra-Torres	Tri-lobe, Envelope, Twin Engine	9600 m^3	Factory	Delivery about January, 1919
CM-5	Chalais-Meudon	Plain Envelope, Twin Engine	9100 m^3	Factory	Delivery about January 1, 1919
CM-6	Chalais-Meudon	Plain Envelope, Twin Engine	9100 m^3	Factory	Delivery about February 2, 1919
ZD-1	Zodiac	Plain Envelope, Twin Engine	9300 m^3	Factory	Delivery about January 1, 1919
ZD-2	Zodiac	Plain Envelope, Twin Engine	9300 m^3	Factory	Delivery about February 1, 1919
ZD-3	Zodiac	Plain Envelope, Twin Engine	9300 m^3	Factory	Delivery about March 1, 1919

The settlement of the outstanding contracts for French Dirigibles were made as follows: The AT-17, CM-5, ZD-1, and ZD-2 were to be completed and turned over to the U.S. Naval Forces at the contracted prices. The orders for the AT-18, CM-6, and ZD-3 were canceled, and an indemnity paid to compensate for the construction work performed on these ships.

Notes:

[1] Van Wyen, Adrian O., *Naval Aviation in World War I,* Naval Aviation News, 1969, G.P.O., Washington, DC

[2] Grossinck, Roy A., *Kite Balloons to Airships....The Navy's Lighter-than-Air Experience*, Superintendent of Documents, Government Printing Office

[3] van Vleet, Clarke, and William J. Armstrong, *United States Naval Aviation 1910-1980*, G.P.O., Washington DC, 1980

[4] Miller Jr., Thomas G. amd Douglas H. Robinson, "How rigid airships in World War I,...." *Cross and Cockade Journal* (U.S.), Volume. 5, No. 1, Pages 97-116

[5] ibid

4

Development of Heavier-Than-Air Craft*

The first airplanes purchased by the Navy were of the pusher design, two of the Curtiss type and one of the Wright type. One of the Curtiss types was an 80 hp seaplane convertible to a land plane configuration, and the other was a 40 hp land plane which was later converted into an 80 hp seaplane. Both of these planes were constructed with a bamboo frame and tail, and came equipped with front as well as tail elevators. These front elevators were soon found to be unnecessary, and were subsequently removed. Each plane was equipped with a single pontoon, as well as with wing tip floats. The Wright was a 32-hp airplane of the usual Wright type, equipped with two propellers. This airplane was later converted to a twin-float seaplane. The speed of the Curtiss seaplanes was about 60 miles per hour, and the Wright about 42 miles per hour. The Curtiss carried 16 gallons of gasoline, and the Wright about 10 gallons. All these seaplanes gave a fairly good performance, considering the state of development at that time. They were all very lightly constructed, and the fact that there were no serious structural failures can probably be traced to the light loadings placed upon their structures.

In the summer of 1912 both a Burgess-Wright seaplane and an improved Curtiss seaplane were delivered to the Navy. In the late autumn of 1912 the first Curtiss flying boat was delivered. This was used for catapult tests and then was sent to Guantanamo, Cuba. During 1913 four more planes were delivered. These were two Curtiss flying boats, one Curtiss amphibian boat (named O.W.L., which stood for "Over Water Over Land"), and one Wright 60 hp seaplane. In addition, in May 1913, the Navy purchased from the Burgess Co. of Marblehead MA, a Model K Flying Boat. Known in the Navy as the D-1, this machine was to be used to conduct experiments associated with various designs of catapult. Such tests were necessary since, as the Navy began to accumulate aircraft from various manufacturers, they began to experience the problem of a lack of uniformity or standardization between the manufacturers in the areas of control systems. In addition to the Wright 2-stick control, there were also the Curtiss yoke control, the rotatable wheel mounted on a moveable shaft, the Deperdussin, and the Nieuport system. While the results of the experiments conducted with the Model K Flying Boat resulted in pilots voicing preference for the Deperdussin system, it would not be until 1916 that the Navy would standardize on its requirements. Early in 1914 three more Curtiss boats of an improved type and a Burgess-Dunne seaplane were delivered. This last named seaplane, designated AH-7, had its wings

The Curtiss AB-2 apparently being prepared for a catapult launch.

Curtiss MF flying boat on display at the Naval Aviation Museum at Pensacola.

Details of the construction of the hull of a Curtiss HS-1.

Curtiss HS-1, photo taken on 29 May 1918. The officer is not identified.

arranged in a V-form and had no tail surfaces. It was inherently very stable, and therefore difficult to maneuver in the air due to the lack of aerodynamic efficiency. It was equipped with a Curtiss 80-horsepower engine. There was also delivered a Burgess flying boat, which was rather similar to the Curtiss type except that the hull was long and narrow, and seats were in tandem instead of side by side.

Prior to the commencement of the war in Europe, contracts were either let or preliminary negotiations for contracts were entered into, for one each of the various types of foreign aeroplanes. Subsequent to the commencement of the war, preliminary negotiations were stopped, and all contracts repudiated by the manufacturers except of that for one Paul Schmitt aeroplane. However, even this plane eventually was not delivered. In the autumn of 1914 two more Curtiss single-float seaplanes were delivered. These were of greater wing surface than the earlier types and had much larger floats.

During 1915 the Navy purchased another Burgess-Dunne and five Curtiss seaplanes. The May 1915 contract with Burgess called for three machines, which were of a distinctive type in that they possessed a high degree of inherent stability. All six of these seaplanes were equipped with the Curtiss OXX motor of 85 hp, and were capable of a speed of about 63 miles per hour. The Burgess Co. believed that they could develop a machine having the required inherent stability with comparatively little loss of aerodynamic efficiency. The first machine to be delivered capsized while being tested, necessitating a more or less complete rebuild of the machine. Following its reconstruction, the machine was found to have undesirable air qualities, which consisted of a decided longitudinal instability at both high and low speeds. The other two machines called for under this contract were held up pending resolution of the problems associated with the first machine.

On 2 September 1915 a contract was let with the Gallaudet Co. for one twin-engine single propeller aeroplane. A distinctively new feature was the incorporation in this machine of the two engines geared together driving a single shaft, to which was secured a single propeller, the axis of which was in the longitudinal axis of the fuse-

Curtiss HS-1L showing how the engine was cranked to start. Personnel are not identified.

Mechanics working on the engine of Curtiss HS 1L No. 2103

Overhead view of a Curtiss H-2 on the water. (source: Sam Richards Collection)

Curtiss HS-2L coming in for a landing.

lage. Delivery of this machine was delayed due in part to the development of this feature, partly due to transmission troubles experienced by the manufacturer, and partly due to the inability of the manufacturer to get a pilot to demonstrate the machine.

On 2 October 1915 a contract was let with the Curtiss Aeroplane Co. for three nacelle hydroplanes. The machines were of a new type. Delivery of the planes took a long time due in part to trouble in designing a float suitable for the machines, and, partly, due to a difficulty in properly balancing the machines. On 19 October 1915 a contract was let with the Curtiss Aeroplane Co. for two Model R hydroaeroplanes. The Model R aeroplane had been successfully constructed by the Curtiss Co. for some time as a land plane, and the company believed that they could adapt this type of machine to water work. A great deal of trouble was experienced in developing floats that were believed suitable for the machine. When a float was designed the machine was sent out for preliminary trials. During the trials the machine was completely wrecked. Prior to the accident, sufficient data had been collected which necessitated a downgrading of both the load carrying capability of the machine and its rate of climb. Contracts were subsequently modified to address these lowered performance characteristics.

In November 1915 the Navy Department, in a sense of frustration over the quality of machines available domestically, the inability of available machines to meet the needs of the Navy, and the schedule of slippages experienced in the procurement of aircraft, undertook the design and construction of a large twin-engine aeroplane—the first machine to be designed and constructed throughout by the Department. A year later the machine was still not ready for fleet operation.

On 16 December 1915 a contract was let with the Martin Co. for two aeroplanes. The first was to be delivered at Pensacola and taken aboard the U.S.S. *North Carolina* to Guantanamo for winter maneuvers with the fleet. Shortly after arrival in Guantanamo the machine was wrecked due to the giving way of the float on a landing. The company was required to modify the design of the float of the second machine before it was accepted.

During 1916, the purchase of aircraft by the Navy was considerably increased, 60 machines being obtained, and in practically all, an improvement in engine power was procured. In the month of January 1916 12 planes were contracted. Different manufacturers produced a variety of machines, a most significant development being the first naval application of the tractor type of configuration.

Curtiss HS-2L.

Enlisted personnel examining a Curtiss HS-2L which has seen better days.

Curtiss HS-1L.

A Curtiss N-9 Gunnery plane taking off—likely at NAS Pensacola.

Fatalities as the result of crashes were immediately reduced with the advent of the tractor type. Among the planes obtained during this year were Thomas, Burgess, Martin, and Sturdevant seaplanes.

On 4 January 1916 two contracts were let, one with the Burgess Co. for six school tractor aeroplanes, and one with the Sturtevant Aeroplane Company, also for six school tractor aeroplanes. The Burgess Co. believed that they could make the required performance using a 100-hp engine. The first machine was completed and tried out, but was found that the weight carrying capacity and the rate of climb was so far under the requirements that the machine could not be accepted. The company then redesigned and rebuilt the fuselage so as to install a motor of 125 hp. The machine was then tried out, and although it was found that the rate of climb was still not as much as was required in the contract, it was sufficient to warrant acceptance, owing to the shortage of aeroplanes in the Navy. In a similar situation, under the contract with Sturtevant, after many delays one of the aeroplanes was tried out, and although the rate of climb was lower than required, it was found to be sufficient to warrant acceptance. Subsequent to its acceptance float, trouble developed showing that the floats were improperly designed. The company was then required to redesign the floats for the remaining machines under the contract.

In June 1916 contracts were let for three more aircraft. The first, with the Standard Aeroplane Corp., was for one single engine

A close up view of the engine mounting, and gas tank installation, of Curtiss HS-2 No. 1551.

Curtiss N-9 No. 213 (No. A216 is on the rudder). Photo was taken 26 January 1918.

Curtiss R-9 No. 895.

Curtiss R-9 No. 958 trainer.

aeroplane of a type that had been satisfactorily demonstrated before the Naval Board. This machine was shipped to Pensacola for final acceptance trials, and during the progress of these trials one float was demolished on a landing. The second contract, also with the Standard Aeroplane Corp., was for one twin-engine aeroplane. The third contract, this one with the Curtiss Aeroplane Company, was for a twin-engine aeroplane. During the progress of its trials the machine was completely demolished.

On 29 August 1916 a contract was let with the Curtiss Aeroplane Company for 30 school tractors. The first machine was tried out before a Naval Board on Hampton Roads, and it was found that the float construction was unsatisfactory in many respects, and several other minor faults were noted. This necessitated changes in float construction, which resulted in an acceptance of the craft.

On 29 August 1916 the Navy had just six aeroplanes in commission. Four of these were at Pensacola, and two were on the *North Carolina*. All the other aircraft, for which contracts had been let, were anywhere from two to 22 months overdue. In the autumn of 1916, the Navy's first production order was placed with the Curtiss Co. for 30 type N-9 training machines. The N-9 was, for all intents and purposes, a Curtiss JN-4B powered by a 100 hp Curtiss OX-6 engine, and having a wing span increased by 10 feet. The increase in span was necessitated by the extra weight resulting from a large center section pontoon and two wing tip pontoons. The increase in span was achieved by applying a wider upper center-section, and fitting in additional lower panels inboard of the standard size outer panels. The successful results of experimental development during earlier years were clearly reflected in the design of aircraft purchased in 1916.

In the early months of 1917, the Navy purchased 11 planes, among which was the Curtiss R-3 seaplane with twin floats, and the H-12 flying boat equipped with two V-2 Curtiss motors, each developing about 200 horsepower.

Upon the declaration of war against Germany it became immediately important to develop aircraft useful for purposes other than mere flying. The suppression of the submarine was an urgency, and for offensive operations against submarines machines of long endurance and of large carrying capacity were immediately necessary. However, the first requirement was for more training machines, and the Curtiss Co. was given an order for 64 more N-9s and 76 of

Curtiss R-9 No. A942 at NAS Rockaway.

Close up view of a unique installation of a Lewis Gun on Curtiss R-9 No. 172.

A Curtiss F-boat at NAS Pensacola.

A Curtiss F-boat at the Curtiss Aviation School, Toronto, Canada, 1915.

a larger type designated R-6. These orders filled the available capacity of the Curtiss Co., which at that time had large orders for training airplanes from both the Army and the British Government. To permit expansion of the training program, additional orders were placed with each of the six other aircraft manufacturers for sample training planes of their own designs. Several satisfactory types were submitted for tests, and orders were planed in the summer of 1917 as follows: Burgess Co. of Marblehead, MA, 12 planes of Burgess design, plus 30 Curtiss N-9s; Boeing Co. of Seattle, 50 planes of Boeing design; Aeromarine Co. of Keyport, NJ, 200 planes of Willard design; and Curtiss Co. of Buffalo, 15 Curtiss Model Fs and 122 Curtiss R-6s. These orders were delivered at a reasonably satisfactory rate, and the training of aviators was at no time held back seriously for a lack of satisfactory training planes.

On 20 June 1917 the first Curtiss R-5 twin float seaplanes assigned to naval service were received at NAS Pensacola. R-types were assigned briefly to cruisers, while some saw service in flight training and were used in many of the early experiments with torpedoes.

Tests marking the beginning of serious Navy interest in launching torpedoes from aircraft were made on 14 August 1917. They were conducted by Lieutenant Edward 0. McDonnell at Huntington, L.I. The first struck the water at a bad angle and ricocheted, nearly striking the plane. Subsequent tests were conducted at Philadelphia. On 24 November 1917, in discussing the development of aircraft torpedoes, the Chief of Naval Operations pointed out that available aircraft could carry a load of not more than 600 pounds, and thus were incapable of delivering by this means an explosive charge large enough to seriously damage a modern warship. This problem of size of an effective charge versus the capabilities of aircraft, retarded torpedo plane development throughout the war.

Shortly after the declaration of hostilities the Navy found it feasible to construct and put into operation its own aircraft factory. It appeared unlikely that existing aircraft plants in the country would be able to cope with the large orders being thrown upon them by the Army and Navy. Therefore, it was reasonable to consider building at once an aircraft factory under Navy ownership.

The Navy had three objectives in establishing such a plant: 1) to manufacture at least a part of Navy aircraft under the direction and control of the Navy Department; 2) to have a plant in which aircraft could be designed and developed under the close direction and supervision of the Navy Department and its bureaus; and 3) to

A Curtiss F-boat at the Curtiss Aviation School, Toronto, Canada, 1915.

Curtiss F-boat No. A2331. Photo taken on 10 June 1918.

Curtiss F-5-L No. 3680.

Manufacture of Curtiss F-5-L at the Naval Aircraft Factory in Philadelphia.

accumulate data by which the Navy could be guided in dealing with questions of cost arising out of contracts with privately owned aircraft factories.

In June 1917, therefore, the Navy Department directed Commander F.G. Coburn, USN, Construction Corps, to make a survey of the situation and report upon a suitable location for, size of, and cost of a naval aircraft factory which would be capable of producing 1,000 training seaplanes a year or their equivalent. Coburn visited various private plants in the country and made a detailed study of the Curtiss Company plant in Buffalo, at that time the only factory in the country that could be considered a quantity-producing plant for airplanes. Upon completion of the tour, Commander Coburn, with Naval Constructor L.M. Henry, wrote a report entitled "Proposed Naval Aircraft Factory." This report, meeting with the approval of the head of the Bureau of Construction and Repair, Admiral David W. Taylor, was forwarded on 10 July 1917 to the Secretary of the Navy, bearing the endorsement and recommendation of Chief Constructor Taylor.

On 27 July the Secretary of the Navy, acting upon the recommendations, approved the project, estimating the cost at $1,000,000. The Philadelphia Navy Yard was selected for the new venture, since ample land was available there and the location was advantageous in terms of labor, material, and transportation. Furthermore, the Delaware River offered a natural facility for testing seaplanes.

Construction was to include a main building for the factory proper and three auxiliary buildings—a dry kiln, dry lumber storehouse, and a boiler house. Commander Coburn estimated the minimum time required putting the factory into operation at 100 days.

The contract was let on 6 August, and the ground broken four days later. Commander Coburn was appointed the first manager of the factory, and reported at the Philadelphia Navy Yard for this duty 27 August 1917. By Executive Order of 23 August 1917, special classes of employees were exempt from competitive Civil Service examination, but others were obtained in accordance with such regulations. Employment posed a difficult problem, particularly at the beginning, for most of the employees, including the superinten-

Manufacture of Curtiss F-5-L a the Naval Aircraft Factory in Philadelphia on 18 September 1918.

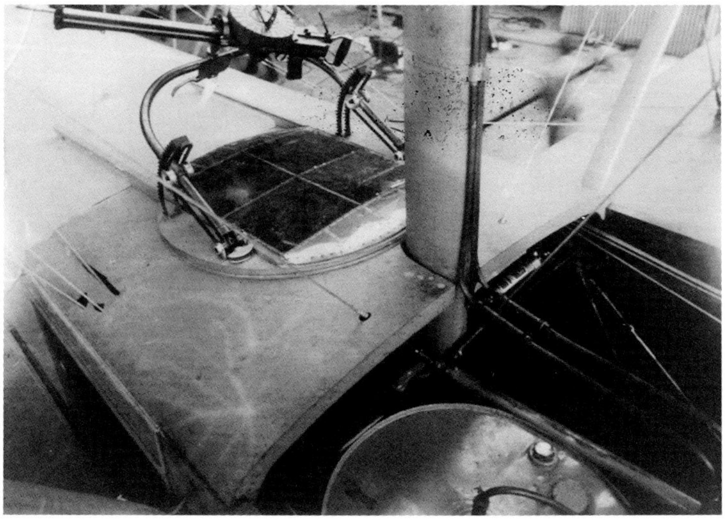

Close up view of the aft scarf mounting and Lewis Gun on a F-5-L. Photo taken 14 July 1918.

Curtiss F-5-L taxiing. Photo taken 20 July 1918.

Ground crew handling a Curtiss H-12. Judging from the lack of armament, lack of a national emblem, and the casual attire of the personnel, the photo was most likely taken at either NAS Pensacola or NAS Key West and was associated with the receipt of a new aircraft. The photo was taken on 17 April 1917.

dents, engineers, inspectors, and foremen, had to be trained to execute their particular tasks. Of 400 engineers and technical men, not more than ten had had previous airplane experience. The first mechanic was employed on 1 October. The first power-driven machinery was put in operation on 16 October, and the entire plant was completed by 28 November 1917, 110 days after breaking ground.

The log of the Naval Aircraft Factory (NAF) indicates that the first women employees went to work in December in the Inspection Department, inspecting turnbuckles. Special efforts were made to use and train women employees, and on 10 April 1918, the women's apprenticeship school opened at the factory. By the end of the war, women made up practically 25% of the entire work force. They were employed on the principle of equal pay with men for equal work.

The original proposal for the NAF had envisioned the building of training planes only, but this plan was quickly revised, since enough trainers were being built by other factories, and what was needed were types of aircraft suitable for antisubmarine patrol and convoy duties. Attempts were made to obtain information from abroad of any successful types in order that their manufacture might be undertaken, and in July 1917, a board of officers was sent to England, France, and Italy to obtain this information first hand. This board, on its return on 1 September 1917, reported that there was no wholly satisfactory foreign seaplane suitable for coastal patrol, and that American types equipped with the new Liberty engine would be superior to any abroad. The joint Army and Navy Technical Board, acting upon this information, and the knowledge that 15 coastal air stations abroad would be operated by the United States Navy, prepared a building program which was approved by the Secretary of the Navy in October 1917.

This initial program provided for 1,185 single Liberty engine flying boats known as the HS-1, and 235 twin Liberty engine flying boats known as the H-16. Provision of but two types with a single type of engine simplified production and maintenance. Two types of flying boats were necessary, as the large boats could not be

Bombsight used on the Curtiss F-5-L.

Curtiss H-12 No. A766.

Curtiss H-12 No. 676 on its step.

constructed in sufficient quantities, were involved in shipping difficulties, and drew too much water for use at certain of the French stations.

The Curtiss HS-1 flying boat was developed from a Curtiss design known as H-14, which was brought out in the summer of 1917. It was a typical Curtiss type of flying boat, having a length of 38 feet and a wingspan of 62 feet. The gross weight in the air of 5,900 pounds included a crew of two men, a machine gun, and two 180-pound bombs. The maximum speed of 87 miles could be maintained for four hours. After production had gotten well underway, information was obtained that the 180-pound bomb were not really effective against submarines, and that heavier bombs as well as a radio set would be needed. In order to permit the carrying of this extra load, it was necessary to increase the wing area. This was done by designing a 6-foot wing panel to be inserted out-board of the engine section on each side. The result of this change was an increase in the span to 74 feet and an increase in the total weight to 6,500 pounds. A larger rudder was also provided for the planes thus modified, and these modified planes were designated model HS-2.

The production of HS-2 flying boats is summarized in the following table:

	Number Ordered	Shipped Abroad	Delivered	Canceled after Armistice
Curtiss A&M Corp.	674	213	674	0
L.W.F. Engineering Co.	300	10	250	50
Standard Aircraft Co.	150	6	80	70
Gallaudet Aircraft Co.	60	0	60	0
Boeing Airplane Co.	50	0	25	25
Total	1238	229	1091	145

Curtiss H-12. The number 52 on the nose is not a Bureau of Aeronautic number and might be a station or squadron number. Personnel are not identified.

Curtiss H-12 No. 152 being towed on 7 April 1918.

Curtiss H-12 in flight.

The other type adopted for production by the Joint Army and Navy Technical Board was the Curtiss H-16 flying boat equipped with twin Liberty engines of 360 horsepower each. This type had been developed during 1915 and 1916 by the Curtiss Co. and the British Admiralty. The original model, as previously discussed, had been the Curtiss *America* of 1914, which was built just prior to the beginning of the war for a proposed Trans-Atlantic flight. The

Curtiss H-12a (a Curtiss H-12 with Rolls-Royce engines) at Felisxtowe, England. (source: Glenn H. Curtiss Museum of Hammondsport)

Sailors planking the bottom of a pontoon of a Curtiss H-16 at the Naval Aircraft Factory in Philadelphia on 10 September 1918.

America was not successful because no high-powered engines were available, but the British Admiralty ordered a number of them and fitted them in England with two French Anzani engines of about 100 horsepower each. In this configuration they were known as the "Little America's," and they were used to patrol submarine areas. Curtiss then designed the H-12, a larger machine on the same lines, which was fitted in England by the Admiralty with twin Rolls-Royce engines. The Admiralty redesigned the hull of the H-12 to provide greater strength, and introduced for the first time the steep Vee bottom with double steps. In the early part of 1917 the Curtiss Co. was given a large order for the British redesigned machines, known in England as F-3, or "Large America," and in the United States as the H-16. This machine was already in production at the Buffalo works of the Curtiss Co. when the U.S. declared war, but the design was configured to mount Rolls-Royce engines. It became necessary to redesign the H-16 to provide for Liberty engines. This redesign of the H-16 involved extensive changes in the plane. Production was started at once, in the absence of trial installation, and by a combination of good luck and good management no serious difficulties developed.

Curtiss H-16 No. 1070 on 10 October 1918.

Curtiss H-16 No. 846.

The H-16 flying boat was 46 feet in length, having a span of 96 feet, and equipped with two 360 horsepower Liberty engines. The empty weight was 7,400 pounds, and the loaded weight was 10,900 pounds. The useful load included a crew of four of five men (pilot, one or two observers, a mechanic, and a wireless operator), a radio, two 230-pound depth bombs, and four machine guns. The maximum speed was 95 miles per hour. At this speed the endurance was four hours, but patrols at cruising speed of nine hours were made in the war zone.

The experimental "gun-tower" on this Curtiss H-16, at NAS Pensacola in 1918, was no great success, but this photo does show how the Lewis Gun as mounted and how it looked in the firing position. The sailor in the hatch demonstrates the standard gun mounting on this aircraft.

The Factory, therefore, began work on the production of Curtiss H-16 twin-engine flying boats. On 12 October the form for the first boat was laid, and the work of ordering material and putting the H-16 into production began. On 17 October actual work on the first boat started, and, on 2 November, the first keel was laid.

Plans for the H-16 had to be completely redrawn to fit the production methods employed by the Factory. While the Curtiss Company's experienced foremen and skilled workmen did not need absolutely clear, detailed drawings of every minor part, the inexperienced NAF employees required complete information. This careful and thorough redrawing of the plans, which required the better part of two months, was the work of the Factory's first Chief Engineer, George R. Wadsworth, a major in the Signal Corps, USA, serving in this capacity while on active duty.

By December 1917, expansion of the planned operating program required an upward revision of scheduled aircraft procurement. The new schedule called for delivery of a total of 864 twin-engined flying boats of the H-16 or similar type by 1 January 1919. The total requirement exceeded not only the number on order, but also the capacity of existing manufacturing plants. An enormous expansion of the NAF was therefore authorized.

It was estimated that $3,250,000 would be required to build the new facilities. Subsequently, an additional $500,000 was needed to cover the cost of hangars and certain waterfront improvements. In addition to the hangar, there was to be a six-story concrete storehouse and a three-story office building; the assembly building was also to be enlarged. When, in June 1918, the original plant was in full production, the new one was very nearly completed. The total space available upon completion was 888,935 square feet, of which 500,000 square feet was used in the manufacture and assembly of aircraft. The rest was devoted to office space and storage.

The assembly building consisted of two parts: a low building 13 feet under the roof trusses for panel shop, varnish, and dope

Curtiss H-16.

Close up of the pilot compartment of a Curtiss H-16.

room, and pontoon manufacture; and a bay—100 feet wide, 51 feet under the trusses, and 680 feet long for final assembly—which was flanked on either side by a bay of equal size, 50 feet wide and 30 feet under the trusses. The 100-foot bay was equipped with two ten-ton, three-motor, overhead traveling electric cranes. Each of the side bays was equipped with a two-and-a-half ton small crane. By the end of the war over 40 acres were occupied by the enlarged plant. A considerable increase in paving, railroad tracks, roadways, etc., was provided for the allotment, which, including the hangar, represented a total investment of a little over $4,000,000.

Almost before this construction program began, the NAF, on 28 February 1918, received an order to produce 100 H-16s in addition to the 50 it was already building. Because there was hardly time to wait for the completion of the new buildings, an ingenious plan of sub-contracting was devised. By it, the facilities of many small manufacturers were put under contract to produce wing panels, boat hulls, and other more minor parts, which were delivered to the Factory for assembly. The first aircraft built at the NAF, H-16 S/N A-1049, was flown for the first time on 27 March, just 228 days after ground was broken and only 151 days after receipt of the original plans. A few days later (2 April), this aircraft and another H-16 were shipped to Killingholme, England, for war service. These were the first of 50 authorized under the Factory's original contract, the last of which was completed on 7 July. By the summer of 1918, when production was at its height, the assembly plant was drawing parts from the Victor Talking Machine Company, seven yacht builders, two furniture factories, and automobile and sheet metal product factories. Except for the two small aircraft shops, all these plants had been drawn into the work by the NAF organization, which maintained offices in each of its contributory plants. In addition to the nearly 3,700 persons directly engaged at the NAF, there were some 7,000 others employed in the manufacture of parts.

Sailors lining up wing panels of a Curtiss H-16 in the Naval Aircraft Factory in Philadelphia on 22 August 1918.

Curtiss H-16 in flight.

A Burgess-built Curtiss N-9H No. 2507 in flight. The machine is powered with an American Hispano-Suiza engine.

Curtiss R-6.

During 1917 the British Admiralty redesigned the H-16 again to produce a boat capable of carrying more depth bombs and possessing greater endurance. A sample machine was successfully developed in the spring of 1918, and the plans thereof were furnished the Navy Department. This machine was designated the model F-5 flying boat. Its 103-foot, 9-inch wingspan was attached to a 49-foot, 4-inch hull. The F-5-L had a gross loaded weight of 13,000 pounds and a maximum speed of 89 miles per hour. Its two Liberty motors developed 360 hp each. The F-5 had an allowable full load of 1,300 pounds and could carry four depth bombs against the two for the H-16, besides having a cruising endurance of 11 hours against 9 for the H-16. The advantages of this flying boat over the H-16 were obvious, and, as the H-16 contracts were completed, it was decided to replace them by orders for F-5 flying boats with the same manufacturers. Before this could be done, however, it was necessary to redesign the British F-5 at the NAF in order to adapt it for quantity production on the assembly system, and in order to use Liberty engines instead of the British Rolls-Royce engines. This redesigned model was designated the F-5-L. The production of H-12s, H-16s, and F-5-Ls is summarized in the following table:

	Number Ordered	Shipped Abroad	Delivered	Canceled after Armistice
Curtiss A&M Corp.	19 H-1	19	0	0
	74 H-16	74	62	0
	410 F-5-L	60	0	350
Curtiss Engineering Corp	50 H-16	50	18	0
Naval Aircraft Factory	150 H-16	150	78	0
	680 F-5-L	137	0	543
Canadian Aeroplane Ltd.	50 F-5-L	30	1	20
Total	1433	520	159	913

Curtiss R-6L at NAS Pensacola.

Another view of Gallaudet No. 59A. This provides a good view of the engine installation of the machine.

land planes exclusively. Before the end of 1917 the Navy entered into an extensive agreement with the French Government for the procurement of 118 seaplanes [D.D., F.B.A., Tellier, and Sopwith] for use at the seaplane stations in France. As delays occurred in the mass production of aircraft in the U.S. the emphasis increased for improving the foreign procurement program for both the Army and the Navy if European factories were to maintain the American bases and aerodromes throughout the winter of 1917-1918 and into the spring of 1918. A plan and an administration was needed for supplying the European manufacturers sufficient raw material to make the sought after aircraft. To meet this situation the Aircraft Production Board sought to establish an administrative agency with authority to deal with raw material and joint procurement problems. Action was taken at the 22 October 1917 meeting of the Board to provide this agency. The Board proposed to the Secretary of War and the Secretary of the Navy that a branch be established in Paris to be known as the Joint Army and Navy Aircraft Committee. This body would represent the aircraft procurement activities of the armed services abroad. On 10 November 1917, Operations cabled Vice Admiral Sims that the resolution of the Aircraft Production Board had been approved by both the Secretary of War and the Secretary of the Navy, and directed him to communicate with Colonel R.C. Bolling in Paris, who was then acting as an unofficial representative of the Board. Difficulties immediately arose on the composition of the Board with the Army demanding a majority representation on the Board.[1] The eventual composition of the Board was: Army—Colonel Bolling, Lieutenant Colonel T.F. Dodds, Lieutenant Colonel E.S. Gorrell, and Captain A.G. Cable; Navy—Captain H.I. Cone, Commander Frank R. McCrary, and Lt. G.R. Fearing (when McCrary was detached to Ireland on 8 February his place on the Board was taken by Captain Thomas T. Craven). Unofficial meetings of the Board took place on both 29 November 1917 and 11 December 1917. No final decisions were reached, however, because of the insistence of Brigadier-General B.D. Foulois, Chief of Air Service, A.E.F., that all recommendations and findings be first reviewed and approved by him. Between 24 December and 9 February 1918 there were no meetings held of this Board. Two informal decisions, however, were made; one of which led directly to the dissolution of the Board. The first informal decision was on the standardization of the Handley-Page and Caproni bombers for night bombing offensives. The second informal decision, made by General Foulois in the absence of Naval input, dealt with the allocation of spruce arriving from the U.S. This question was the issue which triggered Captain Cone to begin to communicate directly to General Foulois about the dissolution of the Board. This inquiry happened to coincide with a similar feeling of the half of Gen. Foulois. The Paris Committee was hence allowed to disappear. The feeling of animosity between the two services in Europe was not resolved by the closing of the Paris Committee. In fact, feelings became even more strained when the A.E.F. learned both of the planned distribution of Liberty engines to the Navy and the planned Navy effort in regards to a land bombing offensive against German naval facilities at Zeebrugge, Ostend, Ghent, and Bruge (the Northern Bombing Group). In light of the failure of the Paris Board, and in an atmosphere of Army hostility for the procurement of land machines by the U.S. Navy, Captain Cone began negotiations in the spring of 1918 for acquiring Italian aircraft. In this endeavor he was aided by Lieutenant John Lansing Callan, USNRF. These negotiations consisted of a series of personnel conferences between the Italian manufacturer and the Navy. The Caproni representatives

A Thomas Bros. machine (either A57 or A58).

A Standard being handled by a beach crew.

A Standard D taxiing on the water. Photo was taken in September 1917.

Another view of a Standard D taxiing on the water. Photo was taken in September 1917.

apparently made attractive promises to Captain Cone, for he concluded that heavy land machines were essential for the Navy's bombing offensive. There had been indications in his correspondence throughout the spring of 1918 that he was not only dissatisfied with the performance of seaplane bombers, but was impressed by the military superiority of heavy land bombers. All these elements led him to believe that the U.S. Navy should purchase Italian Caproni's. Such discussions were consistent with a 15 November 1916 recommendation of the General Board for the purchase abroad of aircraft. Initial Italian interest in providing such aircraft to the Navy culminated in a specific Italian offer late in 1917. This offer, however, was complicated by the administrative problem of the Paris Committee. By April 1918 the Navy was prepared to finalize the agreement for the procurement of Caproni aircraft in Italy. On 7 April Captain Cone requested permission to place contracts in Italy, and this authority was granted on 20 April.[2]

The disbandment of the Paris Committee of the Aircraft Production Board strongly influenced the Navy's preparation, begun in the spring of 1918, for the bombardment of German positions along the channel. On 10 March the General Board recommended the establishment of a force of land aircraft to be flown by Navy and Marine personnel in over-water flights. This project eventually took form as the Northern Bombing Group. The fighting strength was at first set at four squadrons. After careful study of this project in conjunction with French and British aviation officers, the Commander of U.S. Naval Aviation Forces concluded that it was not feasible. The use of 200 planes for day and night bombing of German submarine bases at Zeebrugge, Ostend, Bruges, and Ghent was advised instead. This suggestion was approved, although the Navy Department pointed out that deliveries of large night bombers could not be made until the fall of 1918. Yet, in order that the project might begin, procurement from European sources was authorized for at least 32 land chasse planes and 40 or more heavy bombers.

Despite the personal animosities that embittered the work of Army and Navy representatives in Italy, the Navy did make a very satisfactory agreement with the Commissary General of Italian Aeronautics. The agreement provided that: 1) The U.S. Naval Aviation Forces, Foreign Service would recommend to Vice Admiral Sims that high priority be given both to purchases and shipments of raw material ordered by the Italian government in the U.S. for the manufacture of aircraft (this was a concession to the Italians for diverting Caproni's; the material referred to was not intended to replace that used in the machines delivered to the Navy; it could be used in any Italian aircraft factory); 2) Sufficient raw material would be shipped to Italy by the U.S. Navy to compensate for supplies diverted to the planes manufactured for U.S. Naval Aviation; 3) The delivery of thirty 600 hp Caproni land bombers was promised during June and July 1918; and 4) An additional 80 bombers of the same type would be delivered in August. All delivery dates were to be specified by 15 June. During September 1918, and in each succeeding month until further notice, 20 Caproni machines were to be made available for U.S. Naval Aviation. The agreement created all sorts of problems with the Army. These problems were not resolved until all procurement was made through the Army-Navy Procurement program. In such a manner, the Army could be assured a share of the Caproni production.

The Bureau of Construction and Repair in the U.S. was slow in assembling the raw materials to be used in constructing the aircraft, and the delay in transshipment from Pauillac to Italy once the material arrived in Europe, proved fatal for production at the Caproni factory. In June 1918 49 600 hp machines had been manufactured (without American assistance); this production rose to 53 machines in July, but for want of materials production fell off to 40 machines

View of the cockpit of a Standard Model D.

View inside the cockpit of a Standard Model D.

in August. Workmen were actually discharged during the summer of 1918. Not withstanding, the Commander of the U.S. Naval Aviation Forces in Italy believed that in July 1918 that if material arrived from America, the factory could manufacture 90 large three-engined 600 hp Caproni's a month.

During 1918, several new types of seaplanes were constructed for the Navy Department, and trials were conducted to determine their suitability either as training or as service machines. The order for each of these seaplanes was placed with the definite purpose of development of some particular need in the future program, if the war had continued.

With reference to training machines of the flying boat type, the Curtiss model F had proved itself the most satisfactory in use, but it was desired to develop a machine of better structural character along the same lines. Encouraged by the Navy Department, the Aeromarine Plane Motor Co. developed its Model 40-A, and the Curtiss Engineering Corp its MF (Modified F) boat, both of which were recommended by the Trial Board for adoption, and contracts were awarded shortly before the armistice.

Several service machines of particular interest, some of which presented a distinct advance in airplane design, were also constructed and tried out in the summer and fall of 1918. Of these the most important were the NC-1, the Curtiss model 18-T (Kirkham Fighter), the Curtiss model HA (Dunkirk Fighter), and the Gallaudet D-4.

Development of large flying boats, later designated NC, was initiated by Chief Constructor David W. Taylor in a memo dated 25 August 1917, which outlined the general requirements of an airplane needed in war and directed his staff to make further investigation. Taylor stated in part: "The United States [Liberty] Motor gives good promise of success, and if we can push ahead on the airplane end, it seems to me the submarine menace could be abated, even if not destroyed, from the air. The ideal solution would be big flying boats, or the equivalent, that would be able to fly across the Atlantic to avoid difficulties of delivery, etc." The NC-1 was a large flying boat, built by the Curtiss Aeroplane Co. under the direction of the Navy Department, which was responsible for the design. It was a biplane having a span of 126 feet for the upper wing and a length of 68-1/2 feet from the bow to the end of the tail surfaces. The normal weight, fully loaded, was 22,000 pounds. It was equipped with three Liberty engines, each located in a nacelle between the wings. On 4 October 1918 the NC-1 made its initial flight at NAS Rockaway with Commander Holden C. Richardson and Lieutenant David H. McCulloch as pilots. The NC-1 made a flight at Rockaway, NY, on 27 November 1918 with 51 men aboard, thereby establishing a world's record for number of passengers carried by an airplane.

The Curtiss Model 18-T, or Kirkham Fighter, was a land machine designed and constructed for the Navy Department by the Curtiss Engineering Corp. based on an order of 30 March 1918. Had the war continued it is likely that this type would have been put into production for use on the Western Front in the protection of the Northern Bombing Group squadrons. It was a 2-seater combat plane having a span of 32 feet and a fully loaded weight of 2,800 pounds. On 19 August the prototype experimental triplane figher, equipped with a Curtiss K-12 engine, made a high speed of 162 miles an hour on trials over a measured course and observed by Naval Constructors Richardson and C.N. Liqued, which established a new world's record for speed.

The Curtiss HA, or Dunkirk Fighter, was a single-pontoon seaplane, equipped with one Liberty engine. It was a 2-seater combat plane brought out in 1918 as an answer to high performance German seaplanes, which were interfering with the bombing operations being conducted by the Navy against German submarine bases on the Belgium coast. It made its first flight at Port Washington, Long Island, with Curtiss test pilot Roland Rohlfs at the controls and Captain Bernard L. Smith, USMC, occupying the second seat on 21 March 1918. Its maximum speed of 125 miles an hour was then a remarkable performance for a seaplane. Due to the change in conditions brought about by the end of the war, the HA was never put into production.

The Gallaudet D-4 was a 2-seater combat seaplane. Carrying its normal load of 434 pounds of ordnance, the plane had a high speed of 119 miles per hour, and at this speed the endurance was two and one half-hours. It was the only gear-driven plane developed during the war by the Navy, and was designed and built by the Gallaudet Aircraft Corp. of East Greenwich, RI. The D-4 was fitted with a single Liberty engine mounted in the fuselage, which drove

Standard H-4-H No. A137.

by means of a ring gear, a propeller that was situated immediately behind the wings. The fuselage, or tail structure, of the plane extended through the center of the ring gear carrying the propeller.

On 24 January 1918 the specifications and blueprints drawn up by the Bureau of Construction and Repair for the Davis Gun carrier were received at the Naval Aircraft Factory. Later designated N-1, this was the first airplane designed and built by the Navy for the attack role. On 22 May 1918, construction of the first N-1 was completed at the NAF.

On 11 August Ensign James B. Taylor made the initial flight in the Loaning M-2 Kitten landplane at Mineola, L.I. Intended for shipboard use, the design was not successful. It was, however, the first monoplane developed under Navy contract and one of the smallest planes ever built for the Navy (empty weight under 300 pounds). Although initially equipped with a British ABC engine, it was designed for the Lawrence 3-cylinder 30 hp engine, which was the forerunner of the American air-cooled radial engine.

Elmer Sperry developed an interest in the gyroscope as early as 1896, and over the next 15 years adopted it to a wide variety of naval applications. By 1911 the concept of a radio-controlled aeroplane began to interest him, using the gyroscope for automatic stabilization. In 1913 the Navy provided assistance in his efforts when Lieutenant P.N.L. Bellinger was the pilot of a flying boat which was used to test and evaluate the concept of a gyroscopic automatic stabilizer. During these trials Sperry's son Lawrence acted as an engineer. In 1914 Lawrence went to Europe and demonstrated his father's invention. On a second trip to Europe the potential application of the gyroscope to military aerial activities was realized, and upon his return to the U.S. he made a number of recommendations to the Navy. In response to these recommendations the Navy Department issued contracts for the development of a number of devices, including: a bombsight; a "base line indicator," which became known as the forerunner of the "turn and bank indicator"; and a gyro compass. In 1916 Elmer Sperry joined forces with Peter Cooper Hewitt in the development of an aerial torpedo, or pilotless airplane. In the summer of 1916 Hewitt and Sperry arranged for a representative of the Navy's Bureau of Ordnance, Lieutenant T.S. Wilkinson, to examine their aerial torpedo. The torpedo consisted of a gyroscopic stabilizer, a directive gyroscope, an aneroid barometer to regulate height, servomotors for control of rudders and ailerons, and a device for distance measuring. These were installed in an airplane which could be catapulted or flown from the water. Under preset controls the plane was designed to climb to a predetermined altitude, fly a preset course, and, after traveling a preset distance, either drop its bombs or dive into the ground. A demonstration of the guided-missile equipment was held on 12 September at Amityville, L.I. Lieutenant Wilkinson reported that the aerial torpedo did not possess a degree of accuracy sufficient to hit a ship, but, because of its range of 50 to 100 miles, it might be of interest to the Army.

The Navy's first guided-missile effort began when the Naval Consulting Board recommended to the Secretary of the Navy, on 14 April 1917, that $50,000 be apportioned to carry on experimental work on aerial torpedoes in the form of automatically controlled aeroplanes, or aerial machines carrying high explosives. Immediately after the declaration of war upon Germany, Sperry began urging the Navy to embark on the development of an aerial torpedo. In this he was supported by the Naval Consulting Board, which requested that the Secretary of the Navy apportion $50,000 to carry out experimental work with aerial torpedoes in the form of automatically controlled machines capable of carrying explosives. With this recommendation, the government included development of a flying bomb, or aerial torpedo, in its war preparations.

The details were settled on 17 May when Elmer and Lawrence Sperry met with Secretary Daniels and other Navy officials. It was determined that the Navy would furnish five N-9 seaplanes and purchase six sets of Sperry automatic control gear. Sperry would construct hangars, furnish testing grounds, and secure a staff. Secretary Daniels approved spending $200,000 on this project, half to be administered by the Bureau of Ordnance and half by a combination of the Bureau of Construction and Repair and the Bureau of Engineering. Once a course of action had been determined, the Sperry's went to work. As they got underway, seven large planes were turned over to them, and a flying field at Copiague, L.I., was obtained. A number of hangars were established there with a Marine guard for security.

Development of the flying bomb involved the solution of several serious problems. It was necessary to obtain a practicable airframe, find means of launching a pilotless vehicle, and make sure that the control mechanism would operate effectively after a pilotless launch. Since these problems were interrelated, difficulties with

Close up view of the engine installation on a Standard Twin-Hydro.

the launching device obscured the aerodynamic inadequacies of the airframe, and both served to blur shortcomings of the control mechanism.

Sperry's initial work dealt with testing and perfecting mechanisms for maintaining course and measuring distance. Test flights in which the pilot took the Navy-furnished N-9 off and then turned control over to an automatic gear commenced in mid-September. This gear, it was reported, would fly the plane to the designated target and drop a bag of sand on command from the distance gear. By mid-November, 30-mile test flights were being made regularly with an error in range of about two miles. In spite of the progress made by Sperry and his associates, the Chief of Naval Operations was not excited about the development of the aerial torpedo. The CNO laid down a policy: "While the flying bomb was to be developed to the point of complete readiness for production, no facilities were to be obligated in order to manufacture it for the Navy." The Bureau of Ordnance therefore sought by some means to obtain airframes and engines in large quantity without interfering with scheduled aircraft production. In addition, the Navy invited Major General George O. Squier, Chief Signal Officer of the Army, to witness a demonstration of the flying bomb. A demonstration of the N-9 flying bomb at Amityville, L.I., was witnessed on 21 November 1917 by Major-General Squier, USA. This observation led the Army to establish a parallel project to be set up by the Army at McCook Field, Dayton, Ohio, although with much greater emphasis upon feasible production and lower costs.

With regard to the airframe, little was done to obtain a more efficient machine until Sperry began demonstrations with the N-9 in September 1917. Then, in October, a rush order was sent to the Curtiss Aeroplane and Motor Company for six N-9 planes of special design with an empty weight of 500 pounds, a top speed of 90 miles per hour, a range of 50 miles, and the capability of carrying an explosive load of 1,000 pounds. The engine was to be as light as possible, and the plane was to be fitted for special control equipment to allow automatic operation. The first of these planes, or "flying bombs," was delivered to the Sperry flying field at Copiagne, Long Island, on 10 November; just within the 30-day deadline specified in the contract. It had never been flown as a piloted craft, nor checked in a wind tunnel. Even had the flying bomb been based upon a proven design, it still would have constituted a radial departure and required additional testing.

A couple of abortive attempts to launch the craft as a flying bomb led to the realization that some knowledge had to be obtained of the craft's flying characteristics. One of the planes was then fitted with a ski-type landing gear and taxied over the ice for the purpose of adjusting the ailerons and elevators. Lawrence Sperry, volunteering to be the test pilot, had the plane fitted with a seat and standard stick control. While taxing for his first takeoff, the plane struck a bank of snow, turned two somersaults, and was completely wrecked. Sperry walked away unhurt. Undaunted, he tried again, and this time got plane #2 into the air. When he cut in his automatic controls, they wrested the plane away from him and turned it over laterally twice. Fortunately, he succeeded in righting it and landing it safely. Clearly, something more was required than a flight test of the airplane. To investigate the flying characteristics of the plane, and still keep it on the ground, Sperry and his assistant, N.W. Dalton, fitted a Marmon automobile with an aeroplane motor and attached it to a frame on which they could fasten the flying bomb. With this rig, they drove over the Long Island Motor Parkway at 80 miles an hour to make a kind of open-air wind tunnel test. Finally, they succeeded in getting what they considered to be satisfactory adjustments to the plane's control surfaces and automatic gear. This led to two launching attempts, one successful and the other unsuccessful. In August and September 1918, two tests of the Curtiss Flying Bomb were made; two flights of 100 yards were achieved before the plane crashed to the ground. Of these, only one was blamed upon the flimsy aircraft structure, but disgust was complete. The Curtiss flying bomb was abandoned in favor of the N-9. In the

Experimental Curtiss seaplane Triplane Type L-2. Powered by a 100 hp OXX engine the Type L-2 was ordered both by the Navy and the Army. The caption to this photo says that it was taken in the basin at NAS Hampton Roads on 15 July 1918. Note, however, that No. 475 was the single Army purchase of this type. (source: Naval Historical Center)

Davis Gun installation on a seaplane.

A close up view of the installation of a Davis Gun on the Navy's N-1 Davis Gun Carrier aircraft. The officer is unidentified.

meantime, the Sperry's had built a model for wind tunnel tests, and these were eventually carried out at the Washington Navy Yard, but not until after the cessation of work with the Curtiss flying bomb.

The problem of launching a pilotless aircraft was as complex as that of determining the flight characteristics of the airframe. The initial Hewitt-Sperry concept was that the device would be launched by catapult or from the surface of the water. In any event, when the Sperry's made the first pilotless tests of the flying bomb late in 1917, they launched it by sliding it down a wire cable. In this launch, a wing was damaged. On the second trial, the plane arose from the wire, but immediately plunged to the ground.

These failures led to the abandonment of the wire-launched apparatus in favor of a more conventional catapult consisting of a 150-foot track. Power was obtained by dropping a three-ton weight from a height of 30 feet. Troubles continued. On the first attempt to use this device, the flying bomb lagged the car, damaged its propeller, and then the plane turned over on its nose. A month later the catapult worked satisfactorily, and the plane seemed to respond to its automatic controls, but proved to be tail-heavy when it took to the air, stalled, side-slipped, and fell to the ground. On 22 September a flywheel catapult, the forerunner of that which was used on the U.S.S. *Lexington* and the U.S.S. *Saratoga*, was used successfully to launch a flying boat.

These failures were followed by the already recounted hair-raising experiences when the flying bomb was put on sled runners. Then came the trials with the Marmon automobile. After the controls were satisfactorily adjusted, a launch was actually made from the car on 6 March 1918. The machine left the car cleanly and flew the thousand yards for which the distance gear had been set, descended, and struck the water with only moderate damage. This was epoch-making in that for the first time in history an unmanned plane had made a smooth stabilized flight in response to automatic control. The feat could not be duplicated on a second attempt, so a decision was made to use a smoother roadway. The Marmon was fitted with railroad wheels, and an idle spur of the Long Island Railroad, four miles east of Farmingdale, was brought into service. A run was made down the track, but before flying speed was obtained, the plane developed sufficient lift to raise the front railroad wheels of the car so that they came free, and another crash resulted.

The deficiencies of these three methods of launching led the Sperry's to try a new type of catapult in which a heavy flywheel was spun at high speed. Through a clutch and drum arrangement the flywheel imparted a constant acceleration to the car carrying the flying bomb. (To perform the detailed design work, the Sperry Company employed a young consulting engineer named Carl L. Norden). This device was not completed until August when its first test ended in failure. Two more trials the next month were only partially successful. After this the N-9 airframe returned to favor. Preparations were finally completed in mid-October; and on the 17th a launch was made. The plane was catapulted cleanly from the

Wing construction at the Naval Aircraft Factory.

field at Copiague. It climbed steadily, flying in a perfectly straight line at an angle of about two degrees to the proposed line of flight. The distance gear had been set for 14,500 yards, but it failed to function, so the plane continued on course and was last seen over NAS Bayshore heading east at a height of about 4,000 feet.

The third area of problems connected with the flying bomb was the stabilization system. In the various unsuccessful attempts to launch the craft, behavior of this gear could not be checked. One of the purposes of the tests on the Marmon automobile had been to observe its functioning at flight speed. Satisfactory settings were made for the one successful flight. The acceleration imparted to the plane by the flywheel catapult would have caused the gyroscope to precess. To prevent this—at least for the last flight—the gyroscopes were not released until the launch was completed. At the same time, additional batteries were provided to insure adequate power for the gyroscopes.

In the next launch, on 26 September 1918, the "flying bomb" made a straight climbing flight of about 100 yards, spiraled, and crashed. Either the stabilization system or the airframe was at fault, and changes were made to both. The stabilization gear, which had been used for all work with the "flying bomb," was abandoned in favor of the four-gyroscope system tested earlier in the N-9. The single gyroscope system adapted from the underwater torpedo gear was retained for course, or azimuth, control in order to operate the vertical rudder. For the successful flight of the N-9 on 17 October this course and stabilization gear functioned satisfactorily. Even so, the Navy requested Carl Norden to examine the various Sperry devices and to recommend improvements. The Navy continued to press its view on how to proceed, and was actually contemplating purchase of new flying-bomb airplanes on its own, rather than through the Sperry's. The flight with the N-9 may have been an effort in part to restore Navy confidence—if so, it was to no avail. Sperry made various attempts to stir up additional enthusiasm by calling the "flying bomb" the "gun of the future," and an important step towards "making war so extremely hazardous and expensive no nation will dare go into it." Despite this, at war's end, the Navy took over from Sperry complete control of the "flying bomb" development.

TABLE 1

Partial Listing of HTA Aircraft Purchased by the Navy prior to 1919[1]

Aircraft Number (First Series)	Model/Type/Name Manufacturer	Power Plant Capacity	Remarks
AH-1 (A-1)	"Triad" Seaplane, Curtiss	70 hp (Curtiss)	July 1911
AH-2 (A-4)	Seaplane, Curtiss	80 hp (Curtiss)	July 1911 from spares
AH-3 (A-3)	Seaplane, Curtiss	80 hp (Curtiss)	October 1912
AH-4 (B-1)	Landplane converted to a seaplane, Wright	40 hp (Sturtevant)	July 1911
AH 5 (B-2)	Seaplane, Wright	50 hp (Wright)	October 1912 from spares
AH-6 (B-3)	Seaplane, Wright	50 hp (Wright)	October 1912 from spares
AH-7	Seaplane, Burgess-Dunne and Curtiss	125 hp (Hall-Scott)	October 1913
AH-8	Seaplane, Curtiss	80 hp	1913
AH-9	Seaplane, Curtiss	80 hp	1913
AH-10	Seaplane, Burgess-Dunne and Curtiss	90 hp (Curtiss)	April 1914
AH 11	Seaplane, Curtiss	80 hp (Curtiss)	April 1914
AH-12	Seaplane, Curtiss	80 hp (Curtiss)	April 1914
AH-13	Seaplane, Curtiss	80 hp (Curtiss)	April 1915
AH-14	Seaplane, Curtiss	90 hp (Curtiss)	April 1915
AH-15	Seaplane, Curtiss	80 hp (Curtiss)	April 1915
AH-16	Seaplane, Curtiss	90 hp (Curtiss)	16 November 1915
AH-17	Seaplane, Curtiss	90 hp (Curtiss)	19 November 1915
AH-18	Seaplane, Curtiss	90 hp (Curtiss)	26 November 1915
AB-1 (C-1)	Flying Boat, Curtiss	70 hp (Curtiss)	December 1912
AB-2 (C-2)	Flying Boat, Curtiss	80 hp (Curtiss)	October 1913
AB-3 (C-3)	Flying Boat, Curtiss	80 hp (Curtiss)	November 1913
AB-4 (C-4)	Flying Boat, Curtiss	80 hp (Curtiss)	November 1913
AB-5 (C-5)	Flying Boat, Curtiss	80 hp (Curtiss)	November 1913
AB-6 (D-1)	Flying Boat, Burgess-Dunne and Curtiss	75 hp (Renault)	May 1913
AB-7 (D-2)	Flying Boat, Burgess-Dunne and Curtiss	75 hp (Renault)	January 1914
AX-1 (E-1)(A-2)	OWL: Bat Boat (experimental convertible, Ex-Curtiss	40 hp Curtiss	July 1911
		80 hp Curtiss	November 1913
A-51 (AH-23)	Seaplane, Wright	60 hp (Wright)	
A-52 (AH-63)	Seaplane, Paul Schmitt, Paris	220-230 hp (Renault)	Delivery Delayed
A-53	Seaplane, Deutsche Flugzeug Worke	100 hp (Benz)	CANCELED

A-54 - A-56	Seaplanes, Burgess-Dunne Co.	140 hp (Sturtevant)	A-54 CANCELED A-55 and A-56 delivered in 1918
A-57 (AH-20)	Seaplanes, Thomas Bros.	140 hp (Sturtevant)	
A-58 (AH-21)	Seaplane, Thomas Bros.	140 hp (Sturtevant)	
A-59 (AH-61)	Seaplane, Gallaudet	130 hp (2/Dusenberg)	One Propeller
A-60	N-9 Seaplane, Curtiss	90 hp (Curtiss OXX)	
A-61 - A-62			
A-63 - A-65	N-9 Seaplane, Curtiss	90 hp (Curtiss OXX)	Same as AH-8
A-66 (AH-62)	Seaplanes, (R-3), Curtiss	160 hp (Curtiss VX)	
A-67 (AH-65)			
A-68 (AH-19)	Seaplane, Martin	125 hp (Hall-Scott)	
A-69 (AH-22)			
A-70 (AH-25)	Seaplane, Burgess -Dunne	90 hp (Curtiss OXX)	
A-71 (AH-26)			
A-72 (AH-27)			
A-73 (AH-28)			
A-74 (AH-29)			
A-75 (AH-31)	Seaplane, Sturtevant	100 hp (Sturtevant)	
A-76 (AH-24)			
A-77 - A-81			
A-82	Experimental Seaplane, Washington Navy Yard	200 hp (2/Curtiss VX)	
A-83 - A-84	Experimental Seaplanes, NAS Pensacola	200 hp (2/Curtiss VX)	
A-85 - A-90	Seaplanes, Curtiss	85-90 hp (Curtiss OXX)	
A-91	Tractor Seaplane, Standard Aero.	125 hp (Hall-Scott)	Rejected
A-92	Twin Tractor Seaplane, Curtiss	125 hp (2/Hall-Scott)	CANCELED
A-93 (AH-64)	Twin JN Tractor Seaplane, Curtiss Aero.	90 hp (2/Curtiss OXX)	Wrecked in trials
A-96		100 hp (Curtiss OXX)	A-96 wrecked
A-97			
A-98			
A-99 (AH-34)			
A-100 (AH-35)			
A-101 (AH-36)			
A-102 (AH-37)[2]			
A-103 (AH-38)			
A-104 (AH-39)			
A-105 (AH-40)[2]	Land version		
A-106 (AH-41)			
A-107 (AH-42)	Land version		
A-108 (AH-43)[2]			
A-109 (AH-44)			
A-110 (AH-45)			
A-111 (AH-46)	Land version		
A-112 (AH-47)			
A-113 (AH-48)	Land version		
A-114 (AH-49)[2]			
A-115 (AH-50)[2]			
A-116 (AH-51)			
A-117 (AH-52)			
A-118 (AH-53)			
A-119 (AH-54)			
A-120 (AH-55)[2]			
A-121 (AH-56)			
A-122 (AH-57)			
A-123 (AH-58)			

A-124 (AH-59)			
A-125 (AH-60)	Seaplanes, N-9, Curtiss A&M		
A-126	Seaplane (Aero) Farman		
A-127	Seaplane (Hydro) Farman (Bordeaux)		A-127 CANCELED
A-128 - A-133	Tractor Seaplanes, Sturtevant	140 hp (Sturtevant)	
A-134 - A-136	SH-4 Seaplanes, Thomas-Morse	100 hp (Curtiss OXX-3)	
A-137 - A-139	H-4-H Seaplanes, Standard Aero.	125 hp (Hall-Scott)	
A-140 - A-141	Speed Scouts: Twin Tractor Seaplanes, Thomas Bros.	125 hp (2/Hall-Scott)	CANCELED
A-142 - A-144	Tractor Seaplane, Aeromarine P&M	100 hp (Hall-Scott)	
A-145 - A-146	H-14 Flying Boats, Curtiss		CANCELED
A-147 - A-148	Tractor Seaplane, Pacific Aero (Boeing)	100 hp (Hall-Scott)	
A-149 - A-150	Speed Scouts, S-4 (Model 10A) Tractor Seaplane	100 hp (Curtiss OXX)	A-150 changed to floats, struck off records 6 August 1919
A-152	H-12 Flying Boat, Curtiss	200 hp (Curtiss V2-3)	
A-153	Experimental Tractor Seaplane, NAS Pensacola		Pensacola Design
A-154	Experimental Tractor Seaplane, NAS Pensacola Washington design		CANCELED
A-155 - A-156	HT-B Tractor Speed Scout, Burgess-Dunne	100 hp (Curtiss OXX-3)	
A-157 - A-159	JN-4B, Curtiss A&M	100 hp (Curtiss OXX)	
A-162 - A-197	R-6 Seaplanes, Curtiss	200 hp (Curtiss V2-3)	
A-198	JN Twin-Engine Seaplane, Curtiss	100 hp (2/Curtiss OXX)	
A-199 - A-200	HT-B Tractor Speed Scout, Burgess-Dunne	100 hp (Curtiss OXX-3)	CANCELED
A-201 - A-234	N-9C Seaplane, Curtiss A&M	100 hp (Curtiss OXX)	
A-288 - A-290	Model R, 2-Place Tractor Seaplanes, Wright-Martin	150 hp (Hall-Scott A-5-a)	
A-291 - A-293	L-2 School Triplanes, Curtiss	100 hp (Curtiss OXX)	
A-294 - A-295	Tractor Seaplanes, Boeing	150 hp (Hall-Scott)	CANCELED
A-296 - A-297	Verville Flying Boats, Verville-General	150 hp (Hall-Scott)	CANCELED
A-298 - A-299	Tractor Seaplane, Boeing		CANCELED
A-300 - A-301	Twin Tractor Seaplane, Gallaudet	150 hp (2/Hall-Scott)	CANCELED
A-302 - A-341	R-6 Seaplanes, Curtiss	200 hp (Curtiss V2-3)	
A-342 - A-371	N-9 Seaplanes, Curtiss	100 hp (Curtiss OXX)	
A-374 - A-379	HT-L Tractors, Burgess Co.	100 hp (Curtiss OXX)	
A-380 - A-385	U-2 Tractor School Seaplanes, Burgess-Dunne	100 hp (Hall-Scott)	
A-386 - A-387	F-Boats, Curtiss	100 hp (Curtiss OXX)	
A-388 - A-389	JN-4s, Curtiss	90 hp (Curtiss OX-2)	
A-390 - A-393	F-Boats, Curtiss	100 hp (Curtiss OXX)	
A-394	CS-1 Baby Seaplane, Sopwith	100 hp Monosaupape	Gift from the British Admiralty
A-395 - A-406	SH-4 Tractor Seaplanes, Thomas-Morse	100 hp (Curtiss OXX)	
A-407	CS-1 Baby Seaplane, Sopwith	100 hp Monosaupape	Gift from the British Admiralty
A-408	F-Boat, Curtiss	100 hp (Curtiss OXX)	
A-409 - A-438	N-9 Seaplanes, Burgess-Dunne	100 hp (Curtiss OXX)	
A-439 - A-441	Tractor Seaplanes, Aeromarine P&M	100 hp (Hall-Scott)	
A-442 - A-444	Tractor Seaplanes, (Monoplane), Loening Aero.	30 hp (Lawrance)	British ABC engine in A-443)
A-445 - A-499	GS-2 Gnome Speed Scouts	100 hp (Gnome)	C&R Design
A-450 - A-499	39-A Seaplanes, Aeromarine P&M	100 hp (Hall-Scott)	Twin-Float
A-500 - A-649	38-B Seaplanes, Aeromarine P&M	100 hp (Curtiss OXX)	Single-Float
A-650 - A-699	C-1 Tractor School Seaplanes, Boeing	100 hp (Hall-Scott)	
A-752 - A-756	F-Boats, Curtiss (L.S. Thompson)	100 hp (Curtiss OXX)	A-752 had two engines
A-757 - A-762	S-5 Tractor Speed Scouts, Thomas-Morse	100 hp (Gnome)	
A-765 - A-783	H-12 Flying Boats, Curtiss A&M	330 hp (2/Liberty)	
A-784 - A-799	H-16 Flying Boats, Curtiss A&M	330 hp (2/Liberty)	

A-800 - A-814	HS-1 Flying Boats, changed to HS-2, Curtiss A&M	330 hp (Liberty)	
A-815	HS-1 Flying Boat, Curtiss A&M, Changed to HS-1L	330 hp (2/Liberty)	CANCELED
A-818 - A-867	H-16 Flying Boats, Curtiss Engineering	330 hp (2/Liberty)	A-839 was a H-16-2
A-868	GS-1 Gnome Scout, Curtiss A&M	100 hp (Gnome)	
A-869 - A-872	CS-1 Baby Seaplanes, Sopwith	100 hp Monosaupape	Gift from the British Government
A-873 - A-994[3]	R-6 and R-9 Seaplanes, Curtiss A&M	R-6 had 330 hp (Liberty) and R-9 had 200 hp (Curtiss V2-3)	A-883 - A-887 and A-901 - A-905 transferred to the Army
A-995 - A-997	JN-4A Twin Tractor Landplanes, Curtiss A&M	100 hp (Curtiss OX-5)	
A-999 - A-1028	N-9 Seaplanes, Burgess Co.	100 hp (Curtiss OXX)	
A-1031 - A-1048	H-16 Flying Boats, Curtiss A&M	330 hp (2/Liberty)	
A-1049 - A-1098	H-16 Flying Boats, Naval Aircraft Factory	330 hp (2/Liberty)	
A-1099 - A-1398[4]	HS-1 Change to HS-2 Flying Boats, LWF Engineering Co.	330 hp (Liberty)	50 CANCELED at random; HS-2L's start at A-1223
A-1399 - A-1478	HS-1 Change to HS-2 Flying Boats, Standard Airc.	330 hp (Liberty)	
A-1479 - A-1548	HS-1 Change to HS-2 Flying Boats, Standard Airc.	330 hp (Liberty)	CANCELED
A-1549 - A-2207	HS-1 Change to HS-2L Flying Boats, Curtiss A&M	330 hp (Liberty)	
A-2217 - A-2276	HS-1 Change to HS-2 Flying Boats, Gallaudet Airc.	330 hp (Liberty)	
A-2277	Experimental Triplane Flying Boat, Curtiss A&M	200 hp (Curtiss V2-3)	Written-off 9 June 1919
A-2278	HA "Dunkirk" Fighter Seaplane, Curtiss Engr. Co.	300 hp (Liberty)	Designed by Capt. B.L. Smith, USMC
A-2279 - A-2280[5]	F-Boats, Curtiss A&M	100 hp (Curtiss OXX)	Purchased from Wrigley
A-2281[5]	F-Boat, Curtiss A&M	100 hp (Curtiss OXX-2)	Purchased from Mitchell
A-2282 - A-2283[5]	N-1 Davis Gun Carriers, Naval Aircraft Factory	330 hp (Liberty)	C&R Design
A-2285-A2290	N-9 Seaplanes, Curtiss A&M	100 hp (Curtiss OXX)	From the Army
A-2286 - A-2290	N-9H Seaplane, Curtiss A&M	150 hp (Wright-Dayton)	
A-2291 - A-2294	NC-1 through NC-4 Patrol Flying Boat, Curtiss Engineering Co.	330 hp (3/Liberty)	NC-3 and NC-4 had four engines
A-2295 - A-2344	F-Boats, Curtiss Engr. Co.	100 hp (Curtiss OXX)	
A-2345 - A-2350	MF Boats (Experimental), Curtiss Engr. Co.	100 hp (Curtiss OXX)	
A-2351 - A-2409	N-9 Seaplanes, Burgess Co.	100 hp (Curtiss OXX)	
A-2410 - A-2572	N-9H Seaplanes, Burgess Co.	150 hp (Hispano-Suiza)	
A-2574 - A-2650	N-9H Seaplanes, Burgess Co.	150 hp (Hispano-Suiza)	
A-2651 - A-2652	F-Boats (Briggs), Alexandria Airc.	150 hp (Hispano-Suiza)	
A-2653 - A-2654	D-4 Light Bombers, Gallaudet	330 hp (Liberty)	
A-3205 - A-3234	JN-4Hs, Curtiss A&M	150 hp (Hispano-Suiza)	From Army
A-3235 - A-3244	Gnome Speed Scouts, Thomas-Morse	100 hp (Gnome)	From Army
A-3245 - A-3324	Tractor Seaplanes, Curtiss		From Army, CANCELED
A-3245 - A-3324	DH-4s, Dayton-Wright	330 hp (Liberty)	Numbers reassigned from canceled contract
A-3325	18-T-1 "Kirkham" Triplane Fighter, Curtiss Engineering Co.	400 hp (Curtiss K-12)	Converted to Seaplane
A-3326	18-T-1 "Kirkham" Triplane Fighter, Curtiss Engineering Co.	400 hp (Curtiss K-12)	
A-3327	F-Boat (Briggs), Alexandria Airc.	100 hp (Curtiss OXX)	
A-3328 - A-3322	F-Boats, Curtiss A&M	100 hp (Curtiss OXX)	Purchased from American Trans-Oceanic Co.
A-3333 - A-3382[6]	F-5-L Flying Boats, Canadian Aeroplane	330 hp (2/Liberty)	A-3363-A-3382 CANCELED
A-3384 - A-3458[7]	DH-4s, Dayton Wright	330 hp (Liberty)	Army Signal Corp.
A-3459 - A3558	H-16 Flying Boats, Naval Aircraft Factory	330 hp (2/Liberty)	
A-3559 - A-4035[8]	F-5-L Flying Boats, Naval Aircraft Factory	330 hp (2/Liberty)	343 were CANCELED

A-4036 - A-4037	F-6 Flying Boats, Naval Aircraft Factory	330 hp (2/Liberty)	Geared Propeller
A-4038	F-5-L Flying Boat, Naval Aircraft Factory	330 hp (2/Liberty)	
A-4039 - A-4078	H-16 Flying Boats, Curtiss A&M	330 hp (2/Liberty)	
A-4079 - A-4108	F-Boats, Curtiss Engr.	100 hp (Curtiss OXX-3)	
A-4110	HA-1 "Dunkirk" Fighter, Curtiss A&M	330 hp (Liberty)	Burned in the air
A-4111	HA-2 "Dunkirk" Fighter, Curtiss A&M	330 hp (Liberty)	
A-4112 - A-4117	JN-4Bs, Curtiss Exhibition Co.	100 hp (Curtiss (OX-5)	
A-4128 - A-4217	JN-4HGs, Curtiss A&M	150 hp (Hispano-Suiza)	From Army
A-4218 - A-4227	E-1 (M Defense Fighters), Standard Aero.	80-100 hp (LeRhone)	From Army
A-4228 - A-4229	HS-2L Flying Boats, Loughead Airc.	330 hp (Liberty)	
A-4230	Flying Boat, Tellier (France)		From French Government
A-4231 - A-4280	HS-2L Flying Boats, Boeing Airplane Co.	330 hp ((Liberty)	A-4256-A-4280 CANCELED
A-4281 - A-4340	F-5 Flying Boats, Curtiss A&M	330 hp (2/Liberty)	
A-4341 - A-4342	N-1 Davis Gun Carriers, Naval Aircraft Factory	330 hp (Liberty)	
A-4343 - A-4346	MF & F Boats, Carolina Aircraft Co.	Curtiss OXX-3	All CANCELED or REJECTED, Veneere hulls
A-4347	C-1-F (1 Float), Boeing Airplane Co.	100 hp (Curtiss OXX-6)	
A-4339 - A-4402	F-Boats, Curtiss Engr.	100 hp (Curtiss OXX-3)	
A-4403 - A-4418	MF-Boats, Curtiss Engr.	100 hp (Curtiss OXX-3)	
A-4419 - A-4449	F-Boats, Curtiss Engr.	100 hp (Curtiss OXX-3)	
A-4470 - A-4819	F-5-L Flying Boats, Curtiss	350 hp (2/Liberty)	CANCELED
A-4820 - A-5019	N-9 Seaplanes, Burgess-Dunne	100 hp (Curtiss OXX)	CANCELED
A-5024	F-Boat (Briggs), Alexandria Aircraft Co.	150 hp (Hispano-Suiza)	
A-5030 - A-5039	N-1 Davis Gun Carriers, Naval Aircraft Factory	330 hp (Liberty)	CANCELED
A-5040 - A-5089	Aero Mod. 40 F-Boats, Aeromarine	100 hp (Curtiss OXX-6)	
A-5090 - A-5239	Aero Mod. F-Boats, Aeromarine	100 hp (Curtiss OXX-6)	CANCELED
A-5243	Night Bomber (Flying Boat), Speery Aircraft	330 hp (Liberty)	
A-5244 - A-5246	Night Bombers (Flying Boat), Speery Aircraft	330 hp (Liberty)	CANCELED
A-5247 - A-5256	Modify 10 F-Boats (Briggs), Alexandria Airc.	150 hp (Hispano-Suiza)	
A-5258	F-Boat, Curtiss	100 hp (Curtiss OXX-6)	
A-5259 - A-5458	F-5-L Flying Boats, Naval Aircraft Factory	330 hp (Liberty)	CANCELED
A-5459 - A-5462	HS-3 Flying Boats, Curtiss Engineering Co.	330 hp (Liberty)	
A-5468	M-3 "Cat"/"Kitten", Loening Aero Engr.	60 hp (Lawrence)	
A-5470 - A-5471	JN-6HG-1s, Curtiss A&M	Hispano-Suiza	From Army
A-5483 - A-5562	MF-Boats, Naval Aircraft Factory	100 hp (Curtiss OXX)	
A-5564 - A-5569	HS-2 Flying Boats (Curtiss), NAS Miami	330 hp (Liberty)	Assembled from spare hulls and salvage material
A-5570 - A-5571	SA-1 (Ships Airplane), Naval Aircraft Factory	60 hp (Lawrence, 3 cyl.)	
A-5572 - A-5573	SA-2 (Ships Airplane), Naval Aircraft Factory	60 hp (Lawrence, 3 cyl.)	
A-5574 - A-5575	Seaplanes, Macchi	180 hp (Isotta-Frachini, V/4B)	From Italian Government
A-5576 - A-5579	TF-1 (NC Tandem) Twin-Engined Fighters, Naval Aircraft Factory	300 hp (2/Hispano-Suiza)	A-5578 had a Packard engine
A-5581 - A-5586	JN-6HG-1s, Curtiss A&M	150 hp (Hispano-Suiza)	
A-5588 - A-5589	S.E. 5s, Curtiss A&M	150 hp (Hispano-Suiza)	Royal Aircraft Factory Design
A-5590 - A-5591	HS-3 Flying Boats, Naval Aircraft Factory	330 hp (Liberty)	
A-5606	LS (Seaplane), Loening Aero. Engr.	300 hp (Hispano-Suiza)	Seaplane version of the M-8
A-5607 - A-5608	LS (Seaplanes), Loening Aero. Engr.	300 hp (Hispano-Suiza)	CANCELED
A-5609 - A-5611	LB Flying Boats Loening Aero. Engr.	300 hp (Hispano-Suiza)	Building Suspended, CANCELED
A-5612 - A-5614	AS-1 Change to AS-2, Aeromarine P&M	330 hp (Hispano-Suiza)	

A-5615 - A-5618	HS-2 Flying Boats, NAS Hampton Roads	330 hp (Liberty)	Erected from spare hulls and material
A-5619	HS-2 Flying Boat, NAS Hampton Roads	330 hp (Liberty)	CANCELED
A-5620 - A-5629	HD-1 Hanroits	Clerget type 0-ZS-8	Modified at the Naval Aircraft Factory

Chapter Notes:

* Much of the material for this chapter is extracted from material written by I.W. Robb and L. Peterson which appeared in the publication entitled *Naval Aviation in Word War I.*

1 Anonymous, *Procurement of Aviation Material in Europe 1917-1918*, undated

2 ibid

3 Shirley, Noel C., "La Guardia, Caproni Bombers, and the U.S. Navy", *Cross and Cockade Journal* (US), Vol.25, No. 2, pages 125-140

Table Notes:

1 The following Statement appears in the Navy Estimates H.R. Hearings 1916, p 864 regarding this listing: "Note. - Since purchase many machines have been modified ... A number of machines have been wrecked partially or completely a number of times and rebuilt, so that it is conservative to estimate that more than 50 new or complete machines have existed." Systematic numbering of aircraft apparently started as "Construction Numbers" (later Bureau Numbers) at A-51.

2 AH numbers are probable, on basis of sequence, but not are verified.

3 This batch of aircraft consisted of both R-6 Seaplanes by Curtiss with V2-3 engines of 200 hp and R-9 Seaplanes with 330 hp Liberty engines. The specific breakdown by number is as follows:

A-873 - A891	R-9
A-892 - A-893	R-6
A-894	R-9
A-895	R-6
A-896 - A-908	R-9
A-909	unidentified
A-910	R-6
A-911 - A-917	R-9
A-918 - A-920	R-6
A-921 - A-924	R-9
A-925	R-6L
A-926 - A-942	R-9
A-943	R-6L
A-944 - A-955	R-9
A-956	R-6
A-957	R-9
A-958 - A-959	R-9
A-960 - A-962	R-9
A-963	R-6L
A-964	R-9
A-965 - A-966	R-6L
A-967 - A-969	R-9
A-970	R-6L
A-971 - A-975	R-6
A-976 - A-990	R-9
A-991	R-6L
A-992 - A-993	R-9
A-994	R-6L

4 Some of this batch of aircraft, which were scheduled for conversion from the HS-1 design to the HS-2 design were subsequently canceled. A partial breakdown between delivered and canceled aircraft is a follows:

Delivered	Canceled
A-1099 - A-115	A-1116
A-1117 - A-1133	A-1134
A-1135 - A-1147	A-1148
A-1149 - A-1191 (A-1171 rebuilt as A-5630)	A-1220
A-1193 - A-1212	A-1220
A-1213 (HS-2 erected from spares)	A-1222
A-1214 - A-1219	A-1228
A-1221	A-1231
A-1223 - A-1230	A-1272
A-1232 (HS-2 erected from spares)	A-1277 - A-1278
A-1233	A-1280
A-1235 - A-1271	A-1287
A-1273 - A-1276	A-1289
A-1279	A-1309
A-1281 - A-1286	A-1313 - A-1314
A-1288	A-1319
A-1290 - A-1308	A-1323
A-1310 - A-1312	A-1325
A-1315 - A-1318	A-1329 - A-1350
A-1320 - A-1322	A-1366
A-1324	
A-1326 - A-1328	
A-1351 - A-1365	
A-1367 - A-1372	

5 Reassigned from previously canceled block of numbers. A-2279 to A-2284 were originally Burgess School Seaplanes, probably U-2 type.

6 A-3333 - A-3360	F-5-L
A-3361 - A-3362	F-3 changed to F-5-L
A-3363 - A-3382	F-5-L Canceled

7 A-3384	DH-4B-xP
A-3385 - A-3392	DH-4
A-3393	DH-4B-1
A-3394	DH-4B-x3
A-3395 -A-3397	DH-4
A-3398	DH-4B-1
A-3399 - A-3401	DH-4B
A-3402	DH-4B-1
A-3403 - A-3344	DH-4
A-3445	DH-4B-1
A-3446 - A-3458	DH-4

8 A-3359 -A-3617	Delivered
A-3618 - A-3658	Canceled
A-3659 - A-3683	Delivered
A-3684 - A3783	Canceled
A-3784 - A-3800	Delivered
A-3801 - A-3863	Canceled
A-3864 - A-3880	Delivered
A-3881	Canceled
A-3882	Delivered
A-3883 - A-3935	Canceled
A-3936 - A-3940	Delivered
A-3941 - A-4008	Canceled
A-4009 - A-4019	Delivered
A-4014 - A-4035	Canceled

5

Marine Corps Aviation[1]

Marine Corps aviation can trace its origin to 22 May 1912, when First Lieutenant Alfred A. Cunningham, USMC, then on duty at the Marine Advanced Base School at Philadelphia,[2] was ordered to join the four Navy pilots at the Naval Aviation Camp at Annapolis. The two organizations, at that time, comprised all there was of naval aviation. Cunningham was subsequently ordered to the Burgess Co. at Marblehead, MA, for flight instruction. This date is recognized as the birth date of Marine Corps Aviation. Shortly thereafter, several enlisted marines were also ordered to aviation duty, forming the nucleus of the eventual Marine Corps Section of naval aviation. This Marine Corps Section was gradually increased, and took part in the naval aviation operations at Vera Cruz, Mexico. On 18 September First Lieutenant Barry L. Smith, USMC, became the second Marine officer to be assigned to flight training when he reported to the Aviation Camp at the Naval Academy.

On 5 October 1913 initial trials of the Navy's first amphibian flying boat, called the O.W.L. (for Over Water Over Land), were completed at Hammondsport by First Lieutenant Smith and Naval Constructor Richardson. This aircraft was the old A-2 modified to its new configuration at the Curtiss plant and newly designated AX-1 to indicate its experimental nature. Because of its subsequent assignment to Smith, the OWL is considered by the Marine Corps as being the first Marine Corps aircraft.[3]

On 6 January 1914 Marine Aviation was established as a separate unit within the envelope classification of "Naval Aviation." The organization consisted of: the promoted First Lieutenant Smith, as OIC, Second Lieutenant W.M. McIlvain, and ten enlisted mechanics who were transferred by the S.S. *Hancock* from Philadelphia to Culebra, Puerto Rico, with the Marine Advance Base Unit. Aircraft with this group included the Navy Flying Boat C-3 and the Navy O.W.L. Boat, or E-1. During this exercise Marine flyers for the first time operated with Marine ground troops. It was at Culebra that Marine pilots first performed open sea reconnaissance missions using aircraft. This group is regarded as a Marine Section at the Navy Flying School at Pensacola, as following its return to Pensacola that was its new designation, effective 5 February 1914.[4] This organization, commanded by Second Lieutenant McIlvain, and now consisting of ten officers and 40 enlisted men, was created by the Commandant of the Marine Corps pursuant to provisions of the Naval Appropriations Act of 1915, which established a Marine Corps aviation involvement limited to 12 officers and 24 men.[5]

At the time of the entrance of the United States in the World War the Marine Corps Section of naval aviation, designated the Marine Aviation Section, consisted of five officers (First Lieutenants Smith, McIlvain, Francis T. Evans, Roy S. Geiger, and David

Francis T. Evans, USMC (Naval Aviator No. 26 and Marine Aviator No. 4). Photo was taken in late 1916 or early 1917 while a 1st Lt., USMC.

Marine Camp at NAS Miami. (source Sam Richards collection)

Photo taken of Sam Richards by a Quartermaster in the rear cockpit of a Curtiss JN-4 while in flight. (source: Sam Richards Collection)

C.S. Brewster), one Warrant Officer, and 30 enlisted men stationed as part of the compliment of the naval air station, Pensacola, FL. The equipment of the Section consisted of four Curtiss Type AH hydroplanes. As the Section expanded, the first Marine Corp Warrant Officer pilot was Walter E. McCaughtry, and the first enlisted pilot was Sergeant James Maguire. On 13 February 1917 the promoted Captain F.T. Evans (Naval Aviator No. 26), USMC, ignoring suicidal predictions, first looped and then spun a Curtiss Jenny N-9 floatplane at Pensacola. 19 years later Evans was to receive the DFC for his contributions to the science of flight.

At the outbreak of hostilities the Marine Aviation Section was in training at the Naval Aeronautic Station at Pensacola as a normal compliment of that station. The Section consisted of seven flying officers, 43 enlisted men, and four Curtiss type AH hydroplanes.

It was realized that a large part of the duties of Marine Corps aviation would require flying landplanes, and hence a combination land and water station was established for Marine Corps flyers at the Marine Barracks at the Navy Yard, Philadelphia. An aviation unit, officially designated the Marine Corps Aeronautic Company, Advanced Base Force, was organized at this new station on 27 April 1917. The promoted Captain Cunningham was in command. It consisted of personnel transferred from the Marine Aviation Section at Pensacola, from other Marine Corps units, and from the Marine Corps Reserve Flying Corps. Training in land flying was immediately begun using the units' two Curtiss R-6 seaplanes, one old Farman landplane, and later two Curtiss JN-4s.[6] On 12 October 1917, the Marine Aeronautic Company, then consisting of 34 Officers and 330 enlisted men, was divided into the following: the First Aviation Squadron, under the now Captain W.M. McIlvain, USMC, and consisting of 24 officers and 237 enlisted men; and the First Marine Aeronautic Company, under the command of Captain Evans, USMC, and consisting of ten officers and 93 enlisted men.

On 14 October 1917, the First Marine Aeronautic Company transferred to Cape May, NJ, and took over the naval station at that place for training in seaplanes and flying boats. It brought with it two R-type Curtiss seaplanes. On 7 December 1917 the First Marine Aeronautic Company, by now composed of 12 officers and 133 enlisted men, was ordered to Naval Base 13, Ponta Delgada,

Marine Flying Field at NAS Miami in 1918. Curtiss "Jenny" aircraft are lined-up on the left.

Sam Richards in the front cockpit of a Curtiss JN-4 at NAS Miami giving a Marine Quartermaster a bit of a flight.

Marine Corps Officers at NAS Miami. 2nd Lt. Sam Richards is in the second row from the bottom and third from left. (source: Sam Richards collection)

Result of aerial gun camera work at NAS Miami. (source: Sam Richards collection)

Azores. The First Marine Aeronautic Company departed from Philadelphia aboard the *Hancock* on 9 January 1918. The U.S. Navy Department, on 16 August 1917, had decided that a naval base was needed in the Azores in order to extend convoy protection and to prevent German submarines from using the islands as refueling bases.[7] The organization arrived at Naval Base 13 (on San Miguel Island) on 21 January, 1918, and initially operated an antisubmarine patrol station of ten R-6 seaplanes and two N-9 seaplanes. Later, these aircraft were replaced by eight HS-2L flying boats. This company was the first completely equipped American aviation unit to leave the United States for service in the war. The promoted Major Evans, on 19 July 1918, was succeeded in command of this unit by Major David L. S. Brewster (Naval Aviator No. 55), who remained in command until the end of the war.[8] Unfortunately, with their aircraft not having radios and limited—except for the HS-2s—to two-hour endurance, their activities were extremely handicapped from the start. The first attack in WWI by a U.S. warplane on a German vessel occurred when 2nd Lt. Walter Poague and his observer, Lt. Amas Booty, in a Curtiss R-6, sighted and attacked a submerged submarine. Their homemade bomb failed to explode. This station was ordered to be abandoned on 24 January 1919, and shortly afterwards the organization returned to the United States, arriving at the Marine flying field, Miami, FL, on 15 March 1919.

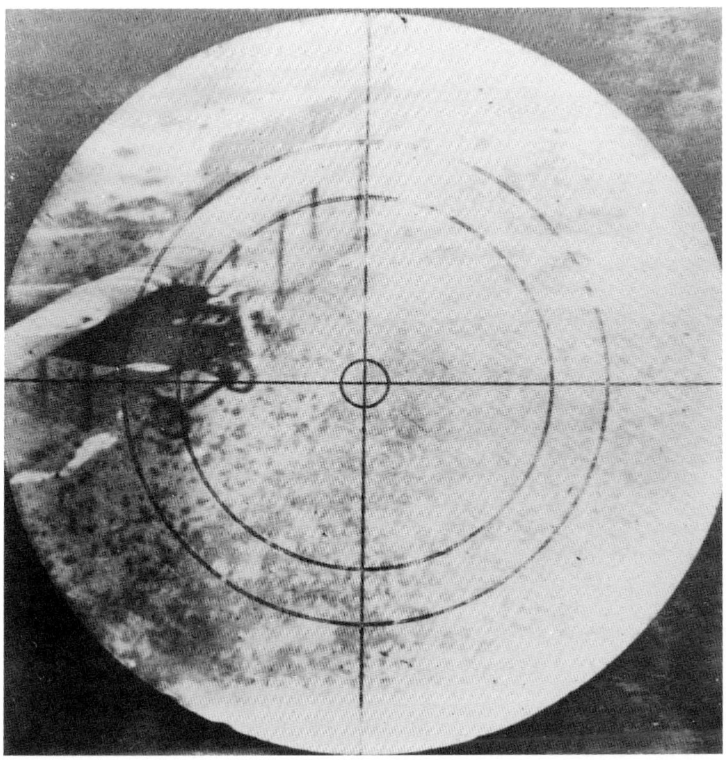

Curtiss F-boat and a Curtiss JN-4D at NAS Miami. (source: Sam Richards collection)

Left: Result of aerial gun camera work at NAS Miami. (source: Sam Richards collection)

Aircraft on the beach at NAS Miami. "F-boats" in foreground and "R-1s" in distance.

Curtiss JN-4 at the Naval Aviation Museum at Pensacola.

On 17 October 1917, the First Aviation Squadron was transferred from the Marine flying field, Philadelphia Navy Yard, to the Army training field (Hazelhurst) at Mineola, Long Island, where further instruction and training was carried on in land flying. On 31 December 1917 the First Aviation Squadron of the Marine Corps, under the command of Captain McIlvain, transferred from Mineola, L.I., to another Army facility at Gerstner Field, Lake Charles, LA, for advanced training in land planes. In March 1918 the Marine flying field at Miami, FL, was established, and on 31 March 1918 the First Aviation Squadron was transferred to that field from Lake Charles, arriving there on 3 April. On 15 April the Marine Aeronautic Detachment and the First Aviation Squadron, each of which had been disbanded on 14 April,[9] were merged at Miami to form the First Marine Aviation Force under the command of the now Major Alfred A. Cunningham.

On 15 December 1917 the Marine Aeronautical Detachment, under the promoted Captain Geiger, was formed at the Marine Barracks, Philadelphia Navy Yard, with four Second Lieutenants and 36 enlisted men. Personnel for this unit came mainly from the First Aviation Squadron. Aircraft consisted of three JN-4s and a Farman. On 10 February 1918 the Marine Aeronautic Detachment, with 11 officers and 40 enlisted men, transferred from the Marine Barracks at the Philadelphia Navy Yard to Miami to set up a Marine Flying Field for landplane training. Aircraft consisted of two Curtiss R-6 seaplanes and one Farman machine. The field, which had been the site of the former Curtiss Aviation School outside of Miami, was adjacent to the Naval Air Station there. Both through the auspices of the Curtiss School and through the efforts of Capt. Cunningham in Washington, DC, the aircraft-situation at the field rapidly grew via the accumulation of Curtiss JN-4s.[10]

Upon the return, in January 1918, of Major Cunningham from observation duty in France, he recommended to the Navy Department the establishing of a Marine Corps land aviation force of not less than four squadrons to operate in the Dunkirk area against submarine bases at Ostend, Zeebrugge, and Bruges. This project was approved by the Secretary of the Navy, and immediate steps were taken to organize this force and secure the necessary equipment. Four squadrons (the Commanding Officers of which were Captains Geiger ["A" Squadron], McIlvain ["B" Squadron—on 16 June], and Roben ["C" Squadron], and First Lieutenant Russell A. Presley ["D" Squadron]) and a headquarters company were organized on 16 June and trained at the Marine Flying Field, Miami, FL. The

Curtiss JN-4 at the Naval Aviation Museum at Pensacola. During the war the U.S. Navy operated 261 of these aircraft.

Curtiss JN-4 at the Naval Aviation Museum at Pensacola.

Curtiss JN-4 of NAS Miami over Florida countryside.

Result of crash of the Curtiss JN-4 of 2nd Lt. Edwin Bertolette. Crash occurred when the JN-4 had its tail clipped by another aircraft.

planes and equipment for this organization were secured from the Army. Before this organization was ordered abroad, a cablegram was received from United States Naval Aviation Headquarters in France recommending that the number of squadrons for this project be doubled, and that these additional squadrons be composed of Navy personnel. This recommendation was approved, and the revised project was called the Northern Bombing Group. The four Marine Corps squadrons hence became known as the Day Wing, Northern Bombing Group.

On 10 July the Force was "detailed for foreign expeditionary shore service." The squadron commanding officers were immediately sent to France to select two sites for operating bases. On 13 July 1918, the First Marine Aviation Force, consisting of squadrons "A," "B," "C," and a Headquarters company left Miami, FL; they embarked on board the S.S. *Dekalb* at New York City for France on 18 July. This organization consisted of 109 officers and 657 enlisted men. On 30 July the *Dekalb* arrived at Brest. Due both to a lack of quarters and a lack of orders for dealing with a contingent of Marine Aviators, the squadrons were obliged to spend their first day in France restricted to their ship.[11] On 1 August the Day Wing disembarked, and proceeded to its aerodromes between Calais and Dunkirk. With their arrival the squadrons were redesignated 7, 8, and 9, respectively. Squadrons "A" and "B" were located at Oye; Squadrons "C" and "D" were assigned to La Fresne; and General Headquarters was at Bois en Ardes.[12] The personnel of the Day Wing were completely organized and ready for service within two weeks after their arrival on French soil. On 5 October 1918, Squadron "D" of the Day Wing, consisting of 42 officers and 183 enlisted men, arrived in France, completing the four squadrons of the Day Wing. Enroute to France, First Lieutenant Donald B. Cowles, the Acting Commanding Officer, died of influenza. Upon the units' arrival at La Fresne he was replaced by the promoted Captain Presley, who resumed his command.

2nd Lt. Sam Richards at NAS Miami.

Marine Corps aviators of the Day Wing performed service both with the British aviation squadrons at the front, due to the scarcity of American planes, and also independently. The type of plane used by the Day Wing were De Haviland 4s and 9s. As originally conceived, the Marine detachment of the Northern Bombing Group was to fly American built D.H.-4 aircraft powered by the 400 hp Liberty engine. Some 72 of these planes had been ordered prior to the departure of the Force from the U.S. It was furthermore planned that the fuselage and engine, sent separately from the U.S., would be mated together in the Assembly & Repair Shops at NAS Pauillac and NAS Eastleigh. To assist in this effort, technical personnel of the Force were assigned to each of these stations to assist in this effort. The first American built D.H.-4 to arrive at La Fresne from Pauillac arrived on 7 September 1918, piloted by First Lieutenant Jesse F. Dunlap (Naval Aviator No. 503), with Gunnery Sergeant Floyd B. Smith as his observer. A difficulty soon arose, however,

Curtiss R-6 No. 505.

Curtiss R-6 No. 505.

due to the fact that more Liberty engines were being received in France than were D.H.-4 fuselages. Fortunately for the Marine Force, at the same time the British had a surplus of D.H. 9 fuselages and a dearth of engines. A little Yankee ingenuity soon resulted in a swap of three "Liberties" for one D.H. 9. Thanks to this effort the Marine Force had, by the end of the war, 20 D.H. 9As and 16 D.H.-4s operational.[13] While Marine aircraft were being received from Pauillac and Eastleigh, arrangements were made wherein three Marine aircrews, with machines, were rotated with Nos. 217 Squadron (D.H.-4) and 218 Squadron (D.H. 9A) RAF. With the German withdrawal from Ostend and Zeebrugge, the original purpose of the Northern Bombing Group no longer existed. This meant that the Day Wing of the Group became an organization looking for a mission.

Marine Corps pilots Captain Francis P. Mulcahy, Captain Robert St. Lytle, and Lieutenant Frank Nelms flew some of the earliest recorded food-dropping missions. On 1 October and on 2 October they made repeated low level runs in the face of German fire and delivered 2600 pounds of food and badly needed supplies to a French Regiment surrounded by German troops near Stadenburg.[14] The first all-Marine effort occurred on 14 October 1918 in the form of a morning bombing raid of seven machines of Squadron "C" from La Fresne, led by Captain Lytle, on the Thielt railway junction. This action coincided with the opening of the Belgian offensive in Flanders. It was on the return trip to La Fresne that actions by Second Lieutenant Ralph Talbot (Naval Aviator No. 456 and No. 802)[15] and Corporal Robinson, during an attack by 12 Fokker D.VIIs and Pfalz D.IIIs, resulted in their being awarded the Medal of Honor. From this date on Day Wing aircraft made raids on Steenbrugge, Eceloo, Ghent, Deynze, and Lokeren. The last Day Wing raid occurred on 27 October. On 26 October an abandoned German field at Knesselaere, Belgium, was chosen as a new field for the Day Wing, as by this date the fields at Oye and La Fresne were too far behind the lines. Only a few operations would be conducted from this forward field before the Armistice. The total number of raids made by Marine Corps personnel was 57, during which 34,000 pounds of bombs were dropped. These raids did considerable damage and brought back valuable information. Some 28 medals were

Curtiss R-6 No. A-337 at NAS Ponto Delgado with the 1st Aero Co., First Marine Aviation Force. (source: Official U.S. Navy Photograph)

Shops and aircraft parking and beaching ramp at Ponto Delgado, Azores. Capt. F.T. Evans was the Commanding Officer of the First Marine Aviation Force.

issued to members of the Day Wing, two of which were the Medal of Honor.[16] It was learned after the armistice that one of these raids resulted in the death of 60 German officers and 300 enlisted men. Four Marine Corps aviators were killed or died of wounds, while 12 enemy aircraft were shot down as a result of these raids. Not all casualties were combat related. On 25 October, at La Fresne field, D.H.-4 D-1 was prepared for a test flight by Second Lieutenant Talbot, with Second Lieutenant Colgate W. Darden, Jr., as a passenger. The machine failed to become airborne, and while the observer was thrown clear, Lieutenant Talbot died in the crash. Additional deaths resulted from illness. As a result of the Spanish Influenza, "C" Squadron was hit with 20 cases on 25 October. By the next day there were 102 cases, and the field was a virtual hospital. Before it was over three officers and five enlisted men would die from the disease. Early in December 1918, the Day Wing received orders to return to the United States and embarked on 6 December on board the S.S. *Mercury* at St. Nazaire, France, arriving at Newport News, VA, on 21 December 1918.

The following table compares the strength of Marine Corps aviation at the outbreak of the war and at the time of the armistice:

	6 April 1917	11 November 1918
Commissioned Officers	4	250
Warrant Officers	1	32
Enlisted men	30	2180

Notes:

[1] Much of the material in this Chapter is based on information in the document Adrian O. Van Wyen's "Naval Aviation in World War I" published in *Naval Aviation News*, 1969

[2] Emmons, Roger M., "Early Flying Marines, *Cross and Cockade Journal* (U.S.), Vol. 22, No. 4

[3] Arthur, Reginald White, *Contact! Careers of Naval Aviators Assigned Numbers 1 to 2000*, Naval Aviation Register, Washington, DC

[4] ibid

[5] ibid

[6] ibid

[7] ibid

[8] ibid

[9] ibid

[10] ibid

[11] Wait, Adam and Noel Shirley, "'Devil Dog' Sam Richards", *Over the Front*, Vol.7, No. 3, pages 195-211

[12] Emmons, Roger M., "The First Marine Aviation Force", *Cross and Cockade Journal* (U.S.), Vol. 6, No. 2

[13] ibid

[14] Van Vleet, Clarke, and William J. Armstrong, *United States Naval Aviation 1910-1980*, Washington, DC

[15] Initially assigned No. 456 by the Navy on 10 April 1918, he was assigned No. 802 by the Marine Corps on 26 May 1918.

[16] Emons, Roger, M., "The First Marine Aviation Force", *Cross and Cockade Journal* (U.S.) Vol. 6, No. 2

6

Naval Aviation in Foreign Service

Naval Aviation Forces in France[1]

On 20 April 1917, the Secretary of the Navy, Josephus Daniels, requested Vice Admiral William Sims in London to make inquiries of the Allies on their plans with respect to Naval Aviation. On 3 July Sims replied that the British had a need for 100 kite balloon units and complete squadrons of seaplanes. On 25 April 1917, and on the same subject, a French mission headed by Rene Viviani, acting on behalf of Marshall Joffre, arrived in Washington. The purpose of this mission was to discuss with the Navy the deployment of naval forces in France. In May 1917, at the request of the French government, the Navy Department decided to send a naval aviation force to France. The first unit to be organized was the "First Aeronautic Detachment, U.S. Navy," which was assembled from men then under training at Pensacola. The unit consisted of seven officers and 122 men under the command of Lieutenant Kenneth Whiting, USN (Naval Aviator No. 16). The unit was spilt into two groups. One group left Pensacola for Baltimore, while the second group left for Hoboken, NJ. The first group boarded the collier U.S.S. *Neptune* in Baltimore. The second group departed for France aboard the collier U.S.S. *Jupiter* (later the first U.S. aircraft carrier, the *Langley*). The *Jupiter* left Hoboken on May 23rd and arrived at Bordeaux on June 7th, while the Ne*ptune* left two days later and arrived at St. Nazaire on June 8th. Compiled from the logs of the *Jupiter* and *Neptune*, the roster of the First Aeronautic Detachment is given in Table 1. In Table 2 is noted the listing of the enlisted men of the First Aero Detachment known to have been designated "Naval Aviators." This detachment was the first American military unit to land in Europe for service ashore. Whiting immediately proceeded to Paris, arriving there on June 13th, and held a conference with Admiral LeBon, French Minister of Marine, and Capitaine de Vaisseau Cazenau, Chief of the French Naval Air Service. At this conference it was decided to send a mission, consisting of French and American Officers, to make an inspection of the French coast for the purpose of locating sites for U.S. Naval Air Stations. It was also decided to establish a School and General Reserve at Lake Heurtin, adjacent to an existing French School. Capitaine de Fregate Laborde, Whiting, Conger, and Captain Smith, the latter began as assistant to the U.S. Naval Attaché in Paris, were appointed members of this mission. After a careful inspection of the French coast, which was completed about the first of July, the mission submitted their recommendations in the form of a report. This formed the basis of an agreement between Whiting and the French Minister of Marine, and was forwarded to the Navy Department for approval via a cable to the Secretary of the Navy on 7 July. Due to a lack of communication within the Navy, all of Whiting's actions were not only performed on the basis of verbal orders, but also without the apparent knowledge of Sims, the Navy Force Commander in London.

Kenneth Whiting, Commanding Officer of the First Aero Detachment. Photo was taken in the 1920's when Whiting, then a full Commander, was associated with the U.S.S. *Langley*. (Source: Naval Historical Center)

TABLE 1

Officers

Lieutenant Kenneth Whiting, Commander
Lieutenant Gratton C. Dichman
Lieutenant (j.g.) Godfrey deC. Chavalier
Lieutenant (j.g.) Virgil C. Griffin
Paymaster Omar D. Conger
Assistant Paymaster Frederick E. Michel
Assistant Surgeon Arthur S. Sinton

Enlisted men

1. Abraham, M.J., Sea. 2c
2. Asion, C., Matt.3c
3. Bauden, L., Matt.3c
4. Baily, D.F., Lds.QM(a)
5. Baker, P.L., Y. 3c
6. Bamrick, E.J., Lds.QM (a)
7. Barrick, T.W., Lds.QM (a)
8 Bensfore, H., Sea. 2c

9 Bishop, A.W., MM.2c
10 Boyulan, C.J. (E.J.) Lds.QM(a)[a]
11. Bracewell, C.E. Lds.QM (a)
12. Brady, T.J., MM. 2c
13. Brown, M.F. (M.E.), Lds.QM(a)
14. Browne, R.R., MM.2c
15. Bruton, L.M. (I.B.) Lds.QM (a)
16. Bunn, W.C. Lds.QM (a)
17. Burnett, C. BM.1c
18. Carson, J.F., Lds.QM (a)
19. Chapin, M.J., Lds.QM(a)
20. Charles, D., Lds.QM(a)
21. Cline, J.C. Lds.QM(a)[b]
22. Conley, D.L., E.2c
23. Counts, E., MM.2c
24. Croswell, G.E. (E.G.), Lds.QM(a)
25. Cunningham, R.C., MM.2c
26. Daniels, W., Matt.3c
27. DeSonier, L.A., Cox.
28. Dickson, S. Lds.QM(a)
29. Edney, H., Matt.3c
30. Elkins, E.M., Lds.QM(a)
31. Elliiott, H.A. Lds.QM(a)
32. Flickinger, C.E., MM. 2c
33. Galllivan, T.J., MM.2c
34. Ganster, J. (X.J.), Lds.QM(a)
35. Garner, D.A. Jr., Lds.QM(a)
36. Gillespie, P.E., Lds.QM(a)
37. Godson, E.E., Lds.QM(a)

38. Goggins, J.E., Lds.QM(a)
39. Gowell, R.M., Lds.QM(a)
40. Haizlett, R., MM. 2c
41. Halstead, F.N. (R.H.) Lds.QM(a)
42. Hammann, C.H., Lds.QM(a)
43. Hanna, L.R., Lds.QM(a)
44. Hardendorf, F.M., Lds.QM(a)

45. Harrell, R.H., Lds.QM(a)
46. Harvie, L.S., BM.2c
47. Hasselman, G.H., Lds.QM(a)
48. Hobt, M.A., Lds.QM(a)
49. Hockett, C.S., Cstd.
50. Hollsena, G.H. (E.H.), Lds.QM(a)

51. Hough, F.M., Lds.QM(a)
52. Huddleston, W.D., Lds.QM(a)
53. Jenkins, J.W., Jr., MM.2c
54. Jernigan, J.D., Jr., Lds.QM(a)
55. Jones, C.R., MM.2c
56. Kanwaring, A.S., Lds.QM(a)
57. Keeip, E.C., MM.2c
58. Lasher, H., Lds.QM(a)
59. Larless, T.L., Lds.QM(a)
60. Leonhardt, T.L., Lds.QM(a)
61. Letzkas, E.A., Lds.QM(a)
62. Lipsey, L.H., Lds.QM(a)
63. Lucy, H.J., PM.1c
64. Manley, G.H. (G.E.), Lds.QM(a)
65. Mansfield, F.R., Lds.QM(a)
66. Mara, R.A., MM.2c
67. Marchant, A.W., CBM.

68. Mmarshburn, D., Lds.QM(a)
69. Marx, J., Lds.QM(a)
70. McKee, J.A., Lds.MM(a)
71. McLaughlin, W.A., Lds.MM(a)
72. Morerro, R., Str. STD.
73. Murphy, A.B., MM.2c
74. Myers, H. Matt.3c
75. Nabors, T.D., MM.2c
76. Neal, A.A., MM.2c
77. Nelson, A.A., MM.2c
78. Nirmaier, E., BM.1c
79. O'Brien, J.H., Lds.QM(a)
80. O'Connor, C.S., CBM.
81. O'Borman, M.E., Y.1c
82. O'Loughlin, L.T., Lds.QM(a)
83. Owen, H. (J.), Lds.QM(a)
84. Parker, R.H., Lds.QM(a)
85. Pearce, C.H., Bkr.1c
86. Petraseck, A.J., E.1cg
87. Porter, L.E., Sea.2c
88. Reichlt, (Reichert), E., BM.1c
89. Roberts, C.B., Lds.QM(a)
90. Robertson, W.R., Sea.2c
91 Rhodes, C.E., Sea.2c
92. Rourke, C.F., Lds.QM(a)
93. San Jose, S., Matt.3c
93. Schneider, W.H., MM.2c
95. Sheely, I.E., MM.2c
95. Shyne, W.W., MM.2c

97. Skagges, A.D., Lds.QM(a)
98. Smith, S.H., Sea.2c
99. Soland, F.F., Lds.QM(a)
100. Specht, E.P., Lds.QM(a)
101. Sprague, G.E., Lds.QM(a)
102. Stample, J.G., MM.2c
103. Stanley, J., Lds.QM(a)

104. Stone, J.B., CMM.
105. Stroupe, Z.A. (Z.R.), MM.2c
106. Sruter (Struder), H.W., Lds.QM(a)
107. Thompson, R.W., GM.1c
108. Thornton, C.H., Lds.QM(a)

109. Thweatt, T.N., Lds.QM(a)
110. Tuttle,, P.H., Lds.QM(a)
111. Underwood, A.M. E.2cg
112. Van Galdr (Galder), E.H., Lds.QM(a)
113. Velie, H.G., Lds.QM(a)
114. Wardwell, C.E., Lds.MM(a)
115. Washburn, C.H., Sea.
116. Weddell, T.H., Lds.QM(a)
117. Wiberg, S.C. (F.C.), Lds.QM(a)
118. Williams, O.E., E.1c
119. Woods, C., Lds.QM(a)
120. Young, F., Lds.QM(a)

Notes:

a. Log entries are handwritten and not always legible. In some instances where a name appears more than once the spelling or initials do not agree; hence, the parenthesized spellings.

b. J.C. Cline, in his history of this Detachment, lists the names of Barton and Jones to bring the compliment up to 122.

Members of the First Aero Detachment prior to departing aboard the U.S.S. *Jupiter*.

TABLE 2

Name	Rating	Rank	NA No.	Date Designated	Date Enrolled
Carson, Julian F.	Lds.QM(a)	Ensign	765	-	10 June 1918
Cline, Joseph C.	Lds.QM(a)	Boatswain	1832	-	7 June 1918
Conley, Delbert L.	E.2c	-	1166	12 September 1918	12 September 1918
DeSonier, Lawrence A.	Cox.	Ensign	762	-	10 June 1918
Elliiott, Harold A.	Lds.QM(a)	Ensign	760	-	10 June 1918
Gallivan, Thomas J.	MM.2c	Ensign	1512	-	2 October 1918
Gillespie, Paul E.	Lds.QM(a)	Ensign	2288	25 March 1918	7 June 1918
Gowell, Robert M.	Lds.QM(a)	Ensign	1847	-	9 June 1918
Hammann, Charles H.	Lds.QM(a)	Ensign	1494	-	14 October 1918
Hardendorf, Foss H.	Lds.QM(a)	Ensign	2456	29 April 1918	8 June 1918
Huddleston, Walter D.	Lds.QM(a)	Ensign	766	-	10 June 1918
Lasher, Herbert	Lds.QM(a)	Ensign	763	-	10 June 1918
Letzkus, Elmer A.	Lds.QM(a)	Ensign	1634	-	25 October 1918
Marchant, Alfred W.	CBM.	Boatswain	2637	19 July 1918	20 July 1918 (Date of Rank)
Nirmaier, Edwin	BM.1c	Ch.Mach.	16749	15 August 1943	French Brevit No. 377
O'Brien, James H.	Lds.QM(a)	Ensign	764	-	10 June 1918
O'Connor, C.J.	CSM.	-	1117 or 2103[a]	-	-
O'Laughlin, Lee T.	Lds.QM(a)	Boatswain	1321	-	19 June 1918
Rhodes, Clifton	Sea. 2c	Ensign	1763	-	3 December 1918
Stanley, John	Lds.QM(a)	Ensign	1495	-	4 October 1918
Thweatt, T.N.	Lds.QM(a)	Ensign	2669	23 June 1918	-
Wardwell, Charles E.	Lds.QM(a)	Ensign	759	-	10 June 1918
Young, Franklin	Lds.QM(a)	Ensign	761	-	10 June 1918

Note: [a] The records are uncertain as to the extent which Naval Aviator No. was used.

In Departmental Memorandum 0p. Air-4874-17 the Navy Department, on 17 September 1917, authorized the establishment of Naval Air Stations in France, namely: Dunkerque (see Appendix Q); L'Aber Vrach (see Appendix K); Brest (see Appendix O); Ile Tudy (see Appendix I); Le Croisic (see Appendix H); Paimboeuf (see Appendix P); Fromentine (see Appendix L); Rochefort, St. Trojan (see Appendix J); Moutchic (see Appendix W); and Pauillac (see Appendix G). Of these stations, all were eventually begun, except for that at Rochefort, which the Navy had planned as a dirigible station, but which the French requested to be ceded back to them in order to make room for dirigible hangars and workshops, which were moved out of Paris by reason of the German Offensive of March 1918. Three of the stations (Dunkerque, Paimboeuf, and Moutchic) were simply to be taken over from the French, while the

Commandant, Instructors, and students of the First Aero Detachment, with their mechanics, at Tours. (source: 80-HAG-5R-6)

The label of this photo reads "First Aero Detachment with instructors at Cranwell" However, there is a good chance that the photo is mislabeled as the instructors appear to be French and Cranwell was an English Station to which only two member of the First Aero Detachment were sent. More likely this is a group photo of member of the First Aero Detachment under instruction at Tours. (source: 80-HAG-5R-3)

French instructors of the First Aero Detachment at Tours. (source: 80-HAG-5R-4)

Students of the First Aero Detachment awaiting instruction at Tours.

Caudron G.III used by members of the First Aero Detachment when training at Tours.

Lt. Virgil Childers Griffin and the Chief Pilot, in a F.B.A. seaplane at St. Raphael. In addition to being Naval Aviator No. 41 Griffin became French Naval Aviator No. 270. St.Raphael was both a school for mechanics and a smooth water training station for seaplane pilots and observers.

Joe Cline of the First Aero Detachment while in training.

NAS Queenstown.

Left to right: Ens. Walter White (Naval Aviator No. 1496), Lt.Cdr. John Lansing Callan, Lt. Erlon Howard Parker (Naval Aviator No. 758), and Lt. Solhaus. (source: Naval Historical Foundation)

remainder were to be constructed as rapidly as materials could be obtained from the United States.

At the same time, the Navy Department ordered Captain Hutch I. Cone, USN, to Paris to assume direct command of all activities in France as Commander, U.S. Naval Aviation Forces, Foreign Service, under the direction of Vice Admiral Sims, in London. Captain Westervelt, Chief Constructor for the Navy, initiated this move on 18 August 1917 when he advised Sims to take a captain to his staff to be in charge of the individual commanders in France and England. Sims asked for an administrator, not necessarily an aviator. He requested Cone, who was then the Superintendent at the Canal Zone and formerly Chief of the Bureau of Steam Engineering. Cone, upon his arrival in England on 27 September 1917, replaced Lieutenant W.A. Edwards as the Aide for Aviation of Sims' Staff. One of Cone's first actions was to offer to cooperate with the RNAS in the building and operation of air stations in England and Ireland. Cone relieved Lieutenant Whiting on 24 October 1917 as the commanding officer, U.S. Naval Forces, Foreign Service. In October, Cone moved his offices from London to Paris, where he remained in direct command of the U.S. Naval Aviation Forces in Foreign Service until 1 August 1918 when he moved his headquarters from Paris to London and became a member of Sims' Staff. While in France, Cone and Captain Thomas T. Craven shared responsibilities. Cone was more involved with the development of Naval Aviation, while Craven undertook responsibilities associated with the daily operations of the activities. As such, there was a split in the reporting chain for these two officers. Cone, because of the technicalities involved with his effort, bypassed the senior naval officer in France, Rear Admiral H. B. Wilson, Commanding Officer of U.S. Naval Forces in France, and instead was responsible directly to Sims; Craven, however, being on Wilson's staff, reported directly to him. On 1 September, in a reorganization of naval aviation forces abroad, the Commander U.S. Naval Aviation Forces, Foreign Service, was assigned to the staff of the Commander, U.S. Naval Forces Operating in European Waters as Aid for Aviation. With this move the naval aviation forces in France were then placed under the command of Wilson on August 1st, and Craven, as Aide for Aviation on

General Caldarera and Capt. De Filippi.

John Lansing Callan and his Italian Chauffeur. (source: Naval Historical Foundation)

NAS Lake Bolsena in 1918. Left to right: Lt. (j.g.) Jack Terry (Medical Officer), Lt. (j.g.) Mark Walton (Executive Officer), and Lt. W.B. Atwater (Commanding Officer). (source: Naval Historical Center)

the staff of Wilson, was then directly charged with all aviation matters in France thereafter until the end of the War. Wilson had assumed command of the Naval Forces in France on 21 October 1917 when he replaced Captain Fletcher. Wilson arrived at his Headquarters in Brest on 1 November 1917.

As combat operations underlined the need for Aviation Intelligence Officers, the Commander, Naval Aviation Forces, Foreign Service, on 19 March 1918, distributed a circular letter defining the duties and functions performed by such officers at Royal Naval Air Stations with the suggestion that provisions for similar services be made at the Naval Air Stations "as may seem expedient." Supplementing letters clarified the duties and functions, and on 31 October it was specifically stated that Aviation Intelligence Officers be specifically trained for such work.

On 21 April 1918, a Memorandum For Organization at Air Stations was submitted for consideration by the Operations Division. The memo proposed that the Naval Air Stations, Foreign Service, be organized and administered on the same principles as relating to Commanding, Executive, and Heads of Departments as is laid down for organization and administration of vessels in the U.S. Naval Regulations and Instructions. The proposed organizational structure was as shown in Table 3. At the time of the Memo the organization at Le Croisic followed closely the general principles laid down by the Memo and were considered suitable to the complement laid down by the Navy Department. The Le Croisic organization, however, did not cover the Navigator, the Radio Officer, the Meteorologist, or the Photographic Officer. It was also believed that the term "Executive Officer" was a more appropriate term to

Rear row (left to right): Capt. Jackson, Lt. Walton, Cdr. Mayo, and Cdr. Cook. Front row (left to right): Capt. Train, Lt. Atwater, V.Adm. H.T. Mayo (Commander-in-Chief of the U.S. Fleet), Italian Lt.Cdr. Caldarera Lt. Cdr. Callan, and an unidentified Lt. Cdr. at NAS Lake Bolsena in November 1918.

Lt. Bill Atwater, in right rear seat of car, on an inspection. (source: Naval Historical Foundation)

Cmdt. Valli and Lt. W.B. Atwater in Venice in July 1918. (source: Naval Historical Foundation)

Formal portrait of V.Adm. H.T. Mayo, Commander-in-Chief of the U.S. Fleet in foreign waters.

use than the then antiquated "Captain of the Yard." Also, the term "Engineer Officer" was used on the Complement List. And lastly, "Chief Pilot" was considered to be an appropriate term to use for the "Officer in Charge of the Flight Department." The Chief Pilot would be the Raid Officer at bombing stations.

V.Adm. H.T. Mayo (Commander-in-Chief) U.S. Fleet) and his staff visiting Monte Graffee. Left to right: Cdr. Leigh Mayes, Capt. Cook, V.Adm. H.T. Mayo, Capt. Jackson, and Capt. Ernest King. Italian officers and two Army officers are not identified. (source: Naval Historical Foundation)

By the middle of 1918, changes in the organizational needs of the naval aviation command structure were beginning to become evident. These changes were necessitated by the fact that the time was rapidly approaching when the U.S. Naval Aviation Forces in Foreign Service would pass from the stage of construction to that of an active organization. In view of the existence of the widely separated and distinct units, Captain Cone, on 22 June 1918, recommended to the Force Commander (Vice Admiral Sims) the following:

a. The officer commanding U.S. Naval Aviation Forces, Foreign Service relinquish his command and become a member of the Staff of the Force Commander.

b. An officer be designated to command U.S. Naval Aviation activities in each area, Italy, Ireland, England, France, and the Northern Bombing Group. The Northern Bombing Group should be a separate unit and not combined with the other English unit located at Killingholme, and should also include the Dunkerque Seaplane Station.

c. In Ireland the Commander of the U.S. Naval Aviation Forces should be on the Staff of the British Commander-in-Chief at Queenstown. In Italy, for the present, the Commander of the U.S. Naval Aviation Forces should serve under the U.S. Naval Attaché at Rome. In France the Commander of the U.S. Naval Aviation Forces should be a member of the Staff of the Commander of the U.S. Naval Forces in France.

TABLE 3

Commanding Officer

Executive Officer

Ordinance
- Armory
- Magazine
- Ord. Instr.

Navigation and Intelligence
- Navigation
- Intelligence
- Radio
  - Communications
  - Pigeons
  - Photography
  - Meteorology
  - Communication Board

Flight
- Flights
- Pilots
- Observers
- Handling
- Crews
- Flight Board

Executive Department
- Guard
- Mail
- Cadre

Repair
- Aircraft
- Carpenter
- Boatswain
- Water Transportation
- Repair Crews

Public Works
- Buildings
- Grounds
- Land and Water Transportation

Supply
- Commissary
- Supply
- Pay

Medical
- Hospital
- Welfare

At large stations Navigation and Intelligence could be divided into:

Navigation
- Navigation
- Meteorology
- Pigeons
- Station Log

Intelligence
- Intelligence
- Communication
- Radio
- Photography

On 26 August 1918 Vice Admiral Sims, in Circular Letter No. 84, ordered the following organizational changes:

1. On 1 September 1918, the Commander of the U.S. Naval Aviation Forces, Foreign Service, will be assigned to the Staff of the Commander, U.S. Naval Forces Operating in European Waters, as Aide for Aviation. As such the Aide for Aviation will be the Chief of the Aviation Section of the Force Commander's Staff.

2. The various U.S. Naval Aviation units in Europe will, after that date, be operated as follows:

a. The Commander, U.S. Naval Forces in France will command all U.S. Naval Air Stations on the West Coast of France. The operations of these stations will be conducted in conjunction with the French authorities. (His mailing address was: Commander, U.S. Naval Forces in France (Aviation), Brest (Finisters), France). This change placed Captain T.T. Craven on the Staff of Rear Admiral Wilson.

b. The Commanding Officer of the U.S. Naval Northern Bombing Group will command that Group and the U.S. Naval Air Station Dunkerque, under the direction of the British Vice-Admiral Commanding the Dover Patrol. He will also command the U.S. Naval Aviation Repair Base at Eastleigh. (The mailing address for this command was: Commanding Officer, Northern Bombing Group, U.S. Naval Aviation Forces, A.P.O. #4, A.E.F.)

c. The Commanding Officer of the U.S. Naval Air Stations in Italy will command those stations under the direction of the Italian District Commanders. (The mailing address for this com-

Aerial view of NAS Porto Corsini. (source: Gregory C. Alegi collection)

Left to right: W.B. Haviland and C.J. Coatsworth in Venice in April 1918. (source: Peter Kilduff Collection)

John Lansing Callan and Capt. Capuzzi in Porto Corsini in July 1918. (source: Naval Historical Foundation)

mand was: Commanding Officer, U.S. Naval Air Stations - Italy, 2, Via St. Susanna, Rome, Italy).

d. The Commanding Officer of the U.S. Naval Air Stations in Ireland (Commander McCrary) will command those stations under the direction of the British Commander-in-Chief, Coast of Ireland. (The mailing address for this command was: Commanding Officer, U.S. Naval Air Stations - Ireland, Queenstown, Ireland.)

e. After 31 August 1918, all mail, cablegrams, and telegrams pertaining to Naval Aviation and which have heretofore been addressed to the Commander of the U.S. Naval Aviation Forces, Foreign Service, shall be addressed to the Force Commander, as in the case of all other correspondence pertaining to Naval activities in Europe.

R. Adm. Wilson was replaced just prior to the end of the War by Rear Admiral W.B. Fletcher, when on 25 September 1918, Wilson was promoted to Vice Admiral. Fletcher assumed command on 20 October 1918. An additional impact of the move was to give the commanders of the aviation units in France, England, Ireland, Italy, and the Northern Bombing Group control and direction over the operations of their stations. This organization remained intact until Captain Cone was seriously injured in the torpedoing of the British steamer *Leinste* on 10 October 1918 while enroute from Kingstown to Hollyhead, Ireland. Vice Admiral Sims, due to the scope of activities then being pursued by the Navy, was forced to replace Cone with the promoted Lieutenant Commander W.A. Edwards. Edwards, who had headed the London Office until Cone moved there, remained in office through the end of the War.

In addition to discussions on the seaplane stations to be established by the Navy in France, there were a number of discussions on the subject of LTA bases held between Navy representatives, French authorities, and representatives of the Astra-Torres Company. On 1 October, at a conference between Lieutenant De Vaisseau Thierry of the Ministry of Marine, Commander Frank R. McCrary, USN, (Naval Aviator No. 91) and Lieutenant Commander Louis H. Maxfield, USN, (Naval Aviator No. 17), arrangements were made for establishing dirigible stations in France.

In addition to the stations previously mentioned, the Navy Department shortly afterward also authorized U.S. Naval Air Stations at Trequier (see Appendix N), Guipavas (see Appendix U), La

Student Officers at NAS Porto Corsini. First row, from left: R.H. Clark, E.L. Smith, C.W. Gates, W. White, A.P. Taliaferro, and K. Stewart. Second row, from left: L.W. Knowles, E.I. Tinkham, C.H. Hammann, J.A. Goggins, and J. Stanley. (source: Naval Historical Center)

Officers Mess at NAS Porto Corsini. (source: Naval Historical Center)

NAS Porto Corsini on 16 November 1918. (source: Peter Kilduff collection)

Hangar #1 at NAS Porto Corsini. (source: Naval Historical Center)

Trinite-sur-Mer (see Appendix R), La Pallice (see Appendix S), Gujan (see Appendix T), and Arcachon (see Appendix M). When the Northern Bombing Group was organized the seaplane station site at Dunkerque was transferred to this unit. Hence, there were fifteen stations in operation or under construction attached to the French unit of U.S. Naval Air Stations at the time of the Armistice. These stations, together with their complement on 11 November 1918, are shown in Table 4. The French stations were selected based upon their assumed roles. The fields of the Northern Bombing Group were intended for aircraft which would offensively attack submarines cruising in the shallow waters off the coast of Belgium, operating from the German submarine bases, and also to operate offensively against the German seaplanes operating from the coast of Belgium. The stations at Trequier, L'Aber Vrach, Brest, Ile Tudy, Le Croisic, Fromentine, St. Trojan, and Arcachon were established as patrol stations. These stations were located with the idea of protecting the ports at which American transports were expected to land, i.e., Brest, St. Nazaire, and Bordeaux. The missions of these stations were defensive in that they denied to the submarine both the advantages of lying close in to the port and of conducting her attack in restricted areas.

Hangar #2 at NAS Porto Corsini in July 1918.

TABLE 4

	Date Put In Operation	**No. of Officers 11 November 1918**	**No. of Men 11 November 1918**
A. Air Stations, Operation			
Trequier	30 September 1918	25	202
L'Aber Vrach	18 July 1918	53	455
Brest	29 October 1918*	188	771
Ile Tudy	28 February 1918	32	357
La Trinite	1 October 1918	10	148
Le Croisic	18 November 1917	42	337
Paimboeuf'	21 March 1918	43	478
Fromentine	19 July 1918	38	356
St. Trojan	19 July 1918	40	345
Pauillac	19 June 1918	220	1305
Moutchic	24 October 1917	93	485
Arcachon	14 September 1918	19	318
B. Air Stations Under Construction			
Guipavas	11 November 1918	25	196
Gujan	never	15	252
La Pallice	never	7	169

* Patrol and convoy system inaugurated

The following are excerpts from a lengthy French and American agreement relative to the employment of Aviation, Department of Brittany:

"THE ROLE OF AVIATION IS AS FOLLOWS:

1. The escorting of convoys
2. Patrolling (Service de Reconnaissance)
3. Answering Allos or SOS signals (Service d'Alerte).

Disposition must permit the following:

1. A continuous surveillance over convoys for the greater part of their course, diminishing, insofar as possible, serial flights which have no military value.
2. A service of patrol when conditions make the presence of submarines seem possible.

Gun pits at NAS Porto Corsini. (source: Naval Historical Center)

NAS Porto Corsini on 16 November 1918. (source: Peter Kilduff collection)

Escorting of the convoys will be conducted as follows:

1. **American Convoys arriving and leaving**: Escorted to the limit practicable with the machines, generally with three successive groups of seaplanes.

2. **Lizard Convoys arriving leaving:** Escorted to the limit practicable with the machines, or until the English aerial escort is met.

3. **Cherbourg Convoys arriving and leaving:**

(a) L'Aber Vrach, from the Four to the meridian of Pontusval

(b) La Penze, from the meridian of Pontusval to that of Sept-Iles

(c) Trequier, from the meridian of Sept-Iles to as far as the planes can practicably convoy, or until a section from Guernsey is met.

4. **Quiberon, Convoys arriving and leaving:** Escorted to the meridian of Glenans or until the section patrolling from the Loire is met.

PATROL SERVICE:

This service will be carried out upon the initiative of station commanders, from information received from any source, when the conditions appear to them deserving of attention. The escorting of convoys being first assured from their own or neighboring bases.

This service may also be prescribed in an emergency by the Prefet Maritime, who will transmit his instructions for American stations through the District Commander (Communications Office, American).

SERVICE D'ALERTE:

This will be assured by keeping a section ready for duty constantly at every station. (Instructions regarding the employment of seaplanes and regarding communications between the different patrol units are given in the following French documents: 1) The order No. 4 of the Vice Admiral, Superior Commandant of the Divisions of Brittany, dated 18 September 1918; 2) D.M. of 1 December 1917 (Method of Bomb Dropping); 3) D.M. of 19 March 1918 (Tactics of Aeroplanes); and 4) D.M. of 12 August 1918 (Escort of Convoys by Aircraft)).

LIGHTER-THAN-AIR:

Military Operations

The two dirigible stations at Guipavas are associated together. The French Station receives all the information regarding the movements of the coastal convoys and transmits these to the American station. The American station will receive information regarding movements of the American convoys, and will transmit these to the French station. Ordinarily, the French station will operate with the

New hospital at NAS Porto Corsini. (source: Naval Historical Center)

Hospital at NAS Porto Corsini. (source: Naval Historical Center)

Aerial view of NAS Porto Corsini taken on 1 September 1918. (source: Peter Kilduff collection)

Macchi M-5 of Ens. Charles Hartwell Ludlow. (source: Peter Kilduff collection)

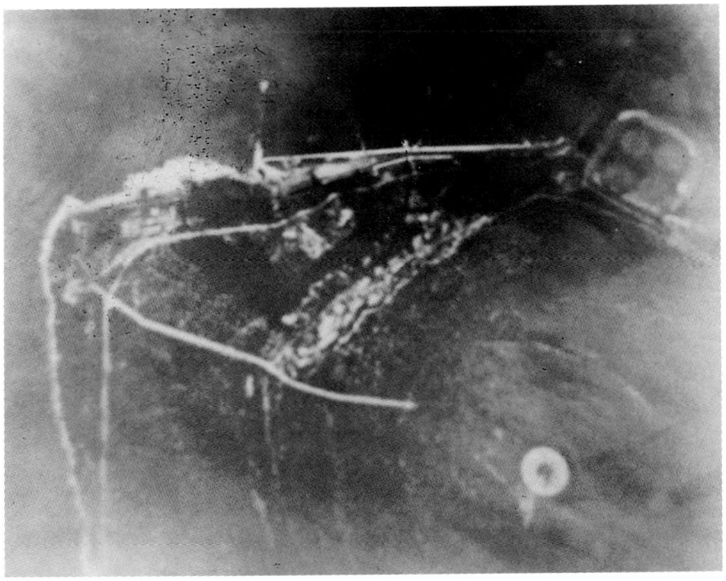

Aerial view of the Austro-Hungarian naval base at Pola, from 2800 meters, taken on 22 October 1918. (source: Peter Kilduff collection)

French convoys and the American station with the American convoys.

Instruction regarding the employment of Dirigibles is given in the following communications:

1. Instruction of November 6th 1917, on the use of dirigibles, by the Rear Admiral, Superior Commandant of the Division of Brittany

2. Permanent order of 21 May 1918, relative to the operating of dirigibles at Guipavas.

INSTRUCTIONS FOR STATION COMMANDERS:

GENERAL PRINCIPLES

1. **Role of Aerial Patrols**

Aerial patrols must provide

(a) Escort of the convoy

(b) Service of the alert

(c) Reconnaissance patrols

NAS Pescara. (Source: Naval Historical Center)

Unidentified personnel at NAS Pescara. (source: Naval Historical Center)

When the alert section starts, you will arrange for the departure of all the section available from which important missions, as the escort of a convoy for example, have not been ordered. These sections, according to circumstances, are sent either together or successively to reinforce or relieve the alert section.

The details of this action being dependent not only on the number of sections of which you can dispose, but also on the number of hours of daylight separating you from the limiting hour—latest hour at which seaplanes can land in water (the hour before which it is necessary that all seaplanes be back at the station). It is possible only to give the following directions:

Try to insure uninterrupted patrol of the suspected zone as long as possible. During the time that the patrol lasts, the submarine can only choose two solutions, both of little advantage for it:

(a) Remain submerged deeply, which will render it harmless.

(b) Resume its traveling depth, which will expose it to receive bombs.

RECONNAISSANCE:

This service consists, when those of a convoy and alert are assured, of sending available sections to patrol in order:

1. To discover, signal and destroy submarines in the spots where there is a presumption of the presence of hostile submarines, according to information received from Intelligence Bureaus, semaphore stations, or ships.

2. To discover mine according to information received.

This service will be provided at the discretion of station commanders when the situation at sea appears to them of interest and the escort of convoys will be assured by their station or the cooperation station. It can be ordered by the Vice Admiral, Prefret Maritime, or by the Commandant of Aerial Patrols as intermediary.

3. The departure of a section.

Seaplanes must always start in a section of two or three units, according to the number of machines available. Whenever a section of three planes is employed, one of them would normally be a cannon seaplane. If this is not done, the section of two planes presents the advantage of permitting a greater number of patrols by the station.

The command of a section should be given to an officer, observer or pilot. The length of patrols of seaplanes, except those who have a mission of limited duration, shall be as long as the material and circumstances permit, without imprudence.

Attack on a submarine

The section flies over the zone where one can find the submarine. In good weather, when a submarine is traveling at attacking depth, the eddies made by its screws reach the surface and form a wake, sometimes very visible and well characterized, the head of which is behind a submarine from 60 to 100 meters.

F.B.A. flying boat used in Italy. (source: Roberto Gentilli)

Maachi M-8. Personnel are not identified. (source: Roberto Gentilli collection)

Italian S.V.A. 7b, the type of machine flown at NAS Lake Bolsena. (source: Roberto Gentilli)

When the submarine comes to the point of increasing its submersion rapidly, the wake stops with a final eddy very strong and behind the real position of the submarine.

It follows from these conditions that it is necessary to launch the bombs from 60 to 100 meters in advance of the eddy, or if the submarine is attacked while traveling submerged, about three seconds after the line of sight has passed over the origin of the eddy. All this is the result of experiences made at Toulon by the Permanent Commission on Submarine Navigation.

It is necessary to state that a submarine submerged does not travel, in general, faster that seven or eight knots. The zone to be watched around the point of an ALLO or SOS is then the interior of a circle having the point as the center and a radius equal to the number of miles obtained by multiplying by eight the fraction of an hour which measures the time elapsed since the initial hour indicated in the radio signal.

Discovery and destruction of submarines

The best altitude to discover submarines submerged, a periscope, or mines varies between 200 and 500 meters. (See D.M. of 29 March 1918).

In principle, one will consider as an enemy every submarine submerged and every submarine on the surface which is not convoyed by an Allied ship carrying the regulation signal or does not make signals on deck or luminous signals. It is necessary to watch carefully all wakes, even of short extent, for they often arise from the motion of the periscope.

It is better to carry two large bombs than several little ones. The absolute rule is that the bombing seaplane shall be armed with two bombs as large as the gear of the plane and the circumstances of flight permit. When one happens to meet a submarine, the planes of their section shall launch all their bombs successively. It is poor calculation to keep any on the chance of again meeting the submarine.

Macchi M-5 chasse machines at NAS Porto Corsini. Notice in the background the dog of Charles Hazeltine Hammann. Also, notice the narrow canal and a M-5 on the rear with an interesting personnel marking. (source: Roberto Gentilli collection)

Wayne Duffett and Giochino Varini in a Macchi L-3. Photo taken on 15 May 1918. (source: Roberto Gentilli collection)

Italian M-8 bombing machine showing an interesting location for the national insignia. (source: Robert Gentilli collection)

Wayne Duffett and Giochino Varini in a Macchi L-3 while in training at NAS Lake Bolsena. (source: Roberto Gentilli collection)

There is a regulation method of attack set for in the D.M. of I December 1917. The altitude of attack is about 100 meters. It is imperative that the bomb shall be dropped beading into the wind. The tactics defined by the Ministerial dispatch of 29 March 1918 prescribe that the plane which first saw the submarine direct the attack and that the other maneuver accordingly. The observer will always have the bars of their sights set for the altitude of attack, 100 meters, and the wind speed of the machine converted into ground speed.

All enemy submarines encountered must be reported as soon as possible by radio, sending an ALLO, or in the fault of that by carrier pigeon, and always by verbal report made upon the return of the station. This station will advise the nearest Bureau de Renseignement and the Commandant of Aerial Patrols of Brittany of its as rapidly as possible. It can happen that you are advised that an Allied submarine will be found on the surface or submerged in a designated part of the zone. You will find in an annex all instructions for this situation.

George Hartwell Ludlow, Hereford, and Wayn Duffet likely at NAS Porto Corsini. (source: Roberto Gentilli collection)

Macchi M-5 No. 13021 "Jeff" at NAS Porto Corsini. Note red-white-blue on the floats. (source: Roberto Gentilli collection)

The officers at Porto Corsini. The officer seated in the center of the front row with the mustache and fur coat is Commanding Officer Lt. Willis B. Haviland. (source: Roberto Gentilli collection)

Close-up view of the wing-tip float of a Macchi seaplane.

Macchi M-5.

Macchi L-3 in flight.

Macchi M-5 in flight.

Unidentified naval aviators in training with the French Army at Avord-Cher. Navy personnel from Moutchic were sent to the French Army Bombing School at Avord after being selected as prospects for the Northern Bombing Group. (source: Official U.S. Navy photograph)

A three-quarter front view of a Marine D.H. 9A in France. The machine is just preparing for a test hop. To the right of the pilot, about to climb into the cockpit, can be seen the scope gun sight, commonly used on Marine aircraft during this period. During combat, many of the Marine aircraft were fitted with Marlin machine guns.

4. Search for mines

Made between 200 and 500 meters altitude. The mines shall be sought above all, in narrow channels and at points of land full of convoys. If there are sweepers about, it is a necessity to signal to them by the signal C.B. 409, or get the details to them by correspondence buoys. One can indicated to them the location exactly by throwing on it one or several phosphorous buoys."

Over a period of time each of the French stations slowly began accumulating a full compliment of men and materials. The first American patrol of the French Coastal Unit of U.S. Naval Aviation was made at Le Croisic on 13 November 1917, and the last at Brest on 13 December 1918 when the Presidential Convoy was met and escorted by American planes and non-rigid airships. The French Coastal Unit, operating for an effective period of nine months, sighted 27 submarines, attacked 25, damaged 12, and probably sank four. In addition, the U.S. airplane stations in France discovered and destroyed a large number of drifting mines. Escorts to convoys were provided and scout patrols were maintained as a matter of regular routine, and whenever a submarine was reported in the patrol area of a U.S. Naval Air Station during hours and weather fit for flying, an alert section of planes was sent in search of the submarine.

In addition to the stations discussed previously, there were a number of proposals made by both French and American officers for an expansion of the Navy operated air stations in France. In particular, France proposed that the Navy take over the operation of French Naval Air Stations at Ajacio on Corsica and at Cette near Nice. Lieutenant Whiting not only agreed with this proposal, but also suggested a broader scope by including proposed stations at Gibraltar and Corfu. All these proposals were rejected by Captain

Another view of the D.H. 9A at Le Fresne aerodrome. A close inspection will show clearly that this aircraft was fitted with the original British prop. Many Marine aircraft flew with British props. After the Armistice, all D.H. 9A's on loan to the First Marine Aviation Force were returned to the RAF.

A side view of a D.H. 9A at the Marine field at Le Fresne in 1918. This model of the D.H. 9A comprised approximately 50% of the unit's aircraft strength. Many of the D.H. 9As were powered with the Liberty engine, and they enjoyed a successful popularity among British flyers who were attached to the unit is liaison duties.

View of an escorting destroyer taken from the ship carrying the First Marine Aviation Force to France. Note the camouflage on the destroyer and the non-rigid airship overhead. (source: Sam Richards collection)

Maj. Alfred A. Cunningham (second from left), Commanding Officer of First Marine Aviation Force with a group of Army and Navy officers. On Cunningham's right is Maj. William M. McIlvain, later C.O. of the Marine's "B" Squadron.

Cone on the grounds that the Navy had insufficient manpower to properly operate any stations beyond those currently committed to.

Heavier-than-Air training

Upon arrival of the First Aeronautic Detachment, 80 men were at once sent, on 22 June 1917, to St. Raphael for training as motor mechanics. The remainder, selected for pilot training, were sent to the Ecole d'Aviation Militaire at Tours. Flight instruction at Tours began on 22 June 1917 on the Caudron machine. On 28 June 1917 Thomas W. Barrett, Lds.QM(a) was killed in a crash at Tours. He thus became the first Navy man killed in France during WWI. After qualifying on the Caudron, pilots were transferred to the French Station at Lake Hourtin for training in seaplanes. The first 21 pilots were transferred to Lake Hourtin on 16 August and began their instruction in the F.B.A. Boat. By the middle of September all 48 pilots had completed the course at Tours. The instruction in the F.B.A. Boats was considered to be completed after a pilot had been in the air for a period of seven hours. By the middle of November the entire detachment had completed this phase of its training. 13 pilots were ordered to Moutchic, and the others to St. Raphael. Of this group 12 were assigned to the U.S. Army school at Issoudun for training in scout planes. After qualifying as scout pilots these men were sent to Scotland for further training in English machines. Upon completion of this course they were assigned to duty with the fighting squadrons at NAS Dunkirk.

The pilots assigned to duty at St. Raphael received the French course of instruction in aerial gunnery and bombing from seaplanes, upon the completion of which they were ordered to Dunkirk, Le Croisic, Ile Tudy, and St. Trojan. Two pilots were sent to Moutchic as instructors.

Dirigible Training[2]

The first dirigible pilots to report for overseas duty were Lieutenant Zachary Lansdowne, USN, (Naval Aviator No. 105) and Lieutenant (j.g.) Ralph Kiely, USN, (Naval Aviator No. 1076), who sailed for England in August 1917. They pursued a course of dirigible training at RNAS Cranwell and were graduated 15 November 1917. Kiely took charge of the Stations, returning to the U.S. in March. Seven Reserve Officers (Dirigible pilots) arrived in France in November 1917 and were temporarily assigned to several French stations. Later, Ensign Hamlen was ordered to Headquarters, Paris, for duty in connection with dirigible operations, schools, and training. The others of this group were ordered to Paimboeuf for duty at that station.

Kite Balloon Training

On 7 March 1918, 22 candidate Kite Balloon pilots arrived at Liverpool and were ordered to RNAS Roehampton, where they received instruction in ballooning. Upon graduation they were distributed to the kite balloon station in France and to Castletown-Berchaven. Ensign Stoppel was ordered to Headquarters, Paris, for duty in connection with kite balloons. In July 1918, kite balloon operations in Ireland were temporarily suspended and the pilots sent to the kite balloon stations in France. When operations were resumed these personnel were returned to Berehaven. Ten more kite balloon pilots arrived from the U.S. in May 1918 and were assigned to the stations of the French Unit.

Lafayette Flying Corps

In January 1918, about 12 American chasse pilots from the Lafayette Flying Corps offered their services to Naval Aviation (eventually 26 such pilots were to join). When released by the French they enrolled as Ensigns and were sent to Moutchic for training in seaplanes to complete their Aviator tests. They were then assigned to various stations in Europe. The addition of such experienced pilots greatly enhanced Naval Aviation in Europe.

Naval Aviation in the British Isles[3]

U.S. Naval Aviation operations in the British Isles, which were a direct result of the negotiations entered into by the mission headed

First Marine Aviation Force in France. Madame Trouille and her daughter pose with the aviators. (source: Defense Dept. Photo CBH 518995)

by James Balfour, which arrived in the United States on 22 April 1917, were carried on by seven naval air stations, two in England and five in Ireland. The two English stations were located at Killingholme and Eastleigh.

Killingholme, located in Lincolnshire on the North Sea, was a patrol station which was established in 1916 by the RFC. By 1917 it had become one the largest bases in England. When negotiations were entered into between the British and the U.S. Navy on the subject of the Navy assuming the responsibility for operating one or more of the stations, the promoted Lieutenant Commander Whiting was sent home to organize such an effort. In May 1918 the collier U.S.S. *Jason* left New York with a contingent of men and supplies, along with the first American seaplanes to be sent to Europe to take over RNAS Killingholme. She arrived in England on 1 June. As an American base it was placed in commission on 20 July 1918 by Whiting, who relieved Wing Commander F.W. Bowhill, RNAS, and who remained in command of the station (Naval Air Stations #14 and #15) until the end of the war. This station was originally intended for the purpose of conducting seaplane patrol offensive operations in Heligoland Blight emphasizing Lighters. This was never carried out due to the objections of the CNO, Admiral Benson. Due to the limited fuel carrying capacity of machines available at that time, patrols of this area were not feasible, and pending the construction of machines capable of this duty, shorter patrols of mine fields and convoy operations were carried on using both the British Short seaplanes, left them by the British, and the American built aircraft assigned to the station. From June 30th until the signing of the Armistice, the Killingholme patrol station convoyed 6243 Allied vessels and covered approximately 60,000 miles in 233 patrols. During this time many of the Killingholme pilots were also loaned to the British forces and were everywhere praised in the highest terms. The casualties at this station were two officers and seven men. Of the ten attacks on enemy submarines made by the Killingholme station, four brought definite results. In two cases, on 9 July and 7 August, a verdict was returned from the Admiralty of "possibly seriously damaged"; on 25 July a submarine was "possibly slightly damaged"; and on 19 July a submarine, the U.B. 10, was attacked. She was sunk later in the day by surface craft. Francis R.V. Lynch (Naval Aviator No.88), while at Killingholme, was credited by the British Admiralty, on 30 July, with the sinking of a U-boat. In addition to conducting reconnaissance and submarine patrols, naval aviators at Killingholme were also used in the aerial defense of England. On 5 August a flying boat piloted by Ensign Ashton W. Hawkins (Naval Aviator No. 128), with Lieutenant (j.g.) George F. Lawrence (Naval Aviator No. 89) as second pilot, took off from Killingholme at 2230 hrs. to patrol a course intercepting a reported Zeppelin raider. They landed at South Shield, England, at 0530 hrs. without sighting any intruder. The planes used at Killingholme were mostly H-16 Flying Boats. At the time of the Armistice 91 officers and 1324 men were attached to the Killingholme station. The base was closed 22 February 1919. During its period of operation there were 233 war flights, totaling 968 hours and covering 66,000 miles, during which over 6000 ships were convoyed.

The Eastleigh station, located about 35 miles from Portsmouth and 4 miles from Southampton, was used for the reception, assembly, and overhaul of planes for the Northern Bombing Group. For this purpose it was splendidly located, as it was only four miles from the port of Southampton, had good rail connections, and was

Capt. Robett Lytle, USMC.

within flying distance of the aerodromes of the Northern Bombing Squadrons across the channel. It was originally designed and built as a reception park for the Royal Air Force, and was transferred to the U.S. Naval Forces about the middle of July 1918. This station also served as a supply depot for Killingholme, as well. The station was commissioned on 23 July 1918 and put in operation on 3 October 1918. On 3 October it had a compliment of 19,820 officers and men and had a capacity of 20,962 men.

In addition to undertaking operations from air stations in England for which command had been ceded to the U.S. Navy, many naval aviators operated under English command from RNAS bases. On 19 March Ensign Stephan Potter (Naval Aviator No. 130), in a formation of flying boats on a long-range reconnaissance of the German coast, was attacked by German seaplanes. Ensign Potter downed one of the attackers and was officially credited as being the first U.S. Naval Aviator to shoot down an enemy seaplane. On 25 March Ensign John F. McNamara, flying out of RNAS Portland, made the first attack on an enemy submarine by a U.S. Naval Aviator. His attack was reported as "apparently successful."

The Irish stations were located at Queenstown, Wexford, Lough Foyle, Whiddy Island, Lough Swilly, and Berehaven, and were organized as a unit under the command of the Commander U.S. Naval Air Stations, Ireland. Commander R. McCrary, USN, assumed command of the U.S. Naval Air Stations, Ireland, on 14 February 1918 and remained in command throughout the War with Headquarters at Queenstown. McCrary, in turn, reported to the British CIC, Admiral Sir Lewis Bayly, who had overall operational control of the joint British-American campaign against the German submarines. The sites for these stations were selected at the request of the British Admiralty and were in accordance with their plan of operation against submarines. The effort expended in establishing these bases in Ireland was not as great as that associated with the French bases. The reasons for this were threefold: 1) Sinn Fein sentiment in Ireland and the subsequent concern over potential involvement of Navy personnel should an event occur on or near an Air Station, 2) Lack of immediate resources both to man and equip additional stations; and 3) The then-current aircraft patrol range limitation of 75 miles. On 8 October 1917 Captain Cone, with Lieutenant Whiting, Paymaster Omar Conger, and Lieutenant Commander F.R.F. Davis, RNAS, toured prospective sites. By 21 October the final sites had been selected with the understanding that the British would be unable to help in any way other than in the construction of shipways and foundations. The compliment of aircraft for these stations was scheduled to be 24 Large Americas (Whiddy Island and Queenstown), along with 58 officers and 498 men each, and 18 Large Americas (Wexford and Lough Foyle), along with 46 officers and 394 men each. These values were based upon the assumption that one-half of the complement of seaplanes would be in operation at any given time, except in extreme weather, and that these seaplanes could scout over areas at least 50 miles to sea from their bases. It was hoped that this operational radius could be expanded to 100 miles. As can be seen from this philosophy, the Navy intended the Irish stations to have both an offensive and a defensive nature. Table 5 lists the Curtiss H-16s delivered to the Irish Stations. In March 1918, construction under the supervision of U.S. Navy civil engineers was commenced. All stations were completed at practically the same time—about the middle of September—and operations began immediately.

The station at Queenstown, which was the principle Irish base, was located on the southwestern section of Queenstown Bay, near the village of Aghada. In addition to being a patrol station, it was also an assembly and repair station, the main training base in Ireland, and a supply depot, as well as the Headquarters of the Commander of U.S. Naval Air Stations in Ireland. The station saw its first U.S. Naval presence in April 1917, when U.S. destroyers arrived there. The British Admiralty started construction of a seaplane base on 15 December 1917. This station supplied aerial patrols for convoys from Cape Clear on the west, south into the English Channel, to the sector covered by the aerial patrols from the north coast of France, and southeast and east to the sectors covered by the stations in the southwest of England and at Wexford. The first U.S. Navy personnel arrived at Queenstown on 6 February 1918. They were quartered in a British Army camp at Aghada. The station was commissioned on 22 February 1918 with Lieutenant Commander Paul J. Peyton (Naval Aviator No. 47) commanding. By 1 April construction work was in full swing. The first seaplanes

U.S. Marine pilot Lt. Edmund Chamberlain who flew with the British.

Marine D.H. 4s.

Marine D.H. 9A E8476 and examples of both 25-lb. and 250-lb. bombs.

arrived on 27 June aboard the S.S. *Cuyama*, with ten more arriving 24 July aboard the S.S. *Kanawha*. On 6 June 1918 it had a compliment of 354 officers and men. The first flight of an H-16 in Ireland from the station was on 3 August with Ensign J.W. Lawrence as pilot. The station was put in operation on 30 September 1918. At the Armistice the station had a compliment of 1398 men and 48 officers. For its history, machines from the station performed the following: conducted 155 flights covering 254 hours; performed 64 patrols covering 198 hours, 45 minutes which covered 11,565 miles; made six convoy escorts; sighted four oil patches; sighted and bombed one submarine wake; and sighted and bombed two oil slicks. All flights from the station ceased on 21 November. The station closed on 10 April 1919.

Marine D.H. 4s of the Northern Bombing Group.

A lineup of Marine D.H. 4s.

Marine Flag being shown off by Maj. Alfred A. Cunningham and Capt. William H. McIlvain

TABLE 5

Curtiss H-16 Flying Boats of the U.S. Navy Delivered to Ireland

A. Flying Boats Received at Queenstown:

Serial Number	Received	Delivered	Assigned NAS	Remarks
A-1071	27-6-18	———	———	Not Completed. Used for Spares
A-1072	27-6-18	25-09-18	Whiddy Island	Wrecked at Whiddy on 22-10-18
A-1073	27-6-18	———	———	Wrecked at Aghada on 12-8-18
A-1074	27-6-18	18-9-18	Wexford	Crashed on Delivery on 18-9-18
A-1075	27-6-18	25-9-18	Queenstown	Wrecked at sea on 4-10-18
A-1076	27-6-18	18-9-18	Wexford	
A-1077	27-6-18	7-9-19	Queenstown	
A-1078	27-6-18	25-9-18	Whiddy Island	
A-1047	24-7-18	———	———	Assembly not completed
A-1048	24-7-18	27-10-18	Queenstown	
A-1078	24-7-18	18-9-18	Wexford	
A-1079	24-7-18	18-9-18	Wexford	
A-820	24-7-18	———	———	Assembly not completed
A-821	24-7-18	———	———	Assembly not completed
A-823	24-7-18	———	———	Assembly not completed
A-824	23-7-18	———	———	Assembly not completed
A-825	24-7-18	———	———	Assembly not completed
A-826	24-7-18	———	———	Assembly not completed
A-829	21-8-18	———	———	Assembly not completed
A-3478	1-9-18	17-10-18	Wexford	
A-3468	1-9-18	4-10-18	Queenstown	
A-3466	1-9-18	24-10-18	Whiddy Island	
A-3465	1-9-18	21-10-18	Lough Foyle	LF-7 Wrecked at sea on 4-11-18
A-3461	1-9-18	21-10-18	Lough Foyle	LF-6
A-4059	1-9-18	———	———	Assembly not completed
A-4054	1-9-18	1 10-18	Queenstown	Wrecked at sea on 12-10-18
A-831	1-9-18	———	———	Assembly not completed
A-4055	1-9-18	———	———	Assembly not completed
A-828	1-9-18	———	———	Assembly not completed
A-1084	1-9-18	24 10 18	Whiddy Island	
A-4044	1-9-18	6-11-18	Wexford	
A-4045	1-9-18	22 10-18	Queenstown	
A-4047	1-9-18	6-11-18	Whiddy Island	
A-4048	1-9-18	9-11-18	Whiddy Island	
A-827	1-9-18	———	———	Assembly not completed
A-4064	1-9-18	———	———	Assembly not completed
A-1080	1-9-18	19-10-18	Queenstown	
A-3550	1-9-18	29-9-18	Queenstown	Wrecked at sea on 8-10-18

B. Flying Boats Received at Lough Foyle

Serial Number	Received	Code	Remarks
A-1059	22-7-18	LF-1	Wrecked at sea on 10-9-18
A-1031	22-7-18	LF-2	
A-819	22-7-18	LF-3	Wrecked at sea on 4-10-18
A-1032	22-7-18	LF-4	
A-799	AA-7-18	LF-5	

Major Douglas B. Roben (left) and Maj. Alfred Cunningham (right) with the U.S. Marine Corps 3rd Squadron.

The seaplane station at Wexford was located at Ferrybank, in Wexford Harbor, on the eastern shore of a wide shallow bay at the southeastern corner of Ireland. Its purpose was to provide convoys and patrols in the sector east of Queenstown over the St.George's Channel (southern entrance of the Irish Sea). Construction at the station was begun in December 1917 under a contract with the British Admiralty. A portion of the concrete hangars was completed, the roads were marked off, and some excavation begun; also, some work had begun in draining the back of what would eventually be the hangars. The first U.S. personnel arrived on 25 February 1918 (eight men under Gunner Rogers). Following this date small drafts of men began to arrive from Queenstown. The station was commissioned on 2 May 1918 under the command of the promoted Lieutenant Commander Herbster, who had arrived at the station on 28 March. On 6 June 1918 it had a compliment of 93 officers and men. By 1 August there were 15 officers and 298 men on the station, short of the total compliment of 50 officers, 450 men, and 18 H-16s. In spite of there never being enough men to build and equip the station as fast as wished, the construction at Wexford established a record for Naval Air Stations in Europe. The station was put into operation on 18 September 1918. The first H-16s arrived at Wexford from NAS Queenstown on 18 September (A-1074, A-1076, A-1078, and A-1079), and patrols were commenced the next day. On 22 September a machine from this station bombed the first submarine. On 11 October a second was attacked; and on 13 October a third submarine was attacked. On 6 November a sixth, and final, H-16 arrived at the station. At the cessation of hostilities the station had a compliment of eight seaplanes and was commanded by Lieutenant John F. McNamara (Naval Aviator No. 199). For its history the H-16s at Wexford made 98 flights of 312 hours duration during which three submarines were attacked.

The seaplane patrol station at Lough Foyle was located on a long narrow arm of the sea on the north coast of Ireland about six miles north of the town of Londonderry. During its construction Gunner H.F. Moseley was in command. This station patrolled the waters in the vicinity of the northern outlet of the Irish Sea. The station was both commissioned and placed in operation on 3 September 1918 (Note: The History of the Lough Foyle station says 20 May) with Commander H.D. Cooke in command, but one week later he was relieved by Lieutenant C.H. Hull (Naval Aviator No. 46). In addition to the aircraft at this station, it was planned to provide two kite balloons. The station compliment was intended to be two officers and 120 men for the balloons. On 6 June 1918 the station had a complement of 118 officers and men. (See Appendix V)

The Whiddy Island seaplane station was located on the eastern side of the island of the same name in Bantry Bay. Designed for a compliment of 60 Officers, 600 men, and 24 aircraft, work on the station was begun, under Admiralty contract, on 16 December 1917. The first U.S. personnel arrived at the site on 12 March. Due to a lack of accommodations they were quartered in Bantry. Naval residence was not established until 27 August. The station was commissioned on 4 July 1918 under the command of Commander J.C. Townsend, and became operational on 25 September with the arrival of two H-16s (A-1072 and A-1078). It was intended that this station furnish patrols and convoys for the waters to the southwest of Ireland. On 22 October H-16 A-1072 crashed in the dark while returning from patrol. The radio operator was killed and the others injured. This was the only fatality in the course of all naval flying activity in Ireland during the war. At the armistice the station consisted of 9 officers and 399 enlisted men. Total flying time for its existence was 64.5 hours.

Berehaven, to the west of Whiddy Island in Bantry Bay, was a kite balloon station where balloons were kept for use in conjunction with Torpedo Boat Destroyers. The station was to have two officers and 157 men for the balloons. The balloons were to be transferred from the shore to the destroyers, made fast, and towed at an altitude of about 500 feet. The station at Berehaven had a rather troubled history. While the British had proposed the American takeover of the station while it was still under construction, Captain Cone opposed it on the grounds that no U.S. destroyers operated in that area of Ireland. A compromise was reached wherein the British agreed to man the station until U.S. operations in Northern Ireland waters begun; then the Navy would take it over. The Navy attempted to abandon Berehaven for Queenstown, as that was where American destroyer flotillas were based; however, the Brit-

Marine D.H. 4s

ish brushed aside that concept on the grounds that construction was too far advanced. Berehaven was located on a sound formed within Bantry Bay behind Bere Island near Castletown. The station was turned over by the RAF on 26 April 1918, Ensign Carl E. Shumway commanding (apparently Shumway was never assigned a Naval Aviator number). Shumway had been commissioned at NAS Rockaway on 30 January 1918 and had been ordered overseas "for kite balloon duty in Ireland." By 9 March 1918 he was a student Naval Aviator at NAS Queenstown and was designated a Kite Balloon pilot on 19 April 1918. On 23 August Shumway was transferred to the U.S. Naval Base at Plymouth to take command of the U.S. Naval Kite Balloon Detachment there. He was subsequently assigned to the S.S.T.S.B.D. Castletown station was put in operation on 21 May 1918. On 6 June 1918 it had a compliment of 81 officers and men.[4] In July 1918 most of the U.S. LTA personnel and kite balloon equipment were transferred to NAS Brest. In late July and early August kite balloon operations at the station became active, this time in support of kite balloon operations aboard the H.M.S. *Flying Fox*. From late August through mid October the station supported kite balloon operations on board the battleships U.S.S. *Utah*, *Nevada*, and *Oklahoma*, which operated out of Bantry Bay. By mid October preparations were begun to move the kite balloon operations out of Berehaven to Queenstown. At the Armistice the station had 16 Kite Balloons on board. The station was decommissioned on 12 February 1919.

Lough Swilly was about 15 miles west of Lough Foyle, and was a kite balloon station which served both American and British destroyers in waters around the north coast of Ireland.[5]

The Admiralty made a proposed expansion of these stations to the Navy's Force Commander on 22 July 1918. This proposal, made by Admiral Lewis Bayly, Commander-in-Chief, Coast of Ireland, would have expanded the seaplane patrol of the west coast of Ireland via the conversion of a 500-ton coasting steamer to an armed seaplane tender. The converted tender was to be capable of handling three seaplanes and would have been under the command of an American Naval Officer. The Navy did not accept this proposal.

The entrance to the Headquarter area of the Marine field at Le Fresne. (source: Sam Richards collection)

A formal portrait of 2nd Lt. Sam Richards taken in a photo salon in Calais. (source: Sam Richards collection)

The following is a summary of operations of the U.S. Naval Air Stations, Ireland:

Total number of flying hours -	761 hours 24 minutes
Distance covered -	45,683 miles
Oil patches sighted -	5
Oil patches bombed -	3
Submarines sighted -	7
Submarines bombed -	7

Two of the submarines bombed were officially credited with having been damaged to such an extent that they had to return to their base. One of these submarines was preparing to attack a large convoy of troop ships. This was a very creditable performance when the facts are taken into consideration that for a large part of the time each station had only two seaplanes in operation and never more than four, that pilots had to be trained, and that the weather conditions are often exceptionally bad all around the Irish coast.

As with the case in France, there were official requests from England for the Navy to assume the operational responsibilities at a number of English Naval Air Stations. Specifically mentioned stations were Gibralter, Alexandria (Egypt), Kingstown (near Dublin), and a proposed dirigible base near Peterhead, Scotland. These proposals were all rejected by Captain Cone on the same basis as the French proposals.

Naval Aviation in Italy[6, 7]

The Navy had originally intended to send students to Italy to learn to fly and then to send them to France for squadron assignment. The Italians initially agreed to this proposal. However, by November 1917 the impact of the war in Italy had become much more grave. On 21 November 1917 the Italian government requested that the United States Naval Aviation activities be extended to Italy, offering to completely equip stations if the United States would man and operate them. To coordinate the formation of these stations Captain H.I. Cone dispatched Lieutenant John Lansing Callan to Rome where he arrived on 19 December 1917. (Callan had learned to fly at the Curtiss school at North Island in 1911. He later became a student of Lieutenant Towers at Pensacola. When Curtiss began construction of the "America" for Rodman Wanamaker's attempt at the London Daily Mail prize for the first transatlantic flight, Callan was sent to the Azores, under an assumed name, to establish a base for fuel and supplies. Following the outbreak of hostilities Callan was sent by Curtiss to Italy as a sales representative of the Curtiss Company. He subsequently returned to the U.S. and eventually volunteered in the Navy.) The day after his arrival he called upon Capitano di Vascello L. De Filippi, the head of Italian Naval Aviation. It was accordingly agreed that the Italian naval air stations at Bolsena (training) and Porto Corsini (Ravenna) and Pescara (operations) should be taken over by the United States. The base at Bolsena had been established late in 1917 and was under the command of Mario Calderare. The Italians would also have liked the U.S. to take over a land-based station at San Severo. This station was to have been equipped with 80 (sic) Caproni aircraft. It would have, as estimated by Callan, required 30 officer pilots, 40 officer observers, ten executive officers, 40 Petty Officer Observers, 130 Petty Officer pilots, and sufficient extra Petty Officers to handle the enlisted working personnel. The total complement required, according to Italian figures, would have been 1364 officers and men. This station was larger than any then planned in France, was for land machines only, and would operate aircraft for which Navy pilots then had no training. Callan recommended that it was probably out of the question for the moment to think of taking it over, and Cone agreed.

2nd Lt. Lawrence A. Shea, a pugnacioius Irishman who, in addition to bombs, would drop bricks obtained from a ruined building near his field. (source: Sam Richards collection)

The plans for the three stations were for stations of nine patrol machines each of the F.B.A. type; six machines of the S.V.A. hydro-chasse type for defending the station against air attacks; and 12 machines of the Macchi single seater flying boat type for escorting the patrol machines and for quick reconnaissance work. The agreement for the takeover of these bases also included the assurance that at each station ten 3" anti-aircraft guns would be mounted and manned by gunners of the Italian Army or Navy. The agreement with the Italians stated:

1. While the seaplane stations at Porto Corsini and Pescara were to be officered, manned, and operated by the U.S. Naval Aviation Forces, Foreign Service, for the purpose of offensive and patrol operations, the stations were to be under the command of the Italian Vice Admiral commanding at Venice. His orders were to be transmitted through the Commander of the Aerial Patrols for that district. For the purpose of the administration of discipline, interior administration, transfer of commissioned and enlisted personnel, and other routine matters, these stations were to be under the direct command of the Commanding Officer for the U.S. Naval Air Stations in Italy;

2. The Italian flying school at Lake Bolsena would continue to receive American students for training, but not over 50 pupils at one time, who, for the purpose of discipline, will be under the command of an American officer, who will, in turn, be under the command of the Station Commander; and

3. The agreement further stipulated that the Italian Navy would supply the stations and school, the necessary supplies and material to equip them and maintain them in operations, including: all the flying machines, motors, spares, accessories, instruments, and armament; all barracks and hangars; all mess and galley gear; and all office equipment and furnishings for quarters. These items would be supplied in accordance with the established allowance for Italian stations. The United States Navy was to provide, either by shipment or purchase, all food, uniforms, personal flying gear, and stationary. It would provide any excess deemed necessary beyond that allowed by the Italian allowance. The Navy was also to provide any items not included in the above mentioned categories, and also any other material it may have which the Italian Navy may have difficulty in obtaining.

In order to carry out the projected activities of the Naval Aviation Forces in Italy, Captain Cone wrote to Commander Charles R. Train, USN, the Naval Attaché in Rome, on 10 May 1918 that he had appointed, effective 25 April 1918, Lieutenant Callan, USNRF, Commanding Officer of U.S. Naval Aviation Forces in Italy. Callan was to report directly to Cone in Paris, and in turn would have reporting to him a Commanding Officer from each of the Naval Air Stations. The Headquarters of the U.S. Naval Aviation Forces in Italy were to be in the American Embassy in Rome. On 14 August 1918, a Lieutenant Commander since May of 1918, Callan wrote a report to the Commander, U.S. Naval Aviation Forces, Foreign Service entitled "Report for Comment on Future Development of U.S. Naval Air Efforts in European Waters." On the 15th of August he submitted a report entitled "Report on Italian Offensive and Defensive Aerial Operations and Necessity for Increasing Same." The thrust of these two reports was that by accentuating the war in Italy the Austrians could be defeated. Such a defeat would cause the collapse of both the Turkish and Bulgarian war efforts. Callan went on to recommend that any increasing of the naval aviation effort in Italy must be accompanied with the appointment of an officer with a rank more senior than that of a Lieutenant Commander. Captain Cone agreed with these recommendations. Subsequently, Callan was relieved on 16 October 1918 by Train, who remained in command of all naval aviation forces in Italy until they were returned to the United States. Callan remained in Italy, having the commanders at Bolsena, Porto Corsini, and Pescara reporting to him. The Commander, U.S. Naval Aviation Forces in Italy, in turn, was under the command of the Commander, U.S. Naval Aviation Forces, Foreign Service, with Headquarters in Paris.

The Bolsena training station was situated on the Lake of Bolsena about 60 miles northwest of Rome. The Porto Corsini station was located on the Adriatic Sea near the town of Ravenna, and the Pescara station was also on the Adriatic near the town of Pescara. The objective of these latter two stations was the Austrian Naval Base at Pola. The original Italian request for aid was approved by the two governments in February 1918.

2nd Lts. Donald N. Whiting (left) and Vincent C. Young (right) next to D.H. 4 "D-8," serial number A3278. (source: Sam Richards collection)

On 19 February 1918 the first American aviation detachment to enter Italy arrived at Bolsena. Two days later the Bolsena training station was officially put in commission as a U.S. Naval Air Station, Lieutenant Calderare of the Italian Navy transferring the command of the American students to Ensign W.B. Atwater, USNRF (Naval Aviator No. 112). On 6 June 1918 the station had a complement of 35 officers and men. Actual instruction of students was started at once. The first flying instructors were Italians, but they gave way to American instructors as soon as the latter become proficient in handling Italian planes. At the beginning F.B.A. Flying Boats equipped with 160 HP Isotta Fraschini motors were used exclusively for instruction purposes, but later some Macchi L-3 and M-5 boats arrived, and thereafter training in these two types was also given. In addition, the Navy at both Lake Bolsena and at Porto Corsini used the Macchi M-8, a large flying boat. One S.V.A. seaplane was sent to the school, but it did not prove satisfactory. The training philosophy at Bolsena was that students started out on the F.B.A. machines and progressed to the L-3 machines. The best of each class was to receive training in the Macchi M-5s. The school policy was that after 12 hours of flight instruction the student was expected to solo. If no solo had occurred after the 14th hour the student was given two more flights of 30 minutes each. If after the second such flight the instructor felt that a solo flight could be made in one to two more hours the student was kept in the program. If the instructor felt that no benefit would be derived from the additional time all flying was terminated and the student reassigned. Ground schoolwork was also organized, and instruction was given in Theory of Flight, Navigation, Engines, Navy Regulations, the Bluejacket's Manual, and Signals. The only casualty of the Bolsena Training Station during its nine months of operation occurred on 20 March 1918 when Clarence A. Nelson, MM lc (A), USN, was killed, in F.B.A. serial 7637, at 1420 hrs. while making his first solo flight. In his memory the town of Bolsena named the road leading from the town to the hangars "Via Nelson." On 22 April J. Stanley, BM 2c received the first Italian flying brevet to be issued at the station. The total number of officers and men who underwent instruction at the Bolsena Training Station was 134, of which 73 completed the course. Upon completing the course of instruction, pilots were sent to combatant air stations in either Italy or France. No complete consolidated roster of names of those who attended the School has been found. Table 6 contains the names which have been compiled both from the daily reports from the School, from the reference noted in endnote 7, and from the J. Lansing Callan collection in the Library of Congress. It is not complete, but it covers the vast majority of personnel assigned there for varying periods during the period of 18 February to 25 December 1918.

On 23 July 1918 the first American aviation personnel arrived at Porto Corsini, which was about 10 miles northeast of Ravena and 70 miles southwest of Venice. These personnel consisted of a detachment of 377 officers and men from Pauillac, France, along with 250 tons of supplies and 35 Italian flying boats, under the command Lieutenant Willis B. Haviland, USNRF (Naval Aviator No. 577). Haviland, formerly of the Lafayette Escadrille, had enrolled in the U.S. Naval Reserve Force Center in Paris on 28 December 1917. He graduated from Moutchic and had served at Dunkirk and with No. 13 (N) Squadron. He had been sent to Lake Bolsena on 2 May to learn to fly the Italian Macchi L-3, M-5, and M-8 flying boats. The following day Haviland took over the Porto Corsini station from the Italians and placed it in commission as a U.S. Naval Air Station. This unit replaced the Italian 263a Squadriglia at the base. In preparing for the arrival of the American contingent Lieutenant Commander Callan had relieved some of the workload from Haviland's shoulders by: 1) Already selecting the pilots for the station; 2) Obtaining the fur-lined flying suits for the station; and 3) Ordering aircraft for the station. (Three machines had been shipped to Porto Corsini by the week of June 24th, two were scheduled to be shipped that week, and four more were to be delivered in seven to ten days. This complement was to complete the first squadron with no spare aircraft.) Callan wrote in July to Haviland indicating that he had made the selection, but suggested that Haviland should select his flight commanders from the older hands currently in France; and, since observers were not being trained at Bolsena, he either had to find good observers in France to bring with him or face the situation of having none upon his arrival in Italy. He also suggested Haviland should not depend upon the Italians for life preservers; these should be obtained in France. Additionally, he suggested that Haviland bring what mess and galley gear he had, and again, not to depend upon the Italians. When Haviland arrived both he and his supply officer were ill. To help out, Callan sent both Ensign White and his Supply Officer to Porto Corsini. On 24 July 1918 the station had a complement of 165 officers and men. While Haviland was ill his Executive Officer, Lieutenant Almour, was in command. The station was put in operation on 21 August 1918. (There is no explanation how 377 men were reduced to 165 in one day.)

The Austrians were apparently aware of the arrival of Americans at Porto Corsini and decided to give them a proper reception, as on 25 July a squadron of enemy planes flew over the camp at midnight and dropped bombs. Luckily, however, they made a mistake as to the location of the station. Although two large bombs landed within 500 yards of the camp, making holes eight meters in diameter and from four to five meters deep, the majority of bombs landed in the marshes and canals further up the coast.

Identification card of 2nd Lt. Sam Richards. The photo was taken at Le Fresne. (source: Sam Richards collection)

2nd Lt. Phillip W. Blood (nicknamed "Bolshevik") who was Sam Richards' tent mate at Le Fresne. (source: Sam Richards collection)

TABLE 6

1. Ens. W.B. Atwater, USNRF, Commanding
2. Ens. D.V. Alvord
3. Ens. ? Baird
4. Ens. C.A. Bates
5. Ens. L.B. Bergen
6. Boatswain R. Budani
7. Ens. E.J. Butchart
8. Ens. J.F. Carson
9. Ens. C.J. Coatsworth
10. Ens. Alva Cushman
11. Ens. J.L. Dean
12. Ens. Alfred Dent Jr.
13. Ens. E.J. Dent
14. Ens. L.A. De Somier
15. Ens. Wayne Duffett
16. Ens. H.A. Elliott
17. Ens. Basil O. Finnegan
18. Ens. T.J. Gallivan
19. Ens. R.V. Grace
20. Boatswain (T) J.H. Green USN
21. Ens R.A. Griswold
22. Ens. W.D. Huddleston
23. Ens D.E. Huger
24. Ens. F.E. Hutcheons
25. Ens. Elmer L. Johansen
26. Ens. George H. Ludlow
27. Asst. Surgeon J.A. Mangiaracina
28. Ens. R.P. Matteissen, USNRF
29. Ens. J.N. O'Brien
30. Ens. Austin Parker
31. Ens. E.H. Parker
32. Ens. H.V. Perren
33. Ens. E. Provost
34. Ens. R.B. Read
35. Ens. Leonard M. Reno
36. Ens. W.B. Rogers
37. Asst. Surgeon S.B. Solhaug
38. Asst. Paymaster Vance Stewart
39. Asst. Surgeon Jack S. Terry, USN
40. Ens J. Vaini
41. Asst. Paymaster S. Vance
42. Boatswain Gioacchino Varini
43. Ens Dudley A. Vorhees
44. Ens F. Young
45. Ens H.A. Young
46. Ens Mark W. Walton, USNRF
47. Ens. C.E. Wordell
48. MM.1c James N. Ashworth (From HQ)
49. QM Richard B. Baily
50. Lds.QM(A) A.A. Baker
51. Ch.Yeo. F.J. Baron
52. PM. O.P. Barrett
53. Lds.QM(a) Chester A. Bates
54. PM. J.O. Bennett
55. QM.2c R.O. Beilley (from Moutchic)
56. QM.1c John W. Bird (from Moutchic)
57. Lds.QM(a) Charles B. Blue
58. Lds.QM(a) E.B. Blue
59. MM.2c Charles Bruno
60. Lds.QM(a) D.D. Chaplin
61. QM.2c H. Christopher (Pauillac)
62. Lds.QM(a) R.H. Clark
63. Lds.QM(a) G.E. Craswell
64. QM.1c Daniel C. Ferguson (Dunkerque)
65. MM T.J. Gallivan
66. Lds.QM(a) D.A. Garner
67. Lds.QM C.W. Gates
68. Lds.QM(a) W.S. Gilmore
69. Lds.QM J.L. Goggins
70. Lds.QM T.H. Gortner
71. Lds.QM(a) Joseph M. Graffis
72. MM.2c F.J. Graham (L'Aber Vrach)
73. Lds.QM(a) J. Gray (dropped)
74. CQM George R Groh (from Moutchic)
75. Lds.QM Charles Hazeltine Hammann
76. QM.2c Ralph R. Harter (Pauillac)
77. MM.2c Howard O. Hazen (Headquarters)
78. Lds.QM(a) E.G. Herendeen
79. Lds.QM(a) E.H. Herendeen
80. Lds.QM(a) Edward W. Kane
81. Lds.QM(a) G.W. Knowles
82. QM.1c Erno F. Landaiche (Dunkerque)
83. MM.2c Robert E. Lee (Le Croisic)
84. QM.2c(a) E.A. Letzkus
85. QM.1c Francis E. Lovejoy (Le Croisic)
86. PHM.2c Thomas M. Lynch
87. QM P. McFuller
88. MM.1c Matt A. Miller (L'Aber Vrach)
89. Lds.QM(a) H. Moyer (Moutchic)
90. QM.2c Francis A. Murray (Le Croisic)
91. MM.2c(a) A.B. Murphy
92. MM.1c Clarence A. Nelson
93. Yeo.3c A.B. Nielsen
94. Lds.QM T.H. O'Connor
95. QM Garland Parner
96. QM.2c R. Parmer (from Ile Tudy)
97. QM.1c C.L. Rawls (from Dunkerque)
98. Lds.QM(a) H.W. Ribinkam
99. Lds.QM(a) R. Ribinkam
100. HA.1c Rodney W. Richardson
101. QM Ernest Roach
102. QM.2c E I Rotch (from Brest)
103. Lds.QM(a) J.L. Rothwell
104. Lds.QM(a) R.W. Sayles
105. Lds.QM(a) E.M. Smith
106. QM.1c Robert H. Smith
107. MM.1c WalterN. South
108. BM.2c J. Stanley
109. Cox.(a) ? Stanley
110. QM.1c(a) Harold Stockwell (Dunkerque)
111. MM.1c Z.R. Strope (Porto Corsini)
112. Lds.QM(a) K. Stuart
113. QM.1c Lewis Suit (from Dunkerque)
114. CQM G.A. Sunderland (Headquarters)
115. Lds.QM(a) Albert P. Talliaferro
116. QM.2c Walter G. Thomas (from St. Trojan)
117. Lds.QM(a) E.I. Tinkham
118. Lds.QM(a) T.H. Wagner
119. QM.2c Elliott S. Walsh (from Le Croisic)
120. QM.1c Charles B. Watson (from Dunkerque)
121. QM.2c R.L. Waugh
122. QM.1c James E. Welch
123. QM.1c P.E. Welch (from Moutchic)
124. QM.2c WalterJ. White
125. Lds.QM(a) G.A. Wilson

Other sources also provide the following names as having been assigned to Bolsena:

Ens. J.M. Grier
QM 2c J.R. Dorman
MM 1c Goerge Graffato
QM Clarrence L. Rawls
QM2c J.B. Bradley
CQM E.T. Enos
AM1c B.T. Higgins
Y1c W.J. Brennan
QM Percy Fuller
Lds. QM Herbert Mayer
QM2c Charles I. Brown
Lds. QM J.L. Goggins

to the Tenete Provenzana Statzione Idrovolanti, Pescara establishing the following sequence of building construction at Pescara: 1) Enlisted Men's' Barracks; 2) New Hangars; 3) Officer Quarters; 4) Provisional Hospital (Farmer's House); 5) Latrine; 6) Wash House; 7) Automobile Garage; 8) Bomb Depot; 9) Barbed Wire Fence; 10) Refugees A.B.C.B.; 11) Fire Engine House; 12) Chief Pilot's House; 13; Administration; 14) Oven; 15; Storehouse; 16) Final Hospital; 17) Recreation Hall; and 18) Other remaining buildings. The chief cause of delay in commissioning this station, however, was not the slow progress of the work of construction, but the lack of airplanes, as the Italian authorities stated that they would be unable to supply any before December 1918. It would have been manifestly unwise to divert any of the few available seaplanes to Pescara before the station at Porto Corsini was properly equipped. On 22 October a small advance party under the command of Ensign Joseph H. Green, USNRF, (Naval Aviator No. 456), was sent to Pescara to prepare the station for the arrival of American Naval Aviation personnel to man the station; but upon signing of the Austrian armistice the project of establishing an air station at Pescara was abandoned.

TABLE 8
PERSONNEL ASSIGNED TO NAS PORTO CORSINI on 11 November 1918

Lieutenant Willis B. Haviland	Commanding Officer		
Lieutenant Goerge W. Almour	Executive Officer		
Lt. J.S. Terry Surgeon	Ens. G. Varini Pilot	Ens. D.D. Chaplin Pilot	
Lt. D.G. Bisson Dentist	Ens. G.H. Ludlow Pilot	Ens. W.S. Gilmore Pilot	
Lt. R.B. Read Chief Pilot	Ens. C.J. Coatsworth Pilot	Ens. H. Gortner Pilot	
Ens. F.H. Phillips Pay Corps	Ens. E.L. Johansen Pilot	Ens. A. P. Taliaferro Pilot	
J.E. Sundberg Pay Clerk	Ens. W. Duffett Pilot	Ens. J. Graffis Pilot	
M.E. Rothenbert Gunner	Ens. A. Parker Pilot	Ens. R.W. Sayles Pilot	
R. Budani Boatswain	Ens. A.W. Smith Pilot	Ens. L.M. Reno Pilot	
A.R. Tiburen Intelligence Officer	Ens. J.M. Grier Pilot	Ens. E. Provost Pilot	
Ens. D.A. Voorhees Engineering Officer	Ens. E.I. Tinkham Pilot	Ens. D.E. Hager Pilot	
A.A. Baker Ordnance Officer	Ens. W. White Pilot	E.M. Smith Pilot	
Ens. C.H. Hamman Pilot	Ens. K. Stuart Pilot	G.W. Knowles Pilot	
	Ens. J. Stanley Pilot	R.A. Clark Pilot	
		C.P. Brewer, "Y" Secretary	
Enlisted Personnel:			
Atkins, John S.	Ayres, Frank H.	Abbot, Lael R.	Bourne, William W.
Abbot, James A.	Allyn, Harold M.	Bawell, Aaurence H.	Boyd Jean A.
Aber, Thomas G.	Anderson, Roy L.	Becker, Machael F.L.	Breedlove, Clifford E.
Atkinson, Leicester E.	Anderson, Robert A.	Berry Charlie S.	Brinker, Walter A.
Atkinson, Willard	Aydelott, Guy W.P.	Bock, William W.	Bartlett, Walter T.
Baylor, Geo. W.	Brown, Charles S.	Cobb, Carrol	Colburn, Walter W.
Bernges, Wilbert M.	Buffington, Earl	Coleman, James S.	Conway, Richard F.
Bickel. Charles S.	Bush, Clyde W.	Corrigan, James P.	Daniels, Stanley
Bourchard, Wilbrod J.	Byron, William O.	Coulson, William M.	DeVoney, Edwin J.
Boyd, Bruce P.	Bennett, John J.	Cramer, Ernest W.	Dougherty, Morgan F.
Boykin, Thomas C.	Bierney, David E.	Culberson, Victory	Davis, John C.
Brewer, Luther G.	Bosse, Gustave H.	Carper, Ray :H.	Doll, Raymond F.
Brocker, Ferdenand C.	Brooks, Myron L.	Cass, Charles E.	Daniels, Shirley K.
Babb, Gordon A.	Baker, Virgil	Charroin, James H.	Davis, Elwood C.
Bailey, Albert W.	Berkihiser, Raymond A.	Clover, Vernon D.	Dickinson, Thomas H.
Belcher, Foy C.	Bonora, Nicholas	Cole, Charles A.	Donohue, Hugh F.
Bishop, Arthur W.	Branhof, George J. Jr.	Collins, Andrew J.	Dalton, Kenneth L.
Blakely, Lester L.	Capron, Earl C.	Coulson, Lake R.	Danner, Albert L.
Branson, James A.	Casson, John E.	Cowperthwaite, Leslie	Davis, Merton A.
Brooks, Clifford B.	Collins, Ernest D.	Cross, Harlan H.	Donnelly, Richard L.
Bruce, Allen F.	Cox, Herbert H.	Carpenter, Charles G.	Davidson, Everette H.
Bugel, Daniel N.	Carndoff, George	Cassell, Wilson H.	Dawson, Edgar H.
Butler, Fred S.	Cierzniewski, J.	Charter, Clyde A.	Dellm, Mirah L.H.
Babcock, Charles L.	Corby, Porter W.	Cole, Ira C.	Darling, Sandford A.
Beckham, William J.	Crawford, Thomas H.	Craven, John W.	Davis, William J.
Beyeler, Chris A.	Campbell, Cyril J.	Calhoun, Cecil G.	DeLeo, Ernest P.
Bishop, Metz	Carr, Clifford H.	Carretto, Emiliio	DeNigris, Giosue
Bower, Chalmers H. Jr.	Chambers, Howard R.	Cerra, Joseph A.	Doane, Henry K.
Brigance, Jack P.	Clark, Floyd I.	Clark, Lynn F.	Duggan, Lawrence D.

Downes, Philip
Evans, Thomas E.
Erro, Salvadore G.
Earll, George D.
Ewan, Frederick H.
Ferry, Francis J.
Flatley, James D.
Frazier, James H.
Fundy, Clarence G.
Fitzpatrick Erwin F.
Frank, John H.
Farwell, Grover C.
Fisher, Terrell W.
Fonda, Jack, C.
Gates, Edward M.
Graves, Harold N.
Gallup, Stephen R.
Gilfoy, Thomas J.
Griffiths, Owen H.
Gabrielle, John J.
Garvin, Ham F.
Gehrke, Fred F.
Gleeson, John J.
Labriola, Frank
Lavsky, Frank A.
Lepore, Dominick E.
McCaul, George A.
McMurray, Chester L.
Marada, Antony S.
Marshall, Edwin H.
Masterbone, Harry R.
Mendelsohn, Lawrence
Meyer, Albert
Mueller, Harry
McClanahan, Clyde V.
Madler, John L.
Marino, Louis L.
Masset, Frank. L. Jr.
Melby, Hilton J.
Merrill, Bertram E.
Montgomery, Robert E.
McCue, Frank J.
Maret, Jack
McCarthy, Kenneth S.
Malpass, Frank C.
Maurer, Irving
McCormick, Ernest B.
Slosser, Daniel C.
Smith, Homer B.
Storrie, George
Sargent, Oscar L.
Sedlaeck, Anton
Spencer, Fred
Spurgeon, Robert G.
Sales James W.
Scheffler, Lloyd W.
Sipes, John B.
Spotts, Harry F.
Starkey, Otis E.
Graham, Silas M.
Green, Dave T.
Garner, George L.
Garvin, Ronald J.
Glahn, James E.
Gleeson, William M.
Granston, William R.
Gross, James B.
Gulas, Henry
Gallagher, John J.
Haggerty, Joseph F.
Hogg, Joseph L.
Howe, John
Harrold, Floyd O.
Houseman, John L.
Huckvale, Robert L.
Hammond, Edward H.
Hopkins, Borgia F.
Hannah, Daniel
Hyndman, William L.
Hedley, William S.
Hellyer, Albert E.
Hornbrook, Dewey S.
McLennon, Daniel J.
McLeod Norman B. Jr.
Mack, George E.
Mehrman, Otto F.
Milana, Blatius L.
Moberly, Cecil
Murphy, Daniel P.
McClave, Edward J.
McKinney, John
MacIver, Norman S.
Mallett, Elbert
Meldrum, Ralph W.
Miller, Stanley W.
Moran, Clifford W.
Nevins, John J.
Nelson, James J.
Nuneviller, William H.
Nichol, Reginald
Nylander, Isaac A.
Nugent, Kenneth M.
Nadeau, Frank G.
Newcomb, Richard C.
Nelso, James J.
Nunns, Charlie S. Jr.
Solibello, Frank
Teirney, Clarence C.
Toland, Morris W.
Tissott, Edward W.
Turner, James R.
Tancre, Roy E.
Tavano, Thomas J.
Tietjen, Jeremiah
Tate, Michael A.
Thomas, John E.
Tutton, Harry, V.
Trobough, Frank J.
Hughes, George G.
Haney, Alexander T.
Hegemann, Adrian
Henderson, Albert W.
Hufmann, Edgar S.
Hunter, John A.
Janutolo, Hugo
Judge, William J.
James, Andrew C.
Jester, Thomas J.
Johnson, Carl E.
Jones, Leon L.
Jenny, Rudolph H.
Jester, Walter H.
Johnson, Henry S.
James, Alvah L.
Kaiser, Bernard
Kinnick, Everett D.
Keyser,k Daniel H.
Koperniak, Peter P.
Kent, Ernest B.
Kirchartz, Charles E.
Kraxberger, Alfred F.W.
Odon, Thomas D.
Onstott, Ferrol
Oyster, George V.
Olson, Oscar E.
Owen, Howard F.
Ogan, Ray L.
O'Rourke, Frank C.
O'Brien, Frank B.
Olson, Arthur C.
Ohnewehr, Clarence H.
Overholt, Donald R.
Ollerton, Frank C.
Paetzell, Russel S.
Pfeifer, John
Plumb, Harry S.
Padgett, Theoaphilus W.
Parrott, Harry L.
Phelps, Earl M.
Potts, Hart
Parker, Paul J.
Payne, William F.
Peterson, Clarence P.
Pierce, Harvey H.
Price, Juddie G.
Underwood, Austin M.
Vandervort, Maurice L.
Venuto, James M.
Vitale, John A.
Vita, Martin
Walton, James D.
Wilson, Dvid R.
Whinney, Charles B.
Wade, Robert D.
Wakefield, Vierre
Wentworth, Paul K.
Whiteside, Charles W.
Koontz. Rea R.
Koch, Lawrence G.
Krummert, Robert W.
Kontowicz, Stanley F.
LeVinness, Gustave
Little, Jesse F.
Lindgren, George E.
Lore, Dallas, D.
Larkin, Frederick O.W.
Larson, George M.
Lauer, Walter A.
Ligon, Rogert F.
Lowe, Oscar H.
Lunt, Percy R.
Large, Clarence E.
Larson, Lester L.
Lauer, Henry D.
Lawson, George G.
Loebs, Ray J.
Lowman, Guy B.
Larson, George A.
Leonard, Rolla A.
Lichtner, William M.
Paris, Clayton F.
Patton, William V.
Perry, Howard T.
Pettijohn, Thomas M.
Pierce, Lloyd B.
Raitt, Charles K.
Richardson, Rodney W.
Rifenberg, Lloyd G.
Rosson, Frank
Reid, Odus
Richter, Oscar M.
Rodes, Charles E.
Russell, Clive E.
Ruppert, Charles L.
Redman, Joe W.
Reed, Jack E.D.
Rudberg, Raymond H.
Rooney, Edmund J.
Richter, Frank E.
Richard, Oscar E.
Rheem, Roscoe H.
Schwartz, Max
Smith, Frank W.
Smith, Walter
Wanger, Ernest J.
Watts, Arno L.
White, Bruce R.
Wieting, Augustus
Williams, Benjamin II
Wilder, Frederick W.
Young, Oliver P.
Young, Harry
Young, Raymond E.
Zingerline, Clarence P.

TABLE 9

ROLL OF HONOR FOR NAS PORTO CORSINI

Name	Date
Ensign James L. Goggins	11 August 1918
Ensign Louis J. Bergen	15 September 1918
Gunner Thomas Murphey	15 September 1918
Csmth (a) George Emmet Killeen	18 September 1918

By orders of Vice Admiral Sims of 8 November no more students were posted to Lake Bolsena. On 15 November orders were received directing a 50% reduction in the personnel. The School was decommissioned by 15 January 1919. Statistics of the Bolsena Station as to the number of machines and amount of flying done are as follows:

Greatest number of machines	18
Number of flights	5540
Actual flying time	2216 hours, 9 minutes

During its existence, 134 American students were trained at this station, 73 of them receiving brevets and moving on to Italian, French, and American operational bases.

The American pilots at Porto Corsini flew 417 combat missions, including 19 bombing operations, 27 reconnaissance and escort flights, four defensive fighter missions, and 367 reconnaissance missions. Pescara was also decommissioned 15 January 1919.

It is interesting to note that even though Captain Cone approved, in January 1918, the assignment of 24 HS-1s and 18 fighter pilots to both Porto Corsini and Pescara, apparently no American-designed aircraft were ever flown by the Navy in Italy.

The "Estaminet" of Marine Squadron 7(A). Personnel are not identified. (source: Sam Richards collection)

The Northern Bombing Group

The concept of a Northern Bombing Group can trace its origins back to a 10 March 1918 Navy Department order to Vice Admiral Sims to prepare for four land fighter squadrons to assist in the bombing of the German submarine facilities at Ostend, Zeeburgge, and Bruges. It was determined that land planes and seaplanes in such a force were incompatible, and that land planes should be used for bombing.

On 17 April Captain Cone cabled Vice Admiral Sims the requirements for such a bombing force. The Northern Bombing Group was thus organized on 30 April 1918 when the Secretary of the Navy approved the plan recommended by the General Board for Air Operations to be undertaken in the Dunkirk-Zebrugge area against German submarine support facilities.[8] The original concept of the Group was for one Day Wing and one Night Wing consisting of six squadrons each, along with one assembly, repair, and supply unit. The squadrons of the Day Wing were to consist of three Flights of six machines each, while those of the Night Wing were to be two Flights of five planes each (Vice Adm. Sims' intention was for the Northern Bombing Group to consist of six squadrons of night bomb-

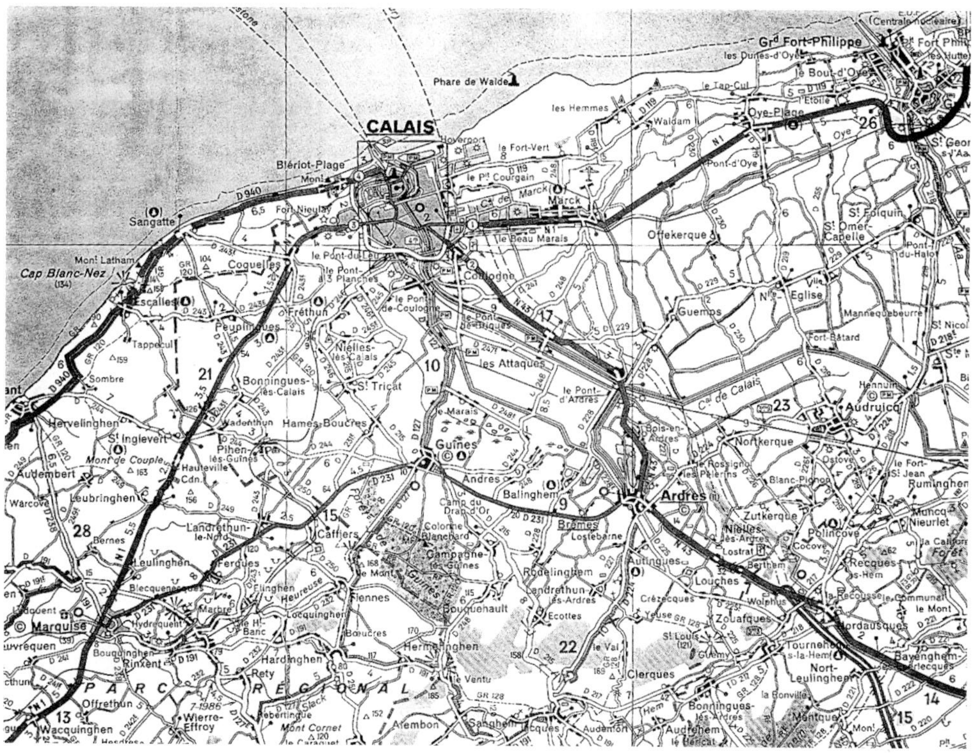

This map and the 'x' mark the location of Le Fresne airfield.

Aerial view of Le Fresne field. Aircraft are visible taxiing in front of the hangars. The field had a slight upward grade towards the right. This was used to give the D.H. 4s a "downhill" run on take-off. The road is the present route D22A. In the upper left-hand corner is the hedge-in are containing farm buildings and Headquarters. (source: Sam Richards collection)

Aerial view of the German Gotha airfield at Ghistelles, Belgium. (source: Sam Richards collection)

ers, with 18 planes per squadron). It was determined that the Night Squadrons would require 90 Caproni or Handley-Page machines with an estimated replacement of 20 machines per month. The Day Squadrons were determined to need 190 D.H. 9 or Bristol F.2B aircraft with an estimated 54 replacements per month. Due to a shortage of aircraft this plan was reduced (Navy Department Cablegram 2416 of 31 May 1918) to four Day and four Night squadrons, with day bombing being assigned to the Marine Corps and night bombing to the Navy. The Group was commanded by Captain D.C. Hanrahan, USN with Headquarters at Antingues, France, and was operated under British control as part of the aviation contingent attached to the Dover Patrol. Antingues was therefore never placed in commission as a naval air station. The aerodromes were located in northern France at St. Inglevert, Campagne Oye, Le Fresne, Sangatte, Spicker, and Alembom. Headquarters were established at Antiques with Marine Headquarters at Bois-en-Ardres. The assembly, repair, and supply base for the organization initially had been planned to be located in France, but this location was reconsidered due to the German Spring Offensive, and was eventually established at Eastleigh, England. Lt. G. deC. Chevalier was appointed Temporary Commanding Officer at Eastleigh on 20 July 1918. From this base the assembled planes were flown across the Channel to the aerodromes, while the supplies were shipped across in barges and by ferry to the port of Calais.

Changes in plans dated 31 May caused Night Squadrons 1 and 2 to use St. Inglevert and 3 and 4 to use Campagne, while Sangatte was used as a dummy field. Day Squadrons 7 and 8 were to operate from Oye; 9 and 10 from La Fresne, with a dummy field at Alembon; and Spicker Field was eliminated.[9]

On 20 June 1918 the first personnel for the Northern Bombing Group were sent from the U.S. Naval Air Station at Pauillac to the aerodrome site at St. Inglevert (this base was commanded by Bob A. Lovett (Naval Aviator No. 66) of the First Yale Unit). St. Inglevert also functioned as a northern repair base for the Marine Day Squadrons, with Guines being used as an advanced repair base. This force of personnel formed the nucleus of Night Squadron No. 1. From this date to the Armistice, personnel, supplies, equipment, and material followed as fast as obtainable, and the organization grew rapidly.

Pilots and observers were placed in aviation schools for intensive training in England, France, and Italy through the courtesy of those governments. Training in France for commissioned pilots and enlisted observers was achieved by sending men at Moutchic to the U.S. Army bombing school at Clermont-Ferrand and to the French Army bombing school at Avord. As soon as the men completed the required school courses they were given additional training in active British squadrons of the Fifth Group, Royal Air Force. Here they were given actual war flights over the German lines. To train

An aerial view of Bruges showing the effect of a bombing raid. (source: Sam Richards collection)

A piece of a piston from a Liberty engine. A souvenir from a 18 October 1918 raid in which Sam Richards' radiator was punctured by shrapnel and the piston cracked from overheating. On the upper portion is scribed "Air Raid 10/18/18". (source: Sam Richards collection)

Marine hangars and aircraft at Le Fresne field. Visible in the distance is the hedged-in area enclosing the farm buildings used as Headquarters. (source: Sam Richards collection)

2nd Lt. Sam Richards holding "Camouflage" in front of his tent at le Fresne. (source: Sam Richards collection)

pilots to fly the Caproni aircraft an agreement was reached with the Italian Government wherein Navy pilots would be trained at the Italian school at Malpensa. On 15 June 1918 Lieutenant (j.g.) S.S. Walker, USNRF, (Naval Aviator No. 86) arrived at Malpensa in command of a detachment of men scheduled to take the Caproni course. These men completed the course and received their brevets after an average flying time of 373.7 minutes. On 13 August 1918 Lieutenant Commander Callan wrote to Captain Cone that Ensign David H. Coddington had successfully completed the course at Malpensa, but had been found unfit for high altitude flying. Callan went on to suggest, and Cone subsequently approved, the assignment of Coddington to Milan to be the Navy's representative in the Army's Caproni acceptance office. In this position Coddington was responsible for equipping and scheduling for ferrying to France of all Caproni aircraft assigned to the Navy for the Northern Bombing Group. Ground personnel were similarly placed in various British squadrons for training purposes. The officers of the Headquarters Staff were temporarily attached to the Group Headquarters of the Fifth Group, RAF, where they received excellent training in operations, intelligence, aerial gunnery, bombs, aerial photography, etc. Advantage was taken of every opportunity to train the entire personnel. Through the courtesy and assistance of Brigadier-General Charles Lamb, commanding the Fifth Group, RAF, this was carried out with such rapidity that the personnel of the Northern Bomb-

2nd Lt. Sam Richards of the U.S.M.C. 3rd Squadron. (source: Sam Richards collection)

2nd Lt. Sam Richards of the Marine Aviation Force of the Northern Bombing Group in his flight suit which was lined with black bear fur. (source: Sam Richards collection)

ing Group were in all respects ready for independent war operation in advance of the receipt of the first planes. In order to fully apply the resources of eager and active aviators in the Night Wing, personnel were loaned out to No. 214 Squadron, RAF, for training and service (beginning in early July), and eventually to single-seat squadrons such as No. 213 Squadron, RAF (Camels), and the Escadrille de St. Pol (SPADs). Lieutenant Artemus L. Gates (Naval Aviator No. 65), the Commanding Officer of NAS Dunkirk, was made POW while flying with No. 213 Squadron, and Lieutenant (j.g.) Kenneth MacLeish (Naval Aviator No. 74) was KIA while flying with this same squadron. Lieutenant (j.g.) David Ingells (Naval Aviator No. 85) was to become the Navy's only WWI ace and winner of the DFC while flying with No. 213 Squadron. His fifth victory, achieved over a six week span, occurred on 24 September while on a test flight in a Camel when he sighted a Rumpler over Nieuport.

On 11 August 1918 the Night Wing of the Northern Bombing Group received its first plane. This was a Caproni Ca.5 (Ca.44) bomber equipped with three F.I.A.T. engines. The plane had been flown from the acceptance field at Fruino, Italy, to the aerodrome at St. Inglevert by the Group's own personnel. The officer in charge of these flights was Lieutenant Commander E.O. McDonnell (Naval Aviator No. 18). The first, and last, raid by a naval Caproni occurred on 15 August when Ensign L.R. Tabor of Air Squadron 1 as first pilot, Ensign Charles Fahey as second pilot, and D.C. Hale as rear gunner made a successful night raid on the submarine shelters at Ostend. The Northern Bombing Group Night Wing attempted no other mission in this type of aircraft, as problems with the aircraft necessitated its transfer to the A&R facility at NAS Eastleigh on 1 October 1918. Hostilities ceased before it could be returned. As additional aircraft of other types were received they were immediately placed in active service. The first day bombing machine, D.H. 4 No. A3295, was received on 7 September 1918.

Due to the scarcity of planes, the operations of the Northern Bombing Group were greatly restricted, and as such the pilots, observers, and gunners of the Group often assisted the British in raids conducted by British squadrons. The German targets, which were the intial objectives of the Northern Bombing Group, were the submarine bases in Belgium up to September 1918. The German submarine activities from Belgian ports ceased at this time, and all raids thereafter were generally on the railway junctions, rail yards, canal and canal docks at Thuront, Thielt, Steenbrugge, Eecloo, Ghent Deyuze, and Loheren, and on ammunition dumps, supply dumps, and aerodromes in connection with the Belgian offensives. These raids were carried out with the view of hindering, as much as pos-

2nd Lt. Sam Richards of the Marine Aviation Force of the Northern Bombing Group is seen apparently fitting a Lewis Gun on D.H. 4 number A3278 "good old D-8." The number D-8 is faintly visible on the fin. This aircraft was brought back to Miami after the war and given number "7". (source: Sam Richards collection)

This Marine D.H. 9A, serial no. E8541, crashed on 16 November 1918 when the landing gear was wiped out. (source: Sam Richards collection)

sible, the retreat of the German ground forces. During this period German aircraft were especially active on the Belgian front, and German planes generally attacked allied planes while on raids.

Marine personnel (see Table 10) were also actively gaining experience via temporary duty with British squadrons (No. 217 Squadron—D.H. 4 or No. 218 Squadron—D.H. 9). As early as 5 September six pilots, including Second Lieutenants Alvin L. Pritchard (Naval Aviator No. 279), Harvey C. Norman (Naval Aviator No. 783), William W. Torrey (Naval Aviator No. 793), and Vincent C. Young (Naval Aviator No. 519), all of "C" Squadron, were rotated through the RAF pilot's pool at Audembert for training and then assignment to either No. 217 or No. 218 Squadrons. On 8 September pilots Captain Robert S. Lytle (Naval Aviator No. 605) and First Lieutenants Herman A. Peterson (Naval Aviator No. 163 1/2) and Arthur H. Wright (Naval Aviator No. 143), along with observer 2nd Lts. Donald N. Whitman, William A. McSorley (Naval Aviator No. 835), and Charles R. Needham (Naval Aviator No. 463), all of "C" Squadron were assigned to No. 218 Squadron, RAF. No. 217 Squadron, RAF, received from "A" Squadron the following pilots: First Lieutenants John G. Kipp (Naval Aviator No. 586), Francis P. Mulcahy (Naval Aviator No. 597), and 2nd Lts. Everett R. Brewer (Naval Aviator No. 585) and Harold C. Major (Naval Aviator No. 604); and the following observers: Second Lieutenant Frederick B. Davy (Naval Aviator Nos. 534 and 771), Sergeant Archie Pascal, and Corporal Thomas C. McCullough. No 218 Squadron received from "B" Squadron the following pilots and observers: First Lieutenants Benjamin L. Harper (Naval Aviator No. 598) and George McLaughin, III (Naval Aviator No. 165), and Second Lieutenants Ford O. Rogers (Naval Aviator No. 560), Frank J. Nelms (Naval Aviator No. 781), Chapin C. Barr (Naval Aviator No. 823), and James K. Noble (Naval Aviator No. 510).

To support the Allied offensive in Flanders (which began on 28 September), Marine Force pilots and observers flew with Nos. 217 and 218 Squadrons, RAF. On 29 September 1918, First Lieu-

"Camouflage," the dog given to 2nd Lt. Sam Richards of the Marine Aviation Force of the Northern Bombing Group by Belgian troops. (source: Sam Richards collection)

D.H. 9A, serial No. E8476. Notice rudder marking "E8472". Apparently this is a replacement part salvaged from an aircraft which had crashed on 29 September 1918. (source: Sam Richards collection)

D.H. 9A E8480 of the Marine Aviation Force of the Northern Bombing Group at Le Fresne. (source: Sam Richards collection)

A view of Le Fresne as it looks today. (Source: Adam Wait collection)

tenant Brewer and Sergeant Harry B. Wershimer were both WIA over Cortemarck. On 29 September Second Lieutenant Chapin C. Barr became the first Marine aviator to be KIA in aerial combat when he bled to death from a leg wound. Also on 29 September First Lieutenant Mulcahy and Corporal McCullough became the first Marines to shoot down an enemy plane when, flying with No. 218 Squadron, they flamed a Fokker D.VII over Cortemarck.

By October the Marine Force was in a position that they could, for the first time, begin to use their own aircraft in raids with the RAF. On 3 October 1918 raids were made against Westende, Nieuport, the railway yards at Ostende, and Lichtervelde. Captain Lytle, with Sergeant Wiman, flew in Marine aircraft No. D-1 in two of these raids with No. 218 Squadron. First Lieutenant Peterson, with Second Lieutenant Edward J. Kennealy (Naval Aviator No. 480), flew with No. 217 Squadron. On 4 October 1918, the team of Lytle and Wiman was replaced by the team of First Lieutenant Talbot and Coporal Robert G. Robinson. Flying aircraft No. D-1, this team flew with No. 218 Squadron on raids to Thourout (4 October), Oroye (5 October), Westende (7 October), and Ardoye (8 October). On the last raid they successfully brought down an attacking plane.

The first all-Marine Force combat mission was made on the morning of 14 October 1918 by "C" Squadron from Le Fresne. Led by Captain Lytle, the target was the railway junction and yards at Thielt, on which 17 bombs totaling 2218 pounds were dropped. On returning, the formation of seven D.H.-4s and D.H. 9As was attacked by eight Fokker D.VIIs and four Pfalz D.IIIs. Second Lieutenant Ralph Talbot and Gunnery Sergeant Robert C. Robinson, in D-1, were both WIA, and both won the Medal of Honor for extraordinary heroism on this and on an earlier raid for engaging enemy aircraft at great odds.

Following the Thielt raid, Day Wing Squadrons made raids on Steenbrugge, Eceloo, Ghent, Deynze, and Lokeren, during which targets consisted of railway yards, canals, supply dumps, and German aerodromes. On 17 October 1918, in a morning raid, Major

2nd Lt. Edwin A Bertolette of the Marine Aviation Force of the Northern Bombing Group. (source: Sam Richards collection)

A D.H. 4 of the 1st Marine Aviation Force in France.

Aerial view of Le Fresne field facing roughly towards the south. A taxiing aircraft is visible in the upper part of the photo left of center.

Douglas B. Roben (Naval Aviator No. 535) of "C" Squadron led a five plane formation in an attack of the railway yards at Steenbrugge. In the afternoon the Marine Force attacked the Ostend Harbor and the Zeeburgge Mole. On 18 October Captain Arthur H. Wright (Naval Aviator No. 148) of "C" Squadron led a formation of seven machines to Eceloo and the Leopold canal. During the raid the German airfield outside of Eceloo was also bombed. Also on this date the Force attacked the railway yards at Sinde. On 19 October a raid on Melle was aborted due to bad weather. During the raid Lieutenants Harvey C. Norman (Naval Aviator No. 783) and Elmer B. Taylor (Naval Aviator No. 1037) were KIA. On 27 October two raids were flown. The first, consisting of six planes, was flown against the railway junction and yards at Lockeren. During this action D-11 (Second Lieutenants Frank Nelms (Naval Aviator No. 781) and John F. Gibbs (Naval Aviator No. 830)) of "B" Squadron was brought down in Holland. The crew was interned for what was left of the War. The second raid, also by "B" Squadron, was a five machine effort aimed against Ghent. Due to the retreat of the German forces, as a result of the success of the Allied offensive, the Northern Bombing Group fields were too far back from the lines.

Third Marine Aero Squadron, 1st Marine Aviation Force, Northern Bombing Group. (source: Sam Richards collection)

A "Line-up for Inspection." D.H. 4s on the left, D.H. 9As on the right.

Marine D.H. 4 line-up. Aircraft directly in front of the hangar is a D.H. 9A.

TABLE 10
Summary of the First Marine Aviation Force
Summary by Squadron

Marine Squadron 'A'
Geiger, Major Roy S. (Commanding)

Pilots

Alder, 2/Lt. Grover C.	Lawson, 2/Lt. Peter R.
Batts, 1/Lt. Walter H.	Leighton, 2/Lt. Delmar
Brewer, 1/Lt. Everett R.	McMurran, 2/Lt. John P.
Clark, 2/Lt. Sidney E.	Major, 1/Lt. Harold C.
Darden Jr., 2/Lt. Colgate W.	Malmar, 2/Lt. Howard B.
Davy, 1/Lt. Frederick B.	Mulcahy, Capt. Francis P.
Dickey, 1/Lt. Paul	Shannon, 2/Lt. Winfield S.
Donovan, 2/Lt. George F.	Stewart Jr., 1/Lt. Maco
Holloway, 2/Lt. Charles T.	Weaver, 2/Lt. John H.
Kipp, Capt. John G.E.	Whitehead, 2/Lt. Marcus A.
Koerbling, 2/Lt. August	

Observers

Abbott, 1/Lt. George M.	Heberer, Cpl. Lee S.
Adams, 1/Lt. Russell S.	Hetwick, Sgt. Joseph M.
Austin, 1/Lt. Joseph W.	Le Master, Sgt. Dean W.
Bettolette, 1/Lt. Edwin A.	McCullough, Cpl. Thomas L.
Collings, 1/Lt. Kenneth B.	Mast, Cpl. Jacob K.
Commstock, 1/Lt. Thomas C.	Paschal, Sgt. Archie
Davis, 1/Lt. Bronson H.	Smith Jr., Cpl. William R.
Josephs, 1/Lt. Walter N.	Sprague, MM.2c George E. (USN)
Beach, Cpl. Wendell N.	Wershiner, Gunnery Sgt.. Harry B.
Clark, MM.2c Howard H. (USN)	Wolf, Cpl. Leo E.

Aerial Gunners

Coggin, Cpl. James K.	West, Cpl. Marion
Fox, Cpl. Lee E.	Wohnhas, Cpl. George F.
Wendt, Cpl. William T.	

Marine Squadron 'B'
McIlvain, Major William H. (Commanding)

Pilots and Observers

Barr, 2/Lt. Chapin C.	Leeper, 2/Lt. Horace W.
Bates, 1/Lt. Clyde N.	Nelms, 2/Lt. Frank J.
Benson, 2/Lt. John O.	Noble, 2/Lt. James K.
Bradford, 1/Lt. Doyle	Paisley, 2/Lt. Robert J.
Breckon, 2/Lt. John P.	Peters, 2/Lt. Chester J.
Chamberlain, Capt. Edmund C.	Pierce, 2/Lt. Walter B.
Edwards, 2/Lt. Daniel M.	Pogue, 2/Lt. Providence L.
Gibbs, 2/Lt. John F.	Powell, 2/Lt. John E.
Harper, Capt. Benjamin L.	Robillard, 1/Lt. Fred S.
Heartfield, 2/Lt. Maurice K.	Rogers, 1/Lt. Ford O.
Hodges Jr., Ens. Charles E. (USN)	Sherman, 2/Lt. Arthur J.
Humphries, 2/Lt. Albert E.	Thompson, 2/Lt. Philip A.
Johnson, Lt.(j.g.) Albert R. (USN)	Trefall, 1/Lt. Melchoir B.
Kragh, 2/Lt. Herbert E.	Van Deusen, 2/Lt. Edward T.
Laughlin III, 1/Lt. George Mc.	Williams, 1/Lt. Trevor C.
Lee, Lt. (j.g.) Delzie R. (USN)	Whitney, 2/Lt. Edwin H.

Observers

Crawford, Cpl. Thomas E.	Loftis, Gunnery Sgt. William H.
Curtis, Cpl. Milton E.	Longfellow, Cpl. Carl W.
Daniels, Cpl. Virgil A.	Martin, Gunnery Sgt. Elda K.
Graham, Cpl. Leon E.	Mulvane, Cpl. John L.
Gravatte, Sgt. Thomas S.	Payne, Cpl. Paul P.
Hughes, Sgt. Herbert	Tatman, CCM Horton E. (USN)
	Winkler, Cpl. Ross W.

Members of the Marine Squadrons of the Northern Bombing Group heading home aboard the U.S.S. *Mercury*. (source: Official U.S. Marine Corps photo)

Caproni Ca.5. (source: Roberto Gentilli collection)

Marine Squadron 'C'
Roben, Major Douglas B. (First Commanding Officer)
Lytle, Captain Robert S. (Second Commanding Officer)

Pilots

Barnwell, 2/Lt. Bunn G.
Barr, 2/Lt. William M.
Dunlap, 1/Lt. Jesse F.
Greenough, Ens. Charles W. (USN)
Head, 1/Lt. William W.
Jones, 2/Lt. Harold A.
Mathews, 2/Lt. Webster A.
Morgan, 2/Lt. George C.
Norman, 2/Lt. Harvey C.
Olsen, 2/Lt. Eyner F.
Peterson, 2/Lt. Herman A.
Pritchard, 2/Lt. Alvin L.
Talbot, Ens. Ralph (USN)
Taylor, Ens. Elmer B. (USN)
Todd, 2/Lt. Charles B.
Wheaton, 2/Lt. Ivan P.
Wright, Capt. Arthur H.
Young, 2/Lt. Vincent C.

Observers

Blood, 2/Lt. Philip W.
Courtney, 2/Lt. Gerald F.
Ingalls, 2/Lt. Edmund H.
Kenealy, 2/Lt. Edward J.
Loring, 2/Lt. Everett O.
McSorley, 2/Lt. William A.
Merriott, 2/Lt. Joy McD.
Needham, 2/Lt. Charles R.
Richards, 2/Lt. Samuel S.
Shea, 2/Lt. Lawrence A.
Taylor, 2/Lt. Caleb W.
Torrey, 2/Lt. William W.
Whiting, 2/Lt. Donald W.
Coffee, Sgt. Leon
Gibson, Sgt. Alfred W.
Jones, MM.1c Jay R. (USN)
Kowalski, Cpl. Walter
Price, Cpl. David F.
Robinson, Cpl. Robert G.
Smith, Cpl. Frank
Turnbull, MM.2c Alva M. (USN)
White, MM.2c Anthony J. (USN)
Wiman, Sgt. Amil

Aerial Gunners

Emmons, Cpl. Roger M.
Shepard, Cpl. Elston H.
Moe, Cpl. John M.

Marine Squadron 'D'
Presley, Captain Russell A. (Commanding)

Pilots

Bennett, 2/Lt. Homer C.
Dunn, 1/Lt. Henry T.
Fleer, 2/Lt. Frank H.
Huhn, 2/Lt. John B.
Jesse, 1/Lt. Herman J.
Kaemmerling, 1/Lt. Gustav H.
Kirwan, 1/Lt. Raymond J.
Kremm, 1/Lt. George F.
Moore, 2/Lt. Robert G.
Reed, 2/Lt. Roland K.
Rhodes, 2/Lt. George M.
Robinson,, 2/Lt. Paul V.
Rodgers, 2/Lt. Francis G.
Shivery, 2/Lt. Andrew K.
Smith, 2/Lt. Blanchard D.
Stanley, 2/Lt. James S.
Stephens, 2/Lt. James S.
Webster, 1/Lt. Clifford L.
Whiteside, 2/Lt. John R.
Willman, 2/Lt. George C.

Observers

Baker, 2/Lt. Henry E.
Burnett, 2/Lt. Chauncey V.
Bushong, 2/Lt. Karl E.
Cain, 2/Lt. Memory H.
Davis, 2/Lt. Neal
Dickerson, 2/Lt. David
Ehret Jr., 2/Lt. Henry S.
Elvidge, 2/Lt. Herbert D.
Ferguson, 2/Lt. William W.
Freland, 2/Lt. Byron B.
McConnell, 2/Lt. William C.
Poythress, 2/Lt. Charles D.
Spencer, 2/Lt. Dwight
Stovall, 1/Lt. Harry E.
Strong, 2/Lt. Howard A.
Woodward Jr., 2/Lt. Dave J.

Aerial Gunners

Bell, Cpl. Earl E.
Briley, Cpl. Lois K.
Griesbach, Cpl. Walter
Heim, Sgt. John LaV.
Pickett, Cpl. Carroll H.
Richter, Sgt. Otto H.

By October 1918 the German retreat from their naval bases along the Belgian coast was such that the Navy was looking for other uses for the Northern Bombing Group. Proposals ranged from moving the Group to the Adriatic area to assigning the Group to the British. The services of the Group were offered to the Army, but General Pershing declined. He did, however, concur with the assignment of the Group to the British Fifth Group, RAF. On 15 October 1918 Vice Admiral Sims agreed to the removal of the Group from the command of the British Vice Admiral at Dover to the Fifth Group RAF. On 26 October an abandoned German aerodrome at Knesselaere was chosen as an advanced field, and Major McIlvain was placed in charge. On 27 October preparations were started to move the remainder of the Group to selected aerodromes in Belgium. At the time of the Armistice one squadron of the Day Wing

U.S. Navy Caproni Ca.5 enroute to the Northern Bombing Group.

Caproni Ca.5 powered with Isotta Fraschini 200-250 hp engines. Note the gunner's pulpit behind the wings.

Caproni Ca. 5 with U.S. roundrel on the forward portion of the fuselage. (source: Gentilli collection)

Bomb racks on a Caproni. (source: Official U.S. Air Force photo)

was completely housed on the aerodrome at Knesselaere, Belgium, while the other Day Wing squadrons were in the process of moving; similarly, the two Night squadrons were housed on the aerodrome at Maria Alta, Belgium. The remaining personnel of the Group had finished preparations for the move. The seaplane station at Dunkirk, which was attached to the Northern Bombing Group, was moved to the Zeebrugge Mole. As German squadrons formerly occupied these aerodromes, and a great quantity of material had been left abandoned when the fields were evacuated, a great quantity of German material was used in housing the squadrons. The movement to new fields had to be accomplished by motor transport over terrible roads for the greater part of the distance, as there were no railroads available.

After the Armistice the squadrons were all moved back to their original aerodromes and from there evacuated to the United States. The complete demobilization of the Group was finished on 10 February 1919. The total force in the field on the date of the Armistice was about 250 officers and 2400 men, and at the Group assembly and repair base at Eastleigh about 220 officers and 2200 men. The total then was around 470 officers and 4600 men for the entire Group.

Aircraft flown by the U.S. Naval Forces in Europe were predominately of European manufacture (with the exception of the D.H.-4s and D.H. 9As flown by the Northern Bombing Group). From France came the Levy-Le Pen, a three place flying boat powered by a 280 hp Renault engine; the Tellier, which was a two-place flying boat powered by a 200 hp Hispano-Suiza engine; the Donnet-Denhaut flying boat, which came in three versions—a trainer, an unarmed two-place machine, and an armed three-place machine, all of which were powered by a 200 hp Hispano-Suiza engine; a Hanroit-DuPont 2, which was a float mounted version of the land plane and which was used solely at NAS Dunkerque; and French manufactured Sopwith 1 1/2 Strutters (used in training). British aircraft used included the F.2A, H-12, and Short 320 aircraft, all of which were used at NAS Killingholme; the D.H.-4 and D.H. 9A used by the Northern Bombing Group; and a few D.H. 6s used for coastal patrol work in the British Isles. And finally, from Italy, the U.S. Navy used Macchi L-3, M-5, M-8, and Caproni Ca.5 aircraft. Tables 11, 12, and 13 provide information on these aircraft.

Demobilization

Upon cessation of hostilities, demobilization became one of the subjects of prime importance. As of New Year's day 1919 the Anti-Submarine and Planning Section had been demobilized entirely at the Naval Headquarters in London. However, the personnel in the other sections still represented a skeleton crew, and a Historical Section had been established. The "thorn in the ointment," so to

Caproni B-15. (source: Official U.S. Air Force photo)

Caproni 900 at Malpensa.

speak, preventing complete demobilization was the contemplated arrival of the Assistant Secretary of the Navy (Franklin Roosevelt), with legal adviser and assistants. This would require a considerable secretarial staff, which would require all personnel that were then at Naval Headquarters to remain until the Assistant Secretary arrived, and it could not be definitely ascertained exactly what personnel would be needed by him.

The status of the air station demobilization, as of 3 February 1919, is shown in Table 14. The general rules of thumb used for the demobilization of officer personnel were: no officers of the regular Navy were being sent to the U.S. without authority of the Force Commander; no officers of the Reserve Force were being sent home whose services could be used to advantage on German ships; and no accounting officers were being permitted to return stateside to settle accounts, but were being retained in the immediate vicinity of the outstanding obligations.

TABLE 11

FRENCH AIRCRAFT FLOWN BY U.S. NAVAL AVIATION UNITS IN EUROPE[10]

Serial Number	From	Date	To
		TELLIER	
10	S.F.A. Dubonnet	29 December 1917	Le Croisic
11	S.F.A. Dubonnet	29 December 1917	Le Croisic
21	Paris	1 February 1918	Moutchic (To Pauillac 17 December 1918)
24	Paris	2 February 1918	Moutchic
25	S.F.A. Dubonnet	9 February 1918	Le Croisic
40	S.F.A. Dubonnet	19 March 1918	Le Croisic to Moutchic
56	Cazaux	22 May 1918	Moutchic
69	Hourtin	4 May 1918	Moutchic
70	Cazaux	20 May 1918	Moutchic (to Pauillac 2 December 1918)
71	S.F.A. Dubonnet	7 October 1918	Le Croisic
72	S.F.A. Dubonnet	5 November 1917	Le Croisic
73	S.F.A. Dubonnet	4 November 1917	Le Croisic
74	S.F.A. Dubonnet	7 October 1917	Le Croisic
86	S.F.A. Dubonnet	4 November 1917	Le Croisic
87*	S.F.A. Dubonnet	17 June 1918	Le Croisic
89	S.F.A. Dubonnet	17 June 1918	Le Croisic
91	S.F.A. Dubonnet	21 June 1918	Le Croisic
93	S.F.A. Dubonnet	21 June 1918	Le Croisic
105	S.F.A. Dubonnet	12 December 1917	Le Croisic
106	S.F.A. Dubonnet	26 December 1917	Le Croisic
111	S.F.A. Dubonnet	12 January 1918	Le Croisic
114	Paris	16 February 1918	Moutchic
116	Paris	4 February 1918	Moutchic
139	S.F.A. Dubonnet	29 March 1918	Le Croisic
140	S.F.A. Dubonnet	3 April 1918	Le Croisic
143	S.F.A. Dubonnet	6 April 1918	Le Croisic
144	S.F.A. Dubonnet	8 April 1918	Le Croisic
145	S.F.A. Dubonnet	8 April 1918	Le Croisic
146	S.F.A. Dubonnet	25 April 1918	Le Croisic
151	S.F.A. Dubonnet	9 November 1918	Le Croisic via Moutchic
153	S.F.A. Dubonnet	16 November 1918	Le Croisic via Moutchic
		LEVY-LE PEN	
GL13	Paris	7 June 1918	Le Croisic to St. Trojan to Le Croisic
GL16	Paris	19 November 1918	Le Croisic to St. Trojan
GL20	Paris	15 June 1918	Le Croisic to St. Trojan to Le Croisic
GL21	Paris	8 June 1918	Le Croisic to St. Trojan to Le Croisic
GL27	Paris	21 June 1918	Le Croisic to U.S. (Became A-5650)
GL28	Paris	17 June 1918	Le Croisic to St. Trojan
GL29	Paris	15 June 1918	Le Croisic to St. Trojan
GL30	Paris	26 June 1918	Le Croisic to St. Trojan to Le Croisic
GL60	Paris	23 June 1918	Le Croisic to St. Trojan to Le Croisic
GL83	Paris	6 August 1918	Le Croisic to St. Trojan
GL84	Paris	16 September 1918	Le Croisic to St. Trojan to U.S. to become A-5651
GL85	Paris	25 July 1918	Le Croisic to St. Trojan

DONNET-DENHAUT

447	French NAS	1 December 1917	Moutchic to Pauillac on 6 December 1917
507	French NAS	5 December 1917	Moutchic to Pauillac on 6 December 1917 to U.S. to become A-5652
809	French Government	22 October 1917	Dunkerque
810	French Government		Dunkerque
812	French Government		Dunkerque
813	French Government		Dunkerque
814	French Government	25 October 1917	Dunkerque
815	French Government	22 October 1917	Dunkerque
816	French Government	26 October 1917	Dunkerque
817	French Government	2 December 1917	Dunkerque
823	French Government	28 December 1917	Dunkerque
825	French Government	31 January 1917	Dunkerque
829	French Government	22 February 1918	Dunkerque
831	French Government	14 February 1918	Dunkerque
832	French Government	14 February 1918	Dunkerque
833	French Government	14 February 1918	Dunkerque
835	French Government	5 March 1918	Dunkerque
840	French Government	13 April 1918	Dunkerque
841	French Government	15 April 1918	Dunkerque
842	French Government	15 April	Dunkerque
843	French Government	15 April 1918	Dunkerque
844	French Government	15 April 1918	Dunkerque
845	French Government	15 April 1918	Dunkerque
846	French Government	15 April	Dunkerque
847	French Government	25 April 1918	Dunkerque
848	French Government	25 April 1918	Dunkerque
849	French Government	25 April 1918	Dunkerque
1150	Paris		Le Croisic to Moutchic
1151	Paris		Le Croisic to Moutchic
1179	Paris	26 December 1917	Moutchic
1180	Paris	26 December 1917	Moutchic
1181	Paris	26 December 1917	Moutchic
1182	Paris	26 December 1917	Moutchic
1193	Paris	21 February 1918	Le Croisic to Ile Tudy
1208	Paris	18 January 1918	Moutchic
1209	Paris	19 January 1918	Moutchic
1210	Paris	19 January 1918	Moutchic to Pauillac on 6 December 1918 to U.S. to become A-5653
1211	Paris	23 January 1918	Moutchic
1217	Paris	19 February 1918	Le Croisic to Ile Tudy as I-24
1218	Paris	21 January 1918	Le Croisic to Ile Tudy to Moutchic to Pauillac
1219	Le Croisic	19 January 1918	Ile. Tudy to Le Croisic
1220	Paris	19 January 1918	Le Croisic to Ile Tudy as I-26
1240	Pairs	20 February 1918	Le Croisic to Ile Tudy to Moutchic to Pauillac
1241	Paris	20 February 1918	Le Croisic to Ile Tudy as I-23
1253	Paris	20 February 1918	Le Croisic to Ile Tudy as I-22
1440	Paris	4 April 1918	Le Croisic to Ile Tudy to Le Croisic
1441	Paris	4 April 1918	Le Croisic to Ile Tudy as I-28
1442	Paris	4 April 1918	Le Croisic to Ile Tudy to Le Croisic
1443	Paris	4 April 1918	Le Croisic to Ile Tudy as I-40
1450	Paris		Ile Tudy as I-35
1451	Paris		Le Croisic to Ile Tudy to Le Croisic
1452	Paris		Ile Tudy as I-31
1453	Paris		Ile Tudy as I-27
1454	Paris	16 April 1918	Le Croisic to Ile Tudy as I-40
1455	Paris	16 April 1918	Le Croisic to Ile Tudy as I-33
1473	Paris		Ile Tudy to Moutchic

TABLE 13[12]
Aircraft of the Northern Bombing Group

Caproni Aircraft[13]

Italian Serial No.	Navy Side No.	Remarks
11597	B-1	Crew of Lambert/Robertson crashed at Bra, Italy on 21 July 1918
11577	B-2	Crew of H. Harris/E. Lewis crashed at Sens, France on 27 July 1918
11598	B-3	At St. Inglevert
11587	B-4	Crew of Kerr/Agar crashed at Paris in July 1918
11562	B-5	Crashed at Dunkerque on 23 August 1918
11590	B-6	Crashed at Mirafiori, Italy on 1 August 1918
11607	B-7	At St. Inglevert
11591	B-8	Caught fire in the air at Mirafiori, Italy (date unspecified)
11560	B-9	Crashed at Brioude, France on 11 August 1918
11592	B-10	No Information
11595	B-11	Crashed at St. Inglevert on 15 September 1918
11599	B-12	At St. Inglevert
11523	B-13	Crashed at Miafiori, Italy on 17 August 1918
11561	B-14	At St. Inglevert
11524	B-15	At Orly, France
11570	B-16	At St. Inglevert
11594	B-17	At St. Inglevert
11593	B-18	At Eastleigh
11589	B-19	Crashed at Dijon, France on 2 September 1918
-	B-20	No Information

D.H.-4 Aircraft

Army Serial	Navy Serial	Side No.	Remarks
32413	A33295	D-1	"C" and "D" Squadrons. Crashed at La Fresne on 25 October 1918
32198	A3260	D-2	"A" and "C" Squadrons. Force landed at Petit Philippi
32387	A3269	D-3	"A", "B", and "C" Squadrons. Forced landed at Pervyse, Belgium on 14 October 1918
32405	A3300	D-4	"A" and "C" Squadrons. Shot down by A.A. during a raid over Melle, Belgium on 22 October 1918
32207	A3280	D-5	"B" and "C" Squadrons
32555	A3262	D-6	"C" Squadron
32318	A3299	D-7	"B" Squadron
32354	A3278	D-8	"C" Squadron. Returned to Miami, FL after WWI where it became Aircraft No. 7
32360	A3260	D-9	"C" Squadron
32199	A3263	D-10	"C" Squadron
32274	A3261	D-11	"C" Squadron. Forced landed in Holland after raid on Lokeres, Belgium on 27 October 1918
32380	A3270	D-12	"C" Squadron
323990	A3279	D-13	"C" Squadron
	A3433	D-14	"C" and "D" Squadrons
	A3432	D-15	"C" and "D" Squadrons
	A3435	D-16	"C" and "D" Squadrons

D.H. 9A Aircraft

Army Serial	Navy Serial	Side No.	Remarks
E 8465	E-1		"A" and "C" Squadrons
E 8477	E-2		"A" and "C" Squadrons
E 8466	E-3		"A" and "B" Squadrons. Crashed at Ghistelles, Belgium on 15 November 1918
E 8472	E-4		"A" Squadron. Crashed on 29 September 1918
E 8475	E-5		"A" and "B" Squadrons
E 8480	E-6		"A" and "B" Squadrons
E 8476	E-7		"A" and "B" Squadrons
E 8469	E-8		"A" and "B" Squadrons
E 8467	E-9		"A" and "B" Squadrons
E 8507	E-10		"A" and "B" Squadrons
E 8502	E-11		"B" and "C" Squadrons
E 8504	E-12		"C" Squadron
E 8506	E-13		"B" and "C" Squadrons
E 8539	E-14		"C" Squadron. Crashed at Knesselaeare, Belgium on 21 November 1918
E 8538	E-15		"C" Squadron
E 8540	E-16		"C" Squadron
E 9874	E-17		"C" Squadron. Aircraft received after the Armistice
E 8478	E-18		"C" Squadron
E 8501	E-19		"C" Squadron
E 8542	E-20		"C" Squadron
E 8541	E-21		"C" Squadron. Aircraft wrecked on 16 November 1918. The same serial number is given for Aircraft
E-22			

The following is a list of Northern Bombing Group D.H.-4s, D.H. 9As, and Caproni aircraft which were ready for service on 11 November 1918:

D.H.-4 D-2, D-6, D-8, D-9, D 10, D-12, D-13, and D-14
D.H. 9A: E-2, E-11, E-12, E-13, E-14, E-15, and E-16
Caproni B-7 and B-17

The Naval Aviation Staff in France at the close of the war. Capt. T.T. Craven is seated in the center of the front row.

TABLE 14

Station	Date of Demobilization	Disposition	Comment
Trequier	19 January 1919	To French Navy	The Bessneau Hangars are being transferred to the U.S. Army while the French barracks will be left intact to be taken over and disposed of by the French (subject to examination for damages). A small sum will be paid the property owner for excavation damages.
Guipavas	13 January 1919	Evacuated	Barracks, lumber, electrical supplies, pipe fittings, and fire apparatus are to be turned over to the U.S. Army. The portable hydrogen plant, with the exception of hydrogen cylinders, will be left on the site to be turned over to the French Government. The estimated cost of this equipment is 465,000 francs. The U.S. will be responsible for restoring the land.
L'Aber Vrach	22 January 1919	Evacuated	Barracks, pipes, electrical stores, fire apparatus, etc. were transferred to the U.S. Army.
Ile Tudy	25 January 1919	Evacuated	All French buildings were returned to their original owners. There was no property damage. Portable barracks were shipped to the U.S. while the U. S. Army took the Bessneau Hangars. The aircraft were shipped to Brest and Pauillac or salvaged at the station.
Le Croisic	28 January 1919	To French Navy	The Bessneau Hangars were transferred to the U.S. Army. The portable buildings were turned over to the U.S. Naval Port Officer at St. Nazaire
Paimboeuf	26 January 1919	To French Navy	LTA craft were deflated and shipped to the U.S. Spare lumber, piping, and fittings were transferred to the U.S. Army.
Fromentine	28 January 1919	Evacuated	The lease of the land was terminated and the owner signed clear of all damage claims. The U.S. Army took custody of the property on the site to provide all necessary transportation.
La Pallice	5 January 1919	To U.S. Army	The Kite Balloons and accessories, together with the hydrogen plant, were shipped to the U.S. The oil tanks on the site were ceded to the French Government.
St. Trojan	29 January 1919	To French Minister of the Interior (Department of the Seine)	All material, including the aircraft, was shipped to the U.S. The contract cost of this station was 1,200,000 francs. Since practically all the work was completed at the site on date of cancellation, the damage claims incident to cancellation of the contract was small.
Pauillac	1 February 1919	To U.S. Army	The French Government requested 726,000 francs for the Army to take over the base.
Moutchic	31 December 1918	To French Army	And in turn, to a private group for use as a tuberculosis sanitarium All Bessneau Hangars were taken down and given to the U.S. Army. The contract cost of this station was 842,000 francs. Damage claims incident to the cancellation of contracts were small as practically all work was completed on the date of cancellation.
Gujan	15 January 1919	Evacuated	All portable buildings were taken down and turned over to the U.S. Army at Bordeaux with lumber salvaged from the portable hangars. All hydrogen equipment was shipped to the U.S. via Pauillac
Arachon	7 January 1919	To French Minister of Interior (Department of the Seine)	All portable barracks were given to the U.S. Army. The material to be sent to the U.S. via Pauillac. The contract for this station was 1,220,000 francs. As work was practically complete on the date of cancellation all claims for damages incident to the cancellation were small.
Dunkerque	2 January 1918	To the Commission on the Relief of Belgium	The Bessneau Hangars were turned over to the Hoover Commission Kite Balloons and hydrogen equipment not taken over by the French Government was sent to the U.S. (approximately 1,000 tons of aviation material was sent to the U.S.). The net cost of the transfer was 692,500 francs.
Brest	15 February 1919	To French Navy	
La Trinite	4 February 1919	Evacuated	Derequisiton of this property was handled for the French Government by the Travaux Hydrauliques.

Northern Bombing Fields	5 February 1919	Evacuated	Material from these fields which was being returned to the U.S. was sent via Antiques
Killingholme	6 January 1919	To British Navy	As the station reverted back to the British indemnification was paid to the U.S. for improvements in the facilities made by the Navy.
Eastleigh	10 April 1919	Unknown	Disposition held in abeyance until arrival of the Assistant Secretary of the Navy. The obligation associated with this station was calculated to be $320,000
Irish Naval Stations			
Berehaven			All aviation equipment to be returned to the U.S. as being collected in Dubln. Final disposition awaited the arrival of the Assistant Secretary of the Navy. During the period of American usage the following total American and British expenditures were encountered:
Dublin			
Lough Foyle			
Queenstown	10 April 1919	203,175	
Wexford	Unknown	116,962	
Whiddy Island	Unknown	114,825	
Italian Naval Air Stations			
Rome			
Lake Bolsena			
Porto Corsini			
Pescara	Unknown	Unknown	Demobilization was scheduled for 15 January 1918
Ponta Delgada	24 January 1919	Evacuated	None

Summary

For its existence the U.S. Naval Air Service in Foreign Service executed 39 attacks on suspected German submarines, 10 of which were considered to have been at least partially successful, 100 tons of high explosives were dropped on enemy targets, and a total of 22,000 flights were made, during which greater than 800,000 nautical miles were patrolled. A force totaling 1,147 officers and 18,308 enlisted men operating 400 airplanes, 50 kite balloons, and three dirigibles expended this effort. The personnel of the Northern Bombing Group dropped a total of 155,998 pounds of bombs on various naval and military objectives in Belgium during their period of service (including those dropped while in the service of the British). For the war the Navy spent approximately $52,256,398 on aviation, $11,250,000 of which was spent on construction of facilities. Table 15 summarizes the activities of the Naval Air Stations in Foreign Service.

TABLE 15
SUMMARY OF ACTIVITY OF NAVAL AIR STATIONS IN FOREIGN SERVICE

Station	**Operations Commenced**	**Aircraft on 11 November 1918**	**Number of Flights**	**Sea Miles Patrolled**	**Number of Officers**	**Number of Men**
Brest (Seaplane)	1 August 1918	30 Seaplanes	221	7355	31	814
Fromentine	9 August 1918	14 Seaplanes	335	38009	31	372
Arachon	1 October 1918‘	7 Seaplanes	106	8727	26	318
L'Aber Vrach	23 September 1918	19 Seaplanes	355	29302	41	458
Ile Tudy	7 March 1918	21 Seaplanes	1238	104877	22	363
Le Croisic	18 November 1917	16 Seaplanes	1045	113324	24	337
St. Trojan	3 July 1918	13 Seaplanes	246	19533	26	343
Trequier	30 September 1918	8 Seaplanes	30	1380	16	266
Dunkerque	18 March 1918	12 Seaplanes	491	45630	30	477
Paimboeuf	15 March 1918	3 Dirigibles	257	48630	30	477
Guipavas	No Operation	1 Dirigible	-	-	15	396
Gujan	No Operation	None	-	-	10	240
Brest (K.B.)	Test Flights	22 K.B.	-	-	18	59
La Trinite	Test Flights	4 K.B.	-	-	5	150
La Pallice	Test Flights	4 K.B.	-	-	9	216
Pauillac	Test Flights					
(2 July 1918)	81 Seaplanes	372	15085	108	4034	
Moutchic	11 November 1917	24 Seaplanes	372	242320	57	493
Queenstown	30 September 1918	64	11568	72	1426	
Lough Foyle	3 September 1918	7 Seaplanes	41	6000	20	432
Wexford	18 September 1918	5 Seaplanes	98	19135	22	405
Whiddy Island	25 September 1918	3 Seaplanes	25	3870	18	400
Castletownbere (Berehaven)	21 May 1918	16 K.B.	Test Flights	-	12	91
Porto Corsini	25 July 1918	17 Seaplanes	743	?	27	360
Bolsena	20 February 1918	8 Seaplanes	5540	Training Flights	11	69
Killingholme	19 February 1918	46 Seaplanes	404	92797	91	1324
Eastleigh	24 September 1918	41 Planes	Test Flights	-	70	1928
Northern Bombing Group	20 July 1918	35 Landplanes	No Patrol Flights	-	294	2154
		Total War Flights			5,671	549,078
		Total Training Flights		16,347	242,320	
		Total	22,038	791,398	1147	18308

Note: The dates and numbers provided in this Table do not exactly agree with similar values given earlier in Table 4. This should not be surprising, due to the unspecified basis used by the various sources in deriving these values. Differences, which may vary by a factor of two to three weeks, should probably be considered to be equivalent until such time as more definitive information is available.

The reference to the Northern Bombing Group having "No Patrol Flights" is perhaps misleading. The concept is used only because of the different nature and intended purpose of the other stations noted in this listing.

Notes:

[1] Much of the material in this section of this Chapter is based on the document entitled *History of U.S. Naval Aviation, Foreign Service, French Unit, 1917-1918*

[2] Grossnick, Roy A., *Kite Balloons to Airships....The Navy's Lighter-than-air Experiments*, G.P.O., Washington, DC

[3] Turnbul, Archibald D, and Clifford L. Lord, *History of the United States Naval Aviation*, Yale University Press

[4] Coletta, Paolo E., *United States Navy and Marine Corps Bases, Overseas*, Greenwood Press

[5] ibid

[6] *History of U.S. Naval Aviation, Foreign Service, French Unit, 1917-1918*

[7] Personal correspondence with Mr. Roberto Gentilli

[8] Arthur, Reginald White, *Contact! Careers of Naval Aviators Assigned Numbers 1 to 2000*, Naval Aviator Register, Washington, DC, 1967

[9] Emons, Roger M., "The First Marine Aviation Force", *Cross and Cockade Journal (US)*, Vol. 6, Number 3

[10] Emmons, Roger M., "The First Marine Aviation Force", *Cross and Cockade Journal (US)*, Vol. 6, No. 2 pages 173-186 and Vol. 6, No. 3, pages 272-292

[11] Material in the Table is taken from the article entitled Naval Aviation Overseas, 1917-1919, Cross and Cockade Journal (U.S.), Vol. 4, No. 1

[12] Material in the Table is taken from the article entitled "Naval Aviation Overseas, 1917-1918", *Cross and Cockade Journal* (U.S.), Vol. 4, No. 1

[13] ibid

[14] Emons, Roger M., "The First Marine Aviation Force", Cross and Cockade Journal (U.S.), Vol. 6, No. 2, pages 173-186, and Vol. 6, No. 3 pages 272-292

Appendix A: Proposed Organization for Aeronautics

May 25, 1916

From: Chief of Naval Operations
To: Bureaus of Construction and Repair
Steam Engineering
Navigation
Ordnance
Yards and Docks

SUBJECT: Proposed Organization for Aeronautics.

1. The Chief of Naval Operations is by law charged with the operations of Aeronautics.
2. The General Board, as with other craft, will advise as to the number and general characteristics of aircraft. The types so advised will be considered by Operations and the data forwarded to the Bureau of Construction and Repair. The Bureau of Construction and Repair will prepare alternative plans and from these certain ones will be selected.
3. After conference with bureau chiefs, the Chief of Naval Operations will decide which craft are to be built by private individuals and which at Navy Yards; and will issue the necessary instructions. The bureaus will then prepare joint requisitions for such craft as are to be manufactured by private individuals; and will issue the necessary instructions to Navy Yards or Stations concerned, relative to the manufacture of such aircraft as are to be built at those yards or stations.
4. The bureaus will assume the same responsibility for repairs and upkeep of aircraft as for the other vessels of the Navy.
5. Repairs to aircraft not exceeding $300.00 may be authorized by the Commandants or yards or stations to which aeronautic allotments are made and by Commanding Officers of ships carrying aircraft.
6. Repairs costing between $300.00 and $500.00 may be authorized by the chiefs of bureaus.
7. Repairs costing more than $500.00 shall be authorized by the Secretary of the Navy.
8. Navy Yards and Stations and aeronautic parent ships shall forward N.S.A. Requisitions direct to the bureaus concerned. Other types of requisitions shall be forwarded to the bureaus concerned via the Navy Department (Operations-Materials).
9. No alterations to aircraft shall be made except as authorized by the bureaus with the approval of the Department.
10. The bureaus shall direct experimental and development work coming under the cognizance of the respective bureaus.
11. Construction, except by private individuals, as provided for above, can be carried out at the Aeronautic Station and the Washington Navy Yard.
12. Repairs to Fleet aircraft can be effected on board ship or at Navy yards, but always under the cognizance of the bureaus concerned.
13. Thus, the duties of the various bureaus should be as follows:

BUREAU OF CONSTRUCTION AND REPAIR

(a) In conjunction with other Bureaus prepare plans for new construction as outlined by the General Board and approved by Operations.

(b) Prepare plans for all structural elements.

(c) Prepare plans for model experiments.

(d) Retain plans of all aircraft.

(e) Keep files of aircraft data showing condition of craft from time to time.

(f) Supply Yards with plans for construction, repair, etc.

(g) Issue necessary instructions to Yards for manufacture, repair, etc. of aircraft.

(h) Make requisition for such material as is required to carry on the work of the Bureau.

BUREAU OF STEAM ENGINEERING

(a) In conjunction with the Bureau of Construction and Repair, prepare plans for new construction as outlined by General Board and approved by Operations.

(b) Prepare plans for power plane experiments.

(c) Retain plans of all different types of powered plane installations of aircraft.

(d) Keep files of power plant data showing conditions of same from time to time.

(e) Supply Yards with plans for construction, repair, etc.

(f) Issue necessary instructions to Yards for manufacture and repair of aircraft power plants.

(g) Make requisition for such material as is required to carry on the work of the Bureau.

BUREAU OF NAVIGATION

(a) In conjunction with the Bureau of Construction and Repair develop plans for new construction.

(b) Prepare experimental charts, diagrams, etc., to facilitate navigation and for experimental instruments under cognizance of the Bureau.

(c) Retain plans of instruments (under cognizance of the Bureau) installation for all aircraft.

(d) Keep files of instrument and equipment data of each aircraft, showing conditions of same from time to time.

(e) Prepare plans for signaling and navigation experiments.

(f) Issue necessary instruction to Yards for repair and installation of Instruments.

(g) Make requisition for such material as is required to carry out the work of the Bureau.

BUREAU OF ORDNANCE

(a) In conjunction with the Bureau of Construction and Repair, develop plans for new construction.

(b) Prepare plans for armament experiments.

(c) Retain plans of all different types of armament installations in aircraft.

(d) Keep files of armament data showing condition of same from time to time.

(e) Supply Yards with Plans for construction, installation, etc.

(f) Issue necessary instructions to Yards for manufacture and repair.

(g) Make requisition for such material as is required to carry out the work of the Bureau.

BUREAU OF YARDS AND DOCKS

(a) Prepare plans for Aeronautic Station and Navy Yard development.

(b) Issue necessary instructions to Aeronautic Stations and Yards for carrying out of plant development.

14. It is desired that the Bureaus make such recommendations relative to the proposed organization as the Bureaus may see fit.

Appendix B: Development of U.S. Navy Aeronautic Station

BuNav File 9321-62

August 3, 1916

From: Commandant.
To: The Secretary of the Navy
Via: Navy Department (Operations-Material)

Subject: Development of U.S. Navy Aeronautic Station.

References: (a) Secretary of the Navy's let. #2192-16 of May 24, 1916.
(b) Bu. Nav. Circular of Jan. 26, 1916.
(c) Comdt's let. 1064-2-10702 of July 11, 1916.

Enclosure: One (1).

1. In compliance with reference (a), the following report is made after conference and careful discussion of this subject with all hands of divisions now at the Station, the aviators now on the *North Carolina*, and the late Lieutenant (j.g.) R.C. Saufley, U.S.N., and the late Civil Engineer J.V. Rockwell, U.S. N. This report, therefore, does not express the views of the undersigned alone; the recommendations are unanimous except in one instance which will be pointed out later.

2. It is believed that the following should be the activities of the Navy Aeronautic Station at Pensacola.

I. AERONAUTIC TRAINING:

(a) The training and qualification of commissioned officers of the Navy (Naval Flying Corps), and Marine Corps, as Naval Aviators.

(b) The training and qualification of enlisted men of the Navy and Marine Corps as Quartermasters (Aeroplanes).

(c) The training and qualification of enlisted men of the Navy (Naval Flying Corps), and Marine Corps, as Airmen and Machinists (Aeronautics).

(d) The training and qualification of enlisted men of the Navy (Naval Flying Corps) as Quartermasters (Dirigible).

(e) The training and qualification of officers of the Navy (Naval Flying Corps) as Navy Air Pilots (Aeroplanes) and Navy Air Pilots (Dirigible).

(f) The development of standards in the following subjects: training of personnel, safety precautions in the operation of aircraft, and the care and preservation of aircraft and aircraft accessories, including forms for all records and reports.

(g) Development, under the cognizance of the Naval War College of Aircraft tactics, by game board methods and actual evaluations.

(h) Postgraduate course in Aeronautics for officers of the Navy and such others as the Department may designate.

II. REPAIRS, REBUILDING AND ALTERATIONS OF AIRCRAFT AS FOLLOWS:

(a) This station's Aircraft equipment.

(b) Fleet aircraft and accessories for such work as is beyond the fleet's capacity at sea.

(c) Aircraft of such other shore stations as may be established for such work as is beyond their capacity to perform economically.

III. DEVELOPMENT OF THE VARIOUS STANDARD TYPES OF AIRCRAFT AND THEIR ACCESSORIES

(a) Aerodynamic work: Wind tunnel and railway tests.

(b) Float tests; model and full size

(c) Brake horsepower and endurance tests of motors.

(d) Dynamic thrust and endurance tests of propellers.

(e) Tensile, bending, compression and she ring (sic) tests of aircraft material.

(f) Design of aircraft and their accessories, except armament.

(g) Preparation of detail specifications for all aeronautic material - raw and finished.

(h) Performance tests of new types of aircraft.

(i) Preparation of performance requirements of new types of aircraft.

IV. (IN TIME OF WAR) COAST PATROL AND RECONNAISSANCE OF THE N.W. GULF DISTRICT

3. The arguments for the foregoing activities (where argument appears necessary) with comments on the required facilities are, under their general headings, as follows: these are followed by remarks on the required organization:

1. AERONAUTIC TRAINING

4. Thus far the Station has been able to carry out the training of officers but little beyond the stage in paragraph 2 (a), which is graduation from the flying school. The first reason for this is a policy that the flying experience to be gained at Pensacola should be limited to the handling of school aeroplanes in flights that start and finish in the smooth waters of Pensacola Bay and the completion of the air pilot's practical education should be elsewhere—presumably in the fleet. That policy, in the opinion of the experienced aviators of the Navy is unsound, and there is much correspondence on file in which the Station has attempted to change it. If it is continued, officers will continue leaving Pensacola after having made only a bare beginning in their aeronautic training; they will have no more flying experience than can be gained at any of the many private flying schools in the country. Until then, the course of training here is extended to include an advanced flying course similar to that recommended herein or failing that, unless the Station is developed for the activities outlined in paragraph 2 III, it would be more economical to abandon the Station entirely and send our student aviators to private schools. There is a large overhead expense in the upkeep of this Station that thus far is not justified by the extent of its aeronautic activities.

5. It is sometimes difficult to draw parallels to aeronautic arguments, but in this case we may say that the present policy of elementary training and no advanced course would correspond to the following:

Graduate Midshipmen from the Naval Academy without giving them the summer practice cruises; their seamanship experience would then be limited to the handling of small boats in the smooth waters of Chesapeake Bay; their navigation experience would be limited to work with artificial horizons. However, in that case the graduate in going to the fleet would not be in danger of paying for his inexperience with his life as may well be the case if aviators leave here for duty in the fleet in accordance with the above policy.

6. As the Station has attempted to point out in prior correspondence, the problem of air navigation out of sight of land is an exceedingly difficult one; more so than navigation of any kind of a surface craft; also, if one misses his "landfall" at sea in an aeroplane his chances of being picked up are small, for his navigation mistake can cause very wide errors and an aeroplane on the water can be seen only a short distance.

7. To those of us who will have to do the actual flying work in the fleet and suffer the penalty for mistakes, it seems indisputable that before going to the Fleet we should be competent to use properly the best available means and methods of air navigation. Here at the Aeronautic Station the training in this line can be progressive and, on account of the shape of the Florida coast, it can be carried on without much danger of loss of aviators and aircraft. In the Fleet the conditions are not suitable for the embryo training in this and various other aeronautic tactics.

8. The greater part of the work in the Fleet will eventually necessitate flying in formation. Certainly the Fleet will be no place for aviators who are not experienced in formation flying where the conditions obviously are such that a very small mistake will be followed by certain destruction of at least two aeroplanes and their occupants. Formation flying training can be given at Pensacola to the best advantage - beginning it with the slower more easily handled school aeroplanes and working up to the larger and faster service types. This for much the same reason that a Naval Officer gets his first training in formation work in steam launches at the Naval Academy before he takes the deck in formation in the Fleet.

9. Officer should not be graduated from Pensacola when they are expert in handling only the school type of aeroplanes; only those who are practical flyers can fully appreciate the difference in the feeling of the controls of aeroplanes of different weights or of different distribution of weights, and their great difference in the way they respond to the controls. To be sure, an aviator who has become expert in one type of aeroplane will not take many days to feel thoroughly at home in another type; but during the time he is adapting himself to the strange aeroplane, it would be courting disaster to assign him to formation flying. At Pensacola before going to the Fleet, the aviator should be given the opportunity to become thoroughly familiar with the high speed and heavy types of aircraft that he will be called upon to use in the fleet. Also, he should be trained here where the facilities are excellent, to handle these types, first in smooth water in the bay, then outside the bay in rough water.

10. It seems hardly necessary to point out that the art of landing an aeroplane in rough water must be acquired progressively and that it will be decidedly a different matter in a slow light weight aeroplane and a high speed or heavy type. Furthermore, after landing on the surface of the water it is quite evident that maneuvering to get alongside a ship at sea will be a far different matter from running in on smooth water to a landing slip in front of a hangar.

11. Experience thus far with the catapult for launching an aeroplane from a ship's deck indicates that as far as the actual flight is concerned, practically no previous experience is necessary; the important part of this operation is adjustment of the catapult before firing; also, when in a rough sea, the proper timing of the shot to avoid bad attitudes of the aeroplane on release. It therefore seems reasonable to ask for the facilities for giving aviators a thorough working knowledge of the catapult before they go to the Fleet to use it. (sic) .....training has been given here is the fact that we have rarely had adequate equipment available. From June 1914 to September 1915 (about 16 months) there was no vessel at the Station for aeronautic purposes other than a coal barge. The *North Carolina* arrived in September 1915 but here aeroplane hoists were not completed and the only catapult available was the crude affair that had already been tested and which, as pointed out by the Station in July 1914, was unsuitable for use aboard ship. However, the apparatus was placed aboard the *North Carolina* and, in spite of makeshift arrangements, was used successfully for three flights; the fourth

resulted in a smash up in which, fortunately, the pilot was not injured. In November 1915, the redesign of the catapult, was finally authorized; the rebuilding was completed in June 9th and tests were completed July 12th. Two days later the *North Carolina* left, and the Station is now without any means of practical instruction with the Catapult or for training in picking up aeroplanes in rough water. It seems logical to state that for the proper aeronautic training of Aviators prior to graduation to the Fleet there should be permanently at this station at least one vessel fitted with a catapult and aeroplane hoists. The vessel need not be of any military value and it is believed it would be desirable to select a vessel of no military value; this both from an economical standpoint and to avoid the possibility of her being sent elsewhere in an emergency, as was the case with the *North Carolina* - absent from the Station for about fourteen months.

12. In November 1915 a detail of Reserve Torpedo Destroyers arrived here for the purpose of assisting in air navigation training and scouting experiments. As the Department discouraged the use of any school aeroplanes in this work, and as only one other aeroplane was available, not much could be done. However, all Naval Aviators then at the Station had at least one scouting flight 75 to 90 miles out of sight of land, and as the experience gave new thought for the solution of this problem it was very valuable. Also those aviators who undertook scouting flights this spring at Guantanamo have stated that they realized their air navigation training here although limited was of great assistance. The departure of the Destroyers from this Station for target practice in April 1915 put an end to our training and experiments in this line; since then the Station has asked for vessels for this work that are of no military value in order that they may be here permanently. The reason for vessels for attendance on this work seem obvious, but it may be said that none may expect mistakes by the beginner in this work that will entail a search for him in surface craft large enough to keep the sea in bad weather.

13. Thus far this Station has developed all standards in training personnel, safety precautions in the operation of aircraft, and the care and preservation of aircraft and their accessories, including forms for all reports and records. It seems reasonable to state that his sort of work should be done at one place to insure uniformity; if the Station is permitted to carry the training of aviators as far as is recommended herein, it will be more convenient to develop the above standards here than in the fleet or in the Department.

14. The development of tactics that relate to aircraft without relation to other units of the fleet, such as evolution of aircraft in formation, search problems, battle tactics against other aircraft, etc., etc., undoubtedly requires careful and progressive development under conditions that will insure a maximum of safety and economy. As there will probably always be available here a sufficient number of small and easily handled aeroplanes, such as are used for schoolwork, it would appear that Pensacola is well adapted for this development. In any case if an aviator is to be well equipped on graduation to the fleet he should be thoroughly conversant with all these matters and should get his first experience by game board methods. Furthermore, it appears essential that the Naval War College should be in touch with everything that is done in this line.

15. It is recognized that certain work with aircraft can be developed only in the fleet; this being the coordination of aircraft tactics with the tactics of other units of the fleet. For example, the employment of aircraft with scouting vessels in search problems; spotting gun fire of divisions (a different problem from spotting for a single ship); the methods of attack on submarines by aircraft and surface craft in cooperation; the methods of using a force of torpedo carrying aeroplanes in conjunction with the battle tactics of the first line ships (a feature that will surely be a very important factor in naval engagements in the not very distant future). Certainly aviators who may be graduated from this station with no more flying experience than that which accords with our former facilities are not at all competent to take up these last mentioned problems. To sum up, it is believed that the course of training for aviators at this Station should be such that on graduation to the fleet they will be fully qualified Navy Air Pilots.

16. At the present the Station has a very satisfactory flying school course for training aviators in the elementary stage, namely, to the point that they are able to pass their flying tests for qualification as Naval Aviators, attain a good understanding of the theory of flight and a good practical knowledge of the aeroplane and its power plant; this is the course authorized is Sec. 2 of reference (b).

17. Our facilities in sight of this part of the course are twelve tractor school aeroplanes under construction, of which the first has been delivered and the remainder will doubtless be ready by the time the hangars now under construction are completed. The housing and handling facilities for aeroplanes under construction are: Building #2; three new hangars not yet completed; and three piers each with two landing slips.

18. Building #27 will house ten (10) school aeroplanes or from five (5) to eight (8) service type aeroplanes (depending on their size). The three new hangars will each house six (6) school aeroplanes. The Department has stated that the Station may expect a quota of thirty-six (36) aeroplanes during the coming fiscal year. On this basis it is recommended that eighteen (18) be of the school type and the remainder be of the service type; this division will allow half for elementary training and the remainder for advanced training and experimental flying. The three new hangars will then just accommodate the school aeroplanes.

19. From prior experience it is estimated that each Instructor can take care of six (6) students in the elementary course and put them into condition for their advanced training in six months provided he has six aeroplanes assigned to him.

20. The most convenient method of taking in students will be three per Instructor per quarter; each Instructor will then average under his charge, three not flying alone and three flying alone; for those not flying alone he would reserve three aeroplanes; one in service, one standing by and one overhauling; for his three student's flying alone he would then have three aeroplanes, one in service, one standby and one overhauling. It is believed that from past experience this will permit an uninterrupted flying school course, and with these facilities we would have an output from the flying school of nine each quarter or thirty-six per annum. In reference (c) a duplication of the three new hangars, water front facilities, etc., has been asked for on the Warrington beach; if this be granted, and

eighteen (18) more school aeroplanes are provided, the capacity of the flying school can be doubled, making it seventy-two per annum.

21. The material required for the elementary course is as follows:-

Eighteen (18) tractor type school aeroplanes as stated above; each with a spare motor and two spare propellers. Twelve (12) aeroplanes of this type are under construction and all will probably be delivered within six weeks.

Four (4) gasoline launches of the type now on the North Carolina; these for towing in aeroplanes with motor trouble or minor accidents; also for first aid work; two continuously on duty on stations in the bay. There are none of these at hand.

Four (4) Viper or similar type speed boats; there are now two on hand, (one requiring extensive repairs), so two (2) additional should be provided. These are required for medical service in event of bad accidents, - two always on duty during flying hours.

One (1) Floating Derrick for picking up wrecked aeroplanes in the bay; on is under construction.

Two (2) motor sailors for general station use; there are two on hand, (one requiring extensive repairs).

Two (2) motor dories for aeroplane towing in shallow water; one now on hand.

22. For housing the eighteen (18) aeroplanes recommended for the advanced course and experimental flying we have Building No. 27 and, if provided, the aviation training ship assigned to this course; the erecting shop, (Building No. 44) will take care of the remainder of these eighteen (18) aeroplanes; those assigned to experimental work would be always housed in Building No. 44.

23. The material required for the advanced course and experimental flying is as follows:

Eighteen (18) service type aeroplanes; the number of these in sight cannot be stated at the present time as it is not known which of those under construction are to be assigned to the station. The two Thomas tractors and the two Burgess Dunne's now at the Station may for the present be considered a part of this eighteen (18), although they will be useful principally for experimental flying.

One (1) aviation training ship fitted with a catapult, aeroplane hoists, and storage facilities similar to the installation on the *North Carolina*. As mentioned before a vessel of no military value will answer for this purpose and would be more economical and less likely to be diverted from this duty. If not a man-of-war, it should be equipped with a broadside battery of eight or ten one pounder, three pounder or six pounder guns to be used for training in spotting and communication. As regards the size of this vessel, the only requirement is sufficient space aft for the catapult installation.

Three (3) seagoing launches for sea patrol work, preferable with gasoline motors and speed of 18 knots; however, pending availability of these, the Navy picket boat type steamers would be fairly satisfactory. These to be equipped with a small radio set. None are on hand.

NOTE: For picking up broken down aeroplanes at sea, if a tug is provided for dirigible work and general stations use, it could be used for this purpose in addition to other duties, when the aeroplane ship was not outside. The three large launches would be used to assist in handling the dirigible as well as for sea patrol work.

24. For the flying school course, with hangar and water front facilities now in sight, we require the following personnel:-

One (1) Officer in Charge of Flying School. There is one now on hand.

Three (3) Flying Instructors; there are two now on hand, not counting the one who is officer in charge; the third can soon be developed here from one of the recently qualified naval aviators at the Station.

One (1) Typewriter for flight and other records of all aeroplanes in elementary flying school, and other clerical work including care of aeronautical library. One yeoman now on hand.

One (1) Janitor for each hangar. There are none now on hand for this purpose; three more will be required when the hangars now under construction are completed.

One (1) Aeroplane crew (enlisted) of four (4) men each for aeroplane in the elementary school; for the eighteen aeroplanes proposed this will require a total of seventy-two (72) enlisted men of which on an average half will be student mechanics; but as a portion of these will be taken from shop work from time to time as the civilian employees in the repair shops become competent to work without instruction by enlisted men, no definite request at this time can be made for additional enlisted men required for aeroplane crews.

One (1) Chief Quartermaster and eight (8) Quartermasters, or seamen, or signalmen for aeroplane lookout duty. None now on hand so all of this detail are requested as soon as practicable. At the present time it is customary to detail one man in each aeroplane crew to keep watch on his aeroplane, but his when the Station has the eighteen school aeroplanes and eighteen service aeroplanes, contemplated will be impracticable unless an extraordinarily large watch tower were built; besides this is objectionable as it interferes with the work of the aeroplane crews, which on the proposed basis of four (4) men per aeroplane is the minimum practicable for taking care of and handling school aeroplanes. If the above lookout detail is provided it is proposed to divide the bay into sectors for observation and establish a more efficient and satisfactory means of observation as well as communication with rescue and towing boats than is at present in use.

One (1) Wrecking Derrick crew consisting of one (1) coxswain, one (1) electrician (for engineer) and two (2) deck hands, seamen ordinary seamen. All these will be required when wrecking derrick is received.

Four (4) Speed Boat crews, each consisting on one (1) coxswain, one (1) machinist 2nd class or engineer, and one (1) deck hand, seamen or ordinary seamen. Two crews now on hand, so two more will be required when the two additional speed boats are provided.

One (1) Sailing Launch crew consisting of one (1) coxswain, one (1) fireman, first class or machinist 2nd class for engineer, and one (1) deck hand seaman or ordinary seaman. All on hand.

Two (2) Motor dory crews each consisting of one (1) coxswain or one (1) seaman. One on hand so one more will be required when the other motor dory is provided.

One (1) Chief Boatswain's Mate for general charge of Station boats; one on hand who will go on retired list shortly; the Bureau of Navigation has already been asked to replace him.

25. The Personnel required for the advanced flying course is as follows:

One (1) Officer in Charge. It is believed that with an output from the elementary flying school of nine students each quarter that one officer, if an experienced flyer, can handle this course; at present there is no suitable officer available at the Station who can be spared from other duties to take charge of this course, and it is therefore most desirable that one of the Navy Air Pilots now on duty elsewhere be ordered here for this work; of these the only ones in my opinion capable of taking charge of this course are:

Lieut. T.G. ELLYSON, U.S.N.
Lieut. J.H. TOWERS, U.S.N.
Lieut. (j.g.). P.N.L. BELLINGER, U.S.N.
Lieut.. (j.g.). G. deC. CHEVALIER, U.S.N.

However, it is believed that in not more than six months after this course is established with the facilities asked for, a suitable relief can be selected from one of the officers graduated from the course. A tentative estimate for the length of this course is six months; later, no doubt, after it is well systematized, it could be shortened considerably.

One (1) Typewriter for aeroplane records, flight report, reports of experiments, etc. None on hand.

One (1) Janitor for Building No. 27. None on hand.

One (1) Complement for aviation training ship. This depends upon the size and character of the vessel provided.

One (1) Aeroplane crew (enlisted) of four (4) men each, for each aeroplane assigned to the advanced course and experimental flying: for the eighteen (18) aeroplanes proposed this will require a total of seventy-two (72) enlisted men. There are no men now assigned to this duty, and the number required cannot be stated for the reason given in remarks after crews for elementary school aeroplanes.

Four (4) Seagoing Launch crews each consisting of one (1) coxswain, one (1) second class machinist for engineering and two (2) deckhands, seamen or ordinary seamen. None on hand; all should be provided when the launches are provided. If steam picket boats are provided each crew will require one additional man, a fireman or coal passer.

26. If the facilities for the elementary course are doubled a certain part of the facilities for the advanced course should also be doubled; namely, eighteen (18) additional service type aeroplanes and the three additions to new hangars now under construction asked for in reference (c). Some of these aeroplanes can be taken care of in the additional aeroplane erecting shop asked for in reference (c). Otherwise the material requirements need not be augmented.

27. As regards material and personnel for dirigible training, in view of the uncertainty as to delivery of the school dirigible under contract, it is not now practicable to make complete recommendations; this will be made subject of a separate letter as soon as practicable.

28. The inclusion of students supplied in accordance with the act for a naval flying corps now under consideration in Congress may necessitate additional instructors for the purpose of training such officers in navigation, deviation of the compass, seamanship, ordnance and gunnery tactics, military law, and such other subjects which are already familiar to the line officers of the Navy ordered here for flying instruction. Until the final passage of the bill it is impracticable to outline the personnel required for such work; furthermore, as such instruction would simply be a duplication of parts of the Naval Academy course, it is possible that these students could be given a special course at that place. For example give them here, upon entry to the service, the elementary flying course of six months; this would weed out those who are not temperamentally and physically suitable for flying, or are not amenable to Navy discipline, or not industrious enough to keep up with the Station course in the theory of flight. Then send them for a year to the Naval Academy, and, if they pass their final examination there, return them here for the advanced flying course, this tentative proposition is suggested to suit the probationary period of two years mentioned in the bill, but it would seem more desirable to be able to give them two years at the Naval Academy instead of one.

II. REPAIRS, REBUILDING AND ALTERATIONS OF AIRCRAFT

29. There appears little need for argument as to the necessity of these activities; however, there has not been unanimous agreement by the heads of divisions as to the extent to which this should be carried; all agree it should eventually cover manufacture of all kinds of structural parts and a minority believe it should include manufacture of motor parts. The Station is now, with the exception of a few tools being negotiated for, well equipped with material facilities for manufacture of structural replacements and experience has been had in all lines of this work. But for manufacture of motor parts a considerable number of necessary special tools and jigs are not on hand, and as there yet is no standard type of aeronautic motor, it appears too early to make investments in tools and jigs that may in a few months be out of date. Furthermore, there are now being organized several motor manufacturing companies with whom we would have much difficulty in competing on account of their excellent resources in shop facilities and engineering talent. The majority of us therefore believe our motor work should be continued as heretofore, using finished material for replacements, and keeping the motor companies advised as to all individual features in their product that appear unreliable.

30. The same arguments are not applied to structural work for the following reasons:-

1st. The really vital part of an aircraft as regards safety is its structure.

2nd. The number of competent aircraft structure engineers in the country is very limited.

3rd. The development of structure manufacturing facilities here is required to provide one of the facilities necessary for activity III which will discussed presently.

31. It should be noted here that the development of a civil force for this work has been slow for the following reasons:-

1st. There has been difficulty in obtaining the necessary clerical and drafting personnel for operation of the planning division; this difficulty will no doubt disappear after the passage of the 1917 appropriation bill which provides for clerical and drafting pay in the aviation appropriation.

2nd. We have had first to educate our commissioned and enlisted force in a line of work that is new to the Navy; then train the civil employees none of whom have had prior experience in aeronautic work.

3rd. The training of the civil force has been slower than if their employment were in a line where errors in work would not be likely to be followed by loss of life.

32. There is therefore still a majority of enlisted men in the repair force for instructing as well as instruction purposes. However, if the Station is allowed the commissioned and Class IV personnel requested elsewhere in this letter, it is believed that within this fiscal year it will be possible to complete the development of the civil shop force.

33. In paragraph I (3) of reference (c) an additional aeroplane erecting shop has been asked for; this will be necessary when the Station has its quota of thirty-six aeroplanes, for even with the number here during the past year there has been congestion in building No. 44, the present aeroplane erecting shop.

34. The Station is now preparing plans and estimates for converting Building No. 29 into a fabric shop; the upper floor for covering the wings and other surfaces; the lower floor, with an exhaust ventilation system, for treating and varnishing fabric, and other varnishing work that requires clean air. No funds out of aviation 1917 are necessary for this purpose as there remains about $14,000 of a continuous appropriation of $15,000 for the modification of this building.

35. The commissioned and Class IV vacancies in the personnel required for this activity are shown in the remarks under Organization.

III. DEVELOPMENT OF THE VARIOUS STANDARD TYPES OF AIRCRAFT AND THEIR ACCESSORIES

36. It should be noted particularly that all the civilian aeronautic engineers in this country have a serious handicap in their design of Naval Aircraft, namely, they are not seamen, and therefore cannot appreciate fully an aircraft's deep-sea requirements. All designs of aeroplanes they have thus far developed for the Navy are nothing more nor less than land aeroplanes fitted with floats instead of wheels and skid; they are therefore, suitable only for comparatively smooth water work and maintenance in a shore hangar instead of being adaptable to deep sea work, launching from a catapult, and maintenance aboard ship. Even the 6000 pound aeroplane manufactured at the Washington Navy Yard is to some extent subject to the same criticism; its float arrangement will be unstable in rough water and a high wind, and also is not the best installation as regards use from the catapult.

37. The British Government recognizing the wide divergence in land and sea aeroplane requirements has, it is reported, arranged that the individual manufacturers shall restrict their product to either one type or the other.

38. When Naval Aircraft have been developed to the point that their standardization in design is on a parity with the standardization in design of other naval craft, then will satisfactory designing be practicable in the Department, or elsewhere, at distances remote from naval air craft operations. In the meantime it is believed that best and most rapid results can be attained by concentration of the majority of the Naval talent available for designing at this station; the reasons for this statement are as follows:

1st. Ideas of a number of active naval flyers can be discussed and consolidated with the ideas of the theoretical designers without recourse to correspondence; as a rule when discussion is by letter there is misunderstanding at both ends and much loss of time in arriving at definite conclusions. In this connection it should be noted that there are here now at least two line officers, active flyers, with designing ability and ideas based on actual sea flying experience; also all other naval aviators at the Station have a thorough grounding in the theory of flight and some will develop designing ability. On the other hand, thus far in Washington, the designing has been practically one-man work. To be sure this has been done by an expert in theory who is also a qualified Air Pilot, but he has had opportunity for very little active flying in the past year and has not yet had any practical experience in sea flying. Furthermore even the best designer is liable to error when he has no competent designer to check his assumptions and computations.

2nd. At this Station there is always a variety of types of aeroplanes in service each of which has some feature, detail or manufacturing process that is worth of incorporation in the standard design or else forms a basis for a new idea. Also the weakness of inconvenience of individual features are directly evident and the means for correction are often self-suggestion to a designer on the spot.

3rd. Facilities for smooth water and sea tests are available at all seasons of the year; new types can be tested without the delay of waiting for suitable weather or shipments of a distant point; also necessary modifications as well as readjustments can be made at once without the delay of reference by correspondence to a distant designing force.

4th. Ample space is available on the Naval Reservation for all laboratory facilities that can be desired for test and research work in connection with designing.

5th. Last but not least, there is the consistent association of the designing force with the active flying, the maintenance of aircraft, and the large and small troubles that appear from day to day. In other words, there is an atmosphere, which affects all concerned from chief designer to copyist draftsman, and this atmosphere is practically nonexistent in Washington.

39. There are now two Naval Constructors who have specialized in the theory of flight and aircraft design, namely Naval Constructors Richardson and Hunsaker. It is recommended that one or

the other be detailed to this Station for duty in charge of aircraft design and development of the laboratory and research facilities that appear desirable at this station. The officer so detailed could have additional duty in supervising the theoretical instruction of all students and could organize a post graduate course for those graduate flyers who demonstrate their adaptability for designing.

40. In reference (c) paragraph 1, items (7) and (8) have been asked for with the above procedure in view. As mentioned therein the railway testing apparatus would provide a facility for test beyond the capabilities of a wind tunnel . the duplication here of the Washington Yard wind tunnel would enlarge the Navy's capacity for work of this character besides providing a Government means for checking the Washington Yard data.

41. It is believed that, at a small expense, one of the speed boats at the Station can be fitted with an attachment that will permit test of float models with reasonable accuracy and at much higher speeds than can be used in the model basin at the Washington Yard. For comparative tests of full size floats, there will always be an aeroplane available.

42. For the necessary tests of raw materials used in aeronautic work a 100,000# Olsen testing machine suitable for 12 foot compression tests and ten foot tension tests; and a 20,000 pound Olsen wire testing machine are ordered; also there is a Kempograph already on hand for testing fabric.

43. A brake horsepower testing stand for the Station is now being manufactured at the Washington Yard and is expected in about six weeks; a building for its installation is completed. The Station is now preparing specifications for 250 H.P. electric motor suitable for testing the strength of propellers. No facilities are at present in sight for dynamic thrust tests of propellers but it is believed they can be devised here without great difficulty.

44. These arguments are not intended to imply that the Navy should absorb all the designing of Naval Aircraft; on the contrary it is believed that the more independent manufacturers we have interested the better will be the product. If a number of independent engineering groups are in competition there will certainly be more rapid perfection of details. But as intimated before, it is believed that the manufacturers are wasting time as well as money until they are shown certain guiding features in Naval Aircraft design that can be developed promptly only by the Navy, and I am convinced that some radical changes in present designs will be found necessary.

45. The Station has already done considerable work in the development of aircraft accessories, the longest job thus far undertaken being the redesign of the catapult installation on the *North Carolina*. If an aviation ship is provided as requested elsewhere in this letter, then the Station will be in a good position to take care of the design work required in connection with standardization of catapult details and also of aeroplane stowage and hoisting apparatus. The Station has had some experience in instrument design, having already produced a very satisfactory type of Incidence Indicator, and is nearing completion of an experimental air speed meter and course protractor that appear promising. Another item in the list of aircraft accessories developed at the Station is the water brake, which it is expected will be tested out before the end of this summer; this in an attachment that will facilitate landing high speed aeroplanes in rough water and also will assist a pilot to make landings at night.

46. The Bureau of Steam Engineering has already taken steps to make this Station the headquarters for design of aircraft radio outfits.

ORGANIZATION REQUIRED

47. The present organization scheme at Pensacola with little alteration will take care of the foregoing activities on any scale desired. At present and ever since the Station has existed, there have been difficulties due to shortages in the commissioned and Class IV personnel; the most serious difficulty being the fact that, with one recent exception, none of the line officers besides the Commandant has had prior experience in Navy business methods ashore. Another difficulty has been the fact that on account of shortage of officers it has always been necessary to assign students to duties that interfere largely with their aeronautic training, both practical and theoretical. The methods of prosecuting work are shown in enclosure A; it will be noted presently that the Inspection force as now organized is, in the aeronautic work, entirely commissioned or enlisted, and it is believed that adherence to this procedure will always be desirable in this work. The Inspectors and sub-inspectors have additional duties as instructors, not only for student officers and men, but also for the civil employees; this far no civil employees have been obtained who have had any previous experience in aeronautic work. The organization of the Station is in the following divisions:

I	Administration Division
II	Flight Division
III	Aero. Planning Division
IV	Yard Planning Division
V	Erecting Division
VI	Motor Division
VII	Radio Division
VIII	Shop Division
IX	Yard Division
X	Supply Division
XI	Accounting Division
XII	Disbursing Division
XIII	Medical Division
XIV	Marine Guard

48. Yard Departments have not been established in view of paragraph 12 of the Secretary of the Navy's letter,- subject: Organization for the continued development of an Aeronautic Service and Establishment of an Aeronautic Station at Pensacola, (not dated; written sometime in Autumn of 1914), which reads, "expect that for the present no yard departments will be organized." It is believed that Station has now developed to the point where it would be appropriate to organize by departments; if this is authorized the only changes necessary in the present organization would be the grouping of certain of the above division into Department, which can be effected without confusion; the organization may then be as follows:-

I. Administration Department
II. Flight Department
III. Manufacture and Repair Department
(1) Aero Planning Division
(2) Erecting Division
(3) Motor Division
(4) Test and Research Division
(5) Radio Division
(6) Shop Division
IV. Public Works Department
(1) Yard Planning Division
(2) Yard Division
V. Supply Department
VI. Accounting Department
VII. Disbursing Department
VIII. Medical Department
IX. Marine Guard

49. The above regrouping need not necessitate any change in sub-division into section or the distribution of personnel shown in paragraph 51. It is recommended for the present that the incumbent as Commandant of the Station be a Navy Air Pilot. this for the reason that all activities here must, for safety as well as efficiency, be subordinate to the work of the station in the air, and the administrative head should have an intimate knowledge of the conditions that are to be met; he must occasionally make decisions between conflicting recommendations of the active flyers that can only be made intelligently when he has had ample flying experience and has a sound theoretical knowledge of flight. Lacking these two qualifications he is dependent on the advice of his subordinates and how well he know which are best qualified to advise him? Furthermore, he has always to contend with the natural inclination of younger officers to ignore risk in operations that concern them personally. An administrative head who is not an active flyer is liable to err in one or the other of the following ways; either he will be so cautious that little progress will be made, or, he will be so bold that lives are sacrificed needlessly.

50. Our most urgent need in personnel is a Planning Superintendent with prior experience in such work and a thorough knowledge of material. The Bureau of Construction and Repair has stated that a Naval Constructor would be ordered as soon as practicable; it is requested that unless this can be done promptly that a suitable line officer be selected for this duty from among those who have had Navy Yard experience since 1909.

51. The commissioned, Class IV, and leading enlisted billets required in the above organization for the activities in sight for the coming year are shown below with the rank or rating of present incumbent in first column to the right and the desired complement in the second column to the right. An asterisk is placed in the right column to indicate billets that cannot be filled from the Station force:

I. ADMINISTRATION DIVISION

Commandant	Lieut.Comdr. (Navy Air Pilot) (Navy Air Pilot)	Commander or Lieut. Comdr.
Aid to Commandant	Lieut.(j.g.) Naval Aviator	Naval Aviator
	(1) Executive Section.	
Captain of the Yard	Lt.Comdr.(Student Naval Aviator)	*Lt.Comdr. (Not under flying orders)
Chief Master at Arms	Chief Master at Arms	Chief Master at Arms
Chief Yeoman	Chief Yeoman	Chief Yeoman
Captain of the Watch	Captain of the Watch	Captain of the Watch
Messenger	Enlisted man	Messenger or messenger boy
	(2) Correspondence Section.	
Inside Superintendent	Lieut. (j.g.) Naval Aviator	Lieut. or Lieut. (j.g.) Naval Aviator
Chief Clerk	———	*Chief Clerk
File	Yeoman 1st Class	*File Clerk
Stenographer	Steno. & Typewriter	Steno. & Typewriter
Mail Clerk	Watchman	*Mail Clerk
(3)	Labor Board	
Senior Member	Lieutenant	Captain of the Yard
Member	Lieut.(j.g.) detached duty.	Aero Planning Supt.
Member	———	Yard Planning Supt.
Clerk	Clerk (authorized)	Clerk

II. FLIGHT DIVISION

Flight Superintendent	———	Lieut.Cmdr. or Lieut Navy Air Pilot
Clerk	———	*Steno. & Typewriter

Clerk	Yeoman 1st Class	*Typewriter
Messenger	Helper, general	*Messenger or Messenger Boy

(1) Flying School

Officer in Charge	Lieut.(j.g.) Navy Air Pilot	Lieut. or Lieut. (j.g.) Naval Aviator
Flying Instructor	Lieut.(j.g.) Navy Air Pilot	Navy Air Pilot or Naval Aviator
Flying Instructor	Lieut.(j.g.) Navy Air Pilot	Navy Air Pilot or Naval Aviator
Flying Instructor	————	Navy Air Pilot or Naval Aviator

(2) Dirigible School

Officer in Charge	Lieut.Cmdr. (Student Naval Aviator)	Navy Air Pilot
Flying Instructor	Lieut. (j.g.) Naval Aviator)	Navy Air Pilot

(3) Advanced Flying Section

Officer in Charge	————	*Navy Air Pilot

(4) Patrol Section

Chief Boatswain's Mate	————	Chief Boatswain's Mate
Chief Quartermaster	————	*Chief Quartermaster

III. AERO PLANNING DIVISION

Planning Supt.	Lieut. (j.g.) Naval Aviator	*Naval Constructor (Not on aeronautic duty)
Ass't Planning Supt.	Lieut. (j.g.) Naval Aviator	Naval Aviator
Ass't Planning Supt.	Chief Machinist	Naval Aviator
Stenographer	Steno. & Typewriter	Steno. & Typewriter (Temporary)

(1) Estimate Section

Chief Planner	Aero. Draftsman	Aero Draftsman
Planner	Chief Machinist Mate	Special Mechanic
Planner	Chief Machinist Mate	Special Mechanic
Planner	Chief Machinist Mate	Special Mechanic
Clerk	Clerk	Clerk
Clerk	————	*Clerk
Typewriter	Typewriter	Typewriter
Messenger	Enlisted man	*Messenger or messenger boy

(2) Drafting Section

Expert Aero. Aid.	Ordnance Draftsman	*Expert Aero Aid
Draftsman	Ship Draftsman	Aero Draftsman
Draftsman	————	*Aero Draftsman
Draftsman	————	*Aero Draftsman
Copyist Draftsman	————	*Copyist Aero Draft.
Copyist Draftsman	————	*Copyist Aero Draft.

NOTE: If Station takes up Aeroplane design, add 4 draftsmen and 2 copyist draftsman to the above.

(3) Progress Section

Progressman	Chief Gunners Mate	*Progressman
Progressman	Blacksmith	*Progressman
Laborer	Laborer	Laborer
Laborer	Laborer	Laborer

IV. YARD PLANNING DIVISION

Planning Supt.	Ass't. Civil Engineer	Ass't. or Civil Engr.
Stenographer	Steno. & Typewriter	Steno. & Typewriter
Messenger	______	*Messenger or messenger boy
	(1) Estimates Section	
Planner	______	Special Mechanic
Clerk	Clerk	Clerk
Clerk	Clerk	Clerk
	(2) Drafting Section	
Draftsman	Structural Steel work drftsn.	*Structural Steel Work draftsman
Draftsman	______	*Structural Steel work draftsman
Copyist Draftsman	______	*Copyist Structural Steel work draftsman
	(3) Progress Section	
Progressman	______	*Progressman
	(4) Contract Section	
Inspector	Ass't. Civil Engineer	Ass't. Civil Engineer
Sub-Inspector	Sub-Inspector	Sub-Inspector

V. ERECTING DIVISION

Inspector in Charge	Lieut. (Navy Air Pilot)	Navy Air Pilot
Ass't. Inspector	Lieut.(j.g.) Naval Aviator	Naval Aviator
Ass't. Inspector	Ensign (Student Naval Aviator)	Naval Aviator
Sub-Inspector	Enlisted man	C.P.O., P.O., or N.C.O.
Sub-Inspector	Enlisted man	C.P.O., P.O., or N.C.O.
Sub-Inspector	Enlisted man	C.P.O., P.O. or N.C.O.
Sub-Inspector	Enlisted man	C.P.O., P.O., or N.C.O.
Quartermaster in Charge	______	*Quartermaster in Charge
Clerk	______	*Steno. & Typewriter
Timekeeper	Helper, general	*Timekeeper
Messenger	Boy	*Messenger or messenger boy

VI. MOTOR DIVISION

Inspector-in-Charge	Lieut.(j.g.) Naval Aviator	Navy Air Pilot
Ass't. Inspector	Lieut.(j.g.) (Student Naval Aviator)	Naval Aviator
Ass't. Inspector	______	Naval Aviator
Sub-Inspector	Enlisted man	C.P.O. or P.O.
Motor Sub-Inspector	Enlisted man	C.P.O. or P.O.
Motor Sub-Inspector	______	C.P.O. or P.O.
Quarterman-in-Charge	Sergeant U.S.M.C.	*Quarterman-in-Charge
Clerk	______	*Typewriter
Timekeeper	Helper, general	Use Erecting Division Timekeeper
Messenger	Enlisted man	*Messenger or messenger boy

VII. TEST DIVISION

Officer-in-Charge	Using Erecting Div. Inspector	*Officer who has specialized in theory of Aeronautic
Clerk	______	*Steno. & Typewriter

VIII. RADIO DIVISION

District Supt.	Lieut. (j.g.) P.G. in Radio (Nay Yd. N.O.)	Lieut. (j.g.) P.G. in Radio
	(1) Aero Radio Section	
Inspector	Expert Radio Aid	Expert Radio Aid
	(2) Radio Station	
Electrician-in-Charge	Chief Electrician (Radio)	Chief Elec. (Radio)

IX. SHOP DIVISION

Inspector-in-Charge	————	*Naval Constructor or line officer not under flying orders
Ass't. Inspector	Chief Carpenter	Chief Carpenter
Ass't. Inspector	Chief Machinist (Ordered)	Chief Machinist
Sub-Inspector	Enlisted man	C.P.O. or P.O.
Sub-Inspector	Enlisted man	C.P.O. or P.O.
Sub-Inspector	Enlisted man	C.P.O. or P.O.
Sub-Inspector	Enlisted man	C.P.O. or P.O.
Sub-Inspector	Enlisted man	C.P.O. or P.O.
Sub-Inspector	Enlisted man	C.P.O. or P.O.
Sub-Inspector	Enlisted man	C.P.O. or P.O.
Sub-Inspector	Enlisted man	C.P.O. or P.O.
Sub-Inspector	Enlisted man	C..P.O. or P.O.
Sub-Inspector	Enlisted man	C.P.O. or P.O.
Shop Foreman	————	*Foreman
Ass't. Foreman	Chief Carpenter's Mate	Master Joiner or (Woodworking trades) Quarterman-in-Charge
Ass't. Foreman	Instrument Maker	Master Mechanic (Metal working trades)
Clerk	————	*Clerk
Timekeeper	————	*Timekeeper
Timekeeper	————	*Timekeeper
Messenger	Enlisted man	*Messenger or messenger boy

X. YARD DIVISION

Public Works Foreman	Quarterman Engine Tender	*Public Works Foreman
Timekeeper	Helper - General	*Timekeeper
	(1) Building and Grounds Section	
Quarterman	————	Quarterman
Inspector	Using Ass't. Civil Engr.	*Instrument man
Ass't. Inspector	————	*Rodman
	(2) Power Plant Section	
Power Plant Foreman	Using Electrical Expert Aid	*Quarterman-Electrician- in-Charge
Inspector	Electrical Expert Aid	Electrical Expert Aid

XI. SUPPLY DIVISION

Supply Officer	P.A. Paymaster	P.A. Master
Ass't. Supply Officer	Pay Clerk	Pay Clerk
Chief Clerk	Chief Clerk	Chief Clerk
Steno. & Typewriter	Steno. & Typewriter	Steno. & Typewriter

	(1) Supply Section	
Clerk (Office)	Clerk	Clerk
Clerk (Office)	Clerk	Clerk
Clerk (Office)	Clerk	Clerk
Clerk (Office)	Clerk	Clerk
Clerk (Storehouse)	Chief Yeoman	Clerk
Clerk (Storehouse)	Yeoman, 2nd Class	Clerk
Store Laborer	Store Laborer	Store Laborer
Store Laborer	Store Laborer	Store Laborer
Shop Store Supervisor	———————	*Shop Store Sup.
	(2) Purchasing Section	
Clerk	Using Chief Clerk	*Clerk

XII. ACCOUNTING DIVISION

Accounting Officer	Using Supply Officer	Use Supply Officer
Clerk	Clerk	Clerk
Clerk	———————	*Clerk

XIII. DISBURSING DIVISION

Disbursing Officer	Ass't. Paymaster	Ass't. Paymaster
Ass't. Disbursing Officer	Pay Clerk	Pay Clerk
	(1) Pay Station	
Clerk	———————	*Clerk
	(2) Commissary Section	
Commissary Steward	Commissary Steward	Commissary Steward
Chief Yeoman	———————	Chief Yeoman
Yeoman, 2nd Class	———————	Yeoman, 2nd Class

XIV. MEDICAL DIVISION

	(1) Dispensary Section	
Medical Officer	P.A. Surgeon	P.A. Surgeon or Surgeon
	(2) Sanitation Section	
Sanitation officer	P.A. Surgeon	P.A. Surgeon

XV. MARINE GUARD

Commanding Officer	Captain, U.S.M.C.	Marine Officer

52. Copies of this letter are attached for the files of the Bureaus of Construction and Repair, Steam Engineering and Navigation. It is realized that some of the matter discussed may require further explanation and I therefore request orders to Washington on temporary duty for consultation on this subject. I request most urgently that none of my recommendations be acted upon unfavorably until I have had a verbal hearing on the Department.

/S/ H.C. Mustin

Appendix C: Organization of Naval Flying Corps

954-12-125995

November 3, 1916

From: Commandant
To: Bureau of Navigation

Subject: Organization of Naval Flying Corps

Reference: BuNav. Let. 5901-610 n6h, of Sept. 21, 1916

Enclosures: (2)

1. In compliance with reference (a) there are submitted herewith suggested regulations for the organization of the Naval Flying Corps. It will be noted that the proposed organization is similar to the organization of the Marine Corps; my reasons for attempting to parallel that highly efficient organization are as follows:

2. The Naval Flying Corps may be regarded as bearing a relation to the Naval Service very much akin to the status of the Marine Corps; as regards interior discipline and management, like the Marine Corps, the Flying Corps as far as the laws permit, should be an independent organization although always an auxiliary to the Naval Force. This for the reason that its major activities are along highly specialized lines distinctly different from the activities of the Naval surface craft. The commissioned personnel require a special training which must be extremely thorough, both for efficiency and the avoidance, even in peace time, of unnecessary loss of life.

3. The operations of the Flying Corps, as regards supply and maintenance, can originate either from the Fleet as a base or from shore bases independent of the Fleet. While basing in the Fleet, detachments of the Flying Corps, like detachments of the Marine Corps, are practically inert until they move from the sea to another element; for its reason for being, the one goes into the air, the other goes ashore.

4. Although the wording in the Naval Flying Corps bill is somewhat obscure, there appears to be no doubt that a Naval Flying Corps has been created by law; whether officers of the Navy and Marine Corps detailed to flying duty are considered in the Corps or simply on duty with the Corps, real efficiency and credit can not be assured unless all officers connected with Naval Aviation are treated as one special group.

5. As regards the material problems of the Flying Corps, it is fortunate that the aviation funds for the coming fiscal year are appropriated to be spent as the Secretary of the Navy may direct. This fact in connection with the creation by law of a Naval Flying Corps, makes it practicable and apparently legal to put Naval Aviation on a sound working basis with a strong centralized authority for its management.

6. The use of the word aircraft in connection with naval aviation seems to have had an unfortunate influence on the progress of the branch of the service work. The Department has apparently regarded aviation units as small ships and has treated their production, maintenance, and accounting accordingly. No one fully appreciates the great differences between aircraft and surface craft until he has absorbed the practical knowledge of aviation that can be gained only be prolonged experience in the air. The whole subject of design, maintenance and operation of aircraft is foreign to the design, maintenance and operation of surface craft; in distributing the material problems of aviation to the Bureaus, the Department has added to some of them a strange and relatively unimportant item of work; also, except in two Bureaus, there is no officer who can give that item his undivided attention.

7. In no other naval activity is there much need of coordination of the natural divisions of the material problems; this on account of the great necessity of avoiding excess weights and the greater necessity of avoiding unnecessary detrimental surfaces. The finished product in aviation material can only be efficient when there is complete harmony in the designs of structure, power plant, and equipment; this harmony can be obtained only when the different designing heads are in close touch with one another under a strong coordinating head. Nominally in Operation there is a coordinating head for the Bureaus' relations with aviation affairs; but there is no one in Operations' with the requisite rank and authority who can give his attention exclusively to this subject; even if there were, the physical separation of the offices concerned makes real coordination extremely difficult; this difficulty is increased by the

newness of all problems connected with naval aviation and the meager resources for production in this country.

8. It might be inadvisable to consider separation of cognizance of aviation affairs from the Bureaus if all the material problems were entirely in line with Bureau work. In aviation munitions there is nothing much really new for the Bureau of Ordnance to consider except reduction in weights; in aviation public works there is still less dissimilarity from the usual work of the Bureau of Yards and Docks; but in the two most important divisions of aviation material. - aircraft structures and power plants. - which are now assigned to the Bureaus of Construction and Repair and Steam Engineering, most of the raw material used as well as the designing problems involved are practically entirely outside the regular lines of those two Bureaus.

9. In outlining an aviation organization in which decisions on designs and control of funds is separated from the Bureaus, total independence of the Bureaus is not contemplated; in fact it seems certain that naval aviation would be a failure under any system without the cooperation of the Bureaus. It is proposed to make use of all design, experimental and product resources of the Bureaus, Navy Yards and Naval Stations in every case where an item of aviation work is closely allied with the regular work and within the resources of those organizations. It is contemplated that the Bureau of Supplies and Accounts will handle the pay accounts of all naval personnel of the Corps and have the same status as material supply and purchasing agent that it has for the Bureaus. Also, it is contemplated that the Bureau of Navigation and Headquarters Marine Corps will bear the same relation to the Personnel of the Flying Corps as they bear to the commissioned and enlisted personnel of the remainder of the Navy and Marine Corps, except it is essential that the Bureau of Navigation and the Commandant of the Marine Corps should delegate such authority to the Commandant of the Flying Corps as will enable him to control the disposition of its personnel.

10 It should be noted here that the present system of Bureau cognizance of aviation material is practically identical with the methods of the fiscal year 1915 when naval aviation existed on such funds as could be spared from current Bureau appropriations. In the following fiscal year a special appropriation (Aeronautics, 1916) made it possible to effect a centralized control of aviation material affairs; but when one reads the attached proposed regulations showing the scope of the work that should be undertaken by the head of aviation, it is easy to see why the then Director of Naval Aeronautics, with only one clerk and occasionally with one officer, and sometimes none, as assistant in his office, - was obliged to turn over much of his work to the Bureau. Careful reading of proposed regulations will also show how really futile it is to expect good results when the officer in Operations with the central authority - no matter how high professional attainments may be - carries aviation affairs as a comparatively insignificant item in the total of his naval duties.

11. The control of aviation affairs is well worth the undivided attention of an officer of adequate rank; this officer should preferably be an aviator; but not necessarily provided he is know to have a talent for coordination and administrative work, and is provided with the necessary number of expert advisors under his direct control.

12. In view of the small number of officers heretofore assigned to aviation duty, in the Department, the proposed number of assistants to the head of aviation will seem large; but in view of the scope of the work that should be undertaken (much of which is now practically untouched) reduction of this number of assistants will surely mean overwork for one or more and the consequent reduction in the general efficiency of the Corps.

13. The attached organization plans has been put in a form similar to the Navy Regulations; it is followed by notes headed with the section number and paragraph referred to. A duplicate copy of the correspondence is forwarded hereto attached with the request that it be forwarded to the Judge Advocate General for his decision as to the legality of the procedure outlined. Another copy has been forwarded direct to the Navy Department (Operation - Material) in view of the fact that the suggested organization involves changes in the present methods of administering the material affairs of Naval Aviation.

14. It should be noted that the proposed organization plan besides being similar to the U.S. Marine Corps organization is very close, in its essentials, to the organization of the Royal Naval Air Service; that service starting on a small scale before the present war, has now expanded to comparatively enormous proportions (2200 officers and 2500 men) and appears to be the most efficient of all aviation organizations in Europe.

s/H.C. MUSTIN

THE NAVAL FLYING CORPS

1. General Regulations

(1) The following duties may be performed by the Naval Flying Corps when so directed by the Secretary

(a) To furnish aviation detachments for duty afloat on vessels of the Navy for service either with the fleets, squadrons, or divisions or on detached service.

(b) To furnish aviation detachments for all aircraft shore stations within and beyond the continental limits of the United States that are under the jurisdiction of the Secretary of the Navy.

(c) To furnish aviation detachments for Marine Corps expeditionary forces.

(d) To supervise the organization, administration, training, equipment and disposition of the Naval Flying Corps and Naval Militia Aviation detachments.

(e) To furnish aviation detachments for temporary duty with the Army, at the request of the Secretary of War, when the personnel and material for this purpose can be spared from the Naval Service.

(2) The Naval Flying Corps shall be at all time subject to the laws and regulations established for the government of the Navy, except when detached for service with the Army; and when so detached shall be subject to the regulations and laws prescribed for the Army.

II. The Commandant of the Naval Flying Corps

(1) The Naval Flying Corps shall be commanded by a line officer of the Navy not below the rank of Commander, detailed to duty in (or with) the Naval Flying Corps, who, while so serving shall have the title: "Commandant, U.S. Naval Flying Corps"; he shall be stationed in Washington, D.C. in offices designated "Headquarters, U.S. Naval Flying Corps," and shall be responsible to the Secretary of the Navy for the general efficiency and discipline of the Corps. When practicable the Commandant shall be a qualified Navy Air Pilot. (See note).

(2) The Commandant shall exercise a general supervision over all expenditures and supplies needed for the maintenance or connected with the management of the corps. It shall be his duty to see that all estimates of appropriations, required for the support and employment of the Corps, are based on proper considerations and made for legal objects.

(3) The Commandant shall exercise a general supervision over the training of the personnel of the Flying Corps and the development of Naval aircraft tactics.

(4) The Commandant under appropriate authority from the Chief of Bureau of Navigation, shall make such distribution of officers and men of the Flying Corps, for duty at the several shore stations, and shall appear to him to be most advantageous for the interests of the Service, and shall from time to time, when required by the Department, furnish detachments for vessels of the Navy, according to the authorized scale of allowance. He shall also, upon proper application, cause vacancies in such detachments to be filled, and shall direct the necessary transfers of officers and men for that purpose.

(5) The Commandant shall make distribution of Naval Aviation material as shall appear to him to be most advantageous for the interests of the service, furnishing the necessary aircraft, with their spare parts, equipment, accessories and supplies to aviation detachments according to the authorized scale of allowances.

(6) The Commandant shall exercise a general supervision over all experimental and research work relating to aviation that is performed by the Navy, and he shall keep in touch with aviation development in material and methods elsewhere, both at home and abroad.

(7) The Commandant shall exercise general supervision over the design of all naval aviation material and shall be responsible to the Secretary of the Navy for the efficiency of the various types of naval aircraft, their accessories and appurtenances.

(8) When any aircraft appurtenance forms a permanent part of the structure of a vessel to the extent that its design and manufacture is under the cognizance of a Bureau, all plans of such appurtenances shall be satisfactory to the Commandant who shall furnish the Bureau concerned with all necessary aviation data required for incorporation in the design.

(9) When any aviation designing or experimental work is within the regular course of any Bureau's facilities, the Commandant shall make request on that Bureau for estimates of the time and cost of the work, accompanying his request with the necessary descriptions and outline plans. Upon receipt from the Bureau of a statement that the work can be undertaken, with the estimate of time and cost, if satisfactory to the Commandant, he shall allot to the Bureau the necessary funds from the aviation appropriation, and the work shall then be undertaken. In such cases all detail plans prepared by the Bureau shall be issued subject to approval of the Commandant.

(10) When any aviation experimental work or production is within the capacity of any navy yard or naval station where it may be desirable to have such work performed, the Commandant shall make request on that yard or station for estimates of cost and time of work, accompanying his request with the necessary description or drawings. Upon receipt from the yard or station of a statement that the work can be undertaken, with the estimate of cost and time, if satisfactory to the Commandant of the Flying Corps, he shall allot to the yard or station the necessary funds from the aviation appropriation, and the work shall then be undertaken.

(11) The Commandant shall take the necessary action, consistent with Naval Laws and regulations, for affecting close cooperation and exchange of ideas with the Army Aviation Section and private manufacturers of aviation material with a view to advancing the efficiency of aviation design and Production. Also, in the same manner, he shall cooperate with the Army Aviation Section and with private manufacturers of aviation material and allied products with a view to mobilization in time of war of all aviation manufacturing resources.

(12) The Commandant whenever called upon to do so shall furnish the Naval War College with the numbers, characteristics and disposition of the various types of naval aircraft in service; also in cooperation with the War College Staff, he shall formulate the tactics of naval aircraft that relate to joint operations with the fleet.

(13) The Commandant shall be ex-officio a member of the Staff of the Chief of Naval Operations.

(14) In the absence of the Commandant, the business of his office shall be conducted by the senior line officer of the Navy stationed therein who shall sign all official papers as "By order of the Commandant."

III. Staff of the Commandant of the Naval Flying Corps

(1) The following Aids shall be assigned to duty in Headquarters of U.S. Naval Flying Corps, on the Staff of the Commandant: Chief of Staff, Aid for Aeroplane Structural Material, Aid for Dirigible and Balloon Structural Material, Aid for Power Plant Material, Aid for Ordnance Material and Equipage, Aid for Expeditionary Forces, and Aid for Naval Reserve Militia Aviation Affairs.

IV. Chief of Staff

(1) The duties of the Chief of Staff, under the Commandant, shall be as follows:

(a) Such supervision of the work of the other Aids to the Commandant in Headquarters as may be necessary for coordinating the divisions of work especially as regards design of aircraft and their accessories and the expenditure of the aviation appropriation.

(b) Preparation of plans for organization, administration and distribution of all aircraft detachments afloat and at shore stations.

(c) Custody of aviation records and files.

(d) Supervision of all matters relating to training of the Flying Corps personnel and the development of Naval Aircraft tactics.

(e) Making all details of personnel and materials.

(f) Such other duties as may be assigned him by the Commandant.

(g) In absence of the Commandant conduct the business of the Corps as
provided in Section II. (4).

(2) The Chief of Staff shall be a line officer of the Navy detailed to duty in (or with) the Naval Flying Corps who is a qualified Navy Air Pilot. (see note)

V. Air for Aeroplane Structural Material

(1) The duties of the Aid for Aeroplane Structural Material, under the Commandant, shall be as follows:

(a) Supervision of all matters pertaining to the design, manufacture, purchase and inspection of all aeroplane structures and accessories, and the experimental work relating thereto.

(b) Compilation of estimates for the part of the aviation appropriation that involve expenditure for the above items.

(c) Supervision of all allotments and requisitions involving expenditures for the above items.

(d) Such other duties as may be assigned by the Commandant.

(2) The Aid for Aeroplane Structural Material shall be an officer of the Navy, detailed to duty in (or with) the Naval Flying Corps, who has specialized in the design of aeroplanes and who is, when practicable, a qualified Navy Air Pilot.

VI. Aid for Dirigible and Balloon Structural Material

(1) The duties of the Aid for Dirigible and Balloon Structural Material, under the Commandant, shall be as follows:

(a) Supervision of all matters pertaining to the design, manufacture, purchase and inspection of all dirigible and balloon structures and accessories and the experimental work relating thereto.

(b) Compilation of estimates for the part of the aviation appropriation that involve expenditures for the above items.

(c) Supervision of all allotments and requisitions involving expenditures for the above items.

(d) Such other duties as may be assigned him by the Commandant.

(2) The Aid for Dirigible and Balloon Structural Material shall be an officer of the Navy, detailed to duty in (or with) the Naval Flying Corps, who has specialized in the design of dirigible and balloons, and who is, when practicable, a qualified Navy Air Pilot.

VII. Aid for Ordnance Material

(1) The duties of the Aid for Power Plant Material, under the Commandant, shall be as follows:

(a) Supervision of all matters pertaining to the design, manufacture, purchase and inspection of all aviation ordnance material and munitions, and of all aerodynamic and navigational instruments connected to each.

(b) Compilation of estimates for the part of the aviation appropriationthat involves expenditures for the above items.

(c) Supervision of allotments and requisitions involving expenditures for the above items.

(d) Such other duties as may be assigned him by the Commandant.

(2) The Aid for Power Plant Material shall be an officer of the Navy detailed to duty in (or with) the Naval Flying Corps who has specialized in the design of aeronautic motors, and is, when practicable, a qualified Navy Air Pilot.

VIII. Aid for Ordnance Material

(1) The duties of the Aid for Ordnance Material, under the Commandant shall be as follows:

(a) Supervision of all matters pertaining to the design, manufacture, purchase and inspection of aviation ordnance material and munitions, and off all aerodynamic and navigational instruments.

(b) Compilation of estimates for the part of the aviation appropriationthat involves expenditures for the above items.

(c) Supervision of allotments and requisitions involving expenditures for the above items.

(d) Such other duties as may be assigned him by the Commandant.

(2) The Aid for Ordnance Material shall be a line officer of the Navy detailed to duty (or with), the Naval Flying Corps who has specialized in aviation ordnance and is when practicable, a qualified Navy Air Pilot.

IX. Air for Expeditionary Forces

(1) The duties of the Aid for Expeditionary Forces, under the Commandant, shall be as follows:

(a) Supervision of all matters relating to equipment, organization and supply of expeditionary forces for service in the field with the Marine Corps or the Army.

(b) Such other duties as may be assigned him by the Commandant.

(2) The Aid for Expeditionary Forces shall be a line officer of the Marine Corps detailed to duty in (or with) the Naval Flying Corps, who is a qualified military aviator.

NOTE XII. (1) (d)

This provides the indispensable men for Flying Corps duty who do not fly or become members of aircraft crews, such as yeomen, and at shore stations, crews of patrol boats, look outs, masters at arms and men in the commissary and messmen branches. The number of these is unlimited in the wording of the Flying Corps Act.

NOTE XII. (1) (e)

Although a considerable portion of the men doing duty with the Flying Corps have no direct connection with aircraft, it is believed that better efficiency and esprit of the Corps will be obtained by considering all in one special group. All should therefore wear the prescribed Corps device which should have additional markings indicating qualifications as Airmen, Machinist Aeronautic, Quartermaster (aeroplane) and Quartermaster (dirigible).

NOTE XIII. (2)

From my experience in command (acting) of the Mississippi and North Carolina in 1914, this appears an equitable as well as necessary ruling for ships equipped with aircraft; if officers assigned to the aviation division are burdened with divisional duties additional to the work required in the proper care and handling of their aircraft, the results will be inefficiency and perhaps unnecessary losses of personnel and material All aircraft are inherently fragile and require constant care and attention to prevent deterioration to unsafe or inefficient conditions even when housed in hangars; in the fleet, where their exposure and treatment will be much more severe the duties of Air Pilots in the care and preservation of the material assigned to them will be very exacting.

NOTE XIV. (1)

This regulation is the equivalent of one of the regulations for the Marine Corps; although it does not accord with existing conditions for naval officers at shore stations, it appears legal in all respects excepting possibly, the implied authority for awarding punishments. For the efficiency of the Corps as a whole, it should be put into effect in so far as the law permits.

Appendix D: Coastal Patrol Stations

NAVY DEPARTMENT Mat.5.E

251-17

Washington,

February 5, 1917

From: Chief of Naval Operations
To: The Secretary of the Navy

SUBJECT: Coastal Patrol Stations

1. It is recommended that aeronautic coastal patrol stations be established at one as follows:

Location	Equipment	Crew Officers	Men
Massachusetts Bay Vicinity	2 Dirigibles	2	
	4 Seaplanes	4	50
Newport Vicinity	2 Dirigibles	2	
	4 Seaplanes	6	58
New York Vicinity	2 Dirigibles	2	
	4 Seaplanes	4	50
Cape May Vicinity	2 Dirigibles	2	
	4 Seaplanes	4	50
Hampton Roads Vicinity	2 Dirigibles	2	
	6 Seaplanes	6	58
Key West Vicinity	2 Dirigibles	2	
	4 Seaplanes	4	50
Galveston Vicinity	2 Dirigibles	2	
	4 Seaplanes	4	50
Canal Zone	2 Dirigibles	2	
	4 Seaplanes	4	50
		52	416

2. There will also be required for each of these stations the following personnel:

1 Doctor
1 Paymaster
1 Cook, wardroom
1 Steward
Mess attendant
Ship cooks
Messmen
Men for boats' crew
Yeomen

3. It is believed that by the time these stations are established and buildings erected there will be sufficient trained personnel from the Pensacola Aeronautic Station to form skeleton organizations of aircraft crews. Naval Militia units of a total of 6 officers and 20 men will also be available. It is anticipated that a certain number of officers and men will enroll in the Naval Reserve Flying Corps and thus be available to assist in filling out the complement of the stations.

4. The buildings required at each station for immediate use would be:

1	Dirigible shed, of sufficient size to house 2 dirigibles130 x 250 feet	$150,000
1	Seaplane shed, to house 6 seaplanes, 75 x 100 x 20 ft. doors	20,000
1	Storehouse, 50 x 75 x 15 feet doors	7,500
1	Machine shop and woodworking shop, equipped	20,000
1	Hydrogen plant and gasometer, 10,000 cu. ft. per hour	45,000
1	Hut, officers quarters, mess room, kitchen, and office 30 x 90 ft.	5,000
2	Huts, men's quarters, each 40 men (Dispensary in 1 Hut) 30 x 90 ft.	10,000
1	Mens' mess Hall and kitchen and bath, 30 x 60 feet	3,000
1	Latrine, divided 10 x 15 feet	1,000
1	Gasoline storehouse, 1000 Gals., 10 x 10 feet	500
1	Runway into water for seaplanes	1,500
1	Dock and shelter for boats, if none available	2,000
		$265,500

Necessary tracking, piping and wiring to furnish transportation, water, light and power from outside sources to buildings, preparing field, and miscellaneous work under Y. & D. (sic.) 35,000

$300,000

5. A land area of at least 1000 x 1200 feet will be required for buildings and fields. At least 200 feet should be on waterfront, and it is desirable to have one whole side on waterfront. A larger field is desired if obtainable.

6. The immediate selection of sites by the Commandants of the various Naval Districts should be undertaken, and officers of extensive aeronautic experience should be ordered to assist the Commandants in this selection. Lieut.Comdr. H.C. Mustin, U.S.N., and Captain A.A. Cunningham, U.S.M.C. are available for this work.

7. The necessary aircraft for these stations have been requested in letters Mat.5-D247 and 248, of February 4, 1917.

8. It is recommended that where no government property is available, the necessary land be leased, with a view to later purchase if desired.

9. In view of the urgent military necessity for these stations it is earnestly recommended that their establishment be approved immediately, in order that plans and construction of the necessary buildings can be undertaken.

ally responsible to the Commandant, First Naval District, and dependent upon that command for support of his operating requirements.

The organizational relationship of the Detachment and its Ground School with the Institute followed the pattern of that already established for the Army School. Overall supervision and responsibility for the program rested with the Commanding Of-

TABLE I

NA[a] Number		**NA[a] Number**	
190	F.G. Allen QM 1/C	426	H.C. Pratt QM 1/C
	J.E. Berry Seaman 2/C	279	A.L. Pritchard QM 1/C
481	F.L. Burk QM 1/C	(e)	G. Richter QM 1/C
201	G. Campo QM 1/C	259	R.A. Powers, Seaman 2/C
360	H.C. Clayton QM 1/C	211	G.T. Roe Seaman 2/C
(f)	H.T. Cutter Seaman 2/C		A.W. Roe Seaman 2/C
(e)	J.A. Eaton Seaman 2/C	200	J.H. Rowen QM 1/C
	L.F. Fowler QM 1/C	217	G.E. Rumill Seaman 2/C
1091	S.A. Freeman QM 1/C	404	H.L. Ryan Seaman 2/C
353	B.M. Greely Seaman 2/C	484	J.M. Sheehan Seaman 2/C
203	L.B Hutchinson Seaman 2/C		W.J. Sheerin Seaman 2/C
182	K.B. Keyes Seaman 2/C	328	W.T. Snow Seaman 2/C
181	R.W. Hyde QM 1/C	186	H.T. Stanley QM 1/C
383	V.T. Leak QM 1/C		F.D. Sullivan QM 1/C
493	H.P. Lewis Seaman 1/C	321	G.N. Swett QM 1/C
205	D.E. Lochman QM 1/C	212	A.P. Teulon Seaman 2/C
204	D.M. Macauley QM 2/C		W. Thompson, Jr. QM 1/C
384	L.K. Marshall QM 1/C	(b)	N. Troutman QM 1/C
492	C.(?) A.(?) McLellan Seaman 2/C	183	A.K. Warren QM 1/C
494	J.M. Miller Seaman 2/C	224	E.A. Wenz Seaman 2/C
369[d]	J.F. Murphy QM 1/C	2258	J.P. Worthington QM 1/c (LTA)
369[d]	J.M. Murphy QM 1/C		R. Van Nests QM 1/C
(f)	D.J. O'Meara QM 1/C		A.H. Yando QM 1/C
(b)	D.C. Pero QM 1/C	402	H.E. West QM 1/C
185	W.L. Peterson QM 1/C		F.W. Prescott QM 1/C

Note: NA Numbers 18-280 indicate Pensacola training while NA Numbers 320 and up indicate Norfolk training.
(a) Naval Aviator Numbers where known.
(b) Commissioned and assigned to aviation duty but no designation is known.
(c) Did not qualify; but was commissioned and was assigned non-flying duties.
(d) Records indicate a John Murphy receiving Naval Aviator Number 369 on Feb. 25, 1918.
(e) Died in an accident at Pensacola.
(f) Unable to qualify at Norfolk and dropped from the program.

ficer. Control over the academic work was vested in an Academic Board consisting of the Commanding Officer, the President of the Academic Board, the Deans of the Departments, and all Institute faculty members serving in the Ground School. The Board was headed by a President appointed by the President of the Institute. Professor Cecil H. Peabody, and later Professor Harrison W. Smith, served in this capacity. The Departments of the School were: a) Signaling, headed by H.N. Carlson; Seamanship and Navigation, by Harrison W. Smith; c) Gunnery, by G.D. Haskill; d) Aeronautic Motors, by Dean A. Fales; e) Aeronautics, by Alexander Klemins; f) Meteorology, by Frank Waldo; and g) Calisthenics, by J.A. MacDonald.[7] Each school had, in general, its own instructing staff. The total number of instructors attached to the Ground School Academic staff was 156, of which the maximum number at one time was 99. 40 men had been or were connected with MIT, either as instructors or as students. The Academic staff of the Inspection School included 24 instructors, all of whom, however, did not teach continuously. 21 of these were associated with the Institute. The Aerography School Academic staff had six instructors during the period of its existence, one of whom was an Institute man. The

Formation of Naval Aviation Cadets at MIT. Personnel unidentified.

Formation of Naval Aviation Cadets at MIT in review. Personnel unidentified

Naval Aviation Cadets at MIT marching.

U.S. Naval Aviation Detachment at MIT in June 1918.

Receiving Ship School Academic Staff was made up of instructors of the Ground School staff. The Examining Board, made up of the President of the Academic Board and three Department Heads, was set up to pass on the qualifications of all students making unsatisfactory progress. The Commanding Officer exercised final authority in judging the fitness of student officers for graduation. With minor modifications in regard to Departments and with some change in personnel, this organization was retained throughout the program, and functioned successfully in spite of its seemingly involved and complicated arrangements.

The organization of the student body was that of a military unit under Cadet and Petty Officers, along lines similar to which the midshipman were organized at the Naval Academy. The Detachment was originally organized as one battalion of four companies of 50 men, each representing a Class. As numbers on board increased, Classes were split into companies of about 50 men, and the organization became that of a regiment of two battalions. At its maximum strength, the Detachment was organized as a brigade of two regiments and three battalions. These units were commanded entirely by Cadet Officers under the immediate supervision of the Drill and Discipline Officer and the Divisional Officers assigned from the staff to each Class. The Cadet Officers for the various companies were chosen from the senior class of the school.[8] Officers were elected each fortnight from the graduating class to govern the students of the school. They were rated as:

- Detachment Commander
- Detachment Adjutant
- Detachment Chief Petty Officer
    - Regimental Commander
    - Regimental Adjutants
        - Battalion Commanders
        - Battalion Adjutants
            - Company Commanders
            - Company Lieutenants
            - Company Ensigns

The first group of men assigned were designated Flight A, the second Flight B, and so on. By the time four flights were on board and Flight A was ready for graduation, this system was changed to make use of these letters constant, each group starting at the lower end as Flight D or E, depending on the length of the course, and

Raising the colors at the U.S. Naval Aviation Detachment at MIT.

Naval Aviation Cadets at MIT awaiting review.

U.S. Naval Aviation Detachment in review at MIT in May 1918.

U.S. Naval Aviation Detachment at MIT Color Guard in June 1918.

progressing every two weeks to the next Flight. By this system "A" was always the senior, or graduating, flight. This change also introduced the practice of assigning a Class number to each entering group, of which there were 34 in all. A Class was graduated and a new one entered every two weeks. The number of men per class began, as noted above, with 50. Increase was gradual, and involved no sudden changes that were sustained.

With Class 7 in October 1917, the number reached into the 60's, and by Class 12 in December went above 100. A typical class roster is presented in Table II. This roster is thought to be from Class 10, which included Company E (26 Nov.-9 Dec.); Company D (10 Dec.-23 Dec.); Company C (24 Dec.-6 Jan.); Company B (7 Jan.-20 Jan.); and Company A (21 Jan.-3 Feb.).

Naval Aviation Cadets at MIT marching in Patriots Day Parade on 16 April 1918.

Flight "A" of the U.S. Naval Aviation Detachment in August 1917. (source: Official U.S. Navy Photograph)

TABLE II

Adams, Russell S. QM 2/C, USN
Ahearn, Wm. J. MM 2/C, USN
Adler, Grover C. QM 2/C, USN
Baird, Cyrus Lds., USN
Bourne, H.G. E 3/C, USN
Carter, Paul Wm. QM 2/C, USN
Cassidy, Robert V. MM 2/C, NRF
Churchill, W.N. Sea. 2/C, NRF
Cunningham, R.M. MM 2/C, USN
Desragnes, H.E. E 3/C, RUSN
Deveas, Samuel H.E. QM 2/C, RUSN
Dichl, Walter S. MM 2/C, USN
Dienner, Robert P. QM 2/C, USN
Donaldson, H.L. MM 2/C, USN
Duckworth, H.L. QM 2/C USN
Dwyer, M.J., Jr. Lds. MM, NRF
Estabrook, H.C. QM 2/C USN
Ernst, H.M. E 3/C, RNRF
Evans, Albert W. QM 2/C, USN
Finch, Velney C. QM 2/C, USN
Fisher, Hewand S. MM 1/C, NRF
Groom, Harry B. Yeo. 3/C, USN
Halpenny, R.E. E 3/C, RUSN
Rollins, Wingate Sea. 2/C, RNF
Rosebourough, J.C. MM 2/C, USN
Sewell, A.T. QM 2/C, USN
Sheldon, Carew E 2/C, USN
Smith, B.D. QM 2/C, USN
Smith, Oliver H. MM 1/C, RNF
Shoper, Harold C. MM 2/C, USN
Svenson, L.G. MM 2/C, USN
Taggart, John E. E 3/C, NRF
Talbot, Robert A. MM 2/C, NRF
Taylor, Caleb. W. QM 2/C, USN
Taylor, William D. QM 2/C USN
Thorpe, Leslie A. QM 2/C, USN
Harris, Fred E 2/C, USN
Haworth, R. MM 2/C, NRF
Hunnington, E.J. MM 2/C, NRF
Ingalls, E.H. QM 2/C, USN
Iseman, J.W. QM 2/C, USN
Jones, Paul S. MM 2/C, NRF
Kennedy, Edward J. QM/2C USN
Laverents, Arthur QM 2/C, USN
MacKnight, K.I. E 3/C RNNV
Martin, Edward MM 2/C, USN
McCalla, R.C. QM 2/C, USN
McCarthy, H. MM 2/C, USN
McCormick, J.S.F. MM 2/C, USN
McDermott, J.J. QM 2/C, USN
McKean, F.D. QM 2/C, USN
Miller, E.H. QM 2/C, USN
Mitchell, E.L. MM 2/C, NRF
Neel, Guy W. QM 2/C, USN
Page, S.C. Jr. E 3/C, USN
Parent, Jos. H. QM 2/C, USN
Perkins, Chas. S. E 2/C, RNRF
Protheroe, O.G. E 2/C, RUSN
Piemeisl, C.J. E 3/C, RUSN
Upton, Vergil M. QM 2/C, USN
Walker, Leslie A. Lds.QM, USN
Whitcomb, H.D. GM 2/C, USN
Whitesidek, J.R. QM 2/C, USN
Whiting, D.N. Sea. 2/C, USN
Williams, R.G. E 3/C, RNRF
Williams, Thomas E. E 3/C, RUSN
Williamson, G.M. QM 2/C, USN
Williamson, R.C. MM 2/C, USN
Wilson, Earl F. QM 2/C, USN
Whitney, Edward H. MM 2/C, NRF
Young, Vincent C. MM 1/C, NRF

Although the climb continued to an early peak of about 150, by February, 1918, the number was almost halved, with the next class only to come back to 150 in April and to remain fairly steady through August. Peak assignment was reached in September of 1918 at slightly over the 200 mark and remained there for the last two classes assigned in October. The total number in attendance at one time ranged roughly from 200 men at the start to about 800 in the final phase.

Unidentified members of the Naval Aviation Cadet Detachment at MIT.

Review of the U.S. Naval Aviation Detachment at MIT in June 1918.

As the number of men in each class increased, classes were divided into sections of from 30 to 35 men to permit small instructional units, and to allow special groupings of certain students when expedient. Those failing to graduate with their class, if retained on board, were assigned to Division X for additional instruction.

Changes in curriculum followed the needs of the service. The course was initially of eight weeks duration, but the addition of new subjects and the expansion of hours allotted to others required its extension to ten weeks, beginning with the class assigned on 15 October 1917. Activation of the Receiving Ship in March, 1918, extended the on-board period another two weeks, but had no immediate effect on the length of the Ground School course itself. Its program, however, covered some of the same subjects as were included in the Ground School, and on 24 June 1918 when these were removed from the basic curriculum, the length of the course was reduced to eight weeks. This course closed in November 1918 when the last of the students on board were transferred to the Ground School. Special provisions for lighter-than-air men were made with Class 22 in May 1918, and required continuing adjustment through the remainder of the program.

Changing requirements were also met by establishing special schools using the facilities of the Institute and the Detachment organization, but set up separately from the basic Ground School. Beginning in October 1917, graduates of the Radio School at Harvard University were assigned for special training as Aerial Observers. This program, which required completion of only part of the Ground School course, was continued until 23 January 1918, when Observer Training was transferred to NAS Miami. A school for Inspectors was also set up in October and ran for one year. An Aerography School, started in December 1917, ran through the program.

The first of 363 Gunnery Sergeants of the Marine Corps were assigned to the school in a group of 25 men on 1 June 1918. When classes reached the 200 mark in August, the normal quota for Marines was established at 40. This Marine Detachment, which was within rather than separate from the Naval Air Detachment, was commanded by Captain Robert J. Archibald, USMC. Its organization required no change in the academic program or instruction schedules.

On 21 September 1918, 20 flight cadets of the Royal Canadian Naval Air Service reported for ground school instruction and were assigned to subsequent classes up to 12 December 1918, when they were all transferred to Headquarters at Ottawa for demobilization. In all, 60 RCNAS Cadets were assigned to the Detachment for training. These men had no local representatives and were handled the same as other ground school students. Although their average age was two years younger than that of the American student officers, their grades were equivalent to those achieved by the American Cadets.

Twenty-six graduates of the Ground School at Dunwoody Industrial Institute, Minneapolis, reported to the Detachment on 13 April 1918. These men had completed instructions practically equivalent to that given at MIT and reported only to take final examinations before being sent to flight training. When training at Dunwoody ended on 25 November 1918, 48 students from its receiving Ship were transferred to MIT for completion of their training. Those expressing desire to finish ground school training were assigned to Class 34.

As the war neared its close, word was received from the Supervisor, Naval Reserve Flying Corps, that more men were under flight instruction than could be handled conveniently at existing fields, and that some reduction in the number of men on board the Detachment was advisable. Accordingly, a special board was convened on 5 November to re-examine the particular qualifications of each man attached to the Receiving Ship. As a result of the decision of this board, some 400 men were transferred to the Receiving Ship at Boston for discharge or other assignment.

On 13 November instructions were received from the Bureau of Navigation concerning the release of all students to inactive duty. Students were to be given their choice of completing their ground training or of going on inactive duty at once. Inactive duty was chosen by 558 men, and their release greatly reduced the number of men in succeeding classes. At this time plans were also made to discontinue the Ground School, and for demobilizing the Detachment upon graduation of the 34th class. By orders of the Bureau the men of this and the preceding class were placed on inactive duty upon graduation and were graduated on 18 January 1919. The total number of students assigned to the Detachment was in excess of 5000, of which about 4448 went on to ground school or one of the special schools, and about 3500 graduated.[9]

The instructional staff expanded as the student body grew. From an initial assignment of ten instructors, the number increased gradually to 48 by the turn of the year, and reached a peak of 99 by August 1918. Over and above this number was a maximum of 22 instructors assigned to the Inspector School and three to the Aerography School. Some of the increase was possible by the assignment of Naval officers and specialists to the School; some was the result of retraining Ground School graduates in an instructional capacity. The Staff was initially composed entirely of civilian members of the Institute faculty, and at the end almost exclusively of Navy per-

Informal photo of unidentified members of the U.S. Naval Aviation Detachment at MIT.

sonnel. This change did not, however, represent a complete withdrawal of the Institute faculty. Many instructors of draft age, and others who expressed a desire to join-up, were commissioned in the Navy and retained on the instructional staff.

After being in session only a little more than a month, the Commanding Officer reported, "Things are going splendidly... in about three weeks the detachment will be working like a machine and... an ordinary seaman will be qualified to handle it."[10] But it was not to be. Changing requirements, changing concepts, and acceleration of the program in the face of problems then unforeseen, would require hard work, ingenuity, and adjustments by both the Institute and the Navy before the machine could run by itself.

Provisions of uniforms caused difficulties from the first. The first group to report reported in sailor whites issued by the First Naval District. By the end of the first week, however, all were in Khakis. These were of a cut similar to the aviation uniform without marks of rank, but with an officer's device on the hat. Questions of cloth and cut for the winter uniform were still very much in the air, and the problem of establishing a good source of supply was not immediately solved.[11] As late as November some men were still reporting to the school in civilian clothes and waiting from ten to 15 days before being outfitted with uniforms.

In a sense, the uniform problem was related to another which was not immediately resolved. Men were enrolled in the USNRF in a variety of ratings and, consequently, there was no uniformity in the rating of men upon reporting to the Detachment. Of the first group, 19 were Seamen 2nd Class, and the remainder were Quartermasters 1st Class. In the second and third groups there was one Quartermaster 1st Class in each, and all the rest were Seamen Seconds. However, the difference was largely theoretical, as all ratings were ignored except for pay purposes, and once a man reported at the Detachment his status became that of a student.

The status of the student body was stabilized in January 1918 when the Bureau of Navigation authorized a change of rating to Chief Quartermaster (Aviation) for all students then on board, regardless of present rating and branch of service.[12] After that time all were given Chief ratings upon reporting unless a higher aviation rating was held at the time.[13] Ratings were not changed during the course of instruction, and upon satisfactory completion of the Ground School the men were transferred to flight stations for elementary training in the same rating. The effect of the change was reflected in the uniform only in regard to the hat, which changed from the officer type to that of a Chief Petty Officer. By February, the uniforms were otherwise the same as those of officers in the Naval Reserve Flying Corps, except that shoulder marks and stripes on the sleeves of the overcoat were omitted.

Three men, all of whom were Naval Aviators, served in command of the Detachment. The pioneer work of organizing the school and setting the precedent fell on Lieutenant Edward H. McKitterick. It was under his command that the curriculum for the Inspector School was developed and the School put into operation. He also completed preliminary arrangements for the Aerology School and supervised the start of its classes. He served six months to 21 December 1917, when he left to commission and take command of the Naval Air Station at Chatham, Massachusetts, and later to go overseas to command the station at Lough Foyle, Ireland. He was relieved by Lieutenant Commander Robert W. Cabaniss, who served approximately seven months before being transferred overseas to command the training station at Moutchic, France. With his arrival a series of orders was published in pamphlet form and furnished to each new arrival. This was a guide to proper conduct, and every rule and regulation it laid down was enforced to the letter:

"**Mail** to insure prompt delivery of mail request your correspondents to use this form of address:

Naval Aviation Detachment
Massachusetts Institute of Technology
Company No. Cambridge, Massachusetts

Give to your correspondents the number of your Company and not the letter, because the number is the same throughout the ten weeks course, while the letter, beginning with E and ending with A, changes each fortnight. The Company entering December 10 is Company No. 11.

Company officers may obtain printed Company Rolls from the Executive Officer or from the Dean. Roll sheets are ready on the Saturday after a Company enters.

The Dean in his office in the Technology Service Building may be consulted about any matters of an academic or general nature. Explanations of Tabular View of Exercises:

E_1 and E_2 represent the first and second weeks of the fortnight during which a Company is E Company; with few exceptions the exercises are the same in weeks No. 1 and No. 2.

Rooms: Numbered from 1 to 15 are in the Tech. Services Building which is just behind Walker Memorial. The other numbered rooms are in the Main Buildings; Building No. 1 is occupied by the Army Aviation; Building No. 2 is directly across the Court from No. 1; Building No. 4 connects No. 2 with the central building under the dome; Building No. 8 constitutes the wing extending easterly from the dome; Building No. 10 is under the dome. In these buildings the numbering of the rooms indicate the building, floor, and room numbers. Thus room No. 4-213 is in Building No. 4 on the second floor. Room 3-370 is directly opposite 4-370 across the court.

Examinations: The class is said to be seated when practicable with a vacant seat on each side of every student. When the class is assigned to two rooms for examination it is to be divided so as best to meet this seating requirement. Proctors will find paper for the examinations in the Dean's Officer; also, the examination questions when needed. Unused paper and the examination papers are to be returned to the office of the Executive Officer. Proctors are responsible for all details of the conduct of the examinations Examination records may be found on the files in the Service build-

U.S. Naval Aviation Detachment at MIT in review, June 1918.

ing. The are ordinarily posted within three days after the examination.

Absence From Examinations Is Not Permitted For Any Other Reason Than Sickness: The Officer of the Day and Company Officers must arrange to have their positions filled during examinations. If necessary applications for relief from duty in order to attend examinations must be made to the Executive Officer.

General Division
(a) Four weeks discipline school
(b) Six weeks ground school

Organization of School (Personnel)
(a) Commanding Officer
2 - Officers Detailed as Instructors
(b) Institute Instructors
(c) Detachment Officers

6:00	AM Reveille	12:55	Retreat
6:15	Formation and Morning Calisthenics	1:00	Lunch Formation
6:40	Retreat from Calisthenics	1:55	School Call
7:00	Breakfast Formation	2:00	6th Recitation Period
7:30	Police Quarters	3:00	7th Recitation Period
8:00	1st Recitation Period	3:55	Drill Call
8:55	Retreat	4:00	Drill Formation
9:00	Sick Call	5:30	Retreat
9:05	2nd Recitation Period	6:00	Dinner
10:00	3rd Recitation Period	7:30 to 9:30	Study Period
11:00	4th Recitation Period	9:55	Tattoo
12:00	5th Recitation Period	10:00	Taps

Routine- Sunday

7:00	AM Reveille	5:30	PM Assembly
7:30	Assembly	9:55	Taps
9:00	Sick Call	10:00	Taps

Liberty Will Be Granted As Follows

From the first to the fourth week inclusive, (Companies "D" and "E") Wednesday, 5 PM to 10 PM, and week-end liberty from Saturday 1 PM to Monday 6 AM reveille formation.

From the fifth to eight week inclusive, (Companies "C" and "B") Monday, Wednesday, and Thursday from 5 PM to 10 PM, and week-end liberty from Saturday I PM to Monday 6 AM reveille formation. Ninth week (Company "A"), Monday, Tuesday, Wednesday, Thursday, and Friday from 5 PM to 10 PM and regular week-end liberty from Saturday 1 PM to Monday 6 AM reveille formation.

Tenth week, (Company "A") 5 PM Monday, Tuesday, Wednesday, Thursday, and Friday until 8 AM the following day.

GENERAL INFORMATION

ORDERS:
The U.S. Marines attached to this station will be saluted and receive the same respect in every way that a Commissioned Officer is entitled to.

As far as possible the men of this detachment will keep out of the sleeping quarters from 8 AM until 11 AM. No one will be allowed to lie on the bunks during this time.

Inspection of quarters will be held by the Commanding Officer or the Executive Officer at 11 AM each day, and the quarters must be clean and in order at that time.

No visitors will be allowed in the barracks after 5 PM except on business, and no visitors under any conditions after 8 PM except unless accompanied by an officer.

Men of this detachment may bowl between the hours of 7:00 AM and 9:45 PM. The use of the alleys must not interfere with classes or studies.

No smoking will be allowed in any building of the Institute except Walker Memorial Building.

All Chief Petty Officers, U.S.N. will report to the Executive Officer at 1:50 PM each day for orders.

Men detailed to this station will report first to the Commandant, First Naval District. They will then go to the District Disbursing Office to arrange for pay and clothing.

Upon arriving at this station they will report to the Executive Officer for registration and assignment to bunks and lockers.

A list of the Company will then be made out immediately. A man selected from the next higher company as Cadet Officer will then take charge.

Hereafter, all orders from the Executive Officer will pass through the Adjutant to the Company Commanders, who will deliver them to their respective Companies, making sure that they are distinctly understood. The Adjutant will report to the Executive Officer daily at 1:30 PM for orders and will deliver them to the Company Commanders in time to be given out to their companies at 4:00 PM. Hereafter, all Companies will use the port stairway when entering or leaving ship. Commissioned Officers and Cadet Officers will use the starboard stairway.

Radiomen will hereafter wear the blue uniforms. Photographers will not be required to purchase uniforms until further notice."

Under his command the Receiving Ship was formally established. At the request of the Institute he was recalled to the school after the close of the program as a member of a Board to determine

Unidentified Naval Aviation Cadets at MIT.

the final settlement of the contract. Lieutenant Commander Cabaniss was succeeded on 9 July 1918 by Lieutenant Harold C. Van Valzah, under whose command the traditions set by his predecessors continued. He remained in command of the school until its close in 1919.

INSTRUCTION FORMAT[14]

The initial instruction program called for a 40 hour week, divided for the first week into Navigation (5 Hrs.), Signals (6 Hrs.), Calisthenics and Boat Drill (5 Hrs.), Drill (5 Hrs.), Navy Regulations (5 Hrs.), Seamanship (6 Hrs.), Study (5 Hrs.), and Examination (3 Hrs.). As each Class progressed toward graduation, the distribution of hours changed, with new subjects being introduced as the total hours required in others was completed, so that a 40-hour week schedule was maintained. The eight week curriculum provided instruction as follows:

Subject	Hours	Subject	Hours
Navigation	24	Theory of Flight	10
Engines	38	Rigging	18
Gunnery	16	Photography	2
Signals	26	Study	54
Radio	6	Examinations	23
Navy Regulations	18	Calisthenics and Boat Drill	24
Electricity	6	Drill	28
Meteorology	6	Liberty	5
Seamanship	16		

TOTAL HOURS - 320

Although this appears a somewhat broader program than called for by the contract, the breadth was more a result of a subject breakdown than the addition of new subjects. Navigation, Navy Regulations, Seamanship, and Drills are the "naval studies" referred to earlier. All others are breakdowns of the Aircraft Engines, Theory of Flight, General Flying, and Signaling and Wireless courses mentioned specifically in the contract.

This program was maintained for the first six classes. In October, the Commanding Officer made a brief visit to the RFC Ground School at the University of Toronto, where he observed classes and had the opportunity to discuss needs in terms of war experience in Europe. As a result, some readjustment of hours was made. This was principally evident in Gunnery, for which time was more than doubled, and in lesser increases in Signals, Rigging, and Navy Regulations. These increases and greater emphasis on physical conditioning, which more than doubled Calisthenics and Drill, combined to bring the total hours of instruction to 428—a load considerably over the 40 hour week established in the early program.

The strain of carrying the extra load was eased when Class 10 reported on October 10th, by extending the program from eight to ten weeks. This still required more than the standard 40 hour week. Further adjustment of hours raised the total to 440 hours beginning in November 1917. For the students, this was not an entirely unbearable load, however, as the net increase of 12 hours was represented by liberty, which had been reduced to zero for Classes 7 through 9. Hours assigned to certain subjects again began to creep upward after the change, but by reducing the hours assigned to others deemed less important, these increases were accomplished without an increase in total hours scheduled. Thus, Navigation, which had started out at 24 hours, soon reached to 52, Signals from 26 to a brief high of 62, and Rigging from 18 to 30 and then to 32. Reductions were accomplished by eliminating scheduled examinations and temporarily abandoning study hours. Compulsory night study was instituted in January 1918 and later reduced to a requirement for the first two weeks for each entering Class, and for all students whose weekly average fell below 2.8.

As course hours became established and the Receiving Ship began to carry the indoctrination load, the program was reduced to an eight week term and held steady at 308 total hours from June 1918 through the remainder of the program. In all there were 12

Band at the U.S. Naval Aviation Detachment at MIT.

Burgess B.P. used in training the cadets at the U.S. Naval Aviation Detachment at MIT. Note tricycle landing gear and side-by-side seating. Since there was no flight instruction at MIT this aircraft was used for other instructional reasons.

different distributions of scheduled hours, the last five of which had only minor variation. A tabular view of the major changes is shown in Table III. Special provisions for prospective Lighter-Than-Air pilots, beginning 27 May 1918 with Class 22, are not shown in Table III. For those students, Theory of Ballooning (22 hours) and Meteorology were also offered, permitting instruction more applicable to future training and careers. The same substitutions were made, with some variance in hours, through all subsequent classes.

Although constant adjustment of schedules presented problems, they were largely administrative and were easily overcome. Changes in course content presented more serious problems, particularly in regard to instructional material. That these too were overcome was due largely to the experience of the instructional staff and the ability of its individual members to adjust to new requirements.

TABLE III
Ground School Schedules (Heavier-than-Air)

Subjects/Class	**8 weeks**		**10 weeks**					**8 weeks**				
	1-6	7-9	10-11	12-13	14-19	20-22	23	24-25	26-27	28-31	32	33-34
Navigation	24	24	29	30	29	40	40	34	34	34	34	34
Engines	38	38	38	44	52	52	50	52	52	52	52	52
Gunnery	16	42	44	50	50	52	50	40	40	40	44	44
Signals	26	37	42	62	49	46	46	50	35	35	33	33
Radio	6	6	8	8	8	8	8	8	8	8	8	8
Navy Regulations	18	30	37	50	37	23	20	20	20	20	20	20
Electricity	6	6	8	8	6	12	12	8	8	8	8	8
Seamanship	16	14	16	18	16	13	13	10	10	10	10	10
Meteorology	6	6	7	8	8	8	8	6	6	6	6	6
Theory of Flight	10	12	12	12	12	14	14	8	8	8	6	8
Rigging	18	24	24	24	30	30	32	32	32	32	30	30
Photography	2	5	5	6	5	5	5	6	-	-	-	-
Study	54	20	36	-	-	-	40	39	39	39	39	39
Exams	23	50	6	-	-	-	-	-	-	-	-	-
Calisthenics	24	49	47	48	45	40	-	-	-	-	-	-
Drill	28	65	67	72	72	59	57	-	-	-	-	-
Liberty	5	-	12	-	17	7	6	-	-	-	-	-
Military Tactics	-	-	-	-	4	6	8	-	-	-	-	-
Aerial Observation	-	-	-	-	-	13	13	-	15	15	16	16
Current Events	-	-	-	-	-	8	8	-				-
Consultation	-	-	-	-	-	8	8	-	-	-	-	-
Wassermann Tests	-	-	-	-	-	4	4	2	2	2	2	2
Athletics	-	-	-	-	-	-	8	7	7	7	7	7
Total Hours	320	428	440	440	440	440	440	308	308	308	308	308

Note: Beginning with Class 20 the title of the Meteorology Class was changed to Aerography

Instructional material in the form of aviation equipment began arriving in late August. The first received was a shipment of aircraft engines from Pensacola, but without tools needed to take them down, and one propeller in very poor condition. They were followed in early September by two freight car loads of miscellaneous equipment. Of all the equipment used by the various academic departments, that of the Rigging Department and of the Engines Department is probably of most interest. The Rigging Department had the following aircraft:

Number	Make	Model	Type
1	Burgess	DU-2	Seaplane
2	Sturtevant	S-5	Seaplane
1	Burgess	B-Scout	Seaplane
3	Aeromobile	Tractor	Seaplane
1	Curtiss	HS-1	Flying Boat
1	Curtiss	N-9	Seaplane

The Engines Department had the following engines:

Number	Make	Model
11	Liberty	12
4	Hall-Scott	A-5
3	Sturtevant	5
9	Curtiss	OXX
1	Curtiss	OX
7	Curtiss	V-2
2	Hispano-Suiza	Rotary
1	Gnome	Rotary
1	Gyro	Rotary
1	Wright	D-8

Although much arrived, much was needed, and a lack of the right kind of equipment made a practical approach to certain subjects more difficult, and, in that respect, also may have affected the quality of the training. A general shortage of up-to-date surplus material was partly responsible, and the reluctance of station commanders to part with still serviceable spare parts may also have contributed; but the lack of material intended specifically for use as a teaching aid was at the root of the problem. Much of what was received was not always adaptable, and changes in course content created a continuing requirement for additional material.

In January, about six months after the school convened, the first shipment of rifles arrived. In that month the Commanding Officer requested materials in an itemized list two pages long and asked that delivery thereof "be expedited much as possible."[15] On 13 February 1918 Lieutenant Commander Cabaniss requested from the Supervisor, Naval Reserve Flying Corps, the following:

150	Copies of "Landing Force and Small Arms"
4	Copies of Navy Regulations
50	Copies of Extracts from Navy Regulations
1000	Copies of "Correspondence in the Naval Service," N.Nav. 405
25	Copies of "Machine Guns," by Capt. Hatcher, USA
50	Copies of Audal's "Automotive Guide"
50	Copies of "Manual of Wireless Telegraphy" by Capt. Robinson, USN
1000	Copies of "Handbook on Lewis Guns," published by Savage Arms Company[16]
25	Copies of "Learning to Fly in the U.S. Army" by Fales
25	Copies of "Military Aeroplanes" by Loerning
150	Copies of the "Bodwitch Practical Navigator"
	Complete service types of radio outfits for aircraft
25	Copies of some standard book on aircraft bombs
25	Copies of "Military and Navy Recognition Book," by Lt. Bunkley, USN

Requests for material continued to be made almost up to the closing date. As late as July 1918, the Commanding Officer took up the problem and emphasized his request for additional navigation equipment by reporting the "proper instruction is now handicapped."[17] The amount accumulated by the close of the school, however, had reached generous proportions. Among other items, the list of equipment being transferred at the close included forty aircraft engines of several types and 14 seaplanes and flying boats, of which only a few were described as "incomplete." Similar difficulties were encountered in the provision of textbooks. Actually, there were no texts in existence for many subjects, and of those that did exist most were too advanced to fit the more practical requirements of the program. One month after instruction began, the Commanding Officer asked to have a shipment of books expedited. Blue Jacket Manuals arrived in late September, and were the only text issued to the students[18] into February. In that and in later months, requests for text and reference books continued without apparent response.

Instruction began with only the barest of outlines as a guide for course content. These were developed by the instructors into lecture notes, which became more elaborate as the work progressed. The first was completed and forwarded to Washington for approval in November, and by the end of the year had been completed for all courses. It was the intention to issue printed copies of these notes as a substitute for texts, but this appears not to have been done until late in the program, if it was done at all.[19]

In spite of the problems and shortcomings, which may have been more apparent than real, the instruction program met its intended purpose. The men received a proper indoctrination into the Navy, and carried with them a background of knowledge basic to their future training. The strong support of the Institute and the willing cooperation of its staff contributed in no small measure to the success of the program.

The rapid expansion of aircraft procurement in the early months of the war was accomplished by an immediate and pressing need for officers qualified to inspect and approve for acceptance the products of various manufacturing plants. This need was initially met by assigning Naval Aviators, who, although untrained in inspection techniques, were well enough acquainted with aircraft structures, components, and working parts to make rapid adjustment to the job. With too few aviators to fill these and other billets where their experience was also needed, the Navy was very soon forced to resort to the assignment of other less experienced officers. They were introduced to the requirements of inspection by working under a qualified inspector, but otherwise learned on the job. The inefficiencies of the apprentice type training during a period when time was a factor in every action, and in an industry which in itself lacked the experience of producing aircraft and aeronautical material in large volume, soon became evident. A special training program seemed the logical answer.

Intent to use the resources of the Ground School to develop qualified inspectors was first revealed to the Commanding Officer on the morning of 22 August 1917, when a newly commissioned Ensign reported to the School with the information that he had come to take the Inspector Course. However disconcerting this may have been to the Commanding Officer, he immediately sent off a letter to Washington expressing both his agreement that such a course would be desirable, and his opinion that it could be made up and handled "without much trouble, providing the Institute agrees." Because no precedent existed for a course of this kind, he proposed that Professor Alexander Klemin and his assistants be asked to work up a course of about six weeks duration with very little work in regular Ground School subjects that had no direct application[20] to inspection. Two weeks later he reported progress on the course outline with the remark "You will have to hand it to the Institute for being on the job in regard to this. They have gone to considerable trouble and I think no little expense in working on their share of the course."[21] On September 15th completed outlines for two courses designed to provide the foundation needed for effective inspectors in the respective areas of Motors and Airplanes were forwarded to Washington for approval. In his covering letter, the Commanding Officer reported a recommendation by the Institute that men be ordered in groups of less than five to permit individual instruction, and that men be selected who were graduates of Engineering Schools and thus had backgrounds needed to pursue the subjects proposed.

The course outlined for Airplane Inspectors was of six weeks duration. It devoted the first two weeks to background studies in the Theory of Flight, Mechanical Principles, Rigging, and Stress and Strength of Fittings. In the third week it emphasized study of material used in aircraft structures, and in the fourth week study of the aircraft itself in relation to all the drawings used in its construction. It set aside the fifth week for visits to factories in the vicinity so that production and fabrication methods could be studied first-hand. During the final week it provided for the important work of making out reports, filling out inspection forms, preparing official correspondence, and learning other administrative duties associated with the inspector assignment. Emphasis was on the practical matters involved in carrying out the work.[22] The Bureau of Construction and Repair approved the course proposed for Airplane Inspectors without change, and reported an immediate need for 20 qualified men, and for another 20 within four or five months. The Bureau of Steam Engineering approved the general recommendations of the course of Motor Inspectors with 23 suggestions for a few minor modifications.[23]

The new courses began on 22 October 1917 with seven students enrolled in each.[24] Prospective Airplane and Motor inspectors took several subjects together, and were separated only for the specialties of their respective lines. The course varied with each class according to the backgrounds and needs of the different groups. Among the subjects covered in the Plane Inspection Course were:

Aeronautical Instruments	Navy Regulations
Airplane Design and Stresses	Physical Measurements
Engine Installation	Propeller Design
General Airplane Construction	Shop Visits
Manuals and Reports	Testing Material
Metallurgy	(Wood and Fabric)
Military Drill	Theory of Flight

In the Engine Inspection Course were:

Aeronautical Engines	Physical Measurements
Aeronautical Instruments	Power Measuring Instruments
Electricity	Propeller Design
Engine Testing	Radiator Design
Manuals and Reports	Shop Visits
Metallurgy	Testing Materials (Metals)
Navy Regulations	Theory of Flight
Military Drill	

The distribution of hours throughout the six weeks of the Inspection course varied with each school according to the availability of instructors and the need of the students. The distribution of time allotted the various subjects was flexible.

On 2 February 1918 the Bureau of Steam Engineering issued the results of its inspection of the first Inspector course and offered the following observations.[25]

A. 1. During the Engine Overhaul and Repair course the men should have received talks on the details of construction, the clearances and tolerances, the methods of inspection, etc.

2. The men should do engine testing themselves and go to outside plants to watch short runs. They should be taught how to bring an engine up to power, to locate troubles, power losses, etc.

3. The lecture on physical measurements should be supplemented by actual practice and by handling of instruments and gauges by students. Lectures were not sufficient.

4. The Electricity Course was theoretical and did not take up actual work in ignition systems. A course with magnetos in operation and ignition troubles should be given.

5. The practical work at factories never allowed the men to see an airplane. Also, more time should be spent in the Sturtevant Company.

6. The Inspector's manuals, correspondence, reports, etc. course was practically omitted.

7. The Power Plant Installation course had the following deficiencies:

a. Since the construction, test, and installation was omitted the men have never seen any accessories.

b. The propeller design and construction area needs to include the study of Specifications.

c. The men have never seen an aerial radiator.

d. There was no discussion on the subject of starting devices (Mechanical and hand) construction and installation.

e. Engine installation, fuel and oil tank installation, and ignition were omitted.

B. A letter was written to the Commanding Officer requesting that a summary of each man be sent to the Bureau of Steam Engineering upon completion of the course. This summary consisted of two words at the most, and none at all in some cases. It has been found that the men were selected almost entirely upon academic standing, from those who had the most experience in business and in engineering work, from those who were experts along certain lines, and from those who were oldest. Those who were not qualified for officers because of low marks in some academic work were recommended for Warrants.

Students enrolled in the first three Inspector Classes began the course without taking the regular Ground School subjects. All succeeding Classes, however, spent the first four weeks in Ground School, and in the remaining weeks devoted full time to the specific requirements of their prospective assignments. Upon completion of the course, the work of actual inspection began at plants producing equipment for the Navy. When the candidates proved themselves efficient in their assignment, they were commissioned as Ensigns.

Difficulties encountered in the program paralleled those experienced in the regular Ground School, particularly in regard to teaching aids. The first enrollment of fourteen students, although slightly above that recommended by the Institute, was hardly enough to produce the estimated 30 inspectors that would be needed within three months. This low enrollment appears to have been not so much the capacity of the school, as it was the failure of the Department to assign men in the required numbers. To fill out the classes, several of those enrolled had been selected by the Commanding Officer from the prospective naval aviators in the student body of the regular Ground School.[26] The first group of nine completed the course in December, and on January 26th 35 Airplane Inspectors were ready for assignment.[27] But for some time the need remained ahead of the production. The urgency of the need, combined with the lack of aeronautical equipment for use as teaching aids, may have had its effect on the quality of training during the initial stage, but as the course progressed the difficulties were ironed out and the school was successful in meeting its objectives.[28] Between the opening of the School and its closing one year later on 22 October 1918, 200 students reported for training. Of these, 167 completed the course successfully, 59 as Motor Inspectors and 114 as Airplane Inspectors (it is believed that 6 men completed both courses), which together provided services essential to the expansion of production and basic to the growth of naval aviation.

The need for special meteorological instruments to measure certain weather phenomena had been expressed by the aviators early in the history of naval aviation, but it took the experience of war to prove the need for officers specially trained in weather forecasting. As a first step toward this training, the Commanding Officer of the Detachment was requested to investigate the possibility of arranging for a training program with Professor Alexander McAdie of the Blue Hill Observatory at Harvard University. He made his preliminary report in November with the comment, "This is undoubtedly an opportunity to obtain information of considerable value for aviation purposes." Only a week later he reported the start of the course with one student enrolled.[29] This course was established on December 22nd as a formal part of the Detachment program at the Institute under the direction of the Commanding Officer. Considerable instruction was given at the Blue Hill Observatory, but classes were also held in the Aerographic Laboratory of the Institute. The course was of six weeks duration, and laid stress on the use of aerographic instruments, the structure of the atmosphere, and methods of forecasting. Because information available regarding the upper strata of the atmosphere was somewhat meager, the students also did a considerable amount of research for the purpose of both improving methods of making weather balloon observations, and to design special aerographic instruments for the Chemical Warfare Department in Washington. The curriculum for the Aerography School included: Aerographic Instruments; Principles of Aerography; Structure of Atmosphere; and Weather Forecasting. The amount of time devoted to these subjects varied.

The course differed radically from the regular Ground School, but with few exceptions all student aerographers first completed the Ground School course. The small size of classes required little formal organization, and hours were flexible. No more than 5 students were on board at any time, and several classes consisted of a lone student.

Eight graduates of this school made up the first detachment of trained aerographers sent in April 1918 to organize and operate an aerography service at naval air stations overseas. In all, 55 men were assigned to the school and 54 graduated, among them Francis W. Reichelderfer, a future head of the U.S. Weather Bureau. The school continued to operate until the Detachment was disestablished in January 1919.

Establishment of the Receiving School on 18 March 1918 solved a problem that had plagued the Program from the beginning. As early as September 1917, the Commanding Officer reported that half of a new Flight arrived two days before orders reassigning the graduates of Flight A were received. Because this put 225 men on board for the 200 bunks available, his only recourse was to send 30 of the men of Flight A on leave—a solution not entirely displeasing to the men.[30] Later he reported difficulty in transferring men after completing the course because transportation was not available on Saturdays, which was the normal arrival day for new flights.[31] Although these difficulties were overcome by the ingenuity, if not the persistence of the Commanding Officer, they carried over for several months and were aggravated by steady growth of the student body. As a solution to this and other problems, the Commanding Officer recommended that students be sent to school two weeks in advance of their scheduled assignment to Ground School and be quartered in a separate building. During those two weeks, he proposed that the students could be vaccinated, outfitted with uniforms, and receive instruction in Navy Regulations, Naval Customs, and Drill. This, he suggested, would permit isolation of new students and thus diminish the chance of spreading contagious disease, would put the students in better physical condition, and give them a proper indoctrination to school procedure. To house these men, he reported the availability of the Mercantile Building located across the street from the Institute's campus. He ended by asking authorization to request the Institute to rent the building and convert it for use.[32]

The subjects of instruction in this school were: Athletics; Boat Drill; Calisthenics; Drill and Discipline; Elementary Aerial Navigation; Elementary Seamanship; Semaphore; and Signaling. The amount of time devoted to these subjects was never definitely fixed. Approval of the plan was recommended to the Bureau of Navigation by the Aviation Office with the admission that, due to error, approximately 65 more students than could be accommodated had been ordered to the next class.[33] The plan was duly approved. The building was leased by the Institute, and alterations as necessary to house 300 student officers were in process by the first of March.

The new school went into operation as scheduled on March 18th under the command of Lieutenant (j.g.) S.W. Sargent. As it developed, the school became a pool where men were held in readiness to fill Ground School quotas; the instruction program was flexible, and the men were held on board from 2 to as many as 6 weeks. During this time they received preliminary instruction, drill, physical training, and medical examinations and treatment, as a result of which the undesirables and those physically unfit were gradually weeded out.

Men of the Receiving Ship were organized into companies, Company I being senior and containing those men farthest along in their training. Every two weeks the senior company was graduated, assigned a Class number, and transferred to the Ground School. The School remained in existence until 19 November 1918, when the last men on board were transferred.

Quarters

When the Detachment came into being at the Institute on 23 July 1917, it quartered and messed in temporary spaces provided in Technology Building No. 1. Early in September, a move was made to the Walker Memorial Building, which was to be the Detachment's home for most of the program. There, the men were quartered on the second and third floors and messed in the cafeteria on the ground floor. At the same time, the administrative and academic headquarters were established in the Stone & Webster Building. Space in the Walker Building was initially quite limited. Only three days after moving in the Commanding Officer reported that no place had been provided for study, and there was scarcely room to write a letter. He suggested that space occupied by the Cadet School of the Naval Militia could be used to great advantage. Acquisition of that space, arranged by the Institute without official action, alleviated this problem.[34] The Detachment was inspected on 15 November by the Commandant, First Naval District, and its space pronounced "satisfactory in every respect." He reported 310 men on board in space that would take care of 450 at 450 cubic feet per man. He found the mess arrangements, which were in the cafeteria run by the Institute, "good," the food of good quality, and the galley and preparation of food satisfactory.[35]

Growth of the student body required further expansion, which was provided in the basement of the Walker Building and by January 1918 reached a maximum capacity of nearly 600 personnel, of which 570 were students. Although this was accompanied by some crowding, the Commanding Officer expressed the opinion that it was not so crowded as to be detrimental to the health of the men. He pointed out, however, that since it was rumored that the Army was planning to close its School of Military Aeronautics at the Institute, the possibility of the Navy taking over the vacated space should be considered. Two weeks later, he reported completion of other arrangements that would permit having a maximum of 600 students in addition to the permanent detail "without the construction of new buildings."[36] In February, the practicability of quartering a maximum of 750 students was under consideration. To meet this increase an addition to the Walker Memorial Building seemed necessary. This idea, however, was abandoned in favor of the erection of a temporary structure that would house 200 men, 50 of which could then be moved out of the basement of Walker. Ground was broken, and the new building was expected to be ready for occupancy by mid-April.[37]

Steady increases in numbers on board underlined the need for consolidating the Medical Department, which in May consisted of two dispensaries and two sick bays maintained in separate buildings a half a mile apart. Construction of a new building to house all medical facilities had the added advantage of releasing space in the Walker Building for quartering more students.[38] This proposal was approved in June, and the building completed in September. In late July, as the Navy was pressing for more classroom space, it was again rumored that the Army School of Military Aeronautics would be closed in September. Although the Institute was planning to use the vacated dormitory space for its own academic program, it was made available to the Navy and occupied in October.

Institute classrooms and laboratories also proved inadequate as the program began to roll. Expansion began in October as the Gas Laboratory was turned over in its entirety to the Detachment use, and a shed for housing seaplanes required in the Rigging Course was under construction. New arrangements for the Laboratory were pronounced "eminently satisfactory." The seaplane shed, intended for use by both Army and Navy classes, provided ample space, the floor area being 150 x 35 feet, with an ell of 150 x 20 feet. Both, however, were soon out grown. Erection of a double hangar for the Rigging Department was requested in March, and plans were drawn up for a new building for the Engine Course in April.

A Report of Inspection made toward the end of the program was indicative of both the extent and the quality of provisions made in this area by the Institute for the Detachment and its program. The Commandant found change in quarters "a very great improvement." The new buildings constructed since his last inspection were "well built and well furnished." Classrooms were "in very good condition, well supplied with models, charts, and everything required for the instruction of the Cadets....An addition has been built to the Gunnery Department allowing more facilities for the instruction of gunnery and bombing and the upper floor is used for an officers' club room. This is most satisfactory...."[39]

Buildings erected by the Institute for use of the Detachment were as shown in Table IV.

TABLE IV

Building	Approximate Date Completed
Airplane Hangar[#]	December 1917
Engine laboratory	June 1918
Engine Test Sheds	June-November 1918
Recreation Building	July 1918
Machine Gun Pits	July 1918
Seaplane Hangar	August 1918
Aerial Observation Building[##]	August 1918
Dispensary and Sick Bay	September 1918
Barracks	September 1918
Gunnery Building	September 1918

[#] Built for joint Army-Navy use

[##] Included two observation ranges and navigation and rigging laboratory

Three contracts were made by the Navy Department with the Massachusetts Institute of Technology to cover the cost of operating the School. These included the Inspector School, but made no special provisions for either the Aerography School or the Receiving Ship. The main features of these contracts were as follows:

First Contract: Effective 23 July to 31 December 1917 with privilege of renewal. Estimated cost $80,000. Required facilities for at least 200 students and a course of 2 months duration. Payment per student was $10.00 per week for the first four weeks and $5.00 per week for the remainder. No provisions were made for subsistence.

Second Contract: Effective 1 January to 30 June 1918 with privilege of renewal. No Estimate of cost. Required facilities for at least 500 men, a Ground School course to 10 weeks, and an Inspector School course for 6 weeks. Payment per student in Ground School was $10.00 per week for the first 5 weeks and $5.00 per week for the remainder; for the Inspector School the cost was $10.00 per week for 6 weeks. Subsistence was set at $1.25 per day per man.

Third Contract: Effective 1 July 1918 to 1 July 1919 with privilege of cancellation. Estimated cost was $500,000. Required facilities for at least 750 men, a Ground School of eight weeks, and an Inspector School of 6 weeks. Payment per student was $7.00 per week for Ground School and $10.00 per week for Inspector School. Subsistence was again $1.25 per day per man. This contract also carried the provision that upon completion the Navy would reimburse the Institute for expenses in excess of operating costs, and that the Institute would return any profits, the amount in either instance to be determined by a Board composed of three members, one appointed by the Institute, one by the Navy, and the third to be selected by both.

On 10 February 1919 Lieutenant Commander Van Valzah reported to the Director of Naval Aviation that "the Detachment under my command is officially closed this date." On the same day, Horace S. Ford, Bursar of the Institute, Captain H.R. Stamford, Institute, and Navy members of the Board to determine final settlement recommended to the Secretary of the Navy that Lieutenant Commander Cabaniss be appointed as the third member. The Board was immediately informed that Lieutenant Commander Cabaniss would be assigned upon his return to the United States.

This Board submitted its report on 12 May 1919, finding as follows: "That on May 15, 1919 there will remain due and payable to the Massachusetts Institute of Tech (sic) by the Navy Department the sum of One Hundred and sixty-nine Thousand Five Hundred and Eighty-two Dollars and Eighty Cents ($169,582.80)." This report, approved and forwarded by the Commandant of the First Naval District on May 13th, was referred to the Bureau of Navigation by the Secretary of the Navy with orders to make final settlement as recommended.

In summary, the following tables summarize the activities conducted at the Institute under the auspices of the Naval Aviation Detachment:

TABLE A (Schools)

General Facts	Totals	Ground School	Inspector School	Aerography School	Receiving Ship School
Opened		23-1-17	1-10-17	22-12-17	18-3-17
Closed		18-1-19	22-10-18	18-1-19	19-11-18
Number of Courses	6	2	2	1	1
Number of Classes	81	34	9	21	17
Total Distribution of Academic Instructors	167[a]	156	24	6	0
M.I.T. Men	57[b]	40	21	1	0

a. Nine Instructors counted twice
b. Four Instructors counted twice

TABLE B (Enrollment)

Scholastic Records	Totals	Ground School	Inspection School	Aerography School	Receiving Ship School
No. of Students	4911[a]	4194	200	55	2978
No. Graduated	3622[b]	3447	167	54	2470
No. Transferred	6-7	329	17	1	350
No. Discharged	298	125	15	0	158
No. Inactive	384	383	1	0	0
No. Academic Failures	95[c]	77	18	0	0

a and b: These Totals corrected for 2516 men counted twice
c: Total includes men in the Transferred and Discharged totals

TABLE D
(Distribution of Student Officers)

Service	Number of Students
U.S. Navy	332
U.S. Navy Reserve Force	3308
U.S. National Naval Volunteers	105
U.S. Marine Corps	295
Royal Canadian Naval Air Service	60
Total	4168

TABLE E
(Distribution of Student Officers from the Receiving Ship)

Records	Number of Students
Entered Ground School	2470
Transferred Elsewhere	350
Discharged (Medical)	18
Discharged (Ineptitude)	140
Total	2978

TABLE F
(Classification of Student Officers)*

Classification	No. of Students
Student Flight Officer, H.T.A.	3572
Student Flight Officer, L.T.A.	252
Student Ground Officer, H.T.A.	132
Student Ground Officer, L.T.A.	2
Student Aerography Officer, H.T.A.	41
Student Aerography Officer, L.T.A.	2
Student Hydrogen Officer, L.T.A.	8
Flight Cadet, R.C.N.A.S., H.T.A.	30
Flight Cadet, R.C.N.A.S., L.T.A.	30
Student Photographers	5
Radio Observers	93
Dunwoody Student Flight Officers	26
Total	4196

*Note again the discrepancy between Naval and Institute enrollment figures

HONOR ROLL

Nineteen Student Officers died while stationed at the Detachment, eleven of whom succumbed in influenza.

Name	Class	Status	Date of Death
Boyer, H.S.	Receiving Ship	Flight Officer	21 September 1918
Cain, O.L.	29	Flight Officer	6 October 1918
Douthitt, R.N.	29	Flight Officer	21 September 1918
Elwood, S.W.	Receiving Ship	Flight Officer	17 September 1918
Fisher, L.H.	30	Flight Officer	21 September 1918
Goodspeed, J.P.	30	Flight Officer	7 October 1918
Hibbard, H.H.	12	Flight Officer	17 March 1918
Krannick, A.C.	22	Flight Officer	29 April 1918
LaFlamme, A.W.	28	Flight Officer	16 June 1918
Noble, E.E.	19	Flight Officer	17 May 1918
Parker, B.	28	Flight Officer	21 September 1918
Picknel, A.H.	18	Flight Officer	18 April 1918
Schneider, A. Jr.	28	Flight Officer	22 September 1918
Scott, W.R.	13	Flight Officer	17 March 1918
Sears, W.	13	Flight Officer	19 February 1918
Snow, L.J. Jr.	30	Flight Officer	30 September 1918
Stem, C.C.	19	Flight Officer	13 May 1918
Treble, H.W.	31	Flight Officer	1 October 1918
Williams, R.C.	19	Radio Observer	1 February 1918

Notes:

[1] Much of this appendix is based upon the paper entitled *The Naval Detachment at the Massachusetts Institute of Technology, World War I,* prepared by A.O. Van Wyen, 1968.

[2] See Sec.Nav. Ltr. MAT 7-AH, 2638-17 of 2 July 1917

[3] Telegram, MacLaurin to Sec.Nav. of 9 July 1917

[4] Memos of telephone conversations, Johnson and Spencer, Op-Air 3-LL, 3017-17, both of 12 July 1917

[5] Sec.Nav. telegram, Op-Air 1-AH, 2952-17 of 12 July 1917 and President MacLaurin's reply of 13 July 1917

[6] Sec.Nav. to BUNAV, Op-Air 3-AH 3017-17 of 14 July 1917

[7] *Technology's War Record*, page 20

[8] CO NAD ltr. to Com. 1st NAD 8640-2, HCV-LC of 30 January 1919

[9] CO NAD ltr. to Comm. 1st NAD 8648-42, HCV-LC of 30 January 1919 reports 5,251 assigned, 4,411 to Ground School and 3,4521 graduated. MIT Report shows 4,911 receiving instruction and about 3,622 graduating. Which of these is correct cannot be determined from available sources, but some of the difference undoubtedly results from counting men more than once because of their attendance at more than one school.

[10] CO NAD ltr. to Lieutenant Johnson, 8 September 1917

[11] CO NAD ltr. to CNO, 31 July 1917

[12] BuNav telegrams to 1st NAD of 7 and 9 January 1919

[13] CO NAD ltr. of 16 January 1918 indicates that this change was made not so much as to standardize the groups as it was to give the men enough money toabuy uniforms without going into debt.

[14] Statistical data in this section are based largely on the report written by Olen C. Morris entitled *Report upon the United States Naval Detachment Massachusetts Institute of Technology, Cambridge Mass. - A survey covering period of its existence from July 23, 1917 to January 18, 1919,* Dated February 1, 1919

[15] CO NAD 790-9, RWC-PC of 8 January 1918

[16] The exclusive reference to the Lewis Gun was based upon the Navy's decision (Ref.: Ltr. dated 25 January 1918 from N.E. Irwin to CO NAD MIT (Op-Air-08333-33) on subject of Machine Gun Instruction) to adopt the Lewis Gun as the moveable gun for all seaplanes operating at Naval Air Stations abroad. The Irwin letter then goes on to state that all instruction on how the Colt and Marlin guns work should be discontinued.

[17] CO NAD ltr. NAD-3549 of 20 July 1918

[18] CO NAD ltr. of 21 August 1917 and 1st Endorsement of 212 February 1918 on Supervisor NRFC ltr., Nav.Air 79-105 of 18 February 1918

[19] Many of these lecture notes may be found in the CNO (Aviation) Records File 088, Boxes 86 and 210 in the National Archives

[20] CO NAD ltr. of 22 August 1917

[21] CO NAD ltr. of 8 September 1917

[22] Enclosure to CO NAD ltr. of 15 September 1917

[23] Bureau of Construction and Repair Endorsement of 6 October 1917 and Bureau of Steam Engineering Endorsement of 1 October 1917

[24] CO NAD Weekly Report of 6 November 1917

[25] Ltr. number 251397-707-Da dated 2 February 1918 from A.T. Atkins {Bureau of Steam Engineering} to Supervisor, Naval Reserve Flying Corps.

[26] CO NAD ltr. of 7 November 1917

[27] CO NAD ltr. of 3 December 1917 and Bureau of Construction and Repair Memo of 15 January 1918

[28] Bureau of Construction and Repair ltr. of 11 January 1918, Bureau of Steam Engineering ltr. of 2 February, Pres. Acd.Bd. ltr. to CO NAD of 8 February, and CO NAD Endorsement of 12 February, all discuss some of the problems and means of overcoming them.

[29] CO NAD ltrs. of 26 November 1917 and 3 December 1917

[30] CO NAD ltr. of 17 September 1917

[31] CO NAD ltrs. of 27 October and 29 October 1917

[32] CO NAD ltr. of 13 February 1918

[33] Aviation in CNO endorsement of 23 February 1918

[34] CO NAD ltrs. of 8 September and 27 September 1917

[35] Rear Admiral A. Ross Report of Inspection, 26 November 1917

[36] CO NAD ltrs. of 3 January and 17 January 1917

[37] CO NAD ltrs. of 15 March and 25 March 1918

[38] Medical Officer, NAD ltr. to 1st Naval District of 17 May 1918

[39] Rear Admiral A. Ross ltr. of Sec.Nav. of 4 December 1918

Appendix F:
Naval Aviation Training at the Dunwoody Industrial Institute

Mr. William Hood Dunwoody, a member of the family who were the owners of the General Foods Company, formed the Dunwoody Industrial Institute in Minneapolis, Minnesota, in 1914. Its charter, then and now, is "A school wherein instruction in the industrial and mechanical arts shall be given free to the youth of Minneapolis and Minnesota without distinction on account of race color and religious prejudice." As the United States edged toward entry into the war the Institute administrators approached the Navy with the idea of offering the Institute as a training facility. On January 6, 1917, it was announced that within a month the Institute was to become a naval training station. It would take companies of men at the Great Lakes Training Station who had enlisted in the Navy as Quartermaster in the Reserve Corp., and who had undergone a week or two of training, and send them to Dunwoody, under the command of Chief Petty Officers and Petty Officers, for skill training. Training was to be provided in the areas of engines and motors, electricity, baking, sheet metal, carpentry, blacksmith, and wireless telegraphy. On June 19, 1917, it was announced that R.Adm. Robert E. Peary, while on a tour of Minneapolis, had stated the intent of the Army and the Navy to establish both an aviation school and a flying field for training candidates for aviation corps. It was felt that such training at the Institute could begin as early as August 15th. Dr. C.A. Prosser, Director of the Institute, informed the Government that the Dunwoody Institute was ready to train groups of 250 or more students in flying, and to provide ten machines that would be required on the condition that the Government later take possession of the machines. On July 1, 1917, the Institute moved to a new and larger location and began military training for enlisted personnel, and August 1st the new plant was ready for operation. On this date naval enlisted personnel also reported. At the Institute the organization of the Navy school was on a department basis. For each department there was in charge a department head. Under the department heads were the individual instructors. Three commissioned naval officers ran the Navy program. The headquarters for the Dunwoody Naval Training Schools was located in a building in downtown Minneapolis a short distance from the Institute. The Navy detachment itself was quartered at the Dunwoody Club and at the two hotels near the school (Ens. F.T. Mayes was in charge of the Hotel Radisson Barracks, Ens. T.H. Patterson was in charge of the Elgin Hotel barracks, and Ens. Kazmarck was in charge of the Dunwoody Naval Club barracks). All responsibility for quartering was under the jurisdiction of the commandant of the schools. The naval training was conducted in parallel with both the Army training program and the normal enrollment of day students at the Institute. Every student was furnished with lesson sheets specifically prepared for navy students. These lesson sheets contained material

Aviation hangar at the Dunwoody Institute. The aircraft appears to be a Burgess-Dunne seaplane.

Aviation Carpenter Mate's class at the Dunwoody Institute

Drill Ground at the Dunwoody Institute.

Carpenter Shop at the Dunwoody Institute.

secured from the Brooklyn Navy Yard, the Navy School at Charleston, and from various flying fields.

The aviation department at the Institute included instruction for riggers (QM (a)), engine mechanics (MM (a)), and wood workers (CM (a)). To help in these areas the Minneapolis Aero Club purchased, and turned over to the Institute, a Curtiss JN-4 and a JN-3 (without motor). The Navy Department secured a Burgess-Dunne seaplane, a new Sturtevant hydroplane, two Lewis machine guns, a Colt machine gun, a Colt automatic pistol, Springfield rifles, a Curtiss OX 90 hp engine, a Sturtevant 8-cylinder 115 hp motor, a 9-cylinder Gnôme 100 hp rotary engine, a 6-cylinder Hall-Scott 100 hp engine, various aeroplane instruments, and surplus miscellaneous parts.

In July Ens. Colby Dodge, Commandant of the U.S. Naval Detachment, presented the idea of a naval aerial detachment to C.W. Gardner, W.W. Eastman, Charles Pillsbury, and Sewall D. Andrews of the Aero Club of Minneapolis. The Aero Club had been formed on August 1, 1917, and Articles of Incorporation were filed on August 8, 1917. The public was requested to donate $25,000 to insure the success of aerial training and the care of aeroplanes. A formal Naval Air Detachment was established 10 August 1917. On August 4, 1917, it was announced that Dr. Posser had been named Director of the National Commission on Vocational Training in Washington. In this position Dr. Prosser would further aid in the expansion of the programs at Dunwoody. On August 24, 1917, Ensign Dodge obtained approval of the Navy Department to enlist 25 men as naval aviator Class 4.

On September 16, 1917, Mr. Sewall D. Andrews, director of the Minneapolis Aero Club, Dr. Prosser, and Congressman Murray Hulbert of New York lobbied the Navy Department for approval of an aerial naval detachment at Dunwoody. By September 23, 1917, it was announced that land plane training only would start, and that it was hoped that later seaplane training could be included on 20 acres near Holdridge, on Lake Minnetonka. The Minneapolis Aero Club planned to construct barracks for housing the members of the new aerial unit, as well as hangars and machine shops in advance of federal funding. The curriculum, for a six to 16 week course, was prepared from information gathered by school representatives sent to: the Bureau of Navigation, Navy Department, Washington, DC; the Navy School of Machinist Mates at Charleston, NC; the Navy School for Electricians at NY; the Navy School for Radio at Harvard University, the Navy Ground School at M.I.T.; the Ground School for Army student pilots at the University of Illinois; the Dayton Electric and Laboratory Company in Dayton, Ohio; the RFC School for pilots at Toronto, Canada; Curtiss Aeroplane Factory at Buffalo, NY; Dayton Wright Aeroplane Factory, Dayton, Ohio; the flying fields at Rantoul, Illinois, Belleville, Illinois, San Antonio, Texas, and Fort Worth, Texas; and the Naval Air Stations at Norfolk and Pensacola. The Naval enrollment in these classes varied from 450 to 550 students. On September 17, 1917, it was announced that command of all recruiting in the naval district embracing Minnesota and North Dakota was being given to Lt. George A. Treadwell, USNRF. Ens. Colby Dodge, USN (retired), was to take charge as Commanding Officer of the Dunwoody naval detail. His Headquarters was to be at Dunwoody.

On October 7, 1917, the Minneapolis newspapers announced that the Aero Club of Minneapolis had leased from C.D. Velie the old Judge M.B. Koon residence at 1600 Harmon Place as the Headquarters of the Aero Club of Minneapolis, and the home of the Dunwoody aerial naval unit. Property owned by Mr. Earle Brown, north of Camden Place, was to be used as the flying field. On October 10th it was announced that the class of student flight officers at Dunwoody had been doubled. An increase up to 300 men at a rate of 50 men per week (with 200 men in class and 100 in the Receiving Ship on a weekly basis) was anticipated. It was planned that 50 students completing their training were to be assigned to the naval

An unidentified group of Aviation Quarter Masters at the Dunwoody Institute.

Study hall at the Dunwoody Institute for Naval Aviator officer students.

air station at Miami for aerial training. On the 22nd the Minneapolis newspapers reported that a selection of 25 men to comprise the naval aerial unit would be made from 38 candidates. Eventually, 25 men out of 153 applicants were selected for the first class. Mr. William F. Brooks, President of the Aero Club of Minneapolis, which was financing the project, visited Toronto, Canada, on the 21st to engage two RFC aviators to serve as instructors at Dunwoody. Furthermore, it was announced that two Liberty engines, furnished by the Government for training purposes, were expected to arrive the following week. On the same date it was announced that Chief Master at Arms William W. Eastman was both to direct and to attend the initial ground school (see Table FA). Eastman, who was to become a qualified naval aviator (No. 1679) following completion of testing at M.I.T., was subsequently promoted to Ensign USNRF and was to return to Dunwoody to command the second ground school. Recruiting for the naval flight program continued through October and right up to the first of November, when instruction began. Mr. W.F. Brooks of the Aero Club of Minneapolis, after three weeks inspecting government flying fields, announced on October 26th the bringing of Lt. J.C. Willard, RFC, to Minneapolis as one of the instructors. Lt. Willard was stated to have served on the Somme and at Verdun.

On November 1, 1917, a four-month period of ground school instruction began. The chief instructor was Capt. A.W. Farmer who, on December 5, 1917, inaugurated the unit by two short flights over Minneapolis in a 150 hp Curtiss biplane. On December 4, 1917, the Minneapolis newspapers announced that the rooster of 25 men for the Dunwoody aerial coastal patrol was completed, and that the men were quartered in the Naval Club Headquarters on Harmon Place. Two Curtiss aeroplanes were at Dunwoody for study. It was further announced that authority had been received for the enrollment of a class of 150 men who had enlisted as Landsman for Mechanician.

On February 11, 1918, it was announced that Cdr. Warren J. Terhune had relieved Ens. Colby Dodge as commandant of the U.S. Naval Training Station in Minneapolis. At this time the station changed from a Detachment to a Training Station. Dodge became the Station's Executive Officer. At its height of operation Dunwoody was second in size only to the Great Lakes Naval Training Base in Illinois. Between August 1, 1917, and August 1, 1918, Dunwoody trained close to 8000 men (2300 for the Navy).

The initial training at Dunwoody for prospective naval aviators was completed in April 1918. Their training had encompassed: Fundamentals of naval service, seamanship, navigation, meteorology, gunnery, rigging, photography, aerial observation, radio, electricity, engines, and theory of flight. Based upon the grade sheets of a number of members of the first class, the training curriculum consisted of the following subjects: Aerography; Electricity; Motors; F.N.S.; Gunnery; Navigation; Rigging; Seamanship; Signaling (Radio); Theory of Flight; Meteorology; Semaphore; Blinker; Calisthenics; Drill; and Aptitude. The graduates were sent to the Naval Ground School at M.I.T. for final examination. Ten of the first graduates were examined at M.I.T. and assigned to naval flying schools, while the remainder were transferred to M.I.T. by about May 15th. After passing 12 written examinations and a physical examination for prospective aviators, the men were detailed to various naval air stations for flight training (see Table FB)

Liberty Motors in the engine shop at the Dunwoody Institute.

Machine shop at the Dunwoody Institute.

Aircraft engine shop at the Dunwoody Institute.

Students trained to fly seaplanes over Lake Minnetonka received training in six phases: 1) Discipline and naval indoctrination; 2) navigation, gunnery, seamanship, meteorology, signals, electricity, photography, and first aid; 3) rigging and structures of aircraft, upkeep, and repairs; 4) gas-engine training and disassembly, overhauling and assembly of engines, trouble-shooting, materials of construction, wood, fabric, and paints; 5) theory of flight; and 6) aircraft instruments.

As in every other city in the country similarly situated, the war recreation activities were organized under, and directed by, the War Camp Community Service of the War Department and Navy Department commissions on training camp activities. The Minneapolis effort was handled by a citizens group who initially established a "hang out" for all service personnel at 1025 Hennepin Ave in February 1918. This site, within a short time, was filled to capacity. Therefore, a new Army-Navy Club House, located at the corner of Hennepin Ave. and Tenth Street, was opened on May 18th. The attendance ranged from 1,000 to 15,000 on weekdays to between 3,000 to 4,000 on Saturdays and Sundays; and on Memorial Day it was nearly 5,000.

The only flying accident at Dunwoody occurred on June 11, 1918, when Norman W. Leslie, aviation mechanic instructor, and Jame Ing, a student aviator, were injured when their plane suffered jammed controls and hit a tree. Neither occupant was hurt.

The Navy was sufficiently pleased with the results of this first class at the Institute that it authorized the formation of a second class of 25 students. This second class enrolled on 15 June 1918 for a ten-week curriculum (see Table FC). It was the last such class to be conducted at Dunwoody. On September 10, 1918, it was announced that the Navy had informed Dunwoody that a gradual slowdown in training was planned, and that in the future training would be provided by the Great Lake Naval Training Base and other military schools. On November 7, 1918, it was announced that training of ten cadets currently in training would end following graduation, and that 25 naval students were scheduled to graduate on November 8th with the remainder to be finished by Christmas. Fifty of the 300 students in the "Receiving Ship" were to be transferred to M.I.T., and the remainder given the opportunity to either transfer to other military branches or to civilian life. Actual naval training at Dunwoody ended on March 1, 1919.

Group photograph of unidentified enlisted personnel at the Dunwoody Institute.

Unidentified student enlisted men at the Dunwoody Institute. The aircraft appears to be a Sturtevant hydroplane. This aircraft was not flown at Dunwoody, but rather was used for other instructional purposes.

TABLE FA
Members of the First Minneapolis Aerial Unit

Milton Bruce	Morris Andrews	C.W. Smith	W.W. Eastman
John C. Flood	C.A. Roedell	Samuel P. Sheldon	David Rittenhouse
Victor Rotering	M.D. Crawford Jr.	B.E. Slyvester	A.A. Trood
J.H., Busnell	George D. Cannon	Torvald Delling	Edgar D. Sageros
Richard B. Grace	Frank B. Aubachek	C.T. Mandeville	L.A. McCarthy
F.P. Peterson	Kenneth B. Salisbury	Charles M. Sanborn	Gordon Tircher
Arthur R. Helm			

TABLE FB
Taken from "The Artisian," assignments were as follows:

Student	**Assigned Base**
Bushnell and Rittenhouse, Jr.	Key West
Torvold Delling and Mandeville	Miami
C.A. Bartholomew	Akron (Balloon Training)
Ratering, Andrews, McCarthy, Roedell, Samuel Sheldon, Brice, Helm, Smith, Flood, A.A. Atwood, Grace, K.B. Salisbury, Frank B. Hubacheck, Sanborn, and Cannon	Pensacola

TABLE FC
Applicants Approved for the Second Course

Truman C. Penny	Armion J. Bruning	Charles H. Carpenter
Donald P. Spurrier	J.E. Schroeder	Harold K. Armstrong
Vincent R. Hunt	Thurman H. Porter	Thamas B. Caldwell
Severt H. Petterson	Elliott W Spalding	Thomas D. Barry
Robert F. Wright	Lewis S. Coryell	Charles W. Greer, Jr.
Earl D. McKay	Ronald H. Joseph	Stevens W. Callaway
John M. Martin	Paul Reverson	Allan E. Greenman
Edmund W. McElligott	Robert W. Olson	James E. O'Malley
Donald D. Stovell	Edgar W. Morrill	Wallace W. Hankins
Oscar William Swanson	Frank P. Bruce	Ivers W. Riley
James K. Lewis		

TABLE FD
Assignment of Various Students Following Graduation (Based upon School Records)

Robert. Fulton Wright	Discharged to accept appointment as Ensign
Roland Homer Joseph	Transferred to NAS Miami as CQM(a)
Totton Peay Heffelfinger	Discharged to accept appointment as Ensign
Wallace Watt Hankin	Transferred to NAS Key West as CQM(a)
Charles Wilbur Greer	Released from active service
Allan Eugene Greenman	Transferred to NAS Key West as CQM(a)
Lewis Sammuel Coryell	Transferred to NAS Key West as a CQM(a)
Donald Kemp Cobb	Transferred to NAS Key West as a CQM(a)
Charles H. Carpenter	Transferred to NAS Key West as a CQM(a)
Steven Ward Callaway	Transferred to NAS Key West as a CQM(a)

Appendix G: Naval Air Station Pauillac[1]

I. Introduction

On September 16, 1917, the Navy Department authorized the establishment of eleven Naval Air Stations in France. One of the sites selected was at Pauillac, on the Grionde River. At NAS Pauillac were to be the receiving barracks, the assembly and repair plant, and the supply depot for the French Coastal Units of U.S. Naval Aviation. It was to Pauillac where personnel and supplies were to be sent upon their arrival overseas for distribution among the various air stations, and where all planes and motors were to be sent for repair and overhaul. Pauillac was selected for this work on account of its central location, its rail connections, the deep-water dock immediately adjoining the site, the climate, and the amount of suitable ground available. In order to adequately discuss the multifaceted activities undertaken by the Navy at Pauillac, the history of the Station will be separated into the categories of activities which were undertaken at the Station (i.e., Construction, Personnel, and Operation—Assembly and Repair, Supply, etc.).

II. Construction

Up to the time that Pauillac started operations as an assembly and repair base for naval aviation in France, the station was virtually a construction camp and a transfer yard for construction supplies to the other Naval Air stations in France. The Public Works Department controlled the former work entirely, and had considerable responsibility in the latter function. From the time the station really began operations as a repair base, however, this department assumed less relative importance in the activities of Pauillac. The record of its physical development and of the other activities of the Navy's Department of Public Works constitute a large part of the 12 month history of the Naval Air Station at Pauillac.

During October 1917, the project of establishing a central repair, assembly, and distribution center at Pauillac had been definitely settled. It was agitated from the first days in France, but upon the arrival of Commander Patton at Pauillac the plot of land belonging to the Bordeaux Chamber of Commerce, together with two buildings thereon, was leased.

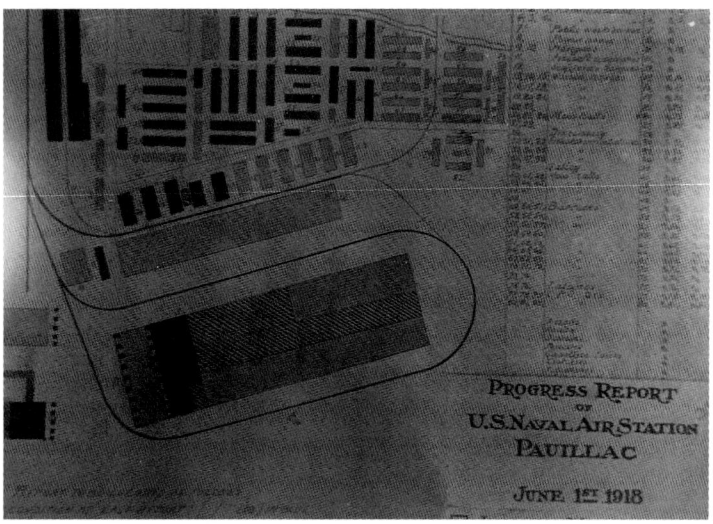

Plot plan of NAS Pauillac taken from the Progress Report on the station issued on 12 June 1918. (source: 80 HAG-5J-9)

Aerial view of NAS Pauillac. (source: Naval Historical Center)

The station was commissioned on December 1, 1917. At that time the only building on the station was one leased from the Bordeaux Chamber of Commerce, known as Building No. 1, and used at that time as offices, crews quarters, mess hall, and galley. The property of the station covered the area bounded on the west by the road, (parallel to the river) from Building No. 1 to the Chanal de Troumpeloup, by the Chanal and the river on the north and east, and by a line from Building No. 1 to the river on the south. It was two weeks later that Lieutenant Commander A.W.K. Billings, (CEC) Public Works Officer for Aviation in France, arrived with Lieutenant Richardson, Civil Engineering Corps (CEC), and Lieutenant (j.g.) H. Burnham to organize a Public Work department. Richardson was detailed as Public Works Officer with Burnham as assistant; preliminary plans for the construction of a Repair Base, with a maximum complement of 1500 men, were decided upon, and Billings returned to Paris Headquarters.

The use of the portable wooden barracks and portable steel frame repair shops, all to be shipped from America, had been previously determined in Washington. The general arrangements and the local problems of water supply, sewage, lights, power, land requirements, dockage facilities, railroad arrangements, and many other such problems were practically all left in the hands of Lieutenant Richardson, subject to the advice and approval of Lieutenant Commander Billings in Paris. One of the first moves was the rental of the French Warehouses known as Warehouses Nos. 1 and 2. The lack of construction materials, however, prevented building activity during the winter, except for the remodeling of the Old Building No. 1, the construction of the small pier for use of a patrol vessel, and some road and railroad work.

In February the land eventually to be occupied by the Assembly and Repair shops, and a little later the land to be occupied by the Warehouses Nos. 3 to 12, the area between them, and the main road leading inland from the village of Trompeloup, were acquired. This permitted the commencement of the work during February for the first two of the provision warehouses, the Public Works Offices, and the foundations for the Assembly and Repair (A&R) Shops. Lieutenant (j.g.) Heuton Byers, (CEC), reported in February as another assistant, along with Lieutenant (j.g.) Burnham, to Lieutenant Richardson. Material commenced to arrive in quantity from the U.S. about this time, as well as additional men for the station.

During the month of March the first five portable barracks were erected, as well as Warehouse Numbers 3, 4, and 5, and the railroad tracks were extended to these warehouses. The steelwork was well started on the repair shop, and work was begun on the foundations for the seaplane hangars. A telephone system and temporary electric light plant were installed and put into operation during this month. The Public Works Department in March had on average 257 men working. It might be said that in this month the construction work of the station actually started. At that time, however, there was no indication that the station would grow to anything like it eventually became.

The program for the Northern Bombing Group was decided upon on about April 1st, and Pauillac was counted upon as the assembly base for this effort. This greatly increased the scope of the station. It was decided to acquire a flying field for land planes, as well as the additional camp space west of the (A&R) Shop, and the whole district eventually occupied by the mess hall and the barracks south and west from it. Construction work was pushed on the erection of barracks to accommodate incoming drafts of men. A permanent sewer system was started, the garage was built, and the roads and railroads were extended. This work was pushed at the expense of repair shop and hangar construction, partly because of the unsettled plans as to the requirements of the latter building, but principally because of the lack of necessary materials and the immediate need of housing the increased complement. In the meantime, the Public Works organization had grown to a force of about 400 men and had been organized with an Electrical Department under Ensign Rodey, and a Plumbing and Miscellaneous Department under Warrant Carpenter Campbell. The outside general construction was organized under various Chief Petty Officers and directed by Lieutenants Byers and Burnham.

During all of this time Lieutenant Richardson had, in addition to his work of organizing the station construction forces here, the same duties on all other French Coastal Air Stations, in his capacity as assistant to Lieutenant Commander Billings. He was obliged to make trips to all stations in France and to see that they received their construction requirements from Pauillac as fast as these could be distributed after arrival from the States. The work figuring out the requirements of all of these stations and the ordering out and recording of all shipments by rail and water was not a small part of the work required of the Public Works Officers at Pauillac. In April Ensign Richards was assigned to duty under the Public Works Officer, chiefly as assistant to Ensign Rodey in the Electrical Department.

The Public Works Department had an average of 515 men per day during the month of May. This was considerably short of the number of men needed to carry on the large amount of work under way, and much night work was necessary toward the last of the month. By the 25th of May the first machine shop in the A&R building was roofed, glassed, and the concrete floor finished so that it was possible to turn that much of the building over to the A&R Department. The entire central section of the building was roofed by the end of the month. The new locomotive crane, which arrived about the first of May, was assembled and put into operation on the 15th. This greatly facilitated the handling of steel, and by the end of May the steelwork for two of the large hangar bays was completed. A large number of portable barracks were erected during this month to accommodate the big increase in the station complement.

The seaplane hangars were pushed night and day by a crew of some 300 men. One hangar, including the concrete floor, was completed by the end of May. Two new small concrete mixers arrived in May and, as up to this time all concrete had been mixed by hand, the arrival of these mixers greatly helped the concrete work on the station. The garage, including the concrete floor, was finished, but as the personnel on the station had increased so rapidly it was turned over to the Executive Department for use as a mess hall. The first two septic tanks were started in May, and considerable sewer line and water main work was accomplished. The construction was continually delayed because of the great difficulty in obtaining gravel and stone for concrete, a considerable quantity of which was necessary to transport by truck a distance of four miles.

About the 3rd of June the requisition of land for the new flying field and the entire west end of the camp was formally put through. Arrangements were also made with Dr. Rascol, the Director of the Lazaret, to allow the Navy use of a strip of land for a road and railroad between the station proper and the flying field. The details of this land requisition work were taken over by Ensign E.R. Metcalf, (CEC), who came to Pauillac at this time from the Paris Headquarters. Word was received at this time of new drafts of men to be expected. This, together with the hot weather conditions, made it imperative to force the work on plumbing and barracks construction and to design and start the work on a large new mess hall. During June all steelwork of the aircraft repair shop was completed except the northern hangar bays. The concreting was carried on so that the two machine shop sections were finished with the exception of part of the floor in the second one. The newly acquired land more than doubled the camp area, so that a considerable revision of sanitary and plumbing layouts had to be planned and carried out. On the ninth of June the first double hangar was completed with its concrete floor and slipway as far as the water edge, so that flying was possible on this date at high tide. Beginning in June, Pauillac rapidly changed over from a strictly construction camp to a producing and manufacturing establishment. The change was very noticeable on every hand. The Public Works Department, although as busy as ever, became less a controlling factor in the stations' activities.

In the month of July the flying field construction, which included a great amount of ditch covering, rolling, and some grading, was speeded up, under the supervision of W.A. Elliot, to take care of the land planes which were expected. Twenty-seven acres had been put into good shape by the end of the month. During the first two weeks of July night work was carried out at the Repair Shop to expedite the completion of concrete floor wanted by the Assembly & Repair Department. By the 13th of the month the two machine shops had been fully completed, and also the first two hangar bays. At the end of the month all the south side hangar bays were done and in full operation, and the north side bays were being concreted and roofed. The Electrical Department wired the repair shops, the new saw mill, and the numerous other buildings, which were accepted during July. The sawmill was practically built and most of its machinery put into operation during the month of July. The necessity for the rapid completion of all septic tanks, latrines, and the new mess hall and garbage incinerator was accentuated by a serious dysentery epidemic about the 1st of July. All this construction was therefore rushed to completion before the end of the month. Sixteen hundred feet of new railroad track was laid in July. The majority of this was in the spur to the oil tanks on the flying field, and included two pile and timber bridges, one 20' and the other 45' long, over the two canals. The number of provision warehouses, which had been gradually increased since March, totaled nine completed buildings by the end of July. All of the permanent living and sanitary conditions, the shops, hangars, traffic, and storage facilities, became operative and were put into full use at this time.

The Assembly & Repair Shops were practically completed during the month of August. Concrete pavements around the shops and between the hangars were also nearly finished this month. During July and August a small group of electrical men assisted the Army Signal Corps on the telephone lines between Pauillac and Bordeaux. During August 14 portable barracks were erected, additional trackage was completed, and 1600 feet of sidewalks finished. The saw mill began the work of resawing, to French specifications, a large order of lumber approximating 300,000 board feet for the replacement of French lumber used in ten Bessaneau hangars ceded by the French Government for the Northern Bombing Group. The work, begun in July, of manufacturing light portable "Trompeloup" barracks was also carried on during August with an average of 29 men building up the portable sections for twenty-five 20' x 60' complete barracks. These buildings were all shipped to other stations, mostly to the Northern Bombing Group. With the coming of Captain Evans, as Commandant of the station, an old French house on the rise back of the station was rented and remodeled for the Commandant's quarters. In August the construction of permanent roads and fences was undertaken, the foundations for the new powerhouse were put in, and the water, sewer, and light systems were greatly extended and practically completed.

The operation of acquiring the remainder of the old village of Trompeloup and the so-called Hotel Tobac was begun in August, although the requisition did not formally go through until September 3rd. This old village, which consisted of a few poor masonry structures and a number of wooden shacks, was entirely cleaned out. The buildings, which could be saved, were all renovated, and the others demolished during September. The Bordeaux telephone line work was finished, and the footing for the self-supporting steel stack and the concrete engine beds all poured. The installation of boilers and machinery was well started by the end of September. The new 100,000-gallon water tank was well up at the end of the month, and construction of motor test sheds had been started at the flying field. During September a great deal of work by way of alterations and additions to buildings, railroad, road, and sidewalks was accomplished.

Colors at NAS Pauillac. (source: Naval Historical Center)

On October 12th, instructions were received from the Force Commander, relative to the establishment of a mine base at Bizerte, Africa, comprising the construction of a camp for one thousand men, with two mine store houses 400' by 180' and one 400' by 80'. All construction materials were to be prepared for shipment by minelayer from Pauillac, and a construction gang of three hundred carefully selected men was there organized. Lieutenant Richardson was temporarily detached from his duties as Public Works Officer of the French Unit, to take charge of the work. In his absence, Lieutenant (j.g.) Forter became the general superintendent. On October 20th, by continuous night and day work, the draft was ready for transfer to Africa with all material and supplies, but due to delays in transportation did not leave Marseilles until October 26th. A few days later, with the minelayer completely loaded and awaiting sailing orders, the project was canceled in view of the approaching cessation of hostilities.

The Public Works Department had, during October, an average of 439 men plus 19 German prisoners at work. The power house machinery was assembled and mostly installed, and the steel stack half completed in October. Many alterations were made, small structures built, and considerable roadwork done. A considerable number of plumbing and sewer items were put in during October. The only large piece of construction carried on was the new Y.M.C.A. Theater. The concrete foundations were in on the first of the month, and at the end of the month the roof was 85% completed.

A week later all work was held up for a day or two following the German capitulation on November 11th. It was decided, however, to continue the Power House and the remodeling of five buildings in the Lazaret for the new Sick Bay, and also the roadwork and the Y.M.C.A. Theater. The Theater was opened Thanksgiving Day. The Power House installation was completed on December 6th and operated on the 7th for the first time. Until then almost all power and light had come from the French Power House of the Societe Grammont.

The work of constructing this station, including land acquisitions, public service, and traffic arrangements with the French, had been entirely handled by Officers who, before the war, were engineering contractors. All had been men who gave up their own business or important positions to enter the service. There was a cooperation and accord to a remarkable degree among all these men working on the construction problems of this and the other French Naval Air Stations. It is important to note that the Navy was unusually fortunate in having a fine class of men able to handle almost every phase of construction work at the station. The mechanics and other men who were on this station were of the very best, and there was always a great spirit and willingness to work well under hard conditions and for very long hours. That this spirit existed among the officers and enlisted personnel was largely responsible for the final completion of the station.

III. Personnel

Ensign R.F. Nourse, USN, Asst. Paymaster R.D. Thomas, and twenty-six enlisted men arrived at the U.S. Naval Air Station at Pauillac, Gironde, on November 27, 1917, and were quartered in a building which had formerly been a French laundry. On February Lieutenant H.B. Cecil, USN, reported and assumed command, and Ensign R.F. Nourse, USN, was appointed Executive Officer.

On April 15th Lieutenant Commander S.L.H. Hazard, USN, was ordered to take command of the Receiving Barracks. The officer personnel on the station on July 1st numbered 109, and there was a total enlisted personnel of 4593 men. Commander J.B. Patton, USN—who was ill—commanded the station, at this time, and Hazard was acting in Command until relieved by Commander F.T. Evans, USN, on July 17th.

About May first Mr. W.T. Spalding, Civilian, arrived from Paris Headquarters for duty in the Public Works Department. He was put in charge of the supply work for the stations outside of Pauillac. Lieutenant Burnham left at the same time for duty with the Northern Bombing Group. Shortly afterwards Mr. S.P. Wing, Civilian, arrived for Paris and was put in charge of a portion of the outside construction.

About June 1st, the strenuous working conditions for Public Work Officers and men were further relieved, both by the arrival of three civil engineer officers and two civilians for temporary duty, and an increase in the working force up to some 800 men. The new men on the Staff were: Lieutenant Knox, who remained at Pauillac several weeks in charge of the rush work on the seaplane hangars; Ensign Fagan, who also remained several weeks in charge of portable building construction; Lieutenant (j.g.) Sam A. Forter, who arrived a little later; Mr. W.A. Elliot, Civilian, who took charge of the work on the flying field, and Mr. Neefus, Civilian, who took charge of septic tank construction and road work. In June, when preparations were being made to evacuate Paris, the officers of the Radio Section were moved to Pauillac, but were returned to Paris on July 15th, 1918. In July, Lieutenant Commander Blankenship was assigned to duty as Personnel Officer, and Lieutenant Jackson placed in charge of Radio Communication with Lieutenant (j.g.) H.W. Kitchin, USN, as Assistant for Radio Material. Lieutenant Warren C. Graham, USNRF, reported on September 23rd, 1918, and assumed charge of the Radio Section.

On the 1st of July the Public Works Department had 1350 men. These were rapidly cut down to a total of 850 men by the 31st. Lieutenant Knox, Ensign Fagan, and Lieutenant Byers were detached and ordered as Public Works Officers at Paimboeuf, Fromentine, Aracachon, and Gujan, respectively; and Lieutenant Richardson was detached for duty as Public Works Officer for the French Coastal Air Stations on Captain Craven's Staff at Brest Headquarters. Lieutenant (j.g.) Forter was made Public Works Officer for Pauillac.

In the month of August the Public Works Department lost the services of two valuable men who had been more than faithful to the large amount of work given to them. Ensign Rodey was taken to the hospital, and for three months remained on the sick list. Mr. W.A. Elliott died of typhoid fever after a brief illness. He was a young man (only 23 years old), an engineering graduate, and had thoroughly made good in his work. He had been recommended for a commission as Ensign in the CEC as a result of his successful work at Pauillac.

In August 1918, with the reorganization of the Aviation Forces, the central Public Works Office was removed to London, with Lieutenant Commander Billings as Chief Public Works Officer. With this move, supervision of the Northern Bombing Project and the English and Irish work became dissociated from the French Unit. In the first week of September the Headquarters for the French Coastal Air Stations were transferred to Brest, with Lieutenant Richardson as the Public Works Officer for the Unit, and Lieutenant (j.g.) Forter appointed Public Works Officer of Pauillac. At Brest, the supervision of the four fuel oil tank depots was placed under Lieutenant Conrad who, as far as concerned this work, became part of the staff organization of the Commander, U.S. Naval Forces in France.

The Assistant Secretary of the Navy, with his party, arrived on August 14th and inspected the grounds. A luncheon was given in the main mess hall, after which the Assistant Secretary addressed the men for a short period before taking his departure. On August 31st, the Brigadier-General Commanding Base 2, U.S. Army, with his Staff, in company with Lieutenant Colonel Clavell of the French Engineers, visited this station. The Commander-in-chief of the Atlantic Fleet and his Staff arrived at Pauillac on October 31, on a two-day inspection visit (See Appendix G-5). A large and successful smoker was given upon this occasion. The following day the Commander-in-chief made a short speech to the men before leaving for the U.S. Naval Air Station at Moutchic.

On the reorganization of the headquarters administration of the Naval Aviation Forces in Europe, Lieutenant Commander Briscoe became Aide for Assembly and Repair on the staff of Captain Cone, Aide for Aviation, to the Commander of the United States Naval Forces Operating in European Waters, with Headquarters in London; and Lieutenant W.B. Jameson was assigned to duty in charge of the Assembly and Repair Division at Pauillac. Lieutenant Commander Briscoe, along with his staff, left for London, and Lieutenant Jameson remained as the Assembly and Repair Officer at Pauillac until September 26th, when he was detached for staff duties at Brest. Lieutenant F.S. Moulton, USNRF, then Personnel Officer of the Department, became the Officer in Charge.

The S.S. *Bella* carried one-half of the construction supplies from NAS Pauillac to the other naval air stations on the French coast. (source: Naval Historical Center)

Mr. Wing, Civilian, who had been in charge of requisitions, special designing work, and of making all reports, left about the first of October to take a commission in the Army Engineer Corps. About the last of October, when the Mediterranean Mine Base project took Lieutenant Richardson, Lieutenant Forter went temporarily to replace him as Public Works Officer for Aviation in France. Ensign Still came down at this time and was acting Public Works Officer at Pauillac for some two or three weeks when he was ordered home with the first draft to leave after the signing of the Armistice. Ensign A.B.C. Scull, (CEC), then succeeded him as acting Public Works Officer about December 1st.

On November 11, 1918, the officers and 3168 enlisted men, shown in Table G-1, were on board. On November 13th a general muster was held, and the Commanding Officer read to the officers and men the congratulatory message sent by the Force Commander on the occasion of the signing of the Armistice. Lieutenant Richardson's return on November 27th relieved Lieutenant (j.g.) Forter from his duties at Brest Headquarters, and he returned to Pauillac and resumed his duties as Public Works Officer.

One of the duties of the Executive Department was that of promotion of athletic activities and the arranging of other entertainment for the men on the station. The Pauillac troupe of entertainers, with the assistance of a very successful band organized from the force, staged numerous shows of a very good quality. An excellent baseball team was maintained, which won consistently, showing a very good average for the season. The best opposing team was the "Grover Cleveland Alexander All-Star Army Baseball Team," then at Bordeaux, against which the Pauillac team once held the score 4-3, Alexander himself pitching for the "All-Stars." The last game of the season also was played with Alexander's All-Star team, on the home grounds, and the score after fourteen innings was 3-2 in favor of the "All-Stars." Boxing bouts were also arranged frequently, there being 13 professional boxers in the ship's company. The football team was organized for the season, and the best game played was against the U.S. Naval Air Station at Moutchic, which was won by a score of 20-0. The Seaman Guard of the station took part in two competitive drills, and in each contest received a large Loving Cup.

Table G-1

COMMANDING	
Captain Frank T. Evans, USN	Commanding
Lieutenant Commander Charlton E. Battle, Jr., USN	Executive Officer
Lieutenant (j.g.) Howard R. Shaw, USNRF	Aide to Commanding Officer
Ensign Courltand Van Clief, USNRF	Aide to Commanding Officer
Ensign Louis R. Metcalfe, (CEC), USNRF	Liaison Officer
Ensign Henry L. Stout, USNRF	Communication Officer
Ensign Edwin E. Bostick, USNRF	Intelligence Officer
EXECUTIVE	
Lieutenant Commander Charlton E. Battle, Jr., USN	Executive Officer

Lieutenant Edmund J.A. Murphy, USN
Lieutenant Ralph F. Nourse, USN
Lieutenant (j.g.) Charles E. Ruttan, USNRF
Lieutenant (j.g.) Louis A. Peterson, USNRF
Lieutenant (j.g.) Francis L. McFadden, USN — Chaplain
Lieutenant (j.g.) Herman R. Newby, USN
Ensign Robert S. Holding, USNRF
Ensign James F. Reilly, USNRF
First Lieutenant Albert B. Sage, USMCR
Chief Carpenter Harold Dillon, USNRF
Boatswain John R.J. Leroy, USN
Gunner (E) Charles F. Hilaire, USN
Machinist Peter B Visco, USNRF
Machinist Alfred F. Geahart, USNRF
The compliment of enlisted men was 1098 men

PUBLIC WORKS
Lieutenant (j.g.) Sam A. Forter, (CEC), USNRF — In Charge
Ensign Joseph F. Still, (CEC), USNRF
Ensign Alfred B.C. Scull (CEC), USNRF
Ensign Reed Walworth, (NCC), USNRF
Machinist Paul D.H. Fisher, USNRF
Carpenter George E. Taylor, USNRF
Gunner L.D. Bond, USNRF
Gunner Charles Stebbins, Jr., USNRF
The compliment of enlisted men was 310 men

SUPPLY
Lieutenant Jacob M. Breger, (PC), USN — In Charge
Lieutenant Arthur B. Poole, (PC), USN
Lieutenant Walter W. Gilmore, (PC), USN
Lieutenant William H. Crap, (PC), USN
Lieutenant (j.g.) Frederick B. Michel, (PC), USNRF
Ensign Clarence S. Powers, (PC), USNRF
Ensign Harold J. Gordon, (PC), USNRF
Ensign Edward Holland, Jr. (PC), USNRF
Ensign Chester T. Darnton, (PC), USNRF
Ensign George L. Aulmann, (PC), USNRF
Ensign Evans D. Steger, (PC) , USN
Ensign Leo V. Flavell, (PC)), USN
Acting Pay Clerk Carl L. Biesy, USN
Acting Pay Clerk Lyle S. Gunn, (PC), USN
Pay Clerk John F. Curtin, USNRF
Lieutenant (j.g.) Austin T. Parkhurst, USNRF
Lieutenant (j.g.) Johnston L. McLeod, USNRF
Ensign Lester W. Capser, USNRF
The compliment of enlisted men was 402 men

ASSEMBLY & REPAIR
Lieutenant Frank S. Moulton, USNRF — In Charge
Lieutenant (j.g.) Arthur M. Goodfellow, USNRF
Lieutenant (j.g.) Francis M. Champlain, USNRF
Lieutenant (j.g.) Ernest C. Marheinake, USN
Lieutenant (j.g.) Charles D. Williams, USNRF
Ensign Walter H. Hill, USNRF
Ensign William V. Richards, USNRF
Ensign Elliott Kauth, USN
Ensign Joseph P. Barchi, USNRF
Ensign Francis A. Wegner, USNRF
Ensign Robert H. Griffin, USNRF
Ensign Carlyle S. Fliedner, USNRF
Ensign W. Overton Snyder, USNRF
Ensign Nathan C. Avery, USNRF
Ensign Louis H. Doyle, USNRF
Ensign Edward J. Giblin, USNRF
Ensign Edgar A. Tygert, USNRF
Ensign Herbert P. Wilder, USNRF
Gunner (R) Roy A. Jones, USN
Machinist Harry W. Dreher, USN
Machinist Edward Dowinig, USNRF
Machinist Edwin A. Krueger, USNRF
Machinist Fred M. Powell, USNRF
Machinist Thomas J. Drummond, USNRF
Machinist John Earl Carter, USNRF
Machinist Neil MacCoull, Jr., USNRF
The complement of enlisted men was 488 men

INSPECTION & TEST DEPARTMENT
Lieutenant Charles P. Mason, USN — In Charge
Lieutenant (j.g.) Reginald D. Thomas, USNRF
Ensign Bernard S. Rodey, USN
Ensign Peter Talbot, USN
The compliment of enlisted men was 53

MEDICAL DEPARTMENT
Commander Harry G. Garrison, (MC), USN — In Charge
Lieutenant Arthur C. Sinton, Jr. (MC), USN
Lieutenant Orville E. Goss, (MC), USN
Lieutenant George E. Kalter, (MC), USN
Lieutenant Thomas F.J. Hanlon, (MC), USN
Lieutenant Otto W. Grisier, (MC), USN
Lieutenant Henry B. Franklin, (MC), USN
Lieutenant George B. Thompson, (MC), USN
Lieutenant (j.g.) Clarence P. Curley, (MC), USN
Lieutenant Charles B. Crawford, (MC), USNRF
Lieutenant (j.g.) Carl L. McLaughlin, (MC), USNRF
Lieutenant Joseph E. Redden, (DC), USNRF
Lieutenant (j.g.) Alwyn Smith, (DC), USNRF
Lieutenant A.G. Twigg, (DC), USNRF
Pharmacist Harold F. Harris, USN
Pharmacist Arthur L. Crowder, USN
The compliment of enlisted men was 49

MARINES
Major John F.S. Norris, USMC — In Charge
Captain Lucina W. Burnhma, USMC
First Lieutenant Chester L. Fordney, USMC
Marine Gunner Thomas F. Malloy, USMC
The compliment of enlisted men was 119

TRAFFIC DEPARTMENT
Lieutenant Frank W. Relyea, USNRF In Charge
Lieutenant Russell D. Thomas, (PC), USN
Lieutenant (J.g.) John C. Sieber, USNRF
Lieutenant Horation S. Ford, USN
Ensign Dennis J. Nerney, USNRF
Ensign Louis J. Goldman, USNRF
Ensign William A. Blanchard, USNRF
Ensign Albert W. Colson, USN
Ensign Arthur R. Robinson, USNRF
Boatswain Robert Huneke, USN
Machinist Sam W. Alston, USN
Machinist George H. Sherbourne, USNRF
The compliment of enlisted men was 520 men

RADIO CONSTRUCTION UNIT
Civil Engineer Arthur C. Eberhard, USN

OTHER UNITS

A. The 88th Company, First Regiment, of the Marine Corps, consisting of 119 men and commanded by Maj. J.F.S. Norris, USMC, was also stationed at Pauillac. This unit had been destined for the Northern Bombing Group, but had been detained at Pauillac when it was learned that they were not required in the northern region.
B. The 312th Company, Horse Drawn Ammunition Train, U.S. Army, was also on duty at Pauillac. Captain H.D Cogdellm, USA, commanded this company of 150 men.
C. There were also 65 enlisted men of the U.S. Army under instruction in Liberty Motors at Pauillac who were under the command of Lieutenant (j.g.) J.J. Percivall, USN

IV. Operations

As stated earlier the station was formally commissioned on December 1, 1917. On the 19th the Commanding Officer assumed command of the Aviation Receiving Station, and on January 1, 1918, the U.S. Naval Base at Pauillac was placed under the same command.

IVa. Assembly and Repair

The establishment of Assembly and Repair activities at the United States Naval Air Station, Pauillac, dates from March 17, 1918, when Lieutenant Commander Benjamin Briscoe, USNRF, Chief of the Assembly and Repair Section, and his staff reported for duty. The buildings that were to house the equipment had just been begun, foundations were being laid, and a few sections of steel for the first of the factory bays had been erected.

It was found desirable to center attention first on the thorough organization of road and water transportation from this base to the proposed Air Stations. The Motor Transportation Department, which at that time was centered here for the Naval Aviation Forces in France, suffered particularly from a shortage of equipment and spare parts, and provision was made to remedy this condition. The officers attached to the A&R Section were assigned as follows: Executive—Lieutenant W.B. Johnson, USNRF; Engineering Officer—Lieutenant (j.g.) R. Stahl, USNRF; Personnel Officer—Ensign R.S. Holding, USNRF; and Secretary—Ensign F.K. Lane, USNRF. As there was as yet no assembly or repair work to be done, and in order to further the construction of the station and the necessary factory buildings, the enlisted personnel were assigned to other departments. As additional men arrived they were classified and detailed for such work, as it was desirable to expedite.

During the German drive in March, a battalion of volunteers was organized on the station, who were to stand by for probable service behind the front lines at the Western Front. There was great disappointment among the men when it was later decided that they would not have an opportunity to fill an active combatant part on the front lines. During the first week of April activities were suspended for a period of about ten days on account of preparations for the mobilization of the station personnel during the German drive on Paris. The need of such special action having passed, normal activities were resumed.

Plans for the Northern Bombing Group Project had been under way for some time, and early in April began to take definite shape, as to Assembly and Repair activities. Lieutenant Commander Briscoe was directed to gather data with reference to location, general proportions, and allied details of the necessary structures and equipment for this project. He made a trip for the purpose with Lieutenant W.B. Jameson and Lieutenant (j.g.) Stahl to Paris and Dunkirk, returning on April 23rd with the data. Shortly thereafter he left for the United States to assist in the procuring of the necessary material and equipment. In the latter part of March 1918, the Northern Bombing Project was launched, and steps were taken to secure building materials and equipment in Europe, rather than to hazard the inevitable delays of dependence upon the U.S. Hangars were secured from the French War Department, to be replaced later by raw materials from the U.S. Experiments were made by the Aviation Forces, as a result of which a highly portable type of canvas tent hangar was developed for housing the Caproni planes. Two such hangars could be transported in one 6-ton truck, as compared with the four trucks and four trailers required for a hangar of similar capacity of the French type. Due to serious delays in the receipt of canvas from the U.S., quantity production of these hangars was barely commencing at Pauillac when the armistice was signed. Experience gained in the construction of the coastal air stations had proved their type far too elaborate, costly, and complete. The success of the Northern Bombing Group depended entirely on the celerity with which the stations could be established and put into operation. The simplest kind of construction was therefore chosen, reducing all equipment and accessories to the purely essential. Plumbing and sewage installations were made using the can system. A very light type of portable barracks, with single sheathing, was devised, which could be erected in four hours and required only three trucks with trailers to transport. A factory for the manufacture of those barracks was established at Pauillac. Lumber was accrued from a timber district adjacent to Bordeaux, being cut by the U.S. Army, and barracks were turned out at the rate of one hundred and twenty lineal feet per day. Lieutenant (j.g.) H. Burnham, USNRF, was appointed Public Works Officer of the Northern Bombing Group, and was detailed to the area of Calais for the supervision of the work. Specially chosen construction crews were organized for this work to accelerate the completion of the construction.

It was originally planned to assemble and test the land bombing planes at Pauillac. Additional property was secured adjacent to the station for use as a flying field, and work was intensively concentrated on the preparation of an area of approximately 50 acres, by clearing, grading, planting, and filling of ditches, etc. When it was determined to change the location of the base to Eastleigh, England, the work was reduced to a smaller area for the testing of only the first planes to be received.

The electrical installation in the Caproni planes of the Northern Bombing Group was assigned to the Radio and Instrument Sections. Radio in this group being used only for landing purposes and for extremely short distance work between planes, the equipment was composed solely of short distance radio and interplane telephone sets. Ground station sets capable of transmitting five miles were ordered from the States for each squadron, making a total of twelve ground radio telephone installations and one hundred fifty short range radio aircraft telephones. On May 29, 1918, the landlines for communication with the Northern Bombing Group were decided upon, and necessary material for this work was ordered.

The first shipment of 12 Liberty motors was received on April 23rd, and ten were shipped out with the seals unbroken. A barracks building was prepared as a temporary motor shop, and the overhaul of these two motors was begun. Additional motors were overhauled in readiness for the first shipment of planes. The first consignment of American-built flying boats, six HS-ls aboard the S.S. *Houston* and two aboard the S.S. *Lake Placid*, arrived at Pauillac on 24 May. The six HS-ls from the *Houston* were unloaded May 25th.

It had become evident that the permanent factory buildings could not be completed in time to immediately begin work on the planes, and two of the hangars were rushed to completion in readiness for the uncrating of the first plane on May 25th. The work of assembling several of the planes was undertaken, and on June 12th the first HS-1 plane was completed. On June 13th, this plane made its first official flight successfully with Lieutenant C.P. Mason, USN (Naval Aviator No. 52), pilot, and Commander J.B. Patton, USN, and Lieutenant W.B. Jameson, USNRF, as passengers. The event signified the first completed result of all the work that had been put into the station. This day was easily the most significant and interesting in the station's history from the standpoint of all men responsible for the work done. The plane was flown to Moutchic on June 18th, arriving in good condition.

Recreation Building at NAS Pauillac under construction. (source: Naval Historical Center)

The first shipment of H-16 planes was received on June 11th. One of these was assembled and flown on July 8th with Lieutenant Mason as pilot and several passengers. A forced landing was made after attaining an altitude of 150 feet, the hull was wrenched in landing, and subsequently damaged in the bow when a motor boat came alongside to take off the pilot and passengers. Early in July the repair shop operations were enlarged and transferred to a partly completed bay of the repair building. The woodworking, welding, sheet metal, and forging shops were installed temporarily, and provisions for the general repair and retipping of propellers was also made.

Executive jurisdiction over the motor transportation features of the Naval Aviation organization was transferred early in July from the A&R Section to a separate transportation organization, but the repair service for the transportation equipment was retained by the A&R Section. In order to hasten shipments from the U.S. to France, a considerable number of planes were carried as deck loads on transports bound for Brest. It was impracticable to re-ship these planes to Pauillac, and a sub-base for the assembly of planes was established, early in July, at the U.S. Naval Air Station, Brest. The assembled aircraft were consigned to air stations near the sub-base and flown to their destinations. The development of the Motor Department proceeded so rapidly that it was necessary to extend this work to an additional building, temporarily. On 15 July, after the completion of the first of the Plane Department buildings, the work of plane assembly was transferred to the new buildings. The transfer of the Motor Department into permanent quarters in the repair shop building was affected gradually a few days later. Lieutenant Commander Briscoe returned late in July, and undertook the final organization of the department and its personnel on the basis of the report of "Organization of Assembly and Repair Activities at Assembly and Repair Stations."

As the complement of the various stations were filled, the production of new planes gradually became secondary to the repair of old ones, which began to arrive in increasing numbers during the latter part of August.

As the principle emphasis of the station changed, personnel were withdrawn from construction and other general work, as required, and assigned to various duties directly connected with the assembly and repair of seaplanes. The personnel employed in this capacity increased from about 20 on the overhaul of the first motors, beginning May 23rd, to 165 on June 1st; 667 on July 1st; 707 on August 1st; 912 on September 1st; and reached a maximum of 936 enlisted men on September 11th. As the increasing needs of other coastal air stations necessitated the transfer of people from Pauillac, a gradual reduction brought the personnel down to 798 by October 1st, and 529 on the first day of November. Up to November 1st, 1918, the total number of motors overhauled was 322, with the total number of seaplanes assembled at 82.

The A&R Department cooperated with the French Military authorities, the U.S. Army, and the U.S. Army Service in furnishing new equipment, in assembling, and in repairing. On 14 September 1918, five Liberty motors, complete with necessary instruments, oil tanks, oil and gas line assembles, and all equipment for the radio system were shipped to the French Authorities; and, on 29 October 1918 five oil gauges, five sets of distributor brushes, and two short oil and gasoline line leads were shipped to French Authorities.

Items shipped to the Aviation Section, Signal Corps, U.S. Army included: To the station at Aulnat, Clermont-Ferrand, France, on 17 October 1918, 100 Liberty motor low compression pistons with rings; on 8 November 1918, 233 Liberty motors, filled with heavy type crankshaft and Army type propeller hubs, in crates; six boxes of spare parts to the base at Romorantin, France; and on 22 November 1918, 200 sets of two each assorted pipes of sheet metal for Liberty motors, also to Romorantin. At the Armistice Pauillac had 173 operating Liberty motors with another 110 undergoing repairs. It was found that the average operating time of the Liberty engine between overhaul periods was 44 hours and 52 minutes (based on 30 engines being overhauled).

Assembly and Repair service was given to the Aviation Section Signal Corps, U.S. Army, when a Nieuport Chasse Plane made a forced landing several miles south of Pauillac. It was brought to this station for repairs on 19 October 1918, requiring a new tailskid, patches on wings, overhauling of a Le Rhône motor, and other small repairs. The plane, after having been repaired, was severely damaged when the pilot on taking off was forced to land in the Gironde River in attempting to fly back to his station on 22 October 1918. This plane was afterwards crated and shipped to the Army base at Bordeaux. Assistance was also given in removing a Sopwith plane fitted with a Clerget 130 h.p. motor from the flying field, where a landing was made, breaking the propeller and causing considerable damage to the motor hood on 3 November 1918. The plane was disassembled and crated for shipment to the United States Army Aviation Base, Bordeaux.

Assembly and Repair service was given to the French Naval Aviation authorities when a Levy-LePen seaplane received on 30 October 1918 was fitted with two new panels and the rigging realigned. Additional service was given, in a special instance, when twelve men were detailed on Sunday, November 17, 1918, for duty at the plant on the Gramnont Electric works at Trompeloup in order to keep up electric power and lighting service, while the employees were afforded an opportunity to celebrate the signing of the Armistice with Germany, on the French National Holiday set on that occasion.

It was at first arranged to have the flying on the station come under a Flight Officer, who, with the pilots, was attached to the Assembly and Repair Department. The Flight Officer and his Staff were detached from the Assembly and Repair Department on 3 September 1918 when the Inspection and Test Department was organized, under the direction of Lieutenant Mason, USN, for the flying and inspection of all machines and aviation equipment. When a machine was reported by the Assembly and Repair Department, ready for flying, it was flown on a test flight by a member of the Inspection and Test Department, which also had charge of the delivery of aircraft to the different coastal air stations. In 572 flights, during which 84 planes (74 HS-1s; four HS-16s; and six HS-2s) were flown 245 hours and 4 minutes flying time, a total of 15,085 knots were covered.

Although difficulties have been for the most part overlooked in the compilation of this history, it is believed advisable here to record some of the more cogent difficulties under which this department worked. The first difficulty experienced was caused by the delay in the completion of the Assembly and Repair shops occasioned by building material not arriving in its proper sequence. This failure prevented the installation of machine tools and delayed the work of organization for the prompt handling of seaplanes on their arrival. It was necessary to assemble the first planes in one of the Beach hangars, the completion of which was accomplished by working 24 hours daily, following the receipt of information that a shipment of seaplanes had been made. No shops for the proper overhaul or test of motors were available, and the overhaul of the first motors was carried out in a section of a portable barracks—the only available building. The second difficulty involved the situation that no spare parts were received with the first motors, and to complete both their overhaul and test and to replace defective parts, it was necessary to take corresponding parts from other engines. A third difficulty was the failure to receive machine tools shipped from the United States, and compelled the station to institute a search at other ports. A number were found in the possession of other units, while some were never located. A fourth difficulty related to the condition in which the first shipment was received. Owing to the poor preparation in the U.S. for ocean transport, it was necessary to remove metal fittings, as no protection was given them before shipment, and to remove water from the cockpits, necessitating the removal of gas tanks, and the cleaning and draining out of hulls. Many definite and absolutely necessary parts for the proper functioning of the seaplanes were missing, such as shortage of batteries, starters, primers, hose-clamps, timer coupling rods, and oil and gas pipe connections. The aileron and rudder leads were often not properly rigged, and these had to be corrected. A fifth difficulty involved the lack of handling trucks, which necessitated their manufacture, securing the material for the purpose in France. A sixth difficulty related to the receipt of motors in bad condition, which compelled the disassembling and overhauling of them before installation. Over 400 motors were received with a 90-degree water connection to the radiator when only a 180-degree connection could be used, and many arrived with broken parts. It was found necessary to repack 75% of the water pumps. Similar conditions had to be overcome with the primers, camshafts housing and intake manifolds. The difficulties found hardest to overcome were occasioned when the missing or broken parts required casting for their manufacture, as no provision had been made for a foundry when the plant was laid out. This applies to such parts as starters, primers, and tubing connections.

The following extract from the progress report for September is quoted:

"Seaplanes began to arrive in France on May 25, 1918, and operations in the shop began on the 26th. Since that time material has continued to arrive from the United States. However, 25% of the hulls were received in a damaged condition; 5% of the nose wires, 50% of the elevator control wires, 30% of the rudder control wires not being long enough.

Many of the panels of the stabilizers were received in a warped condition; ailerons, hinges not in line. Thirty percent of the rudders did not have the proper clearance and a large percent of the struts were warped. It might be also be noted that until recently handling trucks and racks of all kinds had to be constructed for moving or storing because of the condition in which they were received.

Only two storage batteries were received prior to the 24th. Nine starters were received in the meantime on the U.S.S. *Prometheus*. These conditions necessitated the removal of the starter after the delivery of the plane and its return to the Station.

During July and August operations were held up for the lack of propellers and after many faulty propellers were received; errors in thickness of hubs, cracks, open seam, and thin trailing edges. Those faults were particularly conspicuous in the Hartzell propellers.

The Westerfelt Board from the United States is at the present time in Pauillac investigating all shortages in material and provision will be made to avoid future shortage when possible.

Delivery has been held up also due to the changes which have been made in the construction of the planes from time to time."

Another interesting extract taken from the progress report of December 12, 1918, is quoted:

"In addition to these increased repairs, it was determined that such improvements as had been recommended by the Bureau would be incorporated in all new planes before shipment, in addition to incorporating all such improvements on planes returned for repairs.

The outlook for November and the succeeding winter months presented a condition which in the judgment of the Commander of the French Unit meant that seaplane operations on the French Coast would be cut down on account of the weather conditions. In order to permit the use to the fullest extent of the equipment and facilities available, it was determined that negotiations be opened with the Army, offering to assist in the overhaul of Liberty motors. The Navy had already offered a portion of the space in its shops to train a quantity of their mechanics for Liberty motor overhaul. This offer was accepted, and early in October, Lieutenant Percival arrived with sixty mechanics for training.

These men were distributed through the various departments, assembling, testing and repairing Liberty motors and such plans as were necessary were outlined for the remainder of their stay, up to the time the armistice was declared. Lieutenant Jameson was ordered to confer with the Army officials at Romorantin early in November and after a conference held with the Commanding Officer at that station, reported to the Commanding Officer of the French Unit on his return just what assistance from us and just how we could best assist them. It was determined to overhaul and repair a number of Liberty motors daily, but the result of this conference was never put into operation as the armistice was signed before the negotiations were fully completed.

The number of men employed in the Assembly & Repair operations at Pauillac in October and the early part of November was somewhat reduced as compared with July, August, and September. This was principally on account of the fact that the seaplane stations on the French coast which were supplied by Pauillac were not 100% completed or 100% operative and were not able to accept 100% equipment. They did have in general, with the exception of Moutchic which was fully completed, 70% of their proposed complete complement and operations were carried out in about the same percentage.

The station was also advised during the month of October regarding a new project, for which 150 men were drawn from the Assembly & Repair Personnel. This number was determined after due consideration to the requirements of the project, the fact that the personnel attached to Assembly & Repair continued as in October, slowing down slightly, on account of the weather conditions and the approaching winter; when it was believed that the operations at the various stations would be much less for several months than they had been during the summer. This permitted the opportunity to assist the Army as the factory had a capacity of continued assembly and repairs the stations operating at their maximum capacity, and it was believed that the operations for the winter months would not exceed 50% of their facilities. Hence any additional assistance which would be given the Army during that time would not only assist them, but would also assist the Navy in keeping its organization properly tuned up and working to capacity. The assembly operations at Brest continued in a similar manner to the operations at Pauillac; but since no provision had been made for the overhaul of motors at Brest their operations consisted of the assembly of the new planes required for the district assigned to the station. Pauillac continued to be their base of supply for new and the overhaul of all Liberty motors, Brest taking the position of a receiving station and acting as a sub-base for the transfer and exchange of Liberty motors required by seaplane operations in that district. Their activities were carried out very successfully and their efficiency greatly increased as the staff became more experienced and more definite information was to the districts requirements were obtained.

The signing of the armistice on November 11th naturally caused a suspension of all assembly operations at Pauillac and Brest, but the repair continued in the usual way until various conferences and following the various orders from Headquarters relating to the disposition of material on hand such changes were made in the organization and operations carried out by Assembly & Repair, as was consistent with the demobilization of the French Units.

The instruction received from Headquarters regarding the disposition of material and its return to the United States or its disposal either to the Army or foreign governments are being followed out with the utmost expedience."

On November 11th, 1918, Pauillac was in a position to take over a great amount of U.S. Army Aviation work, and an estimate had been made to turn out five complete Army airplanes per day.

IVb. Supply

The evolvement and operation of the Supply Department at NAS Pauillac was directly connected with the development of the Supply Department for all U.S. Naval Activities headquartered in Paris. The Supply Department at Pauillac was directed by Paymaster F.B Colby, USN, and had the general charge of all supplies, their distribution, and handling for the U.S. Naval Air Stations in France, along with a great portion of the supplies of the Northern Bombing Group, as well as the U.S. Naval Air Station, Porto Corsini, Italy, which was entirely equipped from Pauillac. Until September 1, 1918, Pauillac also supplied the U.S. naval Air Stations in Ireland and England.

The Supply organization of Naval Aviation Forces, Foreign Service technically came into existence on the 12th of May, 1917, when Past Assistant Paymaster Omar D. Conger, USN, and Assistant Paymaster F.E. Michel, USNRF, were ordered to duty in France. There was not the faintest conception of what was to be done abroad. It was only known that 120 men were to be ordered at the same time; but as to where the organization would be located and what should be required in the way of storage and equipment could only be guessed.

To supply all material from the U.S. would, for many months, be impossible, but it was not thought that the time to elapse between hoped for and actual deliveries would be as wide as developed. The First Aeronautical Detachment sized up the situation in this fashion:

1. The United States had neither a seaplane nor an engine adequate for the purpose for which seaplanes were to be used.

2. The construction of seaplane hangars and portable houses, due to a lack of development of this industry in the States, would take at least six months.

3. War preparations in the States were not developed sufficiently to permit a hope that necessary materials and workmen for building the stations could be gotten to France in less than six months.

These were initial difficulties, which, as the larger problems, determined the plan of action. Methods to be adopted for their solution had to take form quickly. It was decided that:

1. The Headquarters of the Supply Department of Naval Aviation would be in Paris.

2. Each station to be organized on the lines of a ship about the same complement as that proposed for the stations (i.e., two hundred men).

3. Station accounts to be handled as on board ship, using the titles "B" and "C" rather than titles "R" and "J" for a military establishment

4. That station requirements should not be filled as such by the distributing centers in the United States, but that a single requisition for the Aviation Forces abroad should be prepared in Paris, and that the stores should be sent to Pauillac for distribution.

5. That a repair, assembly, and distribution center be required.

6. The best place on the entire French coast for the location of a repair and distribution center was Pauillac, on the Gironde, on ground to the north of Trompeloup dock of the Bordeaux Chamber of Commerce.

Early in November, the offices of the U.S. Naval Aviation in France were moved from 23 Rue de la Paix to the Hotel d'Iena, at 4 Place d'Iena, Paris. The reporting to the Aide for Material and Supplies on the Staff of the Force Commander, whose duties were to include the coordination of all supply matters in France to those of the Naval Supply Bases at Brest and Pauillac, and between the various supply activities of all stations, ships, and units, relieved the Aviation Unit of all disbursements to be made in Paris. Accounts of the men at the various schools were no longer to be carried on the rolls in Paris, but by the Supply Officer on duty at the Station. Assistant Paymaster Michel had been disbursing for the Supply Officer to scattered detachments of aviation. When Pay Officers were assigned to stations accounts were transferred to them. Officers who reported during November were assigned to Moutchic, Le Croisic, Rochefort, Ile Tudy, and Pauillac.

It was in Paris that the markets in England, France, and neutral countries were known by either the Army or Navy officials. This was particularly true of technical Aviation materials. Stations were urged to make exceptional cases of articles to be procured locally. Paris could give the best results from the point of view of time. The strong Central Control was adhered to until late in February, when Paris as the center of supply began to divide its duties with Pauillac. On the situation in February 25th, the Supply Officer said:

"This decentralization has so far progressed, that now all requisitions for supplies which are at Pauillac are sent there directly without any reference to Paris."

When, on the 4th of June, all sections were hurriedly moved to USNAS Pauillac, the decentralization was complete. Known there as branch headquarters, it was a purely temporary organization, which existed for the purpose of combining with station of 16 planes and 200 men. It was similar to the one forwarded in July, supplementing it by listing small tools and quantities of materials which would be allowed in greater detail. It was understood that articles enumerated in the allowance list would be assembled and shipped from the United States without further reference to France, and as soon as a station was authorized its allowance would be assembled in the United States and shipped together with the allowed complement. These lists represented a type rather than a hard and fast allowance of any station, and varied as the number of men and machines varied. Thus, a station of four hundred men and thirty-two machines would have approximately twice the equipment shown in the allowance list. This applied particularly to articles which were issued in units sufficient for one man, such as flying clothes, wind proof clothing, and mess gear. Pauillac was to make these automatic shipments. For larger items, such as lathes, boats, etc., distribution was made according to local conditions. At first Paris directed all issues, but early in February 1918, Pauillac assumed full control. No shipment was made on this allowance list as authority without first securing the approval of the Department at Pauillac having cognizance over that class of stock. Frequent trips up and down the coast, and conferences and correspondence as to the requirements of the stations for material peculiar to aviation, kept the central supply base advised. After April 15th ordnance, instruments, and accessories were the only articles distributed on the order of the Unit Headquarters.

When a shipment would be received from the United States it would be distributed in accordance with the need as known at the base or made known by Paris, without further reference to the particular station. This resulted in the careful allotment of a limited stock, which was safeguarded due to the uncertainty of the market and time between arrival of Aviation cargoes. Automatic shipment on the basis of a type allowance list supported by the known advance made by the station, followed by requisitions for special supplies as needed was throughout the period of operations the advisable policy. The type allowance list, though never followed as a fixed limit, was a valuable guide.

By the end of November 1917 a Supply Officer had reported to care for shipments then beginning to arrive from the States. Without warehouses, he was called upon to keep material outgoing as much as possible to prevent losses through exposure, which was secondary as compared with station needs, especially for galley and mess gear.

Early in January the first Officer personnel of the Supply Department, as organized in the U.S. by Lieutenant Commander Briscoe, reported. When these men arrived it was made known that an organization complete in all respects had been planned in the States. The requisitions for material to be needed in France had been made previous to the departure of these men. One month later the Supply Officer as designated by the Navy Department reported for this duty. Early in February Paymaster F. B. Colby was assigned to duty as Supply Officer at Pauillac, but not until July 1st were the two offices under the same Commanding Officer. From that date, neighboring stations did not have direct relations with the Bordeaux office; they applied to Pauillac first, that office taking the necessary action to supply the material. Thus, open purchases were curtailed, and competition, which had materially increased prices, was diminished.

On January 25th, Pauillac was assigned the duty of maintaining a stock of patrol and other naval vessel material. Especially designated Patrol Force stock was held in store in a warehouse set aside for that purpose, with requisitions for general supplies and service being filled from stock. Thus, patrol vessels based on the Gironde drew coal and water at Pauillac, getting whatever provisions, clothing, small stores, and canteen stores needed, and then proceeded to Bordeaux if any purchases were to be made. The Port Officer handled purchases at Bordeaux. Pauillac would maintain its stock and secure supplies by:

(1) Requisition on the United States—this to be the usual process, allowing six months for material to arrive.
(2) Cession from the French Government—to be an exceptional case.
(3) By purchase in Bordeaux or Paris
(4) Cession from the U.S. Army—emergency only
(5) Cession or purchase in England
(6) Transfer from another Naval Base—in emergency

Requisitions in the U.S. had been made by the Bureaus concerned to fill the type allowance lists. To these were added the ones made by the A&R organization, which arrived at Pauillac in January 1918, and requisitions made by the Supply Officer, U.S. Naval Aviation Forces in Foreign Service (i.e. Paris). By the middle of September it became known that most of the allowance list material had been shipped, hence little more of this sort could be expected. At that time, of the requisitions sent to the U.S. for filling it was not known positively that more than ten percent had been filled. If requisitions were merged with Bureau requisitions, or if they were canceled or filled, was never known at Pauillac. Marking systems were used which were not understood so far as identification with a Paris or Pauillac requisition was concerned. Not until late in August 1918 did advice of shipment notices begin to arrive at the base. Stores were coming, but no one knew by whom they were ordered or how much more could be expected. Upon Pauillac's ability to supply would depend the whole success of the supply organization, but this base lacked definite data as to what was enroute, since four distinct organizations had been requesting supplies from it. That they were stored on the station made an adjustment possible. The station was in actual competition with neighboring stations whose requests passed through the Bordeaux U.S. Navy Disbursing and Purchasing Office for purchases in the Bordeaux market. Until July 1st, that office handled the needs of the neighboring stations.

During the summer, the extent of Aviation purchases in this district caused the Bordeaux office to become less of a Purchasing Pay Office and more of an Aviation Office. After the establishment of a Purchasing Pay Officer at Bordeaux permission was granted Pauillac for making purchases in which the element of time was paramount.

When as a matter of policy or because of the state of the market it was desirable to purchase or obtain cession elsewhere than in France, the approval of the Assistant Aide for Material and Supplies, whose offices were in Paris, was obtained. Nothing could be secured outside of France without his approval, and after May 10, 1918, nothing could be obtained in France above a certain monetary value without it. His duties were to be familiar with the state of the market and to prevent waste through competition between various branches of the Navy.

By the middle of June stock at the base began to be in good shape. But then the Northern Bombing Group received its stores there, with an officer assigned to care for its distribution who was not responsible to the Supply Officer of the station. This, combined with the fact that the squadrons as a fighting unit had priority over the requests of all stations, tended to reduce to a noticeable degree the station stock, at the same time discouraging the whole station by having a separate supply organization on the station and using the warehouses without being responsible to the station Supply Officer. This situation became less annoying by the end of the summer. It was then that representatives from all stations visited the stations to take away stores necessary for their operations.

The U.S. Army, in time of urgent necessity, was the best friend of the Aviation Forces and individual Air Stations. It was their policy from the start to control all transfers from Paris; this was never deviated from, though the Stations frequently requested independent action. Efforts were made by stations to deal with U.S. Army officials directly, but these efforts failed. Pauillac's effort—a typical one, was to secure permission in the Bordeaux district—and on July 31, 1918, received this reply:

"After conference with the Aide for Material and Supplies U. S. Naval Forces in France, it is found that it will be impossible to make at Pauillac, or Bordeaux arrangements for cessions will go through and be handled by the Purchasing Office, Paris."

One month later the Supply Officer issued a further order limiting relations with the Army. It read in part:

"The Aide for Material and Supplies has advised that the Army desires to reduce the smallest possible amount, issues of stores to the U. S. Navy. In fact there has been an Army order issued to the effect that no supplies should be issued to the Navy except upon request of the Senior Naval Officer present in France, and in any case whatsoever, material must be replaced in kind within sixty days. This does not include items as provisions, gasoline and such stores which we have an agreement with the Army to supply certain stations in large quantities. This order has not been enforced by the Army, but in view of the fact that they desire such an arrangement and also as it is desired that the Navy should be self-supporting, it is requested that requests be made on the Army only as a last resort and after other sources have been tried."

A source of supply which in early days proved of assistance as to general stores, C&S, and Canteen were transports entering the Loire River. At that time the stations were in construction stage, when little material special to Aviation, except for Dunkirk, was necessary. Encouraging this, Commanding Officers were instructed early in December 1917 that such supplies as might be obtained by transfer in ports or from Army officials in the immediate vicinity should be made.

"It is very much desired that supplies as may be obtained from the vessels arriving from the United States and about to return thereto shall be obtained in as large quantity as possible, even though they may not be used by the stations which secures the supplies. As we are at present situated it is practically an impossibility to secure too many provisions, canteen stores, clothing, and small stores. In the event that any station becomes cramped for storage space shipment orders will be issued for the disposal of the surplus stock, and no stock will be too great for some time."

Insofar as this order referred to dealing with Army officials it seemed to be contradictory. However, local quartermasters and engineers who knew of a station's needs intimately were often willing to expend for its use articles asked for.

To distribute supplies along the French coast from Dunkerque to Arcachon necessary for the construction of 15 (France plus Ireland) Air Stations, and later to supply these stations when in full operation presented a transportation problem of no mean proportion.

1. To accomplish this the Supply Department must face the overtaxed Railroad system.

2. Compared with the transportation problems of the larger warring Organizations in France, those of the U.S. Naval Aviation Forces appeared to the railway authorities of minor importance.

3. Navy lines of transportation were running coastwise and at right angles to the systems, making it impossible to absorb naval supplies in the general run of traffic moving eastward. This rendered the transportation organization of other American Units of little value.

4. Freight cars were obtained only in small and insufficient quantities, due to these conditions it early became evident that Naval Aviation would be obliged to resort to coastwise transportation.

The S.S. *Bella*, a vessel of 750 tons belonging to the Bella Steamship Corporation, was finally purchased and detailed to this duty. It was taken over at Bordeaux on the 22nd of February, going into commission late in March 1918. About the same time another steamer was located, of similar type, the S.S. *Necknes* with a net tonnage of 250 tons and drawing 8 feet of water. It was requisitioned by the French Government for the use of Naval Aviation, under charter of March 15, 1918. These two ships offered an admirable solution of a portion of the transportation problems, as the smaller could enter the harbor of any of the Air Stations, whereas the *Bella,* drawing 15 feet of water, had access to the deeper channels. Both vessels had a speed of approximately ten knots and could make from Pauillac two complete trips along the coast each month, insuring a movement of approximately 2500 tons shipping per month.

It was considered advisable in March 1918 to call on the Army for an officer experienced in transportation and port operations to organize a transportation department for the Navy. Captain C.E. Carson, RTC, for several months superintendent of the Army railway lines of communication between the port of St. Nazaire and Saumur, was detailed, and under the title of General Superintendent Transportation with jurisdiction and supervision over all rail and coastwise transportation, organized a department of Transportation. The forces of the Supply Department at the various bases and ports were utilized to carry on the work of this department, and with coordination with the Army, were successful in securing engines for switching service and a fair share of the available railway equipment.

Since the Aviation Supply Base was established at Pauillac in November 1917, the tonnage handled at that port up to October 31, 1918, was as follows:

	Received	**Forwarded**
By water	119,721.78	25,148.23
By rail	30,510.43	14,112.07

This does not take into account a large amount of freight handled by auto trucks, which, in the absence of railway and water transportation, played no small part in transporting material and supplies from this station.

Lieutenant F.W. Relyea, USNRF, was in charge of the Transportation Department until relieved, on account of sickness, by Lieutenant R.D. Thomas, (PC), USN, about September 1, 1918. This department was charged with the management and operation of the railroads, the loading and unloading of ships, and the general handling and shipping of supplies after they passed from the Supply

Hangars under construction at NAS Pauillac. (source: Naval Historical Center)

Department. This department figured very largely in the operation of the station. It handled satisfactorily various physical conditions that made operations extremely difficult. It was hindered by lack of complete control of the Port of Pauillac, and by the continual interference of the French, who were using the same tracks and dock. The handling of this material and the movement of materials incident to the necessities of the Assembly and Repair shops at Pauillac required the service of four or five switch engines, working day and night. Because of the necessarily sharp curves in the yard tracks at Pauillac, only small switch engines could be used. In addition to two U.S. Navy engines received from the United States, the Army furnished three small engines for this service. The car equipment at the station consisted of 30 thirty-ton U.S. Navy flat cars and 85 ten-ton French flat cars, used only in local switching between the docks and the supply yard. Table G-2 is a statement of the work accomplished by this department.

TABLE G-2

	RAIL SHIPMENTS		**WATER SHIPMENTS**	
	RECEIVED	**DISPATCHED**	**RECEIVED**	**DISPATCHED**
Dec. 1917	1,050,000	395,000	395,000	————
Jan. 1918	387,863	479,679	4,043,760	103.250
Feb. 1918	1,201.043	1,019.048	4,452.200	225.000
Mar. 1918	576.338	888.215	7,721.300	1,147.690
April 1918	1,814.395	1,225.020	5,678.300	1.544.270
May 1918	650.625	1,2-5.446	25,783.150	1,461.720
June 1918	863.019	1,541.978	13,569.240	1,169.870
July 1918	4,007.217	1,952.147	1,120.090	1.520.520
Aug. 1918	2,045.313	1,049.138	16,085.100	8,998.850
Sept. 1918	16,062.266	3,176.005	18,430.000	463.790
Oct. 1918	7,852.350	1,575.200	21,644.750	8,013.270
Total	30,510.429	14,112.075	119,721.780	24,648.230

Total Tonnage received by water	119,721.780
Total Tonnage received by rail	30,510.429
GRAND TOTAL	150,232.209
Total Tonnage dispatched by water	25,148.230
Total Tonnage dispatched by rail	14,112.075
GRAND TOTAL	39,260.305
Tons received by rail and water	150,232.209
Tons dispatched by rail and water	39,260.306
TOTAL TONNAGE HANDLED	189,492.515

The following report covers the tonnage through this station for the Northern Bombing Group:

Total amount of provisions received—approximately 1168 1/2 tons
Value of stores received—$290,486.23
Miscellaneous supplied of the Northern Bombing Unit to the extent of 4500 tons handled and shipped to their base.

A&R Shops under construction at NAS Pauillac.

D.H.-4s at NAS Pauillac. The U.S. Army not only had mechanics at Pauillac undergoing training on the Liberty engine, but also had its Liberty engines repaired here by the Navy. (source: 80 HAG-5J-6)

PROVISIONS

From U.S.A.	$289,182.54	To Other Supply Officers	$287,226.28
From S.O. Pauillac	922.04	Expended on surveys	2,699.90
By appraisal survey	381.65	To S.O. Pauillac	560.05
Total receipts	$290,486.23	Total Expenditures	$290,486.23

CLOTHING & SMALL STORES

From U.S.A.	$265,998.49	To Other Supply Officers	$275,070.14
By appraisal survey	122.00	Expended on survey	496.91
Gain by adj. of price	9,470.95	To S.O. Pauillac	24.39
	$275,591.44		$275,591.44

CANTEEN

From U.S.A.	$117,918.78	To Other Supply Officers	$116,565.15
By credit invoice	109.80	S.O. Pauillac	286.65
By appraisal survey	80.04	Survey	1,129.62
Overcharge rebilled back	127.20		
Total	$118,108.62		$118,108.62

PROVISIONS

RECEIVED
From U.S. Supply Officer, Pauillac and by appraisal—approximately 1168 1/2 tons

EXPENDED
By shipments to other Supply Officers, by Survey, and to Supply Officer, Pauillac—1168 1/2 tons

CLOTHING AND SMALL STORES
Received from U.S.A. and Appraisal Survey, approximately 75 tons
Expended by shipments to other Supply Officers and by Survey—75 tons

CANTEEN
Received from U.S.A. and appraisal survey—approximately 325 1/2 tons
Expended by shipments to other Supply Officers and by survey—325 1/2 tons
The Navy and Marine Air Squadrons of the Northern Bombing Group received via the following ships the following materials:

RECAPITULATION

	Pkgs.	Cu.Ft.	Pounds
DOCHRA	40,978	84,515	3,154,419
HOUSTON	3,335	10,489	428,097
PENSACOLA	10,2273	76,436	618,400
RAPPAHANNOCK	61,101	176,315	4,115,583
MALANG	5,436	53,399	1,285,583
NEWPORT NEWS	1,218	———	56,045
BESOEKI	621	13,428	246,541
PENSACOLA	———	9,460	87,019
TOTALS	122,962	242,042	9,991,360

IVc. Medical Department

The efficiency of the Medical Department was manifested in September 1918, during the influenza epidemic which spread over the greater portion of Europe. With an average complement of 4400 men, a total of 11 men died from influenza, out of 550 cases which were admitted to the Sick Bay. Based upon the history of the station, reports from the medical officer of the station, and extracts from reports and letters sent to Senior Medical Officer at U.S. Naval Base Hospital #5, Brest, Pauillac incurred a total of 31 deaths during its existence (three classified as Accidental and 28 classified as Natural Causes). Of these deaths, the three which were accidental were the result of men riding on top of a car enroute from Brest. Three died in Army Hospitals. Additional deaths at the station were: eight subjects of friendly forces; one civilian; and three Army personnel. Two additional reports were submitted, one dated January 1, 1919, in reply to Aviation Circular #110 of January 15, 1919. This reports the burial of 40 men of the U.S. Navy in the vicinity of Pauillac and eight subjects of friendly nations. The second was the Sanitary Report for Pauillac to the Bureau of Medicine and Surgery, dated January 15, 1919. From this report the following is quoted: "Our dead are buried in a Pauillac cemetery in a plot assigned to us. We have there 38, which include about 18 from other ships." From February 1, 1918, until the signing of the Armistice, an average of 3000 men per month answered sick call and were examined and treated by the Medical Officers. One hundred and twelve major operations and 200 minor operations were performed. The other Air Stations in the district transferred their operative cases to Pauillac for surgical treatment. Thirty-two foreigners were given medical and surgical attention at this station. One Medical Officer, one hospital corpsman, and one yeoman were assigned to permanent duty in connection with sanitation. A fluctuating working party was detailed for this duty from time to time, to carry out the proposed plans. As a result of constant endeavor, at the close of activities the conditions of the station, in this respect, were satisfactory.

V. Conclusion

It was clearly the purpose to make the Air Stations in Europe become in every respect self sustaining; to accomplish this it was necessary that requisitions be sent frequently to the States, and that supplies might be coming to the Base without interruption. The degree to which this ideal was reached is a measure of the success of the Supply organization. With the exceptions of certain ordnance equipment and instruments, practically everything was being received from the States at the time of cessation of hostilities. Naturally, those things which were necessary for operating French-made planes in use at five Air Stations must be gotten from the French.

That the Supply on the basis of the allowance list was not coordinated with the number of men in France may be attributed to many causes, which in the U.S. retarded shipment. To pronounce as a complete success the work of the supply organization would be unfair. It was not in every respect a perfect and smooth running Section. Interruptions and frequent changes in the detail of administration as put into force by those organizations that had control of the market of materials and supplies in France, were not conducive to the highest satisfaction. This was the situation as far as the securing of material in the local market was concerned. After May 10, the interests of the Navy and Aviation so far as purchase was concerned were under the direction of one Officer, but there is little doubt that had Naval Aviation been forced from the start not to cooperate, but to work under and as a part of the U.S. Army purchase machinery, there would have been less anxiety. In an effort to run their own little entertainment, the Navy encountered obstacles which would not have appeared, had they considered themselves as a part of the Army purchase organization. The market was well combed by this board. Partial independence proved expensive in time. There was too much opportunity to shift responsibilities.

From the supply standpoint, for the expeditious delivery of materials, the Base at Pauillac was misplaced. Transportation was bad enough, but to attempt to supply stations so far north as were Treguier, L'Aber Vrach, Guipavas, and Brest was a difficult project. Pauillac was on the west bank of the Grionde, necessitating a loss of time in the transfer of shipments through Bordeaux, while the stations of Gujan, Arcachon, and Moutchic were forced to rely upon motor transportation to an increasing degree. The *Bella* and the *Mecknes* did much to offset this loss, but that Pauillac was misplaced there is in slight doubt if only viewed from the standpoint of transportation. That it may have been the most logical point available is not questioned. Expediency is not an advisable policy in all cases.

Supply Base, as a result of its position, was out of touch with the Headquarters at Paris, as well as Brest; it was started and then permitted to grow without careful direction of its efforts. By early June its stock had come to be well balanced, but then the Northern Bombing Group Squadrons were permitted to take anything that was desired without a question being raised by the Base. The bombers got what they wanted, but Coastal Air Stations did not, and this resulted in a policy of search to be made by representatives of the various stations in order to secure material desired.

The Supply situation was never ideal. No one knew what was coming from the States, for shipment orders did not begin to arrive from the Navy Department until late in the fall. It was evident that there was a lack of coordination between the States and the Forces in France, but everyone was anxious to be of service, and if he failed it was only because his efforts were misdirected.

VI. Demobilization

Upon cessation of hostilities demobilization planing was begun. The question of land damages was handled by the Headquarters Office, Brest, in collaboration with the Legal Aide in Paris, and an attempt to expedite the derequisitioning of the flying field made through the French Minister. The French Navy requested that all properties be derequisitioned and all claims settled to date, and that the property be then rerequisitioned by the Minister of War and then be transferred to the U.S. Army. This involved payment of the following items as estimated by the French:

(a) Annual rental of grounds	118,600 francs
(b) Rental of Buildings	18,000 francs
(c) Purchase of French Buildings	217,000 francs
(d) Indemnities for commercial damage and loss of produce	373,000 francs
Total	726,600 francs

An attempt was made to avoid such procedure and to permit the U.S. Army to take over the property with all obligations liquidated upon termination of its occupancy.

With the establishment in February, 1919, of the Paris Naval Board on Claims, the final approval of all claims and adjustments not already settled rested with that body. All claims and matters involving obligation on the part of the U.S. Navy, arising from the demobilization of the Aviation Forces, had been carefully examined by the Commanding Officer of the station, and, in such cases where expert investigation was required, by a Board of Appraisal composed of Lieutenant Richardson and Lieutenant Conrad of the Public Works Department, and Lieutenant Commander R.W. Schumann (PC), USN. Every effort was made to accomplish just and equitable settlements, rather than have numerous cases taken to the French Courts for adjustment, though such action in certain instances, where the owners of property were insistent on making excessive demands, was inevitable. The U.S. Army agreed, in taking over the station at Pauillac, to assume the settlement and payment, under the Indemnity Act, of claims and indemnities due to the occupancy of the properties by the Aviation Forces, thereby relieving the U.S. Navy of very considerable litigation.

The total cost for Pauillac came to:

Cost of U.S. Improvements	$829,157.00
Value of U.S. Material liquidated	651,812.00
Cost	$177,345.00

The station complete was taken over by the U.S. Army, following demobilization on February 1, 1919, to be used as a point of embarkation for troops returning to the United States. It was admirably suited for this purpose, having excellent quarters and deep water to the dock. The Navy temporarily retained living quarters at Pauillac for the nucleus crews for German vessels then being assembled in France.

APPENDIX G-1
SHIPPING DATA ON SEAPLANES
PAUILLAC AIR STATION, PAUILLAC, FRANCE

Machine Number	Type	Arrival Date	Assembly Date	Delivery Date	Destination
A-808	HS-1	5-24-18	7-24-18	7-26-18	Moutchic
A-809	HS-1	5-24-18	7-3-18	7-6-18	Pauillac
A-810	HS-1	5-24-18	6-18-18	6-18-18	Moutchic
A-811	HS-1	5-24-18	6-22-18	6-29-18	Fromentine
A-812	HS-1	5-24-18	8-12-18	8-20-18	Moutchic
A-813	HS-1	6-24-18	— arrived damaged —		Moutchic
A-863	HS-1	8-9-18	-	-	Fromentine
A-864	HS-1	6-7-18	8-4-18	8-10-18	Arcachon
A-1061	H-16	6-11-18	7-8-18	-	-
A-1065	H-16	6-11-18	9-2-18	9-26-18	St. Trojan
A-1415	HS-2	10-4—18	-	-	St. Trojan
A-1554	HS-1	6-24-18	8-4-18	8-10-18	Arcachon
A-1555	HS-1	7-18-18	8-20-18	8-25-18	Arcachon
A-1556	HS-1	6-7-18	7-13-18	1-16-18	Fromentine
A-1557	HS-1	6-7-18	8-10-18	8-12-18	Arcachon
A-1558	HS-1	6-2-18	7-30-18	8-1-18	Fromentine
A-1559	HS-1	-	7-18-18	7-25-18	Fromentine
A-1560	HS-1	6-7-18	7-14-18	7-16-18	Fromentine
A-1562	HS-1	3-20-18	— arrived damaged —		Fromentine
A-1567	HS-1	8-8-18	-	-	St. Trojan
A-1568	HS-1	7-18-18	8-30-18	8-31-18	Arcachon
A-1569	HS-1	7-18-18	8-14-18	8-27-18	Moutchic
A-1573	HS-1	6-18-18	— arrived damaged —		Arcachon
A-1574	HS-1	6-23-18	8-2-18	8-10-18	Moutchic
A-1575	HS-1	5-25-18	6-13-18	6-18-18	Moutchic
A-1576	HS-1	7-1-18	7-24-18	7-26-18	Fromentine
A-1578	HS-1	7-1-18	7-19-18	7-26-18	Fromentine
A-1579	HS-1	6-2-18	7-22-18	7-22-18	Arcachon
A-158(?)	HS-1	7-30-18	9-5-18	9-5-18	Arcachon
A-1582	HS-1	6-7-18	8-8-18	8-12-18	Fromentine
A-1583	HS-1	5-24-18	6-22-18	6-29-18	Fromentine
A-1585	HS-1	7-30-18	9-20-18	9-25-18	Fromentine
A-1586	HS-1	6-7-18	8-1-18	8-1-18	Arcachon
A-1587	HS-1	7-25-18	8-12-18	8-12-18	Fromentine
A-1588	HS-1	7-1-18	7-16-18	7-16-18	Arcachon
A-1594	HS-1	7-26-18	9-5-18	9-5-18	Fromentine
A-1595	HS-1	7-26-18	9-20-18	9-21-18	Fromentine
A-1596	HS-1	7-26-18	8-28-18	8-29-18	Fromentine
A-1597	HS-1	7-26-18	8-26-18	8-27-18	Moutchic
A-1601	HS-1	8-30-18	-	-	Moutchic
A-1609	HS-1	8-30-18	-	-	Moutchic
A-1610	HS-1	8-30-18	-	-	Moutchic
A-1615	HS-1	8-30-18	9-17-18	9-17-18	St. Trojan
A-1621	HS-1	7-26-18	9-30-18	10-2-18	Fromentine
A-1622	HS-1	7-26-18	11-5-18	11-8-18	Arcachon
A-1623	HS-1	7-26-18	8-28-18	8-29-18	Fromentine
A-1624	HS-1	7-26-18	9-2-18	9-14-18	Fromentine
A-1625	HS-1	6-26-18	-	-	-
A-1626	HS-1	7-26-18	8-31-18	9-14-18	Fromentine

A-1627	HS-1	7-26-18	10-23-18	10-23-18	Moutchic
A-xxxx	HS-1	7-26-18	8-28-18	8-31-18	St. Trojan
A-1631	HS-1	7-26-18	8-24-18	8-23-18(sic)	Arcachon
A-1632	HS-1	7-26-18	8-19-18	8-20-18	Moutchic
A-1640	HS-1	7-26-18	8-23-18	8-27-18	Arcachon
A-1641	HS-1	7-26-18	-	-	-
A-1671	HS-1	8-19-18	10-3-18	10-5-18	Fromentine
A-1743	HS-1	8-3-18	10-17-18	10-29-18	Fromentine
A-1745	HS-1	8-3-18	8-26-18	8-29-18	Moutchic
A-1747	HS-1	8-30-18	10-23-18	10-24-18	Moutchic
A-1748	HS-1	8-30-18	11-3-18	11-5-18	Arcachon
A-1749	HS-1	8-30-18	9-22-18	10-22-18	Moutchic
A-1750	HS-1	8-3-18	8-24-18	8-27-18	Arcachon
A-1751	HS-1	8-3-18	9-9-18	9-26-18	Moutchic
A-1752	HS-1	8-30-18	9-17-18	9-17-18	St. Trojan
A-1756	HS-1	8-30-18	-	-	-
A-1775	HS-1	-	10-1-18	10-2-18	Fromentine
A-1776	HS-1	8-19-18	9-21-18	9-24-18	Moutchic
A-1777	HS-1	-	9-13-18	9-17-18	Moutchic
A-1782	HS-1	8-19-18	-	-	-
A-1783	HS-1	8-19-18	11-11-18	-	-
A-1784	HS-1	8-19-18	10-1-18	10-2-18	Fromentine
A-1785	HS-1	8-19-18	10-17-18	11-2-18	Arcachon
A-1786	HS-1	8-19-18	9-15-18	9-17-18	Moutchic
A-1787	HS-1	8-19-18	10-1-18	10-2-18	Fromentine
A-1788	HS-1	8-19-18	10-23-18	10-23-18	Moutchic
A-1789	HS-1	8-19-18	9-15-18	9-17-18	Moutchic
A-1793	HS-1	8-19-18	9-15-18	9-17-18	-
A-1794	HS-1	8-19-18	9-15-18	9-17-18	St. Trojan
A-1795	HS-1	8-19-18	9-15-18	9-17-18	St. Trojan
A-1796	HS-1	8-19-18	9-16-18	9-17-18	Moutchic
A-1797	HS-1	8-19-18	10-4-18	10-4-18	Moutchic
A-1798	HS-1	8-19-18	9-12-18	9-13-18	Arcachon
A-1799	HS-1	8-19-18	9-14-18	9-17-18	Moutchic
A-1800	HS-1	8-19-18	9-19-18	9-21-18	Fromentine
A-1801	HS-1	8-19-18	9-20-18	9-26-18	Moutchic
A-1802	HS-1	8-19-18	9-17-18	9-17-18	Moutchic
A-1952	HS-2	10-4-18	10-15-18	10-18 18	-
A-1953	HS-2	10-7-18	10-30-18	11-12-18	-
A-1954	HS-2	10-12-18	-	-	St. Trojan
A-1956	HS-2	10-4-18	-	-	Brest
A-1959	HS-2	10-18	11-11-18	-	-
A-1952	HS-2	10-10-18	-	-	-

APPENDIX G-2
U.S. NAVAL AVIATION, FOREIGN SERVICE
FRENCH UNIT
ENLISTED PERSONNEL AT NAS PAUILLAC
AT TIME OF DEMOBILIZATION ORDER

Rate	Allowed	On-Hand
B.M.	149	143
G.M.	70	52
Q.M.	220	172
Sea.	2296	854
Spec. Mech.	305	16
E.(G)	213	47
E.(R)	58	22
C.M.	840	342
S.F.	0	28
P. & F.	30	10
S.M.M.	12	4
S.K.	65	80
M.M.	931	533
B. Smith	95	116
C. Smith	129	58
Yeo.	254	243
P.M. & H.A.	69	47
Com. Stw.	2	2
S.C.	60	69
BKRS.	23	28
MATT.	0	30
O.G. & S.	0	8
PRINT.	39	15
FIREMAN	0	38
PAINT.	25	6
BUG.	0	3
MUS.	0	25
TOTAL	5885	2985

Photo labeled as Lt. Ruttman and Cdr. Cabaniss, however, the officer on the right is thought to be Lt. C.E. Ruttan. Cabaniss was the second Commanding Officer of the Naval Aviation Detachment prior to assignment overseas. (source: 80-HAG-5F-8)

APPENDIX G-3
STATISTICAL DATA
U.S. NAVAL AIR STATION PAUILLAC, GIRONDE, FRANCE
From July 15, 1918 To November 11, 1918

Week Ending	Flights Made	Total Knots	Flying Time	Aircraft at Station	Aircraft in Commission	Flying Personnel
July 6	10	180	3:11	19 HS-1, 2 H-16	1 HS-1	3
July 13	10	180	2:44	14 HS-1, 2 H-16	3 HS-1	3
July 20	8	780	12;54	19 HS-1, 2 H-16	3 HS-1	3
July 27	11	330	5:25	31 HS-1, 2 H-16	3 HS-1	1
August 3	18	2250	37:04	29 HS-1, 2 H-16	1 HS-1	10
August 10	12	390	6:25	33 HS-1, 4 H-16	2 HS-1	10
August 17	43	870	14:36	32 HS-1, 4 H-16 4 D.H.-4	2 HS-1	10
August 24	20	390	6:17	50 HS-1, 2 H-16 4 D.H. 4, 1 L.P.	1 HS-1	10

August 31	29	1470	29:19	52 HS-1, 2 H-16 4 D.H. 4, 1 L.P.	1 HS-1, 3 D.H. 4	12
September 7	17	450	7:38	49 HS-1, 2 H-16 1 D.H. 4, 1 G.L. 29	3 HS-1	22
September 14	31	870	14:28	48 HS-1, 2 H-16 1 D.H. 4, 1 G.L. 29	1 HS-1	50
September 21	332	1140	19:02	30 HS-1, 2 H-16 1 D.H. 4, 1 G.L. 29	1 HS-1	10
September 28	18	690	11:12	36 HS-1, 1 H-16, 1 D.H. 4, 1 G.L. 29	0	9
October 5	22	1290	8:15	39 HS-1, 4 HS-2 1 H-16	1 HS-1	9
October 12	17	510	8:15	38 HS-1, 7 HS-2 1 H-16	1 HS-1	7
October 19	13	450	7:23	43 HS-1, 6 HS-2 1 H-16	3 HS-1	8
October 26	29	810	12:37	3 HS-1, 6 HS-2 1 H-16	5 HS-1	3
November 2	11	650	10:36	72 HS-1, 6 HS-2 4 H-16	3 HS-1	6
November 9	17	760	13:37	74 HS-1, 6 HS-2 4 H-16	3 HS-1	6
To November 11	4	625	5:12	74 HS-1, 6 HS-2 1 H-16	2 HS-1	6
Total	572	15085	245:04			

APPENDIX G-4
U.S. NAVAL AVIATION FORCES, FOREIGN SERVICE, FRENCH UNIT
RADIO SECTION STATUS (NAS PAUILLAC)

Personnel	On-Hand	In-Store
Radio Officers	2	-
Radio Gunners	1	-
Chief Elect.	3	-
Ground Operators	12	-
Compass Operators	-	-
Radio Men as Observers	-	-
Radio Mechanics	9	-
Landwire Operators	5	-
Material		
French Air Transmitter	-	-
British Air Transmitter	-	28
American Air Transmitter	-	13
Shore Station	-	3
French Air Receiver	-	1
British Air Receiver	-	-
American Air Receiver	-	4
Shore Station Radio Compass	-	-

APPENDIX G-5
INSPECTION REPORT ON NAS PAUILLAC

17 November, 1918.

From: Commander in Chief
To. Secretary of the Navy (OPERATIONS).

Subject: Report on inspection of U.S. Naval Air Station, Pauillac, France.

1. The U.S. Naval Air Station at Pauillac, France, Captain F.T. Evans, U.S. Navy, Commanding, was inspected by the Commander in Chief accompanied by his staff on 30-31 October 1918.

2. Unlike the other air stations inspected (with the exception of Moutchic), this is not an operating station, but is the supply base to the U.S. coastal air stations in France and for the Northern Bombing projects, and also occupies the position of receiving ship for the above stations.

3. **Organization**

The present Commanding Officer assumed command on 17 July 1918.

The station operates directly under the command of the Commander U.S. Naval Air Forces in France and is independent of the

Commander of the Rochefort District, in which district it is located. It was apparent that close cooperation is had with the U.S. Army officials of Bordeaux, to whom assistance in material is rendered and from whom material is obtained when necessary. It was stated by the Commanding Officer that the station was about to undertake the overhaul of airplane motors for the Army.

The general scheme of organization of the station is as follows:

Commanding Officer, Executive Officer (general supervisor) and department heads—Executive, Supply, Assembly and Repair, Inspection and Test, Transport, Public Works, and Medical. The General Supervisor (Executive) coordinates the various departments.

The duties of the different sections of the organization are so decentralized that there is a proper division of authority and responsibility, but it was apparent that the organization was comparatively new and that it is only now beginning to function properly. The Commanding Officer does not charge himself with details in any of heads of departments, but generally speaking, the heads of departments are very junior in rank and it was evident that a great many of their decisions are made by the Commanding Officer and that the forceful personality of this officer is felt throughout the various activities of the station with good results.

The organization provides for reasonable expansion and seems to be limited only by the capacities of the several heads of departments, who should be officers of greater experience. That is assuming that both men and material in sufficient numbers and quantity are furnished.

To make the organizations more efficient the officers of the station recommend an increase in the number of line officers of the Regular Navy and a permanent working force of enlisted men or prisoners. The first mentioned should be decided by the Department using the necessity for these officers afloat as a basis. The addition of several regular service officers to the station might improve the organization, but it is believed that the duties which these officers would be called upon to perform could be handled by properly selected reserve officers and that the regular service officers could be utilized to better advantage afloat. As to the second recommendation, namely, that a permanent working force be allowed, it is thought that this is a matter of extreme importance and that a compliment (ship's company) be allowed containing non-rated men in sufficient numbers to perform the labor necessary in discharging cargoes, etc. The advantage of the utilization of prisoners of war in large numbers for this purpose is questionable.

4. **Executive Department**

In addition to his duties as general supervisor, the executive officer, a Lieutenant Commander of the regular service, is charged with the general control of personnel, its housing, patrols, amusements and recreation, liberty, etc., and in his capacity of Senior Aide to the Commanding Officer, of communications.

The personnel problem at this station is a very serious one on account of the constant calls made on the station to furnish personnel to the operating air stations in France. These calls for men, together with the uncertainty of arrival of replacement drafts, gives the station a constantly varying complement making it difficult to make plans for work and often seriously slowing the discharge of steamer cargoes and other urgent work. A great deal of difficulty has been encountered in keeping men on the station who have been specially trained to important duties. This applies as well to officers who are being constantly withdrawn.

It was noted that in a number of instances rated men were being used in duties suited to non-rated men. Compliance with the request for a non-rated working force will release these men to perform the duties of their ratings.

The enlisted personnel are comfortably housed and from all appearances the morale is high. There is ample liberty and recreation and the officers of the station cooperate to provide amusements.

The commissary and messing arrangements are not satisfactory; the food was not well served and was cold. When the station is up to complement it is necessary to have two sittings at each meal. At the time of the inspection the complement was so reduced that there was but one sitting. The officers of the station have this in hand and will undoubtedly provide increased messing space if it again becomes necessary.

The uniform and general appearance of the personnel is satisfactory.

5. **Supply Department**

The function of the station makes the efficiency of the supply department of prime importance and a great many complaints from other air stations on account of non-receipt of material are attributable to the former lack of organization and constantly shifting personnel of this department and to the lack of cooperation between the supply and other departments of the station. Apparently no proper check of supplies was made between the ship in which they arrived and the storehouses. It also appeared to have been the custom for various departments to claim their supplies direct upon discharge from the ships and the supply officer had no record of such supplies. Much material which was badly needed at other stations and for the assembly of planes at this station, and which was made the subject of considerable correspondence with the Department, was subsequently located in open storage about the station.

At the time of the inspection matters had considerably improved and the new organization which was being put into effect by the Supply Officer, together with better cooperation with other departments, should entirely correct the faults which formerly existed.

Personnel acquainted with cargo handling and transportation are needed.

6. **Assembly and Repair Department**

This department is well organized, has a most satisfactory plant, and is functioning in an efficient manner. The lack of doors and glass for windows in the assembly hangars will interfere with the assembly of planes when cold weather arrives.

The assembly and repair department overhauls and assembles all airplanes delivered in France, turning them over to the test department for test. It also repairs all planes, engines, etc. returned to Pauillac from operating stations where the repairs are of such a nature that they cannot be undertaken by the operating station. At the time of the inspection practically all boats under repair belonged to the school at Moutchic. One Army plane, which had crashed near the station, was also being repaired.

It was noted that there were approximately sixty enlisted men of the Army employed in the shops of the assembly department. These men were sent to the station under an arrangement with the Army for instruction.

There is a large supply of engines and engine spare parts on hand. It was stated that four hundred Liberty Engines had just been received but as they were fitted with the Army hub they could not be used in the Navy plane, the HS-1. Steps were being taken to convert these engines.

It was also noted that there were approximately sixteen HS-1 boats on the station, which could not be completed, due to lack of tachometers, gasoline lines and oil tanks. This is due to the above boats having been robbed of these parts to furnish spare parts to stations in operation. These spare parts have not been replaced due to the non-receipt of spare parts from home at the expected rate of delivery.

7. **Inspection and Test Department**

This department inspects and tests all material which has been assembled or repaired by the Assembly and Repair Department. It appears to be well organized and efficient. Facilities were at hand for the test of motors and these were being expanded at the time of the inspection. The boats are actually flown after assembly and repair and are delivered only after they have been pronounced satisfactory by this department. The completed boats are flown to the stations to which consigned when this is practicable.

8. **Transportation Department**

This department is organized to discharge the cargo of ships to transport the material to store, to transship material intended for other stations and to handle all other motor and rail transportation.

Working under the Transportation Department at the time of the inspection were some two hundred Army stevedores and a company (Searchlight Company) of Marines. Connected with the Department was a Captain in the Army who was designated as Railroad Transportation Officer. All matters relating to the use of French railways are handled through this officer.

As far as could be observed the Transportation Department was functioning efficiently. They were handicapped at the time of inspection by the lack of a suitable discharge platform which produced difficulty in sorting stores as they were discharged from the ships.

Men with railroad experience are needed in this department, a yardmaster with two assistants being especially necessary. There should also be sent six to eight officers with experience in cargo handling, to work cargo into and out of steamers at docks.

All of the Yard railway transportation is manned by enlisted men of the Navy.

The Transportation Department reports very careless loading of steamers at home, heavy stores being placed on top of delicate machinery, caustic soda so stored as to leak out and destroy valuable material, etc.

The motor transport is well handled, well-equipped garage and repair facilities being provided.

9. **Medical Department**

The sanitary conditions on the station are considered excellent. The health of the personnel has also been excellent, except for an epidemic of Spanish influenza, which was very efficiently handled by the Medical Department.

10. **Public Works Department**

The public buildings, roads and other improvements on the station speak well for the work of this department. Practically all building has been completed with the exception of the power house, water tank and Y.M.C.A. buildings, which are nearing completion.

11. It is a recommendation that steps be taken with a view to expediting the removal of the menace from possible explosion of powder which is unloaded by the French Government at the same dock as the supplies for the air station and often left in the yard in freight cars. It is understood that this matter has already been taken up with the French Government.

This station should be placed under the general control of the Commander of the District in which it is located. At present it operates directly under the Commander U.S. Naval Forces in France, at Brest.

It is the Commander in Chief's opinion that the station is now well organized and that under the present administration it will produce excellent results.

/s/ H.T. MAYO

Notes:

[1] Much of the material forming the basis for the history of this station comes from the work entitled *History of U.S. Naval Aviation Foreign Service, French Unit, 1917-1918*

Appendix H: NAS Le Croisic[1]

I. CONSTRUCTION

Le Croisic was the first U.S. Naval Air Station to be organized in France. It was the first completed, and the first to operate.

Le Croisic is a small fishing village of about 3000 inhabitants, situated on the "Bale de Croisic" about 18 miles from St. Nazaire. The harbor is sheltered by a sea wall and thus afforded a safe anchorage for fishing vessels. During the occupancy of the station by the U.S. Navy, a spirit of great friendship existed between the inhabitants of Le Croisic and the American personnel. It was found unnecessary to establish a military police in the town for the reason that no differences or disturbances occurred.

Previous to the arrival of the Americans the French authorities had established an aviation station in Le Croisic, which was called a "Poste de Combat." It consisted of one Bessonneau hangar with a crane to lower seaplanes, quarters for about 20 men, a Wireless station, and a house in which to keep and train pigeons. Operations had been carried on in a perfunctory manner, as the pilots of the station were those who had seen active service at the Front and were sent there to rest before returning.

Early in July the U.S. Naval authorities in Paris visited Le Croisic and decided to build a station, but objected to the site of the French "Poste de Combat," as the space was not large enough. Two small islands, called "Les Petit et Grand Joncheres," were chosen. These islands previously had been used by fishermen as a place to dry their nets and belonged to the village of Le Croisic. The smaller of the two islands was connected to the mainland by a very strongly built iron bridge. No U.S. enlisted men were available for construction, and the building of the station was actually commenced on 26 July 1917, when 19 German prisoners were obtained to build a heavy, wooden bridge to connect the two islands, which are located between the Place des Armos, Fort de Lenigo, and the Quai de La Motte. They also started to level the ground preparatory to erecting hangars and barracks. Carpenter's shop, wash house, machine shop, general store house, gasoline house, and a Bessonneau hangar were soon under construction. Two Tellier seaplanes arrived on 6 October 1917 and were stored on the mainland.

The hangar used by the French was placed on the island, where within a few days a seaplane was assembled. The difficulty of securing tools delayed the work, but some were obtained from the French and work advanced rapidly. The station was put into Operation on 11 November 1917 and Commissioned on 23 November 1917. By 6 June 1918 it had a compliment of 330 personnel.

II. PERSONNEL

On 5 October 1917, Ensign Rufus H. Bush, USN (Naval Aviator No. 1774), arrived to take charge of construction work for the U.S. Navy, and four days later the first detachment of 61 men reported. As the barracks were not completed, they were quartered in the hospital of St. Jean de Dieu, about one-quarter of a mile from the station. This hospital was leased from the patriotic priests for the sum of one franc a year.

On 29 October 1917, pilots Ensigns Kenneth R. Smith, USNRF (Naval Aviator No. 87), Samuel S. Walker, USNRF (Naval Aviator No. 86), and Reginald D. Coombe, USNRF (Naval Aviator No. 92), arrived and assisted in the work of construction. Thirteen enlisted men, two of whom were pilots and eleven observers, arrived the same day, some of them direct from the States and others from the French flying Schools at Tours and St. Raphael (Note: The enlisted men were members of what had been the First Aeronautic Detachment).

The men were transferred from the hospital and quartered in the new barracks on the last day of October. Several of the large empty seaplane crates were made habitable and used as mess halls.

French Tellier seaplane of the type flown by the Navy at NAS Le Croisic.

On the first day of November 1917, Assistant Paymaster J.C. Bequette, USN, arrived and was assigned to duty as Supply Officer. Previous to his arrival, Paymaster Bertaux of the French Navy had been stationed at Le Croisic, and through his able assistance many things necessary for the construction of the station were secured. He remained for a time after Paymaster Bequette arrived and assisted him in his work. On 3 November Lieutenant John Lansing Callan, USNRF (Naval Aviator No. 1442), reported at the station and relieved Ensign Bush of command. The same day Ensign Henry H. Landon, USNRF (Naval Aviator No. 93), pilot, reported with 100 men who were quartered in the hospital of St. Jean de Dieu until 5 November, when permanent barracks were completed. Lieutenant William Corry, USN (Naval Aviator No. 23), reported on 7 November and relieved Lieutenant Callan as Commanding Officer.

On 23 November the station was formally commissioned. The flagpole had been obtained after some difficulty, and the French colors hoisted to the top; the day of the ceremony, these were replaced by the Stars and Stripes. French and American guards of honor lined up on the parade ground facing the mainland, and the band from the 17th Engineers, at St. Nazaire, assisted. Captaine E'Estrenes, Commandant of the Centre of Aviation of Lorient, read the order concerning the taking over of the station by the American Government, and Lieutenant Corry, Commanding Officer of the station, accepted the station on behalf of the U.S. Government. Personnel on the station as of this date were as follows:

Lieutenant W.M. Corry, USN	Commanding Officer
Ensign R.H. Bush, USN	Executive Officer
Ensign H.H. Landon, USNRF	Chief Pilot
Ensign R.G. Coombe, USNRF	Pilot
Ensign S.S. Walker, USNRF	Pilot
Ensign K.R. Smith, USNRF	Pilot
Assistant Surgeon C. Wheatley, USN	Medical Officer
Assistant Paymaster J.C. Bequette, USN	Supply Officer
299 Enlisted men	

Dr. Murkland, formerly President of the University of New Hampshire, was the Secretary designated to represent the Y.M.C.A. at Le Croisic. He desired to have a building constructed on the island for the men to use as a reading room and for entertainment. As a lack of space made this impossible, a theater building in Le Croisic was leased. This building, just across from the island and directly opposite the bridges on the mainland, had formerly been operated as a cinema called the Salle Jeanne d'Arc. This building belonged to an N. L'Able Clenet, Curate of Le Croisic. Negotiations through the assistance of the French authorities resulted in the leasing of this building for a mess hall and galley. Moving pictures were shown for the entertainment of the men several nights a week. Electric lights were installed, and basketball and handball courts were rigged. Many very good entertainments and concerts were given there by the Y.M.C.A. Among the entertainers was Miss Elsie Janis, who visited the station on 11 April 1918. Church services were held here and were largely attended. After Dr. Murkland was detached, A.J. Mitchell was sent to take his place; but, on account of ill health, he was transferred to the United States and was succeeded by Mr. J.L. Moody, a member of the Navy Y.M.C.A., who became very popular with the men. Several minstrels were given, in one of which, given on May 5th and 6th, Lieutenant Corry was interlocutor. This performance was very successful, and afterwards visited several Army camps in St. Nazaire and Base Hospital No. 101. Natives of Le Croisic were frequently invited by the sailors to attend these entertainments, and wounded French soldiers from the nearby hospital were always welcome.

At the time of the Armistice 337 enlisted men and the officers shown in Table H-1 were on board.

III. OPERATIONS

A seaplane was assembled in the old French hangar during October 1917, and early in November three others were ready for test flights. Though the first flight at this station was made on 13 November 1917, it was not until five days later that the first patrol flight was made and operations were officially started with six French seaplanes of the Tellier type. This flight was the first American patrol of the French Coastal Unit. From that date patrol and convoy flights were made regularly, weather permitting. As the communication facilities were very poor at this time, the time and position of passing convoys were very uncertain, and since there were no adjoining Air Stations with which to cooperate in escorting the convoys along the coast, long flights were necessary.

TABLE H-1

Lieutenant Wm. Masek,, USN	Commanding Officer
Lieutenant Rufus H. Bush, USN	Executive Officer
Ensign Walter W. Wigman, USNRF	
Ensign Frederick H. Becker, USNRF	Pilot
Ensign Frederick E. King, USNRF	Pilot
Ensign Robert T. Whitehouse, USNRF	Pilot
Ensign Harold L. Ryan, USNRF	Pilot
Ensign Sidney Pedott, USNRF	
Ensign Richard L. Farelly, USNRF	
Ensign Samuel G. Clowell, USNRF	
Ensign George E. Craswell, USNRF	
Lieutenant (j.g.) David Ferguson, Jr., USN	Medical Corps
Lieutenant Alfred G. Tinney, USN	Medical Corps
Ensign Ralph G. Gates, USNRF	Pay Corps
Lieutenant Louis E. Thornton, USNRF	Civil Engineer Corps
Boatswain (T) Alfred W. Marchant, USN	
Gunner (T) (O) John McNamara, USN	
Gunner (T) (O) Gunder Z. Johnston, USN	
Gunner (R) Erik E. Bolin, USNRF	
Machinist (T) Robert Farris, USN	
Machinist (T) Robert N. Wilkinson, USN	
Carpenter (T) Milton DeMilt, USN	
Lieutenant (j.g.) C.M. Pouchan	Argentine Navy
Ensign Rallier du Batty	French Navy
Louis Bafflier (Interpreter)	French Navy

A breakdown of the enlisted personnel at NAS Le Croisic at the time of the Armistice is as follows:

Rate	Allowed	On-Hand
B.M.	8	2
G.M.	5	4
Q.M.	67	20
Sea.	99	112
Spec. Mech.	2	0
E.(G)	9	5
E.(R)	8	12
C.M.	14	21
S.F.	0	9
P.&F.	2	0
S.M.M.	1	0
S.K.	0	2
M.M.	100	87
B.Smith	2	2
C.Smith	12	0
Yeo.	12	16
P.M.&H.A.	7	4
COM.STW.	1	1
S.C.	8	8
BKRS.	2	4
MATT.	12	8
PRINT.	0	0
FIREMAN	0	0
PAINT.	0	5
BUG.	1	1
MUS.	0	0
OC&S.	2	0

At the commencement of patrol and convoy flights, an "Alert Section" consisting of one-fourth of the total handling crews, two observers, and two pilots were put on watch. They stood watch from daylight to darkness, always holding two planes in readiness, with bombs attached and all instruments and equipment either in the planes or close at hand, so that it was but a matter of five minutes to lower the planes and get off the water in case a submarine warning was received.

On 20 November 1917, when two German mines were reported off Les Grande Cardinaux, two seaplanes were sent out and the district was thoroughly patrolled, but the mines were not discovered. Later, four submarines were sighted south of Belle Isle and two planes were sent out on patrol. One seaplane of this sector, piloted by Ensign K.R. Smith, USNRF, with N. Wilkinson, Elc.Mec., and Brady, MM2c, failed to return. Word was telephoned to all stations along the coast, to Lorient, to Paris, and to the French semaphore stations, with the result that many patrol boats, vedettes, and destroyers were sent out in search of the crew. No word was received, however, until 24 November, when at 1600 hrs. a telephone message was received from La Pallice that the crew of the seaplane had been picked up 25 miles southeast of Rochembonne by a French destroyer and were being taken to La Pallice. The plane had had to land during its patrol and had been very badly damaged by the landing, and after almost two days in the water it sank a few minutes after the crew had been taken off. The men were in very bad condition from exposure but recovered. The following is the personal account of Ensign Smith regarding the incident:

"Weather conditions were not ideal for flying, clouds being very low and quite a sea running.

After leaving Le Croisic, we started South steering course 195. On reaching Ile D'Yeu, we found our drift to be considerably to the East. After picking up Point Breton on Ile D'Yeu, we sighted a four-masted bark in Ballast with auxiliary engine to the N.E. We circled over her a number of times, increasing our radius on each turn until we were nearly out of sight of Ile Y'Deu. After searching the shore for mines and submarines, returned to Pt. Breton. From Pt. Breton we steered course 29 for 45 minutes. We then headed due east for 30 minutes at an altitude of 50 meters. Motor died and we were forced to make a tail to wind landing. We found it possible to land Tellier in rough water. Dispatched at 3.30 P.M. pigeon with the following message: 'Left Ile D'Yeu at 1:10 p.m. headed 29 for 45 minutes. Then direct east 30 min. had to come down, big sea running. Send all aid.' Following is a personal log kept by me. 'lit on water about 3.00 p.m. Did not give up hope. Sent pigeon out with message. Sea very rough. Could not tell for certain our location. We took watches during the night. One bailed while the other 2 slept. As we could not get motor started we thought over all possible things that could happen to it. Wilkinson found left gas tank had not been feeding, too late to fix it as we could not see. Passed a very uncertain night. We know they would do all possible things to help us.

Sent pigeon at 7:40 A.M. and message as follows: 'Sighted last night 2 light houses on starboard bow which we considered Ile D'Yeu. Cannot see land, but we are probably 20 miles S.W. of Ile D'Yeu. Send torpedo boats and aeroplanes. Have no food. We are taking in water, we are not positive of our location but are going to sea. Send help. If you should not find us say we died game to the end.'

Put in a new spark plug, cleaned magneto, shifted gasoline from left to right tank. We were all so seasick that we could not work to best advantage. Bailed water out of boat. Wilkinson finally got motor started at 11.40 a.m. Saw hydroplane and "blimp" to the North of us. Did not give up hope. Beautiful day. Got motor going and started to taxi towards Ile D'Yeu. We were not making much headway on account of the sea. Our left pontoon had filled with water. Finally decided our only hope was to try to get machine off the water. As a result of trying, I broke left wing and got ourselves into a hell of a scrape. Things began to look black. There was no finding fault with anyone. Could not help marveling at the morale of the men. It was a case of heroic bravery on their part to see their only hope smashed. We took watches during the night by first laying on the wing, then bailing, then sleeping. Wilkinson turned to and got ready to cast adrift the left wing. We had anxious moments of ship rolling over. No one faltered or failed to do his part. We all decided to die game to the end. As a result no one ate or drank water. Wings began to crumble. We all decided to let it stay on as long as possible. Sea began to grow bigger towards evening, and the water began to come in. We all hoped that we would be able to ride out the night. Very comfortable night, and we were all growing very weak. Very long night. Our hopes were beginning to go very low, but no one showed it."

Saturday, Nov. 24, 1917. "Day finally came. Wing getting near to boat as it crumbled. It was heart-rending. We had to bail and stay out on wing-tip. As waves came over we began to feel lower and lower. It was finally decided to cast off wing and let what might come. We tried to get other wing ready to be cast off, but we could not get off nuts as we were so weak and tools were very inadequate. We were going over gradually on the starboard side. We were all on port side trying to keep her righted. We then saw there was no hope of us staying up much longer unless we could get wing off. We had just about given up everything when Wilkinson let out a yell that something was in sight. We were not able to believe our eyes. We thought it was a submarine, but we did not care. If it was a submarine we hoped it would blow us up and end it all."

As a result of this experience it was ordered that Navy planes were no longer to go on patrol by themselves, they were to carry sufficient rations, and they were to carry life saving equipment.

On 4 December, a seaplane made a forced landing while on patrol. The crew was picked up and the plane taken in tow by the S.S. *Anderson*, and returned to the station. On 8 December Ensign K.R. Smith, pilot, and Q.M. 3c Frank Brady, observer, sighted a submarine Northeast of Belle Isle. They circled around and approached close, but it was recognized as a French submarine. On 27 April 1918 Thomas Weddell, Lds.QM., pilot, with R.S. Waugh, Q.M.2c, observer, sighted an oil spot. Two bombs were dropped, both of which exploded. On 8 May 1918, Ensign P.E. Gillespie, pilot, with Gunner M.E. Rothenberg, observer, sighted an oil spot. Two bombs were dropped, both of which exploded. At 2045 hrs. on 30 May 1918 Ensign S.S. Walker, pilot, and Q.M. 2c R.S. Waugh, observer, discovered a floating mine two miles northwest of the lighthouse at La Banche. Two bombs were dropped, and the mine destroyed. On 1 June 1918 Thomas Weddell, Lds.QM, pilot, and Gunner M.E. Rothenberg, observer, sighted a drifting boat, which they suspected might cover mines. They dropped a phosphorous buoy to destroyers, who investigated, after which one bomb was dropped. Nothing occurred. On 25 June 1918 a seaplane from Le Croisic left in answer to an "allo signal," and a suspicious wake was perceived. After having carefully explored the region, and escorting a ship through this sector, a large spot of oil was sighted, about five miles from the suspicious wake previously seen. An F bomb was dropped, but nothing else was observed, and the plane was forced to return to the base because of motor trouble. On 22 October 1918 Ensign Robert T. Whitehouse, pilot, with Q.M. lc N. Barrett, observer, sighted a commotion northeast of Belle Isle. They approached and circled. Two bombs were dropped, one of which exploded. Exploding long range shells from French shore batteries caused commotion.

An unidentified machinist mate and Ens. Frecerick Harrison Becker (Naval Aviator No. 309) in front of a Tellier seaplane at NAS Le Croisic.

As long as the planes were new, forced landings were very few, but continuous long flights and rough seas soon began to show their effects upon the planes, and occasional forced landings at sea far from base, when there were no motor boats to tow them back, would at times delay efficient operations.

Patrols and convoys were soon commenced on a regular schedule to protect the coastal shipping. The communication system at that time was very bad, but for those convoys for which notification was made there was able protection. During the month of September 1918, a convoy was reported in the sector, and although weather was foggy and the visibility poor, two planes went on patrol. An Admiral of the French Navy who happened to be aboard the largest ship in the convoy reported to Commendant Vaschalde an account of the work of the Le Croisic station as follows:

Brest, France, Sept. 23, 1918

From: Vice Admiral Schwerer, High Commander of the Britany Divisions
To: Division Chief of Patrols of Loire, Lorient
Commandant:
On Sept. 19th, while I was escorting the southbound convoy, having left Quiberon in the morning, I had the pleasure of noticing that sections of American seaplanes from Le Croisic flew over the convoy in quite a remarkable way from 7 a.m., the time of our leaving, until after 5 p.m., when we were about fifteen miles south of Ile d'Yeu.

These sections very carefully secured a continuous protection that I would like to see supplied everywhere; that is to say, with scouting flights ahead of the convoy's route as far as six to ten miles and then return, and scouting flights on each side of the convoy....

On the following day, the 20th, when coming back from La Pallice I went to meet the northbound convoy, and seaplanes from Le Croisic station were convoying this one also.

I should feel obliged if you would kindly transmit my best felicitations to the American station at Le Croisic. The facts of which I have been witness show that, contrary to the apprehensions expressed by Commandant Vaschalde in the note you communicated to me, the continuous protection of the convoys from Quiberon and Ile d'Yeu appears to be secure.

In the neighboring sectors I did not see a single seaplane to continue the convoying.

I am now looking for some means to quickly inform the Le Croisic Sables and La Pallice stations to the passage of the convoys at certain points. This section does not appear to be necessary for the sector between Penmarch and Quiberon, as the convoys are always in sight of the semaphores.

(Signed) Schwerer"

After the station had really begun operations, the French made many visits with American Intelligence men in reference to reported espionage and signals said to be shown in and around the district of Le Croisic.

On 4 March, a seaplane piloted by Boatswain Joseph Cline (Naval Aviator No. 1832), with F. Lovejoy as observer, started on patrol, and just as the plane left the water the bomb on the port side became detached and fell, striking the water and exploding. The explosion caused the other bomb to discharge. The fuselage just aft of the pilot seat was completely destroyed, as well as the engine and motor. The machine was completely cut in two, but fortunately neither the pilot nor observer were injured.

After the station began to operate, it was used as an assembly base of Tellier, D.D., and Le Pen seaplanes.

A fatal accident occurred at the station on 1 July 1918 when T.M. Weddell, pilot, and E.C. Kneip, observer, were killed when one wing of their plane collapsed, and the machine fell in a nosedive. These were the only fatalities that occurred at the station.

As soon as more machines, equipment, spares, and hangar space were received more efficient work was carried out. Radio installations on shore and in planes enabled the Intelligence Officer to keep better knowledge of the position of the seaplanes on patrol; and with the completion of the machine shop and carpenter shop, worn engines and damaged planes were quickly put back in commission.

On 1 October 1918, an "allo" from the station at Paimboeuf was received. Urgent assistance was needed. Although it was dark, two pilots and an observer volunteered to go out. Two planes were immediately equipped and lowered, and a third hooked on to the crane in readiness. In less than eight minutes the two planes were taxing on the water. Owing to complete darkness and low water, one of them piled high and dry on a sand bar. The third machine with another pilot was at once lowered and was soon outside of the breakwater, heading south on the "step." It was by this time pitch dark, and before the planes could arrive at the position of the reported combat between submarine and dirigible, the submarine had submerged.

Based upon U.S. Naval Aviation Intelligence Reports, the following table provides a summary of the patrols flown from NAS Le Croisic:

Ens. Rufus Harrison Bush (Naval Aviator No. 1774) at NAS Le Croisic.

In May 1918 the French Unit of the U.S. Naval Aviation Forces, Foreign Service began a series of Aerographic observations at various stations in France. Le Croisic was chosen as one of those stations. The officer placed in charge of the Le Croisic aerographic section was Ensign C.N. Keyser, USNRF. Weather data obtained at the Le Croisic observatory was shared not only with other Naval Air Stations, but also with British and French stations. By the time of demobilization the Le Croisic activities were functioning out of an office set up on the top floor of the vacant hospital building. Because of both the difficulties in obtaining the needed instruments with which to carry out this type of work and the rudimentary nature of aerograpby at that time, the Le Croisic station aerographic

U.S. NAVAL AVIATION (SEAPLANE) CONVOY PATROLS

	Feb.	Mar.	Apr.	May	June	July	Aug.	Sept.	Oct.	Nov.
Convoys Reported		5	13		14	14	14	30	40	8
Convoys Sighted		5	13		14	14	14	30	40	8
Convoys Escorted			11		8	10	8	36	26	6
Days Fit for Flying	20	20	21	18	21	24	18	18		5

equipment consisted only of a barograph, three types of thermometers, sondage equipment, and a Stevenson Screen.

NAS Le Croisic was the biggest user of pigeons of any of the Naval Air Stations of the French Unit of the U.S. Naval Aviation Forces, Foreign Service. Judging from the records available, Le Croisic appears to have been the central distribution facility for pigeons to other Naval Air Stations. This is based upon the fact that NAS Le Croisic was assigned 175 pigeons, of which 140 were trained; yet for the period of Nov. 1917 through Oct. 1918, NAS Le Croisic carried 3943 pigeons. Of the pigeons carried, some 70 were in fact used to carry messages.

The French were very appreciative of the efforts of the naval personnel at Le Croisic. In particular, taken from French reports, citations were given the station for action both on 30 March 1918 when, at 2045 hrs. a plane from the station destroyed a floating mine near La Banche buoy, and again on 25 June 1918, when at 1910 hrs. a plane from Le Croisic bombed an oil spot near La Banche buoy. Of particular interest is the observation made by the French in a letter to the Commandant des Petrovilles Acriennes de La Loire: "It is realized that the recompenses are very little in comparison with the great service rendered by the U.S. Naval Aviation Forces.

1. We have never been free to give citations, as at first the laws of the U.S. Navy prohibited the awarding of Croix de Guerre to their valiant officers and sailors. Later, however, consent was obtained from the U.S. Navy Department.

2. I have to call attention to the appreciation of the French authorities to the services of Lt.Cdr. Corry who has so brilliantly organized the U.S. Navy at Le Croisic."

Operations were suspended for the most part on 12 November 1918, on receipt of telegraphic instructions to that effect.

IV. DEMOBILIZATION

After 11 November plans were made for the demobilization of the French Unit. On 23 November the instructions of the Force Commander relative to demobilization were sent to all Air Stations. For NAS Le Croisic this meant that by I January 1919 the Force Commander could write to the Chief of Naval Operations that the "Bessonneau hangars are being taken down for transfer to the United States Army. Portable buildings are being dismantled and will be turned over to the United States Naval Port Officer at St. Nazaire. A Commission has visited this station from the Ministry of the Interior with a view to taking it over. It is reported that the impression of this Commission was favorable, but no definite decision has yet been arrived at relative to the transfer of this station to the French Government."

Demobilization was completed on 28 January 1919, material having been disposed of and personnel transferred in accordance with the instructions of Headquarters. By 1 February 1919 all naval personnel had left Le Croisic, and the U.S. Navy was awaiting the appointment of the members of a French Commission which was to take over the station. Information had been received from the Commandant des Patrouilles of the Loire that the French navy would take the station into custody and dispose of it finally to the account of the U.S. Government. As of 1 March 1919 the total cost to the U.S. Navy of NAS Le Croisic was as follows:

Cost of U.S. Improvements (including Cost of Labor and Transportation on French Contracts)	$124,962.00
Value of U.S. Material liquidated	31,215.00
Total Cost (subject to considerable further deduction for French buildings to be sold to the municipality, the exact price of which had not yet been determined.	$93,747.00

TABLE A
STATISTICAL DATA
U.S. Naval Air Station, (Seaplane)
Le CROISIC, Loire-Inferieure, France
From 18 November 1917 To 11 November 1918

Wk. End.	**Flights Made**	**Total Knots**	**Flying Time (Hr.)**	**Suitable Flying Time (Hr.)**	**Aircraft on Station**	**Aircraft in Comsn**	**Flying Personnel**
1917							
18 Nov.	26	1698	28:28	25	6 T	4 T	9
25 Nov.	23	2395	39:55	25	6 T, 2 DD	5 T	9
2 Dec.	15	620	10:20	30	6 T, 2 DD	3 T	9
9 Dec.	14	605	10:05	30	6 T, 2 DD	3 T	9
16 Dec.	12	440	7:20	15	6 T, 2 DD	3 T	10
23 Dec. 8	8	468	7:48	13	7 T, 2 DD	3 T	10
30 Dec.	13	704	11:45	16	7 T, 2 DD	5 T	12
1918							
6 Jan.	5	355	5:55	10	7 T, 4 DD	4 T	12
13 Jan.	22	1076	17:56	31	7 T, 2 DD	6 T	14
20 Jan.	9	500	8:20	5	6 T, 5 DD	3 T	14
27 Jan.	19	694	11:34	10	6 T, 3 DD	4 T, 3 DD	14
3 Feb.	28	2096	34:56	30	6 T, 3 DD	6 T, 3 DD	19
10 Feb.	18	1693	28:13	37	6 T, 3 DD	4 T, 1 DD	20

Wk. End.	Flights Made	Total Knots	Flying Time (Hr.)	Suitable Flying Time (Hr.)	Aircraft on Station	Aircraft in Comsn	Flying Personnel
17 Feb.	23	2189	36:29	25	8 T, 4 DD	5 T, 2 DD	19
24 Feb.	42	3038	50:38	40	8 T, 4 DD	5 T, 2 DD	19
3 Mar.	14	1000	16:40	15	10 T, 4 DD	4 T, 2 DD	19
10 Mar.	12	2050	34:20	46	10 T, 4 DD	3 T, 1 DD	19
13 Mar.	13	1105	18:25	37	8 T, 4 DD	3 T, 2 DD	19
24 Mar.	22	2890	48:10	33	9 T, 3 DD	4 T	18
31 Mar.	18	1460	24:20	34	9 T, 3 DD	4 T	18
6 April	14	725	12:05	38	11 T, 5 DD	5 T	19
13 April	11	1900	31:40	25	14 T, 4 DD	7 T	19
20 April	15	1140	19:00	24	14 T, 5 DD	9 T	19
27 April	26	2035	33:55	23	15 T, ? DD	11 T	20
5 May	24	4270	71:10	25	15 T, 3 DD	10 T	20
11 May	28	2385	39:45	26	15 T, 3 DD	10 T	19
18 May	42	7095	118:30	56	14 T, 2 DD	11 T	19
25 May	25	4960	82:40	38	14 T, 1 DD	8 T	18
1 June	14	2815	46:50	23	14 T, 8 T		18
8 June	16	3915	65:15	59	14 T, 2 LP	7 T	22
15 June	18	3055	50:55	50	13 T, 3 LP	5 T	22
22 June	9	1295	21:33	17	16 T, 5 LP	4 T	22
29 June	30	4525	75:25	51	16 T, 4 T	22	
6 July	16	1270	21:14	26	15 T, 4 LP	4 T	17
13 July	19	1585	26:25	27	15 T, 4 LP	4 T	15
20 July	23	1395	223:15	24	15 T, 2 LP	4 T	17
27 July	13	1030	17:10	18	15 T, 3 LP	6 T	18
3 Aug.	47	4145	69:05	46	10 T, 2 LP	4 T	21
10 Aug.	33	1395	23:15	28	10 T, 3 LP	7 T	20
17 Aug.	24	2735	45:35	42	10 T, 4 LP	5 T	23
24 Aug.			— data not entered for this date —				
31 Aug.	19	3265	54:25	27	10 T, 3 LP	8 T	23
7 Sept.	23	3640	60:40	38	9 T, 3 LP	5 T	22
14 Sept.	7	625	1-:25	10	9 T, 3 LP	5 T	23
21 Sept.	21	4815	80:15	48	9 T, 2 LP	6 T	23
28 Sept.	14	2075	34:35	19	9 T, 2 LP	5 T	23
5 Oct.	32	4170	69:30	35	9 T, 1 LP	5 T	23
12 Oct.	0	0	0	0	9 T, 1 LP	7 T	23
19 Oct.	23	2065	34:25	19	8 T, 1 LP	2 T	19
26 Oct.	22	2555	42:35	29	8 T, 1 LP	5 T, 2 DD	20
2 Nov.	26	2250	37:50	34	9 T, 1 LP	3 T, 2 DD	21
9 Nov.	21	1483	25:05	14	6 T, 4 DD	4 T	221
To 11 Nov.	10	2300	38:20	17	7 T, 4 DD, 5 LP	5 T, 2 DD, 4 LP	221
TOTAL	1045	112,324	1890:19	1522			

Key: T - Tellier; LP - Levy le Pen; and DD - Donnet Donhaut

Note: As of 11 November 1918 Le Croisic had the following consignment of aircraft:

7 Tellier
4 Donnet Donhaut
5 Levy le Pen
1 HS-2

Notes:

[1] Much of the material in this Appendix is taken from the document entitled *History of U.S. Naval Aviation in Foreign Service, French Unit, 1917 and 1918.*

Appendix I: NAS Ile Tudy[1]

I. CONSTRUCTION

At the Station at Ile Tudy, on 30 November 1917, there was one French built hangar, a radio station, and a sardine factory, the latter doing duty as a barracks. When the first draft of 100 men arrived on 9 December 1917, they at once began to assist the French sailors in repairing this factory. A French contractor was in charge of making the following alterations and improvements: 1) Building offices for Administration; 2) Installing lavatories and shower rooms; 3) Installing tanks with necessary pipes and fixtures; and 4) Installing two 112 kW generators and necessary wiring and lights for the building. In addition to this, a contract was given to build the following: 1) a machine shop; 2) a carpenter shop; 3) a store house; 4) a garage; and 5) a stone oil house. The bulk of this work was actually done by the station force, however, and was completed early in March 1918, at which time the French personnel were withdrawn from the station.

On 27 February 1918, foundation sites for the Bessonneau hangars were laid out and the work of erecting was started. The building of a bomb house and the laying of cement floors in shops were begun, and roads about the station were laid out. Grading for the erection of barracks was also undertaken. This work was particularly difficult because of the quantities of sand that had to be drawn from the beach with the few wheelbarrows available, in order to fill the many large holes. By the end of March, hangars #2 and #3 were completed. During April work proceeded on the following: erection of gasoline tank; American timber hangar, 214' x 93'; digging a well for potable water two kilometers from the station; construction of new concrete runway across the main road; and a Y.M.C.A. tent. A great many difficulties had to be overcome in these new constructions. There was scarcely any stone near the station for making concrete, and it was necessary to search the surrounding countryside in order to obtain a sufficient supply. That which was collected had to be broken by the crew with hammers, and the cement mixed by hand. Moreover, it was necessary to withdraw the men, from time to time, in order to keep the landing runway in condition, as the rising and lowering of the tide washed away the sand from under the rails.

In May 1918, because of the timely arrival of urgently needed material, work continued more rapidly on the projects already under way. On 11 May the first shipment of timber arrived for new double hangars. The first hardware for hangars arrived on 16 May, and the following day uprights were cut. No material was available to make a "gin-pole," with which to erect the trusses, but an old mast found on the beach, which had evidently floated in from some wrecked steamer, was put into use as a satisfactory substitute. Ten badly needed wheelbarrows arrived on 26 May. This more than tripled the number of available wheelbarrows at the site.

On 1 June Bessonneau Hangar #4 was started, and on 21 June the concrete runway for seaplanes was begun. All construction work was done by the general detail until 28 June when the first construction unit arrived. On the following day, portable barracks were received to take the place of the tents, and these were all assembled by 1 July. More barracks were received on 5 July, and after their erection men of the station occupied them. Construction, up to 20 July, was in the charge of Ensign Lemanski, the Executive Officer, but on this date Warrant Carpenter F.D. MacDonald from the Public Works Department took over the responsibilities for all construction.

Aerial view of NAS Ile Trudy. (source: Naval Historical Center)

Probably the biggest work was the concreting of the hangar floors, apron, and runway. The concrete apron, which was 160 feet wide and 50 feet long, was started in March, but work was discontinued on it from time to time, owing to a lack of material and proper facilities. Only a few French shovels of very poor quality were available, but a concrete mixer was supplied in August. No running water was available, but a gas tank was raised on ties and connected with the mixer. After considerable searching, a gravel bed of excellent quality was found near Plemeur, some 15 miles from the station. A truck was started transporting it to the station, and it soon proved to be less expensive than getting stone from a quarry and cracking it by hand. With two trucks and a lot of sweat, 16 tons a day could be hauled with only the cost of the gasoline and wear and tear on the trucks. The mixer was capable of pouring 1000 square feet per day. The concrete runway was 20' wide and about 1240' long. Only a small section of a sidewall (two 20' sections) could be laid in a day, owing to the tide. This necessitated the pouring of walls one day and the floor the next, and because of the flatness of the beach, which rose less than one foot per 100 ft., the further out the runway was extended, the slower was the progress. At the time of demobilization, there were about 675' laid, the runway being 60% completed. This allowed the HS-1 seaplanes to be launched at half tide. At the cessation of hostilities it was over 79% complete

In the latter part of August it was decided to raise the four Bessonneau hangars, to allow sufficient clearance to store two HS-1s in each, as these hangars had only been designed to house small French seaplanes. This was done by building concrete piers about 5.5 feet long under each post, making a total of 42 piers to a hangar. The first hangar was raised on 30 September, and the next two were finished on 1 November. These hangars were raised by bracing the posts, and with a crew of 200 men, lifting on the stays and struts. After the hangars were raised, a concrete strip 20' wide was poured from each hangar to the apron.

A 40' water tower, with a 12,000 gallon tank, was erected in August. A 2.5-inch iron pipe was connected with the tank, and at the lower end of the pipe a hose coupling was fastened, so that this water supply could be used in case of fire. The tank was filled by the use of a fire engine.

Due to the fact that roofing paper and many parts of the portable buildings were not received, the following buildings were not completed prior to demobilization: Radio house, Radio shed, Officers' quarters, Officers' wardroom, and C.P.O. barracks.

Barracks and hangars at NAS Ile Trudy. (source: Naval Historical Center)

II. PERSONNEL

On 30 November 1917, Lieutenant John Lansing Callan, USNRF, Assistant Paymaster W.T. Hopkins, USN, and one seaman arrived at Ile Tudy. On 9 December Ensign Norman Cabot, NNV, arrived at the station with a draft of 100 men and relieved Lieutenant Callan of his command. On 12 December Lieutenant B.F. Holding, M.C., USN, reported to the station for duty. On 8 February Ensign Cabot was relieved of command by Lieutenant C.E. Sugden, USCG.

III. OPERATIONS

On 14 March 1918, the U.S. Naval Air Station at Ile Tudy, Finistere, was commissioned, and the National Ensign hoisted. At this time, construction and operations on the station passed into the hands of the U.S. Naval Forces, although the French Commander of Aerial Patrols at Lorient still exercised supervision over operations. At this time the station personnel were: Lieutenant C.E. Sugden, USCG; Lieutenant W.T. Hopkins, Pay Corps, USN; Ensign K.R. Smith, USNRF; Lieutenant B.F. Holding, M.C., USN; Acting Pay Clerk (T) H.J. Taylor, USN; Gunner (E)(T) M.S. Brainard, USN; and 186 enlisted men.

This station was situated at a very important point. Two convoys daily passed through its sector, which extended from Raz de Sein on the north, to Ile Verte on the south. From Raz de Sein to Penmarch, the water is deeper near the shore, free from reefs and bars seaward, and well suited to submarines. The majority of the "allos" received were from this region. The sector was marked off into squares 25 miles on a side, and then further subdivided into squares of five miles on a side. By this means planes were able to report position every half-hour and be quickly and accurately located. Communications were maintained with the shore bases by radio and pigeons, and with vessels by message buoys, phosphorus buoys, Very pistols, and the blinker system for ordinary signaling.

A section of two planes escorted each convoy. As the sector was too large to be covered entirely by two planes, it was necessary to send out another section to relieve the first, when the convoy was approximately halfway through the area. This necessitated using at least eight planes per day for convoy work alone, two sections with northbound and two with southbound convoys. In addition to this, there was always a section known as the "Alert" ready to take the air from daybreak to dark in response to any "allos" received. When the convoy was picked up, the planes would first circle over it. Then, while one plane would remain around the convoy the other would fly as far as 10 to 15 miles ahead, zig-zagging broadly on both sides of the course of the convoy. This plane would return, again circle over the convoy, repeating the same maneuver again and again. Before leaving a convoy, the planes circled a last time in its neighborhood. In this way the convoy was well protected from surprise.

The French semaphore stations were of great assistance in supplying information regarding the convoys, their whereabouts, and the position of the planes and any accidents. With each message they also gave a local weather report.

On 28 February 1918 the station was ready to operate, and a section of planes was ordered out at 1100 hrs. in answer to an "allo."

The first machine to leave the water attempted to climb too rapidly and crashed, killing pilot L.S. Harvey, BMlc, USN, and the observer, A.D. Skaggs, Lds.QM(A), USN.

The first attack on an enemy submarine by planes from this station occurred on 23 April 1918. At 1033 hrs. a section of two planes, No. I-25 with pilot R.H. Harrell, QMlc(A), USN (Naval Aviator No. 2721), with observer H.W. Studer, QM2s(A), USN, and No. I-22 with pilot Ensign Smith, USNRF, with observer G.E. Williams, C.E., USN, left on a convoy flight. They joined the southbound convoy of about 20 ships, six miles northwest of Pointe de Penmarch. As the weather was foggy, they went to the rear of the convoy to look for any straggling ships, then began a wide circle in the offing and headed parallel to the ships. A very white wake was sighted, made either by a periscope or the top of the wheelhouse of a submarine moving rapidly. The observers noticed water disturbance, which paralleled the convoy, consisting of bubbles of air and oil. The plane piloted by Ensign Smith dropped two bombs, one at 1150 hrs. and the second at 1152 hrs., of which the first landed on the fore part of the disturbance, and the second ten feet ahead. After the explosion of the two bombs, disturbances and bubbles appeared. As nothing else was seen, the other plane did not release its bombs, but dropped a phosphorous buoy and circled over the spot. During this time, the first plane went to meet the American destroyer U.S.S. *Stewart*, which was heading for the spot. The seaplane dropped a correspondence buoy, informing her of the location of the enemy, and of the attack. The *Stewart* arrived at the spot, followed soon after by the French gunboat *Ardente,* and dropped three depth charges. Small wreckage and particles of sea growth and oil were seen coming to the surface. The two machines returned to the station, after having sighted, twelve miles south of Penmarch, the northbound convoy of 16 ships. The convoy passed soon afterwards, without being attacked. The day after this, when seaplanes were circling over the place, a large spot of oil was seen on the surface of the water. Of the 5th and 6th of May, this spot could still be seen. Ensign Smith and Observer Williams were officially credited by the French Naval authorities with having sunk a submarine, were cited in the order of the day, and were awarded the Croix de Guerre.

On 5 July 1918, seaplanes DD No. I-27 piloted by Ensign H.J. Rowen (Naval Aviator No. 200), and DD No. I-28 piloted by C.J. Boylan, QMlc(A), with observers H.S. Ropke, MMlc(A), and L.W. Wintsch, QM2c(A), left the base in answer to an "allo" off Point L'Ervilly. One plane circled over the spot, where a smoke buoy had been dropped, and a streak as usually seen in the wake of a vessel could be seen. Both planes released their two bombs, one failing to explode. Several minutes after the bombs were dropped, a great disturbance of water occurred, and a small amount of oil was seen in the center of the disturbed water.

An attack on a submarine took place on 3 August 1918. A DD seaplane, No. I-28 piloted by C.J. Boylan, QMlc(A), USN, with observer L.W. Wintsch, QM2c(A), USN, left the station at 1615 hours in response to an "allo." At 1640 hours, when about six miles north of Pointe de Penmarch, a large spot of oil and what appeared to be a periscope was sighted. The latter immediately disappeared. When they arrived directly over the spot, converging wakes were seen coming to the surface, and two bombs were dropped, causing a quantity of oil, bubbles, and debris to appear. A seaplane, DD No. I-22, piloted by Ensign M.H. Bailey, USNRF (Naval Aviator No. 313), with observer G. Wolff, E2c(A), and a plane, DD No. I-35, piloted by Boatswain L.T. O'Loughlin, USNRF, with observer R. Haizlett, MMle(A), which had left the station in response to the "allo," arrived two or three minutes later. Trawlers were firing shots, and a long trail of oil was seen, near one end of which were observed two sets of bubbles very near together. Each of these machines dropped two bombs, and a great quantity of bubbles and oil arose immediately. The planes circled the spot for a while, and some wreckage was seen.

On 27 August 1918 (Note: Author dates thia as 27 September), another attack was made on what appeared to be an enemy submarine. A plane, DD No. I-27, piloted by Ensign H.S. Pou, USNRF (Naval Aviator No. 435), with observer H.A. Ropke, MMlc(A), USN, and a plane, DD No. I-28 piloted by C.J. Boylan, QMlc(A), USN, with observer L.W. Wintsch, QM2c(A), USN, left on convoy duty at 1500 hours. While patrolling about two miles southeast of Pointe de Penmarch, an oil streak was seen, and fresh bursting oil bubbles were observed rising in two streams about one yard apart. Two bombs were dropped in line with the bubbles of oil, causing large oil bubbles to come to the surface, the film of oil spreading rapidly. No further information could be ascertained concerning this attack or the cause of the oil.

In response to an "allo" from two miles northwest of Pointe de Penmarch on 10 August two planes, DD No. I-28, piloted by P.H. Tuttle, QM2c(A), USN, with observer B.J. Maurer, QM2c(A), USN, and DD No. I-32, piloted by Ensign R.H. Harrell, USNRF, with observer D.F. Bailley, QM2c(A), USN, left station at 1315 hours. About 1335 hours, when three miles north of Pointe de Penmarch, each plane dropped one bomb on a spot where the water appeared to be disturbed. Patrol boats in the vicinity dropped depth charges and opened fire on the spot where a smoke buoy had been dropped after bombing. A slight amount of oil appeared as a result of this attack.

At 1435 hours on 27 September a seaplane, DD No. I-29 with Ensign Pou, USNRF, pilot, and observer H.F. Duffy, QM2c(A), USN, and one plane, DD No. I-34, with pilot P.H. Tuttle, QM2c(A), USN, and observer Otis Wherly, QMlc(A), USN, left the station on patrol to escort a northbound convoy. When about four miles south of Penmarch three trawlers were seen hovering close to shore and apparently firing on a mine. Immediately after the arrival of the patrol section the three trawlers steamed southeast in good formation. A dark spot was observed about eight miles south of Penmarch at 1255 hours. A smoke bomb and two bombs were dropped on the spot, and a violent explosion took place, the shock of which considerably affected the seaplanes, and caused oil to come to the surface. A message buoy was dropped to the leading trawler, and the planes returned to the station.

On 22 October 1918, a flight section composed of an HS-1 seaplane, No. I-7, piloted by Ensign P.A. Sweeney, USNRF (Naval Aviator No. 561), with D.F. Bailey, QM2c(A), USN, as observer, and an HS-1, I-15, piloted by Ensign E. Dent, USNRF (Naval Aviator No. 315), with observer H.A. Ropke, MMlc(A), USN, bombed a suspicious oil spot while convoying a southbound convoy two miles south of Penmarch. The bombs failed to function. On the same day, an hour later, a mine was bombed and exploded eight miles southwest of Penmarch by a seaplane, DD No. I-29, piloted by Ensign Pou, USNRF, with observer H.F. Duffy, QM2c(A), USN. In the afternoon of the same day a section composed of an HS-1, No. I-7, piloted by Ensign F.A. Sweeney, USNRF, with D.F. Baily as Observer, and an HS-1, No. I-15, piloted by Ensign E. Dent, with H.A. Ropke as observer, left the base at 1300 hrs. and went to the spot where the bombs had been dropped in the morning. An oil wake was seen and bombed at 1430 hrs. by both planes. Three bombs hit exactly in the path of the oil streaks, and functioned properly. A submarine had been heard up to that time by means of listening devices on a French boat, and after the bombs had been dropped, large quantities of oil and some debris came to the surface. The submarine was not heard after this, and the commandant of the French patrol boat *Leger* asserted that the submarine was destroyed.

On 26 October, HS-1 No. I-15, piloted by Ensign W.G. Sprague, USNRF, with observer Ropke, sighted an oil wake four miles southwest of Penmarch and dropped two bombs immediately. Four minutes later HS-1 No. I-14, piloted by Ensign Dent, with observer Bailey, dropped two bombs on the same spot. Quantities of oil rose to the surface and spread over a large area. At 1150 hrs. a plane, No. I-21, piloted by Ensign H.J. Rowen, USNRF, with observer Bailey, dropped two bombs approximately in the same place, because of a great amount of oil which could be seen on the surface. Later advises from the French indicated that the bombs dropped by the plane piloted by Ensign Sprague sunk the submarine. On returning from this flight, the plane piloted by Ensign Sprague went into a nosedive from a flat spiral. Ensign Sprague was killed, and observer Ropke severely injured.

Upon making a landing on 28 October an HS-1, No. I-12, struck a spar buoy, killing the pilot Ensign Pou, and injuring Banks, MM2c(A), USN. The third man in the machine, J.H. Young, MMlc(A), USN, escaped uninjured and fought valiantly with the flames, trying to extinguish the fire which had started and prevent the flames from reaching Ens. Pou and J.R. Banks.

On no occasion was a convoy attacked in this station's sector while accompanied by seaplanes, and planes never saw submarines on the surface. With an average of nine pilots, ten observers, and sixteen planes, 2043 hours of flying were put in throughout the eight and one-half months of operation. Approximately 6,900 vessels were escorted safely through the sector without the loss of a single ship, and 117,000 miles were covered. Out of 54 "allos" reported in the sector, 16 attacks were made, two submarines apparently sunk, one probably sunk, and one mine destroyed. Seaplanes from French stations of Lorient and Camaret were rescued, towed in from the sea, and repaired when necessary. About 15 such rescues were made. When hostilities ceased there were on board 363 enlisted men and the following officers:

Town of Ile Trudy, a hangar of the station, and a Kite Balloon in the air. (source: 80 HAG-2)

Captain C.E. Sugden, USCG	Commanding Officer
Lieutenant (j.g.) (G)(T) J.A. Lemanski, USN	Executive Officer
Ensign H.J. Rowen, USNRF	Chief Pilot
Ensign E.E. Dent, USNRF	Asst. Chief Pilot
Ensign L.S. Peck, USNRF	Ordnance Officer
Ensign P.J. Callahan, USNRF	Intelligence Officer
Ensign C.S. Payne, Jr. USNRF	Aerographic Officer
Ensign P.A. Sweeney, USNRF	Pilot
Ensign E.D. Fageros, USNRF	Pilot
Ensign E.L. Smith, USNRF	Pilot
Ensign J.M. Daniel, USNRF	Pilot
Ensign R.H. Wettach, USNRF	Pilot
Ensign V.F. Rotering, USNRF	Pilot
Gunner (O)(T) F.B. Byrne, USN	Acting Ordnance Officer
Gunner (E)(T) H.S. Brainare, USN	Radio Officer
Machinist E.J. Rowen, USNRF	Engineer Officer
Machinist M.M. McMaster, USNRF	Transportation Officer
Carpenter F.B. MacDonald, USNRF	Public Works Officer
Lieutenant B.F. Holding, USN, Med. Corps	Medical Officer
Lieutenant V.W. Shields, USN, Med. Corps	Medical Officer
Lieutenant W.T. Hopkins, USN, Pay Corps	Supply Officer
Acting Pay Clerk (T) H.J. Taylor, USN	Supply Department
363 enlisted men	

During the nine months of active operations at Ile Tudy, citations and Cruise de Guerre were awarded from the French Navy to the following men:

Ensign K.B. Smith, USNRF
Ensign W.G. Sprague, USNRF
Ensign E.S. Pou, USNRF
O.E. Williams, C.E., USN
H A. Ropke, MM1c (A), USN

Table I-1 provides operational statistics associated with NAS Ile Tudy.

IV. DEMOBILIZATION

Operations at NAS Ile Tudy were suspended, pursuant to orders dated 12 November. By 25 January 1919 Ile Tudy was completely dismantled and placed out of commission, the material and personnel having been transferred in accordance with the instructions from Naval Headquarters in Paris. All French buildings were returned to the original owners, and there were no property damages. All barracks were taken over by the U.S. Army.

TABLE I-1
NAS Ile Tudy
U.S. Naval Air Station (Seaplane) ILE TUDY, Finistere, France
From 23 February 1918 To 11 November 1918

Wk. End.	Flights Made	Total Knots	Flying Time (Hr.)	Suitable Flying Time (Hr.)	Aircraft on Station	Aircraft in Comsn	Flying Personnel
23 Feb.	-	-	-	-	2	2	5
2 Mar.	-	-	-	-	3	3	5
9 Mar	4	158	3:08	No Record	3	3	5
16 Mar.	11	585	11:42	No Record	3	3	6
23 Mar.	14	1062	21:14	No Record	4	4	7
4 April	0	0	0	None	4	3	8
13 April	16	1129	22:36	42	7	6	11
20 April	18	1449	28:58	15	9	5	15
27 April	42	3649	72:58	60	9	5	15
4 May	35	2869	57:23	51	13	8	23
11 May	16	1604	32:04	33	13	6	23
18 May	34	3941	78:29	35	14	9	25
25 May	39	4138	82:45	46	16	9	25
1 June	26	6257	125:05	61	16	8	23
8 June	41	3107	57:56	57	16	7	19
15 June	28	2340	46:46	33	16	8	21
22 June	29	2521	50:25	22	16	8	23
29 June	60	6269	125:05	62	16	7	23
6 July	52	6036	120:40	60	16	9	23
13 July	27	1733	34:40	23	17	9	23
20 July	34	1841	28:20	18	16	12	20
27 July	52	2888	52:30	20	16	10	19
3 Aug.	59	4777	990:00	40	16	9	21
10 Aug.	57	5109	102:00	28	16	10	21
17 Aug.	59	5048	100:55	60	16	8	19
24 Aug.	43	3751	75:00	38	15	9	18
31 Aug.	67	4715	94:15	52	15	6	18
7 Sept.	45	2693	53:50	38	14 DD 4 HS-1	1 2	18
14 Sept.	9	175	3:30	3	14 DD, 8 HS 1	7 6	18
21 Sept.	40	3604	74:55	34	14 DD 11 HS-1	7 4	18
28 Sept.	36	1967	39:15	20	14 DD 11 HS-1	7 4	18
5 Oct.	45	2922	58:25	37	14 DD 13 HS-1	6 1	23
12 Oct.	26	1338	26:45	15	4 DD 12 HS-1	3 2	23
19 Oct.	42	33250	64:55	39	6 DD 13 HS-1	3 2	23
26 Oct.	44	3543	66:30	35	4 DD 20 HS-1	4 8	19
2 Nov.	18	2060	31:34	21	4 DD 18 HS-1	4 5	21
9 Nov.	38	3733	65:15	30	3 DD 19 HS-1	1 11	37
11 Nov.	13	1509	21:20	13	2 DD 19 HS-1	1 10	18
TOTAL	1238	104,877	2043:29	1140			

Notes:
[1] Material for this Appendix has been gathered from the document entitled *History of U.S. Naval Aviation, Foreign Service, French Unit, 1917-1918*

Appendix J: NAS St. Trojan[1]

I. CONSTRUCTION

The necessary property for the U.S. Naval Air Station, St. Trojan, was secured partly by leases made by the French Navy, and partly by a loan from the Department des Eaux et Forets. The contracts for the construction were made by the French Marine with Delvert and Company. In October 1917, Lieutenant Darchis of the French Navy was sent with a draft of 15 men to the site to prepare to receive the French contractor and the Algerian laborers, and also to act as supervisor in the interest of the French Government. At that time, the only buildings on the station were two knock-down barracks, one of which was used as quarters for 15 French enlisted men, as an office for Lieutenant Darchis, and as a storeroom, while in the other one, 20 Algerians (*Kabyls*) were quartered. Delvert and Company started construction work on the old pier and the mess hall, and the Kabyls were set to work clearing the land of trees, excavating, and grading.

The most feasible way to transport materials to St. Trojan was to ship to Le Chapus by rail, then to transport by motor sailor direct to the pier at the station. It was impossible, at that time, to bring material overland on the island, due to an impassible stretch approximately a mile long adjacent to the station. The most urgent work was the completion of the pier, and the laying of moorings for boats in the channel.

In January 1918 the seawall and the hangar foundations were started. The plans for the station called for 20 buildings, and the date for the completion of the station was set as 16 June 1918. The contractor, however, was greatly hampered by difficulties in securing transportation for his materials, although special efforts were made to expedite shipments, and by the scarcity of labor. In particular, the shortage of cement for the seawall threatened to cause serious delay, until the U.S. Navy furnished this item in various amounts, which finally aggregated to 200 tons. Considerable difficulty was experienced with the laborers, as most of the *Kabyls* were diseased, and their capacity for work was very small. They had no inclination to work, and at the slightest provocation would go on strike.

In order to expedite the work of construction, the enlisted men were put directly on the work of the station with the French contractor, their labor being hired at eighty centimes per hour per man. This proved a solution to the labor problem, and during February, the work progressed. By the 25th of March, sufficient quarters had been built to accommodate the personnel, and the transfer from the village of St. Trojan to the station was completed in six days.

By the first of May the crew's barracks and the majority of the shops were finished by the French contractor, while the American detachment was working on the 1200 yards of road to the camp, the hangar, and the hangar aprons. Materials for the first hangar arrived by the *Mecknes* on 18 May, and the assembling was at once begun. All erection of the frames was done by hand, and in one day as many as seven 107' trusses were placed. The station was ready for operation upon completion of the hangar and the first slipway, on 20 July. The *Kabyls* were gradually shipped out as the buildings neared completion, and the enlisted men were turned to wireless towers, water piping, fire protection, and gasoline storage. At this time the only delay was caused by lack of sufficient materials, due to the impossibility of securing adequate transportation from Pauillac. All construction work was sufficiently far advanced by the middle of June to have permitted aircraft operations at that time.

Aerial view of NAS St. Trojan.

II. PERSONNEL

On 8 November 1917, Assistant Paymaster J.M. Bregar, USN, reported to the Commander of Aerial Patrols in the Gironde Section as Supply Officer for the U.S. Naval Air Stations at Rochefort and St. Trojan. On the decision to recede Rochefort to the French, Paymaster Bregar's entire time was devoted to St. Trojan. The first draft of 35 men arrived on 29 January, and as of 3 February Gunner L.N. Phinney, USN, took command. 50 men soon increased the American detachment. They were quartered in the little town of St. Trojan two miles distant, and daily marched to and from the station. Lieutenant V.C. Griffin. USN (Naval Aviator No. 41), relieved Gunner Phinney as Commanding Officer on 11 March.

In early September 1918, the station was attacked by an epidemic of influenza, which caused the death of one officer and five men, and incapacitated 210 men for various periods. This epidemic lasted for about three weeks, and there were days when the station was unable to carry on operations because of it.

On 11 November 1918 343 enlisted men and the following officers were at the station:

Lieutenant Commander V.C. Griffin, USN	Commanding Officer
Lieutenant J.D. Ross, USNRF	Executive Officer
Lieutenant F.H. Clements, Medical Corps, USN	Medical Officer
Lieutenant (j.g.) T.J. O'Brien, Medical Corps, USNRF	Asst. to Medical Officer
Lieutenant (j.g.) C.A. Hawkins, USNRF	Chief Pilot
Lieutenant (j.g.) J.V. Farwell, USNRF	Ordnance Officer
Lieutenant (j.g.) H.T. Stanley, USNRF	Pilot
Ensign J.S. Buchanan, USNRF	Pilot
Ensign V.T. Leak, USNRF	Pilot
Ensign H.C. Sargent, USNRF	Pilot
Ensign W.W. Bell, USNRF	Pilot
Ensign W.M. Barr, USNRF	Pilot
Ensign R.B. Clark, USNRF	Pilot
Ensign R.H. Hyde, USNRF	Pilot
Ensign W.S. Grooch, USNRF	Pilot
Ensign J.G. Hallett, USNRF	Pilot
Ensign T.T. Barr Jr., USNRF	Pilot
Gunner (T) J.N. Phinney, USN	Radio Officer
Ensign W. Reiner, Civil Engineer Corps, USN	Public Works Officer
Ensign E.A. Cain, Pay Corps, USNRF	Supply Officer
Ensign C.A. Brinkman, Pay Corps, USN	Asst. to Supply Officer
Ensign B. Rhodes, USNRF	Engineer Officer
Machinist C.J. Lee, USNRF	Asst. to Engineer Officer
Machinist J.L. MacIver, USNRF	Transportation Officer
Ensign A.L. Theard, USNRF	Intelligence Officer
Lieutenant (j.g.) E.K. Busse, Dental Corps, USNRF	Dental Officer

III. OPERATION

On 29 June 1918, the first two seaplanes were flown to this station from Le Croisic, where they had been assembled. There were French planes manufactured by the Ley-Le Pen Company and equipped with one 280 H.P. Renault engine.

On 14 July the French formally ceded the station to the U.S. Navy, and on 19 July the first convoy flight was made from this station by seaplanes piloted by Ensign W.M. Barr, USNRF (Naval Aviator No. 381), and Quartermaster G.H. Hasselman. Convoy and patrol flights were made regularly thereafter. The motors used in the planes had been overhauled two or three times, and it was therefore very difficult to keep them in good condition. No bomb carrying gear was received with these planes, and it was necessary to install gear furnished by the French, which had been designed for another type of seaplane. This involved considerable labor, and caused the loss of many flight hours.

On 20 August the first and only fatal accident of this station occurred. A seaplane piloted by Ensign E.B. Barry, USNRF (Naval Aviator No. 421), was blown up on the slipway while about to leave for patrol. Three men were killed instantly—the pilot, M.H. Holley, QM2c(A), and E.J. Vrath, E13c(R); L.F. Tucker, QM2c(A), and J.C. Richardson MM2c, died the same day, and on the following day J.J McVeigh, QM2c(A), succumbed. Two months later an eighth man died of injuries from this accident—E.W. Stoker, CMM. Sixteen other members of the handling crew received injuries of more or less serious nature. The cause of the explosion, as ascertained by a Court of Inquiry, was a defective bomb carrying gear, and certain changes were made before resuming operations.

Due to the geographic location of St. Trojan and the courses and channels followed by ships in passing through the sector covered by seaplanes from this station, it was decided, at a conference with the French District Commander, that reconnaissance flights were more valuable than convoy flights, and this idea was carried out in operations.

The first attack on a submarine by planes from this station was made on 6 September 1918. An "allo" was received at 0930 hours, reporting a submarine in a position about 20 miles from the station. The alert section was sent out, and a seaplane piloted by Ensign V.T. Leak (Naval Aviator No. 383) attacked a submarine without success at 1022 hours. The accompanying seaplane, piloted by Ens. R.B. Clark (Naval Aviator No. 420), was unable to get into a position to attack.

Curtiss H-16 seaplane at NAS St. Trojan. (source: Naval Historical Center)

On 26 September, one H-16 seaplane was delivered to the station, but was never flown on patrol because of the lack of bomb gear, the necessity of rebuilding steps and plugging leaks in the hull, and the inability to procure material for any of these repairs. During October, additional HS-1 seaplanes and spare parts for French seaplanes and motors were received, thus making it possible to increase the flying time.

The fourth Liberty Loan Campaign was opened at NAS St. Trojan on 26 September, and the ship's company subscribed the sum of $28,350.

On 26 October four bombs were dropped by seaplanes from this station on a suspicious wake. The submarine was later sighted in the vicinity by a French seaplane from a neighboring station.

On 11 November operations were suspended in accordance with instructions received from Naval Headquarters in Paris. Table J-1 provides statistical data associated with the flight operations from NAS St. Trojan.

IV. DEMOBILIZATION

On 13 November demobilization began, and the station went out of commission on 19 January 1919. St. Trojan was taken over by the Minister of the Interior. The contract cost of this station was about 1,200,000 francs. It was found that the damage claim incident to cancellation of the station was small.

TABLE J-1
NAS St. Trojan, Charente Inferieure, France
U.S. Naval Air Station (Seaplane)
From 6 July 1918 To 11 November 1918

Wk. End.	**Flights Made**	**Total Knots**	**Flying Time (Hr.)**	**Suitable Flying Time (Hr.)**	**Aircraft on Station**	**Aircraft in Comsn**	**Flying Personnel**
6 July	7	180	2:50	21	4 GL	3	14
13 July	1	30	0:30	53	4 H-16	1 H-16	14
20 July	5	300	4:45	40	7 GL	4 GL	16
27 July	13	1350	22:01	38	7 GL	4 GL	18
3 August	12	1170	19:34	38	8 GL	5 GL	20
10 August	9	1440	23:45	32	8 LP	4 LP	21
17 August	10	510	8:22	72	7 LP	3 LP	21
24 August	2	60	0:55	62	6 LP	5 LP	19
31 August	4	60	0:51	70	6 LP	2 HS-1	19
						2 HS-1	
7 September	19	1530	25:20	60	6 LP	2 HS-1	19
						4 LP	
						1 HS-1	
14 September	8	480	7:55	23	6 LP	1 HS-1	19
						5 LP	
21 September	19	1230	20:20	44	7 LP	5 HS-1	19
						3 LP	
						1 HS-1	
28 September	26	1050	17:09	38	7 LP	1 H-16	19
					2 HS-1	5 LP	
5 October	22	2850	47:03	46	7 LP	1 H-16	19
					3 HS-1	6 LP	
12 October	5	180	3:00	15	7 LP	1 H-16	18
					3 HS-1	Not Indicated	
19 October	19	910	14:37	32	6 LP	1 H-16	20
					1 HS-2	5 LP	
						3 HS-1	
26 October	25	1680	28:00	44	6 LP	5 HS-1	18
						1 H-16	
					1 HS-2	4 LP	
						5 HS-1	
2 November	27	2600	58:12	44	6 LP	6 HS-1	19
						1 H-16	
					1 HS-2	4 LP	
						4 HS-1	

Wk. End.	Flights Made	Total Knots	Flying Time (Hr.)	Suitable Flying Time (Hr.)	Aircraft on Station	Aircraft in Comsn	Flying Personnel
9 November	8	535	9:00	16	4 LP	6 HS-1	18
						1 H-16	
					1 HS-2	4 LP	
						6 HS-1	
11 November	5	1388	14:28	8	4 LP	6 HS-1	20
						1 H-16	
						1 HS-2	
					1 P.S.	1 LP	
						6 HS-1	
TOTAL	245	19533	323:37	796			

Note: 1. Both the designators of GL and LP refer to Levy Le Pen aircraft.
2. The designator H and HS refer to Curtiss aircraft
3. The designator P.S. refers to a Paul Schmidt aircraft.

Notes:

[1] Material forming this Appendix predominately comes from the document entitled *History of U.S. Naval Aviation, Foreign Service, French Unit, 1917-1918*

Appendix K: NAS L'Aber Vrach[1]

I. CONSTRUCTION

The station was the seventh to go into construction and the sixth to go into operation. The mission of the station was to provide aerial support over the shipping lanes forming the western approaches to the English Channel. The U.S. Naval Air Station L'Aber Vrach, Finistere, France, was situated on a small island called "Ile d'Ehre" in the harbor of Vrach. The station was one and a half miles south of the large ILE VIERGE Light House, which marks the southern entrance to the English Channel. A party of U.S. Naval Aviation representatives, of whom Lieutenant Commander Whiting was the senior member, selected the site. It was 21 miles north of Brest, and is connected with that city by a fairly good highway and a narrow gauge railway.

On 27 January a small shipment of handtools and foul weather clothing arrived from Brest. A work party was sent to the nearby town of Lannilis to purchase sufficient building material to construct a tool shed on the island. The first construction work commenced when three fishing boats with 34 naval personnel left L'Aber Vrach for the island at 0800 hrs. on 29 January. The next day two Frenchmen appeared with a letter from the French Commandant at Brest stating that they were archeologists and requesting permission to inspect some monuments on the island for the purpose of preserving them. Several piles of loose rocks on the island were declared to be very ancient, and a request was made not to disturb them. The naval personnel honored this request. The men were daily ferried to and from the island in a sailboat hired from local fishermen. One of the first structures upon which work was commenced was a boat landing on the island. As portable barracks were not at once received from the United States, it was necessary to secure tents and barracks locally, so that the men could live on the station. In the later part of February, 25 tents were received as a loan from the U.S. Army and three French wooden portable barracks were transported in fishing boats from l'Aber Vrach to the island, and when they had been erected, the men were quartered and messed on the site of the Air Station.

Great difficulty was experienced in obtaining tools and material. In order to obtain lumber, a detail of men was sent to a sawmill in the town of Lannilie, 5 kilometers from l'Aber Vrach, where they sawed such logs as could be found. At the same time, work was being carried on at the boat pier and the aeroplane runway. Both of these projects necessitated the construction of large stone walls, the stone for which had to be collected and carried by the men on their shoulders. Gradually, tools and small quantities of lumber were received from the American Naval Base at Brest and the Aviation Supply Base at Pauillac.

Before 1March the tents had been pitched on the island and most of the men moved from the town to the island. Sentries were posted from 1000 hrs. to 0800 hrs.

After the personnel were quartered on the island it was found that a considerable portion of the manpower available was required for transportation of the necessary provisions and water to the island. All fresh water was brought from l'Aber Vrach in gasoline drums. Later, two 1200 gallon steel tanks were placed on an old barge, which had been rented for transporting water. One well was dug in the very center of Ile d'Ehre, and at 26 feet an abundant supply of briny seawater was found. The presence of salt water was explained by the fact that under a rock crust there was a layer of very coarse sand through which the seawater flowed freely. Later, a well was dug on the mainland to the northeast of d'Ehre, and there a supply of water was found which, however, was too brackish for drinking purposes, but was satisfactory for washing and cooking. A pipe was laid from this well to the island, and thus the water problem was completely solved.

On the first of March a 20-foot motor dory was received. This was of great service in that it could tow the native boats laden with the provisions and material, as well as transport the personnel to and from the island. A 36 ft. motor sailing launch, a 40 ft. motor sailing launch, another dory, a 50 ft. motor sailing launch, and a 35 ft. captain's barge were later received. With these motor boats on hand use of the sailboats was discontinued.

On 30 March 1918, all work constructing the station was abruptly halted by urgent orders from U.S. Naval Aviation Headquarters in Paris to organize the personnel into a military battalion. Rifles and other military equipment were received from Brest to equip the battalion, and military drills were immediately commenced. The drill field used was the area initially leveled off in

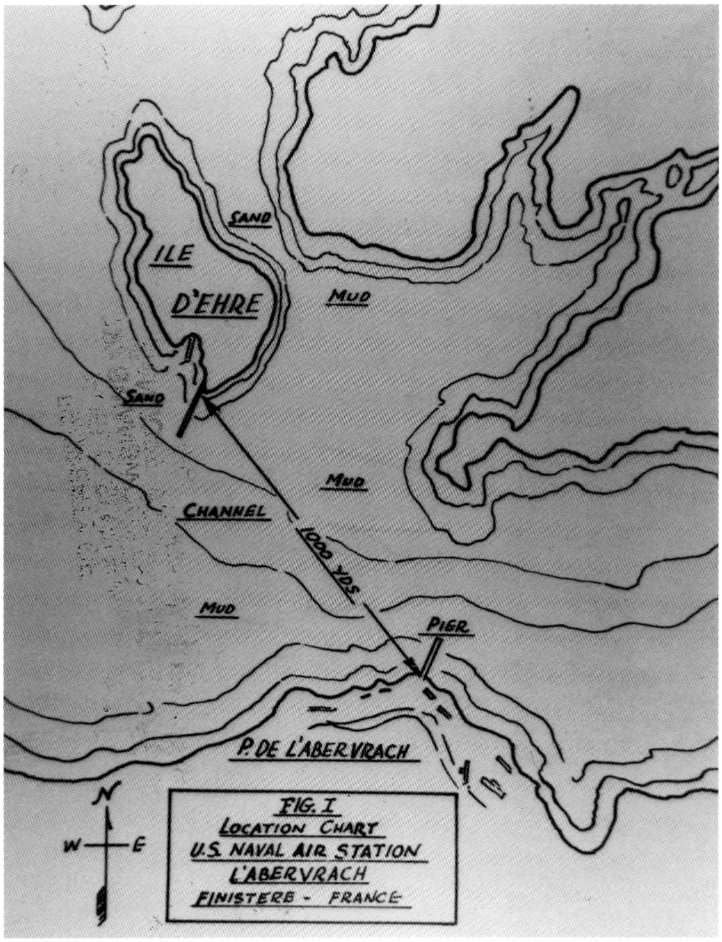

Location Chart, U.S. Naval Air Station L'Aber Vrach, Finistere, France.

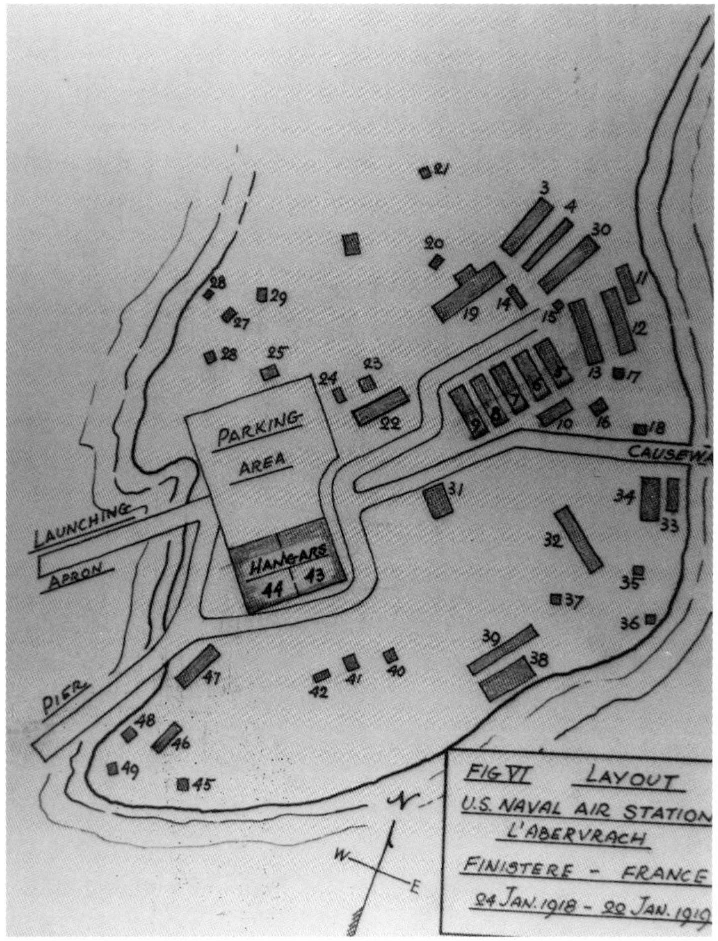

Layout, U.S. Naval Air Station L'Aber Vrach, Finistere, France.

front of the hangars, which was to be used to park aircraft. This emergency lasted for 10 days when orders were received to resume construction of the station.

Material for the seaplane hangars and wooden barracks was received in small shipments from Pauillac. For transporting this material from Pauillac to the various Air Stations, two small coastwise steamers, the S.S. *Bella* and the S.S. *Meknes*, had been procured. Neither of these steamers could unload in this port, and it was therefore necessary to send men from this station to Brest for the purpose of unloading these steamers and loading materials on to the narrow gauge railway, by which it was brought to l'Aber Vrach.

The construction gangs became so expert that in 4 hours a portable building, 20 ft. by 107 ft., could be completely erected and ready for occupancy. Materiel for the seaplane hangars came in the form of coarse lumber. With an assortment of French handsaws,

NAS L'Aber Vrach showing radio towers. (source: Naval Historical Center)

NAS L'Aber Vrach. (source: Naval Historical Center)

NAS L'Aber Vrach. (source: Naval Historical Center)

View of Isle Vierge, with its 292 ft. lighthouse, which was the landmark for NAS L'Aber Vrach. Photo taken on 28 October 1918. (source: 11-SC-30995)

French augers, and a few American carpenters' tools, which had been procured from the transports arriving at Brest, the construction of the hangar proceeded.

The trusses for the hangars were constructed on the ground and hoisted into place by manpower. This was no small undertaking, as the trusses were tremendous structures. The work of placing these trusses was entrusted to Chief Boatswain's Mate John H. Bray, USN. Bray borrowed a gin-pole, got his tackle together, and developed a speed of four trusses hoisted and secured in place in one day. On 16 June a double hangar, 214 ft. by 93 ft., was completed.

Cement and a small mechanical concrete mixer were received from the Army Supply Depot at Brest. A seaplane runway, 14 ft. wide and 240 ft. long, and a boat pier, 14 ft. wide and 180 ft. long, were concerted, as well as the floor of the double hangar and an area in front of the hangar, 214 ft. long and 112 ft. wide.

On 18 October, a new double wire American telephone and telegraph line from this station to Brest was completed. It gave direct telephone and telegraph connection with the Flag Officer in Brest, and this insured accurate and rapid communication regarding movements of convoys, enemy submarines, reports, etc.

On 11 November the construction of the station had been completed. The wireless station, consisting of two 120 ft. masts, 2 kW sending sets, one receiving set, and one radio direction finder, was also ready for operation. The seaplane runway had been concreted down to the low water level, permitting the launching of planes at all but extreme low tides, and the boat pier had been completed to such a stage that there was a good concrete wharf. All the personnel were comfortably housed for the winter, and everything was ready for continuous operations.

II. PERSONNEL

Gunner (T.R.) Carlton Arthur McKelvey, USN, arrived at l'Aber Vrach to take command on 24 January 1918. Accompanying him from Brest was Lieutenant C.P. Conrad, Asst. Civil Engineer, USN, who had with him the plans and specifications for the construction of the new air station. The next day Gunner McKelvey and Lieutenant Conrad visited the island, and stakes were driven to denote the locations of the planned structures; they then returned to L'Aber Vrach, where Conrad departed for Brest. On 26 January Chief Carpenter's Mate Milton DeMilt, USN, arrived in l'Aber Vrach by rail. With him was a draft of 37 men who were immediately quartered in the town's only hotel. The next day Gunner McKelvy interviewed each man to determine both their official skills, as well as their unofficial skills. They were then organized into groups or di-

NAS L'Aber Vrach runway and harbor with flying boats at anchor on 28 October 1918. (source: 11-SC-30992)

View of NAS L'Aber Vrach from 10,000 ft. taken on 28 October 1918. (source: 11-SC-30996)

Left to right: Ens. Rufus H. Bush (first C.O. at L'Aber Vrach and in charge of instruction), Ens. Kenneth R. Smith, Ens. Samuel S. Walker, Ens. Reginald D. Coombe, Asst. Paymaster J.C. Beguette, Ens. Henry H. Landon, Lt. William H. Corry (C.O. as of 7 November 1917), Louis Baffier (French Army instructor who remained at the station up until the armistice) and Asst. Surgeon C. Wheatley. Photo was taken on day of commissioning of the station (27 November 1917)

visions along the line of a ship's company. At that time Ile d'Ehre was nothing but a lonely weather-beaten rocky island, the surface of which was cut into small plots by rock and mud-walls. The entire shoreline of the island was covered with boulders, which made approach dangerous when the sea was rough. It would have been difficult to find a more desolate and hopeless task than the first draft found comforting them upon their arrival at l'Aber Vrach. During the first week at l'Aber Vrach Ensign John W. Nears, Supply Officer; Dr. Harmon, M.C.; and Charles F. Flannery, Pay Clerk, arrived and reported for duty. These officers were urgently needed to handle the details of ordering and receiving supplies, disbursing funds, and attending to the health and medical needs of the personnel. About the middle of February another drat of men reported to the station. These men were also quartered in the hotel, which was now full to capacity.

On 26 April Lieutenant Henry B. Cecil, USN (Naval Aviator No. 42), relieved Gunner McKelvey as Commanding Officer, and Gunner McKelvey assumed the duties of Executive Officer and continued in general charge of construction. At that time the personnel consisted of the Commanding Officer, Executive Officer, a Medical Officer, a Supply Officer, and 178 men of various ratings. All except an office force and the chauffeurs were quartered on the island. Throughout the spring and early summer, men and officers worked from daylight until dark with a spirit that never failed. Gradually Ile d'Ehre began to assume the appearance of a Naval Air Station. In the latter part of May the officers established an officers' tent village on the island. A bath was secured through the medium of a small French tub, together with a coffee heater, and a wine cask being used as a retainer of the water. This was a great convenience, as a hot bath was something that could not be obtained in the large towns of Finistere.

From the time the Americans first arrived, their relations with the populace were of the best. The men were given liberty daily from 1800 hours to 2130 hours, and the inhabitants treated them cordially at all times. They were Bretons of the sternest type, and they were amazed at the manner in which the Americans accomplished their business. They were invited to attend the moving pictures and the theatrical performances at the Y.M.C.A. hut, and these were entirely new experiences to the majority of them. Previous to the arrival of the American detachment, there had not been even a telephone anywhere in the vicinity.

On several occasions the Medical Officers rendered much needed medical assistance to the inhabitants. On one occasion a frantic mother brought a child with a dislocated hip to be cared for. Another baby about to die was saved by a timely operation in the Sick Bay. This created such an impression that the local churches set aside one day on which everyone prayed for the welfare of the doctors and Americans. In addition to the above, the officers and men became interested in rendering assistance to the peasants in the vicinity who seemed threatened with starvation. A campaign of relief was started on the island, and 3700 francs were collected to be distributed to the needy families. This work created a wonderful friendship between the natives and the Americans.

On 1 June 1918 Lieutenant (j.g.) Aymar Johnson, National Naval Volunteers, reported for duty as Executive Officer. Gunner McKelvy then assumed the duties of Radio Officer. At this time there were 12 officers and 273 men on the station.

In the latter part of February, a Y.M.C.A. Secretary was assigned to l'Aber Vrach. Mr. W.O. Davies of Chicago reported for this duty in July and remained until the armistice was signed. To him is due great credit for the welfare and contentment of the personnel. Through his efforts the Y.M.C.A. tent was replaced by a wooden building 30 ft. by 150 ft., with a reading and writing room 30 ft. by 50 ft. attached. The station carpenters and bricklayers employed all their talents in erecting this building. They constructed a stage with electric footlights, and they built an old-fashioned fireplace that was the joy and comfort of everyone. In the reading and writing room an abundant supply of stationary, magazines, books,

Unidentified enlisted personnel in front of the Post Office at NAS L'Aber Vrach. (source: Naval Historical Center)

Hangars at NAS L'Aver Vrach. (source: 80-HAG-5D-8)

Hangars and flying boats at NAS L'Aber Vrach.

etc., was always at hand. A standard billiard table was also installed, and Moving Pictures were shown three times a week, while twice a week troupes of entertainers performed at the station.

A station minstrel troupe with a band as orchestra, which proved to be a great success, was organized at this lonely post. Upon the request of the Y.M.C.A. authorities, it gave performances at the Brest Air Station, at the Brest Army Camp, at the Y.M.C.A. hut in Brest, and the Naval Air Station Ile Tudy. Upon request the orchestra played at a number of dances and soirees at various places in Finistere.

Athletic teams were organized, and in spite of the fact that there was not a clean level spot within 10 miles of the station that was large enough for a baseball diamond, the teams from l'Aber Vrach competed for honors in the Brest League and were considered fairly successful.

On 11 November there were 29 pilots, 14 enlisted observers, 15 ground officers, and 476 men on the station.

Cecil, Henry B., Lieutenant Commander USN	Commanding Officer
Johnson, Aymar, Lieutenant USNVF	Executive Officer
Craig, John F., Lieutenant USNRF	Armament Officer
Enos, George, Lieutenant (j.g.), USN (T)	Chief Pilot
Kindell, Norlan M., Ensign USNRF	Assistant Chief Pilot
Burrows, Julina S., Ensign USNRF	Intelligence Officer
Baker, Virgil P., Ensign USNRF	Engineer Officer
Lang, Fred H., Ensign USNRF	Transportation Officer
MacRae, Donald C., Ensign USNRF	Meteorologist
Tree, Ronald T., Ensign USNRF	Pilot
Wright, Webster M., Ensign USNRF	Pilot
Trail, Oscar, Ensign USNRF	Pilot
Whitney, Richard T., Ensign USNRF	Pilot
Thompson, Willis, D., Ensign USNRF	Pilot
Clarke, Edwin, K., Ensign USNRF	Pilot
Laferty, Edgar B., Ensign USNRF	Pilot
Hartley, Francis Jr., Ensign USNRF	Pilot
Keddie, Edward A., Ensign USNRF	Pilot
Boot, Harry E., Ensign USNRF	Pilot
O'Brien, Andrew, Ensign USNRF	Pilot
Rogers, William A., Ensign USNRF	Pilot
Neale, Raymond M., Ensign USNRF	Pilot
Parvin, John I., Ensign USNRF	Pilot
Morford, James R., Ensign USNRF	Pilot
Hoffman, Roger G., Ensign USNRF	Pilot
Thackray, George E., Ensign USNRF	Pilot
Poyntz, Pierce C., Ensign USNRF	Pilot
Corry, Arthur, Ensign USNRF	Pilot
Jennigns, Albert G., Ensign USNRF	Pilot
Lough, James C. Lieutenant (j.g.), D.C., USN	Dental Officer
Neely, Ashton E., Lieutenant M.C, USN	Medical Officer

Hangars and aircraft at NAS L'Aber Vrach.

Pulling a Curtiss HS-1 up on a runway after a four hour patrol. Photo taken at NAS L'Aber Vrach on 28 October 1918. (source: 11-SC-30993)

Lebensohn, James E., Lieutenant M.C., USN — Relieving Medical Officer
Mears, John W., Ensign P.C., USNRF — Supply Officer
Landreth, Lucius S., Ensign P.C., USNRF — Relieving Supply Officer
Flannery, Charles T., Pay Clerk USNRF — Assistant Supply Officer
McKelvey, Carlton A., Gunner (R) USN (T) — Radio Officer
Bundy, Ralph E., Gunner (E) USN (T) — Electrical Officer
Sefton, Benjamin E., Carpenter USNRF — Public Works Officer
Mowbray, Chauncy C., Machinist USNRF — Assistant Engineer Officer

III. OPERATIONS

On 16 February, a German submarine appeared off the harbor in plain view of the island, but as nothing worth wasting shells on could be seen, it peacefully steamed away. The natives reported that before the establishment of this station, it was a common occurrence to see German submarines shelling sailing craft or attacking powerboats just off the coast.

On 4 June 1918 the American Flag was hoisted with appropriate ceremonies. Also in June a rescue party from the station, in a large motor launch, gave assistance to a French seaplane which had crashed off the coast of Finistere

On 18 July 1918 the first American seaplane arrived. It was an HS-1 flying boat, which had been received at Brest, assembled there, and flown to the station by Lieutenant Commander H.B. Cecil, USN. As the first shipments from the United States were short of a number of essential parts, it was necessary to take off the first plane the Liberty motor starting device, Liberty motor switches, and various other accessories, and to take these to Brest for installation on another plane before that could be flown to this station. In this way it was possible to transport the planes and to make the necessary operative changes at the station when the material arrived. This procedure was followed until 14 August.

On 2 September there were ten planes on hand, four of which were ready for operation, and military activities were begun. These planes were equipped with Liberty motors having light crankshafts, and as three of these shafts broke during flights, it became necessary to suspend operations until heavy crankshafts were installed in all seaplanes.

The American Clarke bombs, which had been supplied for use at this station, were discovered to be defective, as three of these bombs had been dropped without exploding, and all Clarke bombs were returned to the United States. French "F" and "G" bombs were received, and the American bomb carrier was modified to carry the French bombs, a safety device being improvised which forestalled any accidental explosions.

On 7 October 1918 military operations were resumed. From that time on, when weather permitted, all convoys passing through the sector of l'Aber Vrach were escorted, and an alert section was kept ready to take to the air at any moment. The patrol and convoy sector as assigned by the French Commandant des Patrouilles Aeriannes de Bretanne and approved by the Commander, U.S. Naval Forces in France, was as follows: From a line 33 miles west to Quessant, North to a point opposite the middle of the English Channel to a point 45 miles north of Ile de Bats. The zone of operation was to a distance of not less than 66 miles from the station, and greater in case of emergency.

Through this zone proceeded all the steamship routes between the Bay of Biscay and Ireland, the Bay of Biscay and England, the coasting route between the northern French ports and the southern French ports, and the northern route of the convoys between the United States and Brest. Daily convoys passed through this sector going toward England, coming from England to France, and proceeding up and down the French coast. The convoys to and from England were usually composed of from 12 to 30 ships. Practically at all times there were one or more convoys in this vicinity. Usually flights from l'Aber Vrach were relieved at about mid-channel by British dirigibles, but flight sections frequently accompanied convoys or patrolled well beyond mid-channel. On 25 October, a section from this station accompanied a convoy to the English coast, crossed over the Lizard for a few minutes, exchanged signals with British land planes, and then returned. From the time the station first started operations, submarines in its sector sank no ships.

A frequent passenger in the planes was the station mascot, a dog named "Buster," who had been given to the station by the local

View of Curtiss HS-1 flying boats and hangars at NAS L'Aber Vrach taken on 28 October 1918. (source: 11-SC-30991

French people. Whenever he heard an airplane motor start he would head for the plane and beg to be taken for a ride. Table K-1 provides a summary of the aerial operations at NAS L'Aber Vrach.

IV. DEMOBILIZATION

By 1600 hrs. on 22 January the station had been completely demobilized and was placed out of commission. The property was derequisitioned. All barracks and hangar lumber was turned over to the U.S. Army.

Curtiss HS-1 (L'Aber Vrach No. 14) in Brest harbor.

TABLE K-1
NAS L'Aber Vrach, Finistere, France
U.S. Naval Air Station (Seaplane)
From 27 July 1918 To 11 November 1918

Wk. End.	Flights Made	Total Knots	Flying Time (Hr.)	Suitable Flying Time (Hr.)	Aircraft on Station	Aircraft in Comsn	Flying Personnel
27 July	15	420	7:12	65	1 HS-1	1 HS-1	9
3 August	5	240	3:55	73	2 HS-1	2 HS-1	19
10 August	11	5990	6:14	51	6 HS-1	2 HS-1	19
17 August	30	1380	22:52	100	7 HS-1	2 HS-1	19
24 August	26	1590	26:36	70	9 HS-1	2 HS-1	19
31 August	14	2310	48:27	67	10 HS-1	3 HS-1	19
7 September	17	3230	53:50	75	16 HS-1	4 HS-1	19
14 September	3	360	5:41	13	12 HS-1	6 HS-1	19
21 September	18	630	10:11	42	12 HS-1	5 HS-1	19
28 September	24	690	11:21	38	15 HS-1	6 HS-1	21
5 October	29	1920	32:00	55	19 HS-1	6 HS-1	21
12 October	11	1560	26:00	15	18 HS-1	6 HS-1	27
19 October	323	2600	40:00	55	18 HS-1	8 HS-1	27
26 October	42	3558	58:58	51	18 HS-1	10 HS-1	32
2 November	33	2315	38:35	16	18 HS-1	12 HS-1	41
9 November	42	5493	91:33	46	19 HS-1	11 HS-1	38
11 November	3	616	10:16	10	19 HS-1	11 HS-1	38
TOTAL	355	29,302	484:11	842			

Curtiss HS-1 in flight at NAS L'Aber Vrach on 28 October 28, 1918. (source: 11-SC-30994)

Notes:

[1] Much of the material contained in this Appendix is taken from the document entitled *History of U.S. Naval Aviation, Foreign Service, French Unit 1917-1918*

Appendix L: NAS Fromentine[1]

I. CONSTRUCTION

The U.S. Naval Air Station at Fromentine was located on a sandy island in the province of Vendee. This island is about 12 miles long and is separated from the mainland by a half-mile stretch of water. The seacoast thereabouts is clear, and the surf breaking on the long beach made aircraft landing there impossible, but the sheltered water between the island and the mainland was entirely suitable for seaplanes. The village of Fromentine is located on the mainland, and is the transfer point for travelers to the island of Fromentine and Ile d'Yeu. On the island of Fromentine, outside the gates of the camp, was the very small village of La Fosse. There was no city of any importance within 35 miles of the station site.

The construction work, under the charge of Assistant Civil Engineer G.D. Ellsworth, USNRF, was commenced on 23 February 1918 when the excavating for a road, the digging of a well, and the building of Hangar No. 1 were begun.

On 6 March tents were set up on the station, and a temporary galley was erected. At this time the men were moved to the station from the temporary barracks in which they had been quartered on the mainland, and from where they had been ferried to the island each day by a small French steamer. By 13 March the roadway through the station was progressing, and three portable French Barracks had been erected. Toward the end of the month the building of the hangar columns and trusses was commenced.

The S.S. *Meknes* arrived on 11 April with a cargo of cement, piping, and roofing paper, and was unloaded by the station personnel in 48 hours. On 11 May the *Meknes* again arrived with a cargo of steel and lumber for the hangars, and upon the receipt of this material the hangar footings were poured and the roadway completed. On 24 May the *Meknes* delivered the balance of material for the hangar and portable warehouses.

Materials sent by rail from Pauillac arrived at Challans and were then transferred to a narrow gauge railroad for transportation to Fromentine, 15 miles away. At Fromentine the cars were switched by hand to a point near the end of the long wharf, and unloaded into wheel carts or wheelbarrows. The material was then moved to the end of the dock and unloaded piece by piece into motor sailing launches, a task complicated by a 17-foot rise or fall in tide. Upon landing at the island, the launches were unloaded and the material carted by truck, and later by tramway, to the station site.

NAS Fromentine from the air. (source: Naval Historical Center)

NAS Fromentine from the air.

Hangars at NAS Fromentine. (source: 80 HAG-5M-1)

Hangars at NAS Fromentine.

On 22 May the little train running between Challans and Fromentine jumped the track about five miles from the station. When the engine and several cars loaded with material for the naval base were thrown across the road, thus blocking transportation, the railroad authorities appealed for assistance, and all trucks which could be spared were sent to the scene of the accident to transport passengers and the most important material. All the articles destined for the station were delivered by truck, and until the road was again in commission, a mail car was run between Fromentine and Challans, carrying both French and American mail.

French labor was employed at this time to assist in unloading the rapidly arriving material and to relieve the Americans from construction work. The party of Frenchmen was composed of old men and young boys, and made a surprising appearance. They accomplished much and were faithful workers.

On 5 June, Ensign P.F. Fagan, USNRF, reported as Public Works Officer, relieving Assistant Civil Engineer G.D. Ellsworth. By 20 June the first hangar was completed, additional barracks were erected, and the concrete footings for hangar #2 were commenced. On 25 October the station was practically finished, with the exception of very minor details.

II. PERSONNEL

On 4 February 1918, Gunner (R) R.J. McGee, USN, arrived at Fromentine and took command of the station. On 29 February the first draft of 41 enlisted men was received and quartered in local hotels until necessary repairs had been made to a "Chateau" rented for barracks. The second and third drafts arrived on 13 March and 18 April, and were quartered in tents on the station site. Lieutenant Commander W.G. Child, USN (Naval Aviator No. 29), relieved Gunner McGee of command on 13 March 1918.

The first casualty of the station occurred on 16 March when H.J. Stretch, QM2c (A), USNRF, while in charge of a draft of men being sent from Pauillac to Fromentine, was taken ill at La Rochelle, and was removed to the Army Hospital, where he later died. He was buried in the American plot of the French cemetery at La Rochelle, in grave No. 1. Coxswain H.H. College was the second member of the Fromentine force to die when a case of pneumonia proved fatal on 24 December 1918. He was buried at St. Nazaire.

On 3 April the first edition of "Plane Talk" was published by the station personnel. Frank L. Morrman, Y1c, had been appointed editor. Later, J.V. Metcalfe, Y1c, and S.M. Haskew, MM2c (A), became the editors, and the paper was issued in printed form of four three-column pages, each week after September. The thirtieth number, a souvenir edition, was published after the armistice had been signed. Copies of this paper were of great interest to the station personnel.

On 26 April Lieutenant Commander W. Capehart, USN (Naval Aviator No. 19), relieved Lieutenant Commander Child as Commanding Officer.

NAS Fromentine. (source: 80 HAG-5M-4)

Hangars at NAS Fromentine with a HS-2L in front of the hangar. (source: Kilduff Collection)

Liberty parties of the enlisted personnel were sent first to the pretty little town of Pornic, and later to Les Sables d'Olonnes, a beautiful summer resort 35 miles down the coast from the station. The men were sent to the city in trucks and allowed 24 hours or more liberty at regular intervals. The residents of these towns always cordially received the men. Liberty parties were at one time arranged to be sent to Ile d'Yeu. It became apparent, however, that the small steamer making the trips was in danger of submarine attack, and these excursions were discontinued.

On 30 June the station force completed the Y.M.C.A. hut, and, with Secretary J.T. Crosser, it became a factor in the life of the station. Entertainment of a varied character were given, including smokers, stage dances, boxing matches, lectures by the officer of the station, etc. Exceptional musical talent found expression in an orchestra and brass band. Baseball and football equipment was furnished, and a well-equipped library was maintained. Classes in French were held, money orders were cashed, money was transmitted to the States, and many other conveniences were arranged for the personnel.

In July an epidemic of Spanish Influenza appeared and 42 cases occurred, each lasting from three to four days. The epidemic was brought under control after a brief, and not serious, visit.

On 5 August five members of the torpedoed ship U.S.S. *Covington* were received at the station, and the tales of adventure at sea fired the personnel with interest. Two days later, a lifeboat bearing the name *Covington* floated into the Bay of Fromentine, in good condition, emergency rations still in its lockers; the advent of this boat was an incident in the quiet life at this isolated station.

In August a little French boy of La Fosse whom the Americans had befriended and nicknamed "Noly," died, and as a tribute, the officers and men of the station attended the funeral in formation, bearing many flowers. This is mentioned as an example of the cordiality existing between the U.S. personnel and the civilian population.

On 16 August Assistant Secretary of the Navy, Franklin D. Roosevelt, visited the station, and at the end of the month an inspection was made by a group of Congressmen. On 29 October Admiral H.S. Mayo and Staff inspected the station, accompanied by the Aide for Aviation.

On 11 November there were 572 enlisted men, and the following officers, on board:

Hangars and HS-2L at NAS Fromentine. (source: Kilduff Collection)

Lieutenant Commander W. Capehart, USN	Commanding Officer
Lieutenant A.D. Warwick, USN	Executive Officer
Lieutenant (j.g.) C.H. McLellon, USN	Ordnance Officer
Carpenter W.E. Fitzgerald, USN	Assistant Public Works Officer
Gunner (R) R.J. McGee, USN	Radio Officer
Machinist J.M. Fixon, USNRF	Engineer Officer
Machinist H.P. Meachon, USNRF	Engineer Department
Ensign J. Wolfe, USNRF	Pilot
Ensign A.E.K. Ellis, USNRF	Pilot
Ensign H.E. West, USNRF	Pilot
Ensign T.T. Roberts, USNRF	Pilot
Ensign C.E. Hubbard, USNRF	Pilot
Ensign T.D. Southworth, USNRF	Pilot
Ensign A.G. Wheeler, USNRF	Pilot
Ensign T.R. Morse, USNRF	Pilot
Ensign N. Boyneston, USNRF	Pilot
Ensign R.H. Harrell, USNRF	Pilot
Ensign M. Butler, USNRF	Pilot
Ensign D.E. O'Neil, USNRF	Pilot
Ensign A.H. Sinclair, USNRF	Pilot
Ensign J.S. Allison, USNRF	Pilot
Ensign C.A. Rowe, USNRF	Pilot
Ensign Paul Watson, USNRF	Pilot
Ensign R.A. Holton, USNRF	Pilot
Ensign J.L. Little, USNRF	Pilot
Gunner (T) B.D. Blade, USN	Ordnance Department
Assistant Surgeon R.D. Bussdicker, M.C., USN	Medical Officer
Assistant Surgeon J.L. Manion, M.C., USN	Medical Department
Lieutenant (j.g.) E.R. Tilley, D.C., USNRF	Dental Officer
Assistant Paymaster C.H. Jernigan, USN	Supply Officer
Acting Pay Clerk A.J.E. Charbonneau, USN	Supply Department

On 29 June two HS-1 seaplanes were delivered from Pauillac, and as there were no launching trucks on the station, they were anchored in the bay. They were carefully attended to each day, and all wires and fittings were kept in good condition. The constructing of launching trucks was begun immediately. By the end of July, eight planes had been delivered, but as some of the principle parts of six of these had to be returned to Pauillac, only two planes were in commission until the last of August. Operations were begun, however, with two planes, and while these were under overhaul, the parts required in other planes were removed, so that flights could be made each day. On 20 July the first shipment of seaplane and hangar tools was received, and after the receipt of the second shipment, the Engineering Department had a very complete set of equipment.

On 6 July, Lieutenant (j.g.) C.H. McClellan, USN, reported after an inspection trip to British Air Stations, and to the French Armory at Morient, and was appointed the Armament Officer. A modified design of the French Corpet bombsight was installed on the HS-1 seaplanes, and daily practice was held with dummy bombs. Ranges for dropping live bombs and for machine gun practice were at a safe distance from the coast, and a range of four targets was constructed at the station.

The first of 200 convoy flights from the station was made on 17 August, and thereafter all north and southbound coastal convoys were escorted through this area by planes. The area was also covered by regular patrol flights, and an "Alert Section" was at all times ready to respond within three minutes to any "allo"" signal received.

On 17 September, while pilot Ensign C.E. Hubbard (Naval Aviator No. 350) and observer Ford were on a patrol flight 15 miles south of Ile d'Yeu, a patrol boat and a destroyer accompanying a convoy were seen to turn back and drop three depth charges. The plane flew across the spot indicated, with bombs armed and ready to be released, but no object was visible from the air.

On 26 September Ensign T.D. Southworth (Naval Aviator No. 389), with observer Megness, sighted a suspicious object three miles off the northwest point of Ile d'Yeu. A smoke bomb was dropped to indicate the position, and a destroyer drew up alongside immediately, but nothing was discerned.

On 2 October Ensign Southworth and observer Megness sighted what was considered to be the wake of a submarine three miles south of Ile d'Yeu. The plane was brought into a position for bombing, but it was discovered that the object sighted was debris from a torpedoed ship. On this same day Ensigns A.G. Wheeler (Naval Aviator No. 361) and Watson (Naval Aviator No. 359), with observers Fogg and Barbe, sighted an oil streak 15 miles south of Ile d'Yeu and dropped bombs. A French destroyer approached and patrolled the spot without results.

On 13 October, Ensigns Southworth and Roberts (Naval Aviator No. 382), with observers Magnell and Stevens, sighted a fresh oil streak 22 miles southwest of Les Sables d'Ollonne. The streak was followed to its western extremity, but nothing was found. Returning to the original spot, it was observed that the oil was fresher than previously and three bombs were dropped. Black bubbles immediately appeared on the surface and continued to rise while the planes hovered in the vicinity. It was later learned that this was the location of a sunken wreck.

On 27 October Ensign Harrell, with observer Wherley, sighted three miles northeast of Ile d'Yeu what was taken to be a periscope disguised under a barrel. Upon closer examination this object was found to be a floating barrel, but it was used as a target for machine gun practice before the plane returned to base. Also on 27 October, planes from this station made flights over Pornis, Noirmoutier, and Port Joinville in order to drop French War Loan circulars over these villages.

Table L-1 summarizes the aviation activities at NAS Fromentine.

IV. DEMOBILIZATION

After the signing of the Armistice instructions were received to discontinue operations. Upon receipt of Aviation Circular Letter No. 84 dated 23 November 1918, demobilization was started. The station was placed out of commission on 28 January 1919, with the personnel having been transferred and the material disposed of in accordance with the instructions from Headquarters. The remaining property on the site was turned over to the custody of the U.S. Army. The lease of the land was terminated, and the owner signed the Navy clear of all damage claims.

TABLE L-1
NAS Fromentine, Vendee, France
U.S. Naval Air Station (Seaplane)
From 10 August 1918 To 11 November 1918

Wk. End.	**Flights Made**	**Total Knots**	**Flying Time (Hr.)**	**Suitable Flying Time (Hr.)**	**Aircraft on Station**	**Aircraft in Comsn**	**Flying Personnel**
10 August	5	270	4:332	14:50	10 HS-1	2 HS-1	14
17 August	5	33	5:13	79:00	10 HS-1	2 HS-1	14
24 August	4	210	3:27	58:00	10 HS-1	2 HS-1	14
31 August	14	870	14:23	75:00	11 HS-1	3 HS-1	14
7 September	16	1230	20:39	75:00	10 HS-1	3 HS-1	16
14 September	11	630	10:17	22:00	10 HS-1	3 HS-1	16
21 September	25	3570	59:22	71:00	14 HS-1	6 HS-1	16
28 September	26	2640	43:51	40:00	11 HS-1	7 HS-1	16
5 October	49	6350	105:01	67:00	11 HS-1	5 HS-1	16
12 October	24	1440	34:34	32:00	12 HS-1	7 HS-1	15
19 October	39	4552	68:42	56:00	12 HS-1	7 HS-1	17
26 October	35	4189	71:28	44:00	12 HS-1	8 HS-1	17
2 November	46	7280	112:32	56:00	14 HS-1	8 HS-1	17
9 November	25	3869	60:45	37:00	14 HS-1	8 HS-1	23
11 November	11	976	16:42	16:00	14 HS-1	6 HS-1	23
TOTAL	335	38,009	631:29	742:50			

Notes:

[1] Much of the material contained in this Appendix is taken from the document entitled *History of Naval Aviation in Foreign Service, French Unit, 1917-1918*

Appendix M: NAS Arachon[1]

I. CONSTRUCTION

A contract was made in the autumn of 1917 by the French Navy, acting on behalf of the U.S. Navy, for the construction of a Naval Seaplane Station at Arachon (Cap Fettet). The property selected for the site consisted chiefly of sand dunes covered with pines, and of low areas subject to inundation at high tide.

On 5 November 1917, ground was broken by the French contractor M. Hauret. At first French laborers, chiefly consisting of old men, women, and young boys, were used; these were later supplemented by Singalese laborers sent by the French Government to aid in the construction.

French methods were employed, and fair progress was made for about three months. Considerable excavating and filling took place, and by 31 January 1918 practically one third of the total area to be leveled and filled had been completed. The foundations for the forge, administration building, and galley were well under way, and there was a considerable quantity of brick, lumber, and cement on hand.

The construction went on quite steadily until about 4 March 1918, when friction arose between the contractor and the Singalese laborers, who demanded an increase in pay of one franc per day. When this demand was not granted these none too enthusiastic workers went on strike. The French laborers were also discontented on account of being unable to obtain but very little bread. Work was delayed until the contractor finally decided to allow his men the demanded increase in pay.

At the end of March construction materials became scarce. The contractor had the much needed materials at the small town of La Teste, about nine kilometers across the Bassin d'Arcachon from Cap Ferret, but was unable to bring it to the station for the want of water transportation. The 18-ton flat-bottomed sailboat available was insufficient to transport enough material to continue construction. As the Navy had no vessel with which to provide assistance, work came to a virtual standstill.

Work had been done on the administration building, the board floor of the hangar apron, the machine shop, the forge, slipways, excavating and leveling, the boardwalk, two mess halls, the galley, and the hospital. The temporary wooden barracks erected by Navy personnel on the hill at the extreme northwest corner of the station were complete except for floors.

From the end of April to 1 July, very little progress was made owing to the shortage of materials. On 25 May 87 men of the station were transferred to Pauillac to aid in construction work at that station. This left Arcachon with only 21 men to guard and carry on the daily routine; construction was delayed until 25 June, when the men loaned to Pauillac returned.

The erecting of hangars was begun the last of June, and the work progressed rapidly. By 1 August one slipway was sufficiently completed to permit planes to be launched for eight hours of every tide, and sufficient hangar space was supplied for the storing of two H-16s or six HS-1s. The apron had been completed to such an extent as to permit the storing of six additional HS-1s. On 27 August both sections of double hangar No. 1 were completed and occupied by ten HS-1 seaplanes; considerable progress also had been made on hangar No. 2, as column foundations were set and filled, six columns had been erected, and seven trusses completed.

Every effort was devoted to work which was absolutely necessary for an early beginning of seaplane operations. No. 2 double hangar was completed about the middle of September. The French contractor had fulfilled the most essential part of his contract, and

Aerial view of NAS Arcachon taken on 17 November 1918.

with a few French laborers and the aid of some Navy personnel was endeavoring to finish the work.

A pine needle road was constructed across the Cape, and considerable difficulty was experienced, since much scrub pine had to be cleared away, and the greatest portion of the road leveled and filled. Electric lighting was installed with temporary leads, as the proper wire could not be obtained. The laying of a pipeline for water outside the station area was begun.

On 10 November 1918 orders were received to discontinue all construction work except that which was absolutely essential for the health and comfort of the men. The French constructor had completed the galley, two mess halls, the hospital, the administration building, the machine and forge shops, the power house, the pump house, two storehouses, two barracks, the armory, the south slipway, two pigeon houses, and a pigeon keepers' barracks. Under construction but not completed were the Post Office, the C.P.O. barracks, three additional barracks, two bathhouses, the carpenter shop, the laundry, sewage system, water line, pier, hangar apron, a magazine, radio tower, the Captain's house, officers' quarters, and electrical installations.

II. PERSONNEL

On 28 January 1918, Ensign R.J. Rodgers, Pay Corps, USNRF, arrived in Arcachon, Gironde, and made an official visit to Capitaine de Corvette de Framond, Commandant les Patrouilles Aeriannes de Biscaye, who made known the situation in regard to the construction of the station. A few days later Lt. H.C. Gebhart, Medical Corps, USN, and Acting Pay Clerk T.A. McDairment, USN, arrived in Arcachon with 20 men. The officers were quartered at the Hotel de France, and the men at a nearby hostelry. On 26 February quarters for the men were established on the site of the station in tents obtained from the Army. The officer personnel at this date were as follows:

Lieutenant L.L. Babbit, USN (Commanding)
Ensign R.J. Rodgers, Pay Corps, USNRF
Lieutenant H.C. Gebhart, MC, USN
Acting Pay Clerk T.A. McDairment (T) USN

Lieutenant H.G. Fuller, USN, assumed command of what was to become the station on 10 April, but he was detached on 10 May. Temporary command of the naval personnel was given to Ensign J.N. Brown, USNRF, who was in that capacity on 8 June 1918 when the station was commissioned. Lieutenant Z.W. Wicks assumed command of the station on 15 June 1918, relieving Ensign Brown.

On 11 November 1918, 312 enlisted men and the following officers were on board:

Lieutenant Z.A. Wicks, USN, Commanding
Lieutenant (j.g.)(T) Frederick Evans, USN, Executive Officer
Lieutenant (j.g.) C.E. Roberts, USNRF
Ensign (NL) (T) Edward Webb, USN
Ensign J.H. Brown, USNRF
Ensign W.S. Estees, USNRF
Ensign Edward S. Brewer, USNRF
Ensign A.M. Campbell, USNRF
Ensign M.H. Bailey, USNRF
Ensign J.L. Rothwell, USNRF
Ensign T.H. Wagner, USNRF
Ensign J.M. Dodd, USNRF
Ensign J.L. Appleby, USNRF
Ensign J.D. West, USNRF
Ensign H.G. Benedict, USNRF
Ensign W.G. McAdoo, USNRF
Lieutenant H.C. Gebhart, Medical Corps, USN
Lieutenant E.A. Sharp, Medical Corps, USNRF
Ensign R.J. Rodgers, Pay Corps, USNRF
M. l'Enseigne de Vaisseau de lere Classe Loranchet—Liaison Officer
Boatswain (A) L.T. O'Loughlin, USNRF
Boatswain (A) G.A. Wilson, USNRF
Gunner (T) J.H. Gowan, USNRF
Machinist M.R. Kondolf, USNRF
Acting Pay Clerk (T) J.E. Moore, USN

III. OPERATIONS

The original plans for the U.S. Naval Air Stations in France called for the establishment of an H-16 seaplane station at Cap Ferret, but due to the nondelivery of planes of this type, HS-1 seaplanes were supplied in their stead. The station was located on the Bassin de Arcachon on the eastern side of the Cape, about three miles from the southern end of the point. On account of prevailing winds from the northwest quadrant, a well-sheltered body of water at this point is offered for the getting away and landing of planes. Due to the fact that there is no road on the edge of the Cape for a distance of about 12 miles, communications and transportation of material were accomplished entirely by water.

On 25 July the Commanding Officer reported to the Commander, U.S. Naval Aviation Forces, Foreign Service, that this station would be ready to operate on 1 August. The first HS-1 planes delivered from the base at Pauillac were equipped with Liberty light crankshaft motors and lacked starters, bomb carriers, releasing gear, bomb sights, machine guns, and turret mounts. On 5 September a machine was delivered on which the starter was left off and the Clarke bomb carrier and releasing gear installed, and on 13 September the twelfth seaplane was received fully equipped. On 14 September the station was ready to operate. One pilot and one observer had reported for duty, but as it was contrary to orders to operate any small seaplane alone, it was impossible to commence operations. Test flights were made in order to have the machines ready for operations when the necessary pilots and equipment should arrive.

During this period the Engineering Officer, Ensign Walker S. Estees, USNRF, experimented with the gasoline feed pump in order to try to overcome its faults. The following alterations were finally recommended in a full report made to Aviation Headquarters, from where orders were given to make these changes standard on all feed pumps: The fan was cut down to the diameter of eight inches, and both edges of each blade were trimmed slightly; holes were bored near the tip of each wing, through which the retaining wire was run and welded in; the fan shaft was also redesigned, and a ball bearing thrust installed to take up the thrust of the fan in place of the thin steel washer in the original design. It was also recommended that oil cups of sufficient size to contain small wicking be installed in the place of those which were supplied by the manufacturer. The knob on the end of the spare throttle was removed in order to avoid the danger of cutting the spark when throttling down. Both seats in the pilot's cockpit were raised two inches. The seat of the second pilot was made to slide back so that it could be shifted back out of the way when the second pilot desired to go forward to the observer's cockpit, in order to assist him in estimating the speed of the plane. The compass, as originally installed in the HS-1 seaplanes, was removed and placed in the observer's cockpit, and a small French compass mounted on a stand was installed on the top of the center of the yoke in the pilot's cockpit. This arrangement gave both the pilot and the observer a clear view of a compass.

As it was impossible to get adequate spare parts, it was necessary to use parts of six of the twelve planes at this station in order to prepare the other six for flying. By 3 October sufficient parts had been received to equip nine planes.

On 1 October the French Naval Aviation Patrol Station at Lake Cazaux, Gironde, five miles southeast of Arcachon, was put out of commission. The Commanding Officer of Arcachon agreed to accommodate at his station two or three seaplanes from the French station at Bayonne. Arrangements were immediately made to obtain from that station a supply of ordnance materials, and the adapting of the Clarke bomb carrier for the French bomb was accomplished by removing the propeller protective cap, and by shifting forward the bomb releasing catch and the after steadying band. A six-inch sheet iron band with a link in each end was used to secure the bomb to the carrier. This device worked very satisfactorily.

On the afternoon of 1 October two DD seaplanes from the French center at Bayonne arrived for patrol work. Therefore, the first operations against German submarines at this station were commenced on 4 October by two French seaplanes temporarily attached to the station, accompanied by one HS-1 seaplane. The zone of operations as allotted to this station extended from Contis Lighthouse (Pt. Julian) on the south to Hourtin Lighthouse in the north, a distance of about 63 nautical miles. The patrol as outlined in accordance with these limits by the Commanding Officer was included between the four points, Hourtin Lighthouse, Contis Lighthouse, and Lat. 44 degrees, 5 minutes, Long. 2 degrees, 15 minutes. Even this small area was greatly reduced, due to the fact that the station was not supplied with craft which could be sent to the aid of seaplanes in distress at sea, and it was deemed expedient not to send planes further than a few miles out of sight of land, except in answer to an "allo." Each day a northbound coastal convoy between St. Jean de Luz and the mouth of the Gironde River entered this area at about 1500 hours. As darkness set in about 1700 hours, the convoy coverage ability from this station was limited to about two hours daily. On 17 October two Ensigns and one Boatswain (A) reported from Moutchic for flying duty, and the local Commandant of Aerial Patrols was notified that Arcachon was capable of carrying on its assignment without aid from the French planes from Bayonne. On 20 October two pilots and two observers reported for duty from Ile Tudy, and additional operations were undertaken.

About 1800 hours on 22 October an "allo" was received from a point north of this station's area. On the morning of 23 October an alert section of two planes was sent out at 0625 hours in order to cover the area of the submarine's reported position. This section was composed of a seaplane piloted by Ensign J.L. Rothwell (Naval Aviator No. 1460), with observer Ensign T.H. Wagner, and one piloted by Boatswain G.A. Wilson (Naval Aviator No. 1463), with observer MMlc (A) Haizlett. At 0710 hours the latter made a forced landing at sea 45 miles northwest of Cap Ferret in a rather heavy sea. The other plane returned to the base immediately to make a report. As the necessary sea-going craft to send after this plane was not on hand, the French submarine patrol base at the mouth of the Gironde, the American District Commander at Rochefort, and the French Naval Aviation Station at Bayonne were notified. Upon the subsequent return to the station of the crew it was learned that their investigation, upon landing at sea, had shown that the gasoline line was blocked with metallic filings. Strainers were cleaned out, but on account of the rough sea it was impossible to remove the carburetors to clear the jets. All attempts to start the motor had failed. By 1000 hours the rough sea had practically destroyed both lower ailerons. The bombs, machine gun, instruments, and everything of weight were thrown overboard in attempting to keep the plane afloat. By means of Very Pistols the attention of a French patrol boat (*Etourdi*) was attracted, and the plane was picked up about 0300 hours on the 24th. The pilot and the observer were taken aboard the patrol boat, and having been in the seaplane for a period of 20 hours were in an exhausted condition. The plane was taken in tow, but in a short time became full of water and sank to the level of the upper wing. The pilot and observer both requested the Captain of the patrol boat to either ram the plane or fire a shot into it in order to make sure of its sinking, but these requests were refused. The plane was cut adrift, and the patrol boat proceeded to St. Jean de Luz, from which place the pilot and observer proceeded on to Arcachon. After an elapse of three days the Commanding Officer at Arcachon received a report from the French Ministry that this plane had been picked up about 12 miles northeast of Cape Machichaco on the Spanish coast by Spanish fishermen, and towed into the port of San Sebastian. The Naval Attaché at Madrid was requested to ship to the United States the engine propeller, instruments, and valuable parts of the plane after the demobilization order went into effect.

On 24 October, while escorting a northbound coastal convoy, a seaplane equipped with a light crankshaft motor, when 20 miles south of the station, threw off the tips of the propeller, and the resulting racing of the motor carried away the crankshaft. The hull and wings of the boat were severely damaged, but it remained afloat, and was towed by one of the ships of the escort to the harbor of La Pallice, 120 miles away. This plane was afterwards towed from La Pallice to the U.S. Naval Air Station, St. Trojan, from where, about a week later, it was taken in tow to be brought to Pauillac for repairs. However, on account of the heavy surf running off the coast, the towline was carried away and the plane was severely damaged and sunk.

At about 1900 hours on 24 October Stephen Joseph Matthews, Seaman, USN, was in the foreword compartment of the 35 foot motor boat (Captain's Barge) with a lantern, breaking out the running lights. One of the other members of the boat's crew noticed that the lantern was acting in a peculiar manner and asked Matthews to pass it out of the hole. Matthews reached for the lantern, and just as he was taking hold of it an explosion occurred. It was impossible to determine the cause of this explosion. However, the opinion was that the gasoline tank, which was located in the next compartment, must have sprung a leak, and the fumes of the gasoline invaded the forward compartment through the supposedly watertight bulkhead, thus forming an explosive atmosphere. The Barge was severely damaged, the forward deck being entirely blown off, the planking on the starboard side being entirely blown away from the stem, and the stem slightly damaged. When the explosion occurred, Matthews was blown out of the forward compartment through the small hatch on the upper deck and fell back into the burning compartment. He then crawled out after being severely burned about the face, neck, and hands. He immediately proceeded to assist the crew in extinguishing the fire, during which operation he noticed that Sgt. Edwards, U.S. Army, stationed at Arcachon, had been knocked unconscious by the concussion of the explosion and had fallen overboard. By quick action, Matthews saved Edwards from drowning and placed him in a wherry which was laying alongside of the Barge, and paddled it ashore himself in spite of the fact that he was severely burned. Stephen Joseph Matthews, Seaman, USN, was specially commended for his action in this affair. The Coxswain of the boat was also slightly injured.

Due to breaking of the light crankshaft motors in planes, all operations with light crankshaft motors were stopped by orders from Headquarters, and as soon as possible planes equipped with heavy crankshafts were delivered to the station, arriving on 26 October. The planes equipped with light crankshaft motors were sent to Pauillac for exchange of motors.

Table M-1 summarizes the aerial activities at NAS Arachon.

On 11 November orders were received to carry out mine search patrols off the mouth of the Gironde, but no mines were sighted. On 14 November orders were received to cease all operations except those necessary to keep planes in efficient condition, and to reduce all test flights to the minimum.

IV. DEMOBILIZATION

On 7 January 1919 Arcachon was placed out of commission as a U.S. Naval Air Station, material and personnel having been transferred. The station was taken over by the Minister of the Interior. The contract cost of the station was 1,200,000 francs. As work was practically complete on the date of cancellation, the claims for damages incident to cancellation of the contracts were small.

TABLE M-1
NAS Arachon, Gironde, France
U.S. Naval Air Station (Seaplane)
From 5 October 1918 To 11 November 1918

Wk. End.	Flights Made	Total Knots	Flying Time (Hr.)	Suitable Flying Time (Hr.)	Aircraft on Station	Aircraft in Comsn	Flying Personnel
5 October	6	6990	11:10	32	12 HS-1	2 DD	
					6 HS-1	1 DD	2
12 October	4	540	8:38	34	12 HS-1	2 DD	
					1 LP	5 HS-1	
					1 DD	1 LP	2
19 October	11	455	7:18	34	12 HS-1	4 HS-1	7
26 October	32	2775	47:30	45	13 HS-1	2 HS-1	9
2 November	26	2210	34:14	40	5 HS-1	3 HS-1	10
9 November	14	995	14:11	21	7 HS-1	4 HS-1	11
11 November	13	1064	15:11	17	7 HS-1	5 HS-1	12
Total	106	8727	138:12	225			

Note: HS indicates Curtiss Flying Boats
DD indicates Donnet-Denhaut Flying Boats
LP indicates Levy Le Pen Flying Boats

Notes:

[1] Much of the material contained in this Appendix is taken from the document entitled *History of Naval Aviation in Foreign Service, French Unit, 1917-1918*

Appendix N: NAS Treguier[1]

I. CONSTRUCTION

The U.S. Naval Air Station, Treguier, was located between the towns of Treguier and Plougiel, about four miles from the coast at the junction of the rivers Grundy and Jaudy, which form the Treguier river at that point. It was thus well protected from coastal storms.

The prevailing winds were southwest, often necessitating cross wind takeoffs and landings. The river was generally smooth, but narrow and winding, and at low tide the rocks and muddy banks projected into the stream, leaving a very narrow and irregular channel. The river marks outlining the channel were approximately 35 feet in width and were extremely difficult to see when landing at dusk or on a cloudy day. There was a normal tide of 29 1/2 feet at the runway. Frequent rain, fog, and low-lying clouds in the late fall and winter—November to April—made flying practically impossible during this period.

Here in May 1917, the French had established a small seaplane station of four Bessonneau hangars, but the small number of temporary buildings, the crude slipway, and incomplete aprons necessitated enlarging the station. The first draft arrived 21 August 1918, and construction was started immediately.

Aerial view of the naval station and town of Treguier.

As Treguier was situated on a narrow gauge railway it was necessary to occasionally send working parties to Guingamp, 22 miles away, to transfer supplies and materials from the standard to the narrow gauge railway. All material was transferred by motor truck from the railway station to camp, a distance of two kilometers. 47 tons of cement, 20 tons of coal, 25,000 feet of lumber, six complete portable barracks, and provisions and supplies were so transferred. Supplies urgently needed were secured from the Base at Brest, 90 miles away.

The completion of the Officers' quarters was delayed until 10 November by the making of a concrete basement, but on 20 October construction was sufficiently advanced for the barracks to be occupied.

During the latter part of September grading was begun for the Mess Hall and Galley, and by the third week in October this work was completed. Owing to the insufficient clearance of the Bessonneau hangars, it was necessary to raise the frames and to excavate to permit housing HS-1 seaplanes, which arrived the lat ter part of September. The total excavation approximated 1290 cubic yards, 20 men occupied this work for 30 days.

On 17 October construction of the barracks was begun and was finished a week later. About this time grading and construction for the new dispensary was begun, and was completed by 8 November. On 12 November the Recreation Hall, begun early in the month, was finished. Due to the difficulty in securing transportation facilities, construction work was continually delayed by the lack of proper equipment, supplies, and materials. Portable building parts, owning to improper handling during shipment, were broken or damaged and needed repairs. The concrete mixing was done entirely by hand. Sand was obtained only from Port Blanc, a distance of six miles. This task of securing occupied five men for 30 days.

On 10 October work was commenced on a pipeline for drinking water, to a spring 3250 feet north of camp. On 17 November the water supply system was completed, and water was brought through a two and one-half inch iron pipe laid in a twelve-foot trench. An auxiliary reservoir for public use was constructed at the station, and the spring was sealed, leaving only a manhole. Three 1000-

Barracks and other buildings at NAS Treguier. (source: Naval Historical Center)

NAS Treguier and the river in front of the station. (source: Naval Historical Center)

gallon reservoirs were also constructed on the hill at camp with temporary connections. Owing to extremely high pressure at points, considerable caution was necessary to insure tight joints. The maximum difference of elevation was 140 feet. Seven men were occupied for 37 days on this work.

The first Officer assigned to duty at Treguier was Lieutenant A.M. Baldwin, USNRF, Commanding Officer, who arrived at the French Aviation Station on 14 August 1918 with orders to supervise the necessary additions to the station and to assume command upon its completion. One carpenter's mate third class and two seamen second class were sent from the U.S. Naval Air Station Brest with a three-ton Packard truck for temporary duty at Treguier. The same month Lieutenant H.E. Bank, M.C. USN, was attached as Medical Officer. During September and October six seaplane pilots arrived at the station.

A draft of 43 enlisted men was transferred from Brest on 21 August, and a draft of 25 men from Moutchic on 30 August. During September a draft of 16 and one of 82 men arrived from Pauillac. A draft of 40 men reported from Guipavas on 20 October.

On 4 October 1918, Dewey Biggs, Bsmth 2c., USNRF, after an illness of eight days, died at this station of Lobar Pneumonia. He was buried in the French Cemetery at Treguier.

Mr. P.W. Jones, the Y.M.C.A. representative assigned to the station, took a personal interest in the welfare of the men, both physically and spiritually. Well-attended church services were held every Sunday morning. Two nights a week moving pictures were shown, and the men were allowed to invite their friends from Treguier. Once a week a troupe of Y.M.C.A. entertainers from Brest gave a show. Three dances were given in the Y.M.C.A building, at two of which the only ladies present were natives of Treguier. In the recreation building a piano was provided, as well as excellent books, magazines, writing paper, envelopes, pens, and ink. Many indoor games were also at the disposal of the personnel.

The river approaching NAS Treguier.

Baseballs, bats, and gloves, footballs, volleyballs, and other athletic gear were part of the "Y" equipment. Visitors at the station were always entertained in the Y.M.C.A. building.

On 11 November 266 men and the following officers were on board:

Baldwin, Augustus M., Lieutenant, USNRF	Commanding Officer
Portz, Warner P., Lieutenant, USN	Executive Officer
Hickey, James J., Lieutenant (j.g.), USN	Liaison Officer
Mathews, Charles E., Ensign, USNRF	Communications Officer
Sweitzer, Edward N., Ensign, USNRF	Engineer Officer
Thweatt, Troy N., Ensign, USNRF	Acting Chief Pilot
Waters, Robert S., Ensign, USNRF	Acting Assistant. Chief Pilot
Gillespie, Paul E., Ensign, USNRF	Seaplane Pilot
Gardner, Gibson, Ensign, USNRF	Seaplane Pilot
Dillon, Theodore F., Ensign, USNRF	Seaplane Pilot
Keyes, Kenneth B., Ensign, USNRF	Seaplane Pilot
Dolan, William R., Gunner (T) USN	Transportation and Radio Officer
Korst, Charles, Gunner (T), USN	Ordnance Officer
Bank, Harry E., Lieutenant M.C., USN	Medical Officer
Hallen, Harry A., Lieutenant (j.g.) D.C., USN	Dental Officer
Smith, Robert M. Jr., Ensign P.C., USNRF	Supply Officer

II. OPERATIONS

Treguier was established as a French Naval Air Station in May 1917 and was taken over by the U.S. Naval Forces in August 1918. The Americans had several opportunities to be of service to the French civil and military authorities. On various occasions French artillery of 57 mm, amounting to six guns and several thousand rounds of ammunition, was transported by the U.S. Personnel from the railroad depot of Treguier, and stored on the station, being later

NAS Trequier and the town of Treguier. (source: Naval Historical Center)

NAS Treguier. (source: Naval Historical Center)

reshipped by railway or carried in trucks to the French Coastal Fort near Plougrescant five miles away. Two guns of large caliber were transported by trucks from this station direct from the railway station to the Fort at Plougrescant.

A number of French sailors, together with bags and hammocks, arriving at this station on a French sub-chaser were transported to the French Destroyer Base, located at Lezardrieux, in trucks.

At the request of the French Army Surgeon in charge of French Hospital No. 56, in Treguier, trucks and crews from this station made 50 trips to haul over 400 wounded German prisoners from the railway depot to the Hospital. The majority of these German wounded were treated by the Surgeon attached to this station.

At the request of the authorities in charge of Belgian Refugee Children located at the town of Plestin, 10 tons of coal was hauled in a truck from this station from the railway at Plouaret to Plestin, a distance of 30 miles

For the French authorities a truckload of gasoline was hauled from Treguier to the town of Trebeurden, and a load of concrete from the depot to the Fort at Plougrescant.

At the request of Mme. Poilpot, President de l'Orphelinet des Arts, two trucks with trailers carried 80 French War Orphans and 3000 kilos of baggage from the town of Trestel to Lannion and Guingamp, a distance of 40 miles. A trip was also made to carry 2000 kilos of baggage and 10 bags of potatoes from Plougrescant to Lannion, a distance of 35 miles.

At the request of the French Air Station at Le Penze, a truck was sent to Lannion to transport a small French touring car, which had met with an accident, to La Penze, 56 miles away. Eight truckloads of scrap wood and lumber supplied by this station were delivered to French Hospitals and to the poor of Trequier.

The first aircraft to arrive on the Station were two HS-1 planes delivered on 24 September 1918, and the first official flight took place on 30 September, by which time 5 planes had been received.

In the morning of 3 October it was reported that a seaplane from the French Station at Le Penze had made a forced landing in the Channel the previous evening, and that a carrier pigeon had just arrived from the wrecked plane giving the approximate location as bearing 45 miles WSW of the Island of Guernsey. The Captain's Barge was sent in search. That morning, and for the preceding 24 hours, a steady gale had been blowing from the north, and as a result of the high sea it was impossible to drive the barge at a greater speed than two to three knots. Allowing for a driftage due to tide and wind, a course was laid for a point four miles due north of "Ile de Bas" light. Owing to heavy head seas and the necessity of battering down all hatches, the two men in the engine room were constantly inhaling gas fumes and shortly became ill, but managed to keep the engine working by alternately crawling into the forward cockpit. At 1430 hours a French destroyer and two French patrol vessels overtook the barge. After an interchange of inquiries as to whether the wrecked plane had been sighted, the barge was headed back to the station, since the greater range of vision and speed of the destroyer and patrol boats would enable them to locate the plane, if still afloat. Ten minutes later, and at a point within a half a mile of the point originally estimated, the destroyer found the plane and rescued the pilot and observer. The barge returned to the station at 1700 hrs. in such condition as to necessitate a general overhaul, the engine having been loosened from its bed by the rough weather encountered. The plane, though practically wrecked, was later washed ashore 15 miles further west.

On 1 November the U.S. Ensign was hoisted and the station was officially reported as having been commissioned.

On 4 November word was received that a French fishing vessel had been dismissed by the storm in the Bale e'Enfer at the entrance of the Treguier river, and had become unmanageable. The

Curtiss HS-1s at NAS Treguier.

NAS Treguier with a hangar under construction.

Group photograph of the personnel at NAS Treguier.

Captain's barge was sent out to locate the vessel, and as the crew succeeded in getting a line aboard her, she was towed into Treguier.

The signing of the Armistice and the cessation of hostilities so soon after the commissioning of the station eliminated the possibility of the performance of those duties which had been the earnest desire of both officers and men to render, with that efficiency assured by the "esprit de corps" of the personnel and the hearty cooperation accorded this station by the entire Staff. Table N-1 summarizes the aviation activities of NAS Treguier.

IV. DEMOBILIZATION

On 19 January 1919 the station reverted to the control of the French Navy and the American personnel were detached, the material having been disposed of in accordance with instructions from Headquarters. The terms of the agreement with the French Navy relative to the disposition of the station were: 1) The French agreed to take back all buildings subject to examination for damage; 2) A small sum was paid the property owner for excavation damage; and 3) No rental changes were made by the French. The Bessonneau hangars and all barracks were turned over to the U.S. Navy. The French hangar remained intact.

TABLE N-1
NAS Treguier, Cotes Du Nord, France
U.S. Naval Air Station (Seaplane)
From 29 September 1917 To 11 November 1918

Wk. End.	Flights Made	Total Knots	Flying Time (Hr.)	Suitable Flying Time (Hr.)	Aircraft on Station	Aircraft in Comsn	Flying Personnel
5 October	1	30	0:25	-	6 HS-1	-	3
12 October	4	150	2:25	-	7 HS-1	-	3
19 October	9	420	6:57	-	7 HS-1	-	4
26 October	2	90	1:38	-	7 HS-1	-	4
2 November	2	60	0:45	-	7 HS-1	-	6
9 November	8	540	9:00	-	7 HS-1	-	6
11 November	4	120	2:00	-	7 HS-1	-	6
Total	30	1410	23:12				

Notes:
[1] Much of the material in this Appendix comes from the document entitled *History of U.S. Naval Aviation, Foreign Service, French Unit 1917-1918*

Appendix O: NAS Brest[1]

I. CONSTRUCTION

The U.S. Naval Air Station at Brest was one of the stations contracted for through the auspices of the French Government.

In January and February 1918 the work at the station consisted of road building, grading, and the construction of portable barracks. Early in March, work was commenced on four barracks to be made from cinder blocks. The station personnel constructed one of these barracks and a C.P.O. barracks, while French contractors built the other three. The inability to obtain material and labor caused the cancellation of the French contract the latter part of August 1918, by which time the contractor had completed the following buildings: two officer's quarters; one wardroom building; one Commanding Officer's house; one transformer house; three crew's barracks; one Mess Hall; and one garage. The following buildings were partly erected by the French contractor and finished by the crew of the station: one C.P.O. quarters; one crew's Barracks, and one garage (constructed from seaplane boxes).

The French contractor laid the foundation piers for three slipways, but the only slipway that was completed, except for about 18 feet, was decked by the Station Force. The second transformer house was partly built by the French but never completed. The French contractor installed the fire system and the washroom fixtures in the crew's barracks. The hangar to be erected by the French never progressed any further than the foundations and one truss framed on the ground. The first buildings to be erected by the crew were portable barracks obtained from the U.S. Army. Later, hospital barracks and Dixie buildings arrived, and the following were erected by the crew: six crew's barracks; one Galley; two Mess Halls; one Sick Bay; two C.P.O. quarters; one Administration Building; one Canteen and Small Stores Building; one Officer's quarters; six latrines; and two storehouses.

Two double seaplane hangars were built; a third was never completed. The two standard radio towers, the radio house and power plant, the Officer of the Day shack, wash house, wing storage building, bomb storage building, machine shop, two tool shops, and one small barracks were built from seaplane and wing section boxes. The concrete aprons, side walks, and roads were laid by the crew. The crew also installed the electric work. Light was obtained from the French 110-volt alternating current. The Station was supplied with water from the tower of St. Anne four miles away.

Brest Harbor and City showing Kite Balloon Station and French Naval College.

NAS Brest from the air. (source: Naval Historical Center)

NAS Brest and harbor.

Entrance to NAS Brest. (source: Naval Historical Center)

The Kite Balloon station was adjacent to the seaplane base; hydrogen gas at this station was to have been supplied under normal conditions from the French Electrolytic plant. The French had, on this station, a 350 cubic meter portable silicon plant for emergency use. The Americans had the right to use this portable plant, furnishing the necessary chemicals and personnel for its operation. A six inch cast iron pipe was installed, connecting this portable plant with the French Nourrice, and a six inch cast iron distributing line from this main header was installed to the three-stall hangar, arrangements being made to take care of the fourth stall. It was planned to connect a high-pressure charging manifold with the existing French compressor, the manifold to be located in a small building erected on the U.S. Naval Air Station property.

All the low-pressure pipe and fittings, drip pots, seals, and connections had been completed by 15 October. High-pressure manifolds were delivered and assembled, and all the necessary high-pressure pipe and fittings were delivered and ready for assembly by 25 October. Of the 211 tons of caustic soda received at this station, 174 tons arrived in such bad condition that it was unfit for further use and it was necessary to dispose of it, leaving 37 tons of caustic soda for use in the manufacture of hydrogen gas. The French arranged to dispose of the sludge by dumping it in the bay.

During the whole time that the station was in commission, its personnel were called upon to do so much outside work that it was very difficult to carry on construction at a normal rate.

II. PERSONNEL

On 7 October 1917, Lieutenant (j.g.) G.R. Romulus, U.S. Navy, arrived at Brest to establish a U.S. Naval Air Station.

The last week in January 1918 the first draft of 50 men was received, and 40 of these were sent to l'Aber Vrach, the remaining ten being quartered in the barracks at the French Torpedo Station. Upon completion of the first barracks, which arrived at this time, the crew was transferred to the station. The first week in February 60 men arrived and were at once put to work on the road approaches.

The first seaplane pilot to report to the station was Lieutenant Commander F.C Dichman, USN (Naval Aviator No. 30), who arrived on 13 February 1918 when he relieved Lieutenant Romulus

NAS Brest on 22 October, 1918. Left to right: Ens. A. Sellared (Personal Aide); Vice Adm. H.B. Wilson, and unidentified. (source: 11-SC-30983)

Personnel at NAS Brest working on the assembly of a Curtiss H-16 flying boat on 2 November 1918. (source: 11-SC-30988)

as Commanding Officer. On 6 June Lieutenant Commander Dichman was detached, and Lieutenant W.M. Corry, USN, reported to assume command.

An epidemic of Spanish Influenza struck the station on 5 July, but had run its course by the 27th, after 147 cases had been admitted to the sick bay. Lieutenant Commander J.C. McEvitt, M.C., USN, was at this time in charge of the Medical Department.

Ensign J.R. Gibson, USNRF, was Balloon Officer until 17 September when he was ordered to the United States for duty, and was succeeded by Ensign R.K. Blakely, USNRF. Ensign Frank S. Smith, USNRF, was Chief Seaplane Pilot at the time of demobilization. On 11 November 1918 the officer personnel included the following:

Lieutenant Commander William M. Corry, USN — Commanding Officer
Lieutenant (j.g.) George J. Romulus, USN — Executive Officer
Lieutenant (j.g.) George H. Turner, USN — Ordnance Officer
Gunner (O) Fred V. Clark, USN — Aide to Ordnance Officer
Lieutenant (j.g.) Forrest V. Wysong, USNRF — Assembly and Repair (A&R) Officer
Machinist Harry R. Abrams, USNRF — Aide to A&R Officer
Machinist John S. Repjke, USNRF — Aide to A&R Officer
Ensign Harry B. Rutledge, USNRF — Engineer Officer
Machinist Thomas J. Charles, USNRF — Transportation Officer
Machinist John H. Stevens, USNRF — Beach Machinist
Lieutenant (j.g.) James N. Byers, C.E.C., USNRF — Public Works Officer
Ensign David L. Brown, USNRF — Intelligence Officer
Ensign Andrew A. Lord, USNRF — Aide to Intelligence Officer
Ensign Edwin T. Fox, USNRF — Aide to Intelligence Officer
Ensign Frank S. Smith, USNRF — Chief Seaplane Pilot
Ensign John W. Ashley, USNRF — Seaplane Pilot
Ensign Benjamin H. Baird, USNRF — Seaplane Pilot
Ensign Dwight S. Barnum, USNRF — Seaplane Pilot
Ensign Henry B. Constable, USNRF — Seaplane Pilot
Ensign Mathew D. Crawford, USNRF — Seaplane Pilot
Ensign Foss W. Hardendorf, USNRF — Seaplane Pilot
Ensign Herbert V. Perron, USNRF — Seaplane Pilot
Ensign Henry W. Rubinkam, USNRF — Seaplane Pilot

Group photo of station personnel at NAS Brest.

Fuselages of Curtiss HS-1L and HS-2L flying boats ready for assembly at NAS Brest on 2 November 1918. (source: 11-SC-30989)

Ensign Otto W. Schlms, USNRF — Seaplane Pilot
Ensign Thomas H. McClure, USNRF — Seaplane Pilot
Boatswain Joseph C. Cline, USNRF — Seaplane Pilot
Ensign Robert K. Blakely, USNRF — Chief Kite Balloon Pilot
Ensign Theodore K. Cook, USNRF — Kite Balloon Pilot
Ensign Guy R. Drumm, USNRF — Kite Balloon Pilot
Ensign Harry A. Duckworth, USNRF — Kite Balloon Pilot
Ensign Joseph W. Green, USNRF — Kite Balloon Pilot
Ensign Everett L. Hazelton, USNRF — Kite Balloon Pilot
Ensign Earl A. Gardner, USNRF — Kite Balloon Pilot
Ensign Robert K. McConnell, USNRF — Kite Balloon Pilot
Ensign Robert McLean Jr., USNRF — Kite Balloon Pilot
Ensign Alan L. Morse, USNRF — Kite Balloon Pilot
Ensign Russell V. Pollard, USNRF — Kite Balloon Pilot
Ensign William H. Partridge, USNRF — Kite Balloon Pilot
Ensign Gerald T. Stanley, USNRF — Kite Balloon Pilot
Ensign Frank E. Temple, USNRF — Kite Balloon Pilot
Ensign Herbert C. Wing, USNRF — Kite Balloon Pilot
Ensign Paul L. Whitney, USNRF — Kite Balloon Pilot
Ensign Aaron L. VanEmden, USNRF — Kite Balloon Pilot
Lieutenant Commander John C. MacEvitt, USNRF, M.C. — Medical Officer
Lieutenant Wilbourt E. Greenwood, M.C., USN — Medical Department
Lieutenant (j.g.) Charles H. Morris, D.C., USN — Dental Officer
Lieutenant (j.g.) Thomas C. Edrington, P.C., USN — Supply Officer
Pay Clerk Harrison W. McGrath, USN — Supply Department
Pay Clerk Joseph L. Foss, USN — Supply Department
Compliment of enlisted men - 786

III. OPERATIONS

Two three-ton English trucks were received from the Army in February and were used night and day hauling barracks, provisions, and drafts of men, both for this and for other stations in the district. The ground covered by these trucks was very hilly and the roads exceptionally rough. Owing to the demand for transportation, the much needed road repairs often times could not be accomplished. 11 trucks were received from America in March and were immedi-

Liberty engine used in flying boats at NAS Brest; photo was taken on 2 November 1918. (source: 11-SC-30990)

Assembled Curtiss HS-2L flying boats at NAS Brest on 2 November 1918. (source: 11-SC-30985)

ately put into service hauling sand, gravel, cement, lumber, and provisions. All trucks were used discharging the *Bella*, which generally took from six to seven days of continuous work. Half of her cargo was taken to Guipavas, which was about seven miles from the docks. Whenever a truck could be spared it was loaned to the Army for duty. During the month of April the "*Bella*" was discharged twice, the "*Astoria*" once, and an English ship once. During this month 28 trucks and six Ford touring cars were received, assembled, and delivered to other stations. All this was outside of the regular work of the station. Trucks were kept busy hauling road rollers and building roads, in addition to keeping up the regular station work. At this time four Ranier trucks, two Fords, and 30 trailers were received and put into immediate use.

During the month of July 1918 portable barracks, hangars, lumber, sand, gravel, and cement were delivered to Guipavas. There was a constant demand for trucks from the Base Supply Officer, so Navy Base Hospital No. 5 was furnished with the trucks, and working parties were daily detailed to the Army for use in transporting troops from Pontanezen Barracks to La Trinite, where a water main was being laid. One light truck was sent to La Trinite daily at noon with food for these soldiers. During the dry weather in August, one truck was detailed to carry water for the Army. One truck was detailed to the Signal Corps of the Army. Assistance was also rendered in unloading Army materials from ships or storehouses. The Headquarters Supply Officers of both the Aviation Section and the regular Army units were continually supplied with working parties and trucks. The working personnel for the building of three fuel oil tanks of seven million pounds capacity of Lannihon were quartered on the station throughout the time these tanks were being constructed, and working parties were also required to haul material for this construction. All vessels arriving at Brest with material and supplies for the Naval Aviation Service were unloaded by the personnel of this station, and to a large extent those vessels also for regular Naval Units. In many cases these personnel also loaded these vessels. The cargoes of 32 ships were handled within a period of nine months—an average of slightly over three ships a month.

The water transportation of the station, consisting of one 35 foot Captain's Barge, one 40 foot motor sailor, one 35 foot motor sailor, one 30 foot motor sailor, and one 24 foot dory were used for towing planes and large barges, discharging ships in the harbor, and for standing by for flying.

Assemblying Curtiss HS-1L and HS-2L flying boats at NAS Brest on 2 November 1918. (source 11-SC-30986)

Assemblying a Curtiss H-16 at NAS Brest.

A Curtiss H-16 at NAS Brest. Personnel are not identified.

A Curtiss flying boat starting out on a patrol from NAS Brest. (source: Naval Historical Center)

On 21 August 1918 the only fatality at this station occurred. An HS-1 seaplane, piloted by Ensign R.F. Clark, USNRF (Naval Aviator No. 196), with Ensign A.E. Boorse (Naval Aviator No. 333) as second pilot and W.F. Redman, MM2c(A), USN, as observer, while on a test flight in the harbor, fell about 400 feet to the water, out of control. All of the crew were killed and the plane wrecked. The cause of the accident was never known.

The assembly of the first H-16 plane was begun on 24 September and was completed in six days; and on 13 October the first HS-2 plane was flown and found satisfactory. On 29 October 1918 regular patrol and convoy work was inaugurated.

A complete 2 kW shore station radio set was received, and the radio personnel immediately began to assist the Public Works Department to build the radio station, which was completed on 31 October. The receiving apparatus was installed and made ready for service. Installation of French sets was commenced on three HS-2 planes, the first of which was ready for testing 3 November. The results were satisfactory, but difficulty was experienced in receiving signals on account of the noise of the motor and the rush of the air. A Simon 1/2 kW transmitter was installed on an H-16 plane by 15 November.

On the night of 1 November a windstorm arose, causing a great deal of damage along the waterfront. The whole force was called out and stood by the hangars all night. No planes were damaged upon this occasion, but on 3 November, in another storm, two planes were slightly damaged.

On 5 November, two planes of the HS-2 type were flown to NAS Killingholme after being assembled at NAS Brest.

On 6 November a HS-1 seaplane, piloted by Ensign R.T. Whitney, USNRF (Naval Aviator No. 393), with Ensign C.K. Schwarar, USNRF (Naval Aviator No. 767), as second pilot, and F.J. O'Rorke, E2c(r), as observer, made a forced landing at sea while on a delivery flight to NAS Ile Tudy. The crew was saved, but the plane was totally wrecked.

The last plane delivered from this station was flown to NAS l'Aber Vrach on 12 November. Up to the time when the armistice

Curtiss HS flying boats at NAS Brest in June 1918.

NAS Brest with various Curtiss flying boats in the hangars. (source: Naval Historical Center)

Enlarging NAS Brest. (source: Naval Historical Center)

was signed, 53 HS-1 and 11 HS-2 planes had been assembled, tested, and delivered from this station.

The photographic personnel remodeled, with the help of the Public Works Department, a certain portion of the old general storeroom into two dark rooms and a workshop. Photographic work was started on 13 November, and photographers were sent to l'Aber Vrach, Guipavas, and Treguier to take official pictures of those stations.

The first Kite Balloon detachment of 40 men and two officers with 12 balloons and accessories arrived in Brest on 4 July 1918 from the U.S. Naval Air Station at Castletownbere, Ireland. Arrangements were made with the French Kite Balloon station at Lanninon, adjoining the U.S. Station, for storeroom and space for housing one inflated balloon. The French also agreed to furnish enough gas for probable needs and to share their transferring and field winch.

The first American balloon (Goodrich type "M") to be flown in France was operated from a French trawler, with a French winch, on 11 July. Several trips of a day's duration were made successfully. Before kite balloons could be operated from destroyers it was necessary to install marionette stands, fair leads, etc., and in some cases the mainmast had to be cut down, so that it would not be fouled by the balloon cable. This work was made possible by the assistance rendered by the destroyers U.S.S. *Prometheus* and *Bridgeport*.

The first trial trip on a destroyer was made on 20 July aboard the destroyer U.S.S. *Cushing*. The Lawrence-Scott electric winch and the balloon equipment functioned properly. After several transfers had been effected by means of a hauling-in line and the Jacob's ladder, the balloon, with four officers and seven men, was put aboard the *Cushing* for a five-day trip. Because of bad weather observation work was possible for only a few hours, but much useful experience was gained. Several other successful balloon trips were made shortly. On 14 August a trip with the Erickson was favored with perfect weather, and 64 hours observation work was carried on from the basket during the 100 hours at sea. On 18 August a trial trip on the U.S.S. *Sigourney* to try out the Lidgewood steam winch was very successful. On 13 November a trial trip on the U.S.S. *Benham* to try out the "R" type of balloon and the Mumford steam winch was also successful. It was decided that a balloon with nose ballooned was not best for use at sea, and that a Mumford winch was best for destroyer use.

On 19 October the balloons and equipment were moved from the French to the U.S. hangar adjoining, and a gas line was rigged between the French plantand and the U.S. hangar. Approximately 300,000 cubic feet of gas were used in inflating and topping up.

On 21 October classes of instruction for enlisted men were started in the following subjects: Theory of Ballooning; Meteorology; Navigation; Navy Rules and Regulations; Winches; Telephones; Hydrogen; Seamanship; First Aid; Signaling (wig-wag, buzzer, semaphore, and blinker); Infantry Drills; and Manual of Arms. These classes were taught by the officers, and were continued until the men were ordered to the United States. A great deal of experimenting in wire rigging for baskets and other suspensions, dropping of parachutes, etc., was carried on successfully. A number of hours were put in with the field winch (le Dion Bouton), which, on account of its location, could be used only on the days when the French did not fly. The Sykes Petrol winch and an old transferring winch were later received, and were completely overhauled before being used. At the time of demobilization, five destroyers were ready for Kite Balloon operations.

Aircraft activities and NAS Brest are summarized in Table O-2.

IV. DEMOBILIZATION

The station was placed out of commission on 15 February 1919, the material having been disposed of and the personnel transferred in accordance with instructions received from Headquarters. The station was transferred to the French Navy at the net price of 692,570 francs as agreed upon by a joint commission of French and American Officers arranging the details of this transaction.

Vice Admiral H.B. Wilson at NAS Brest on 22 October 1918. (source: 11-SC-39881

TABLE O-2
NAS Brest, Finistere, France
U.S. Naval Air Station (Seaplane)
From 3 August 1918 To 11 November 1918

Wk. End.	Flights Made	Total Knots	Flying Time (Hr.)	Suitable Flying Time (Hr.)	Aircraft on Station	Aircraft in Comsn	Flying Personnel
3 August	4	240	3:40	—	73 HS-1 3 H-16	0	18
10 August	8	240	4:00	16	71 HS-1 3 HS-2	0	25
17 August	29	780	12:52	54	71 HS-1 3 HS-2	1 HS-1	19
24 August	18	450	7:07	32	69 HS-1 3 H-16	2 HS-1	18
31 August	5	120	1:45	14	70 HS-1 3 H-16	1 HS-1	18
7 September	12	330	5:28	6	67 HS-1 3 H-16	2 HS-1	19
14 September	12	330	5:28	—	64 HS-1 6 H-16	0	20
21 September	12	240	3:44	—	59 HS-1 6 H-16	1 HS-1	18
28 September	17	720	12:00	26	54 HS-1 14 HS-2	1 HS-1	22
5 October	14	480	7:48	22	47 HS-1 14 HS-2 14 H-16	0	21
12 October	3	60	1:00	—	27 HS-1 12 HS-2 14 H-16	0	24
19 October	10	390	6:00	12	20 HS-1 14 HS-2 14 II-16	2 HS-2	27
26 October	17	5990	10:07	42	16 HS-1 14 HS-2 14 H-16	1 HS-1 2 HS-2	34
2 November	9	520	8:32	10	15 HS-1 14 HS-2 14 II-16	3 IIS-2	13
9 November	25	1565	26:43	20	4 HS-1 12 HS-2 14 H-16	3 HS-2	23
11 November	18	—-	4:59	—	4 HS-1 12 HS-2 14 H-16	3 HS-2	23
Total	211	7355	125:53	264			

Notes:

[1] Much of the material in this Appendix is taken from the document entitled *History of U.S. Naval Aviation in Foreign Service, French Unit, 1917 and 1918*

Appendix P: NAS Paimboeuf[1]

I. CONSTRUCTION

When the U.S. Naval Air Station at Paimboeuf was taken over from the French on 1 March 1918, the equipment was very primitive. It consisted of a steel-skeleton canvas covered hangar, a gas plant, a nourrice, electrical and shipfitters' shop, a radio shack with two 80 ft. towers, five barracks, officers' quarters, a mess hall, an office building, a sick bay, three storage shacks, a galley, a bake shop, a brig, a wash house, two concrete dugouts, and a concrete storage tank for water. A gasoline motor on the station furnished a limited amount of electric light.

Work was immediately begun on a drainage system, roads, repairs, and general station improvements. The location of the new hangar was laid out, and grading was begun. The detail and construction equipment consisted of 30 men, 50 shovels, 6 wooden wheelbarrows, 10 clay picks, and two narrow-gauge dump cars, with 16 pieces of track. Two French trucks were used for hauling sand and rock for the road building. Excavating was begun for the laying of a four-inch sewer pipe in a ditch in front of the station, as the French had arranged for the sewage in an open trench on both sides of the road.

In April a 650 ton cargo of lumber and bolts for the new hangar arrived on the S.S. *Bella*. The French began the framing of the doors for the small hangar, and six men of the naval personnel were loaned to assist. Trusses were assembled, and frames for two new barracks were erected. The digging of a well was begun, but was abandoned when water was not struck at ten feet. Most of the time of the personnel, during this month, was given to the unloading of lumber, rock, cement, and other materials, and to the bettering of the living conditions.

In May the excavation of the hangar piers and the grading was continued. A third well was dug 300 yards southwest of the camp, and a good spring found. A 750-ton cargo of lumber and American tools was received, and a temporary warehouse was erected on the hangar site. With the completion of two new barracks, all the men were comfortably housed on the station. On 10 May the Y.M.C.A. hut was commenced. A pump shed was built and the pump installed, and a pipeline was laid from the location of the gashouse to the new hangar site. The first hangar piers were poured the last day of May, ten cubic yards of concrete being mixed and poured by hand.

Aerial view of NAS Paimbeouf.

Aerial view of NAS Paimbeouf.

Dirigible hangar under construction at NAS Paimbeouf. (source: 80 HAG-5G-5)

Dirigible hangar at NAS Paimbeouf.

In June, the first work done was the assembling of parts for the new hangar frame, and the unpacking and assembling of Dixie barracks. During this month, continual flying hampered construction in some measure, but the work later progressed more smoothly because of the arrival of new drafts of men for construction duty. By 27 June the first great hangar frame was assembled.

On 1 July Civil Engineer J.H. Knox, USNRF, reported and assumed the duties of Public Works Officer for the station. The rigging on the new hangar was immediately begun, and the barracks were hastily erected to accommodate a new draft of 149 men. Four cars of lumber arrived at this time, and also a nine cubic foot power concrete mixer supplanted the old hand mixing process, and thus greatly facilitated the work. The well was cased with concrete, and a mess hall, three Dixie barracks, a galley, a dispensary annex, and a cold storage house were completed. On 24 July the first frame of the new hangar was raised in place, and before the end of the month three trusses for the hangar were erected and 50 percent of the hangar lumber was framed.

The only mishap during the entire construction of this station was the breaking of arch No. 13 of the new hangar on 2 August on account of a faulty casting in the hoist clutch. The hangar progressed rapidly at this stage, as all available labor was concentrated on this work. A brick bake oven was built during this month, with a capacity of 90 loafs, the new well was deepened to increase the flow, and additional barracks, a mess hall, and a warehouse were built.

In the month of September, the work on the hangar was continued, and an aerial hydrogen line to Ursine 3 was commenced. Fifteen hundred feet of piping was laid from the well to the camp, a new coal bin was built of handmade cement blocks, and work was begun transforming an old Chateau on a hill into an Aerography Bureau. The first two avant-porte windshields were completed, but were never raised. The new water tower was finally secured in its new position near the fire pump house, and the pipeline was connected. The doors of the small hangar, upon which the French had been working since April, were now completed with the assistance of naval personnel.

Hydrogen was furnished by one 600 cubic meter semi-portable ferro-silicon plant. The adjacent chemical plant supplied approxi-

Dirigible hangar under construction at NAS Paimbeouf. (source: Naval Historical Center)

Zodiac Vedette at NAS Paimbeouf.

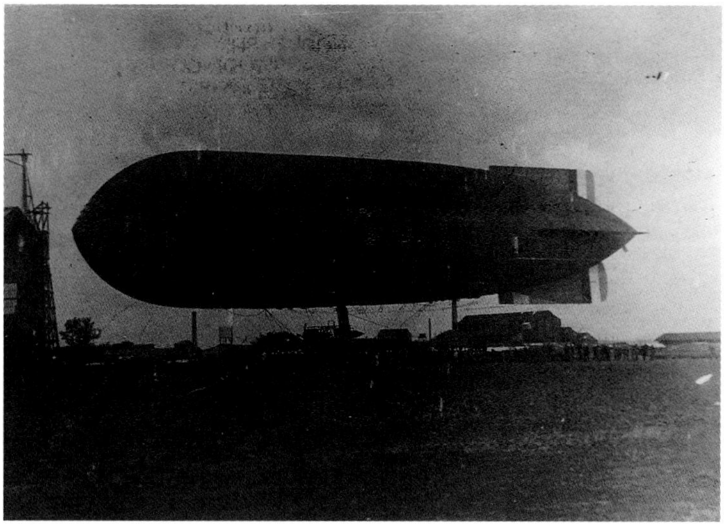

Dirigible AT-13 at NAS Paimbeouf. (source 80 HAG-5K-2)

mately 600 cubic meters of hydrogen gas in cylinders per day. A two-inch pipeline was installed between this plant and the nourrice to eliminate the handling of cylinders. The plans called for the erection of a new hydrogen building and sludge tanks to accommodate both the old and new semi-portable ferro-silicon plants, but although the new plant had been erected on foundations on 30 October, and the floor completed, no work was done on the building or tanks. The new six-inch cast iron piping was about 60% completed at the close of operations. The liquid from the temporary tank ran directly to the sea through a trench, and the same procedure was planned for the new sludge tanks, the solid being buried on the station ground.

During October a new 10,000-gallon water tower was erected, and ditches were dug for the station sewage system and for the laying of fire-pipe line to the Loire River. The 206 avant-porte footings were completed on 19 October. The coarse rock used in their construction, as well as that for the roads used in their construction and for the roads in general, was broken by two old Frenchmen and an old Frenchwoman. This is an example of the difficulties encountered. Three old sections of the hangar roof were replaced with new, and the roofing of the hangar with corrugated iron slabs and asbestos shingles was commenced. In November this work was nearly finished, but was delayed on account of materials.

On 11 November orders were received from Headquarters to discontinue all construction except that necessary for the health and comfort of the personnel.

Continual operating had hindered steady construction work. The station was considerably isolated by inadequate and uncertain transportation, shipments were long delayed, and the whole was complicated by a radical increase in the building program contemplated by the French. Particular difficulty was experienced with sewage and drainage problems. Choosing petty officers and selecting men according to their abilities and experience was relatively simple, and to keep up their enthusiasm was a matter of understanding; therefore, in spite of bad weather and a lack of equipment, the work progressed, carried always ahead of schedule by the wonderful stamina, willingness, and spirit of the men in the service.

II. PERSONNEL

The occupation of the station at Paimboeuf by U.S. Naval personnel was very gradual. On 10 November 1917, Lieutenant F.P. Culbert, USN (Naval Aviator No. 94), was assigned to the station for actual flying with the French. On 30 November the first American detachment of three officers and 17 men reported to Lieutenant

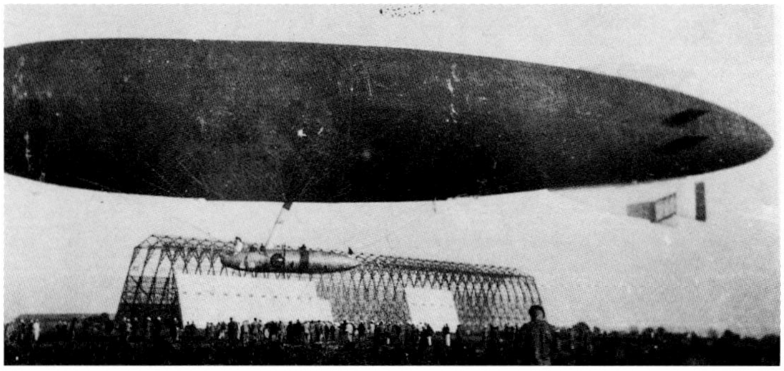

"Capt. Caussin" ascending at NAS Paimbeouf. (source: Naval Historical Center)

Dirigible AT-13 at NAS Paimbeouf. (source 80 HAG-5K-2)

Culbert for duty. On 4 January 1918 Lieutenant Commander L.H. Maxfield, USN (Naval Aviator No. 17), arrived from Rochefort and took over the command of the American detachment on the station. With the arrival of a draft of 28 men from Rochefort and 64 men from Moutchic, the Americans began to supplant the French personnel, and from time to time, as further drafts were received, additional French personnel were withdrawn for other purposes.

When the station was commissioned as a U.S. Naval Air Station of 1 March 1918, 205 enlisted men and the following officers were on board:

Lieutenant Commander L.H. Maxfield, USN	Commanding Officer (Pilot)
Lieutenant F.P. Culbert, USN	Executive Officer (Pilot)
Ensign A.B. Talbot, USNRF	Commanding AT-1
Ensign C.G. Little, USNRF	Commanding VZ-3
Ensign W.P. Whitehouse, USNRF	Meteorology and Radio Officer (Pilot)
Ensign R.M. Strader, USNRF	Gas Plant and Hangar Officer (Pilot)
Ensign A.D. Brewer, USNRF	Engineer Officer (Pilot)
Ensign P. Delano, USNRF	Watch Officer (Pilot)
Assistant Surgeon W.R. Taylor, M.C.	Medical Officer
Assistant Paymaster T.A Durnham, USN	Supply Officer
Pay Clerk E.G. Ross, USN	Supply Department
Civil Engineer G.D. Ellsworth, USN	Public Works Officer

On 5 February 1918 Mr. W. Hammond reported as a Y.M.C.A. Secretary. The first moving pictures were shown in old No. 1 Barracks on 20 March. On 4 April the station force planted a vegetable garden, which later proved very successful, in an effort to assist in the movement to economize food and soil. On 4 May "Uncle Joe" Huntington arrived at Paimboeuf to replace Mr. Hammond, and soon won the regard of everybody. The Y.M.C.A. hut was opened on 18 June, and the opportunity for recreation which it offered brought an immediate change in the aspect of the camp. Several vaudeville performances were given, many evening talks, and at times moving pictures were shown. On 19 July, when "Uncle Joe" Huntington left the station, he also left many friends. Mr. W.A. Hearn took up his duties of serving the men. On 25 July the famous "Carola Band" visited the station, and the concert given was greatly appreciated. On 27 July a professional hypnotist gave an interesting entertainment. On 1 September the Fromentine Jazz Band gave a performance, and on 8 October the jazz band organized on the station gave its first concert. On 28 October Mr. J.C. Glover replaced Mr. Hearn.

Dirigibles at NAS Paimbeouf. Zodiac Vedette is closest to the camera. (source 80 HAG-5K-4)

The station baseball team was a unit of great interest to both the officers and men. The first game played against the Le Croisic team, on 23 March, was won 5-4. On 12 May, Le Croisic defeated Paimboeuf 7-3. On 19 May, in a game against the Fromentine team, the Paimboeufians were victors 2-0. The first game played against the "Amex-League" was with the 17th Engineers, and was won 5-0, but on 2 June, the 19th Engineers defeated Paimboeuf 13-5. On 10 June, a successful game was played against the 25th Engineers, 5-3, and also on 16 June against Company M, 14-6. On the 23rd Paimboeuf defeated Base Hospital No. 101 by a score of 6-1. 7 July a game was won from the 17th Engineers 3-1, and on 21 July the Reception Park won a game 5-4. 18 July Company M was again defeated 10-0. On 25 July the team lost to Le Croisic, 10-3, but on the 25th defeated Le Croisic in a doubleheader, 4-0 and 2-1. The Naval Battery team made a victory on 2 August, 6-1.

On 28 July a little child fell from the wharf at Paimboeuf into the Loire River at a point where the river is quite rapid. Herman Marcus, Csmthlc, USN, happened to be working nearby, and by jumping in after her succeeded in rescuing her. The Commander U.S. Naval Forces in Europe commended him for his bravery.

The first edition of the "Gas Valve," a single sheet semimonthly periodical prepared by the station personnel, was published on 16 August. The second edition was issued in two sheets and contained cartoons of station activities. This paper was very popular, and proved a successful expression of the life of the camp.

On 17 August the Assistant Secretary of the Navy visited the station and made a flight in the "AT-l."

On 3 September the first fatality occurred at the station. The motors of the "AT-13" were being tested for flight, in the presence of three officers and the crew when N.H. Lamport, Sea.2C, USNRF, a member of the crew, intent upon some errand, ran around the nacelle and into the propeller. He was instantly killed, and was buried at the Base Hospital Cemetery, St. Nazaire.

On 16 October, N.C. Vinson, Sea.2c, USNRF, was thrown from a truck which was rounding a sharp turn in the road and fell on his head, sustaining a fracture of the skull. Five days later he died from the effects of the injury. On the same day J.A. Junz, SF2c, USNRF, died from a lingering malaria in the Base Hospital at St. Nazaire. The military funerals of both were held on 21 October in that town.

On 26 September C.T. Lupien, Sea.2c, USNRF, was commended by the French Commander of Aerial Patrols of the Loire Section for his ability and industry in aiding the French in the construction of the small hangar.

On 28 October, the Commander-in-Chief of the Atlantic Fleet, with Staff, visited the station, and on 2 November, the Director of Naval Aeronautics arrived for an inspection.

On 11 November the officers attached to the station were as follows:

Lieutenant F.P. Culbert, USN Commanding Officer (Pilot)
Lieutenant (j.g.) B.L. Moulthrop, USNRF Executive Officer (Pilot)
Lieutenant Commander J.P. Norfleet, USN Attached temporarily for inspection of dirigibles and methods of operation
Lieutenant (j.g.) R.M. Strader, USNRF Captain P-4 (AT-13)
Lieutenant (j.g.) W.P. Whitehouse, USNRF Chief Pilot
Lieutenant (j.g.) J.J. Quinn, USNRF Intelligence Department
Lieutenant (j.g.) M.Q. Corbett, USNRF Second Officer P-4
Ensign A.C. Burnham, USNRF Captain P-5 (VZ-13)
Ensign D.H. Merrill, USNRF Captain P-3 (VZ-7)
Ensign M.J. McDermott, USNRF Junior Officer P-3
Ensign T.R. Punnett, USNRF Junior Officer P-4
Ensign R.R. Norris, USNRF Junior Officer P-4
Ensign A. Gardner, USNRF Pilot, Editor of the paper ("Gas Valve")
Ensign J.B. Anderson, USNRF Aerographic Officer
Ensign R.F. Taylor, USNRF Hydrogen Gas and Hangar Officer
Ensign A. Byork, USNRF Assistant Hydrogen Officer
Ensign A.B. Leonard, USNRF Intelligence Officer
Ensign H.L. Goldspeed, USNRF Divisional Officer (Pilot)
Ensign E.B. Park, USNRF Divisional Officer (Pilot)
Ensign R.L. Piper, USNRF Ordnance Officer (Pilot)
Ensign T.I. Morrow, USNRF Divisional Officer (Pilot)
Ensign F.L. Moorman, USNRF Intelligence Department
Ensign J.S.F. McCormick, USNRF Transportation Officer (Pilot)
Lieutenant W.R. Taylor, M.C., USNRF Medical Officer
Lieutenant J.L. Pierce, M.C., USNRF Medical Officer
Lieutenant J.L. Durham, Pay Corps, USN Supply Officer
Pay Clerk W.P. Pebworth, USNRF Supply Department
Lieutenant J.H .Knox, Civil Eng. Crops., USNRF Public Works Officer
Machinist (A) F.K. Tone, USN Engineer Officer
Machinist (T) C.M. Wilson, USNRF Assistant Engineer Officer

The compliment of enlisted men on the station at this time was 377 divided as follows:

Department of Public Works	169
Supply Department	73
Engineering Department	70
Seaman Guard	42
Ship's Crew	37

The remaining men were divided among the Hospital Corps., Aerography Department, Radio Department, and the different offices.

On Thanksgiving Day a suitable celebration was held. Many officers and a large number of soldiers of the 309th Engineers, St. Nazaire, Red Cross nurses, and Y.M.C.A. girls from St. Nazaire, Nantes, and Savenay were invited, and almost the entire French Population of Paimboeuf and the surrounding country attended in full force. The entire station force of Le Croisic was invited to settle the old rivalry in athletics by a cross-country race and a football game before the celebration. Paimboeuf scored a victory, winning the race 12-35, and defeating Le Croisic's football team by a 22-0 score. During the afternoon the band from the 309th Engineers performed in the big hangar, and moving pictures were shown in the Y.M.C.A. hut. At dusk, the Kaiser's effigy was burned in a huge bonfire, and the evening ended with a vaudeville performance by the personnel of the station.

III. OPERATION

On 2 December 1917 permission was obtained for Lt. Culbert, one Reserve Officer, and two enlisted men to receive flying instruction in French ships at this station, and the first preparations were made for the taking over of the station by the Americans. On 20 January a portion of the hangar roof was blown off during a storm, and U.S. Naval personnel made the necessary repairs under dangerous conditions, in order to prevent damage to the dirigible housed in the hangar. This work was highly commended by the French authorities. On 30 January an Astra Torres dirigible, called the "AT-l," arrived from Rochefort with Americans comprising part of the crew, and on 3 February a Zodiac Vedette dirigible called the "VZ-3" was transferred to Paimboeuf from the French station at Guipavas. The first patrols were made on 24 February 1918.

The station was gradually ceded to the Americans, and the period of transition from French to American was one of dual control. By the cessation on 1 March 1918, of the "AT-l" the U.S. Naval Aviation Forces, Foreign Service, obtained its first dirigible, and, on the same date, the American flag was hoisted over the hangar with that of the French. The first flight of the "AT-l" under American control was made on 3 March. On 20 March the "VZ-3" was ceded, and at this time the French Commander of Aerial Patrols of the Loire Section, Commandant Vaschalde, and the U.S. Naval District Commander, Captain T.P. Magruder, paid a formal visit to the station, and the control passed to American hands. The following day, the first flight of the "VZ-3" under American control was made.

On 12 April the "AT-l" was deflated and a new bag was substituted. The entire operation took 43 days, one day less than the same operation in the hands of the trained French crew at Rochefort.

On 17 April, the "VZ-3" was transferred to Rochefort, in order to prepare the hangar to receive the French dirigible "Capitaine Caussin," which had been sent to Paris for repairs. This ship arrived the following day, with American officers in the crew.

NAS Paimbeouf football team. Personnel are not identified.

On 24 April, the Third Liberty Loan Drive was terminated, and the subscriptions taken at Paimboeuf placed this station in second place, in proportion to the number of men on board.

On 25 April an accident occurred to the "Capitaine Caussin" during a patrol flight. A gas valve failed to close after valving, and as the gas escaped the ship became increasingly heavy, lost pressure, became uncontrollable, and dove into the sea from 100 meters. Two members of the crew were thrown into the water in their heavy flying suits, and would have drowned had not Lieutenant Commander Maxfield and Lieutenant F.P. Culbert (Naval Aviator No. 94) jumped from the ship and aided them until rescued. The "Capitaine Caussin," under the guidance of Ensign Delano and the French Commandant Leroy, drifted to the beach and was dismantled by the crew, being later packed on trucks and returned to the station. The behavior of the entire crew in this emergency was highly commendable. Maxfield and Culbert each received a French Life Saving Medal from the French Minister of Marine, and Maxfield was commended by the Secretary of the Navy and awarded a gold life saving medal. Culbert was also commended by the Secretary of the Navy. On 1 May, when the hangar had been prepared, the "VZ-3" was returned from Rochefort.

On 5 June, a fire broke out in Ursine #3, and the whole powder factory was in danger of explosion. The fire was extinguished with the aid of the Paimboeuf station force, and commendation was received from the French civil authorities. This is only one instance of assistance given to the civilian population by the personnel of this station.

On 7 June the establishment of an aerographic center at Paimboeuf was begun. On 8 June the "VZ-7" was transferred to Paimboeuf from Paris. On the 9th satisfactory tests of a submarine listening device were made aboard the "AT-1." On 18 June the "AT-1" made a successful landing in a 16-mph wind, without drag-rope, as the rope was broken in the first attempt to land. Later in the month the same ship made a 25 2/3-hour flight, the longest on record in France for a ship of its type. Lieutenant Culbert and Ensigns M.P. Delano (Naval Aviator No. 104), A.O. Brewer (Naval Aviator No. 103), and T.E. McCracken (Naval Aviator No. betwen 606 and 609), as well as the enlisted men of the crew were commended for this performance by the French Minister of Marine. The "VZ-3" and the "VZ-7" broke records for the Vedette type by making patrol flights of nine hours.

It was in this month that a conference was held at this station consisting of the commanding officers of the coastal stations to draw up a plan for the internal organization of a Naval Air Station. This plan was put into practice at all the stations, and unity in their organization was obtained.

On 25 July the inflation of the bag of the "Capitaine Caussin" was begun. On 27 August it was found that the fabric was unsafe, and the bag was deflated and returned to Paris.

On 30 August the "AT-13" was transferred from Paris to Paimboeuf and was added to the station equipment. During the first week in August the "AT-1" was surveyed, and thereafter was used only on instruction flights. On 10 September this ship was deflated to be sent to the United Stated. On 26 September the "VZ-3" was transferred to Rochefort and retransferred to the French, it having become no longer serviceable for patrol.

During August Ensign A. Gardner (Naval Aviator No. 1093) made 17 flights in the "VZ-7," covering 164 hours, 55 minutes flying time, including record patrols, and received a citation for this excellent work. He and his crew were again commended by Vice Admiral Aubry, Commander in Chief of the Prefet Maritime, for having flown 71 hours during the month of September, thus tripling the best French record for this type of ship.

On 1 October a submarine attacked the "AT-13." The "AT-13" (P-4) left the station at 0715 hours to patrol in the northern sector. At 1100 hours it picked up the southbound convoy from Brest and conducted it to port, and about dusk, with some available hours of patrol still left she steered for the northbound La Pallice convoy, shooting two shots on the way from her 47 mm gun at a rock off Haedik for practice. On the second shot the firing spring broke. At 1730 hours she picked up the La Pallice-Quiberon convoy. The following official report of subsequent events is quoted: "Ship circled convoy, then saw two storms from the north, northeastward, and left convoy to dodge between the storms. At 18 hours Greenwich, sighted suspicious object to the northward. At about a mile distant object was made out to be enemy submarine, which immediately opened fire. Shrapnel used. Ship turned and headed for convoy. Thirteen other bursts near the ship. Apparently no damage done. Dirigible rejoined convoy, returning to station at 20 hour 20 minutes."

The camp was thrown into a turmoil of excitement, which fostered the long patrols of the month. The touch of real fighting was there, but though the ships faithfully searched every scrap of coastline during the remainder of the month, no submarine was again encountered.

On 3 October the inflation of the new bag of the "Capitaine Caussin" was begun and was finished in forty hours, this work establishing a record. Successful trial flights were made during the month.

On 5 October Lieutenant Culbert assumed the duties of Commanding Officer, when Lieutenant Commander Maxfield was detached for duty in America after an inspection trip in Italy and England.

On 19 October, after the Fourth Liberty Loan Drive, it was announced that $54,200 had been subscribed from this station, an average of $99.81 per man. On this date the "Capitaine Caussin" was transferred to Guipavas for operation by the personnel of the U.S. Naval Air Station at that site. On 28 October, a seaman guard of 42 men was established, and the station was divided into nine posts.

The new Vedette, the "VZ-13," was transferred from Paris on the 25th and became part of the station equipment. She flew every day thereafter until 5 November, when on returning heavy from patrol after dark she crashed into a tree and had to be deflated. No one was injured in the crash.

During the month of October the station had just begun to strike its pace in flying. Out of 21 flying days during the month the "P-4" flew 20, totaling 200 hours 30 minutes. This record was only beaten by Mediterranean station Aubagne that totaled 222 hours. 29 October the "P-4" made a flight of 15 hours, eight of which were spent with convoy, and the following day left again on a flight of 12 hours 10 minutes. For this excellent work, Lieutenant (j.g.) R.M. Strader, USNRF, the crew of the "P-4," and the Commanding Officer of the station were commended in a letter by Vice Admiral Aubry, the Commander-in-Chief of the Perfect Maritime.

With the signing of the Armistice the two Vedettes were deflated for shipment to the United States. The larger ship, the "AT-13," was kept in commission until December when she flew to Guipavas to form part of the escort of the President on 13 December. Then on 16 December she returned to Paimboeuf and was deflated.

IV. DEMOBILIZATION

On 28 January 1919, on the completion of demobilization this station was placed out of commission and reverted back to the French Navy. A commission convened on 14 January, and with the advice of the Commandant des Patrovilles of the Loire District arranged for the transfer. The steel and canvas, one small hangar, and also the French barrack building were taken over by the French. The American camp buildings were taken over by the U.S. Army. The large American dirigible hangar was sold to a French civilian contractor.

TABLE P-1
NAS Paimboeuf, Loire-Inferieure, France
U.S. Naval Air Station (Dirigible)
From 2 March 1918 To 11 November 1918

Wk. End.	**Flights Made**	**Total Knots**	**Flying Time (Hr.)**	**Suitable Flying Time (Hr.)**	**Aircraft on Station**	**Aircraft in Comsn**	**Flying Personnel**
2 March	—	—	—	—	—	—	18
9 March	7	1217	40:20	30	1 AT	1 AT	18
16 March	8	1320	44:07	60	1 AT 1 VZ	1 AT 1 VZ	18
23 March	3	535	20:18	8	1 AT 1 VZ	1 AT 1 VZ	17
30 March	2	196	7:35	10	1 AT 1 VZ	1 AT 1 VZ	16
6 April	4	570	21:17	25	1 AT 1 VZ	1 AT 1 VZ	16
13 April	3	172	5:22	6	1 AT 1 VZ	1 AT 1 VZ	16
20 April	3	750	17:45	21	1 AT 1 CM	1 CM	15
27 April	3	940	24:30	40	1 AT 1 CM	1 CM	24
4 May	3	207	9:00	10	1 AT 1 VZ	1 VZ	17
11 May	6	242	11:55	13	1 At 1 VZ	1 AT 1 VZ	17
18 May	2	231	6:47	41	1 AT 1 VZ	1 VZ	22
25 May	3	38	1:10	41	1 AT 1 VZ	1 VZ	22
1 June	6	189	5:34	10	1 AT 1 VZ	1 VZ	22
8 June	8	1002	28:40	24	1 AT 1 AT	2 VZ 2 VZ	22
15 June	10	3098	71:22	35	1 AT 1 AT	2 VZ 2 VZ	25
22 June	6	1465	443:45	20	1 AT 1 AT	2 VZ 2 VZ	25

29 June	10	2950	85:01	36	1 AT 1 AT	2 VZ 2 VZ	25
6 July	8	2276	65:03	30	1 AT 2 VZ 1 CM	1 At 2 VZ	24
13 July	3	1770	28:45	10	1 AT 2 VZ 1 CM	1 At 2 VZ	24
20 July	6	995	27:51	20	1 AT 2 VZ 1 CM	1 At 2 VZ	35
27 July	6	1015	36:37	30	1 AT 2 VZ	1 At 2 VZ	38
3 August	8	918	30:49	30	1 AT 2 VZ	—	30
10 August	15	1359	38:32	30	1 AT 2 VZ 1 CM	1 At 2 VZ	30
17 August	24	2357	86:332	55	1 AT 2 VZ 1 CM	1 AT 2 VZ	30
24 August	9	1396	63:43	50	1 AT 2 VZ 1 CM	1 AT 2 VZ	 29
31 August	7	2210	68:42	50	2 AT 2 VZ	1 AT 2 VZ	29
7 September	6	1095	41:55	35	2 AT 2 VZ	1 AT 1 VZ	37
14 September	4	1235	39:40	20	2 AT 2 VZ	1 AT 1 VZ	38
21 September	3	725	22:15	25	1 AT 2 VZ	1 AT 1 AT	40
28 September	7	1040	34:20	25	1 AT 1 VZ	1 AT 1 VZ	38
5 October	10	2338	79:25	54	1 AT 1 VZ 1 CM	1 AT 1 VZ	35
12 October	3	425	17:30	10	1 AT 1 VZ 1 CM	—	35
19 October	10	1513	56:55	40	1 AT 1 VZ 1 CM	1 AT 1 VZ	35
26 October	11	2925	96:25	50	1 AT 2 VZ	1 AT 2 VZ	38
2 November	19	4586	152:45	55	1 AT 2 VZ	1 AT 2 VZ	35
9 November	9	2266	74:48	37	1 AT 2 VZ	1 AT 2 VZ	36
11 November	4	995	31:10	20	1 AT 2 VZ	1 AT 2 VZ	36
TOTAL	257	48561	1538:30	1106			

Notes:

[1] Much of the material contained in this appendix is taken from the document entitled *History of Naval Aviation, Foreign Service, French Unit, 1917 and 1918*

Appendix Q: NAS Dunkirk

The concept of a U.S. Naval Air Station at Dunkirk can be traced back to 18 June 1917 when Lieutenant Kenneth Whiting proposed the site for an American air base. At that time Whiting had in mind a base for naval land planes whose target would be the German submarine facilities at Zeebrugge, Ostend, and Bruges. The concept of naval land planes performing tactical bombing activities on the Western Front was sufficiently radical at that time that nothing was done about establishing a base at Dunkirk for several months. During this period the scope of activities and the charter of the proposed station were modified.

Construction by the French on an American seaplane station started on 20 July; by 25 September barracks and other facilities had been completed. The first plane arrived on 1 October. Dunkirk was thus the first U.S. NAS established in France. The layout of the station was such that a fieldstone quay about 200 yards in length, and approximately 10-15 ft. in height jutted out into the English Channel. The area between the quay and the shore established the takeoff and landing areas for the aircraft based at the station. Sitting on top of the quay were wooden derrick-cranes, with a vertical mast imbedded in the quay, each with a boom hinged at the base of the mast. Each aircraft was stored astride a two-wheeled wooden dolly, each bearing a 3-digit number, usually matching the side number of the aircraft. The derrick-cranes picked up the aircraft from either the quay or the water and moved them from one location to the other. Approximately 50 yards inshore from the edge of the quay were hangars, each with a bowstring-arched roof. In the fall of 1917 Lieutenant Godfrey deC. Chevalier, USN, under orders from Captain H.I. Cone, arrived at Dunkirk with 100 men and with orders to establish a seaplane station at that location, whose objective was the support of the British and French aviation authorities in their patrol of the English Channel and the North Sea. When the British suggested a U.S. takeover of their station at Dunkirk Captain Cone agreed. It was intended that the station would have the same anti-submarine patrol duties as those assigned to the other American naval air stations in France and Ireland. On 24 November Lieutenant Artemus L. Gates, USNRF (Naval Aviator No. 65), arrived at Dunkirk with some 50 enlisted men. On 1 January 1918 Lieutenant Chevalier (Naval Aviator No. 7) was able to place NAS Dunkirk in commission, even though there were no seaplane pilots yet assigned to the station. The transition from a British base to an American base was expedited by the fact that Vice Admiral Sir R.H.S. Bacon, the English Commander of the naval activities in the English Channel, did not feel that flying boats were suitable craft for submarine patrol. It was for this reason that, on 1 Febru-

Hangars and aircraft at NAS Dunkirk.

Hanriot HD-2 at NAS Dunkirk.

Gun pits at NAS Dunkirk. The use of the German cross is of interest.

Ensign George Clark Moseley in his Hanriot HD-2 on the seawall at NAS Dunkirk. Moseley enlisted in the NNV on 6 April 1917. He was discharged in June 1917 and enlisted in the Foreign Legion on 10 July 1917. Trained at Avord and Pau he received his brevet on 20 October 1917. He served in Spa 150. He enrolled in the U.S. Navy as an Ensign in the NRFC in Paris on 4 February 1918.

ary, the British seaplane base at Dunkirk was transferred to the U.S. Navy. The German response to the American takeover of the British base was violent; the air station came under long-range artillery fire and was frequently bombed.

The initial allocation of aircraft at the station consisted of French Donnet-Denhaut 8 flying boats. The reason for this was that not only was the narrow harbor at Dunkirk unsuitable for the large U.S. machines, but also the U.S. machines were considered unsuitable for operations either over the North Sea, or in direct contact with the German machines at Ostend, Zeebrugge, and Bruges. It was soon realized that the DD 8 aircraft were vulnerable to German fighters based along the Flanders coast. On 24 January Capt. A.A. Cunningham, USMC, suggested that his Corps. provide fighter protection to the seaplanes. Instead, the navy opted to assign French Hanroit HD-2 fighting seaplanes to the base as protection for the DD 8s. The eventual allotment of aircraft to the station consisted of eight DD 8s and ten HD-2s. The HD-2s accompanied the DD 8s on almost 500 patrols. However, no German aircraft were encountered during any of these missions.

One of the early fatalities at Dunkirk occurred on 26 February when Ensign Curtis Read, USNRF (Naval Aviator No. 83), went up for his first practice flight in a French DD seaplane, just two days after his arrival at the station. Twenty minutes into the flight, at 1020 hours, the plane crashed. Pulled from the wreckage, Read died at 1110 hrs. Read thus was the first U.S. Naval Aviator to be killed in France. The body of his Observer, Petty Officer Eichelberger, was not found until July 8th.

NAS Dunkirk was fortunate enough to receive the services of some very experienced pilots. As American citizens who had been serving with the French began to opt for American service, since the U.S. was now in the war, several of these men decided to volunteer for the U.S. Navy. From this group Dunkirk was fortunate to receive Lieutenant Willis Bradley Haviland, formerly of Esc. N.124, David Edward Judd (Naval Aviator No. 565), formerly of Spa. 3,

Hanriot HD-2 at NAS Dunkirk. Personnel are not identified.

Hanriot HD-2 at NAS Dunkirk. The pilot is not identified.

Spencer (left) and George Clark Moseley in flight training.

and Ralph Loomis (Naval Aviator No. 578). Haviland arrived at Dunkirk in February 1918 and replaced Lieutenant Gates as Chief Pilot (Haviland became Naval Aviator No. 577 on 1 February 1918 at NAS Moutchic; Lieutenant Gates being reassigned as Intelligence Officer. Haviland remained as Chief Pilot until 1 April 1918 when he was ordered to Italy. Upon his departure, Gates once again became Chief Pilot at Dunkirk.

At the end of March, when the German "Operation Michael" began, Lieutenant Chevalier offered to the British his men, his pilots, and all of his equipment. The offer was accepted, with pilots Lieutenants Haviland, D.S. Ingalls (Naval Aviator No. 85), K. MacLeish (Naval Aviator No. 74), and E.T. Smith (Naval Aviator No. 126) being specifically "loaned" to No. 13 Squadron, RFC, at Bergues, to fly Sopwith Camels. At the same time Lieutenant Gates was loaned to No. 12 Squadron, RNAS, also at Bergues, to fly D.H. 4s. These men were to be on loan to the British until 19 April. It was not until 20 April that the station returned to American command.

Ensign David Edward Judd at NAS Dunkirk. Judd was an ambulance driver with the American Field Service in France. He transferred to the French Foreign Legion on 2 June 1917 and took his flight training at Avord and Pau. He transferred to naval aviation in Paris on 19 January 1918.

As the Navy's plans for the Northern Bombing Group were being implemented, the need for fighter protection aircraft became a high priority. To provide for such a necessity, the seaplane capability of the Dunkirk base was supplanted by its assignment to the Northern Bombing Group as a scout station. On 1 July the promoted Lieutenant Commander Gates replaced Lieutenant Chevalier as Commanding Officer at Dunkirk when Chevalier left to take command of the Assembly and Repair bast at Eastleigh.

Left to right: Wellman, a Sengalese guard, and David Judd. Photo taken at Pau.

A Hanriot HD-2 at NAS Dunkirk following a German bombing raid on the station.. Personnel are not identified.

A crashed Hanriot HD-2 at Dunkirk.

On 13 August 1918 Ensign Julian F. Carson (Naval Aviator No. 765), while on patrol over the channel in DD 8 No. 825, and escorted by two HD-2s, sighted a submarine which was on the surface. Upon challenging the sub it proceeded to open fire on Ensign Carson's plane, hitting it in several locations and driving him off. The two HD-2s attacked and cleared the deck of the submarine, permitting Ens. Carson to again attack. Aligning himself for a bombing attack on the submarine, Carson's bombs scored hits on the submarine while it was in the act of submerging. Soon after the explosion of the bombs the submarine rose to the surface at a sharp "bow-up" angle, and then slowly slid, stern first, under the waves. Ensign Carson was credited by the French with the sinking of the submarine and was awarded the Croix de Guerre. On 22 August Lieutenant Commander Gates successfully came to the rescue of a British Handley-Page which had been shot down near Dunkirk and was still under shellfire. For this action Vice Admiral Sims recommended him for the Medal of Honor, but Gates was instead awarded the D.S.M. While still commanding officer at Dunkirk Gates volunteered to fly with a French fighter squadron based at Dunkirk. On 4 October 1918 Gates, on his second chasse patrol, was shot down and made a POW.

NAS Dunkirk was decommissioned on 1 January 1919.

David S. Ingalls.

"Di" Gates at NAS Dunkirk.

Lt. Artemus "Di" Gates and Ens. George Clark Moseley at NAS Dunkirk

Lt. Artemus "Di" Gates (seated) as a POW. Others are unidentified.

Irving Sheely, Observer/Gunlayer, in the cockpit of a Donnet-Denhaut at NAS Dunkirk. (source: Larry Sheely collection)

A French Donnet Denhaut seaplane, fittted with a 160 hp AM engine, lifts off the waters from its base at Dunkirk in early September 1916.

Appendix R: NAS La Trinite[1]

I. CONSTRUCTION

The U.S. Naval Air Station was situated in the small fishing village of La Trinite-sur-Mer, about four miles distant from the town of Carnac, on an inlet in the Bay of Morbihan. Plouharnel, six miles from La Trinite, was the nearest railroad station. The intended objective of the station was to be a base for dirigibles.

On 14 March 1918, preliminary arrangements were made locally for the establishment of the station. Five summer villas were leased for barracks, and the French Navy proceeded to secure the property necessary for the station by lease and requisition. Work was immediately commenced under the handicap of insufficient personnel and lack of equipment. Sand for roads and paths was carried from the adjacent beach in large dishpans—part of the mess gear equipment. Due to the scarcity of Naval Civil Engineers, personnel, and construction materials, and arrangement was made on 28 March with the French Navy whereby the Trevaux Hydrauliques agreed to furnish a Supervisional Engineer, and such labor and material as were available.

On 8 April, the Commander of the Aerial Patrols of the Loire Section sent Commissaire Bertaux of the French Navy to assist in completing all arrangements for the rental of houses and land. Also on this date a five-ton Pierce Arrow truck belonging to the French Government was loaned for use at the station. On the following day, a civilian engineer arrived with thirty Bulgar prisoners, and work was begun on a seawall. Toward the end of the month, the masonry work was begun on this seawall by seven civilian masons. A road through the station was commenced when six wooden wheelbarrows, seven shovels, five picks, and two sledgehammers had been obtained as a loan from the village of Carnac. Assistant Naval Constructor R. Walworth, USNRF, reported for duty on 23 April and was appointed Public Works Officer for the station.

On 24 April, a 350 cubic meter portable ferro-silicon plant for the production of hydrogen was received from Paris; a four inch gas distributing liner of welded wrought iron pipe was laid, connecting the hydrogen plant to the hangar. The hydrogen plant, sludge tanks, all low pressure piping, valves, and fittings were installed and ready for operation by 1 October. One 1500 cubic foot hydrogen compressor was to have been installed at this station for the charging of hydrogen cylinders. High pressure manifolds, piping, valves, and fittings were received and ready for installation by 1

Aerial view of NAS La Trinite.

Aerial view of La Trinite and the railroad. (source: Naval Historical Center)

Preparing a Kite Balloon for accession at NAS La Trinite. (source: 80 HAG-5G-6)

Unidentified Officers at NAS La Trinite.

November, but the compressor did not arrive from the U.S. Considerable difficulty was experienced in the disposal of hydrogen sludge, owing to the presence of valuable oyster beds in the immediate proximity of the hydrogen plant. It was found necessary to install a pipeline, a half-mile in length, to carry the sludge to the opposite side of the peninsula.

Telephone lines were installed, and communications were established with the Naval Headquarters at Paris. The first six carloads of construction materials arrived on 29 April, and the excavating for the main foundations was immediately begun. On 1 July 75 more Bulgar prisoners were put to work excavating for the hangar site.

On the first of August a four-stall steel balloon hangar was received from Pauillac. Its erection was immediately commenced, and was completed about 1 September. The seawall and the road from the pier to the hangar site were completed the latter part of September, and the station was reported to be ready for operations on 1 October.

II. PERSONNEL

Lieutenant (j.g.) R.D. Patterson, CEC, arrived at the station on 14 March 1918 and was in command until his detachment on account of illness the latter part of the month. The first draft, consisting of 30 men, arrived on 24 March, and was quartered in one of the villas already procured. A temporary galley was hastily set up, and arrangements were made with the local bakery for a sufficient supply of bread, which was made with flour supplied by the Navy. The water of the local wells was found to be undrinkable, but the city water from a spring in the center of town and pumped to the waterfront was found to be excellent.

On 20 March the American Naval District Commander, the Commander of Aerial Patrols of the Loire Section, and Monsieur Haelling, an engineer of the Travaux Hydrauliques, held a conference at the station. Lieutenant (j.g.) Patterson turned over to the latter all construction plans, and the command of the station to Lieutenant H.E. Martin, MC, USN, who, in turn, was relieved on 10 April by Gunner C.M. Johnson, USN.

A 300 cubic feet per hour portable hydrogen generator plant. Such a unit was standard for both NAS La Trinite and NAS La Pallice. The individual is not identified.

A standard Navy Hydrogen Charging Manifold, with a 20 cylinder capacity, used at NAS La Trinite.

On the evening of 17 April an American ship, the S.S. *Florence B*, loaded with powder for the French Government was blown up in the Bay of Quiberon. The cause of the accident was unknown. Many bodies were afterwards recovered but were never identified. The French buried one body in the cemetery of Loemariaquer, another on Ile aux Moines, and five unidentified bodies were buried on Haedik by the American authorities at Lorient. During the summer the personnel of La Trinite marked all the graves with suitable headboards.

By 3 July 150 enlisted men were on board, and of these 70 were transferred to the United States shortly after the armistice was signed; the remainder being held to demobilize the station.

On 11 November the following officers were at La Trinite:

Gunner C.M. Johnson, USN	Commanding Officer
Lieutenant H.E. Martin, MC, USN	Medical Officer
Ensign L.N. Thompson, PC, USNRF	Supply Officer
Ensign G.F. Pursel, USNRF	Hydrogen Officer
Ensign H.C. Harris, USNRF	Balloon Pilot

III. OPERATIONS

On the 25th of April, the French dirigible "Capitaine Caussin," flying from the U.S. Naval Air Station at Paimboeuf, was forced to land in Quiberon Bay. The officers and crew were picked up and cared for at La Trinite, and the balloon and nacelle were salvaged, being sent to Paimboeuf by truck on the following day.

The first balloon received at this station was inflated from hydrogen bottles on the 18th of October, and the second on the 8th of November. Many flights were made for practice and instruction purposes, but no operations were carried out at sea on account of the lack of a towing boat. The station was ready to operate two months before the cessation of hostilities.

IV. DEMOBILIZATION

The work of demobilization was completed on 5 February 1919 and the site evacuated. The property was derequisitioned. The hangar was turned over to the U.S. Army.

Notes:

[1] Much of the material in this appendix is taken from the work *History of U.S. Naval Aviation in Foreign Service, French Unit, 1917-1918*

Appendix S: NAS La Pallice[1]

I. CONSTRUCTION

The United States Naval Air Station at La Pallice was located near La Rochelle, one of the most important ports on the west coast of France. It was intended that this station be a kite balloon base for destroyers entering convoys in the area.

In May 1918, the site of the station was a field of uncut wheat, and, as the ground for the station had been requisitioned by the French Government from civilian inhabitants, it was necessary to delay the starting of construction until 23 June, in order to allow the former owners to remove their property.

The nonreceipt of materials seriously hampered the building of the station. The first barracks were begun on 23 June and were erected in three days. The dispensary, mess hall and galley, garage buildings, oil house, additional barracks, administration building, storehouse, armory building, canteen building, hydrogen plant, and hangar were subsequently erected.

Hydrogen gas was to have been furnished at this station by one 350 cubic meter ferro-silicon plant. The plant had been completely installed by 15 November on the floor of the hydrogen building, but the building was never erected. A low-pressure six-inch cast iron pipe connecting the gas plant with the hangar was 90% completed at the cessation of hostilities; sludge tanks had also been installed. All high-pressure manifolds, pipes, valves, and fittings had been delivered at this station by 25 October. The one 1500-foot compressor to be installed at this station for the charging of hydrogen cylinders was never received. The liquid sludge was to be conducted through a small six-inch pipe to the main sewer leading to the sea from a chemical plant adjacent to the station. Permission was granted to make this connection. The solid was to have been removed and dumped into the sea.

NAS La Pallice.

II. PERSONNEL

Assistant Paymaster Douglas Barnes, USNRF, reported for duty on 5 May 1918, and a month later four officers and 32 enlisted men of various ratings reported. Gunner L.J. Peiffer, USN, was commanding officer at this time, with Assistant Surgeon L.H. Williams, USN, as Medical Officer, Assistant Paymaster Douglas Barnes, USNRF, as Supply Officer, and Machinist J.E. Gordy, USNRF, as Public Works Officer.

On 17 June Lieutenant (j.g.) J.H. Dashiell, USNRF, relieved Gunner Peiffer of Command.

On 11 November, 216 enlisted men and the following officers were attached to the station:

Lieutenant (j.g.) J.H Dashiell, USNRF	Commanding Officer
Ensign Lester C. Winslow, USNRF	Executive Officer
Ensign Joseph Le Doan, USNRF	Hydrogen Officer
Ensign Ronald Z. Mickey, USNRF	Kite Balloon Officer
Ensign Edwin S. Kant, USNRF	Kite Balloon Officer
Machinist Jonathan E. Grody, USNRF	Public Works Officer
Carpenter Albert S. Osterbery, USNRF	Assistant Public Works Officer
Lieutenant Louis M. Williams, M.C., USN	Medical Officer
Lieutenant Leonard G. Hoffman, P.C., USN	Supply Officer

III. OPERATIONS

La Pallice was never commissioned, as it was still under construction at the time of the Armistice.

During the course of its career the station had opportunity to render some outside assistance to the village. Commander C.L. Hand, Port Officer at Rochefort, praised the work done by officers and men of the station in fighting a sodium nitrate fire in La Pallice on the 27th of August. The assistance provided the French by the station personnel and saved much property and many lives.

IV. DEMOBILIZATION

On 5 January 1919 La Pallice was transferred to the U.S. Army, the material having been disposed of and the personnel transferred in accordance with instructions received from Naval Headquarters in Paris. The Travaux Hydrauliques derequisitioned the property not taken over by the Army. The oil tanks on the site were ceded to the French Government.

Notes:

[1] Much of the material included in this Appendix is taken from the document entitled *History of U.S. Naval Aviation in Foreign Service, French Unit, 1917-1918*

Appendix T: NAS Gujan[1]

I. CONSTRUCTION

The United States Naval Air Station Gujan-Mestras (which was intended to be a dirigible station) never progressed beyond the constructional phase. From February to the middle of July very little construction was accomplished, the only work being the making of preliminary roads and the excavating for the foundation piers and windshields. A draft of all but 21 men from this station was sent to Pauillac for duty from 24 May to 27 June.

Some construction on foundations was accomplished by hand between the first and sixteenth of July. On the 16th, a concrete mixer was received, and work progressed more satisfactorily. While the foundations were being poured, the trusses were framed. This was a slow process due to the lack of all equipment but hand tools. Lack of men and material were a continual impediment to progress, but even with the station's limited personnel it was necessary to send one truck and 16 men to Pauillac for temporary duty in order to get material loaded onto the cars at that station. Before 11 November 19 trusses had been assembled and erected during 28 working days.

Hydrogen was to have been supplied at this station by one 600 cubic meter semi-portable ferro-silicon plant. This plant had been installed on foundations, but at the cessation of hostilities the building for the unit had not yet been erected. The six-inch cast iron pipe connecting the hydrogen plant with the hangar was 50% completed.

II. ORGANIZATION

On 2 February 1918, the first draft of three officers and eight enlisted men arrived and was quartered temporarily in a Sardine Factory at Mestras. Gunner J.H. Gowan, USN, was in charge of this detachment. The station was commissioned on 3 February. On 11 November 240 men and the following officers were on board:

Lieutenant L.L. Battitt, USN	Commanding Officer
Lieutenant R.J. Miller, USN	Executive Officer
Ensign C.H. Breyman, USNRF	Pilot
Ensign E.D. McKean, USNRF	Pilot
Ensign J.W. Hill, USNRF	Pilot and Transportation Officer
Ensign A.M. Crawford, USNRF	Hydrogen and Engineering Officer
Gunner A.L. Hartigan, USN	
Lieutenant E.D. Hardin, USN	Medical Officer
Lieutenant A. Rembert, USN	Supply Officer
Ensign J.H. Kyger, USN	Assistant to the Supply Officer

Aerial view of NAS Gujan. (source: Naval Historical Center)

Aerial view of NAS Gujan. (source: Naval Historical Center)

Aerial view of NAS Gujan. (source: Naval Historical Center)

Hangar under construction at NAS Gujan.

III. OPERATIONS

In the summer of 1918 an epidemic of Spanish influenza visited the station, but was soon controlled by the untiring efforts of Dr. Hardin, who also, on numerous occasions, gave prompt assistance to the natives of the village.

The station was commissioned on 3 February. Though far from completed, instruction of the personnel was undertaken, and three times a week officers of the station, with the aid of blackboard illustrations, gave lectures. This instruction was along general lines of the dirigible branch of naval aviation.

On the afternoon of 9 July the station personnel responded with fire apparatus to a call from a nearby town where a fire in a lumberyard had gotten beyond the control of the village firefighters. The sailors, under the personal direction of their commanding officer, succeeded in getting the flames under control after several hours. On several other occasions, fires were extinguished by the stations' force in Gujan-Mestras and La Hume.

Group photograph of personnel at NAS Gujan taken on 17 November 1918.

Hangar construction at NAS Gujan. (source 80 HAG 5N-6)

Barracks, flag pole, and hangar under construction at NAS Gujan.

Administrative Offices at NAS Gujan. (source: 80 HAG-5N-3)

Barracks at NAS Gujan. (source: Naval Historical Center)

IV. DEMOBILIZATION

Upon receipt of the order to demobilize the material was disposed of and the personnel transferred in accordance with instructions from Naval Headquarters in Paris. The station was placed out of commission on 15 January 1919. The U.S. Army took over the custody of the lumber and barracks on the site, and the Travaux Hydrauliques derequisitioned the property.

Notes:

[1] Much of the material contained in this Appendix is taken from the document entitled *History of U/S/ Naval Aviation, Foreign Service, French Unit, 1917 and 1918*

Unidentified Officers, believed to be Commanding Officer Lt. L.L. Battitt and his staff at NAS Gujan.

Appendix U: NAS Guipavas[1]

I. CONSTRUCTION

Because of the geographically strategic location for the protection of convoys, the establishment of a U.S. Naval Dirigible Station in the vicinity of Brest was especially requested by the French Navy. After a careful survey of the surrounding country by a commission of American and French Naval Officers, it was determined that the most advantageous site would be immediately adjacent to the French Dirigible station at Guipavas. By such a consolidation, it was possible to limit the amount of project to be requisitioned and to share the French landing field, thus avoiding extensive clearing and grading.

The first officer assigned to duty in connection with the construction of this station arrived on 28 January 1918, but no work could be started until 11 March, owing to a lack of materials. Upon the receipt of the first draft, which arrived without bags or hammocks, the officer in charge was forced to billet the men with the residents of the village of Guipavas until tents were pitched on the station five days later. Stores and construction material were kept in a storehouse in the village of Guipavas for this purpose.

On 8 March a portable barracks was received and was immediately erected. This necessitated considerable grading, filling in of mud holes, and turning over of turnip fields.

It was necessary that a 700-ft. road be constructed from the main highway to the hangar site, and construction of this road was immediately commenced. Owing to the continual rains, it had to be made permanent and was laid with rocks, which were obtained from the adjacent quarry and crushed at the French Station.

On 10 April four portable barracks were loaned by the French Army. The following day a shipload of lumber for the hangar arrived on the U.S.S. *Bella*, and was unloaded and delivered on the campsite by the station force. A detail was turned to excavating and preparing for the erection of the barracks. Because of dense growth of underbrush and being crisscrossed at several places with earth hedges three feet high, it was necessary to remove these before a system of streets and roads could be laid out.

On 17 April a 70-ton shipment of cement was delivered and stored in one of the barracks buildings loaned by the French. At about this time two French laborers were loaned the station by the officials of the adjoining French Air Station to dig wells.

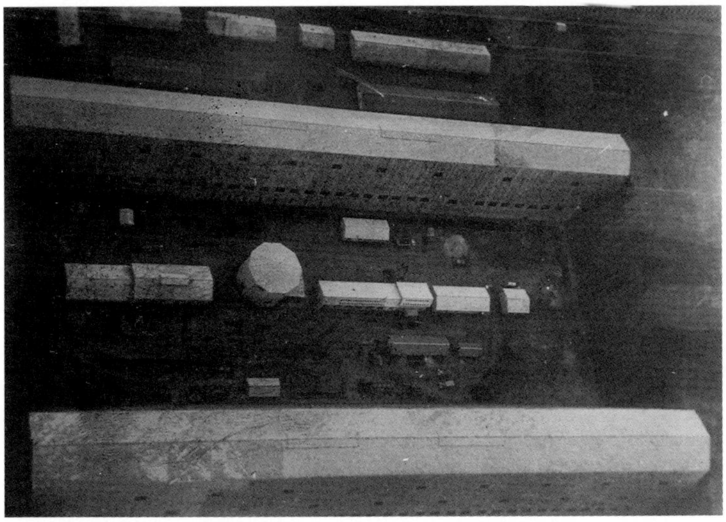

NAS Guipavas from the air. (source: 80 HAG-5P-15)

Hangars at NAS Guipavas. (source: Naval Historical Center)

NAS Guipavas from the air. Item in the foreground appears to be a wind barrier or shield to minimize damage to the airships entering and leaving their sheds.

The "Capt. Cassin" ascending at NAS Guipavas. (source: Naval Historical Center)

On 23 June, the first truss of the hangar was raised and bolted into place. From that time on those trusses went up at the average of one a day, except for a period of three weeks when construction was practically held up on account of failure to receive material from the Supply Base. This time was used in covering the hangar with asbestos covering and tin sheeting for the roof, as well as constructing avant-porte trusses.

On 1 July five enlisted men's barracks were completed, one of which was being used temporarily as the mess hall. The officer's barracks were also erected and almost completely furnished. Three trusses had been raised on the hangar site, and the floor graded for 21 bays. 144 piers for trusses had been excavated, and into 119 of these had been poured the concrete foundations. The hangar storehouse was 90% complete, and little work was left on the permanent road from the main highway to the hangar site. On account of the fact that material for the administration building had not yet been received, the administrative offices were located in the ends of the barracks, partitioned off from the men's sleeping quarters. The sick bay was still located in the tent loaned the station by the Red Cross Society.

At the end of July seven barracks were completed, six wells dug for both drinking water and fire protection, and camp roads 90% completed. All cement piers were placed for the remainder of the trusses, the floor of the hangars was graded for 32 bays, the machine shop was 80% completed, and 200 feet of the water mains laid on the camp site. Considering the fact that the station had to maintain a crew on the rock crusher, get the rock from the nearby quarry, deliver it to the crusher, and later from the crusher to the hangar site, the construction progress was satisfactory.

During the month of August work on the campsite progressed, but that on the hangar site was not satisfactory, on account of the failure to receive material for the construction of the trusses. Dur-

The nacelle of the "Capt. Cassin" leaving its hangar at NAS Guipavas. (source: Naval Historical Center)

"Capt. Caussin" preparing to ascend at NAS Guipavas.

The "Capt. Caussin" in her hangar at NAS Guipavas. (source: Naval Historical Center)

The "Capt. Caussin" nearly clear of her hangar at NAS Guipavas. (source: Naval Historical Center)

ing the month the Hydrogen plant was nearly completed, the dock of the hangar had been graded for a distance of four more bays, the machine shop had been erected, the generator set installed, and the water tower and tank erected, although the entire ship's crew had been engaged for nearly a week in unloading two ship loads of material at Brest.

The "Capt. Caussin" in her hangar at NAS Guipavas.

During the month of September the hydrogen plant was completed, and a total of 800 feet of water main laid. The new mess hall and galley were erected and fitted out, the septic tank for the sewage system was completed, and two new barracks were completed. All tents were struck, and the whole ship's crew moved into barracks. By 1 October the system of water mains was completed, the water tank erected on a tower, a pump installed, and the administration building completed. The hydrogen plant was in working order. One hangar door was erected, complete except for sheathing. A total of 33 trusses were raised, and 23 bays of the hangar were covered with asbestos.

During the month of October the raised roadway from the campsite to the hangar was completed. The raising of this roadway was made necessary on account of the heavy rains, which completely inundated the swampy land between the two sites. The bomb house at this time was almost finished, and cold showers were installed in both the officers and enlisted men's latrines. The meteorology house, a building but recently authorized for the station, was about half completed, and two-thirds of the ship's crew were engaged during the latter part of the month in unloading another shipload of material for the station.

By 11 November all that was left to complete were the following: Camp Site (roads, walkways, wiring, telephone system, Y.M.C.A. building, foundation posts for two garages, the Meteorology house, drainage system, garage, and wash house); and Hangar site (repair of hangar road, walkway to hangar site, bomb house, and erection of two trusses for the west door). The station had facilities for housing comfortably a personnel compliment of 400 men. The hangar was ready to house a ship, except for the door at the west end. This work was being rushed as rapidly as possible with depleted personnel in order to be ready for the reception of the "Capitaine Caussin" when that ship was officially taken over by the U.S. Navy.

NAS Guipavas with a hangar under construction. (source: Naval Historical Center)

II. PERSONNEL

The history of the U.S. Naval Air Station at Guipavas, Finistere, France, dates from 29 January 1918 when Ensign Glenn E. Round, Pay Corps, USNRF, arrived pursuant to his assignment to duty in connection with the construction of the station. Ensign Round, together with Assistant Civil Engineer C.P. Conrad, USN, Public Works Officer, inspected the site of the proposed station, then an expanse of mud and turnip fields.

On 26 February 1918 Pay Clerk J.M. Lieber, USN, reported for duty. On 10 March a draft of 49 men reported with one 3 ton and one 3/4-ton truck. On 15 March Lieutenant (j.g.) E.D. Andrews, Medical Corps, USN, reported for duty. On 27 March 39 men were received, and on 9 April 48 men arrived. On 11 April Carpenter Stuart B. Scruggs, USNRF, reported from Brest for temporary duty as Construction Officer. On 12 April Lieutenant J.F. Maloney, USN, reported as Commanding Officer of the station. Shortly after, 83 men reported aboard to assist with the construction work. Until 1 July, small details of from one to five men of special ratings reported. On 14 April five officers were detached from Brest and reported to Guipavas for temporary duty. On 15 July Ensign H.W. Rugg, USNRF, and Ensign W.A. Stumpf, USNRF, reported for duty: the former was assigned to the duties of Executive Officer, and the latter as Hydrogen Officer.

On 5 August a draft of 48 men was detailed from the U.S.S. *Carola* for temporary duty and placed in the construction gangs. On 15 September the station was called upon for a detail of 55 men to assist in the construction of the telephone line for French Coastal Air Stations. On 25 September, Lieutenant (j.g.) C.G. Little, USNRF (Naval Aviator No. 102), and Ensign T.E. McCracken, USNRF, reported for duty. Upon their arrival the five kite balloon operators who had been on temporary duty since 3 July were detached and returned to the Brest Air Station. One week later Ensign A.A. Bailey, USNRF (Naval Aviator No. 1086), reported for duty, also with flying orders.

On 25 September an epidemic of influenza struck the station, and 35 cases were reported for treatment on that day. The sick bay was found to be too small, and one of the barracks was fitted up as a hospital. There were a total of 98 cases during the epidemic, none of which resulted in a death. Four showed complications of pneumonia and were transferred to U.S. Naval Base Hospital No. 5, but were later returned to duty. Lieutenant Greenwood, Medical Corps., USN, reported for temporary duty as Medical Officer from the Brest Air Station during the epidemic, and stayed until the two regular Medical Officers of the station had recovered from the influenza.

In October a draft of 18 men was transferred to Pauillac for further transfer to the Mediterranean Mine Base. On 19 October Ensign C.M. Keyser, USNRF, reported for duty as Meteorological Officer. On 23 October a draft of 45 men arrived from Paimboeuf for duty. On this date Carpenter Scruggs and Lieutenant Andrews, Medical Corps, were detached, the former for duty at the U.S. Mine Base at Bizerte, Algeria, the latter for medical duty with the Naval Railway Battery No. 1, and Lieutenant (j.g.) G.H. Carpenter, USNRF (Naval Aviator No. 543), reported for duty with the "Capitaine Caussin," the dirigible bought from the French. On the 28th, Ensign George F. Baker, USNRF, reported for duty from Moutchic and was assigned as Ordnance Officer. On 30 October, 40 men were transferred to the U.S. Naval Air Station, Treguier, for duty.

On 30 October, Lieutenant Commander Z. Lansdowne, USN (Naval Aviator No. 103), relieved Lieutenant J.F. Maloney, USN (Naval Aviator No. 105), as Commanding Officer of this station, and the latter was detached to command a U.S. Naval Air Station in Ireland.

On 1 November Lieutenant (j.g.) A.D. Brewer (Naval Aviator No. 103), Lighter-than-air pilot, reported for duty at this station. On 6 November Leon Adolph Griffin, Chief Yeoman, USNRF, took oath and acceptance of office as Ensign, Class 4, USNRF, for general service. On 8 November Ensign Paul F. Pagan, Civil Engineer, USNRF, reported from Fromentine and was assigned as Construction Officer. On the same date Lieutenant (j.g.) M.P. Delano, USNRF, reported from Paimboeuf for duty and was assigned as commanding officer of the "Capitaine Caussin" when it should be taken over from the French. On 11 November Lieutenant (j.g.) Julian Peabody, USNRF, reported from Paimboeuf to relieve Ensign McCracken as Intelligence Officer, as the latter had been ordered to England for duty.

On 11 November, the muster of officers and ship's complement was as follows:

Lansdowne, Z., Lieutenant Commander, USN — Commanding Officer

Golden, Waldo E., Lieutenant M.C., USN — Medical Officer

The "Capt. Caussin" ascending at NAS Guipavas. (source: Naval Historical Center)

Little, Chas. G., Lieutenant (j.g.), USNRF
Chief Pilot and Watch and Divisional Officer
Carpenter, Grant H., Lieutenant (j.g.), USNRF
Pilot and Watch and Divisional Officer
Peabody, Julian, Lieutenant (j.g.), USNRF Intelligence Officer
Brewer, Arthur D., Lieutenant (j.g.), USNRF
Transportation Officer
Delano, Merril P., Lieutenant (j.g.), USNRF
Commanding Officer "Capitaine Caussin"
Rugg, Edward V., Ensign, USNRF Executive Officer
Round, Glenn E., Ensign Pay Corps, USNRF Supply Officer
Keyser, Clarence N., Ensign, USNRF Meteorological Officer
Baker, George F., Ensign, USNRF
Ordnance, Watch and Divisional Officer
Bailey, Albert A., Ensign, USNRF
Pilot, Watch, and Divisional Officer
Stumpf, William A., Ensign, USNRF Hydrogen Officer
Pagan Paul F., Ensign, Civil Eng. Corps., USNRF
Public Works Officer
Lieber, Josephus M., Pay Clerk (T), USNRF
Assistant Supply Officer

The enlisted men complement of the station was 396 men.

On 15 November 50% of the enlisted personnel were transferred to the Receiving Ship at New York. On 20 November, the following officers of the USNRF received orders to proceed to New York: Lieutenant (j.g.) A.D. Brewer, Lieutenant (j.g.) G.H Carpenter, Ensign C.F. Baker, and Ensign A. Griffin.

The personnel at all times maintained the most cordial relations with the personnel of the adjoining French station, as well as with the civilian authorities. The Medical Officer on one or two occasions gave medical attention to civilians of the village of Guipavas in cases of minor accidents. On 4 July the officers and men took up a purse, and 100 children from Guipavas were invited to the station for the holiday; a ball game was staged, after which the children were served candy and cakes.

A baseball team was organized on the station, and a successful season was planned, the team finishing third in the league. A football team was started and ably coached by Lieutenant Carpenter. One game was planned with the U.S. Base Hospital No. 5, but three days later the demobilization order was received and a part of the team was transferred.

Close up of a hangar at NAS Guipavas. (source Naval Historical Center)

Y.M.C.A. Secretary Robert E. Sellars had reported for duty when tents were the only shelter, and remained up to the time of demobilization. He assisted ably in keeping the crew in high spirits, and was willing at all times to carry on the enormous amount of work necessary for the construction of the station in the disagreeable climate and weather that is characteristic of Finistere. Classes in French were conducted semiweekly for the men of the station.

III. OPERATIONS

The station was ready to operate on 11 November 1918. The French dirigible "Capitaine Caussin" was housed in the French hangar upon its arrival from Paimboeuf, and the pilots and crew made numerous flights from this station. This dirigible was officially taken over by the United States Naval Forces on 23 November, and was thereafter maintained and operated by the personnel of this station, though still housed in the French hangar.

In November 1918, investigation was made as to the advisability of conducting experiments in minesweeping with the dirigible. The British sweeps suggested for this purpose were designed for use with surface craft and were not suitable for work with dirigibles. It would have been necessary to have extensive alterations made on the dirigible before such operations could be attempted. The Force Commander was advised in detail of the impracticability of the proposed experiment, and instructions to proceed with it were withdrawn.

On 13 December President Wilson arrived at Brest, and the "Capitaine Caussin" was one of the aerial escorts which met the U.S.S. *George Washington* outside the harbor and escorted her to port. From this dirigible were taken the majority of the aerial pictures of the event. On the following day the deflation of the "Caussin" was begun, and she was shipped to the United States in January.

IV. DEMOBILIZATION

The work of demobilization was started on 14 December 1918, immediately after the arrival of the President of the United States. The material was disposed of and the personnel transferred in accordance with instruction received from Naval Headquarters in Paris. The campsite was completely cleared and the buildings turned over to the U.S. Army. The station was placed out of commission on 13 January 1919. The complete hangar site, dirigible hangar, and hydrogen plant were transferred to the French at a total price of 465,600 francs, as arrived upon by the joint French and American Commission. The derequisitioning of the property not being taken over by the French Navy proceeded in negotiation with the original owner of the land.

Notes:

[1] Much of the material in this Appendix is taken from the document entitled *History of U.S. Naval Aviation in Foreign Service, French Unit, 1917 and 1918*

Appendix V: NAS Lough Foyle[1]

The U.S. Government representatives selected Lough Foyle as a site for a proposed station some time before actual construction began. The location was 18 miles inland from the open sea on the northwest shore of the lake, at a point not far distant from the mouth of the Foyle River.

Geographically, the site was ideal; certainly no station presented a more pleasing appearance after completion, particularly from the air. The meteorological conditions, however, were always a matter of contention, as high wind velocity, heavy cloud strata, and rain seriously interfered with efficient air activities.

The contract for erecting the buildings necessary for a seaplane station was placed with the British Admiralty, work commencing on 5 January 1918. Civilian labor was employed, supplemented on 26 February by seven carpenter's mates of the U.S. Naval Aviation Forces, commanded by Gunner H.F. Moseley, USN.

On 12 March, and at various times later, other men of the naval service arrived, so that by 7 June all civilian labor was dismissed, following a strike, and the work was carried on entirely by enlisted personnel.

At first much difficulty was experienced in the transportation of building materials to the station from Londonderry, the nearest hauling point, nine miles inland. The arrival of several motor trucks, the first of English manufacture being driven from the U.S. Naval Air Station on 27 March, and two Tyler trucks eventually alleviated this on 10 April.

In the spring good weather prevailed, and by 1 May the slipway was ready for launching seaplanes and the concrete apron for the hangars was completed. In addition, eleven buildings were ready for occupancy, including one galley, one gasoline storage, one officers' barracks, and eight barracks for the enlisted men. Ensign E.A. Whaley, C.E., USN, reported to Lough Foyle on 3 May. On 7 May the first material was hauled 35 miles to Malin Head for the construction of the Meteorological Station. On 11 May a Cadillac touring car was received, along with three motorcycles with sidecars. On 13 May Boatswain A.J. Raymond, USN, relieved Gunner H.F. Moseley, USN, as Commanding Officer of the station. He, in turn, was relieved on 17 May by Commander H.D. Cooke, USN, as Commanding Officer. On 18 May well drilling equipment purchased at Newton-Hamilton and conveyed to the station arrived in order to ensure a proper water supply. On 20 May the U.S. flag was officially hoisted on the new water tower. On 22 May Captain Thomas T. Craven, USN (on the Staff of the Commanding Officer, U.S. Naval Forces in France), and Commander R. McCrary (Commanding Officer of the U.S. Naval Air Stations, Ireland) visited the station, accompanied by several British and U.S. Naval Officers. On 24 May the new water tank was completed and filled. On 30 May the first station baseball game was held on the Parade Ground, in celebration of Decoration Day. And finally, on 31 May, the Rev. John Brown, of Pensacola, FL—the Y.M.C.A. Secretary for the station—formally opened the temporary Y.M.C.A. hut.

By 1 June some 37 buildings had been completed on the station. On 5 June Y.M.C.A. Secretary Taylor arrived. On 6 June Captain Dodge, RAF, inspected the Station. On 7 June civilian labor struck for higher wages. This act resulted in their eventual dismissal. On 9 June extremely high winds demolished a garage on the station. On 10 June the Commanding Officer and Admiral Miller, RN, held an inspection of the station. On 12 June a 24-foot whaleboat and two dinghies were purchased for the purpose of conveying supplies to flying boats anchored to buoys in the harbor. On 15 June a consignment of 72 pigeons from England was received at the station. On 16 June three canvas buoys were placed in shore from the deep-water channel by English trawlers. On 19 June Ensign G.W. Shaw (Naval Aviator No. 171), USNRF, reported for duty from Killingholme, England. Ensign Shaw was the first pilot at Lough Foyle. Accompanying Ensign Shaw was another pilot, Ensign J.B. Anderson, USNRF. On 21 June Lieutenant C.N. Meador, M.C., USN, reported for duty at the station. On 23 June Lieutenant C.T. Hull, USN (Naval Aviator No. 46), and Ensign W.C. Hindle, USNRF, reported for duty. On 24 June the station's Intelligence Department was put into commission following the arrival of Lieutenant Linkins, USN (Naval Aviator No. 225), and Ensign G.G. Zabriskie, USNRF, the latter reporting for permanent duty. On 27 June Ensign D.B. Alvord, USNRF (Naval Aviator No. 182), reported for duty. On 28 June Ensigns D.M. McCauly, C.L. Ostridge (Naval Aviator No. 231), A.N. Hyde, and K.B. Keyes, USNRF, all reported for duty.

By July all construction work was rapidly nearing completion, the sewage system was installed, and electric wiring to all parts of the station was nearly finished. The formal commissioning of the station, under the command of Commander Cooke, was carried out at noon on 1 July. All officers and men attended, the personnel being reviewed by Admiral Miller, RN, Lieutenant Commander Wyndam, RN, and Lieutenant Commander Bates, RN. On 2 July Ensigns K.B. Keyes, A.N. Hyde, and D.M. McCauley, USNRF, were all detached and transferred to France for duty there. On 3 July Ensign J. Perrin, USNRF (Naval Aviator No. 202), reported for duty. The Independence Day was celebrated in a gala fashion, with sports during the day and a dance at night, under the auspices of the Welfare Committee. Civilian friends from Londonderry were invited, and the Y.M.C.A. building was filled to its capacity. On 6 July Ensign M.A. Hoffer, USNRF (Naval Aviator No. 194), reported at the station for duty. On 7 July the Y.M.C.A. formally opened, services being held by Rev. Brown, and a short address by Mr. O'Hagan, the American Consul in Londonderry. In the afternoon Lieutenant Jamison, USNRF, Lieutenant J. Mitchell, USNRF, and Lieutenant Commander Briscoe, USN, inspected the station. Commander Cooke was detached from the station, being replaced as commanding officer by Lieutenant Hull, USN, with Ensign Shaw as Executive Officer. On 10 July civilian stenographers were employed as part of the office staff. On 12 July Pay Inspector Victor Jackson, USN, and Lieutenant (j.g.) Carpenter inspected the Supply Department. On 13 July Lieutenant Commander Copeland, C.E., inspected the station. Also, the first shipment of seaplane parts arrived at the station on this date. On 17 July Ensign A.P. Teulon, USNRF (Naval Aviator No. 212), reported, and Ensign Zabriskie, representing the Intelligence Department, was ordered to British Naval Headquarters, Lough Swilly. On 20 July men and trucks were detailed to unload flying boats at Londonderry, the first ones to arrive at the station. On 27 July the second hangar was completed at the station, and on 31 July a second shipment of flying boats arrived. By this time all the buildings on the station were practically completed, and attention was now centered on flying.

On 1 August Assistant Naval Constructor Lieutenant F.J. Wilson, USN, reported to organize the Repair Department and to conduct the assembling and repairing of seaplanes. On 5 August the first shipment of ammunition arrived and was stored in the magazine, under the supervision of Ensign D.B. Alvord, USN. On 8 August Lieutenant E.H. McKitterick reported to the station, replacing Lieutenant Hull as Commanding Officer. On 11 August a motor launch was obtained through the British Admiralty, to act as a tender for the station's seaplanes. On 12 August Hull was detached from the station. On 20 August Lieutenant Commander Odlin officially inspected the Supply Department. Also on this date the station Radio Receiving Set was put in first class order, and messages received with Queenstown and France. From this time on daily messages were received from both locations. On 21 August Ensign L.A. Hodgdon, USNRF (Naval Aviator No. 661), reported for duty. On 22 August Ensign F.A. Rosenberger, USNRF (Naval Aviator No. 1507), reported for duty. On 27 August Lieutenant F.J. Wilson, C.C., USN, was ordered to the station as Executive Officer, replacing Ensign Shaw. The organization was now in good working order. On the last day of the month Ensign W.C. McCreery, USNRF, reported for duty. Originally sent as an aerographer, scarcity of officers compelled his assignment as Intelligence Officer. He held this position until relieved by Ensign M.A. Hoffer. Also, on the same day Ensign J.S. Thompson (Naval Aviator No. 650) reported for duty. The second field day and entertainment given by the Welfare Committee was held on the 31st. Highlights included sports in the afternoon and a dinner and musical play "Shove Off" in the evening. Civilians from neighboring points were invited, and the occasion was a grand success. The day was saddened by the death of E.J. Reilly, CMlc, at 2125 hours of pneumonia, which had been contacted in the line of duty.

On 2 September funeral services conducted by Rev. John Brown were held according to Naval Regulations for CMlc Reilly. A second service was held at the Catholic Church, Ture, where the remains were escorted thence to Queenstown by F.B. Reid, SFlc, USNRF. This was also the date Ensign G.S. Montgomery (Naval Aviator No. 300) reported for duty. Until this time no bombs had been attached to the planes, owing to difficulty in loading English bombs, but on this date all details were explained and made clear by an English Sergeant, who was sent by the RAF at Omagh. On 5 September Ensign E.B. Dewey, P.C., USNRF, was detached with orders to report to Queenstown. On 15 September an informal dance was held in the Y.M.C.A. hall for personnel and guests. Also on this date, Ensign Robb Gover, USNRF (Naval Aviator No. 173), reported for duty. On 16 September orders detaching Ensigns G.W. Shaw and F.A. Rosenberger, USNRF, were delivered. Also, Ensigns C.L. Ostridge, D.B. Alvord, and L.A. Hodgdon were ordered to Queenstown for temporary duty. On 18 September William E. Kelly, Boilermaker, USNRF, was drowned in an accident. His funeral was held on 21 September.

By 1 October construction commenced on hangar No. 3. This hangar was 98% complete by the armistice. On 2 October Commander Smead, USN, Commander Westerveldt, USN, Lieutenant Commander Pickering, USN, Lieutenant Bush, USNRF, Paymaster Jones, USN, and Lieutenant (j.g.) Stinson, USNRF, arrived at the station on an inspection tour. On 5 September L.F. 3 was wrecked at Warren Point Light, and Ensign H C. Fisher, P.C., USNRF, reported for duty. On 7 October the Commanding Officer and Lieutenant Commander Odin left for Queenstown for temporary duty, in accordance with orders. The station's Executive Officer acted for Lieutenant McKitterick while he was away. On 10 October the S.S. *Otranto* was in a collision with another vessel off the Irish coast while transporting U.S. Army troops. Six of the survivors, in a destitute condition, were brought to the station, where medical assistance was rendered to them. On 12 October Commander R. McCrary arrived on the station on a tour of inspection. Also, "Aces Up," another original Welfare Committee production, was presented to a large audience in the Y.M.C.A. hut. On 20 October Montgomery and Glover left for Queenstown to ferry two additional seaplanes to Lough Foyle. On 22 October Montgomery, Gover, Hodgdon, and Ostridge returned from Queenstown with planes for the station. On 28 October Lieutenant Commander N.R. Sullivan, M.C., reported for temporary duty as Lieutenant R.D. Elliot, M.C., was dangerously ill. On this date Lieutenant Commander Sullivan returned to Queenstown. On 29 October Lieutenant John A. Nunn, M.C., reported for duty as Senior Medical Officer.

On 6 November Commander Sutherland, RN, visited the station and delivered a lecture to pilots on German and English mines. With the surrender of Turkey and Austria a signal was received from Queenstown ordering flying to be cut down by 50%. On 11 November an Official Signal was received from Vice Admiral Miller, RN station, that the armistice had been signed and that all hostilities were to cease. General Quarters sounded, and all men assembled in front of the hangars and cheered enthusiastically upon hearing of the signing of the armistice. Dinner to the Commanding Officer and other officers was given at 1900 hours in the C.P.O. mess. On 18 November Lieutenant Elliot, having recovered from illness, was detached from the station with orders to proceed to Queenstown for temporary duty. All construction work stopped, and officers and men waited anxiously for word to dismantle the station. During the interim Captain Irwin, Commander R. McCrary, and Lieutenant Kirkpatrick, USN, arrived on a tour of inspection. On 25 November a Peace Banquet and dance was held. This was the final entertainment by the station Welfare Committee.

On 2 December the first draft of 300 men returned to the U.S. On 5 December Major McArthur and Lieutenant Braddock inspected the station for the RAF. Lieutenant Commander L.A. Odlin, P.C., arrived on tour of inspection. The Commanding Officer, with Lieutenant Commander Odlin, left the station, motoring to Dublin. On 6 December the Commanding Officer returned from Dublin. Ensigns C.L. Ostridge, A.P. Teulon, R. Gover, J.S. Thompson, and W.C. McCreery reported on the station for temporary duty. Lieutenant F.J. Wilson, C.C., USN, was ordered to relieve Lieutenant Commander (T) E.H. McKitterick, USN, as Commanding Officer, the latter to proceed to Portland, England, for passage to the United States. On 7 December the following officers were detached and ordered to proceed to Portland, England, for passage to the United States: McKitterick; Ensign John Perrin, USNRF; Ensign M.A. Hofer, USNRF; Ensign J.S. Thompson, USNRF; Ensign W.C. McCreery, USNRF; Boatswain A.G. Raymond, USN; and Gunner H.F. Moseley, USN. On 8 December Ensign A.P. Teulon, USNRF, was ordered as station Executive Officer. On 9 December Major Mulville, RAF, Captain Cutler, RAF, Captain Spink, RAF, Lieutenant (j.g.) Ellsworth, USN, and Civil Engineer Shires inspected the station, the Commanding Officer later accompanying them to the British Naval Base at Buncrana. On 11 December Ensign Montgomery, USNRF, was detached from the station and ordered to proceed to the U.S. Naval Hospital, White Point. On 12 December the station's supply of ammunition was sent to Aghada under guard of five men, in the charge of a Chief Petty Officer. On 31 December one three ton Packard truck and one six-ton Packard truck left for the U.S. Naval Aviation Shipping Depot, Dublin. The Commanding Officer, accompanied by Capt. E.H. Jackson, RAF, and Ens. MacFarlin, USN, inspected the U.S. Naval Meteorological Station at Malin Head. On 14 December Lieutenant Commander N.R. Sullivan, M.C., USN, reported to inspect the station's Medical Department.

The administrative work on the station was conducted as planned for all American Stations. It included some 20 divisions with the Commanding Officer in charge of all, and the Executive Officer and Officer of the Day generally responsible. The Captain of the Yard was responsible for his branch. Following came all heads of departments with their allotted offices, which at first were rather scattered, but later were all situated in or near the Administration Building. The offices of both the Commanding Officer and the Executive Officer were located in this building. Partitioned off, but in the same building was the Officer of the Day's Office, conveniently located for routine work coming under this duty.

In the executive building, and connected by a hall to the Captain's Office, was the Intelligence Office. This office was first in commission on 15 August. The office was in reality a plotting room, well equipped with six large map and chart boards covering the wall. In the middle was a large table for laying off courses on charts, as well as a desk, safe, and charts. One board was reserved for bulletins and general information, on which were also posted all messages received each day—weather reports, diagrams of patrols, and bulletins for pilots. The weather reports were sent from the U.S. Meteorological Station at Malin Head, the most northerly point in Ireland. The Meteorological Station was a substation of Lough Foyle and was successfully built and maintained with much difficulty. It was situated on a mountain of extreme height, 37 miles from the station, and accessible only over bad roads. Weather reports came in every six hours from Malin Head, and also twice a day from the English Naval Base at Buncrana.

The communication was a great drawback, for this station had neither a private wire to the U.S. Naval Headquarters at Queenstown, nor to the Admiralty at Buncrana. The Irish telephones were very poor, and during a wind or storm were sure to be out of order because of trees falling and short-circuiting the wires, or else breaking them completely. At such times it would often be days before the telephone was again in operation—only one being installed on the entire station. Telegrams were as slow as the mails, and there was no quick delivery after they left Londonderry. Often messages had to be relayed through various exchanges, and as there were Malin Head, Queenstown, and Buncrana to be kept in constant communication, the Intelligence Department had a difficult task in accomplishing its work.

By 20 August the allowance of codebooks was received, corrected and up to date. The Intelligence Department kept an officer detailed at Buncrana who kept the station informed on all movements of submarines, convoys, and other necessary data, which he obtained from the British Admiralty. This data was kept on the wall charts so that pilots could obtain all information at a glance. Fixes of submarines were plotted on a large square chart by means of pins with pieces of paper attached, giving all data, such as the date and time a fix was made, and course and call signs, if possible. The positions of all allied submarines entering the Lough Foyle patrol area were thus followed until they passed out of the area. On another wall chart, all convoys were plotted with their course and time given. On a third chart an up-to-date war map was kept with the battlefront designated by pins, and with all the latest war news. Before each patrol the Intelligence Officer gave the pilot all the necessary information and a blue print chart by which he traced his course as he flew, marking down in pencil his position, bombs dropped, ships sighted, convoy sighted, etc. By filing these charts and issuing a new one for every patrol, an accurate account of all flights was on record. The Intelligence Officer was kept in direct contact with the planes by means of wireless and pigeons. A private telephone connected with the Radio Hut and Intelligence Office ensured that all messages were telephoned over, at once. Files were kept of all data. The radio was fairly efficient, seaplanes receiving within 40 miles radius without difficulty and the station receiving much farther. The seaplane sets, however, gave much trouble.

Between the Intelligence Office and the Transportation Office was the Engineer Office. Here was kept all the data concerning "Liberty" motors, such as charts of flying hours, overhauls made with dates, location of motors, adjustments, horsepower, test stand results, fuel consumption, type of crankshaft, etc.

The Supply Department occupied an office in the Administration Building, and in it were kept the pay, purchasing, and miscellaneous accounts.

Across the street from the Administration Building, the Captain of the Yard had an office from which he supervised all operations in the yard, checked materials received, etc.

Near the Captain of the Yard's Office was the Crafting and Planning Office, where all plans were drawn, work estimated, and where all technical data was filed and kept.

The pigeon loft was begun on 25 May and completed 10 June. It faced due south and was constructed to hold 72 birds, and a compartment for two men. The 72 birds arrived on 15 June and were given their first flight 12 days later. In a few weeks' time the birds had become accustomed to their surroundings and were ready for training. First the birds were taken only a short distance and then released, but this distance was gradually increased, and the birds became accustomed to all the neighboring country, especially the shot lines. The birds were trained up to a distance of 70 miles, on coastlines from each side of the Lough, after which they were taken up in seaplanes for further training. During the early patrols many birds were released at various points. After each bird had found its way home in good time from several trips, the bird was ready for use for regular patrol work. In this training many birds were lost, due to hawks or through loss of direction. The birds rendered valuable service and displayed much speed.

The Photographic Department was located next to the Intelligence Office. Here, all pictures taken on patrol were developed, and all records of photographic supplies, plates, pictures, etc., were kept.

Between the hangars and the Captain's Office was situated the Squadron Commander's Office. Here all records and data relative to planes were kept, and from which the daily reports were obtained.

The duty Flight Officer had his office on the beach between two hangars. Here all records pertaining to the beach work were kept. Under him were all the boat crews, signal force, motor launches, etc. At times of flying there was always a pilot on the beach and a hospital apprentice.

The Commissary Department was put in operation in June, but was unsatisfactory owing to poor equipment. Most of the cooking had to be done outside in the continual rain. On 4 July a big meal was served to the station personnel and guests. The galley was constantly in operation, serving cocoa, sandwiches, eggs, etc., to all men on duty either day or night. Later, all cooking was done inside, which materially increased the efficiency of the department.

The Medical Department on the station was very satisfactory indeed. It came into existence on 20 March 1918, being then situated in Londonderry, and from that date cared for every sick and injured man. On 1 June the hospital on the station was put in commission. There were 100 admissions to the hospital since it had opened, and for a camp of 445 men, was extremely low. Assistant Surgeon Elliot had charge at first, with Asst. Surgeon C.N. Meador, USN, arriving in June. Later Lieutenant J.A. Nunn, M.C., USN, relieved Surgeon Elliot. There were only two deaths on the station, one from accidental drowning and one from pneumonia.

Across from the Administration Building was situated the Ordnance Officer's Office. Here was kept data and records concerning all ammunition, firearms, and bombs. The inexperience of the men was keenly felt in this division. Trouble was experienced with the bomb racks and bomb releases, and lack of material further held up the operations. The safety pins were never removed from the bombs until the plane was just leaving the slipway or starting from the buoy. Bombs were of the 2.5-second delay type, and proved very effective. Delay in getting bombsights necessitated improvising substitutes until those ordered finally arrived. This is an example of the countless difficulties that were constantly arising, all of which were handled by inexperienced men. The magazine was near the hangars, yet far enough away to prevent danger in case of fire. Very's lights were used for signaling, 25 being included for plane armament and guard use.

The first working plan of the Irish stations, like those in France, called for a Central Repair Base (at Queenstown), where all motor work, except minor repairs and adjustments, was to have been done. The transportation difficulties, however, made this method impracticable for Lough Foyle unless sufficient spare motors were available. The first shipment of five seaplanes and ten motors arrived 23 July. Two of these motors were of the "Scupper" type, the manufacture of which had been discontinued earlier in the year. In view of the fact that there were no spare parts on the station, it was decided to use these motors as spares for the other eight. To do at least some of the overhaul work at this station, work on the motor room and test shed was rushed as fast as possible. No "Liberty" tool kits had been received on the station, the only tools on hand being those in the small toolboxes shipped with each seaplane. However, these tools were of improper design and could not be used. Accordingly, the greater part of the tools for motor work were made on the Station until "Liberty" kits arrived. Following receipt of orders from Headquarters to overhaul all motors before use, motors were taken from the seaplanes and sent to the motor overhaul shop. Motors Nos. 220 and 118 were the first overhauled, the work being accomplished with all possible haste consistent with safety; 138 man hours being required. As the test shed had not been entirely finished at this time, these two motors were installed in planes and given beach tests. The first flight was made on 21 August and was entirely successful, from which date motor overhauls were performed regularly at an average of 169 man-hours per motor. 27 complete over-

bomb racks and made ready for flight. It was a test flight first, then after everything was found to be satisfactory, it was turned into an instruction flight, lasting three hours 15 minutes. About 50 landings were made. During August 65 gallons of gasoline was consumed per flying hour, the average length of flight was two hours, and the total flying hours for the month was seven hours, 44 minutes.

On 3 September the first patrol flight from NAS Lough Foyle was carried out with seaplane L.F. 1. It was up for four hours and carried bombs for the first time. This was also the first patrol carried out by any American Station in Ireland. Ensign Teulon was first pilot, with Ensign J. Perrin as second pilot. Upon returning, the plane made a second patrol of three hours and 35 minutes, making a total of seven hours and 35 minutes for the day. On the second patrol, an altitude of 2500 feet was reached. On 4 September L.F. 1 again made a patrol, this time of 3.25 hours. There was a very strong northeast wind, and the port wing pontoon was damaged in landing. Seaplane L.F. 2 was taken on a test flight of 40 minutes. Ensign Teulon was the pilot, with Ensign Montgomeryl, Jr., as second pilot. On 6 September seaplane L.F. 1 again went on patrol and was forced to land at sea because of low oil pressure. On resuming flight, the pressure was found to drop again, so the plane landed after being up for just an hour. Seaplane L.F. 2 on the same day was used for an instruction flight of one hour and 40 minutes. On 7 September seaplanes L.F. 1 and L.F. 2 were made ready for flights. For the week two patrols were carried out and one discontinued. Weather was unfavorable for flying.

On 9 September an American convoy was escorted for the first time. Seaplane L.F. 2, piloted by Ensign Montgomery, picked up the convoy and escorted it in. Clouds and rainsqualls were troublesome. After the pilot had left the convoy he was forced to land because of engine trouble, and was towed in by the station motor launch, which was sent in response to pigeon messages. Seaplane L.F. 1, piloted by Ensign Teulon, picked up the same convoy and escorted it through the station area. On 10 September the radio generator hold down bolts on seaplane L.F. 1 became loose while the plane was on convoy duty, with Ensign Montgomery as first pilot. In taking off—after landing to remedy the trouble—the starboard propeller was broken by the heavy sea, and the boat hull damaged beyond repair in consequence. The plane was towed into Portsmouth Harbor and later to the station. On 13 September an instruction flight was made in seaplane L.F. 2, with Ensign Teulon as first pilot and Ensign Hofer as second pilot. For this flight boat L.F. 1 had to be used for much needed spare parts. During the week one patrol was carried out, two convoys through and a third attempted, but abandoned because of an accident. In no case was the weather favorable for flying, and on two days it made flying impossible. The following week there was only a half-day suitable for flying. On 17 September, in spite of bad weather, seaplane L.F. 3, equipped with some of the parts of seaplane L.F. 1, made a test flight of 28 minutes, piloted by Ensign Teulon. On 20 September seaplane L.F. 3, while on a patrol of four hours and 25 minutes, attempted to drop bombs, but the release failed to work, due to "U" bolts being too tight. This trouble was remedied, and the releasing apparatus was tested out on 26 September by the Squadron Commander Teulon as first pilot, and Ensign Montgomery as second pilot when two bombs were dropped to test the releasing mechanism. Only one hour of suitable flying time was available during the week, the days being spent in changing to a better type of radiator. On 29 September two flights were made, the first of which was a patrol flight of 55 minutes carried out in seaplane L.F. 3, with Montgomery and Ensign Perrin as pilots; trouble being experienced with the oil thermometer. Teulon made the second, a two-hour instruction flight, as pilot, and Ensign Robb Gover as second pilot. During September 16 flights were made, with a total flying time of 33 hours and five minutes, during which time Ensign Teulon piloted for 25 hours. Ten patrol flights were made, with an average of two and one-half hours each. 53 gallons of gas was consumed per flying hour. Bad weather and a lack of materials held up flying considerably.

On 4 October Ensign Montgomery, upon returning from escorting a merchant convoy, and while in a left bank, had his port motor stop. This resulted in a slide slip from 1,000 ft. to 300 ft. The flying boat was by then too near the shore to flatten out and make a good landing. The plane subsequently landed on the water with great force at an estimated 90 mph. The plane was beached, and salvage commenced on the wreck. There were no casualties. During the first week in October there were three days possible for flying, and only two suitable for flying. Nevertheless, eight convoy patrols were made and one other between periods of bad weather. On 11 October a patrol flight was made in L.F. 2 with Ensigns Montgomery and Hofer as pilots. Also, an instruction flight of one hour was flown in the same plane, conducted by Montgomery, with Ensign Gover as second pilot. On 12 October Gover, with Ensign Hofer, carried out a short test flight in L.F. 4 as second pilot. On this date seaplane L.F. 2 made a patrol flight of 3.5 hours, with Montgomery as pilot and Ensign J.B. Thompson as second pilot. L.F. 4 also made a short patrol flight, piloted by Gover with Hofer as second pilot. The following week there was a heavy storm, the U.S. Meteorological Station at Malin Head recording the wind as 99 and 97 mph on two successive days. Parts from wrecked seaplane L.F. 3 were put into seaplane L.F. 4, making her ready for use. On 13 October the H.M.S. *Leviathan* was escorted through the station area, with a 50-mph wind blowing, which made flying difficult. This was done by seaplane L.F. 2, with Montgomery as pilot and Gover as second pilot. On 16 October seaplane L.F. 4 was used for a short patrol flight, with Montgomery as pilot and Gover as second pilot. On 17 October L.F. 4, with the same pilots, was launched, but flight was not carried out because of weather conditions. On 18 October seaplane L.F. 4, in a thick fog and heavy weather, and following a storm, was used on patrol duty—Montgomery, pilot, Gover, second pilot. On 19 October Ensign G.S. Montgomery, in seaplane L.F. 4, while escorting a 32 ship convoy, sighted and successfully bombed a hostile submarine which was about to attack the convoy. Both bombs functioned, one striking 30 feet to the right of the periscope and the other 10 feet forward. Undoubtedly at least one ship in the convoy was saved by the timely bombing. Bubbles and oil appeared on the spot, and recognition was received later in a letter from Admiral Sims. Up to this time a new record was made for duration of patrols at all Irish Stations, the time being five hours and 13 minutes. During the flight the weather was thick and rainy, and as the plane had no compass the work was carried on with great difficulty. On 20 October an instruction flight was conducted in seaplane L.F. 2 by Montgomery, Jr., and Hofer, as second pilot. On 22 October Montgomery, first pilot, and Hofer, second pilot, carried out a three-hour patrol flight in L.F. 4. A floating mine and wreckage were sighted and position recorded. On 23 October 18 hours, 43 minutes of flying time were achieved. Two seaplanes were ferried up from Queenstown. Montgomery, with Ensign C.L. Ostridge, piloted boat L.F. 6 as second pilot. Gover, with Ensign L.A. Hodgdon, piloted boat L.F. 7 as second pilot. Both planes took additional gasoline and oil at Wexford. On 24 October seaplane L.F. 2, with Ensign Teulon as first pilot and Ensign Perrin as second pilot, sighted and bombed a suspicious oil patch while on a special emergency patrol to look for submarines which had been reported in the area of the station. On 25 October Ensigns Thompson and Hodgdon, in seaplane L.F. 4, had engine trouble while coming in from a patrol, but were towed in by the station's motor launch, sent out in response to a pigeon message. On 26 October, Montgomery, in seaplane L.F. 2, made a new station record for duration of patrol of six hours and five minutes, exceeding the previous Lough Foyle record and establishing a new one for all Irish Stations. A patrol was made in seaplane L.F. 7, with Montgomery, Jr., as pilot and Ostridge as second pilot. On 27 October seaplane L.F. 2 was used to escort a convoy, with Ensign Thompson as first pilot and Ensign Hodgdon as second pilot. On 31 October seaplane L.F. 6 made a test flight, with Teulon as pilot and the Commanding Officer as a passenger. During October 23 flights were made, with a total flying time of 65 hours, 51 minutes. This included 15 patrols, with an average patrol of three hours 20 minutes. More flights could have been accomplished, but the condition of the slipway, being out of water at low tide, interfered.

On 3 November seaplane L.F. 6, with Ensign Montgomery, Jr., as pilot and Ensign Ostridge as second pilot, made a patrol of 6 hours and bombed suspicious oil patches. Seaplane L.F. 4 also conveyed a convoy on the same day, with Ensign Thompson as pilot and Ensign Perrin as second pilot. On 4 November a lightweight crankshaft in the port motor of seaplane L.F. 7 (Montgomery first pilot and Ensign Hodgdon second pilot) broke while off the Mull of Cantyre, Scotland. It was towed into Campbletown and placed in charge of the Thames Submarine Depot in good condition. A storm arose, and the boat was dashed ashore—a total wreck—the pieces being conveyed to the station on a tug some days later. This same storm also caused seaplanes L.F. 6 and L.F. 4 to break away from their mooring, when they were washed on the beach a short distance north of the station; the damage was slight. On 6 November Ensign Gover, first pilot, and Ensign Perrin, second pilot, made a short patrol flight with seaplane L.F. 6. On this date orders were received at the station to reduce flying operations. On 11 November seaplane L.F. 2 was used for a flight with Ensign Thompson as pilot. On 12 November seaplane L.F. 5 made a short test flight, with Ensign Teulon as pilot, along with Lieutenant F.J. Wilson, C.C., USN. On 30 November a test flight was made with seaplane L.F. 4 with Ensign Teulon as pilot and accompanied by the Commanding Officer.

The log of the station indicates a total flying time for station aircraft of 130 hours and 33 minutes. A total of 99 hours, six minutes was spent on 41 separate patrols. 31 hours 27 minutes was spent on 12 instructional flights, and nine test flights were carried out. The station was decommissioned 22 February 1919.

Notes:

[1] Much of the material contained in this Appendix comes from the document entitled *War Diary and History of the United States Naval Air Station, Lough Foyle, Ireland*

Appendix W: NAS Moutchic-Lacanau[1]

The activities of U.S. Naval Aviation in France, and the history of the U.S. Naval Air Station at Moutchic-Lacanau, began with the landing at Pauillac and St. Nazaire of the First Aeronautic Detachment of the U.S. Navy. Members of this Detachment had been chosen at Pensacola, and the two sections had crossed the Atlantic in the U.S.S. *Juptier* and the U.S.S. *Neptune*, respectively. The whole detachment, composed largely of machinist's mates and quartermasters, was commanded by Lieutenant Kenneth Whiting, USN, who proceeded at once to Paris and established Headquarters there. Lieutenant (j.g.) V.C. Griffin, USN, was in charge of the party, which landed on 9 June 1917, from the *Neptune* at St. Nazaire, and Lieutenant G.C. Dichman, USN, of the other party, which on June 10, 1917, landed from the *Jupiter* at Pauillac. The Quartermasters from each party, under Dichman, received instruction in the French Army Flying School at Tours. Their preliminary instruction completed, as many as could be accommodated were sent to learn smooth-water flying in seaplanes at the French School of Naval Aviation at Hourtin, and finally, to be trained on rougher water, to the French Naval School for Pilots and Observers at St. Raphael on the Mediterranean. Upon completion of this general schedule which, however, was not followed in the case of every individual, nearly all the Quartermasters of the original detachment were sent to Moutchic. The mechanics, after a course at St. Raphael under the command of Griffin, were also nearly all sent to Moutchic, which thus became the mother station of U.S. Naval Aviation in France.

Meantime, while the personnel of the Detachment were thus being trained to establish an American Instruction Station in France, the station itself was begun on 17 July 1917 when Lieutenant John Lansing Callan, USNRF, arrived at Moutchic in command of three men, E. Reichell, BMlc, D.A. Garner, Lds. QM, and J. Stanley, Lds. QM, all U.S. Navy. Lieutenant Callan took charge of the ground previously selected on the Lake of Lacanau four miles from the Ocean, half a mile from the Railway Station of Moutchic, and 32 miles from Bordeaux. 12 miles to the North was the Lake of Hourtin, while about forty miles to the South was the French School of Aerial Gunnery at Cazaux. Both of these schools were to contribute largely to the early training of the personnel of the Station at Moutchic. Cazaux, in particular, under Commandant Marzae of the French Army, exercised a powerful influence over the policies and methods of the American School.

NAS Moutchic from the air.

Instructional aircraft in front of hangars at NAS Moutchic.

Barracks at NAS Moutchic.

Barracks at NAS Moutchic.

At the time of Lieutenant Callan's arrival, a rough road along the shores of the lake was the only sign of human habitation on the ground to be covered by the Air Station. The pine forests, which covered the dunes for miles around, ran almost to the water's edge, and there were only a few scattered huts and villas anywhere in the vicinity. The arrival on 31 August of the 54 mechanics and observers who had been trained at St. Raphael, followed on 11 September by that of 11 men who had been trained at Tours, was the real beginning of the Station. On 9 October, a new draft of 33 were received from the United States, and on 15 October 27 more arrived from Brest. During this period several officers also reported for duty, including: Assistant Paymaster Michel, USN, on 8 September, who established the Pay and Supply Department; Assistant Surgeon Sinton, USNRF, attached as Medical Officer 11 September; and Ensign (T) H. Jorgenson, USN, on 10 October. During this tim drafts or small parties of officers and men were frequently sent to Cazaux for instruction as pilots and observers, the first draft of men being transferred to Cazaux 2 September.

The station remained under the command of Lieutenant Callan until 22 October. During these first three months progress was made principally in construction, which included pitching and flooring tents, digging wells, making temporary roads and paths of moss and pine-needles, erecting three Bessonneau hangars, and assembling five F.B.A. flying boats. The construction of the station had been entrusted by the French Navy for the account of the U.S. Navy to M. Georges Hauret, a French civilian contractor who also built the U.S. Naval Air Stations at Arcachon and St. Trojan. But as a result of the scarcity of civilian labor, and even more because of transportation difficulties caused by the urgent need of rolling stock at the front, it was frequently found necessary to supplement civilian labor with Navy labor in order to hasten badly needed construction. The first cars of lumber arrived and were unloaded the last of July 1917, and on 2 August a French surveyor began laying off the station. Tents were erected for the first large draft (54 men) from Detachment, and the well was prepared to be used for drinking water. Work was begun on a pier for the platform and on the breakwater.

Administrative Offices at NAS Moutchic.

Armory at NAS Moutchic.

F.B.A. flying boat used at NAS Moutchic by members of the First Aero Detachment.

The first Bessonneau hangar was completed and the telephone installed on 22 September, and shortly afterwards hangars Nos. 2 and 3, and Runway No. 1, were finished. It is interesting to note that in spite of the level of activity at this time planned for Moutchic, it was not until 8 February 1918, in a letter from the French Ministry of the Navy to Captain H.I. Cone, Commanding Office U.S. Naval Aviation in Foreign Service, that a formal acceptance of the proposal for the development of an Air Station at Moutchic was received. The progress of the work was very slow, and 15 months after its commencement was still incomplete. Consequently, during all the fall and part of the winter of 1917-1918 the men lived and ate in tents, and later in huts rudely constructed from airplane boxes. The winter climate, though the temperature never went very low—the lake only froze over once or twice—was damp and the cold penetrating, as the only available fuel was sticks and pine-cones gathered in the forest.

While the establishment of the station was thus being carried on, in the face of difficulties of various natures, there was comparatively little scope for the performance of its function as a school. On 27 September 1917, Ensign R.A. Lovett, USNRF (Naval Aviator No. 66), made the first flight in seaplane F.B.A. No. 295, the assembling of which he had directed. This flight lasted eight minutes. Another flight was made the same day of six minutes, without an observer or mechanic, using sandbags as ballast. The same officer made trial flights in F.B.A.s on 16 October, 18 October, and 22 October. There was, however, no routine flying or aerial instruction until 24 October 1917. On 22 October Lieutenant Dichman, USN, who had previously been in charge of instruction at Tours, Hourtin, and St. Raphael, relieved Lieutenant Callan as Commanding Officer, and Ensign (T) H. Jorgenson, USN, was made executive officer, a duty which he retained up to the time of demobilization. Dichman remained in Command of the Station until 6 February 1918. Under his command, construction was carried forward in the face of the same difficulties which had confronted it from the first. The prominent features of the history of this period were the commencement of the instruction, which was the ultimate function of the Station, and the thorough systematizing by Ensign Jorgenson of all that pertained to enlisted personnel and routine. Physical exercises were inaugurated, and the guard was thoroughly organized and instructed.

Morning orders were written regularly, and an increased amount of attention was given to the log. It was at this time also that bunkhouses were improvised from airplane boxes, and the men thus saved from the hardships and ill-health attendant upon a damp and cold winter spent in tents. Sanitary regulations were strictly enforced, quarantines were resorted to when necessary, and in spite of the insufficient accommodations, the health of the camp was excellent.

The station may be said to have been commissioned 24 October 1917, since on that date instruction was begun. The instruction at this time consisted of: 1) Ground School (which consisted of Navigation, Gunnery, Signaling, Aeroplanes, Motors, and Navy Regulations); 2) Solo flights for pilots; and 3) Flights for pilots and observers (passages). In order to give flying instruction in F.B.A.s—the only planes then on the station—double controls were brought in and installed in the planes by the station mechanics. There was no gunnery range, and no attempt was made to teach bombing by the use of dummy bombs. In fact, the whole course was that of a flying school, rather than of a bombing and gunnery school. This policy was not to be changed for several months. The commissioned students who took this initial course were: Ensign Archibald G. McIlwaine, USNRF (Naval Aviator No. 82), and afterwards Chief Pilot; Ensign Beach, USNRF (Naval Aviator No. 75), afterward Engineering Officer; and Ensigns N. Cabot, D.S. Ingalls (Naval Aviator No. 85), G.S. Fearing, and H.H. Landon (Naval Aviator No. 93), all USNRF, who were later sent out to patrol stations.

About this time Moutchic began to exercise its function of supplying patrol stations with trained personnel, three commissioned pilots and thirteen men being sent on 27 October to the new station of Le Croisic, Loire-Inferieure. Moutchic continued to be a finishing school. A group of enlisted men was sent every six weeks to the Gunnery School at Cazaux for observer's training. Men awaiting the opportunity for training as pilots were also sent there for this instruction. Six groups in all were sent to Cazaux. By February 1918, approximately 60 men trained in aerial gunnery became available at Moutchic.

In January 1918, about 12 American chasse pilots from the Lafayette Flying Corps offered their services to Naval Aviation. Several of these had seen service over the lines, and it was evident that they would be valuable for chasse work at Dunkerque. When released by the French they were enrolled as Ensigns and sent to Moutchic for training in seaplanes to complete their Aviator's tests.

Formation of men at NAS Moutchic.

From this time on Ensigns who had been commissioned in the schools in the United States arrived in increasing numbers, and the course at Moutchic began to assume importance in the overseas training of American naval aviators who had hitherto relied entirely upon French Schools or English Patrol Stations for their instruction. This became true in an even stronger sense when, on 17 January 1918, Lieutenant Bartlett was attached to this station as bombing and Gunnery Officer, and with a class of 11 pilots and 11 observers, inaugurated the first bombing course. This officer had studied English methods, and for about two months had been a Cazaux, where he became familiar with the improvements in aerial gunnery that the French had been able to produce in four years of intensive research. Under his direction a gunnery range has immediately begun, and on 28 January the first dummy bomb, modeled after the French 75-kilo bomb, was dropped, inaugurating the most important feature of the course.

During all this period, and until about 1 July, French planes were used exclusively in instruction. F.B.A.s, the first type, were gradually discarded for DDs and Telliers, the first DD being received 1 December, and the first Tellier, 1 February. These two types of planes, though for patrol work they had some grave defects, were found excellent for instruction purposes, and in this respect surpassed the American planes which finally replaced them.

On 6 February Lieutenant Dichman was relieved as Commanding Officer by Lieutenant Bartlett. Ensign Jorgenson remained as Executive Officer. The period of foundation and preparation may now be said to have ended, and the school to have begun its real work. Pilots arrived from the United States to complete their training, and Moutchic's real function as a school began to appear. The Instruction Department under Ensign C.D. Murray, USNRF, showed the effects of that officer's thorough training in all the English schools. The range was completed, and the Batchelor Mirror and the towed target, constructed to resemble a submarine, were introduced. At all times the preponderance of the Instruction Department over all the others was emphasized as being the end to which all other departments were the means. This policy soon began to show its effects in inventions and improvements made in bombing and gunnery. J.H. Dalen, CMM (latter Ensign Dalen, USNRF), invented and standardized a breast-plate-butt stock by means of which the availability of the Lewis gun for aerial shooting was increased many fold. B.R. Ailsworth, CCM, invented a small dummy bomb of light wood and cement, which was so simple that it could be expended without appreciable loss. This was an important device, as the dummy bombs formerly used had been so elaborate that they had to be recovered by divers. The importance of this invention and that of a bomb-dropper to fit the new bomb can hardly be overestimated, since an unlimited supply of bombs was the basis of the great improvements in the bombing course.

Buildings and hangars at NAS Moutchic.

The gunnery course under Ensign C.R. Parks, USNRF, who was trained at Cazaux, and who visited all the English Aerial Gunnery Schools, was also built up and finally made at least the equal of similar courses in the Allied Services. A training course for Aviation Intelligence Officers, including the Ground School and several specialized courses, was introduced into the Instruction Department, with Lieutenant (j.g.) P.S. Lincoln, USNRF, who also taught navigation, as Instructor. Closer and more cordial relations were established with neighboring French units, and with all the French military and civil authorities. French instructors and experts visited the school, and ideas and methods were exchanged with great freedom and good effect. Several instructors were sent to England to visit the training centers there and study English techniques in bombing and gunnery. English officers visited the station and made and received suggestions. In March 1918 the German spring offensive initiated a flurry of action on the part of naval personnel. On 30 March 1918 Vice Admiral Sims, Commander, U.S. Naval Air Forces Operating in European Waters, issued the following cable:

"In order to be prepared for possible necessity of reinforcement to the utmost of our capacity the allied army now fighting in France, please make up immediate survey of your floating forces, your forces on shore, and Naval Aviation forces in France, to determine how many men could be sent to the Western Front to do transport and other auxiliary work. No man either qualified or in training actual flying should be included in any such expedition nor should ships or stations be so depleted in personnel as not to operate efficiently. Prepare plan for concentrating this force for its organization and command, assuming that it would be employed in conjunction with British or French troops behind the front. French Ministry of Marine is being communicated with to secure their consent to this proposed employment of forces now operating in conjunction with French Navy. The plan is not definitely adopted but should the military situation become critical every possible assistance must be rendered by American military and Naval forces, and it is necessary to have a scheme worked out in advance. Unquote. Consult French Ministry and secure their consent to temporary release our Naval personnel as outlined in foregoing dispatch 02130 1751"

A copy of this cable was sent from the headquarters for U.S. Naval Aviation Forces, Foreign Service, in Paris, to all stations, along with a directive to proceed to organize the force which could be released from each station upon a basis of 50 men to the section, 100 men to a company, and four companies to a battalion. Captain Cone sent the following specific cable to Moutchic:

March 30, 1918.

"In order to be prepared for possible necessity of reinforcing to the utmost of our capacity the allied army now fighting in France advise what personnel available to be sent to the Western front to do transport and other auxiliary work period No man either qualified or in training actual flying to be included nor should station be so depleted in personnel as not to operate efficiently period In this emergency construction work at stations would be arrested temporarily."

By 3 April 1918 there were about 7000 naval personnel available in France to implement these orders. Detailed plans for the implementation of these directives included not only the assemblage of effected personnel, but also the planned relocation of the Headquarters for Naval Aviation Personnel in Foreign Service from Paris to Orleans. In the event such a move was necessary, cars and trucks from Moutchic were to rendezvous at the Hotel De Ville in Poitiers. All these plans were given a lower priority, however, upon receipt of the following cablegram:

April 3, 1918.

"Vice Admiral Bebon and General Foch consider that present circumstances do not call for presence at front of this force since they have at hand all forces needed period If such condition should arise General Foch will certainly call upon Admiral Sims and will accept offer period General Foch thanks Admiral Sims most warmly for this new proof of the ardor with which the United States participates in the war period Minister of War and the Minister of Marine were informed of the offer period Above opinions are those of General Foch and Admiral Debon who are in accord period It is not deemed advisable to assemble and hold in readiness this force for possible use within fortnight 15303."

On numerous occasions when fires broke out in the vast pine forests which border the whole of the coast near Moutchic, the station force gave valuable help to the local civilians, who, deprived of most of their foresters by the Army, and without American assistance, were unable to fight the fires lighted, sometimes undoubtedly by Spanish incendiaries. Letters stating appreciation for the efforts expended by station personnel while fighting such fires were received by the station commander on 20 July 1918 from the Domaine De Lacanau, and on 10 September 1918 from Director of the French Service Des Baux et Forets.

During May and July 1918 a draft of 77 radio electricians, who, in accordance with a policy recently decided upon at Washington, were to be trained as observers, were received from the United States, where they had already been trained in bombing and gunnery at Miami. The men in this draft, one group of 12 which was received on 27 May, and a third group of 38, being received on 13 July, were accordingly assigned as observers to a commissioned pilot and trained in bombing and gunnery.

By 1 July, the Administration, Instruction, and Engineering buildings, the armory, five hangars, the bunkhouses, the mess halls, the sickbay, the head, and the wash houses with hot and cold showers had all been completed and were in use. As there were yet no officer's quarters on the station, the officers under instruction lived at Lacanau-Ocean, four miles away, and were carried in trucks to and from the station. About half the crew each weekend had liberty in Bordeaux, and the remainder had five-hour local liberty on Sundays. Under the direction of Acting Pay Clerk C.W. Fox, USN, Athletic Officer, a volunteer orchestra was organized and equipped, theatrical entertainments were given, and boxing was highly developed among the station force. American planes equipped with Liberty Motors soon arrived. Two Curtiss HS-1 Flying Boats had been received at Moutchic and had been tested by the Instructors from the points of view of flying, bombing, gunnery, and engineering, and their defects, especially the faulty cockpits, had been criticized in reports and recommendations for changes made. There were on the station at the time, 16 planes for instruction purposes, two HS-1s, six Telliers, and eight DDs. On account of the bumpiness of the air caused by midday heat, flying was begun at 0430 hrs., discontinued at 1030 hrs., resumed at 1500 hrs., and finished at 2030 hrs. The Instruction Department, of which on July 23 Ensign E.L. Van Houten, USNRF (Naval Aviator No. 269), himself a product of the school, had taken charge, included:

1. A ground course lasting one week and embracing:
    - (a) Navigation
    - (b) Meteorology
    - (c) Recognition of ship silhouettes
    - (d) Theory of bombing
    - (e) Mechanism of bombs
    - (f) Use of carrier pigeons (a total of 10 homing pigeons were used in the training of pilots and observers)
    - (g) Signaling
2. A Gunnery course lasting approximately two weeks, and embracing:
    - (a) Theory of deflection
    - (b) The mechanism of the Lewis Gun
    - (c) The cleaning of jams
    - (d) Target practice on the range
    - (e) Target practice from the air

3. A bombing course lasting approximately two weeks and embracing:
    - (a) Passages
    - (b) Batchelor Mirror work
    - (c) Dummy bombing
    - (d) Surprise bombing
    - (e) Bombing a towed target made to represent a submarine

Each student dropped one hundred bombs before completing this course.

A salient feature of the station was the remarkable morale which existed equally among students and enlisted men, and which was a product of excellent living conditions, hard work, a strong Executive Department, and, indirectly, of the knowledge by the entire personnel that the School, and consequently the Station, were accomplishing important and increasing results.

Barracks at NAS Moutchic.

Meanwhile, what was known as the Northern Bombing Project, for naval personnel to do night bombing in land machines on the Belgian submarine ports, was conceived and elaborated. Commissioned pilots and enlisted observers were at once sent from Moutchic to the U.S. Army Bombing School at Clermont-Ferrand, and the French Army Bombing School at Avord, for special courses in bombing. Drafts of enlisted men were also sent to help establish the centers for the squadrons in July, August, and September.

When the U.S. Naval Aviation Service also commenced activities in Italy with the opening of a Flying School at Lake Bolsena, pilots and observers trained in bombing and gunnery were supplied from Moutchic to the Station at Porto Corsini, which was occupied 24 July. Both of these activities, however, were secondary to the Station's real function of supplying the Naval Air Stations along the French coast with personnel trained to fight submarines, and the instruction continued to be directed primarily to this end.

On 14 August, Lieutenant Bartlett was relieved as Commanding Officer by Lieutenant Commander R.W. Cabaniss, USN. Lieutenant Bartlett was sent back to the United States to give expert advice, from the point of view of practical needs in France, on the fundamental training of pilots and observers there. During the six months of his command, the instruction had been developed from very simple beginnings into a practical and effective training in anti-submarine warfare. The School had trained and sent out to active duty 104 commissioned and 103 enlisted students, and every American heavier-than-air station on the French coast included among its personnel officers and men trained at Moutchic.

Under Lieutenant Commander Cabaniss, who already had experience as Commanding Officer of the Ground School at the Massachusetts Institute of Technology, a successful effort was made to intensify the flying and thereby produce results more rapidly than before. This policy was made at once necessary by the great increase in the number of students who were sent to Moutchic from the United States, and practicable because of the change of seasons, which allowed more flying in the middle of the day. But the new policy was used primarily on the argument that since actual patrolling must not be dependent upon the weather, students who were being trained for patrolling should be taught to practice to bomb in bad weather as well as good. The old policy had been based on the argument that since no one could learn the technique of bombing if the instruction was given while the weather was rough, the best results would be obtained by teaching students this technique so thoroughly in smooth air that they would be able to use it even in bad weather. One result of the new policy was that an increasing number of students were trained, and that the number of hours in the air was also greatly increased. More attention was now also paid to the strict observance of Navy Regulations, and such points as military appearance and etiquette. Correctness in carrying out all formations was emphasized. The Station was modeled as nearly as possible along the lines suggested by the Paimboeuf Conference of Commanding Officers of Patrol Stations, held in July 1918. A policy of decentralization was followed, some of the responsibility which had hithertofore been centered in the Executive Officer being placed upon Heads of Departments, and a separate Transportation Department was created. The Station force was organized as a regiment of two battalions, and there were three daily regimental formations, a daily inspection, and a weekly review.

According to a further change in policy at Washington about this time, no more enlisted men were to be trained as observers, the commissioned pilots being trained to act interchangeably as observers and pilots. This decision, however, was in turn reversed when fifty radio electricians arrived on 9 September to be trained as gunners in H-16s, followed on 4 November by another class of enlisted men, all of whom were to be given the observer's course.

The abrupt ending of hostilities on 11 November found the Station thoroughly organized and equipped, with 23 permanent officers, 24 officers under instruction, and 483 enlisted men (See Table W-1). There were 24 planes on the Station, 11 of which were HS-1s, which—since about the beginning of September—had been used almost exclusively in bombing instruction. The roads around and through the camp had been finished, and the construction was, at last, practically complete. After the receipt of instructions to demobilize, the material not being taken over by the French was disposed of and the personnel transferred as directed by Headquarters. At 0900 hrs. on 31 November 1918, the station at Moutchic went out of commission. The station was taken over by the French Army, a commission appointed in Bordeaux arranging the details of the transaction. On receipt of authority from the Director of Travaux

A French F.B.A. seaplane.

Hydrauliques at Rochefort, the rifle range and the other remaining property were derequisitioned. The contract cost of this station was 842,000 francs. It was anticipated that the damage claims incident to the cancellation would be small, as practically all work was completed on the date of cancellation. For its brief period of existence the Naval Air Station at Moutchic cost the U.S. government $159,295.00. The breakdown of this expense was as follows:

a) Cost of improvements (including charges for labor and transportation on French contract) $202,095.00
b) Value of improvements liquidated 42,800.00
c) Cost (Subject of considerable further deduction for French buildings to be sold to the Ministry of War the exact price of which had not been determined on March 1 $159,295.00

During its period of operation there were a total of 14 fatalities at Moutchic. Five were due to natural causes, and nine were due to accidents, all of which were related to aircraft crashes.

It is safe to say that when the history of the Station ended with the departure on 24 November of the first draft of 200 men for demobilization in the United States, it was in a position to continue its work with increasing efficiency and usefulness.

French F.B.A. Type C seaplane.

TABLE W-1
Officers and Student Pilots Onboard NAS Moutchic
as of 11 November 1918

Cabaniss, Robert W., Commander, USN	Commanding Officer
Jorgenson, Herman, Lieutenant (j.g.) (T)(G), USN	Executive Officer
Van Houten, Eugene L., Ensign, USNRF	Officer in Charge of Instruction and Ordnance Officer
Mayo, Thomas F., Ensign, USNRF	Intelligence Officer and Aide to the C.O.
Roche, Francis J. Ensign, USNRF	Instruction Officer
Tribken, Irving, B., Ensign, USNRF	Transportation Officer
Townsend, Charles H., Ensign, USNRF	Chief Pilot
Batchelor, Henry A., Ensign, USNRF	Engineer Officer
Stribling, Harrly A.L., Ensign, USNRF	Instruction Officer
Letzkue, Elmer A., Ensign, USNRF	Instruction Officer
Affleck, William R., Ensign, USNRF	Instruction Officer
Dalen, John H., Ensign, USNRF	Instruction Officer
Palmer, Thomas R., Ensign, USNRF	Assistant Chief Pilot
Miller, George C., Ensign, USNRF	Instruction Officer
Clark, A.B., Lieutenant, USN	Pay Corps.
Kuhlmann, A.E., Lieutenant (j.g.), USN	Medical Corps.
Biffar, H.M., Lieutenant (j.g.), USN	Medical Corps.
Kenyon, E.M., Lieutenant (j.g.), USNRF	Dental Corps.
Breen, J.W., Gunner (T), USN	Assistant Ordnance Officer
Byrne, O.J., Gunner (T), USN	Radio Officer
Stroud, R.H., Acting Pay Clerk, USN	Pay Corps.
Doyle, P., Gunner (E) (T), USN	Public Works Officer
Stone, J.D., Machinist (A) (T), USN	Assistant Engineering Officer
Norton, Ansel, N., Ensign, USNRF	Under Instruction in Gunnery and Bombing
Pottinger, Earl H., Ensign, USNRF	"
Smith, William P., Ensign, USNRF	"
Stewarat, Vance, Ensign, USNRF	"
Van Deren, Frank, Ensign, USNRF	"
Wolfe, Alexander M., Ensign, USNRF	"
Williams, Chauncy L., Ensign, USNRF	"
Waggoner, Carl E., Ensign, USNRF	"
Warner, Herbert R., Ensign, USNRF	"
Williamsosn, Richard L., Ensign, USNRF	"
Wright, Floyd H., Ensign, USNRF	"
Austin, Raymond M., Ensign, USNRF	"
Burke, James F., Ensign, USNRF	"
Burrags, Walter S., Ensign, USNRF	"
Bard, William H., Ensign, USNRF	"
Bowers, Anderson, Ensign, USNRF	"
Bullen, William G., Ensign, USNRF	"
Cantwell, William H., Ensign, USNRF	"
Gaty, Theodore H., Ensign, USNRF	"
Haggarty, Alfred C., Ensign, USNRF	"
Hastings, Eugene T., Ensign, USNRF	"

TABLE W-2
Statistical Data U.S. Naval Air Station (Seaplane)
Moutchic, Lacanau, France
From November 11, 1917 To November 11, 1918

Wk. End.	Flights Made	Total Knots	Flying Time (Hr.)	Suitable Flying Time (Hr.)	Aircraft on Station	Aircraft in Comsn	Flying Personnel
1917							
11 November	83	19:54	1200	8	6	No Record	No Record
18 November	206	43:212	2600	10	7	"	"
25 November	171	49:11	2940	17	7	"	"
2 December	122	39:54	2400	10	7	'	'
9 December	191	62:19	3750	11	8	"	"
16 December	296	90:54	5460	12	8	"	"
23 December	105	38:31	2360	12	8	"	"
30 December	17:53	1080	13	9	"	"	"
1918							
7 January	24	5:48	360	13	8	No Record	No Record
14 January	18	7:40	480	12	7	"	"
21 January	64	23:00	1380	17	11	"	18
28 January	137	45:20	2730	14	9	"	18
4 February	149	55:10	3300	16	10	'	18
11 February	132	47:15	2850	17	11	"	22
18 February	65	20:03	1800	17	13	"	24
25 February	58	16:47	1020	16	12	"	24
4 March	60	17:07	1050	22	13	"	20
11 March	90	36:07	2160	22	10	'	45
18 March	174	61:48	3720	22	8	"	45
25 March	157	50:39	3060	22	10	"	46
1 April	139	46:05	2760	19	10	"	46
8 April	153	53:56	3230	112	11	"	46
15 April	187	62:35	3750	16	8	"	46
22 April	164	50:14	3030	16	12	"	42
29 April	220	69:55	4200	16	12	"	36
6 May	203	84:24	5080	16	11	"	—
11 May	174	65:09	3930	3 SOP	—	32	—
18 May	234	74:44	4500	3 SOP 4 T 1 FBA 11 DD	13	55	11
25 May	—	—	—	—	—	—	—
1 June	261	86:21	5160	3 SOP 6 T 1 FBA 2 GL 10 DD	13	35	—
8 June	229	99:38	5940	3 SOP 6 T 1 FBA 1 GL	10	39	90
15 June	199	76:23	4590	1 GL 8 DD 3 SOP 6 T 1 FBA	9	38	124

22 June	177	60:14	3600	21	2	33	124
29 June	302	127:28	7650	20 SOP	5 SOP	83	122
6 July	173	67:34	3950	2 HS-2 2 SOP 6 T 8 DD 1 GL	7	45	11
13 July	352	103:54	6240	19 SOP	8	40	92
20 July	300	88:35	5310	2 HS-1 3 SOP 6 DD	8	44	98
27 July	208	64:18	3870	4 HS-1	9	35	106
3 August	227	56:28	3390	2 HS-1 3 SOP 6 DD	6	28	114
10 August	164	37:46	2250	2 HS-1 2 SOP 6 T 6 DD	5	21	109
17 August	139	45:10	2700	3 HS-1 2 SOP 6 T 5 DD	6	32	96
24 August	235	72:41	4380	4 HS-1 2 SOP 9 T 6 DD	7	45	115
31 August	238	99:48	6000	6 HS-1 2 SOP 6 T 9 DD	12	56	107
7 September	256	109:05	6640	7 HS-1 2 SOP 6 T 9 DD	11	57	18
14 September	129	35:28	3300	6 HS-1 2 SOP 6 T 6 DD	12	19	18
21 September	406	183:25	11040	13 HS-1 2 SOP 6 T 5 DD	17	66	22
28 September	468	226:10	13560	16 HS-1 2 SOP 6 T 5 DD	21	56	22
5 October	499	223:43	13440	10 HS-1 2 SOP 6 T 5 DD	13	72	19
12 October	430	187:42	11280	9 HS-1 2 SOP 6 T 5 DD	17	43	19

19 October	350	153:18	9180	10 HS-1 4 SOP 6 T 5 DD	13	39	23
26 October	461	194:11	11640	13 HS-1 2 SOP 6 T 5 DD	18	73	22
2 November	407	210:15	12050	11 HS-1 2 SOP 6 T 5 DD	11	52	22
9 November	333	158:53	9540	11 HS-1 2 SOP 6 T 5 DD	13	40	22
11 November	33	14:35	90	11 HS-1 2 SOP 6 T 5 DD	15	18	22
Total	10,807	4,049:37	242,320				

TABLE W-3
U.S. Naval Aviation, Foreign Service, French Unit
Enlisted Personnel At NAS Moutchic
At Time of Demobilization Order

11 November 1918

Rate	**Allowed**	**On Hand**
B.M.	8	23
G.M.	17	5
Sea.	28	47
Spec. Mech.	77	159
E.(G)	2	0
E.(R)	6	2
C.M.	0	11
S.F.	15	44
P.&F.	2	15
S.M.M.	2	0
S.K.	1	0
M.M.	55	109
B.Smith	1	3
C.Smith	2	2
Yeo.	14	20
P.M.& H.A.	5	7
COM.STW.	1	2
S.C.	8	8
BKRS.	2	2
MATT.	8	16
O.C. & S.	2	1
PRINT.	1	1
FIREMAN	0	0
PAINT.	1	1
BUG.	1	1
MUS.	0	1

Attachment W-1

INSPECTION REPORT ON NAS MOUTCHIC

UNITED STATES ATLANTIC FLEET
THE COMMANDER IN CHIEF

Paris, France
18 November 1918

From: Commander in Chief
To: Secretary of the Navy (OPERATIONS).
Subject: Report on U.S. Naval Air Station, Moutchic-Lacanau, Gironde, France.

1. The U.S. Naval Air Station at Moutchic was inspected by the Commander in Chief and Staff on 31 October 1918. The inspection consisted of a thorough inspection of the station and of an inspection and review of the personnel.

2. Moutchic is not an operating air station in the strict sense of the term, But is an aviation, bombing and gunnery school under the direct supervision of Commander U.S. Naval Forces in France (Aviation). It is well situated on Lake Lacanau in the Gironde, weather and air conditions being favorable for the extensive flying which is necessary in performing its mission as a school. The Lake, however, would probably prove too limited in area to take care of any considerable expansion in the activities of the station.

3. This station easily surpasses any other inspected in the military appearance and bearing of its personnel and there are many evidences of a healthy state of discipline for which credit is due to the Commanding Officer, Commander R.W. Cabaniss, U.S.N., particularly in view of the inexperience of his assistant officers and of the constantly change personnel.

4. The station is well planned and the Buildings are of at least a semi-permanent nature. The enlisted personnel are excellently housed and except for the lack of stoves, which have been requested should marke their quarters very comfortable. The quarters for student officers are satisfactory and suitable quarters are in course of construction for the chief petty officers. There are not suitable quarters for the permanent officers, such personnel occupy private dwellings, which they have rented and which are considered inadequate. A Y.M.C.A. building is in course of construction to replace an old and unsatisfactory building not being utilized:

5. At present the HS-1 planes have to be anchored out or made fast to the shore, as the hangars are not large enough to admit a machine of this size. The present hangars are to be raised and an additional one is being built which will take the HS-1 planes, but there is not sufficient space in which to located hangars enough to care for the ultimate complement of machines which is placed at eighteen HS-1 planes and five Telleirs. Apparently no particular damage is done by anchoring these machines out, except that after a while they become more or less waterlogged and difficult to fly.

6. Difficulty has been experienced in disposing of sewage. The Public works Department of the station is undertaking the installation of a new sewer system. Use is made of a cesspool and it is probable that an additional one will be required.

7. All major repairs to the planes of this station are made at Pauillac, although Moutchic is well equipped to take care of minor repairs and its workshops are well planned and efficient.

8. The officers and instruction buildings seem to be adequate and the mess halls are both excellent in construction and scrupulously clean.

9. The system of instruction of pilots is thorough, the maximum possible amount of flying, bombing and machine gun practice being required, together with class room theoretical instruction. An excellent feature of this is the discussion of the dummy bombing patterns with the pilots who made them, the observations and plotting being done by personnel in the three stands erected for this purpose in the Lake. It is believed that more instruction in day visual signals could be given, using the Aldis lamp. It was also noted that personnel are being sent to the station for the purpose of obtaining instruction in radio for use in seaplanes and that the apparatus is on the station, yet no instruction is provided due to the prohibition of the use of radio by the Force Commander on account of possible interference with French Stations. This instruction should be undertaken, and by using the proper tuning no interference will result.

10. Machine gun practice is carried out on shore at the target range and in the air at a submarine target, at shadows of other seaplanes and at silhouettes of seaplanes anchored in the Lake. There is an extensive plant for the manufacture of dummy (concrete) bombs of which there is an ample supply for the practice in this branch of instruction.

11. Although this station is thoroughly efficient, and it is believed that is has been useful in the training of pilots in the past, it is the Commander in Chief's belief, that in view of the fact that practically all the air stations in France are now beginning to operate and especially as comparatively well trained pilots are now being received from home, this station should be discontinued.

/s/ H.T. MAYO

Copies to:
OPERATIONS
OPERATIONS (Aviation)
Comdr., U.S. Naval Forces, Europe
Comdr., U.S. Naval Forces (Aviation)
Comdr., U.S. Naval Air Station, Moutchic
Comdr., U.S. Naval Forces, France

Notes:

[1] Much of the materil in this Appendix is taken from the report entitled History of U.S. Naval Aviation, Foreign *Service, French Unit, 1917 and 1918*

Appendix X: NAS Eastleigh[1]

I. Formation

The U.S. Naval Air Station at Eastleigh existed solely due to the Navy's effort with the Northern Bombing Group. The Navy originally intended to establish all the stations of this Group along the coast of France, or up immediately behind the battle line of the early months of 1918. The first Supply and Distribution Base was established at St. Ingleverte in a wheat field, some 700 miles from the nearest established U.S. Naval Aviation Repair Base (NAS Pauillac), and a half a mile west of Calais—just five miles from the Channel. The first contingent of men arrived at St. Ingleverte on 3 July 1918 following a long and tiring motor lorrie trip from Pauillac. They were the vanguard of the contingent of men assigned to undertake the construction of the facilities of the Northern Bombing Group. Well in advance of the establishment of St. Ingleverte, the Navy had begun the work of planning for the operations of the Northern Bombing Group. Part of this planning involved the establishment of the Group's bases. One concept of this facet of the program involved the necessity for a well-equipped assembly and repair base. A site for this plant had been previously surveyed, and the location fixed some 50 miles or more behind the lines. However, late in June 1918 there was considerable alarm, based on the events of 21 March 1918, that the Germans might break through along the French coast and overrun the Pas de Calais, the area originally selected for the repair and assembly base. It was therefore considered advisable to seek out another location more isolated from night disturbances and the possibility of capture for a base where skilled mechanics could labor practically immune from German interference. St. Ingleverte was left as a facility chartered with the distribution of aircraft arriving for the Northern Bombing Group squadrons.

The task then became one of selecting a suitable site for the erection of a large, well-equipped assembly and repair base to serve the whole Northern Bombing Group with its delivery-distribution point at St. Ingleverte. With the French coast eliminated from consideration, the other side of the Channel attracted the U.S. Board of Survey. A Committee of Investigation, comprising Captain Hanrahan, Lieutenant Commander Briscoe, Lieutenant Billings, and others, after a long search, met the disappointment of being unable to find an available site adjacent to the coast of France that was within ferrying distance to St. Ingleverte. An appeal was made to the British Air Ministry for one of their sites on the southern coast of England. Fortunately, the Air Ministry came forward and offered a desirable site. On July 4, 1918, in reply to the letter from the Air Ministry, the same Survey Board, together with some British officers, proceeded from Paris to look the site over. Arriving at Eastleigh, they found an RAF Acceptance Base about half-completed. They decided at once to take it over.

Lieutenant George deC. Chevalier, Commanding Officer of Dunkirk, became Commanding Officer of the new base, and Lieutenant Frederick N. Bolles was appointed as Public Works Officer. They landed in Eastleigh together on 23 July 1918. A few days later Paymaster J.S. Masters and "Doc" York, the first Medical Officer, arrived. Living quarters with modern conveniences had not yet been constructed on the Station, which then floated on a sea of mud, so it was necessary for the first arrivals to establish themselves at the Junction Hotel, Eastleigh. Two taxicabs were hired as a means of transportation to and from the Station for the first 30 days.

The problems which confronted these pioneer officers were numerous; chief among which was the construction of one of the most elaborate and important units of the whole Northern Bombing Group and its equipment. With no material on hand, and a very limited, intangible supply available, and with no crew, and only a pocket-edition typewriter belonging to Lieutenant Bolles, the task of submitting plans and obtaining the approval of officers located in comfortable headquarters was begun.

Appeals for materials were made, and the inevitable fight was on between the Supply Department and those upon whom rested the responsibility for actually getting the work done. Appeals being ineffective, demands were made, and afterwards authority was assumed, material located, and possession obtained by means of all sorts of schemes and devices. Among the examples of resourcefulness which might be cited was the borrowing of 150 tons of cement and five carloads of roofing felt from different sources, employing nothing more than the combined persuasive power of several officers and Earle L. Holms, CSM, who made the expedition of work and the housing of the men their immediate paramount duty to their

Country. A small quantity of cement was secured through the usual channels. The shortage of cement and entire lack of roofing paper would have brought to a halt all construction work at a time when the very activity of the Station might have been halted, and pneumonia was threatening to seriously decimate the ranks of the men. Similar direct methods were pursued in obtaining shafting pulleys, etc., the lack of which prevented the actual operation of what little machinery Assembly and Repair (A&R) had been able to obtain.

A frequent occurrence was the unheralded arrival of sundry drafts of men—sometimes hundreds in number, other times filtering in two or three stragglers at a time who usually arrived at unheard-of hours of the night, or frequently unannounced. As in many other critical moments in the experience of those in command of Overseas Forces, the spirit of Clara Barton appeared to ward off and prevent what seemed to be inevitable suffering. One day, when Commanding Officer Chevalier and Lieutenant Bolles were absolutely at their wits end—the Rest Camp being full to overflowing and unwilling to take more men from the Station—a Red Cross representative appeared on the scene as though he were an angel from heaven and inquired whether or not the Station could use some Red Cross tents. The announcement of this good fortune, however, brought more men and, as badly as men were needed to "carry on" the work, it seemed that the packing boxes and all the scrap lumber in England would be exhausted before the full compliment for the Station was housed. At its peak of operation NAS Eastleigh had a compliment of nearly 2200 NCOs and enlisted men.

Lieutenant Chevalier was advanced to the rank of Lieutenant Commander and detached from technical staff duty, almost coincident with the placing of the Station on an actual operating basis. His replacement was Commander Bayard T. Bulmer, a non-aviator who arrived at the station on 21 September and assumed command the next day. Commander Bulmer appears to have been selected to command NAS Eastleigh based on the fact that for two and a half years he had been Shop Superintendent and Overseer of the New and Repair Work at the Charlestown Navy Yard in Boston.

In late September influenza struck Eastleigh. Before it abated 21 men would die of the disease.

II. Organization

NAS Eastleigh was organized along the formal lines of a Naval Air Station. Under the Commanding Officer was an Executive Department (headed by Lieutenant Joseph F. Dunn) which was responsible for the day-to-day functioning of the Station. Lt. Dunn arrived at Eastleigh after being First Lieutenant at NAS Miami and Executive Officer of a squadron of the Northern Bombing Group in the field. Individual and specialized departments were organized as follows: Public Works Department (Lieutenant Bolles); A&R Department (Lieutenant O. W. Howard); Flight Department (initially Lieutenant Kenneth MacLeish); Medical Department (Lieutenant (j.g.) E.W. York, followed by Lieutenant A.R. Neal, and finally Lieutenant Commander Frederick Ceres); Transportation Department (Ensign Carl C. Francis); Supply Department (Lieutenant Josiah G. Venter); Disbursing Department (Lieutenant Thomas A. Henry); and Commissary Division (Pay Clerk Charles J. Wacker).

The A&R Department was the sole reason for the existence of NAS Eastleigh. The Station's only A&R Officer was Lieutenant O.W. Howard. Howard received his commission as Ensign in the Illinois Naval Militia in 1911, and on 1 February was made Commanding Officer of the Seventh Division, Illinois Naval Militia. He was commissioned Lieutenant in the USNNV on 4 February 1917. Prior to his arrival at Eastleigh he had been Executive Officer aboard the U.S.S. *Massachusetts*, Executive Officer of the U.S. Naval Training Camp for Seamen at Philadelphia, and Mechanical Superintendent at the U.S. Naval Aircraft Factory at Philadelphia. Serving at various times under Howard were: Lieutenant (j.g.) Austin E. Potter (Engineer-in-Charge Fiat and Caproni Divisions); Lieutenant (j.g.) William H. Dernell (Material Officer); Ensign Charles M. Hick (Asst. A&R Officer); Ensign George Harris Britt (Engineer Officer); Ensign Douglas W. Brooks (Superintendent Metal Shops and Liberty Divisions); Ensign George H. Bray (Superintendent Fiat Division); Ensign Warren Clements (Superintendent Wood Shops Division); Ensign S.D. Hallagan (Superintendent Plane Assembly); Ensign George R. Canty (Officer Manager); Ensign George T. Tavenner (Beach Officer); Ensign Roy D. Young (Personnel Officer); Ensign Edwin W. Cooney (Personnel Officer); Machinist F.L. Bixby (Assistant Superintendent Plane Assembly); Machinist Burt Blackstock (Superintendent Motor Lorry Division); Machinist Roy Burleigh (Ignition Division); Machinist Lyman W. Callard (Chief Draftsman); Machinist James F. Crum (Foreman, Metal Shop); Machinist Francis Gatchet (Assistant Superintendent, Liberty Division); Machinist Harwood J. Gilbert (Assistant Superintendent Fiat Division); Machinist Harry Jaeckel (Assistant Superintendent Liberty Division); Machinist M.F. McHugh (Ordnance Officer); Machinist Enoch McPeake (Foreman Machine Division); Machinist Frederick Rueckeert (Superintendent Motor Testing Division); Machinist Van Allen Soule (Inspector, Fiat Division); Carpenter R.R. Huntley (Assistant Material Officer); and Carpenter E.F. Rouillon (Caproni Division).

The Flight Department was the immediate connecting link between A&R and the actual bombing operations of the Northern Bombing Group. All airplanes were delivered to this Department for flight testing, at the successful conclusion of which they were sent over the English Channel to Northern France, this flight usually taking about one and one-half hours for D.H.-4s and D.H.-9s, and slightly longer for the D.H.-6s. Lieutenant MacLeish was Eastleigh's first Flight Officer. Upon his assignment to France Lieutenant MacLeish's place was taken by Lieutenant (j.g.) Ingalls. In September Captain William McIlvain was temporarily assigned to Eastleigh. His function was to expedite the shipment of material to the Day Wing of the Northern Bombing Group. Following the signing of the Armistice Lieutenant Ingalls was permitted to return to the U.S. Ensign William Brockwell (Naval Aviator No. 334) then became Flight Officer. During its existence the Flight Department consisted of the following staff: Lieutenant (j.g.) R.G. Coombie (Naval Aviator No. 92) (Instructor, Flight Department); Ensign R.L. Loomis (Naval Aviator No. 578) (Ferry Pilot); Ensign J.C. Newlin Jr. (Naval Aviator No. 312) (Ferry Pilot); Ensign Earl Schoonmaker (Naval Aviator No. 388) (Ferry Pilot); Ensign John Warburton (Naval Aviator No. 163) (Ferry Pilot); Ensign W.M. West (Naval Aviator No. 280 1/2) (Ferry Pilot); Machinist Einar Boydler (Naval Aviator No. 1736) (Instructor, Flight Department); and Machinist William Miller (Naval Aviator No. 1735) (Instructor, Flight Department).

III. OPERATION

The A&R function at NAS Eastleigh lasted only for a period of about two and a half months. Starting from nothing, the assembly and repair of aircraft was soon operating with a double shift of operators. Production was so successful that for three days during the second month activities actually had to be suspended due to a lack of facilities in France to house the aircraft that Eastleigh was sending. The work at Eastleigh was of such a high quality that of all the aircraft sent over to France, only two machines were reported as being out of alignment upon their arrival. Subsequent investigation found that in each case the ferry pilots had indulged in some extra-curricular activities with the machines enroute to their destination.

The majority of work performed within the A&R Department involved the assembly of D.H.-4 aircraft and the preparation of Liberty "Twelve" engines. Of this effort, most of the work of the men was directed in the preparation of the engines, as there was a shortage of airframes to assemble. In fact, because of this shortage, coupled with an excess of British D.H. 9 airframes, considerable time at Eastleigh was spent preparing Liberty engines for the British. This was done as part of a swap arranged by the Navy with the British, wherein U.S. engines were being swapped for British airframes. For the most part the work of preparing the airframes and engines went smoothly. The only significant points of difficulty which arose with this work were in the areas of adapting the British machine gun synchronizing gear to the Liberty engine and the Marlin machine guns, and in adapting Signal Corps propeller hubs to the Navy design of the plane. Each of these problems was successfully overcome.

It was absolutely necessary that all Liberty engines, upon receipt, be completely disassembled, reassembled, inspected, and tested before use in an aircraft. In its initial state Eastleigh lacked motor test stands. Therefore, with a little ingenuity, the following procedure was adopted. Before assembling the wings the machine was run out of the hangar, its wheels blocked and the tail weighed with sand bags, while the motor was completely installed with all auxiliaries, and connected by hose with the Station's water supply. The motor then was run at full speed, using a full-sized propeller to hold down the motor. In a relatively short time the first temporary test stand was available, and subsequent motors could be subjected to longer testing times. Eventually permanent test stands were constructed. By the end of hostilities permanent test stands Nos. 1 and 2 were in operation, and Nos. 3 and 4 were under construction. By this time the motor test crews were working 18 hours a day with both a day and a night crew. On 15 November the word was given to cease testing and to dismantle all motor test stands. Within two hours three test stands, each with a motor in-test, were completely stripped of everything except controls, sheds, and the framework of the stands. These same stands had taken some two weeks to construct.

As part of the proposed plan for the Northern Bombing Group the Navy had purchased three-engined Caproni bombers from Italy. These machines were intended to be prepared at Eastleigh prior to becoming operational. The first of these machines, B-18, arrived at Eastleigh on 1 October 1918. The Fiat motors were removed, disassembled, and reassembled, after the correction of deficiencies. One of the motors was then given an eight hour running on the engine test stand with satisfactory results. Attention was then given to the airframe of the Caproni. The motor beds were rebraced, and the gasoline system was redesigned so that the feed would be entirely via gravity, rather than varying pressure. The work on this machine was not completed in sufficient time for the machine to be ferried to France.

IV. Conclusion

The first draft of men to leave NAS Eastleigh departed on 2 December 1918 at 1830 hrs. A second draft departed at 2045 hrs, and a third draft departed at 2145 hrs. A fourth draft of 600 men was left at the Station on guard duty. The departing personnel boarded trains for Liverpool. The next morning they all boarded the S.S. *Leviathan.* On Wednesday the S.S. *Leviathan* pulled out into the Mersey, bound for Brest. For three days the ship waited at Brest for coal. Finally, on Sunday, at 1430 hrs. she steamed out of the harbor bound for home.

During its history 21 men stationed at NAS Eastleigh died. They were:

Machinist James W. McMeekin, USNRF
Arcival, Henry, Alexander, Sea.2
Benson, John Mayo, LQM
Bettisworth, Arthur Rolland, CM2
Britt, George, LQM
Burch, James Madison, LE(R)
Claude, Elmer Samuel, Sea.
Dean, George Franklin, LE(R)
Johnnston, Eruy Alvin, LE(R)
Kerr, John Braden F3
Kronek, Fred Charles, AS
Lortz, Harold Ray, Sea.2
McNeely, Claude Johnson, CM2
Orange, Barrett Carlisle, LE(R)
Radford, Carroll Herber, LE(R)
Reindl, Eric John, AS
Schohn, Eugene Charles, Sea.2
Swinnerton, David, SC2
Vance, David Graham, MM1
Waltrip, Hobart Theodore CM2

Notes:

[1] Much of the material in this Appendix is taken from the document entitled *The Battle of Eastleigh* published by Frederick N. Bolle

Appendix Y: NAS Killingholme[1]

I. CONSTRUCTION

Killingholme was one of two sites selected by the Navy for the location of a Naval Air Station in England. The town had little to recommend for itself, other than being in a strategic location for potential aerial operations from the English east coast against Germany. Early in the war (1916) the RFC selected the site as a base for such operations. Over a period of time the RNAS took over the base, intending to use it as a base for aerial operations in the Heligoland Blight. However, it was soon found that the technical shortcomings of the aircraft then in use precluded such activities. That being the case, the base was reconstituted as a patrol station for shipping, mine detection, and anti-submarine patrols in the North Sea. Killingholme rapidly became the center of great shipping activities; convoys were constantly passing up and down the coast; it was within striking distance of the lines of submarine travel; and, moreover, German Zeppelins in their raids on the English coast often overflew the base. By pushing the patrols out on somewhat extended flights, great assistance could be rendered to the fleet maneuvers and observations from this base. When a British and American joint board decided that the U.S. would cooperate in patrolling the North Sea, a portion of the existing air stations at Killingholme was selected to be converted into an American station. In December 1917, Commander Kenneth Whiting, who was then in Europe, was ordered home for the purpose of organizing the necessary personnel, and to obtain the equipment to operate the station by the Navy.

II. PERSONNEL

A U.S. Navy presence at Killingholme can be traced back to a draft of 40 enlisted men, under the command of Ensign Richard H. McCann (Naval Aviator No. 147), who left NAS Miami for the Signal Corps. training field at Fort Worth, Texas, on 31 January 1918. These men, mostly radiomen, arrived at Taliaferro Field, Texas, on 4 February 1918. After three weeks of training they left for Philadelphia on 25 February. Some of the men used this travel as an opportunity to take some furlough time. The group reported to the Philadelphia Navy Yard on 27 February. On 12 March the group left Philadelphia and traveled to New York, where they sailed on the S.S. New York, out of pier 62, for England. On 19 March the destroyers U.S.S. *Shaw* and *Cunningham* met the ship, and on 21

Aerial view of NAS Killingholme.

Aerial view of NAS Killingholme showing part of the store hangars and the rest of the hangars and building at the end of the camp.

Ground level view of NAS Killingholme showing the hangars and structures.

Aerial view of NAS Killingholme showing the central part of the station with various buildings and tents.

March she docked in Liverpool. From this port the group was immediately sent to Killingholme, where they arrived on 22 March at 0600 hrs. Due to a lack of facilities, the draft of men, under Ensign Thomas Henry Murphy (Naval Aviator No. 51), was quartered in the Recreational Hall until huts could be assigned. The American flag was first raised at Killingholme on 2 April 1918. In command of the Naval Air Unit at Killingholme at that time was Lieutenant Commander Carl Townsend Hull (Naval Aviator No. 46). Over a period of time, naval personnel continued to straggle into the station. Carr F. Pross and P. Edward Rollhaus, following the departure of Hubinger and Wickes from the U.S. on 22 March on an oil tanker via the Orkney Islands, met Harold C. Hubinger and Wickes in Hull on 12 April.

Men and material were dispatched from time to time, but it was not until 11 May 1918 that the collier U.S.S. *Jason* left New York with a large force of men, a cargo of supplies, and the first American seaplanes to be sent to Europe. She arrived on June 1, whereupon the necessary additional buildings to house the men and accommodate the planes were promptly erected, and steps taken to relieve the British forces at the station. Twenty-eight buildings, lacking only plumbing and wiring, were built with green crews in 30 days. The work progressed so rapidly that on 20 July, Commander Whiting relieved Wing Commander F.W. Bowhill, RNAS (RAF), who had served with great distinction in the war. By this time the compliment of navy men at the station had increased to 1,500 men, and the station was ready for full operation.

Five Navy men died while on duty at the station. They were:

Elec.3c Robert Evans Richardson	11 October
Ensign Benjamin Lee	28 October
Ensign Charles McG. Tyson	11 October
Raymond G. Fisher	28 October
MM 2c Bennett Sergai	11 October

III. OPERATIONS

Operations from the station involving U.S. personnel began very shortly after the establishment of a naval presence. Initially, these activities were associated with naval crews flying with their RAF counterparts in the English machines assigned to the station.

Hangars and flying field at NAS Killingholme. (source: Naval Historical Center No. 6901)

Third row of hangars containing machine shops and mess hall when the old mess hall at NAS Killingholme became too small.

Exterior view of the Mess Hall at NAS Killingholme.

As H-16 machines began to arrive flights were conducted on both the English machines, which had been left at the station following the departure of the RAF, and the new Navy machines. The following are excerpts from a combination of sources, including the diary of P. Edward Rollhaus, which relate to aerial operations at the station:

5 April: Elvin S. Wright, in a Short 320 flown by an English Sub-Lieutenant, experienced a forced landing off Filey. The machine had to be towed to shore by a destroyer.

12 April: Zeppelin alerts were sounded at 2200 hrs., 2400 hrs., and at 0200 hrs. Some bombs were dropped in fields near East Halton.

26 April: There was a report of 12 German ships out in the North Sea. A large number of planes from the station were sent out to look for them.

1 May: Elvin Stanley Wright was on patrol with Ensign James Phelan (NA No. 220) in a Short. A bomb was dropped just for fun. Upon returning to the station the crew had a hard time explaining the loss of the bomb to the English.

10 May: Lt. Pattinson, RAF, in a station F.2A, encountered a zeppelin over the North Sea. Unfortunately, the zeppelin climbed too fast for the F.2A and escaped.

18 May: A very busy day for the station personnel. Elvin Wright and Ensign Francis Gerald Allen (Naval Aviator No. 190) had a forced landing in a Short off Withensea. They were rescued and put up for the night in Officer's Quarters. Schuyler C. Page crashed in the North Sea about 40 miles off shore and was subsequently picked up. And two men were brought to the station in an exhausted condition. Their blimp had fallen in the sea some four days earlier, and they had just been rescued.

23 May: Seven men from the station attempted to recover a Short pontoon. The tide was too strong for the rowboat they were in, and a motor launch had to be sent out to haul them in.

28 May: a Short 320, with Navy personnel as crew, does a 5 hr. 20 minute North Sea patrol.

31 May: the *Jason* docked at Immingham. She was escorted in by a H-12 with Lieutenant Commander Carl Hull and Edward I. Klaus in the crew. Aboard the ship was an $18,000,000 cargo, including 22 H-16 planes (there were 26 more aircraft as a station compliment).

8 June: Carr F. Pross, James E. Dwyer, Joseph W. Urner, and Wm. L. Nelson had a close call when, in waders pulling in a F.2A, they were knocked off the slipway in a heavy tide. Fortunately, they were all rescued.

While the station was still under joint control, pilots Captain Munday, RAF, and Ensign George Edwin Rumill (Naval Aviator No. 217) sighted a periscope 15 miles east of Spurn. The periscope disappeared immediately, and the plane, upon arriving at the position, noticed a disturbance of the water, as if the submarine were lying on the bottom, and bubbles were seen to rise to the surface. Two bombs were dropped, whereupon more bubbles as well as oil came to the surface. No further results were observed, but owing to lack of fuel the seaplane was compelled to put back to base.

Left to right: Lt. Martin Kelly, Lt.(j.g.) Watson, and WO Campbell at NAS Killingholme. (source: 80-HAG-5B-28)

NAS Killingholme station personnel at formation. Even though this appears to be a dress parade note the two pilots in the flying togs in the front row. (source: 80-HAG-5B-3)

NAS Killingholme football team. Personnel are not identified.

9 June: Lieutenant Commander Kenneth Whiting assumed command of the U.S. Navy contingent at Killingholme. Lieutenant B.G. Leighton was the Executive Officer. (Note: Inconsistent with previous date of 20 July)

10 June: an English H-12 crashed. Ensign William Jackson (Naval Aviator No. 272) injured his head and hip.

13 June: A Flying Boat, with Lieutenant Cleeve, RAF, as pilot and Ensign Francis Allen as second pilot, sighted a submarine's wake. They immediately dropped two bombs in the line of the wake, whereupon oil and wreckage came to the surface, but the submarine continued on its course. Destroyers were signaled, and depth bombs brought more oil and wreckage to view. The submarine was not sighted again.

9 July: H-12 #4336 (Ensign John Jay Schieffelin (Naval Aviator No. 124), Ens. John Francis Staub (Naval Aviator No. 263), Dudley Bernstein, and Rollhaus, who was substituting for John Edward Taggart who was ill) was on convoy patrol at 1915 hrs. escorting a convoy of 30 ships. An oil patch was sighted off Hornsea and bombed. Escorting destroyers dropped depth charges, with the oil patch increasing in size. This is the first instance in which an O.P. "Urgent Priority" message was sent by a flying boat from the U.S. Naval AviatorS at Killingholme. According to Admiralty records the submarine was classified as "seriously damaged."

11 July: H-12 No. 4343 (Ensign James Edwin Baum (Naval Aviator No. 226), Ensign George Rumill, Birtch, and Ed Rollhaus) left on patrol at 1900 hrs. Off Flamborough Head their aileron controls broke; the ailerons hung down and flapped, Ensign Baum spun the control wheel freely, and the cabane struts of the machine collapsed from slip pressure with the machine dropping like a leaf. Baum made a luck landing. The crew sent off pigeons, but they did not home at night. Baum decided to taxi into shore and go down the coast. He tried to make landing and established blinker communications above Withernsea. They requested aid, but the people on shore thought it was a German decoy and fired shots in the dark. The crew returned back out to sea and taxied south to Humber and Killingholme. They arrived back at the base after 0900 hrs. on the 12th.

Ordinance Storeroom at NAS Killingholme. (source: Naval Historical Center)

Curtiss H-16 at NAS Killingholme fitted with a 520-lb. bomb.

12 July: Ensign Martin Dwyer (Naval Aviator No. 999) and his crew went out at 2000 hrs. in an F.2A. They crashed on takeoff and had to return to the station with a damaged hull.

H-12 #4336 (Ensign Pardridge and his crew) damaged a wing in landing. There were no injuries.

Lieutenant George Francklyn Lawrence (Naval Aviator No. 89), Ensign George Seward Hodges (Naval Aviator No. 253), Harry S. Pelton, and Harrison D. Brailsford, while on patrol, sighted and bombed a submarine. Official credit was given.

18 July: A Naval AviatorS Killingholme Short 320 Flying Boat did a ship convoy patrol of 4 hrs. 55 minutes.

19 July: H-12 #4336 (Lieutenant Aston William Hawkins (Naval Aviator #128), Ensign McDonald, Massina, and Edward J. Klaus) had a forced landing 40 miles off Whitby. Their hull was cracked, and a trawler picked them up.

Ensign John Jay Schieffelin and Ensign Roger Wilson Cutler (Naval Aviator No. 371) and their crew, including "Ned" Taggart, bombed a submarine that was on the surface 25 miles off Whitby. After the explosion the submarine's screws were seen to rise and almost break the surface, then the submarine disappeared. No further movement was discerned, and the plane returned to the station. The submarine was not put out of service, however, for later in the day she attempted to attack a convoy, but was repulsed by a motor launch which dropped depth charges, forcing the submarine to the surface. In the fight which ensued, a destroyer rammed the submarine, which was unable to submerge, and after being rammed again, she capsized and sank.

24 July: A Torpedo defense was sounded at 2300 hrs. Zeppelins were reported in the air. Three planes were readied, but none were sent out.

5 August: Two zeppelins were reported at 1930 hr. H-12 "Convert" went up at 2230 hrs. with Ashton Hawkins and Lieutenant Edward Klaus in the crew. Due to poor visibility nothing was sighted. The H-12 landed at 0530 hrs. on the 6th at South Shields, some 100 miles from Killingholme.

6 August: A Fire Call was sounded at midnight. H-12 "Convert" burned in the hangar. The wings of two H-16s were also burned. Smith, Gunners Mate 2c, was burned while taking bombs off the plane while it was afire.

10 August: Zeppelins were reported 100 miles off the coast. Three machines from the station went out, but only one was successful in staying up (Captain Pattinson, RAF, with Ensign Ashton Hawkins, who almost went to Heligoland).

11 August: Captain Pattinson (RAF) and Lieutenant Lawrence (USNRF), while on patrol, sighted a zeppelin about 50 miles off the Dutch coast. They gave chase, but the zeppelin out-climbed them.

12 August: A Fire Call was sounded at 1400 hrs. Wickes was working on a radio set when gas fumes in the hull exploded. Wickes and Kemp were very badly burned on their face and arms. Wickes' recovery extended over a long time, and Harry Kemp was unable to return to duty.

18 August: Ensign Henry C. Geiger and the crew of #785 had a forced landing and were towed back by a trawler. Ed Rollhaus and crew returned from convoy patrol early due to engine trouble.

21 August: H-12 #1062, with Walter I. Pardridge in the crew, sighted and bombed a submarine off Withernsea. A Trawler also dropped depth charges.

3 September: While on patrol H-16 #788 had a valve, welded to the gravity gas tank in the upper wing, crack loose, causing gas to drain out of the tank. The crew had to spend the rest of the trip home standing on the fuselage to hold the valve against the tank in order to have enough gas to feed the engines.

8 September: Ensign John Scheffelin was promoted to Lieutenant j.g. grade and commended for damaging a submarine on 9 July. Harold C. Hubinger, while on patrol duty escorting a convoy, saw a ship in the convoy sunk by a torpedo. The submarine was not located. On a subsequent patrol Rollhaus noted the huge amount of floating lumber that looked like matchsticks on the North Sea.

17 September: H-16 #788 (Ensign Dick McCann, Ensign Clarence Howard "Henry" Geyer (Naval Aviator No. 254), Benjamin P. Thomas, and Ed Rollhaus) left in a fog at 0600 hrs. They rose to 2000 ft. to clear the oncoming storm but got caught, and the plane was tossed about badly. They made an attempt to land, but crashed, and the gas tanks went through the bottom of the boat (their altimeter was off 400 ft.). The yoke ripped off McCann's thumbnail. Rollhaus received secondary "dry" burns from soaking in gasoline. The plane kept afloat by the buoyancy of the lower wings. Eventually the machine was towed to Paull by a barge. The plane was written off. Leighton apologized to McCann for sending the plane out in such weather.

1 October: Ensign Benjamin "Bennie" Lee (Naval Aviator No. 137) and crew, including Harry A. Grant, took a Liberty boat to 10,200 ft. at the rate of 1,000 ft. in five minutes. The gas pump froze. So did Harvey, who, thinking it was only a short test hop, did not get his flying gear, and went up with only working blues to keep him warm.

11 October: The Order for the Day specified the following: "Flight Duty Officer"—Ensign William Jackson; Officer of the Day—Ensign McDonald. H-16s may expect calls as follows: K-42 (Ensign Knight Barry Owen (Naval Aviator No. 737 and crew); K-21 (Ensign Dick McCann and crew); K-38 (Ensign Stanley Thompson Curran (Naval Aviator No. 287) and crew); K-28 (Ensign George E. Rumill and crew); K-39 (Ensign Francis G. Allen and crew); K-16 (Ensign Alexander Clinton Zabriskie (Naval Aviator No. 314) and crew); and K-43 (Ensign Raymond Loring Atwood (Naval Aviator No. 292) and crew). Shorts on call as follows: 1373—Ensign Malcolm Stevenson (Naval Aviator No. 499) with Millard, QM2c, and 1702—Ensign Lewis Hughes Lee (Naval Aviator No. 109) with Waite, QM2c. H-16 K-38 (Lieutenant (j.g.) Stanley T. Curran (Naval Aviator No. 287), Lieutenant Charles McG. Tyson (Naval Aviator No. 260), Bennett Sergai (Engineer), and Robert Richardson (Radio)) took off at 0625 hrs. on a mine laying operation. Near Immingham the engine stopped and the plane went into a spin. Coming out of the spin, the tail failed. The machine crashed at 0700 hr. in the Humber River, with Curran being rescued by a motor lorry. Tyson, Sergai, and Richardson were killed in the crash.

14 October: H-16 K-21 (Ensign McCann, Ensign Clarence Geyer, Benjamin J. Thomas, and Ed Rollhaus) left the station at 0600 hrs. and headed straight out to sea. The radiators failed, and

with the loss of water the engines overheated. The crew headed back to shore and spent the night at Scarborough.

28 October: The Order of the Day specified the following: "Flight Duty Officer"—Ensign Raymond L. Atwood; Officer of the Day—Ensign William Jackson; 1st Crew (Convoy Patrol 0600 Hrs. K-7 (Lieutenant Dick McCann, Ensign Clarence H. Geyer, Benjamin H. Thomas [Engineer], and Ed Rollhaus [Radio]); 2nd Crew—K-1 (Ensign Alexander C. Zabriskie, Ensign Foye Shumway, Ledward [Engineer], and Harvey A. Grant [Radio]); 3rd Crew—K-6 (Ensign George E. Rumill, Ensign Townsley, Gimpel [Engineer], and Carr Fred Pross [Radio]); Special F.2A Patrol at 0630 hrs.—1st Crew—8685 (Lieutenant (j.g.) John Jay Schieffelin, Ensign John Willis Hines (Naval Aviator No. 338), Johnathan W. Cullen [Engineer], and James E. Taggart [Radio]); 2nd Crew—4082 (Lieutenant Lawrence, Ensign MacDonald, Cote [Engineer], and James Harvey Frink [Radio]); 3rd Crew—4067 (Ensign Benjamin Lee, Ensign Joshua Garrison, Jr. (Naval Aviator No. 261), R.S. Fisher [Engineer], and Fred Harris [Radio]); and Stand-by boat K-29 (Ensign Charles Frederick Kunkel (Naval Aviator No. 273), Lieutenant Roger Weinberg [Engineer], and Harold C. Wilson Cutler (Naval Aviator No. 371) Hubinger [Radio]).

Three H-16s took off for Dundee, Scotland. #4067 (Ensign Lee, Ensign Garrison, Harris, and Fisher) was seen to bank very steeply and sideslip from about 600 feet to 200 feet, then bank again and crash, starboard wing first, at 1245 hrs. into the Humber River. A few minutes later the petrol on the surface of the water caught fire. The other two planes landed nearby. Harris received a heavy blow on the jaw, and saw Fisher, whose foot was caught, unable to pull him out from above. Harris dove under the wreckage and pulled him downward to release the foot, and brought Fisher to the surface. Garrison came up, and Harris grabbed him, also. He then treaded water until a trawler threw a line. Fisher was held by his gloved hand, and in catching the rope his hand slipped out of the glove and the current took him down. Ives and Hawkins landed their planes, and the co-pilots—G.S. Hodges and R.H. McCann—dove overboard into the flaming petrol and wreckage for the crew. Pardridge was on one of these planes and began to strip, but his pilot requested him not to dive over. Hodges and McCann were not able to find Lee and Fisher. They were chilled in the cold water and somewhat burned. McCann and Hodges were awarded the Distinguished Service Medal for their efforts outside their line of duty.

29 October: Three planes took off for Scotland at 1200 hrs. The pilots were Ensign Paul Frost Ives (Naval Aviator No. 195), Ensign Alexander Hawkins, and Lieutenant (j.g.) Schieffelin; second pilots were Ensign Wilcox, Ensign McCann, and Ensign James Baum; and radio operators were Pardridge, Frink, and Taggart.

30 October: H-16 machine from the station made a recorded time flight of nine hours thirty-eight minutes. The crew were Ensign Stanley Carmichael Kennedy (Naval Aviator No. 302), Ensign Francis G. Allen, Foye Shumaker, and Belvin. They made one landing, so continuous time granted was cut to nine hours.

For its operational history (beginning 20 July 1918), the summary of station operations is as follows: sea miles patrolled—57,647; hours of flying—968; number of flights—233; average length of flight—4 hours, 10 minutes; forced landings—35; and number of ships convoyed—6,243.

IV. CONCLUSION

During its period of operation some 6,243 ships were convoyed; the distance covered in 233 war patrols, totaling 968 flying hours, was nearly 60,000 miles, not including test flights or experiments. For several weeks when German submarines were believed to come to the surface under the cover of darkness to recharge their storage batteries, nightly patrols were conducted on seven and eight hour patrols. In January 1920 Secretary of the Navy Josephus Daniels accepted a Gift of about $30,000 from Britain as a Memorial to the Dover Patrol and the part which NAS Killingholme played in that effort.

Many of the personnel stationed at Killingholme were recognized for their contribution to the war effort. Distinguished Service Medals were awarded for heroism to Richard H. McCann and G.S. Hodges. Navy Crosses were won by Dudley Bernstein, David C. Hale, Ensign Benjamin Lee, Ensign Lewis H. Lee, Schuyler C. Page, P. Eduard Rollhaus, Lieutenant j.g. John Jay Schieffelin, John F. Staub, John Edward Taggett, Lieutenant Commander Kenneth Whiting, and H.M. Wilcox. And Letters of Commendation, for heroism, were issued to Ensign Francis G. Allen, Ensign Raymond L. Atwood, Jonathan W. Cullen, Ensign Stanley T. Curran, Ensign Roger W. Cutler, Chauncey A. Galloupe, Ensign Clarence H. Geyer, Rettig A. Griswold, Theodore P. Grosvenor, Ashton W. Hawkins, John W. Hines, Kenneth B. Hodges, Ens. Paul P. Ives, Ensign Stanley C. Kennedy, Edward J. Klaus, Thomas H. Murphy, Ensign Knight B. Owen, Ensign Walter I. Pardridge, Leonard A. Welty, and Ensign Alexander C. Zabriskie.

V. DEMOBILIZATION

At the Armistice the compliment of the station was 91 officers and 1324 men. The first draft of men (491) left the station in late November. A second draft (500) of men left at 0950 hrs. on 1 December 1918. They traveled to Liverpool, where they boarded the S.S. *Leviathan* for the trip home. Aboard the *Leviathan* they found the first draft of Killingholme men, under the command of Lieutenant Tom Murphy. The base was closed on 22 February 1919, with the property reverting back to the British Government.

Notes:

[1] Much of the material in this Appendix is taken from: a) *Flying Officers of the U.S.N.*, published by Naval Aviation War Book Committee, Washington, D.C.; and b) the Killingholme Fly Paper, Vol. 2

Appendix Z: Naval Aviation Training at the University of Washington

The University of Washington, prior to the entry of the United States into the war, had a tradition of student military training. The Board of Regents of the University authorized the President of the University, on 16 March 1917, to "offer the use of university buildings and grounds for military, nursing, and other activities, in the event of war...." Prior to April 1917 the Reserve Officers Training Corps had a full Regimental organization of 12 companies and 801 men. On 28 April the Board of Regents authorized the President "at his discretion" to grant faculty leaves of absence for detachment service on war affairs. On 18 May the President of the University was authorized to offer the use of certain on-campus buildings and drill space for naval training purposes. During the 1917-1918 academic year the university's ROTC program was combined with other existing programs (specialty courses and a Non-Commissioned Officer Training Program) into a College of Naval, Military, and Aeronautical Science. The purpose of this reorganization was to increase the effectiveness of the war training being provided the students of the university. The College was organized under Major William T. Pattern, professor of military science and tactics of the ROTC as acting director. Curriculum for the new College was to be effective the summer of 1918 quarter.

On 8 September 1917 University President Henry Suzzallo wrote to Captain C.C. Marsh, Chief, Division, Naval Militia Affairs, a letter on the subject of "Training in Aerodynamics for Naval Militia." In this letter President Suzzallo "offered the facilities of the University, on behalf of the Regents and Faculty of the University of Washington for the training of squads of the National Naval Volunteers currently located at the Naval Training Camp located on the campus and for the training of selected men from the Aviation Division, First Brigade, Naval Militia of Washington, recently established by Adjutant General Thompson, in that preparatory work necessary to the complete training of hydroplane pilots, and their associate mechanics." The letter then went on to describe the advantages of the location, the university equipment available for such a school, the teaching staff available to work in the school, and the cooperative working agreement the university had with the Boeing Company for the operation of an aviation laboratory on the campus.

It was not until March 1918 that the Navy Department was able to act on this offer. But, between 17 March 1918 and 23 March 1918 there was a flurry of telegrams between President Suzzallo of the University, Captain Miller Freeman, Naval Training Station, University Campus, Admiral R.E. Coontz, Commandant, Navy Yard, Bremerton, Washington, William E. Boeing, Dean John T. Condon of the University, and Lieutenant R.D. Kirkpatrick of the Navy, the culmination of which was agreement between the Navy and the University regarding the formation of a formal Naval Aviation Ground School on the campus of the University.

The announcement of the creation of a Ground School was made on 1 May 1918. On 11 June 1918 a Naval Aviation Ground School was formally organized at the University. This was in advance of the signing of the formal contract between the University and the Bureau of Navigation on 29 June 1918. Ground School had as its purpose the training in basic scientific and technical courses of future officers. The school at the University was under the control of the 13th Naval District, then located in Bremerton, Washington. The school was commanded by Lieutenant James Campbell Montford, U.S.N. (Naval Aviator 35). Montford was a graduate of the U.S. Naval Academy Class of 1912. The cost to the Navy for this school was established to be "not more than $1500.00 per month." The school was intended to handle all men enlisting west of the Rocky Mountains for instruction in aviation, and was designed for a course of eight weeks duration being introduced every two weeks. Men assigned to the school were enlisted at chief quartermasters. The students were to be intertwined into squads of 40, with a new group being introduced every two weeks. It was the intent of the school to graduate 200 men at a time. The course of instruction, oriented toward ground work in aviation, consisted of drill, aerial navigation, aerial gunnery, bombing, signaling, rigging of aircraft, theory of flight, both theoretical and practical work with aviation engines, seamanship, calisthenics, and radio. Graduates of the ground school were assigned to NAS San Diego for preliminary flight training. Upon successful completion of their flying tests at San Diego the men were commissioned as ensigns in the Navy

The Navy, besides Lt. Montford, provided nine ensigns and nine petty officers from Atlantic Coast stations to act as instructors.

The ensigns included Harry F. Fletcher, Ralph A. Fletcher, Hugh McConnell, George B. Markle, John B. Moller (Naval Aviator 2077), William McEwen, Wallace S. Thomas (Naval Aviator 2093), Russell, H. White (Naval Aviator 972), and Frank A. Zunio, Jr. (Naval Aviator 152)

While an exact listing of all the students enrolled in the University Naval Aviation Ground School awaits further research, it is known that the 19 graduates of the second aviation class (Company 2) from the Ground School were as follows:[1]

R.A. Brant
L.W. Brummitt
W.H. Coombs
R.H. Myers
E.R. Paul
L.F. Price
M.A. Conway
G.E.W. Davis
J.F. Deuds
E.W. Frederick
C.C. Heed
W.I. Jones
R.J.. Mellen
H. Saxby
A.J. Schaefer
A.M. Smith
I.K. Worth
O.J. Wood
H. Wylie

At the time of this graduation there were four other Companies undergoing training.

In its history the school would receive 522 applicants, the average enrollment would be 450, and it would have 101 men completing its curriculum. The School was terminated in January 1919.

Notes:

[1] This listing is taken from the 13 June 1918 issue of the Seattle Times. The same subject is covered in the Seattle Post Intelligence with a slightly different listing (i.e., Bremitt, Combs, Jones and Schaefer are not listed, but the names of Brown, Larkin, Shepard, and McConnell are)

Bibliography

Published Books

Abbott, Willis J., *Blue Jackets of 1918*, Dodd, Mead, and Co., Inc.

Arthur, Reginald White, *Contact! Careers of Naval Aviators Assigned Numbers 1 to 2000*, Naval Aviator Register, Washington, DC

Bingham, Hiram, *An Explorer in the Air Service*, Yale Press

Bowers, Peter M., *Curtiss Aircraft 1907-1947*, Naval Institute Press

Caidin, Martin, *Golden Wings*, Randon House

Casey, Louis S., *Curtiss: The Hammondsport Era 1907-1915*, Crown Publications Inc.

Colette, Paolo E., *United States Navy and Marine Corps Bases, Domestic*, Greenwood Press

Colette, Paolo E., *United States Navy and Marine Corps Bases, Overseas*, Greenwood Press

Collins, Francis A., *Naval Heroes of Today*, The Century Co.

Foss, William O. *The United States Navy in Hampton Roads*. The Donning Co.

Gordon, Dennis, *Lafayette Escadrille Pilot Biographies*, The Doughboy Historical Society

Knott, Richard C., Capt. (Rt.) USN, *The Naval Aviation Guide,* Naval Institute Press

Hubbard, Joseph, *On the Coast of France*, A.C. McClurg and Co.

James, Henry J. *German Subs in Yankee Waters*, Gotham House

Paine, Ralph D., *The First Yale Unit "A Story of Naval Aviation" 1916-1917 (Vol. 1*), The Riverside Press

Paine, Ralph D., *The First Yale Unit "A Story of Naval Aviation" 1916-1917 (Vol. 2)*, The Riverside Press

Pearce, George F., *The United States Navy in Pensacola*, University of Florida Press

Raliegh, Sir Walter and H.A. Jones, *The War in the Air, Being the Story of the Part Played in the Great War by the Royal Air Force*, Vol. 4, page 74, Oxford Press

Reynolds, Clark G., *Admiral John H. Towers*, Naval Institute Press

Rossano, Geoffrey L., *The Prince of Honor; The World War One Letters of Naval Aviator Kenneth MacLeish*, Naval Institute Press

Sims, R.Adm. William Sowden, *Victory at Sea*, Doubleday Page & Co.

Trumbull, Archibald D. and Clifford L. Lord, *History of the United States Naval Aviation*, Yale University Press

van Duers, George, *Anchors in the Sky*, Presidio Press

van Vleet, Clarke and William J. Armstrong, *United States Naval Aviation 1910-1980*, U.S. Government Printing Office, Washington DC, 1981

Wise, S.F., *Canadian Airmen and the First World War, The Official History of the Royal Canadian Air Force, Volume 1,* University of Toronto Press, page 604

Official Publications and Published Documents

Anonymous, *Activities of the Bureau of Yards and Docks, Navy Department, World War I 1917-1918*, Government Printing Office

Anonymous, "The First Navy Dirigible," *World War I Aero*, Vol. 141, August 1993, pages 47-53

Bowers, Peter M., "The Curtiss JN-4," *Profile Publications* Ltd.

Bruce, J.M., "The Hanroit HD-1," *Profile Publications* Ltd.

Bulletin, University of Washington, "*The Fifteenth Biennial Report of the Board of Regents of the University of Washington to the Governor of Washington*," No. 124, January 1919

Butler, Jaravis, "The General Board of the Navy," *U.S. Naval Institute Proceedings*, Vol. 52, No. 8, Whole No. 330, pages 700-705

Casari, Robert. "U.S. Purchasing Commission for Aircraft." *Cross & Cockade Journal* (US) Vol. 9, No. 4, Pages 283-286.

Charlton, Capt. A.M. "Man-lifting Kites in the Navy," *U.S. Naval Institute Proceedings*, Vol. 64, No. 10, Whole No. 428, Pages 1452-1455

Dater, H.M., *Aviation and Seapower*. 1952.

Dwelle, D.C., "The Davis Gun," *Cross & Cockade Journal* (US), Vol. 6 No. 1, Pages 76-84

Duncan, Donald B. and Dater H.M. "Administrative History of U.S. Naval Aviation," *Air Affairs, An International Quarterly,* Summer 1947, Vol. 1, No. 4 .

Edwards, Lt.Cdr. W. Atlee, "The U.S. Naval Air Force in Action, 1917-1918," *U.S. Naval Institute Proceedings*, Vol. 48, No. 11, Whole No. 237, Pages 1863-1182

Emons, Roger M., "Early Flying Marines," *Cross & Cockade Journal (US)*, Vol. 22, No. 4, pages 358-368

Emons, Roger M., "The First Marine Aviation Force." *Cross & Cockade Journal* (US), Vol. 6, Vol. 2 Pages 173-186 and Vol. 6, No. 3 Pages 272-292.

Featherston, Cdr. Frank H. "A.E.O.D., A History and a Heritage," *U.S. Naval Institute Proceedings*, Vol. 104, No. 2, Whole Number 780, 1968, Pages 33-45.

Foxworth, Tom, "Curtiss Transatlantic Effort of 1914; or Wanamaker's Wonderbird, *World War I Aero*, Vol. 134, Pages 38-55

Gemeinhardt, M/Sgt. Fritz, "Flying Boats, U.S. Marine Corps," *World War 1 Aero*, No. 109, April 1986, Pages 22-41

Gemeinhardt, M/Sgt. Fritz, "Curtiss R-6 World War I Aero, No. 162, November 1988, Pages 26-30

Gould, Bartlett, "Burgess Pt. VIII," *World War I Aero*, Volume 133, August 1991

Gould, Bartlett, "Burgess Pt. IX," *World War I Aero*, Volume 135, February 1992

Gould, Bartlett, "Three of a Kind," *World War I Aero*, Vol. 130, November 1990, Pages 25-32

Grossinck, Roy A., *Kite Balloons to Airships...The Navy's Lighter-than-Air Experience*. Superintendent of Documents, Govt. Printing Office, Washington DC

Hunsaker, Cdr. J.C., "The Navy's First Airship," *U.S. Naval Institute Proceedings*, Vol. 45, No. 8, Whole No. 198, Pages 1347-1368

Holcombe, David C., "Evolution of the Curtiss Pusher Part V(d)," *World War I Aero*, Volume 161, page 29

Layman, Richard, "Naval Kite Trials," *Warships 1994*, Conway Maritime Press, 1994

Mathews, Lt.(j.g.) Charles, "U.S. Naval Air Stations in Canada in 1918," *Canadian Aviation Historical Society Journal*, Winter 1989

Miller, Lt.(j.g.) H.B., "Shooting the Catapult," *U.S. Naval Institute Proceedings*, Vol. 59, No. 4, Whole No. 362, Pages 544-554

Miller Jr., Thomas G. and Robinson, Douglas H., "Nonrigid Airships in World War I," *Cross and Cockade Journal (US)*, Vol. 5, No. 1, Pages 97-116

Morris, Olen C., *Report Upon the United States Naval Detachment Massachusetts Institute of Technology Cambridge, Mass. - A Survey Covering Period of its Existence from July 23, 1917 to January 18, 191,*. February 1, 1919

Mustin, H.C. *Development of U.S. Navy Aeronautic Station*, 1916.

Mustin, H.C. *Organization of Naval Flying Corps*, 1916.

"Naval Aviation Overseas, 1917-1918." *Cross & Cockade Journal* (US) Vol. 4, No. 1, Pages 52-83.

"Naval Aviation Overseas - I. Establishment, *Sea Power*, May 1921

"Naval Aviation Overseas - II. Organization, *Sea Power*, June 1921

"Naval Aviation Overseas - III. Operation, *Sea Power*, July 1921

Nelson, Stephen, "Italian Naval Aircraft," *Cross & Cockade Journal*, (US) Vol. 5, No. 3, 1964

Rankin, Lt.Cdr. Robert H., "DN-1, The U.S. Navy's First Dirigible," *U.S. Naval Institute Proceedings*, Vol. 83, No. 18, Whole No. 656, Pages 1144-1145

Ray, Thomas, "Naval Aviation, The Beginning," *U.S. Naval Institute Proceedings*, Vol. 97, No. 1, Whole No. 815, Pages 32-42

Ray, Thomas, "The First Three," *U.S. Naval Institute Proceedings*, Vol. 97, No. 7, Whole No. 821, Pages 34-43

Ray, Thomas, "Annapolis: The Navy's First Aerodrome," *U.S. Naval Institute Proceedings*, Vol. 97, No. 10, Whole No. 824, Pages 34-41

Ryan, Capt. Paul B., "Ten Day at Veracruz," *U.S. Naval Institute Proceedings*, Vol. 98, No. 6, Whole No. 832, Pages 65-73

Sheely, Lawrence D. "Irving Edward Sheely - Naval Observer," *Over theFront*, Vol. 3, No. 2 Pages 99-133

Shirley, Noel C., "A Brief History of U.S. Naval Dirigible Stations in France," *Over the Front Journal,* Vol. 2 No. 4, Pages 356-370

Shirley, Noel C., "John Lansing Callan, Naval Aviation Pioneer," *Over the Front Journal*. Vol. 2, No. 4, Pages 180-185

Shirley, Noel C., "La Guardia, Caproni Bombers, and the U.S. Navy," *Cross & Cockade Journal* (US), Vol. 25, No. 2, Pages 125-140

Sitz, Capt. W.H. USMC, *A History of U.S. Naval Aviation*. Technical Note 18, Series of 1930, United States Navy Department, Bureau of Aeronautics. *Technology's War Record*, Page 20

Tegler, John. "Birthplace of Naval Aviation," *Air Classics*, May 1986, *The- Artisan*, Vol. III, No. 9, June 1918

Tucker, CWO-4 Lester B. (Ret.), "The First U.S. Navy Combat Aircrew Wings—Who May Know?" *Trading Post*, April-June 11992

United States Naval Aviation 1910-1970, U.S. Government Printing Office, Washington, DC. *U.S. Naval Air Station Wexford*, Edited by Lt.(j.g.) T.B. Tillotson

Vaeth, Lt. J. Gordon, "Daughter of the Stars," *U. S. Naval Institute Proceedings*, No. 99, No. 9, Whole No. 847, Pages 62-69

Van Wyen, Adrian 0. "Naval Aviation in World War I." *Naval Aviation News*, 1969.

Van Wyen, Adrian 0., "The Naval Detachment at the Massachusetts Institute of Technology, World War I," *Naval Aviation News,* July 1967

Vincent, Charles Helm. "Birth of the Liberty Engine." *Cross & Cockade Journal* (US), Vol. 10, No. 4, Pages 350-354.

Wheeler, Gerald E., "Naval Aviation's First Year," *U.S. Naval Institute Proceedings*, Vol. 87, No. 5, Whole No. 699, Pages 88-95

Wait, Adam and Noel Shirley, "'Devil Dog' Sam Richards," *Over the Front*, Vol. 7, No. 3, pages 195-211

Wilson, H.B., *An Account of the Operations of the American Navy in France During the War with Germany*

Woodhouse, Henry, "The Torpedo Plane," *U.S. Naval Institute Proceedings*, Vol. 45, No. 5, Whole No. 195, Pages 742-752

——— *World War 1 Aero*, Vol. 105, Pages 69-71

Ziegler Jr., Lt.Cdr. S.J., "The Naval Aircraft Factory," *U.S. Naval Institute Proceedings*, Vol. 52, No. 1, Whole No. 275, Pages 83-94

Unpublished Documents

Anonymous, *Procurement of Aviation Material in Europe 1917-1918*, undated

Aviation Circular, May 1, 1917 BuNav file 5901-77, National Archives

Cline, J.C. *The First Aeronautic Detachment*

History of the United States Naval Air Station Ile-Tudy, Finistere (France)

Imprimerie A. Jaoven-Mmee Chauet Bargain, Succ. 1918

Letter, H.E. Coffin to Sec.Nav. dated June 22, 1917

Letter, OP Air 2935-17 of July 10, 1917

Letter, Sec.Nav. MAT 7-AH, 2638-17, dated July 13, 1917

Letter, War Department, Office of Signal Officer to Operations (Aviation) dated July 13, 1917

Letter, Sec.Nav. to BuNav, Op Air 3-AH 3071-17, dated July 14, 1917

Letter, CO NAD to CNO, dated July 31, 1917

Letter, CO NAD of August 8, 1917

Letter, CO NAD of August 22, 1917

Letter, CO NAD to Lt. Johnson, dated September 8, 1917

Letter, CO NAD of September 8, 1917

Letter, CO NAD of September 15, 1917

Letter, CO NAD of September 17, 1917

Letters, CO NAD of October 27, 1917 and October 29, 1917

Letter, CO NAD, dated November 7, 1917

Letters, CO NAD, dated November 26, 1917 and December 3, 1917

Letter, CO NAD, dated December 13, 1917

Letters, CO NAD, dated January 3, 1917 and January 17, 1917

Letter, CO NAD, dated January 16, 1917

Letter, CO NAD 790-9, RWC-PC of January 18, 1918

Letter from N.E. Irwin to CO NAD MIT (OP Air - 088-33) of January 25, 1918, on the subject of Machine Gun Instruction.

Letter 251397-707-Da from A.T. Atkins (Bureau of Steam Engineering) to Supervisor Naval Reserve Flying Corps, dated February 2, 1918.

Letter, CO NAD, dated February 13, 1918

Letter, CO NAD, dated August 21, 1917 and First Endorsement dated February 21, 1918 on subject of Supervisor NFRC letter Nav.Air 79-105 of February 18, 1918

Letters, CO NAD, dated March 15, 1918 and March 25, 1918

Letter Medical Officer NAD to 1st Naval District, dated May 17, 1918

Letter R.Adm. A. Ross to Sec.Nav., dated December 9, 1918

Letter CO NAD to Comm. 1st ND, NAD 8648-2, HCV-LC dated January 30, 1919

Letter CO NAD to Comm. 1st ND, NAD 8648-42, HCV-LC dated January 30, 1919

Lord, Lt.Cdr. Clifford L. *The History of Naval Aviation, 1898-1939*

Lewis, Henry P., *"Massachusetts and Naval Aviation 1917"*

Lewis, Henry P., *"The Sguantum Story"*

Memorandum (MAT.5E) of 24 Oct. 1916 to Capt. J.S. McKean, USN, on the subject of *"Memo re aeronautic work from 1 Jan. 16 to 1 Nov. 16"*

McKelvey, Carlton A., *Construction of the U.S. Naval Air Station l'Aber Vrach, France, World War I*, 1963

NAVAIR 00-OP-1 *United States Naval Aviation 1910-1970*

Norris, Olen C., *Report upon the United States Naval Aviation Detachment Massachusetts Institute of Technology, Cambridge Mass.*, 1 Feb. 19

Sec.Nav. Telegram OP Air 1-AH, 2952-17 of July 12, 1917

Telegram, Maclaurin to Sec.Nav. of July 7, 1917

Telegrams, BuNav to 1st ND of July 7, 1918 and July 9, 1918

The Naval Air Detachment at the Massachusetts Institute of Technology, World War I, Aviation History, Office of DCNO(Air)

RAF Fortnightly Summaries of No. 5 Group, Dover Patrol 16 Sept. 19 to 30 Sept. 18 and from I Oct. 18 to 15 Oct. 18.

Memo of telephone conversations, Johnson and Spencer OP AIr 3-LL, 3017-17 and 3051-17

Report of Inspection of R.Adm. A. Ross, dated November 26, 1917

War Diary and History of the United States Naval Air Station, Lough Foyle, Ireland

Weekly Report of the CO NAD of November 16, 1917

Newspapers

Seattle Times, 13 June 1918, page 14

Seattle Times, 6 September 1918,

Seattle Post-Intelligence, 6 September 1918, Page 2

Hearings

Statement by R.Adm. J.S. McKean, Subcommittee on Naval Affairs, U.S. Senate 66th Congress, April 29, 1920

Memoirs

Cline, Joe C. "First Naval Aviation Unit in France." *Naval Aviation News*, June 1967.

Halstead, J. Sterling. "A Mission to the Royal Flying Corps.", *U.S. Naval Institute Proceedings*, Vol. 91, No. 2, Whole No. 744, Pages 78-94.

Lewis, Henry P. *The Story of Flight A, 1917-1918 and Recollection of its Members*